LEISURE, WOMEN, AND GENDER

LEISURE, WOMEN, AND GENDER

EDITED BY

VALERIA J. FREYSINGER, SUSAN M. SHAW, KARLA A. HENDERSON,
AND M. DEBORAH BIALESCHKI

VENTURE PUBLISHING, INC.

Library of Congress Catalogue Card Number 2013932741
ISBN-10: 1-892132-98-2
ISBN-13: 978-1-892132-98-7

TABLE OF CONTENTS

CONTRIBUTORS

Cara Aitchison: I am Head of The Moray House School of Education at the University of Edinburgh in Scotland, where I hold a Chair in Social and Environmental Justice. From 2008 to 2010, I was Dean of the Faculty of Education and Sport at the University of Bedfordshire, and from 2003 to 2008, I was Professor in Human Geography and Director of the Centre for Leisure, Tourism, and Society at the University of the West of England, Bristol. My research interests cohere around two themes: social inclusion in leisure and sport with a primary interest in gender relations, and sustainable development in leisure and tourism, with a particular interest in the role of tourism in integrated rural development. (Cara.Aitchison@ed.ac.uk)

Denise M. Anderson: I am an Associate Professor in the Department of Parks, Recreation, and Tourism Management at Clemson University. My research interests are centered on the role of recreation and leisure in the lives of girls and women in multiple settings including sport. My own passion for sport has led me to examine the circumstances girls and women continue to work through to experience the highs and lows of sport I experienced on many playing fields. My own leisure these days has been influenced by my young son but still includes hiking, baking (and tasting), boating, and seeing the world through new eyes again. (dander2@clemson.edu)

Leandra A. Bedini: I am a Professor in the Therapeutic Recreation concentration of the Department of Recreation, Tourism, and Hospitality Management at the University of North Carolina at Greensboro. My interests in scholarship relate to understanding the leisure of disenfranchised groups, specifically family caregivers, as well as girls and women with disabilities. I also like to teach how to use magic as a therapeutic intervention for people with disabilities. My personal leisure interests include playing softball (lifelong activity), reading mysteries, hiking and exploring nature, bicycling, and socializing with friends and family. (bedini@uncg.edu)

Lisbeth A. Berbary: I am an Assistant Professor of Qualitative Research Methodology at the University of Memphis. I earned my Ph.D. in Leisure Studies with graduate certificates in both qualitative research and women's studies. My overall line of inquiry deconstructs discursive expectations and social consequences of traditional and non-dominant performances of self within community leisure spaces. I am particularly drawn to creative analytic practices to represent my research because I feel it is important to make research findings accessible to community members. For fun I enjoy throwing dinner parties for friends, walking my dogs, sitting in the sun with a pop-culture magazine, doing yoga, and creating art. (laberbary@gmail.com)

Liza Berdychevsky: I am a Ph.D. student working with Dr. Heather Gibson in the Department of Tourism, Recreation, and Sport Management at the University of Florida. My main research interests are located at the intersection of gender, tourism, and leisure, with a focus on female tourist experiences, motivations, and constraints, liminoid effect, performativity, existential authenticity, and sexual behavior in tourism. I love dancing, swimming, and diving, and I consider the beach to be the best place to think and rest. (liza@hhp.ufl.edu)

M. Deborah Bialeschki: I am the Director of Research for the American Camp Association and a Professor Emeritus from the University of North Carolina, Chapel Hill. My research interests include youth development, the value of outdoor experiences, systems for evidence-based evaluation, and the leisure experiences of girls and women. I believe research is only as good as the practice it supports and that practice is only as good as the research that guides it. My own leisure is often focused on participating in volunteer opportunities, playing in the community band, doing almost anything in the outdoors, spending time with family and friends (including four-legged furry ones), and continuing my quest for the perfect s'more. (moon@email.unc.edu)

Fern M. Delamere: I am a Professor in the Department of Applied Human Sciences at Concordia University in Montreal, Canada. My scholarship interests are leisure, gender, disability, and digitally mediated leisure behaviors. My research is qualitative and inter-disciplinary, crossing the boundaries of leisure, game studies, and media communication studies. My leisure passions are varied, exceeding the bounds of my physical (cycling, swimming, walking my dog, and gardening), cerebral (reading, graphic design, photography, and playing guitar) and social (social networks–virtual and in-person, family gathering, and culinary play) worlds. (fern.delamere@gmail.com)

Rylee A. Dionigi: I am the Associate Head of the School of Human Movement Studies at Charles Sturt University, Bathurst, Australia. I am a qualitative researcher interested in exploring the personal and cultural meanings of exercise and sports participation in later life. I have published in the fields of sport sociology, aging and physical activity, sport and exercise psychology, and leisure studies. I have met so many interesting, insightful, and positive people through my interviews with research participants and my ongoing collaboration with colleagues. I also enjoy life with my family and friends, especially my husband, Claudio, and my beautiful children, Giordano and Lorena. (rdionigi@csu.edu.au)

Shanly Dixon: I am a Ph.D. candidate in the Humanities Doctoral Program in Interdisciplinary Studies in Society and Culture at Concordia University in Montreal, where I draw upon the disciplines of sociology, communication, and education to explore young people's engagement with digital culture. I teach a range of courses in digital culture, sociology, mass media, and popular culture at John Abbott College and Concordia University. Because much of my research involves hanging out with young people, playing or watching them play, or talking to them about play, most of the time my work feels like play.

Valeria J. Freysinger: I am an Associate Professor in the Department of Kinesiology and Health at Miami University of Ohio. My research and teaching focus on leisure across the course of life (particularly mid- and later life), gendered experiences/practices of leisure and aging, social (in)equality in leisure and aging, and qualitative research methods. As a graduate student at the University of Wisconsin, I was inspired by the work of Sue, Karla, and Deb, and I continue to be inspired by them today. Traveling, reading, being with friends and family, hiking, and bicycling are what I love to do at my leisure. (freysivj@muohio.edu)

Wendy Frisby: I am a Professor in the School of Human Kinetics at the University of British Columbia in Vancouver, Canada. My research interests lie in the areas of poverty, community-based recreation and health promotion, organizational theory, and feminist participatory action research. I am most fortunate to have worked collaboratively with women living below the poverty line, a number of community partners, graduate students, and colleagues over the years from whom I am continually learning. Reading, playing bridge, socializing, cooking, walking the beautiful North Shore Mountains with my partner and Jackson (our golden retriever), and staying in touch with my globetrotting children via Skype are my favorite things to do in my leisure time. (frisby@interchange.ubc.ca)

Simone Fullagar: I am an Associate Professor in the Department of Tourism, Leisure, Hotel, and Sport Management at Griffith University, Australia. As an interdisciplinary sociologist, I have undertaken a range of qualitative research projects that explore the sociocultural dimensions of leisure, sport and tourism, health and well-being, gender equity, diverse families, and sustainable practices. From a leisure-studies perspective, I find researching social problems, such as depression and recovery or healthy family lifestyles, offers the challenge of identifying how power relations both regulate and generate experiences of freedom. Currently I am combining my passion for cycling and sustainable leisure/travel with research into women's experiences of cycle touring. (S.Fullagar@griffith.edu.au)

Jacqueline Gahagan: I am a Professor of Health Promotion in the School of Health and Human Performance and hold cross-appointments in Community Health and Epidemiology, Nursing, Gender and Women's Studies, and International Development Studies. I am also the founding Director of the Gender and Health Promotion Studies Unit at Dalhousie University. My current research projects are related to gender and HIV prevention, access to health services among rural males, community-based research ethics, and sexual health indicators. I am a founding member of WOW! Women On Water—a community-based health promotion project to encourage women to take up the sport of sailing in Nova Scotia. (Jacqueline.Gahagan@dal.ca)

Heather J. Gibson: I am an Associate Professor in the Department of Tourism, Recreation, and Sport Management at the University of Florida. I am interested in the meanings people hold regarding their favorite forms of leisure (including sport and tourism) with a view to understanding how such participation contributes to their health and well-being, particularly in later life. I love to be physically active. Being outside, walking, skiing, and cycling in all types of weather is what I like to do, although blue skies and sunshine are preferred! (hgibson@hhp.ufl.edu)

Audrey R. Giles: I am an Associate Professor in the School of Human Kinetics at the University of Ottawa. I conduct feminist, poststructural, and typically ethnographic research with Aboriginal peoples, especially women, in Northern Canada. My interdisciplinary research touches on all of the following areas in some way: leisure studies, sport, physical activity, health, anthropology, Aboriginal studies, and women's studies. I have a particular interest in writing and teaching about qualitative research methodologies. My spare time is spent running with the best training partners in the world: my dogs. (audrey.giles@uottawa.ca)

Maureen Harrington: I was born in London, Ontario, Canada and have lived in Queensland, Australia since 1995. I obtained a Ph.D. in Sociology from University of California, Santa Barbara (1988) and am now a Senior Lecturer in the Department of Tourism, Leisure, Hotel, and Sport Management at Griffith University. My research areas are volunteerism in leisure events and sport, women's work, leisure, and active and health policy. My present research is in the area of family leisure, children's sport, healthy lifestyles, and notions of risk. When not studying other people's leisure, I enjoy working in my herb garden and raising German Roller canaries, which are much sought after by other breeders across Australia. (m.harrington@griffith.edu.au)

Karla A. Henderson: I am a Professor in the Department of Parks, Recreation, and Tourism Management at North Carolina State University. My interests in scholarship relate to leisure behavior, gender and diversity, youth development through organized camp programs, physical activity promotion, and research methods (particularly related to qualitative data). I have had wonderful opportunities during my career to meet colleagues from all over the world at various conferences and professional meetings. I am passionate in my leisure about running, hiking in the Rocky Mountains, playing my trumpet, socializing with friends, and writing. (karla_henderson@ncsu.edu)

Ray Hibbins: I am a sociologist with research specialization is migration, gender, ethnicity, and sexuality. I have published in journals concerned with transnationalism, migration, entrepreneurship, leisure, and masculinities, and have written book chapters and co-edited books in these areas. Recently I became involved in research on internationalization of the curriculum, the attributes of global citizenship, sustainability, and transformational learning. I am chair of the Cultural Diversity and Internationalization Community of Practice at Griffith University in Australia and have conducted symposia on language issues and multifaith issues in the classroom. I enjoy listening to live performances of world and classical music, bushwalking, and visiting art galleries. (r.hibbins@griffith.edu.au)

Margo Hilbrecht: I am the Associate Director, Research for the Canadian Index of Wellbeing at the University of Waterloo. My research interests focus on time use, leisure, wellbeing, and the work-family interface. I am especially interested in what happens to family life when parents' work routines are at odds with children's school and activity schedules. My current research examines self-employment and how it affects time with family, time for personal leisure, and perceptions of quality of life. I enjoy spending time outdoors, taking vacations with my family, visiting galleries and museums, and eating good food prepared by someone else. (mhilbrec@uoguelph.ca)

Shewanee Howard: I am an Assistant Professor in the Department of Health Promotion and Physical Education at Ithaca College and have been teaching at the secondary and collegiate level for over ten years. I have studied abroad and co-directed a study abroad program in international health. My teaching experiences include the areas of psychoactive drugs, human sexuality, and minority health disparities. I received my doctorate from Miami University, where I examined black women's experiences of teaching in the black female body at predominately white institutions. Current research interests include topics that discuss the intersections of race, age, class, sexuality, and the challenges black women face teaching in the academy. I look forward to developing a global service-learning program in the Caribbean. (howard@ithaca.edu)

Susan L. Hutchinson: I am an Associate Professor in the School of Health and Human Performance at Dalhousie University in Halifax, Nova Scotia. My research focuses on leisure's role in coping with chronic health conditions. Time with my son Cole and my book (and wine) group are both important to me. As a graduate student at the University of Georgia, I was awestruck to meet Karla Henderson, Val Freysinger, Sue Shaw, Deb Bialeschki, and Leandra Bedini at my first Leisure Research Symposium. That was over ten years ago, but I continue to be awestruck. I am honored to contribute to this new volume. (Susan.Hutchinson@dal.ca)

Corey W. Johnson: I am an Associate Professor in Counseling and Human Development Services and the Institute for Women's Studies. I teach courses in leisure history/philosophy, research methods, and experiential education. My qualitative inquiry focuses attention on non-dominant populations in the cultural contexts of leisure, providing important insight into the discriminatory practices and experiences that marginalized people often encounter in mainstream leisure settings. My leisure includes horseback riding, traveling abroad with my husband Yancey, and hiking, camping, cooking, playing with my dogs Foucault and Butler and torturing my kitty-cat Eve. (cwjohns@uga.edu)

Fiona Jordan: I am the Postgraduate Scheme Director of the Bristol Business School at the University of the West of England in the UK. My research interests focus on the experiences of women traveling alone, the links between tourism and body image, and exploring representations of tourism in popular cultural forms such as women's and men's lifestyle magazines. As you might expect given my academic interests, I enjoy traveling and am fortunate enough to be able to do plenty in both my work and social life. (Fiona.Jordan@uwe.ac.uk)

Tess Kay: I entered leisure research in 1981—and never left! Since then, although much of my work has had a sports focus, all of it has been underpinned by a fundamental belief that studying leisure provides a unique and exceptionally powerful way of understanding everyday life. I am particularly fascinated by the relationship between leisure, family, and cultural identity. The opportunities I have had to work with colleagues in diverse global regions exploring these issues have been truly life-enhancing experiences. (tess.kay@brunel.ac.uk)

B. Dana Kivel: I am an Associate Professor and Chair of the Department of Recreation, Parks, and Tourism Administration at California State University, Sacramento. My scholarly interests include identity formation, LGBT youth, identity and ideology, issues of leisure and social change, and social justice. I have a herd of cats. I love Bikram yoga, and I'm very active in my neighborhood, working with neighbors and allies to strengthen one of the oldest and most disenfranchised communities in Sacramento. (kivelb@saclink.csus.edu)

Sherryl Kleinman: I've been a Professor in the Department of Sociology at the University of North Carolina, Chapel Hill for 30 years. My work is qualitative, and I've studied many settings and groups through the lens of symbolic interactionism: a seminary, a holistic health center, detectives, and medical students. My latest book is Feminist Fieldwork Analysis (Sage, 2007). I've published creative nonfiction and poetry, attending workshops in the U.S. and in Paris—a city that reminds me of my hometown of Montreal. I thought of myself as a textual rather than a visual person until last summer, when I bought a digital camera. The literal lens has given me a new look on the world.

Kevin D. Lyons: I am a Senior Lecturer and Head of Leisure and Tourism Studies at the University of Newcastle, Australia. My research interests over the past 15 years have focused primarily upon community and outdoor leisure services, with an ongoing interest in gender and leisure. My research interests recently have shifted toward the area of youth development through tourism, which has involved research on young adults who participate in volunteer tourism and international cultural exchange experiences. I have long loved to travel to far-flung places but am developing a great appreciation for the simple pleasures of rediscovering my local neighborhood when I go for bicycle rides with my young son. (kevin.lyons@newcastle.edu.au)

Diana Parry: I am an Associate Professor in the Department of Recreation and Leisure Studies at the University of Waterloo. Using a feminist lens, my research explores the personal and political links between women's leisure and women's health, broadly defined. My research privileges women's standpoints and aims to create social change and enact social justice by challenging the medical model of scholarship. (dcparry@uwaterloo.ca)

Amanda L. Paule-Koba: I am currently an Assistant Professor in Sport Management in the School of Human Movement, Sport, and Leisure Studies at Bowling Green State University. My primary research areas are gender equity policies, Title IX, and issues in intercollegiate athletics. Specifically, I examine areas in which reform is needed in collegiate athletics, such as the NCAA Division I recruitment process and academic clustering of athletes. I am passionate about working toward creating a better environment for collegiate and high school athletes in the United States. (apaule@bgsu.edu)

Catherine A. Roster: I am an Associate Professor in the Department of Marketing and Information Decision Sciences at Anderson School of Management, The University of New Mexico. My scholarly research examines how self-identity impacts decisions to acquire, perpetuate, or discontinue involvement with objects or consumption experiences, with special emphasis on related factors such as macro-level societal norms and micro-level interpersonal influences. I also conduct methodological studies that explore data quality and quantity issues associated with Internet surveys. I enjoy camping, white-water rafting, and geocaching in the mountains close to my home. (roster@mgt.unm.edu)

Diane M. Samdahl: I am a Professor in the Recreation and Leisure Studies Program at the University of Georgia. I also serve on the faculty for the Institute for Gender Studies and the Qualitative Inquiry Program. My background is in sociology. My early studies of outdoor recreation were a catalyst that helped me see the gendered nature of leisure spaces and spurred my interest in studying women's leisure. More recently, I have studied the ways leisure mirrors and maintains social inequities, as well as the potential within leisure to reshape cultural norms and discourse. Away from work, I enjoy spending time with my dogs and cats, wonderful friends, and good books. (dsamdahl@uga.edu)

Dorothy L. Schmalz: I am an Assistant Professor in Parks, Recreation, and Tourism Management at Clemson University. My research interests include the effects of stereotypes and social stigma on participation in recreation and leisure activities from the perspective of those who are subjects of stereotypes and those who possess and impose stereotypes. I would also like to explore how a change in perspective about individual differences can positively affect development, and the relationship between hobby cooking and health. In my own leisure, I enjoy cooking, a glass of wine with friends and family, running, and participating in triathlons. (schmalz@clemson.edu)

Sheila Scraton: I am an Emeritus Professor at Leeds Metropolitan University, having recently retired from being Professor of Leisure and Feminist Studies and Pro-Vice-Chancellor (research). My research interests include all aspects of gender power relations in sport, leisure, and physical education, feminist theories, women and football (soccer), older women and leisure, and the complex intersections of social categories, particularly gender, race, ethnicity, and age. My own leisure has always involved activity and my soul can be found amongst the mountains, lakes, and rivers where I love to walk (with my new knees!) and have wonderful memories of mountaineering, climbing, and canoeing. Being a granny is now also very special. (S.J.Scraton@leedsmet.ac.uk)

Charlene S. Shannon: I am an Associate Professor in the Faculty of Kinesiology at the University of New Brunswick in Canada. My research has focused on women's leisure, links between leisure and health, and parental influence on children's leisure. I am the Leisure Education Coordinator for the Paediatric Lifestyle Management Program at UNB, and I work to empower parents of children who are overweight or obese to facilitate changes in child and family leisure behaviors. I have recently returned to a leisure activity I quit when I was 14—dance—and am enjoying tap, jazz, and hip-hop classes. (cshannon@unb.ca)

Susan M. Shaw: I am a Professor in the Department of Recreation and Leisure Studies at the University of Waterloo, Canada. My research revolves around the many interconnections between work, family, and leisure, and the gendered nature of those connections. I have long been interested not only in how leisure and leisure practices reflect inequalities at individual and societal levels but also how leisure and leisure research can contribute to social change and social justice. I look forward to adding new interests and new adventures, as well as more leisure and more time for family, in my retirement years. (sshaw@uwaterloo.ca)

Kimberly J. Shinew: I am a Professor in the Department of Recreation, Sport, and Tourism at the University of Illinois at Urbana-Champaign. My research focuses on studying marginalized populations. Most of this research has examined the leisure behavior of African Americans and Latino(a)s. I seek to delineate the complex relationships between race/ethnicity and leisure behavior and services. I also examine issues affecting the leisure behavior and services of women. I strive to highlight the factors that can make leisure and leisure services problematic for these groups. In my leisure, I enjoy traveling, hiking, running, climbing, and camping with my family. (shinew@ad.uiuc.edu)

Monika Stodolska: I am an Associate Professor in the Department of Recreation, Sport and Tourism at the University of Illinois. My research focuses on leisure behavior of ethnic and racial minorities and on constraints on leisure. In my studies, I explore the effects of race and ethnicity on leisure behavior of recent immigrants, the adaptation processes among minority groups, transnational networks among immigrants, discrimination in leisure settings, physical activity among minority populations, and the use of natural environments for leisure. In my free time, I love to hike in the Rocky Mountains, ski, and travel. (stodolsk@uiuc.edu)

Anne-Marie Sullivan: I am an Associate Professor in the School of Human Kinetics and Recreation at Memorial University of Newfoundland. My teaching includes ethics in recreation service delivery, therapeutic recreation, leadership, and group dynamics. I am interested in family leisure, particularly the impact of life events on leisure engagement for the individual as well as the family unit. I also hope to examine how leisure education may be used to provide assistance for individuals facing such events. My own leisure revolves around my three young daughters and enabling them to "practice what I preach," and someday soon I hope to find more time to devote to my own interests. (am.sullivan@mun.ca)

Susan Tirone: I am an Associate Professor in the School of Health and Human Performance with a cross-appointment in the College of Sustainability at Dalhousie University in Halifax, Nova Scotia, Canada. My recent research focuses on leisure experiences of families and youth who are marginalized by poverty, race, and ethnicity, and by ability/disability status, and on the diverse experiences of the communities of marginalized groups. In my leisure I enjoy time with family and friends, my book club and choir, rug hooking, and walks along the shores and coastal barrens in the community where I live. (susan.tirone@dal.ca)

Dawn Trussell: I am an Assistant Professor in the Department of Recreation and Leisure Studies at Brock University. My research focuses on diverse social contexts and issues of power and social inclusion, particularly related to constructs of gender, family, age, and rurality. I also have a keen interest in methodological issues in the research process when working with vulnerable and socially marginalized populations (i.e., children, youth, and those living in poverty). In my leisure time, you will find me on the volleyball court, canoeing, and hiking backcountry trails in the mountains. (dtrussell@brocku.ca)

Beccy Watson: I am a Principal Lecturer in the Carnegie Faculty of Sport, Education, and Leisure at Leeds Metropolitan University, UK. My teaching includes sociology of leisure and sport across undergraduate and postgraduate levels, and my research students at the Ph.D. level reflect the dynamic and multidisciplinary nature of all that contributes to leisure and sport studies. I am particularly interested in the interrelationships and intersections between gender and social relations including race, ethnicity, and aging. I am currently one of the managing editors of Leisure Studies, which enables me to have lively and current engagement with our field. I live right in the city but I am outdoors at every opportunity. I walk and cycle everywhere, as I don't have a car by choice—it's part of a (possible) radical future. (R.Watson@leedsmet.ac.uk)

PREFACE

Leisure, Women, and Gender is part of an ongoing examination that explores and elaborates issues of leisure for girls and women. The book is both an update of *A Leisure of One's Own: A Feminist Perspective on Women's Leisure* (1989) and *Both Gains and Gaps: Feminist Perspectives on Women's Leisure* (1996) and a departure from these earlier works, in its process and structure. Specifically, in this volume, rather than writing *about* the research that others are doing, we invited some of those researchers to talk about how they came to study leisure, women, and gender; what they have learned from their research; and to reflect on directions for future research. Hence, organizationally and structurally it falls in the "middle ground" between a coauthored and an edited book: it mixes writing by the book's editors with the voices of invited scholars, who contribute central and additional perspectives regarding the topics.

We undertook this collaborative project because although recognition of the gendered realities of girls' and women's lives seems to be evident in most Western societies, and literature about women and leisure has grown in the disciplines of leisure sciences/studies, questions can be raised about the changes that have occurred and the new opportunities that are emerging. Has "progress" been made in girls' and women's access to recreation and leisure, are we witnessing a stalled revolution, or is it a bit of both? Further, although women's leisure remains central to this book, in contrast to our previous books, a critical analysis of girls' and women's leisure from the perspective of gender relations is centered. This perspective led to changes in how the subject of women's leisure is thought about and studied, as well as attention to emerging research on the gendered nature of men's leisure lives. Insight into the power that gender (as well as age, race/ethnicity, sexual orientation, age, social class, and able-bodiedness) has in shaping the lives of both males and females can help explain the meanings and values of leisure for all individuals and for society more broadly.

Hence, the purpose of this book is to present a critical analysis of the research to date and propose directions for the future study of leisure, women, and gender. Previous analyses that we offered focused primarily on social-psychological perspectives and gender *differences*, with some acknowledgment of broader sociological and cultural analyses. In this book, we purposely structure a broader analysis. The guiding metaphor for this book (both conceptually and structurally/organizationally) is the *matryoshka*, the (originally) female Russian "stacking doll" that is constituted of many layered figures. The matryoshka expresses our vision of girls'/women's lives, in that each figure can be seen as representing individual, social-historical, cultural, or political "selves."

At the same time, the matryoshka constitutes a complete entity, meaningless without its many bodies and representative of the intersections of the personal, social, historical, cultural, and political. This metaphor can also be extended to a conceptualization of gendered relations that ultimately cannot be understood separately from race, age, class, sexuality, and able-bodiedness. Hence, in this book we explore some of the many practices and contexts of girls' and women's lives, and the gendering of *all* of our lives. At the same time, we recognize that the separate sections, chapters/readings, and discussions that comprise the book inevitably intersect in many ways that the organization of this text cannot capture. The book is organized by five sections: background and context; personal lives; lives in social contexts; culture, power and politics; and ways forward. In these sections, the book's authors, as well as the voices of some of those conducting research on women, gender relations, and leisure are heard. While we frame and provide some context, the research, stories, and critical reflections of various scholars illuminate and provide depth and breadth for each section.

Further, this book is situated unabashedly within a feminist framework. Although some individuals have argued that "feminism is dead" and too many people believe feminist perspectives are no longer needed, we believe that the principles of feminism continue to be relevant. As long as sexism exists, women around the world are oppressed, and patriarchy dominates the world's cultures, a commitment to feminist issues is vital.

The thesis of this book is that people's lives (both women's and men's) may be enriched through opportunities for leisure. Examining and reflecting on gender relations empowers individuals to work for personal and social changes that will do much to enhance the leisure lives of women and men. We hope this book provides a synthesis of where an understanding of women, gender, and leisure is after the first decade of the twenty-first century, and will provide a framework for future activism as well as future research. Most of the chapters and discussion in the book focus on Western cultures, since this is where research on women, gender, and leisure has been concentrated to date. Nevertheless, we have included discussion on other cultures where possible, and we hope that the text itself will stimulate an interest in research within diverse cultures and around the globe.

Although the primary audience for this book is graduate students, researchers, and senior undergraduates, we have written it in a way that also makes it accessible to a wider audience. We explain the terminology used and incorporate examples that illustrate concepts and theories. We seek to put together the most current thinking about leisure issues relevant to girls/women and boys/men as we introduce ideas and provide a lens for examining the meanings, experiences, and practices of leisure.

Clearly, many people are responsible for this book—colleagues, mentors, friends, and family—and this holds for every contributing author to this book. We cannot begin to acknowledge all the individuals who, at different times and at different places in our lives, have contributed to this book. The matryoshka may be the most apt metaphor to show how each of us has been influenced by so many others and by the culture and historical moment in which we live.

We foresee that this book will be the last one that we will write together, but we look forward to other scholars continuing to examine these topics as long as gender inequity exists in any culture in the world. Despite the distance we have come and how much our understanding has increased, much work still needs to be done. Hence, this book is both a summary of our understanding about leisure, women, and gender and a call for future explorations of this topic.

SECTION 1
SETTING A CONTEXT

Chapter 1
Introduction:
Constructing a Framework

Valeria J. Freysinger, Susan M. Shaw, Karla A. Henderson, and M. Deborah Bialeschki

This book is about leisure, women, and gender. All three topics are important individually, but in this book we examine the meanings and importance of their intersections. Leisure is a relatively recent concept in Western cultures, although in Asia, people used symbols for leisure centuries ago (Lui, Yeh, Chick, & Zinn, 2008). Ancient Greek philosophers also discussed the cultural ideal of leisure as early as the first century A.D. This Greek ideal, however, pertained to aristocratic or free males only and shaped the lives of the many female and non-aristocratic others whose labor made this leisure possible. The *study* of leisure, however, is largely a twentieth-century phenomenon. Yet until the 1980s, the topic of women and leisure was mostly unexamined. In fact, we maintain that even into the twenty-first century, a focused analysis of leisure, women, and gender remains an important area for exploration.

Many gains have been made in women's lives and in understanding women, gender, and leisure since research on this topic began over 25 years ago. At the same time, gaps are still evident. While many countries have passed laws to make discrimination against women in various aspects of society illegal, one only has to read the daily newspaper or go online to see that such discrimination still exists. Over 20 years, ago, Hochschild and Machung (1989) brought attention to the *second shift* that women who worked outside the home faced when they came home and also had predominant responsibility for household labor and childrearing. They coined the term *leisure gap* because of their finding that "just as there is a wage gap between men and women in the workplace, there is a general 'leisure' gap between them at home" (p. 4). This gap continues today, as illustrated by a number of chapters in this volume. However, not only do some differences exist between females and males in the amount of time available for leisure, as Hochschild and Machung suggested, but gaps of various kinds important to leisure also exist *among* women. Women who are poor, for instance, may face different leisure gaps than women gainfully employed in professional jobs; most women in England experience life in a much different way than most women in Tanzania. At the same time, women have fought and sought to find leisure in their lives, and the participation of girls and women in various leisure pursuits seems to be increasing universally.

Gender influences everybody's life from the time he or she emerges as a baby into the world until his or her dying days. Children are taught and negotiate an "appropriate" gender identity (both consciously and unconsciously) from the first day forward, through the clothing they wear, the ways they are encouraged (or not) to use their bodies, and the toys they want/are given. Gendered *discourses*, or the ways in which "being female/feminine" and "being male/masculine" are talked about, practiced, and enacted, are both implicit and explicit in people's lives. Gender in all its manifestations (e.g., bodily practices, emotional expression) is also enacted in play, recreation, and leisure, as many chapters in this volume illustrate.

Gender is relational; that is, it is constructed and reconstructed in relation to and interaction with other individuals within the contexts of society, culture, and history. Leisure offers a venue not only for the reproduction, but also for the resistance and transformation of gender (Shaw, 2001). The lives of all men and women are gendered, but beyond this, they are also differentiated by race, class, sexual orientation, age, and cultural background. Hence, while we find commonalities among many women and between women and men, we also find diversity and difference, as well as inequality. We contend that all individuals should have the opportunity to seek meaning, identity, and a high quality of life—however those are defined—and that leisure potentially plays an important role in this regard.

The purpose of this book is to examine these many issues by presenting a critical analysis of research and proposing directions for the future study of leisure, women, and gender. The five sections of the book address background and context, personal lives, lives in social contexts, power, culture, and politics, and ways forward. This first section of the book sets the foundation for subsequent sections by discussing the ideas that inform our discussion of leisure, women, and gender, as well as by acknowledging the assumptions that underlie those ideas. This first chapter starts to do this through a discussion of girls' and women's lives today, the intersection of leisure, gender, and culture, the centrality of gender relations, and different ways of thinking about leisure.

GIRLS' AND WOMEN'S LIVES TODAY

What are some of ways gender makes a difference in girls' and women's lives and leisure? Finding reliable data on girls' and women's lives to answer this question and that document trends, changes, and progress can be a challenge. At the United Nations (UN) World Conference on Women, held in China in 1995, the Beijing Platform for Action was developed and adopted. An important part of the action plan was to gather longitudinal statistical data from UN member states throughout the world to document and monitor progress (or lack thereof) towards gender equity. The purpose was to use these data to promote social policy and action at national and international levels that would improve women's lives. Since that time, data have been collected every five years on issues ranging from demographic information (births, marriages, divorces, households, etc.) to education and literacy, work and wages, and health. Data are available for each reporting country, grouped according to six geographic regions (Africa, North America, South America, Asia, Europe, and Oceania). This major undertaking by the UN has been hampered by the lack of availability of gender-based data on some issues from some countries. Nevertheless, based on the most recent statistics available (United Nations, 2006), some, albeit limited, progress towards equity is evident.

One example of progress in the UN report relates to school enrollment. In most of North and South America, Asia, Europe and Oceania, girls' rates of enrollment in secondary education (high school) are similar to boys' level of participation. At the post-secondary (tertiary) level, girls' rates of participation tend to be lower than boys' in many countries, but female enrollment has actually increased in a number of Western industrialized nations where enrollment in university programs (undergraduate) is higher for women than for men. According to Paula Dobriansky (2006), Under Secretary for Democracy and Global Affairs at the UN, government programs that provide scholarships and stipends that help poor families send their daughters to school have improved the status of girls' education in countries such as Bangladesh, Brazil, Colombia, Kenya, and Mexico.

Of course, these data need to be treated with caution because of the lack of information from some countries and because of the low levels of access to education for either gender in some regions of the world. Illiteracy remains a problem, particularly in parts of Asia and Africa, and when the problem exists, rates of illiteracy are higher for women than for men. Specifically, while it is estimated that one-sixth of the world's population is illiterate, two-thirds of the illiterate are female (Dobriansky, 2006). In some instances it is only the wealthy—and boys from wealthy, upper-class families—who receive adequate education. Yet it is estimated that worldwide "for every year beyond fourth grade that girls attend school, wages rise 20%, child death drops 10%, and family size drops 20%." Specifically, research in Africa indicates that "agricultural yields" can be increased by more than 20% by investing in women's education (Women's Funding Network, 2009).

The data on other indices of gender equity also provide a mixed picture in terms of the current status of women. Among those countries reporting data on women's economic activity, women's level of participation in the paid labor force tends to be about 50% or less of men's participation level. That is, men are twice as likely to have *paid* jobs. In those countries reporting relatively high rates of female labor force participation, for example in Europe, many more women than men work part time. Further, even among full-time workers, there is a persistent wage gap, with women receiving less income than men. For example, in the United States, which has one of the highest rates of female employment, the latest data (full-time employees only) show women's median annual earnings as a percentage of men's earnings hovers around 78% (IWPR, 2009). While this is up from the 62% that women earned compared to men in the 1960s, a gap still exists. Moreover, a study of the wage gap among college graduates in the U.S. reported that among recent university graduates, women's salaries averaged only 80% of the salaries of their male counterparts, and this gap increased and women dropped further behind in the years following graduation (AAUW, 2007). The authors of this study controlled for a range of factors, including hours of work, occupation, and parenthood. They concluded that, "a large portion of the gender pay gap is not explained by women's choices or characteristics" (AAUW, 2007, p. 2). Similar research with similar findings has been conducted in other countries, such as Canada and the United Kingdom (e.g., Statistics Canada, 2006). Given gender differences in employment and wages, and the feminization of poverty around the world, it is perhaps not surprising then that the World Food Organization reports that 7 out of 10 of the world's hungry are women and girls (Women's Funding Network, 2009).

This income inequity does not affect all women equally, and there is considerable evidence that women of color and women with disabilities face higher rates of income discrimination wherever they live in the world. For example, aboriginal women and visible minority women in Canada have lower incomes than women of white heritage (Statistics Canada, 2006). In the U.S., African American women earn only 69 cents for every $1.00 earned by men, and Latinas earn only 59 cents in comparison to their male counterparts for each dollar earned by men (NOW, 2009). As a result, the risk of living in poverty is higher for women than for men, and it is particularly high for women of color (Women of Color Policy Network, 2009). Parental status and marital status also influence the risk of poverty among women (but not among men), with single-parent mothers all too often finding it extremely difficult to escape the poverty trap.

Another ongoing gender equity issue is that of health. Women, on average, have higher life expectancy than men, but women have higher rates of disability (perhaps because they live longer) and higher rates of hospitalization (United Nations, 2006). For women, reproductive health is a major concern. Many women, however, do not receive adequate reproductive or prenatal care (United Nations, 2006), which puts their reproductive choice, their health, and the health of their children at risk. While reproductive medical technologies that are available in some parts of the world may be seen as progress and a boon to women's health, some note that "women's health is put at risk with inadequately studied pharmaceuticals and technologies, women's bodies are increasingly medicalized in these biomedical processes, and women are under increasing pressures to produce particular types of children, whether they be of a particular sex or ability" (Jesudason, 2006). In parts of Africa, there remains a tragic HIV/AIDS epidemic, despite the fact that medications and treatments have successfully stemmed the tide of this disease in the West. Moreover, in parts of Africa with a high incidence of HIV/AIDS, women have higher rates of infection and higher death rates due to AIDS or AIDS-related complications than men. Another ongoing problem in all parts of the world is violence against women, particularly partner violence, family violence, human trafficking, and war-zone violence. Physical and sexual assault and abuse are associated with a range of health-related problems. For example, violence against women is one factor that helps to explain why women are more likely than men to struggle with mental health issues (Statistics Canada, 2006).

It is evident from the comparative statistical data that progress towards gender equity is painstakingly slow. Moreover, these problems are much more severe for some women compared to others, based on race, class, ability/disability, societal norms, values, and ideologies. Women who live in the "majority world" (i.e., the non-Western world, or the less wealthy parts of the world where most of the world's population lives) often face a multitude of challenges, although these are not always well understood because of the lack of research and data. This is not to say that women in the "minority" (or Western, industrialized, wealthy) world no longer face equity issues. Despite some progress, women in these more privileged nations still face the wage gap, work-related problems, fear of violence, and expectations about responsibilities for household labor and childcare. One issue that has been given particular attention over the years, as noted previously, is that of *work-life balance* (Hochschild & Machung, 1989). In particular, evidence of the increasingly high levels of time stress, role overload, and work-family conflict, especially among employed mothers and/or women who care for other dependent family members, continues to be found (Bedini, this volume; Zuzanek, 2004). This is related to increasing hours of paid work, changing work cultures, and the increasing responsibilities of parenthood (Harrington, this volume; Lyonette & Clark, 2009; Shaw, 2008). Employed women with children have always worked a *double shift* (Hochschild & Machung, 1989), but now both components of that double workload appear to be increasing. While large numbers of women have entered the work force in recent decades, there has been comparatively little change in the gendered distribution of household and family responsibilities. At the same time, governmental social policies have not kept pace with the need for social and community services (such as maternity, parental, and family leave), and the provision of affordable and accessible childcare. These services are lacking not only in the parts of the world with fewer economic resources, but also in many wealthier nations, such as the United States.

Linked to the lack of "women-friendly" policies or policies that promote gender equity, is the lack of women with political power. The UN data show that women are underrepresented in national or state governments throughout the world (United Nations, 2006). Looking at each UN-defined region, the average percentage of parliamentary seats held by women (among reporting countries or areas) is 33% in South America (based on 11 countries or areas reporting), 21% in Europe (40 countries), 20% in Asia (41 countries), 17% in North America (21 countries), 13% in Africa (49 countries), and 6% in Oceania (13 countries or areas). The states with the highest representation of women in parliament are Sweden at 45%, and Denmark and Finland at 38%. Nine countries or areas reported zero representation of women, including Kuwait, Saudi Arabia, the Solomon Islands, and Tonga. Countries around the world also evidence many contradictions in the political status of girls and women. For example, in India where Indira Gandhi became an influential leader in the later 20th century, female infants "were routinely killed or starved because they were deemed less valuable than boys" (Jesudason, 2006). Thus it is clear that global gender equity at the political level, as well as at the economic and social levels, remains an elusive goal.

This brief overview of some of the gender equity issues that national and international agencies and researchers are continuing to document clearly has relevance for the discussion of leisure, women, and gender that we are engaging in through this book. The notion of *leisure in society* (Coalter, 1999) highlights the *embeddedness* of leisure and the impossibility of separating leisure from the personal, social, cultural, economic, and political components of everyday life. Access to work, education, and healthcare, as well as freedom from poverty, racism, heterosexism, ageism, and ableism, and the violence and stress these engender, all affect opportunities and choices, including opportunities for leisure, as a number of chapters in this volume present (Anderson; Howard, this volume). Continuing inequities based on gender indicate the importance of a gender-based analysis of leisure, and also one that is sensitive to diversity and inequities among girls and women, and boys and men.

THE INTERSECTION OF LEISURE, GENDER, AND CULTURE

The challenges that women and girls face with regard to everyday life and leisure are experienced at different levels. On an individual level, women and girls (and men and boys) can face discrimination and harassment in the workplace, at school, in the community, and in leisure. Racism, sexism, and heterosexism, as well as negative attitudes to disability, can prevent or limit participation in leisure and can also limit the freedom of individuals for self-expression and positive identity development through leisure. Boys who are interested in activities that do not fit their culture's traditional, dominant definitions of masculinity may be particularly likely to be stigmatized by others (Johnson, Kivel & Johnson; Schmalz, this volume). Opportunities for girls in so-called "masculine" activities increased in Western societies in particular in recent years, through the enactment of Title IX in the United States and human rights legislation in other countries. Yet, opportunities remain unequal (Paule-Koba, this volume), and there is evidence of an increasing problem for girls related to the pressures to conform to a particular "feminine" image that idealizes very low body weights and/or a sexualized appearance at least among some populations/cultures in some countries (Shannon, this volume). These issues cause some children and teens to turn away from desired activity and/or to feel uncomfortable about their participation (James, 2000). For women, difficulties associated with work and family responsibilities, health, stress, and economic resources can limit leisure participation, especially among those who are caring for young children or other dependent family members (Frisby; Sullivan, this volume). There is evidence, too, that the movement towards *involved fatherhood* (Kay, 2009a; Shaw, 2008) and men's increased participation in childcare activities, has increased the time stress and lack of leisure for some men as well (Duxbury & Higgins, 2009).

Given these various challenges, it is clearly important to understand the individual leisure experiences, meanings, and challenges for girls, boys, women, and men in different life situations. Understanding these experiences can be an important stimulus for change. Nevertheless, there are limits to a focus on experience and change at an individual level only. The influence of social contexts and cultural factors also need to be taken into account. Sometimes individual-level understanding tends to locate the problem *within* the individual and tends to encourage the individual to adapt to the "system." This is evident in the growing "self-help" book industry, which has been highly lucrative in North America and elsewhere. For researchers, though, seeking to bring about societal as well as individual change, an understanding of different social and interactional contexts is also needed, as well as an understanding of broader societal influences, ideologies, and discourses.

Many of the challenges that individuals face in terms of their leisure arise out of, or are shaped by, life contexts. Social interactions at home, at work, or at school may be supportive and helpful, enhancing opportunities for leisure and self-development, or they may be difficult, stressful, and constraining. Most likely, they are a complex mix of both positive and negative interactions and meanings (Trussell, this volume). Community relationships also affect individuals and families in terms of acceptance and inclusion and/or rejection and social isolation. There may or may not be community support for women from diverse backgrounds who face challenges at home or in their everyday lives (Shinew & Stodolska, this volume). And there may or may not be neighborhood-based opportunities for leisure, relaxation, and social engagement. In any case, the importance of social context suggests the need to better understand the variety of interpersonal interactions and negotiations that occur in different leisure settings.

Consideration of societal contexts is also central to researchers concerned about understanding leisure meanings and leisure practices and working towards gender equity within the leisure sphere. By bringing together notions of power, culture, ideologies, and discourse, a broad perspective on the politics of leisure is possible, which provides additional insight into ways in which inequities in leisure are reproduced and resisted at various levels (Dionigi; Gibson, Jordan, & Berdychevsky; Roster, this volume). One approach for feminist researchers is through a focus on patriarchy and the role that patriarchal beliefs and relations of power play in the perpetuation of inequalities linked to education, work, income, health, and human rights (Fullagar, this volume). This approach points to the devaluation of women and of the feminine in patriarchal societies. At the same time, researchers face the challenge of recognizing diversity within patriarchal oppression (Giles, this volume). That is, other axes of power also need to be incorporated into the analysis, including power relations associated with race, class, cultural background, sexual orientation, ability/disability, and age.

A related approach is working to unmask culturally constructed ideologies of domination, inferiorization, and oppression. This includes understanding how ideologies associated with sexism, racism, heterosexism, and other "isms" are perpetuated and how these dominant ideas influence behaviors, attitudes, and access to resources. A way to do this is to explore how societal ideologies influence leisure policies, and how these policies, in turn, affect opportunities and participation, i.e., how ideologies influence leisure. Another way is through analysis of different media (e.g., television, movies, video games, fashion shows, newspapers, magazines) to document the ways in which media representations reinforce and/or challenge dominant beliefs about femininity or masculinity (Delamere & Dixon, this volume). That is, the focus is on the various different and contradictory ways in which leisure practices (such as watching television or playing video games) can influence societal ideologies or beliefs.

The idea of discourse is central here too, since discourse, or the ways in which everyday issues are talked about, practiced, and enacted, have a powerful influence on the conceptualizations and beliefs that come to be associated with those issues. Sherryl Kleinman's chapter on "Why Sexist Language Matters" provides a compelling argument for the need to become aware of the political and ideological power of everyday language and how the words that we use are not trivial, but have potentially damaging and/or empowering consequences. This understanding of language and everyday discourse can help to link our personal experiences of leisure and leisure activities with social and interactional contexts, and such understanding can also show how these experiences relate to societal ideologies and culturally based systems of belief.

Our point here is not to value one type of research over another but rather to emphasize the wide range of research approaches, issues, topics and perspectives that make up the body of feminist research on leisure (Aitchison, this volume). Clearly, research about personal lives, social contexts, power, culture, and politics can make distinct contributions to understanding but must also be considered as a whole. Indeed, it is sometimes difficult to separate these three areas of concern. What can be seen to tie these different approaches together is a gender-relations approach that recognizes that notions about gender are constructed and reconstructed, reproduced and resisted at all levels of social life. Further, challenges at one level of practice can and do have repercussions for other levels (Sullivan, 2004). Thus, through this book we sought to not only present research using different approaches and focus on different topics, but to illustrate the interconnections within the growing body of research on women, gender, and leisure. At the same time, the research presented is, in multiple ways, a *select* and thus incomplete representation of research in this area.

GENDER RELATIONS

Discussing girls and women and their leisure in the twenty-first century requires that the notion of *gender relations* be central to the discussion.

Some research, focusing solely on women, has been partially effective in making women's lives visible and calling attention to the androcentric nature of traditional history. The concept of gender relations, however, allows for an understanding of the constructed and reconstructed lives of both males and females within the broader context of culture and history. The study of gender relations provides an analysis of relationships of power, of how and why gendered discourses advantage/empower some and disadvantage/disempower others. Gender is relational in that it is produced, reproduced, and sometimes contested/resisted and transformed in everyday interactions with individual others, society, and culture. Gender relations are based on cultural distinctions that have been made of biological sex, and these distinctions may constrain or enable leisure for women and men.

When biological sex is perceived at birth as female or male, numerous social and cultural expectations are immediately put onto the child. One's biological sex leads to a lifetime of relationships and expectations, opportunities and constraints, based on gender. That is, gender is an ongoing process rather than an inborn biological trait. People learn and transform gender, they *do* or *perform* gender, in every context of their lives. Both women and men begin *doing* gender very early and continue with those performances throughout life. While some males and females resist dominant gender ideologies, gender remains a *practice* that shapes everyone's lives (Kimmel, 2004; West & Zimmerman, 1991). At the macro level, gender is evident as a set of structured power relations that are enacted through law, legislation, and policy. At the micro level, gender relations are produced and reproduced by the everyday activities, interactions, and practices of individuals (Scraton & Watson, this volume).

Gender scholarship addresses the complexity and fluidity of the practices and discourses, the expectations, roles, and behavior that we enact in being female and male. Further, as Deem (1986) suggested, "gender is emphatically not 'a woman's problem!'" (p. 30). Put in another way, gender is a discourse that shapes everyone's life and that we all contribute to, negotiate, accommodate, and transform.

Gender theory may focus on gender roles, identities, relations, socialization, or whatever the yardstick for the measurement or conceptualization of gender happens to be. The relationship of gender to leisure is interactive. In other words, leisure may provide a way for women or men to embody and/or resist the discourses of gender. In terms of the former, gender is enacted in an individual's leisure when, for example, expectations of femininity and motherhood prevail or masculinity and physical strength are emphasized and considered the norm. When and how this occurs is the focus of a number of the chapters of this book.

NOTIONS OF LEISURE

Leisure studies is a contemporary area of inquiry, although, as noted previously, the concept of leisure was addressed originally by ancient Eastern, as well as early Greek, philosophers. Leisure is thought about and studied in a number of different ways. These various notions of leisure reflect larger ideological differences among those who conduct research on this subject. In addition, understandings of leisure occur in the larger context of knowledge production across fields of study. While we feel that it is important to briefly address the different notions of leisure here, the scholarship presented in the remainder of this book perhaps more powerfully illustrates the diverse and fluid thinking about leisure.

"Traditional" Ways of Studying Leisure

Free time, *discretionary activity* or *recreation*, and *individual experience* have been the ways leisure has been traditionally defined in industrialized societies (particularly North American societies). These notions of leisure are useful in documenting differences between groups of individuals, but they also *may* essentialize, dichotomize, de-contextualize, and de-politicize leisure. They arose out of the push for empiricism, objectivity, and quantification in research, policy, and practice.

For example, *leisure as time* refers to discretionary periods in one's life that are available to do whatever one wishes. Leisure is the time beyond that needed to do work or daily maintenance activities. 'Leisure' was initially defined simply as "free time" that typically meant non-work (non-paid labor) time. However, some feminists have objected to the definition of leisure as non-work time because it assumes that all work is paid work. Some women, as well as some men, are not part of the workforce, so considering leisure only as the opposite of paid work negates important unpaid activity such as maintaining a household, childrearing, community volunteer activities, and personal care. Further, only examining leisure as a particular type of time leaves out individuals' experience of time (e.g., freedom and a sense of a lack of entitlement to, or guilt about, free time), meanings they associate with time, opportunities available, and the perceived and actual amount of time available—all factors that affect whether individuals even perceive the time as leisure as well as their enjoyment of it.

When leisure has been studied as *activity*, it typically has focused on *what* recreation pursuits or "play" are done by various individuals (and groups of individuals) during free time and *how frequently*. In the sense of activity, "recreation" and "leisure" often have been used interchangeably. It is assumed that this activity generally is pursued for its own sake and for fun, and it is also assumed that such activity is positive and beneficial for the individual and/or society. As with time, leisure as activity is relatively easy to measure because it is quantifiable. However, in defining "leisure" as activity, it is often assumed that time is available for activity participation, that these types of opportunities exist for everyone, and that all consider the same activities to be leisure. As studies of gender and leisure (including several chapters in this volume) have shown, none of these assumptions is necessarily so.

In reaction to the limitations of definitions of leisure as time and activity, leisure as individual experience, as perception and state of mind, became a common way to conceptualize leisure. In this definition, importance was placed on the perception of freedom of choice as a prerequisite for leisure. Leisure as experience suggested that what a person did or when a person did it was not what mattered. What mattered was how an individual felt about an experience. Leisure from a state-of-mind perspective is defined by the *perception of* free choice, that something is done for its own sake, and a sense of control (Henderson et al., 2001). Wimbush and Talbot (1988) described, however, that for women all leisure is a *relative* freedom because of how gender is constructed. The same might be said for some men as well because *choice* is framed by more than gender. While quantitative scales and methods (e.g., Experience Sampling Method) have been developed to assess leisure as perception or state of mind, qualitative research methods seem to be a more useful approach, as evidenced by a number of chapters in this volume. This research highlights the often positive experiences and emotions of leisure—enjoyment and pleasure, satisfaction, relatedness, and improved mental health, to name a few (Hutchinson; Parry, this volume). Further, qualitative research has highlighted that separating individuals from the contexts of their lives tells only part of the story about leisure, women, and gender.

Leisure as/in Context

Definitions of leisure as free time, discretionary activity, and experience focus primarily on the individual. These definitions of leisure often separate leisure from other contexts of human activity, and they are how leisure is commonly studied in the U.S. (Coalter, 1999). Coalter noted that leisure is *in* society and therefore connotes a greater social-cultural context than suggested by some of the more personal-individual definitions of leisure as free time, activity, or state of mind. More recently, and particularly outside of North America, leisure as experience in context, a social construction (i.e., as legitimated pleasure), and/or discursive practice have been given attention.

For example, one area that has received attention is the physical environment (the places and spaces) and cultural contexts that give leisure importance. According to Tuan (1977), the concept of space has absolute and relative dimensions with concrete boundaries. Place is perceptually and socially produced by individuals. Thus, spaces become places when they mean something significant. The physical place may be less important, however, than the meanings that people attach to places in their minds as they participate in leisure. Wearing (1998) described how women may experience public spaces in different ways than men and the ways in which that experience impacts women's leisure. Skeggs (1999) explored how gay bars are leisure places for the enactment of gender but are used and experienced by gay women and men, and straight women, in different ways—that is, gender intersects with other identities in shaping the meanings of space. Others have found that because people's homes represent many aspects of their lives, they may or may not be viewed as places for leisure, and this perspective may be truer for women if they do not have a "room of their own" for leisure (Hilbrecht, this volume). That is, leisure is constructed as individuals interact with ever-changing social situations and cultural contexts.

Leisure as part of culture calls for an integrated view of leisure; a view that conceptualizes leisure as occurring, and gaining meaning, in time and space. *Individual preferences* are not independent of social and cultural practices and discourses. People often "choose" activities based on social experiences, what others around them are doing, and the cultural community of their lived experiences (see chapters by Berbary and Samdahl, this volume). Further, social norms and mores are enacted, negotiated, and sometimes resisted in leisure, and they certainly shape gendered leisure. The symbolic meanings of leisure often come from accommodation to a culture (Tirone & Gahagan, this volume). As discussed by Rojek (1989), leisure time and space are continually made and remade by the actions of people in their social worlds.

The cultural embeddedness of leisure results in further challenges to defining leisure with any degree of consensus. Iwasaki and colleagues (Iwasaki, Nishino, Onda, & Bowling, 2007) described how problematic constructing a notion of leisure is from a global, and particularly linguistic, perspective. These authors asserted that "leisure" is an ethnocentric term used mostly in North American and European thinking that evokes the dominance and intrusion of Western thinking. While not using the term "leisure" may be one way to resolve some misunderstandings, not having a term may also make interpretations of leisure a challenging process.

The Complexity of Leisure

All these notions of leisure suggest the complexity of the construct. Leisure clearly can be thought about and studied in more than one way. The thinking about how leisure should be defined evolves and is disrupted as ways of producing knowledge and dominant discourses change. Certainly, understanding leisure, women, and gender with the traditional approaches of time, activity, and experience, provide particular insights. At the same time, the ideas of multiple identities, the reflexive self, the breakdown of clear divisions between work and leisure, and the ambiguous and contradictory aspects of postmodern existence resonate with many researchers (e.g., Rojek, 1995), including feminist scholars (e.g., Wearing, 1998) who have been critical of traditional definitions of leisure. The various ways of envisioning leisure indicate what is problematic about *essentializing*, or suggesting only one way to think about, leisure (Aitchison, 2000a). Understanding leisure requires "both-and" rather than "either-or" thinking. This is the tension that exists among the variety of definitions and the idea of commonality of experience that is often sought in order to advocate for a group such as women. However, we believe that accounting for the situations and subjectivities of individuals as well as the possibility of shared experiences among individuals continues to be a challenge worth addressing. Hence, how leisure is described socioculturally as well as *in situ* (Henderson, 2006) is important.

Recognizing that definitions of leisure and interpretations of its meanings will always be incomplete and fluid should not stifle putting new ideas forward and continuing to analyze the what, how, and why of leisure. Wrestling with diverse and often ideologically incompatible notions of leisure is only one of the challenges those who study and talk about leisure face, but it is a challenge all the contributors to this book ably meet/explore in their respective chapters.

CONCLUSIONS

Women's and men's leisure is not just individual experiences nor merely a social practice, but both of these and more. Understandings of women's leisure require an examination of gender as relational. The perspective of gender relations also highlights that gender is "not [only] a woman's problem" (Deem, 1992). That is, gender shapes men's lives and leisure as well, and different men are affected differently (Hibbins, this volume). In addition, this perspective reminds us that "men can be feminists, too" (Lyons, this volume). The ideologies, discourses, practices, social institutions, and institutionalized sexism that inform and frame leisure must be taken into account and explored. Finally, research continues to document the myriad ways that girls and women are disadvantaged worldwide, at the same time that it indicates stark differences among women within any country and between women who live in the "majority world" and those who live in the "minority world" (Kay, this volume).

Feminists seek to illuminate such differences. They advocate for equity and justice and for women (and all people) to have control over their lives. Leisure, at least in Western cultures, can be seen as one area of life that is associated with greater freedom of choice, and thus leisure provides a potential context for empowerment. Leisure has the potential to facilitate self-development, liberation, and change in many aspects of people's lives. However, as a gendered discursive practice, leisure also has the potential for continued exclusion and oppression, for disempowerment. This complexity of women's/gendered leisure is illustrated by the other chapters in this section and the diversity of research approaches and topics presented by the contributors to this book.

REFERENCES

Aitchison, C. C. (2000a). Poststructural feminist theories of representing others: A response to the "crisis" in leisure studies discourse. *Leisure Studies, 19*(3), 127–144.

American Association of University Women (AAUW). (2007). *Behind the pay gap*. Washington, DC: American Association of University Women. Retrieved from http://www.aauw.org/learn/research/behind-PayGap.cfm

Coalter, F. (1999). Leisure sciences and leisure studies: The challenge of meaning. In E. L. Jackson & T. L. Burton (Eds.), *Leisure studies: Prospects for the twenty-first century* (pp. 507–522). State College, PA: Venture Publishing, Inc.

Deem, R. (1986). *All work and no play? The sociology of women and leisure.* Milton Keynes, UK: Open University Press.

Dobriansky, P. (2006, September 25). The education of girls in the developing world. Retrieved from http://www.ungei.org/news/247-1140.html

Duxbury, L., & Higgins, C. (2002). *The 2001 national work-life conflict study: Final report*. Ottawa, ON: Health Canada.

Duxbury, L., & Higgins, C. (2009). *Work-life conflict in the new millennium: Key recommendations from the 2001 National Work-Life Conflict Study*. Ottawa, ON: Canadian Policy Research Networks.

Henderson, K. A. (2006). False dichotomies and leisure research. *Leisure Studies, 25*(4), 391–395.

Henderson, K. A., Bialeschki, M. D., Hemingway, J., Hodges, J. S., Kivel, B., & Sessoms, H. D. (2001). *Introduction to recreation and leisure services* (8th ed.). State College, PA: Venture Publishing, Inc.

Henderson, K. A., Bialeschki, M. D., Shaw, S. M., & Freysinger, V. J. (1996). *Both gains and gaps: Feminist perspectives on women's leisure*. State College, PA: Venture Publishing, Inc.

Hochschild, A., & Machung, A. (1989). *The second shift: Working parents and the revolution at home*. New York, NY: Viking.

Institute for Women's Policy Research (IWPR). (2009). *The gender wage gap: 2008*. Washington, DC: Institute for Women's Policy Research. Retrieved from http://www.iwpr.org

Iwasaki, Y., Nishino, H., Onda, T., & Bowling, C. (2007). Leisure research in a global world: Time to reverse the Western domination of leisure research? *Leisure Sciences, 29*, 113–117.

James, K. (2000). "You can feel them looking at you": The experiences of adolescent girls at swimming pools. *Journal of Leisure Research, 32*, 262–280.

Jesudason, S. (2006). The future of violence against women: Human rights and the new genetics. *Women's Funding Network*. Retrieved from http://www.womensfundingnetwork.org

Kay, T. A. (2009a). *Fathering through sport and leisure*. London, UK: Routledge.

Kimmel, M. S. (2004). *The gendered society* (2nd ed.). New York, NY: Oxford University Press.

Lui, H., Yeh, C., Chick, G., & Zinn, H. (2008). An exploration of meanings of leisure: A Chinese perspective. *Leisure Sciences, 30*(1), 87–92.

Lyonette, C., & Clark, M. (2009). *Unsocial hours: Unsocial families? Working time and family wellbeing.* Cambridge, UK: Relationships Foundation.

National Organization for Women (NOW). (2009). *Women deserve equal pay.* Washington, DC: National Organization for Women. Retrieved from http://www.now.org/issues/economic/factsheet.html

Neulinger, J. (1974). *The psychology of leisure.* Springfield, IL: Charles Thomas.

Rojek, C. (1989). Leisure time and leisure space. In C. Rojek (Ed.), *Leisure for Leisure: Critical Essays* (pp. 191–204). London, UK: Macmillan.

Rojek, C. (1995). *Decentring leisure.* London, UK: Sage.

Shaw, S. M. (2001). Conceptualizing resistance: Women's leisure as political practice. *Journal of Leisure Research, 33*(2), 186–201.

Shaw, S. M. (2008). Family leisure and changing ideologies of parenthood. *Sociology Compass, 2*(2), 688–703.

Skeggs, B. (1999). Matter of place: Visibility and sexualities in leisure spaces. *Leisure Studies, 18,* 213–232.

Statistics Canada. (2006). *Women in Canada.* Ottawa, ON: Social and Aboriginal Statistics Division, Statistics Canada.

Sullivan, O. (2004). Changing gender practices within the household: A theoretical perspective. *Gender and Society, 18*(2), 207–222.

Tuan, Y. (1977). *Space and place: The perspective of experience.* Minneapolis, MN: University of Minnesota Press.

United Nations. (2006). *The world's women 2005: Progress in statistics.* New York, NY: Economic and Social Affairs, United Nations.

Wearing, B. (1998). *Leisure and feminist theory.* Thousand Oaks, CA: Sage.

West, C., & Zimmerman, D. H. (1991). Doing gender. In J. Lorber & S. A. Farrell (Eds.), *The social construction of gender* (pp. 13–37). Newbury Park, CA: Sage.

Wimbush, E., & Talbot, M. (1988). *Relative freedoms: Women and leisure.* Milton Keynes, UK: Open University Press.

Women of Color Policy Network. (2009). *Race, Gender, and the Recession.* Retrieved from http://wagner.nyu.edu/wocpn

Women's Funding Network. (2009). Retrieved from http://www.womens-fundingnetwork.org

Zuzanek, J. (2004). Work, leisure, time-pressure, and stress. In J. T. Haworth & A. J. Veal (Eds.), *Work and leisure* (pp. 123–144). East Sussex, UK: Routledge.

CHAPTER 2
WHY SEXIST LANGUAGE MATTERS

SHERRYL KLEINMAN

Reprinted with permission from *Qualitative Sociology,* *25*(2), 299–304.

For 11 years, I've been teaching a sociology course at the University of North Carolina on gender inequality. I cover such topics as the wage gap, the "second shift" (the disproportionate amount of housework and child-care that heterosexual women do at home), the equation of women's worth with physical attractiveness, the sexualizing of women in the media, lack of reproductive rights for women (especially poor women), sexual harassment, and men's violence against women. But the issue that both female and male students have the most trouble understanding—or, as I see it, share a strong unwillingness to understand—is sexist language.

I'm not referring to such words as "bitch," "whore," and "slut." What I focus on instead are words that most people consider just fine: male (so-called) generics. Some of these words refer to persons occupying a position: postman, chairman, freshman, congressman, fireman. Other words refer to the entire universe of human beings: "mankind" or "he." Then we've got manpower, man-made lakes, and "oh, man, where did I leave my keys?" There's "manning" the tables in a country where we learn that "all men are created equal."

The most insidious, from my observations, is the popular expression "you guys." People like to tell me it's a regional term. But I've heard it in Chapel Hill, New York, Chicago, San Francisco, and Montreal. I've seen it in print in national magazines, newsletters, and books. I've heard it on television and in films. And even if it were regional, that doesn't make it right. I bet we can all think of a lot of practices in our home regions we'd like to get rid of.

Try making up a female-based generic, such as "freshwoman," and us-ing it with a group of male students or calling your male boss "chairwoman." Then again, don't. There could be serious consequences for referring to a man as a woman—a term that still means "lesser" in our society. If not, why do men get so upset at the idea of being called women?

What's the big deal? Why does all this "man-ning" and "guys-ing" deserve a place on my list of items of gender inequality?

The answer is because male-based generics are another indicator—and, more importantly, a *reinforcer*—of a system in which "man" in the abstract and men in the flesh are privileged over women. Some say that language merely reflects reality and so we should ignore our words and work on changing the unequal gender arrangements that are reflected in our language. Well, yes, in part.

It's no accident that "man" is the anchor in our language and "woman" is not. And of course we should make social changes all over the place. But the words we use can also reinforce current realities when they are sexist (or racist or heterosexist). Words are the tools of thought. We can use words to maintain the status quo or to think in new ways—which in turn creates the possibility of a new *reality*. It makes a difference if I think of myself as a "girl" or a "woman"; it makes a difference if we talk about "Negroes" or "African Americans." Do we want a truly inclusive language or one that just pretends?

For a moment, imagine a world—as the philosopher Douglas R. Hofstadter did in his 1986 satire on sexist language—where people used generics based on race rather than gender. In that world, people would use "freshwhite," "chairwhite," and yes, "you whiteys." People of color would hear "all Whites are created equal"—and be expected to feel included. In an addendum to his article, Hofstadter says that he wrote "A Person Paper on Purity in Language" to shock readers: only by substituting "white" for "man" does it become easy to see the pervasiveness of male-based generics and to recognize that using "man" for all human beings is wrong. Yet, women are expected to feel flattered by "freshman," "chairman," and "you guys."

And why do so many women cling to "freshman," "chairman," and "you guys?"

I think it's because women want to be included in the term that refers to the higher-status group: men. But while being labeled "one of the guys" might make women *feel* included, it's only a guise of inclusion, not the reality. If women were really included we wouldn't have to disappear into the word "guys."

At the same time that women in my classes throw around "you guys"—even here in the southern United States, where "y'all" is an alternative—they call themselves "girls." I'm not sure if this has gotten worse over the years or I've just noticed it more. When I was an undergraduate in the early to mid-1970s, we wanted to be women. Who would take us seriously at college or at work if we were "girls"? To many of my students today, "woman" is old enough to be "over the hill." A "girl" is youthful and thus more attractive to men than a "woman." Since they like the term so much, I suggest that we rename Women's Studies "Girls' Studies." And since the Women's Center on campus provides services for them, why not call it "The Girls' Center." They laugh. "Girls" sounds ridiculous, they say. The students begin to see that "girl"—as a label for twenty-one-year-olds—is infantilizing, not flattering.

"Girl" and "you guys" aren't the only linguistic problems on campus. A few years ago, Bob, a student in my class, said that his fraternity is now open to women as well as men and that a controversy had erupted over whether to continue to use the term "brother" to refer to all fraternity members, or to use "sister" for female members. Almost all the women in his fraternity, he said, voted to be called "brother" rather than "sister." As with "you guys," the women wanted to take on the word that has more value. Yet the practice of using "brother" reinforces the idea that a real member of the group is a brother (i.e., a man). I asked what would happen if he had suggested that all fraternity members be called sisters rather than brothers, or that they rename the fraternity a sorority. Everyone laughed at the absurdity of this suggestion. Exactly. Yet it is not absurd, but acceptable, to call women by the term "guys" or "brothers."

Since the "fraternity" Bob referred to is no longer exclusively male, and since gender is no longer a criterion for membership, I asked him how he thought others might react if he suggested they substitute "association" or "society" for "fraternity." Perhaps they could call both men and women "members," or, if students preferred a more informal term, "friends?"

"Yes, that makes sense," Bob told us. "But, I just don't think they'll go for it." He paused. "I'm not sure why."

We talked as a class about why this simple solution might meet with resistance. We concluded that many men would resist losing these linguistic signifiers of male superiority, and many women would resist losing the valued maleness implied by "brother" and "fraternity." "Member" would feel like a drop in status for both women and men!

The students, like most people who use male "generics," don't have bad intentions. But as sociologists, we know that it's important to look at the *consequences*. All those "man" words—said many times a day by millions of people every day—cumulatively reinforce the message that men are the standard and that women should be subsumed by the male category.

I worry about what people with the best of intentions are teaching our children. A colleague's five-year-old daughter recently left her classroom crying, after a teacher said, "What do you guys think?" She thought the teacher didn't care about what *she* thought. When the teacher told her that, of course, she was included, her tears stopped. But what was the lesson?

She learned that her opinion as a girl mattered only when she's a guy. She learned that men are the norm.

A friend's six-year-old son refused to believe that the female firefighter who came to his school to talk to the class—dressed in uniform—actually fought fires. The firefighter repeatedly referred to herself as a "fireman." Despite the protests of the teacher and the firefighter, the boy would not be convinced. "A fire*man* can't be a woman," he said. His mother, who is fastidious in her use of nonsexist language, had a tough time doing damage control.

So, is it any surprise that the worst insult a boy can hurl at another boy is "girl"?

We know from history that making a group invisible makes it easier for the powerful to do what they want with members of that group. Perhaps that's why linguists use the strong language of "symbolic annihilation" to refer to the disappearance of women into male-based terms. And we know, from too many past and current studies, that far too many men are doing "what they want" with women. Most of us can see a link between calling women "sluts" and "whores" and men's sexual violence against women. We need to recognize that making women linguistically a subset of man/men through terms like "mankind" and "guys" also makes women into objects. If we, as women, aren't worthy of such true generics as "first-year," "chair," or "you all," then how can we expect to be paid a "man's wage," be respected as people rather than objects (sexual or otherwise) on the job and at home, be treated as equals rather than servers or caretakers of others, be considered responsible enough to make our own decisions about reproduction, and define who and what we want as sexual beings? If we aren't even deserving of our place in humanity in language, why should we expect to be treated as decent human beings otherwise?

Some people tell me that making English nonsexist is a slippery slope. As one colleague said to me, "Soon we'll have to say waitperson, which sounds awful. We won't be able to 'man' the table at Orientation. And we'll become 'fellowpersons' at the Institute!" I told him that "server" works well. We can "staff" the table. And why not use "scholars" instead of "fellows"? We've got a big language to roam in. Let's have fun figuring out how to speak and write without making "man" the center. If sliding down that slope takes us to a place where we speak nonsexist English, I'm ready for the ride.

And this doesn't mean that every word with "m-e-n" in it is a problem. Menstruation and mending are fine. Making amends is good, too. There's only a problem when "men," as part of a word, is meant to refer to everyone (freshmen, chairmen, and so on).

Now and then someone says that I should work on more important issues—like men's violence against women—rather than on "trivial" issues like language. Well, I work on lots of issues. But that's not the point. Working against sexist language *is* working against men's violence against women. It's one step. If we cringe at "freshwhite" and "you whiteys" and would protest such terms with loud voices, then why don't we work as hard at changing "freshman" and "you guys"? Don't women deserve it? That women primarily exist in language as "girls" (children), "sluts" (sex objects) and "guys" (a subset of men) makes it less of a surprise that we still have a long list of gendered inequalities to fix.

We've got to work on *every* item on the list. Language is one we can work on right now, if we're willing. It's easier to start saying "you all," "y'all," or "you folks" instead of "you guys" than to change the wage gap tomorrow.

And what might help us make changes in our language? About a year ago I was complaining, as usual, about the "you guys" problem. "What we need is a card that explains why we don't want to be called guys!" Smita Varia, a veteran of my gender course, said, "Let's write one."

And so we did. Smita enlisted T. Christian Helms, another former student, to design a graphic for the card. You can access the layout of this business-sized card from our website: www.youall.freeservers.com. Make lots of copies. Give the cards to friends and ask them to think about sexist language. Leave one with a big tip after you've been "you guysed" during a meal. The card explains the problem and offers alternatives.

And institutional change is also possible. Some universities have adopted "first-year student" (instead of "freshman") because some students and faculty got angry about the male-based generics embedded in university documents. The American Psychological Association has a policy of using only inclusive language in their publications. Wherever you work or play, get together with other progressive people and suggest that your organization use "chair" instead of "chairman," "Ms." instead of "Mrs." or "Miss," "humankind" instead of "mankind," and "she or he" instead of "he." In my experience, members of some activist groups think sexist language is less important than other issues. But if we're going to work on social change, shouldn't we start by practicing nonsexist English among ourselves? Let's begin creating *now* the kind of society we want to live in later.

Nonsexist English is a resource we have at the tip of our tongues. Let's start using it.

References

Hofstadter, D. R. (1986). A person paper on purity in language. In D. H. Hofstadter, *Metamagical themas: A questing for the essence of mind and pattern* (pp. 159–167). New York, NY: Bantam.

"Hey, you guys!"

Imagine someone walking up to a group of guys and saying, "Hey, girls, how're ya doing?" We doubt they'd be amused! So isn't it weird that women are supposed to accept—even like—being called "one of the guys"? We're also supposed to like "freshman," "chairman," and "mankind."

Get over it, some people say. Those words are generic. They apply to everyone. But then how come so-called generics are always male?

What if generics ended in "white" (as in "freshwhite," "chairwhite," and "Hey, you whiteys!")? Would people of color like being called "one of the whites"? We don't think so.

The term "guys" makes women invisible by lumping them in with men. Let's quit doing that. When you're talking to a group of customers, gender doesn't really matter, so why not replace "you guys" with "you all," "folks," or "y'all." Or simply say "what can I get you?" That would take care of us all.

Thanks for your help.

Chapter 3
Many Voices: Historical Perspectives on Women's Leisure

Valeria J. Freysinger, Susan M. Shaw, Karla A. Henderson, and M. Deborah Bialeschki

What has more feelingly and pragmatically been said by people of color, by white women, by lesbians and gay men, by people with roots in the industrial or rural working class is that without our own history we are unable to imagine a future because we are deprived of the precious resource of knowing where we come from: the valor and the waverings, the visions and defeats of those who went before us. (Rich, 1986, p. 141)

Women have always worked, whether inside or outside of the home, and had leisure, whether plentiful or constrained. Yet the written record of women's experiences of leisure and work, and of their lives in general, is relatively limited. When analyzing the past two hundred years of primarily U.S.-American history, what can be seen is that the leisure of women is often misunderstood, understood only in relation to that of men, or even obscured, which is particularly true for the leisure of women of color, lesbians, and other marginalized groups. Historical "oversights" and inaccuracies often exist because of social definitions of appropriate activities for girls and women, and for girls and women of different backgrounds. Activities pursued by women for pleasure and enjoyment that were not a part of these social definitions (e.g., sex, sewing circles, sport) were not necessarily considered leisure by historians and thus overlooked. To further complicate issues, activities often associated with women and assumed to be leisure (e.g., caring for children, holiday dinners) were in reality not necessarily or always leisure. Additionally, only the leisure of the most visible and privileged group (i.e., white, middle-class, heterosexual women) has generally been described. Therefore, examples of primarily white women involved in the arts, physical activities, and hobbies are found to some extent in U.S. history (e.g., Dulles, 1965). Histories of industrialization and the emergence of *cheap amusements* such as dance halls, amusement parks, and movie theaters have included reference to working-class women's increased access to these new forms of leisure, or pleasure and choice (Peiss, 1986). Yet much is left unsaid and under-documented.

Leisure both shapes and reflects the cultural values of a society. In ancient Greece and more recently in the late 1800s in Great Britain and North America, a system of slavery or working-class labor made leisure possible for the upper classes that did not have to work to live. At other times, such as during the Protestant Reformation, leisure was equated with "idle time" and was condemned by religions that valorized work. Women were both subject to and part of such historical contexts, and additional circumstances existed that influenced their leisure. For example, women generally had inferior status in patriarchal societies starting in ancient Greece where, according to Plato, even a poor man had a slave—his wife. In Victorian Britain and North America of the late 1800s, women faced expectations and restrictions (e.g., perceptions of femininity, lack of economic independence, motherhood responsibilities) that often adversely affected their leisure. At the same time, the lives of upper-class women, "ladies of leisure," were made possible by the labor of working-class women and men, and indentured servants and slaves. In other words, the history of women's leisure is not a simple history. Rather, it is characterized by many consistencies *and* contradictions.

This chapter offers an historical perspective on women's leisure from both a "difference among women" and "differences between women and men" perspective. It also highlights the nuance and complexity of, and some of the historical considerations that have influenced (and continue to influence), women's lives and their leisure. It explores the pluralism and resulting diversities of women's lives, as well as the inequalities that can arise from these. It aims to provide examples of differences in leisure among women as well as how "men as a group" have oppressed the leisure of "women as a group." Considering how women experienced leisure in the past may provide insights into how similar, as well as how very different, women's lives and leisure are today.

Specifically, this chapter highlights some historical issues that are important to understanding women's leisure today. The topics range from the personal to the institutional, and from self and family to group and society. While many of these issues and topics are particular to the United States, some have parallels in other countries. All provide examples of how and why an understanding of history is important. Historical categories used to frame this chapter include the influences of the Victorian ideal of woman, notions of the ideal family, women's work, women's involvement in social reforms and voluntary organizations, and the early women's movement on women's leisure. First, however, how women's history is done, and the importance of doing women's history, are briefly discussed.

DOING WOMEN'S HISTORY

While knowledge about women's leisure has been growing in visibility in the past 20 years, the history of leisure largely has been a history of men's leisure. "Traditional" history generally conceptualizes the past in terms of the politics of power and conflict over material resources and ideological supremacy, so is framed around issues that structure men's lives and hegemonic notions of masculinity/femininity. The history of women, however, demands a different conceptualization and periodization than political history (Lerner, 1975). While it is not possible to separate women's history totally from that of men's, women's lives have been shaped not only by their engagement in and exclusion from the *public* sphere, including sites of paid labor and political life, but also dominated by the *private sphere*, or the world of reproduction, childrearing, and family caretaking, even when they were engaged in full-time work. Women's history tends to focus on a different set of social circumstances and issues, though even in such history, women who do not marry, have children, or conform to heteronormative ideals are often less visible.

Women's historical work can be likened to playing jazz (Brown, 1991). In jazz, each of the individual voices can go its own way but is held together by its relationship to others. When engaged in women's historical work, everyone "talks at once," with the effect of multiple rhythms played simultaneously. The people, their experiences, and the settings do not occur in isolation but in concert with other events and people. Historians studying women's lives often try to move away from traditional history by giving voice to the diversity of women who shaped history. Women's history is concerned with understanding how race, class, ethnicity, and sexuality have influenced women's and men's lives. Scholars of women's history face some of the same challenges of inclusion and representation faced by feminist theorists, however, and have approached women's history in multiple ways.

Women can be incorporated into history through a discussion of *notable* women or by looking at the contributions made by women in general. A focus on notable women certainly illuminates the abilities, achievements, and contributions of influential women. However, often the concept of noteworthiness is defined by patriarchal standards, and thus this approach often does not tell about the activities in which most women engaged, nor the significance of women's everyday activities to society (Lerner, 1975). *Contribution history* applies questions from traditional history to women and fits women's part into the empty spaces. The problem is that women's "contributions" are uncritically presented. For example, during World War II, many women in the countries who were part of the war were heavily involved in supporting the war effort through their work in industry. However, the capabilities of these women in the labor market were largely ignored when the United States, for example, returned to a peacetime economy and women were exhorted to return to hearth and home in order to make employment available to men. Thus, the contributions of women, while noted in traditional history, were not put in the context of what the patriarchal society needed at that particular time.

Another way to analyze the experience of women from a historical perspective is to consider the cultural context. Culture does not refer solely to behavior but rather to patterns of values, thinking, and beliefs that underlie behavior as a result of everyday experience (Luschen, 1974). Culture consists of gender beliefs, norms, and signs that construct what is "true" or acceptable for women and men. For example, Peiss (1986) described the culture of, and Victorian culture's influence on, white working-class young women in New York City by detailing the perceptions held about these women and how they engaged in the *acceptable* forms of recreation available to them.

The role of culture in the history of leisure, women, and gender is complicated because socially sanctioned expressions of femininity and masculinity are relative. They differ from era to era, from culture to culture, and from group to group within any given society. In addition to the fluidity of gender, cultural notions and practices of social class, race, ethnicity, age, sexual orientation, and able-bodiedness intersect with gender to define women's lives and leisure. In the past, some historians addressing "women's culture" viewed women's development of group identity and psychological autonomy as a way that women create themselves and actively construct social lives regardless of the larger culture (e.g., DuBois, Buhle, Kaplan, Lerner, & Smith-Rosenberg, 1980). Today, historians of women's lives are likely to question the notion of *women's culture* and its essentialist overtones, and to think of women's lives as discursive practices inseparable from the larger culture (Millward, 2007; Smith, 2010).

To meet the goal of restoring women to history that Kelly (1984) called for more than two decades ago, the historical context of women's lives must be examined. Perhaps a different historical approach to understanding women's leisure is needed—an approach that centers women as active agents of history rather than subjects and sidebars. Over the past 30 years, women's history has become an accepted area of academic study. Interest also emerged around areas such as lesbian history and the history of masculinity (e.g., Faderman, 1991; Katz, 1992; Kimmel, 1996a; Kimmel & Aronson, 2003). Feminism has been the foundation for many of these explorations. Still, Bennett (2006) asserted that we continue to see "patriarchal equilibrium" in that "women's low status vis-à-vis men has remained remarkably unchanged" (p. 4). This critical feminist problem cannot be ignored. An analysis of the past, understanding the changes (or lack thereof) in women's lives, and how women, men, and gender are enacted help to address this problem.

THE IMPORTANCE OF A FOCUS ON *WOMEN'S* HISTORY

In early feminist research, *women* were often centered. However, some claim that in the 1980s a shift from *women* to *gender* began to some extent, as a way to find political acceptability, because gender seemed less threatening and less exclusive than women (Mies, 2007). In addition, some scholars moved from a focus on *women* to a focus on *gender* because of new ways of thinking about women and the relational analysis gender suggests. That is, a focus on women *or* women and men *or* gender shifts the lens, the frame of thinking, and the kinds of questions that are asked and thus the insights that are gained. A feminist viewpoint focused on women provides an important lens for understanding how history informs current leisure issues for women. Bennett (2006) articulated in her research that women's history actually includes gender history and has a strong feminist connotation, with the advantage that women might be seen as "being a sort of mother—not a single mother, but a co-parenting mother—of gender history, the history of masculinities, and the history of sexualities" (p. 19). Although the term *women* may be theoretically challenging, both because of the diversity of women and fluid notions of womanhood, it is useful to the extent that it signifies opportunities and challenges that matter in a given context of time and place. In this chapter, the term *women* refers to the shared experiences as well as the differences in girls' and women's leisure within historical contexts, rather than serving as a way to universalize and minimize differences in their experiences. Acknowledging differences among women offers a way to increase understanding and promotes a unified—but not unitary—category of women (Bennett, 2006; Keenan, 2004). Although historical differences exist based on class, race, age, and sexuality, the characteristic of being female has consistently resulted in certain disadvantages due to patriarchal structures and practices. An examination of several historical issues illustrates this contention.

THE VICTORIAN IMAGE OF IDEAL WOMANHOOD

Women generally have been perceived as the weaker sex. Often this belief was based on the perception of absolute and universal biological/structural differences between women and men—specifically, women's narrower and smaller shoulders and broader pelvic girdles. Perhaps nowhere were these perceptions more apparent than during the Victorian era. These perceived differences were believed to make "running, throwing, striking, and climbing activities more difficult for her than the typical man" (Bowers, 1934). These average physical differences between the sexes were often attributed to Mother Nature or biological inevitability, and many myths developed to explain them. Perhaps the most pervasive myth to evolve was that of *female goodness* (Williams, 1977).

The myth of female goodness created an image of the ideal woman, assumed to be of white heritage and upper-class standing, as an ethereal person. She was put on a pedestal somewhere above the realities of life (Gerber, Felshin, Berlin, & Wyrick, 1974). This ideal was praised in endless writings and from pulpits, which brought pressure on all women to behave according to this image. To defy it was to be unwomanly. Hence, working-class women and women of color were believed to comprise a separate category of women, a category of individuals who were "less than" and "lacking" as women.

This Victorian ideal, and the behaviors required by much leisure, were often antithetical to each other. For example, leisure experiences involving physical exertion did not allow *gentility*. Physical activities connoted vigor, while the ideal woman was supposed to be delicate. Leisure occurring outside the home that allowed for expression of emotions also conflicted with the ideal woman's propriety and modesty. Passivity, obedience to her husband, circumspection, and most of all, a particular physical attractiveness, were deemed necessary to maintain the Victorian image of womanhood. By avoiding exercise, cultivating a pale face and *hourglass* figure, and "being incapable" of strenuous physical, intellectual, or emotional labor, a woman gave the appearance of gentility. To have facial color, muscular strength, and "coarse" features was a sign of both having to work for a living and a lack of femininity (Gerber et al., 1974).

The concept of the Victorian woman was not just the standard for evaluating femininity among upper-class white women. As noted, working-class women's "womanliness" was also judged according to this standard. Women of color were largely regarded as existing outside of this standard; hence, they were constructed as "others" due not only to gender, but also to race. At the same time, they were still held to this Victorian ideal and influenced by it. For example, women of color were sensitive to the desirable "pale skin" promoted by the ideal and lighter-skinned women of color were perceived as more intelligent, refined, and desirable as house-workers (Peterson-Lewis, 1993). The traditional African aesthetics around hair were also altered because of these ideals. For example, elaborate hairstyles symbolic of particular African heritages were abandoned in the United States during this time. Women of African heritage often wore scarves to cover their hair, and later, some women of color straightened their hair to fit the idealized notions of womanhood set for white women.

Expectations for women's physical characteristics and dress also reflected the desired ideal. Veblen (1899) believed that women's delicate and diminutive hands and feet and slender waist were seen as proof that a woman was incapable of useful effort and must be supported in idleness by her "owner" (i.e., husband, if married; or father, brother, or other male relative, if not married), which served as evidence of his strength. Veblen's view of the ideal woman reflected his criticism of capitalist society. He indicated that "in the modern civilized scheme of life the woman is still, in theory, the economic dependent of the man—she is still the man's chattel" (p. 222).

The dress expected of women was lamented by women who wanted to engage in physically active leisure activities. Women were to stay almost entirely covered from head to toe, and long skirts with layers of petticoats and corsets were the norm. Fashion not only hindered exercise but contributed to health problems and the preservation of the idea that women were the weaker sex. For example, medical research conducted by Dickinson (1887) showed that the corset exerted pressure—between 30 and 80 pounds—which weakened the abdominal wall and damaged the liver. While women were certainly held back by their own image of themselves and the precept that how their bodies looked was more important than how they felt (Kaplan, 1979), middle-class and higher-status women also often faced serious consequences for deviating from societal expectations. For example, an "ovariotomy," or surgical removal of the ovaries, could be prescribed if a woman was seen as eating too much, having too much of an interest in sex, or being "intractable" and uncooperative (Ehrenreich & English, 1973).

Yet some women defied the restrictions of dress and behavior and risked being perceived as less than womanly to pursue their leisure interests. Eleonora Sears, for example, in the early twentieth century, participated in men's sports such as polo and shooting as well as tennis, squash, and equestrian events. She was one of the first well-known women to appear publicly in pants with short hair, riding astride on her polo pony (Cahn, 1994). Mary Schaffer (1911), one of the explorers of the Canadian Rockies in the early 1900s, commented:

> Why must they settle so absolutely upon the fact that the lover of the hills and the wilderness drops the dainty ways and habits with the conventional garments and becomes something of coarser mould? Can the free air sully, can the birds teach us words we should not hear, can it be possible to see in such a summer's outing, one sight as painful as the daily ones of poverty, degradation, and depravity of a great city? (p. 14)

However, many physicians and other "experts" believed that women were physically and biologically incapable of participating in physical activity and sport (Cahn, 1994). Three social practices in particular reinforced the perceptions of women's weakness and caused them medical problems: (a) girls were usually confined to the house and not allowed to run, jump, and play actively; (b) tight lacing of corsets caused biological ailments; and (c) few acceptable forms of birth control were available other than being "sick," which only further contributed to the public image of women's general weakness and frailty. In addition, the unhealthy conditions of the times (e.g., polluted air, poor diet, crowded and unsanitary conditions in the cities) often compromised women's well-being (Gerber et al., 1974). Further, a major medical concern was "pelvic disturbances" as a result of "over-activity." Physical activity such as running, jumping, and skipping was viewed as having a harmful effect on reproduction and the reproductive potential of girls by "shaking up" the uterus and ovaries. Many people were also convinced that falls were inherently more dangerous for females because they might affect menstruation.

The supposed physical effects of physical activity were not the only concern. Some medical practitioners at the time believed the emotional strain of physical or intellectual leisure experiences could be injurious to the mental well-being of women. For example, Bax (1913) believed that women should not pursue physical leisure experiences because women were physiologically less well-developed than, and mentally inferior to, men. Even many women who believed that physical leisure experiences should be an option, believed that special care needed to be taken to avoid strains that could undermine either their physical or emotional stability (Bowers, 1934); hence, girls' "half-court" basketball that was played into the 1960s in the United States.

Gradually, the eighteenth- and nineteenth-century Victorian ideology surrounding women's place and the definition of femininity began to be less restrictive. Many of these changes grew from other social developments, such as women's involvement in the paid labor force, a redefinition of family and changing marital relationships, and the feminist movement (Mandle, 1979; Peiss, 1986).

THE IDEAL FAMILY

People have specific roles that they are expected to fulfill based on the gendered expectations and values of the society. For all women, this social indoctrination has restricted their choices to a greater degree than for men. Further, some women have been restricted more than other women. One such institution is family. Historically, for most girls, the world was the domestic circle of their family. Society ascribed to women the functions of childrearing and family nurturing. Until the latter half of the 1900s, in many countries around the world, formal education was not seen as necessary for girls to fulfill their life roles, and often education was perceived as in competition with domestic roles. Women's education was typically sporadic, if at all, and often interrupted. Women's capacity for reproduction was, and in most societies still is, seen as primary and perhaps even "sacred" because society needs women to bear children. Before the twentieth century, most women fully internalized the wife/mother role, perhaps because they perceived themselves as helpless to do anything else. Most women were told they should be interested and absorbed in maternal functions and not the outside world (Blackwell, 1875/1972). Therefore, women were legitimately visible in three ways: they married, they gave birth, and they died (Ulrich, 1979). Because the meaning of women's lives and leisure has been, and continues to be, tied to family, how family is thought about today cannot be separated from how it was constructed during the past.

Family can be thought about in at least two ways: family as a social and economic institution, and family as an ideology. Since the mid-1800s, family as a social and economic institution has been organized around households on the basis of close kinship relations that reflected a division of labor between the male (i.e., breadwinner) and the female (i.e., childrearer). However, family as ideology is often stronger than the reality of the institution (Barrett & McIntosh, 1991). For example, the ideological model of a traditional nuclear family has been promoted as "the family" in North America. At the same time, in many countries, both the socially constructed institution and ideology of family have gone through significant changes. Today, males are not the only, or primary, breadwinners. Nuclear families are neither the reality for, or desired by, many. Yet at the same time, many people in North America lament the "breakdown" of the family and wish to return to the traditional family of bygone days. What such nostalgia ignores are at least two facts. First, it ignores the extent to which the ideal of the traditional family produces a particular social organization of sexuality, intimacy, reproduction, motherhood, division of labor, and division of gender itself (Thorne, 1992). For example, during the mid-1800s, the Victorian middle/upper-class white family was seen and expected to represent the ideal family. In this family, women's roles became redefined around domesticity rather than economic production, men were relegated to the public sphere of paid employment, and children were thought to need an extended period for childhood in which they could play and thrive on the gentle maternal guidance rather than the patriarchal authoritarianism of the past (Coontz, 1988, 1992). While representing the social ideology of the family, the reality for most families was different. The majority of women and children worked in factories or on farms, and white women often hired household help (a sign of middle-class status) to accomplish the domestic tasks and the expanded responsibilities of childrearing. This help was usually provided by recently immigrated women who were seen as ethnic minorities, as well as African American women who after slavery had few other employment opportunities.

Further, notions of the "good old days" of the traditional nuclear family also ignore the fact that such a family structure was little more than a *blip* in human history (Coontz, 1992). In the United States, it is an ideology of family that was produced after the Depression of the 1930s and World War II, and continues today as one of the most powerful visions of family. During this time the extended families common in most of human history gave way to the rise of the ideal of the nuclear family. This organization of the family was needed by capitalist economies, and was made possible by social and economic policies that encouraged newly married couples to strike out on their own, establish single family dwellings, and move to the suburbs where they could escape the elder generation (Coontz, 1992). The U.S. government in the "boom years" of post-WWII was generous with the educational benefits, housing loans, highway construction, and job training that set the stage for family values and strategies that assumed cheap energy, low-interest loans, educational and occupational opportunities, and steady employment. These opportunities resulted in early marriages and childbearing, consumer debt, and extensive residential patterns. These changes produced the values of the 1950s family that emphasized producing a world of satisfaction, amusement, and creativity within the nuclear family to meet family members' personal needs (May, 1988). Childcare absorbed more than twice the amount of mothers' time as in the 1920s, and the time spent in housework actually increased despite the availability of labor-saving devices. At the same time, men were encouraged for the first time to root some of their identity and self-image in familial and parental roles (Coontz, 1992).

The ideal family of the Victorian era and post-WWII, however, did not exist for everyone in the United States. Many groups, for example, Native Americans and those whose ancestry was Japanese, Eastern European, Chinese, or Mexican, faced *structural inequalities* that made this ideal impossible, or it was an ideal inconsistent with their cultural heritage. For example, until the mid-1860s, many African Americans lived in slavery except for those individuals who were "free" and living in the North. For Southern slaves, the concept of family held by Whites apparently did not apply, because white slave owners continually broke up their family units by selling family members to another owner. After emancipation, many black families' experiences paralleled those of other poor, working-class families, but with the additional burden of racial discrimination. Indeed, for poor and racial- and ethnic-minority individuals in the United States across the first half of the twentieth century, this notion of family was not reflective of how family was constructed either ideologically or institutionally. The opportunities that produced the ideal family of 1950s United States were available primarily to middle and upper-class Whites and were often inconsistent with other notions of family. However, while the ideal of family was not generally available to or desired by those who were not white or affluent, they were still held to this standard and labeled dysfunctional when they did not conform.

This construction of womanhood that centered on the family had consequences for women's leisure. For many, leisure experiences were viewed as an extension of their mandated sex-roles and were unstructured, self-initiated, and generally connected with home and family duties. In the past, some used this gendered construction of family to explain gender differences in leisure. For example, Bowers (1934) contended that as the roles of homemakers and mothers were fulfilled, white women in particular often had few opportunities for social cooperation and teamwork. Thus, they were seen to differ in interests and tastes from men, who generally experienced competition and cooperative activities in the hunt, in tribal life, in war, and in the industrialized system. Historically, almost all women had to make leisure secondary to the needs of the family. Family was an important component, both positive and negative, for women's leisure and continues today to exert great influence on women's lives, regardless of social class, race, or other life conditions as the recent research presented in a number of chapters in this volume illustrates.

WORK IN RELATION TO WOMEN'S LEISURE

The previous discussion has shown how much of *women's work* was privatized within the household. Women who were relatively affluent were often not involved in visible labor or market activity, or their involvement was tangential. Scheduling of education, job training, and paid work was developed to fit the male life cycle (Lerner, 1977). The separation of the domestic, private sphere of women from the economic, public sphere of men has much to do with the inferior status of women historically (Lenz & Myerhoff, 1985; Rosaldo, 1974). Throughout history, however, some women defied social expectations. For example, working- (and some middle-) class white women and many women of color explicitly stepped outside what was expected when they worked outside the home even though they had young children. Other women involved themselves as volunteers in social reforms such as women's suffrage and the temperance movement, but carried out these activities within the context of their family responsibilities. These women defied women's sole commitment to the family, although social and economic policies did not exist to support their need or desire to work. Indeed in the second half of the nineteenth century, Elizabeth Blackwell (1875/1972), the first woman in the United States to graduate from medical school, encouraged women not to claim maternity as a barrier to their own self-achievement. She contended that the time had come to repudiate the idea that marriage and a practical life-work were incompatible. For working-class white women and many women of color, of course, the combination of marriage and paid work had always been a reality.

Prior to industrial society in the United States, for those who were free (i.e., not enslaved), the family often functioned as an economic unit. For example, in the agrarian setting everyone in the family contributed to the production of food. With the industrial revolution, however, men went to the public sphere of the marketplace while middle- and upper-class women continued to work at home. Fatherhood became connected with a man's successful performance in labor as a way to show he could provide for his family. In contrast, more affluent women became separated from the activities most valued by a society that measured value in monetary terms. Work in the home was not valued because it was not paid, and yet this is what women were to aspire to. This condition was a double jeopardy for many ethnic minority women and women of color who had no choice but to work outside the home. Many of these women found that domestic jobs were available, but were extremely low-paying because of the low status associated with this type of work, as well as because of racial and ethnic discrimination. At the same time, many Whites saw their work outside of the home as an indication that they were not "good" mothers (nor were white ethnic minority men or men of color seen as capable economic providers). Marriage and motherhood remained the socially approved *career* for most women regardless of class or race. This shift in the value of women's and men's roles was evident in the United States as well as other parts of the newly industrialized Western world.

The changes because of industrialization sharpened class distinctions among women. Many middle-class women began to enjoy the benefits of fathers' and husbands' increasing wealth. They had more relief from household drudgery and greater educational opportunities. They became *ladies of leisure* and epitomized the ideal toward which all women were supposed to aspire (Lerner, 1977). Such a woman was the social ornament that proved a man's success—her idleness, her delicacy, her childlike ignorance of reality gave a man *class* that money alone could not provide (Ehrenreich & English, 1973).

Throughout the industrial revolution, the labor of lower-class women was required to make possible a growing middle class. Unlike men, however, entry into paid work did not mean improvement of women's status. For employed women, industrialization meant a day of double burdens. Outside work was added to home and childcare responsibilities. Further, women often felt guilty for working outside the home and rationalized that the work was only temporary (Lerner, 1977). This cultural rationalization provided an excuse for employers to pay women less than men. As temporary help and as females, the feeling was that these women only required *pin money* (that is, a little extra cash or "allowance" for personal purchases that were seen as "luxuries," such as pins). Thus, work designated as *women's work* became characterized by poor pay, low status, and no security. According to Lerner (1977), industrialization yielded one positive outcome for women. Because of the demands of industrial society, some women were able to overcome the educational discrimination that had kept them subordinate. When they faced obstacles to entering into professions, these women organized separate female institutions such as women's colleges, seminaries, and medical training schools. In the process, a *new woman* evolved who became economically independent and whose feminist consciousness found expression in the demands for rights and the organization of groups that worked for social change.

As industry became more mechanized, sex differences in physical strength should have become increasingly irrelevant to occupational qualifications and perceptions of work as appropriate for women. This was generally not the case, though perceptions of sex differences in physical strength were shown to be unfounded during wars. The U.S. Civil War proved the arbitrariness of assigned sex roles related to work. Some women moved from the confines of their homes to engage in demanding previously male-defined work, such as managing farms and plantations (Welch & Lerch, 1981). During the years of World War II, women in many of the Allied nations filled jobs formerly held by men such as munitions workers, welders, and builders. "Rosie the Riveter" was part of a national campaign exhorting women to enter the workplace to support the war effort. Yet, after each of these wars, patriarchal policies and values (e.g., female passivity, dependence, nurturance, submissiveness, subordination) returned. Work and leisure activities that were incompatible with these values were seen as a threat to power relations between the sexes, that were predicated at the most basic level on male strength and female weakness (Lenskyj, 1986).

The implications of unpaid and paid labor for women's leisure are many. First, the popular definition of leisure centered on the idea that leisure was a needed opportunity to recuperate from time spent at work. The non-work or free time of paid workers gave them the right to leisure in order to relax and recuperate so that they could return to work refreshed and more productive. This definition of leisure was problematic for women who were unpaid workers in the home. Their "free" time from paid work was filled with unpaid household and childcare work. These homemakers were often perceived as not earning the right to leisure because they were not making valued financial contributions to the family. Therefore, leisure was an experience seen as existing outside the realm of women's rights or needs. Housewives often felt guilty for wanting to take time for themselves. Their need or desire for leisure as recuperation was not easily justified. Leisure experiences requiring money were difficult for most homemakers because they were struggling just to feed and care for their children, were economically dependent, and often did not have responsibility for controlling household money even if they had earned it.

Another common misperception of women who worked full-time and unpaid in the home was that all of their time was leisure. The work they were doing was not linked to a cash product, and it happened within the private sphere of home. A homemaker's free time was to be filled with activities such as childcare, cooking, and cleaning. These activities were to be done "*at* her leisure" or perhaps more accurately, "*as* her leisure." However, this assumption that homemakers did nothing or only pleasurable activities of their choosing was inaccurate for most women.

Yet some women who worked exclusively within their homes found opportunities for leisure, or at least made their daily obligatory activities as leisure-like as possible. Women often used household obligations as a way to fulfill leisure needs. For example, in agricultural areas, cornhusking, maple sugar gathering, harvesting, quilting bees, and other sewing tasks provided women with practical forms of enjoyment. These activities were at least in part recreational because they gave women an opportunity to socialize with other women and get out of their own homes, and to get their work done in a pleasant and enjoyable way.

For women who were employed outside the home, leisure experiences remained primarily home-based and home-centered. By the end of the nineteenth century, however, long hours of work and "unhealthy" leisure pursuits led to a concern for the quality of life, especially for men. This concern was heightened with the onset of WWI, when many men were found to be unfit for military service. Some companies (e.g., Kellogg in Battle Creek, Michigan) started employee recreation programs in which some women participated. Formal employee recreation programs were the result of changing social forces, increased education, and an acceptance of leisure. Industries supported employee recreation in the early 1900s to promote loyalty, fellowship, high morale, and physical and mental health among their employees (Tober, 1988). Although female workers continued to face restrictions because of sex-role expectations, they were able to be involved in some programs. However, most of these programs were racially segregated for both women and men.

A good example of the relationship between gender, paid employment, and leisure can be found in the young working girls employed in the mills and factories at the turn of the century in the United States. As the industrial revolution progressed, working-class constructions of gender were influenced by the changing organization and meaning of leisure itself. Specifically, the ongoing development of capitalism affected the organization of work and time, and intensified the commercialization of leisure in the late nineteenth and early twentieth centuries. This commercialization provided new *cheap amusements*. The young single women working in the mills and factories were one such market. Yet, for these young wage-earning women, separate and autonomous leisure was problematic. The cultural ideologies about women's roles did not support this conception of womanhood or leisure, while their working status within the capitalist economy encouraged this orientation. Their pursuit of leisure led them to the newly emerging forms of commercial recreation such as dance halls, amusement parks, and movie theaters. These cheap amusements became the place where a working-class variant of the New Woman emerged. This New Woman linked the heterosocial culture to a sense of modernity, individuality, and personal style (Peiss, 1986). The leisure pursuits of single working-class women, however, usually ceased with marriage and motherhood. This example shows that while leisure activities may affirm the cultural patterns embedded in other social institutions (e.g., work) they may also offer an arena for the articulation of different values and behaviors (Peiss, 1986).

The leisure norm for working women, nevertheless, was similar to women working within the home, in that their leisure experiences were scarce. The leisure that did occur in women's lives at this time was often linked to other life aspects such as work and family responsibilities, social obligations, and economic considerations. Regardless of whether women worked for pay because of choice or necessity, or without pay in the home, the leisure and the free time that many men had access to were not seen as the right of most women. Thus, many women sought ways to create social change, and in so doing, legitimized their free time.

SOCIAL REFORM MOVEMENTS

The emergence of social movements all over the world, such as the woman's rights or anti-slavery movement, has frequently been dependent on a class of educated women with free time and leisure (Lerner, 1979). Women in such movements called upon the *leisured class of women* to take upon them-selves what some saw as the *world's highest work*. In the 1870s in the United States, Blackwell (1875/1972) called upon the rich, married women, the childless wives, and the old wives (the latter two groups in earlier days were despised and set side) to become the standard-bearers of a higher culture. She challenged these women who had leisure not to fritter it away for themselves and to use it to make positive changes in the world. These educated *leisured* women shaped history not only through their economic lives, but through community-building and politics. Women built com-munity life as members of families, as conveyers of cultural and religious values, and as founders and supporters of organizations and institutions working for social and political change (Lerner, 1977).

In the United States, the late 1800s and early 1900s were years filled with social reforms, and women were instrumental to the success of many of these movements. These movements were often based on compassion, spirituality, and concern for improving the quality of family life—particu-larly for the waves of immigrants from Europe and emancipated southern Blacks migrating north for jobs and a better life. For many women, the transition from the private sphere of the home to the public sphere of political action was tenuous, yet justifiable when viewed as an extension of the prescribed roles of women related to caregiving (e.g., prohibition, laws against child labor, voting rights). Educated white middle class wives probably benefited most from the newfound freedoms, the advances in industrialization and technology, and leisure activities.

The impulse for organizing seemed to arise whenever an urgent so-cial need was perceived and remained unmet. Social issues and movements such as the Women's Christian Temperance Union, anti-slavery, settlement houses, birth control, the American Equal Rights Association, and the National Woman Suffrage Association, were examples of types of *righteous* concerns and organizations that women felt were within their realm of ac-tion. The growth of women's clubs and especially women's involvement in the abolition (anti-slavery) movement were central to the emergence of the first American feminist movement. Through such activities, many women gained autonomy without being perceived as deviating from prescribed sex roles.

A common setting for many of these social reform activities was the church. The private sphere of the home was the only domain of influence for most women, but as *moral guardians of society*, many women found the more public sphere of the church a comfortable setting in which to conduct their social work. The church became a place for self-help, leader-ship roles, and social welfare efforts (Higginbotham, 1993). These efforts were apparent in black churches at the turn of the century. These churches came to signify a public space that was denied to African Americans in the rest of the community. These churches often contained schools, libraries, restaurants, concert halls, insurance companies, vocational training, and athletic clubs that catered to a membership broader than that of individual churches. The church connected black women's spirituality with their social activism. The decades of activism within the church set the stage for the secular club movement at the turn of the twentieth century and provided many black women with organizational and leadership skills that had long-lasting influence.

Another aspect of women's involvement in church work was the unlikely sisterhood that developed between northern white church-women and southern black women. For example, during this time of Jim Crow when discriminatory laws served to separate Blacks from Whites (1876–1965), northern Baptist women articulated a set of values that were counter to the trends of the 1890s and were the foundation for the belief that women were spiritually responsible for the advancement of race and gender interests (Higginbotham, 1993). This common cause prompted interracial interaction between the women as they developed projects to transcend the oppression that encompassed schools, churches, homes, and other organizational settings.

African American women working together was an example of how the traditions of the African American community resulted in social reform. The virtual absence of social welfare institutions in many southern U.S. communities and the frequent exclusion of Blacks prompted black women to organize clubs to found orphanages, old folks' homes, day-care centers, nursery schools, and other educational institutions (Williams, 1900). For example, in 1938 in Philadelphia, Marion Turner Stubbs Thomas, building on an idea of Louise Truitt Jackson Dench, founded *Jack and Jill of America*, "an African American organization of mothers who nurture future leaders by strengthening children 2–19." According to Thomas, "To us as mothers, it [Jack and Jill] has become a means of furthering an inherent and natural desire . . . to bestow upon our children all the opportunities possible for a normal and graceful approach to a beautiful adulthood" (www.jack-and-jill.org). Black educational organizations such as these often became the centers for community organizations, women's activities, and a network of supporting institutions. The black community turned to their voluntary associations to resolve their own internal problems and not as a way to imitate white society (S. J. Shaw, 1991).

The establishment and growth of women's clubs and organizations was a social movement that had ties to leisure for many women in the United States. These clubs often had a focused purpose such as literary clubs, garden clubs, or homemaker clubs. The programs were often much broader, however, and at times operated from the activist perspective of *woman's work for women* (Higginbotham, 1993). Recreation was sometimes the starting point for some of these clubs and organizations, which eventually broadened their focus toward other social concerns. The focus expanded to include children's clubs for recreation and day care and also attracted children's mothers to other activities (Lerner, 1979). These ventures brought the women closer together, gave them confidence in their own abilities, and inspired them to look for other community problems to solve. The social movements were largely a result of women using their free time to create positive social change. The outcomes of these movements in providing meaningful leisure as well as a better quality of life were beneficial to different racial groups, all socioeconomic groups, and to both women and men. Although many social movements were influential, one of the most important for women was the women's movement.

THE EARLY WOMEN'S MOVEMENT

The early (i.e., first) women's movement of the nineteenth century occurred worldwide, and in the United States this movement was the result of social factors and concerns converging. As noted previously, during the Civil War, many women succeeded in positions formerly occupied by men, many women from all racial and ethnic groups were involved in the public sphere through social reform movements, and some women were allowed expanded educational opportunities. At the same time, some women began to question the contradictions in their lives. Some women with the inclination and time to organize were motivated to work to extend rights for all women. The groundwork was set for historic change in women's lives.

Two philosophical divisions emerged during these early years: a suffrage focus and a feminist focus. The single-issue suffrage groups were primarily concerned with getting the right to vote extended to women. The feminist group was broader in its goals and approaches. The lack of the right to vote was only one of many critical issues that these feminists believed all women faced. They also believed that rights such as women's control over reproduction, equal opportunity in work, and education were denied to many women because of patriarchy. As a consequence of being denied these rights they believed that women's autonomy often was sacrificed. These feminists formed organizations such as the American Equal Rights Association, as well as informal feminist groups such as the Heterodoxy luncheon group in New York City (Schwartz, 1982).

At times, members from these two major divisions worked together. At other times, the more conservative suffrage groups did not become involved with, and often did not even support, the issues of the feminist movement. The feminist movement was too radical for some women and men. Feminists were suggesting changes that brought into question some of the most basic underpinnings of society such as the church, the family, and the law. On occasion, the ideological differences were so great that some suffragists slowed the feminist movement by isolating activists and leaving them open to charges of deviancy, which discouraged women from involvement. Feminists' *radical* demands for equality and for freedom from oppression came from the women themselves and not through the government, the educational system, religious institutions, or professional groups (Williams, 1977). Even though the feminist movement lost prominence after suffrage was granted to women, into the twentieth century it continued to spread and legitimize a new image of women, family, and marriage, and developed an alternative set of ideals and values. The movement enabled women to overcome obstacles and to move on to other issues central to their, and others', lives and well-being. Women's achievements were likely a combination of circumstance and individual fortitude. For example, women like Amelia Earhart, who was born into an affluent and noted family in Atchison, Kansas, pursued her dream of flying by resisting stereotypes (i.e., flying was seen as a male pursuit) and developing the self-determination, independence, and mental strength to achieve her goals in the 1920s (Backus, 1982). In the mid-twentieth century, Rosa Parks, by refusing to give up her seat on the bus to a white man, provided a rallying point around which to move demands for racial equality forward. Native American and First Nation women were central to the work of the American Indian Movement (AIM) in the 1960s and 1970s in North America by seeking "to turn the attention of Indian people toward a renewal of spirituality" in order to reverse the destruction of their people, lands, and culture (Wittstock & Salinas, n.d.).

Early suffrage and feminist movements advanced opportunities for women's leisure even though leisure was not a primary focus of the major women's organizations. Still, most of the groups did give some attention to the leisure needs of women, particularly for physical activity. For example, the clothing that women were expected to wear (e.g., corsets, delicate fabrics, heavy petticoats and hoop skirts or bustles, and high heels) were finally seen as a detriment to physical activity and the health of women (Welch & Lerch, 1981).

At the National Woman Suffrage Association Convention in 1893, Haven gave a speech on "The Girl of the Future" and predicted that women would have some leisure for recreation (Anthony & Harper, 1902). In the autumn of 1920, representatives of the National Woman Suffrage Association, the National Women's Trade Union, the Young Women's Christian Association, the National Women's Christian Temperance Union, and the General Federation of Women's Clubs agreed to promote physical health and recommended use of recreation centers for educating women about the importance of emotional as well as physical health (Goodsell, 1923).

From these women's movements came major societal changes. Women were granted the right to vote and increased freedoms in private and public spheres of life. The Victorian notion of the *ideal woman* began to wane. However, feminist issues, such as equal pay for equal work, reproductive rights, educational opportunities, continued to exist. In the 1960s they gained new visibility in the United States with the second wave of the women's movement and the Civil Rights (and other) movements that once again confronted gender (and race) inequalities in leisure, family, and work in the private and public spheres of life.

SUMMARY/CONCLUSION

As illustrated throughout this chapter, the leisure of women has been heavily influenced by patriarchal structures that dictated sex roles, family structures and practices, work opportunities, and ideologies of ideal womanhood. At times these structures have been overly repressive and oppressive of women in all aspects of their lives. At other times, when demanded by women or needed by the society, these strict expectations have eased. And sometimes they have been transformed by the actions of individuals and groups of women and men committed to social justice—as well as by chance and circumstance. Women then were allowed more freedom in which to grow personally and collectively and develop their own leisure apart from patriarchal definitions. The advancements were sometimes slow, yet, the striving for rights in all aspects of women's lives, including leisure, continued to progress. When Gertrude Ederle swam the English Channel in 1926, Carrie Chapman Catt, a leading suffragette, said, "It is a far cry from swimming the Channel to the days to which my memory goes back, when it was thought that women could not throw a ball or even walk very far down the street without feeling faint" ("How a Girl," 1926, p. 56). Clearly, progress has been made, while at the same time there is much yet to be done, as many of the chapters in this volume attest. As we continue to move forward, we do not leave the past behind— hence, the importance of understanding the history of women's leisure that this chapter provides.

REFERENCES

Anthony, S. B., & Harper, I. H. (Eds.) (1902). History of woman suffrage (vol. 4). Rochester: Susan B. Anthony. (Cited in Welch, P., & Lerch, H. [1981]. *History of American physical education and sport* (p. 86). Springfield, IL: Charles C. Thomas).

Backus, J. L. (1982). *Letters from Amelia, 1901–1937*. Boston, MA: Beacon.

Barrett, M., & McIntosh, M. (1991). *The antisocial family* (2nd ed.). London, UK: Verso.

Bax, E. B. (1913). *The fraud of feminism*. London, UK: Grant Richards.

Bennett, J. M. (2006). *History matters: Patriarchy and the challenge of feminism*. Philadelphia, PA: University of Pennsylvania Press.

Blackwell, E. B. (1972). On marriage and work. In N. F. Cott (Ed.), *Root of bitterness*. New York, NY: E. P. Dutton. (Original work published in 1875.)

Bowers, E. (1934). *Recreation for girls and women*. New York, NY: A. S. Barnes.

Brown, E. B. (1991). Polyrhythms and improvization: Lessons for women's history. *History Workshop Journal, 31*, 85–90.

Cahn, S. K. (1994). *Coming on strong: Gender and sexuality in twentieth-century women's sport*. New York, NY: The Free Press.

Coontz, S. (1988). *The social origins of private life: A history of American families, 1600–1900*. New York, NY: Verso.

Coontz, S. (1992). *The way we never were: American families and the nostalgia trap*. New York, NY: Basic.

Dickinson, R. L. (1887). The corset. *New York Medical Journal, 11*(5), 14–28.

Duberman, M., Vicinus, M., & Chauncey, G. (Eds.) (1989). *Hidden from history: Reclaiming the gay & lesbian past*. New York, NY: Meridian.

DuBois, E., Buhle, M. J., Kaplan, T., Lerner, G., & Smith-Rosenberg, C. (1980). Politics and culture in women's history: A symposium. *Feminist Studies, 6*(1), 29.

Dulles, R. F. (1965). *A history of recreation: America learns to play*. New York, NY: Appleton-Century-Crofts.

Ehrenreich, B., & English, D. (1973). *Complaints and disorders: The sexual politics of sickness*. New York, NY: The Feminist Press.

Faderman, L. (1991). *Odd girls and twilight lovers: A history of lesbian life in 20th century America.* New York, NY: Penguin.

Gerber, E., Felshin, J., Berlin, P., & Wyrick, W. (Eds.) (1974). *The American woman in sport.* Reading, MA: Addison-Wesley.

Goodsell, W. (1923). *The education of women: Its social background and its problems.* New York, NY: MacMillian.

Higginbotham, E. B. (1993). *Righteous discontent: The women's movement in the Black Baptist church 1880–1920.* Cambridge, MA: Harvard University Press.

How a girl beat Leander at the Hero game. (1926, August 21). *The Literary Digest, 90,* 52–67.

Jack and Jill of America, Inc. (2010). Retrieved from www.jack-and-jill.org

Kaplan, J. (1979). *Women and sports.* New York, NY: Viking.

Katz, J. N. (1992). *Gay American history: Lesbians and gay men in the USA* (2nd ed.). New York, NY: Meridian.

Keenan, D. (2004). Race, gender, and other differences in feminist theory. In T. A. Meade & M. E. Wiesner-Hanks (Eds.), *A companion to gender history* (pp. 110–128). Oxford, UK: Blackwell.

Kelly, J. (1984). *Women, history, and theory: The essays of Joan Kelly.* Chicago, IL: University of Chicago Press.

Kimmel, M. S. (1996a). *Manhood in America: A cultural history.* New York, NY: The Free Press.

Kimmel, M. S., & Aronson, A. (2003). *Men and masculinities: A social, cultural, and historical encyclopedia.* ABC-CLIO.

Lenskyj, H. (1986). *Out of bounds: Women, sport, and sexuality.* Toronto, ON: The Women's Press.

Lenz, E., & Myerhoff, B. (1985). *The feminization of America.* Los Angeles, CA: Jeremy P. Tarcher.

Lerner, G. (1975). Placing women in history: Definitions and challenges. *Feminist Studies, 3*(1–2), 5–14.

Lerner, G. (1977). *The female experience: An American documentary.* Indianapolis, IN: Bobbs-Merrill.

Lerner, G. (1979). *The majority finds its past: Placing women in history.* New York, NY: Oxford University Press.

Luschen, G. (1974). The interdependence of sport and culture. In G. Sage (Ed.), *Sport and American society* (2nd ed.). Reading, MA: Addison-Wesley.

Mandle, J. (1979). *Women and social change in America.* Princeton, NJ: Princeton Book.

May, E. T. (1988). *Homeward bound: American families in the Cold War era.* New York, NY: Basic.

Mies, M. (2007). A global feminist perspective on research. In S. N. Hesse-Biber (Ed.), *Handbook of feminist research: Theory and praxis* (pp. 663–668). Thousand Oaks, CA: Sage.

Millward, J. (2007). More history than myth: African American women's history since the publication of 'Ar'n't I a Woman?'. *Journal of Women's History, 19*(2), 161–167.

Peiss, K. (1986). *Cheap amusements: Working women and leisure in turn-of-the-century New York.* Philadelphia, PA: Temple University Press.

Peterson-Lewis, S. (1993). Aesthetic practices among African American women. In K. Welsh-Asante (Ed.), *The African aesthetic: Keeper of the traditions* (pp. 103–142). Westport, CT: Greenwood.

Rich, A. (1986). Resisting amnesia: History and personal life. *Blood, bread, and poetry: Selected prose 1979–1985.* New York, NY: W.W. Norton.

Rosaldo, M. Z. (1974). Women, culture and society: A theoretical overview. In M. Z. Rosaldo & L. Lamphere (Eds.), *Women, culture, and society* (pp. 17–42). Stanford, CA: Stanford University Press.

Schaffer, M. T. S. (1911). *Old Indian trails of the Canadian Rockies*. New York, NY: The Knickerbocker Press.

Schwartz, J. (1982). *Radical feminists of heterodoxy: Greenwich Village, 1912–1940*. Lebanon, NH: New Victoria.

Shaw, S. J. (1991). Black club women and the creation of the National Association of Colored Women. *Journal of Women's History, 3*(2), 10–25.

Smith, B. G. (2010). Women's history: A retrospective from the United States. *Signs: Journal of Women in Culture & Society, 35*(3), 723–747.

Thorne, B. (1992). Feminism and the family: Two decades of thought. In B. Thorne & M. Yalom (Eds.), *Rethinking the family* (pp. 3–30). Boston, MA: Northeastern University Press.

Tober, P. (1988). Historical perspective: Evolution of employee services and recreation. *Employee Services Management, 31*(1), 11–16.

Ulrich, L. T. (1979). Virtuous women found. In N. Cott & E. Plack (Eds.), *A Heritage of her own* (pp. 58–80). New York, NY: Simon & Schuster.

Veblen, T. (1899). *The theory of the leisure class*. New York, NY: Viking.

Welch, P., & Lerch, H. (1981). *History of American physical education and sport*. Springfield, IL: Charles C. Thomas.

Williams, F. B. (1900). The club movement among colored women of America. In B. T. Washington, N. B. Wood, & F. B. Williams (Eds.), *A New Negro for a new century* (p. 383). Chicago, IL: American Publishing House.

Williams, J. (1977). *Psychology of women*. New York, NY: W. W. Norton.

Wittstock, L. W., & Salinas, E. J. (n.d.). *A brief history of the American Indian Movement*. Website of the American Indian Movement Grand Governing Council. Retrieved from http://www.aimovement.org

CHAPTER 4
REFLECTIONS ON THE ROLE OF MEN IN A FEMINIST LEISURE STUDIES

KEVIN D. LYONS

I have engaged with feminism in leisure studies somewhat sporadically over the past two decades. Initially, I was a graduate student who completed a course that focused on women, gender, and leisure. That experience presented to me a different way of viewing leisure, as it highlighted the dominance of an androcentric focus in leisure studies at that time (e.g., Henderson, Bialeschki, Shaw, & Freysinger, 1996; Wearing, 1998). Although I found that course and the feminist scholarship refreshing, as a man I also found it disquieting. This discomfort came largely from a question that I have sought to answer over the past two decades. What is the role of men in a feminist leisure studies?

My sporadic engagement with feminist theory reflects my oscillating attempts to embrace two key extreme responses to men in feminism. On one hand is the perspective that men are neither needed nor wanted in feminist studies. I was recently reminded of this perspective. When preparing my thoughts for this chapter, I revisited Klein's (1983) work, in which she argues forcefully that "there is no room for men in Women's Studies whatsoever" (p. 413). I am tempted to reflect upon such a provocative view from well over two decades ago as part of a battle that has long been won. However, this conclusion would understate a foundational reality that is alive and well today: that men are still either directly or indirectly responsible for women's oppression in the twenty-first century. Indeed, some male scholars have suggested the futility of men attempting to be brought on board feminism, claiming "a man's relation to feminism is an impossible one . . . no matter how sincere, sympathetic or whatever, we are always also in a male position" (Heath, 1987, p. 1). Such a view, however, sits in direct contrast with the position that feminism is not the sole property of women (Denner, 2001). Rather, it is a way of seeing the world that both men and women need to embrace.

Henderson's (1994a) work suggested that these two perspectives might be located on the evolutionary continuum that follows the trajectory of a feminist phase theory laid out by Tetreault (cited in Henderson). The first phase Tetreault defined as *male scholarship* was manifested in the patriarchal ideologies that dominated both leisure research and social research more broadly and was taken to be the essential truth on the subject. This phase was challenged by a feminist critique of a predominantly androcentric approach to leisure research, which had until the early 1980s rendered the leisure experiences of women largely invisible. Subsequent research published on leisure and gender sought to address this invisibility. As the voices of feminist scholars began to rise, androcentric views of leisure were challenged. The second phase of the evolution described by Tetreault as *compensatory scholarship* was evident in the *add women and stir* approach to understanding gender and leisure, which remained largely male-defined but also acknowledged that women should be considered. Henderson suggested that Tetreault's description of the third phase of the evolution as *bifocal scholarship* was embraced by feminist leisure scholars as they examined differences between men's and women's leisure. The fourth phase of Tetreault's theory, *feminist scholarship*, encompassed research that sought to understand the experiences of women in leisure and the impacts of oppression upon their leisure. The first three phases coincided with the growing voice of radical feminism, which recognized the threat that men can and will co-opt feminism.

Henderson (1994a) recognized that Tetreault's final phase, described as *new scholarship*, challenged broad assumptions about viewing leisure as a universal experience and that "no one female or male voice exists" (p. 1). This new scholarship led to research focusing on "the different experiences that women and men as gendered subjects have in leisure" (Henderson, 1994a, p. 2), and even wider perspectives. Implied in this new scholarship is the recognition men could make significant contributions by asking questions from their "individual gendered perspective" (Henderson et al., 1996, p. 216). This yet-to-be-fully-realized phase clearly suggests men play a necessary role not in, but parallel to, a feminist leisure studies.

Although feminist phase theory provides a valuable historical justification for the inclusion of men's voices, it fails to capture the way such a trajectory has played out in men's responses to a feminist leisure studies that impede progression to a new scholarship. The remainder of this chapter examines men's responses. This attempt was inspired by reading Wearing's (1998) influential book, *Leisure and Feminist Theory*, where she critiqued what she saw as key masculinist responses to feminism. Her work, particularly the chapter on leisure and masculinity, examined the many ways men have reacted to and attempted to engage with feminist theory.

However, the take-home message from Wearing's chapter for me was that although a growing body of research produced by male scholars considers men's engagement with feminist theory, their work remains entrenched in "masculine perceptions of social and personal situations" (p. 86). Such perceptions are rife in men's studies literature. However, I feel this message underestimates the nuances of how men have responded to a feminist leisure studies. Teasing out these responses specifically as they have emerged in leisure studies is an important step toward finding a way forward.

MEN'S RESPONSE TO FEMINISM

When faced with the issues raised by feminist thought in the past two decades, men have responded in ways that are worth examining. These responses help show why the task of locating men in feminist leisure studies has been challenging. While Klein (1983) suggested that men involved in women's studies could be categorized as self-appointed "experts," "ignoramuses," or "poor dears" (p. 414), others have been less provocative. Heath (1987) suggested that men respond to feminism based on either fear and/ or desire. Based on my own observations over the past decade, as both a leisure-studies student and academic and through my formal and informal interactions in the field, I suggest that these two categories should be expanded into the following four response types: justifying, gatekeeping, tokenism, and empathizing.

Rather than trying to pigeonhole other researchers, I draw on hypothetical illustrations and examples from other work, but I primarily draw upon examples from my own research to show these responses in action. That I can draw out examples of these types from my own work may simply reflect the way I have changed as an individual over time. However, I would argue that while I am to some extent an agent of my own actions, I have been influenced by the structural changes that have surrounded me during my career. Therefore, I feel my own work is both emblematic and symptomatic of broader trends.

Justifying

In light of the mounting evidence that clearly supports that men have oppressed women, a reaction from men is inevitable. The defensive reaction is driven by the notion that men may be the overall cause of oppression, yet individuals should not necessarily be blamed (Blood, Tuttle, & Lukey, 1995; Felson & Felson, 1993). This logic gave rise to the idea that men are also oppressed (Kimmel, 1993). The men's movement was born out of this logic, creating an environment where men have used the feminist approach to defend themselves (Paul, 1993).

Defensively justifying involves responding to feminism in part by arguing that men have changed and that the women's movement has not recognized these changes. Astrachan (1986) described this response when pointing out that men are increasingly more willing to be involved in less manly behaviors such as crying in public and changing diapers. Studies that attempt to show the injustices men must endure due to the feminist movement also typify the defensive response. This reaction might hypothetically manifest as research that is conducted to see how men's leisure has been affected by the gradual increase in the number of women who enter traditionally male activities such as rugby and boxing (Paule-Koba on Title IX, this volume), or it may manifest as research that examines how men who are primary caretakers in the family experience the same problems in accessing leisure as do women in similar circumstances.

In reflecting back on my own work on non-resident fatherhood with a colleague (Jenkins & Lyons, 2006), I can see evidence of adopting this response. The following excerpt from that work captures this justifying:

Men have traditionally enjoyed the bulk of privileges in a variety of social contexts, including leisure. It is not surprising therefore that men are rarely considered as a group with specific needs and are typically not singled out as such in the leisure research literature. A large body of literature that has emerged over the past three decades that examines leisure and gender has primarily focused on women. (p. 223)

In addition:

The misleading, if not derogatory, label "Disneyland dad" has been applied to non-resident fathers, implying that these fathers attempt to buy the love of their children. Other labels include "deadbeat" or "missing in action." Stereotypes like these imply that the absence and sporadic leisure-based and indulgent interactions of non-resident fathers are a product of individual choice. They tend to trivialize the leisure interactions of non-resident fathers and fail to consider that these leisure interactions are often shaped by legislation, particular family structures, and a range of other moderating and mediating variables mentioned above. (p. 228)

Although there are specific instances and examples where men's experiences and needs have been overlooked as feminism emerged as the dominant position in the study of gender and leisure, our analysis overlooked the more macro-social trends that continue to structurally disadvantage women. This oversight is not unique. This defensiveness may have inspired men to examine themselves more carefully, yet I doubt whether it actually assists in reducing women's oppression. If anything, it is likely to contribute to oppression by positioning women as the cause for men's perceived disadvantage—a position that has been criticized as dangerously anti-feminist (Frye, 1995; Paul, 1993).

Gatekeeping

Another response is gatekeeping, described as a type of response based on a genuine desire to support women. Christian (1994) exemplified this idea in his book on the making of anti-sexist men:

> Men interested in gender are, not unreasonably, suspected of wanting to muscle-in on scarce teaching posts and research funds. I was conscious of this throughout this research and for this reason, despite being urged by a female head of department, I refrained from applying for research funding which might have gone to women researchers. (p. 17)

The power to make the decision about whether women should have a voice or access to a resource does little to address the source of that power. Kimmel (2000) captured this sentiment: "Men's power over women is relatively straightforward. It is the aggregate power of men as a group to determine the distribution of rewards in society" (p. 30).

As a man, I am part of the *aggregate that determines*. In my work, I can see moments when I have been gatekeeping. This behavior was particularly evident when I argued that men should be leading the way in deconstructing our own masculinities:

> This dearth is evident in an upcoming special issue of *Leisure Studies Journal* dedicated to the issue of fatherhood. This special issue is guest edited by a woman, and the contributions are largely from women. Another example is a recent encyclopedia on outdoor recreation and leisure that included an entry on men written by a woman. While feminist scholars undertaking these tasks should be applauded, this work needs to be coming from male scholars. It is our voices and our perspectives that can make a difference. Indeed some leading feminist scholars have been calling for such work from men in the field for over a decade. (Lyons, 2006, pp. 307–308)

With the benefit of hindsight, the subtext in this passage is one that seeks to control women who are researching the experiences of men. The patronizing tone I evoked by saying women scholars' work should be applauded, reeks of the next type of response—tokenism.

Tokenism

Tokenism is a political response by men that seeks to support feminist positions largely because it is politically advantageous and correct to do so. Women's rights were a well-publicized hot potato a couple of decades ago, when many men were afraid to challenge prevailing ideas on the subject for fear of being sanctioned. This fear resulted in many men supporting equality between the sexes, but doing so mechanically (Horowitz, 1993). This tokenism might manifest as men studying women's experiences, as was the case for me when I was studying Australian women's experiences as international camp staff in American summer camps (Lyons, 2004). I found that the women interviewed struggled to find cultural identity markers of Australia that were not male-dominated. The focus of my research seemed quite worthwhile, but the decision-making process behind it revealed, in retrospect, a tokenistic treatment of women as subjects.

My research on international staff was part of a larger study that examined the experiences of both men and women. I chose to do a secondary analysis of the data to examine the experiences of women as a focused study. Although this practice is legitimate in research, my motivation was to some degree driven by the recognition that such a study would be well received at an upcoming leisure studies conference in a session on women and leisure. At the time I recall thinking that this presentation would help me to develop my credentials as someone who promotes the feminist cause—something that I felt was a politically expedient position and would ensure that I was not considered a dinosaur by the growing ranks of influential feminist scholars in leisure research.

Empathizing

The typologies I described above were largely motivated by fear—the fear of being misunderstood and labeled, the fear of being left behind, and the fear of losing power. The fourth type of response is an empathetic one that is motivated by desire. To understand this response, contextualizing it within the popular cultural context through which it developed is important.

In the 1980s, popular media suggested that a new style of man had emerged in response to the women's rights movement of the previous decade. Heath (1987) argued that these men were typically self-proclaimed feminists who ran the risk of dismissing their own maleness. These sensitive men were charged by other men with *selling out* to women (Stoltenberg, 1993). These *sensitive new-age guys* of the 1980s and 1990s underwent some reimagining after being scorned and parodied by song writers and popular media and have reemerged as more postmodern, edgy, and appropriately ambiguous *metrosexuals*. These broader lifestyle patterns have also infiltrated the scholarly arena, where finding male academics acting sensitively and empathetically in their research is relatively commonplace.

However, the response I am referring to is one that involves men actively changing their behavior regardless of negative consequences because they see value for themselves as well as for women (Blood et al., 1995). The empathizer is motivated by the desire to have what women have, and attempts to become more like a woman by finding his feminine side (Greely, 1993). The empathizer makes no excuses or justifications for a patriarchal society. Underlying the fashionability of this type of response, however, is the desire to become more like a woman by finding the woman within. Kimmel (2000) criticized this response and argued that men who seek to discover their feminine side attempt to de-gender themselves. This effort is impossible, according to Kimmel, as everything a man does expresses his masculinity. Although the de-gendering of traits may be desirable, this process needs to be done without de-gendering people. While I cannot identify any one specific example of empathizing from my previous work, I am currently pondering whether my involvement in this ongoing dialogue with feminism, including my contribution of this chapter, is in some ways an example of me acting as an empathizer.

TOWARD A NEW SCHOLARSHIP

Each of the responses described in this chapter leads ultimately to the reinforcement of men's power over women. Whether the response is motivated by the need to appease guilt, maintain political astuteness, control through power, or a desire to have what women have, each position is nonetheless motivated by the needs of men. This need-base is an undeniable component of human motivation but will do little to move feminist leisure studies forward. Based on these typologies, I offer a position that echoes Heath (1987), who suggested that men cannot become feminists. As a man I will never live the experience of a woman and will, therefore, never be in the position to be a feminist. Nor should I! Feminism requires an ability to read the world as a woman and to experience the *political as personal*. Actions such as defending, gatekeeping, patronizing, and empathizing will alter nothing in this regard.

So I am back to the beginning—what is the role of men in a feminist leisure studies? In pondering this question, I engaged in an introspective exercise and found myself guilty, as I have illustrated above, of some combination of the four types of responses outlined. Perhaps my interest in engaging with feminist leisure studies has been fueled by my genuine empathy toward women and the inequities women face regarding leisure. Perhaps it has been fed by a desire to ensure that I would not be seen as standing in the way of activism undertaken by women in the field. Perhaps I was interested in ensuring I was seen as politically correct in my actions, or perhaps it was simply a means to make certain that I could defend myself against charges of contributing to this inequity. If all attempts to act are likely to become acts of colonization and co-optation based on male needs, does this mean that I should give up and leave feminist leisure to women? Clearly, this response is inadequate as it will lead only to justifying the status quo.

The answer is best found by first recognizing that men cannot be feminists, which does not preclude men from acting in ways that empower themselves without drawing that empowerment at the expense of women. A major starting point for such action is for men in the leisure field to begin deconstructing masculinity as played out in men's leisure and, by extension, in the patriarchal society in which we live. Men subordinating their deconstruction to the deconstruction of women will not sufficiently limit patriarchal domination. Men deconstructing masculinity is complementary to feminism without actually being feminist. Importantly, this action of deconstructing masculinity allows men to break free of the roles that reproduce oppression over women.

Examples of this work largely began to emerge a decade or more ago. At that time, men explored aspects of gender-based analysis of leisure constraints (Jackson & Henderson, 1995); leisure, gender, and power relations (Rojek, 1997); leisure and homosexual identities (Markwell, 2002); and gendered sport and leisure (Rowe & McKay, 2003). More recently, however, such work has been relatively scarce in leisure research. Perhaps this inertia is the product of not knowing how to respond to a feminist leisure studies. More likely it is because such work requires significant emotional engagement with one's own masculinity. Nevertheless, the need for such research is important.

Areas of research that fit this new or, more accurately, renewed scholarship include how masculinity plays out in the leisure interactions of fathers and their children and issues associated with male role–modeling, such as how unchecked notions of masculinity as aggressive and dominant behavior have led to a crisis in boyhood. Other areas prime for research include men's health and wellness matters, parenting skills, suicide and violence prevention, depression, and loneliness and isolation. All of these topics are real experiences for men and boys, yet they rarely receive attention in the leisure studies literature.

I see the future as laden with possibility. As a male scholar interested in feminism, my responses to feminism have inadvertently encroached upon and perhaps interrupted the evolutionary progression toward a new feminist scholarship. Men can and should play a role in reigniting that progression not by responding to feminism, but by focusing upon studying their own gendered perspectives as important. To that end, I have developed the following postulates that speak specifically to male scholars and students of leisure studies.

- We need to gather our knowledge in such a way that the outcomes of that knowledge contribute to the equitable distribution of gendered power that is central to a feminist critique of leisure.

- We need to conduct research in our field from our subjectively gendered perspective.

- We need to examine how our masculinity is constructed in a way that limits access to alternative leisure experiences.

- We need to conduct research that examines the way the ideology of masculinity limits the ability to live life free of the constructs of *macho* and *manly*.

- We need to conduct research that deconstructs masculinity so that men can free themselves from the necessity to oppress women and co-opt feminism.

The issues raised in this chapter are situated in a broader theoretical frame of gendered leisure that will more fully complete the picture of a *new feminist scholarship* in leisure research. This new scholarship will not and cannot be fully realized without including the gendered perspectives of men.

REFERENCES

Astrachan, A. (1986). *How men feel: Their response to women's demands for equality and power.* Garden City, NY: Anchor Press/Doubleday.

Blood, P., Tuttle, A., & Lukey, G. (1995). Understanding and fighting sexism: A call to men. In M. L. Andersen & P. H. Collins (Eds.), *Race, class, and gender: An anthology* (pp. 202–219). New York, NY: Wadsworth.

Christian, H. (1994). *The making of anti-sexist men*. London, UK: Routledge.

Denner, J. (2001). The gap between feminist theory and practice: Lessons from teenage women in California. *Feminism & Psychology, 11*, 162–166.

Felson, R. B., & Felson, S. R. (1993). Predicaments of men and women. *Society, 30*(6), 16–20.

Frye, M. (1995). Oppression. In M. L. Andersen & P. H. Collins (Eds.), *Race, class, and gender: An anthology* (pp. 19–37). New York, NY: Wadsworth.

Greely, A. M. (1993). Necessity of feminism. *Society, 30*(6), 12–15.

Heath, S. (1987). Male feminism. In A. Jardine & P. Smith (Eds.), *Men in feminism* (pp. 1–32). New York, NY: Methuen.

Henderson, K. A. (1994a). Broadening an understanding of women, gender, and leisure. *Journal of Leisure Research, 26*(1), 1–3.

Henderson, K. A., Bialeschki, M. D., Shaw, S. M., & Freysinger, V. J. (1996). *Both gains and gaps: Feminist perspectives on women's leisure*. State College, PA: Venture Publishing, Inc.

Horowitz, I. L. (1993). Domesticating ideology. *Society, 30*(6), 41–45.

Jackson, E. L., & Henderson, K. A. (1995). Gender-based analysis of leisure constraints, *Leisure Sciences, 17*(1), 31–51.

Jenkins, J. & Lyons, K. D. (2006). Non-resident fathers' leisure with their children. *Leisure Studies, 25*(2), 219–232.

Kimmel, M. S. (1993). Invisible masculinity. *Society, 30*(6), 28–35.

Kimmel, M. S. (2000). *The gendered society*. New York, NY: Oxford University Press.

Klein, R. D. (1983). The "men problem" in women's studies: The expert, the ignoramus and the poor dear. *Women's Studies International Forum, 6*(4), 413–421.

Lyons, K. D. (2004). "We are not all Crocodile Hunters": Exploring the working holiday experiences of Australian women abroad. Abstracts from the *2004 World Leisure Congress*. Brisbane, Australia.

Lyons, K. D. (2006). Wolves among sheep? The role of men in a feminist leisure studies. *Leisure Sciences, 28*(3), 305–309.

Markwell, K. (2002). Mardi Gras tourism and the construction of Sydney as an international gay and lesbian city, *GLQ: A Journal of Lesbian and Gay Studies, 8*(1–2), 81–99.

Paul, E. F. (1993). Silly men, banal men. *Society, 30*(6), 36–40.

Rojek, C. (1997). "Leisure" in the writings of Walter Benjamin. *Leisure Studies, 16*(3), 155–172.

Rowe, D., & McKay, J. (2003). A man's game: sport and masculinities. In S. Tomsen & M. Donaldson (Eds.), *Male trouble: Looking at Australian masculinities*, (pp. 200–216). Melbourne, Australia: Pluto.

Stoltenberg, J. (1993). *The end of manhood: A book for men of conscience.* New York, NY: Dutton.

Wearing, B. (1998). *Leisure and feminist theory.* Thousand Oaks, CA: Sage.

CHAPTER 5
FEMINIST THEORIES: A DIVERSITY OF CONTRIBUTIONS AND PERSPECTIVES

VALERIA J. FREYSINGER, SUSAN M. SHAW, KARLA A. HENDERSON, AND M. DEBORAH BIALESCHKI

There is no doubt that feminist scholarship is controversial. Feminist research challenges taken-for-granted beliefs about women and about the naturalization of gender and gendered lives within society. Further, feminist scholarship is fundamentally activist, arguing for social change, for gender equity, and for the empowerment of women. It seeks to change not only deeply rooted attitudes and behaviors but also social, economic, and political practice. As a result, feminist perspectives have garnered both support and opposition from the media, from different generations of women and men, and from the public in general.

Within the academic world, the political nature of feminist research was evident as early as the 1960s, as what is often seen as the first generation of feminist scholars drew attention to the androcentric bias inherent within both biological science and social science research (Hesse-Biber, 2007). These early feminist researchers, sometimes known as feminist empiricists, questioned the assumptions and methods underlying existing scholarship in many different fields. Their work helped to reveal the political nature of research, and the ways in which underlying assumptions and beliefs inevitably influence the kinds of questions that researchers ask, as well as the methodological and interpretive approaches they adopt (Mies, 2007). This, in turn, helped to explain changing attitudes towards feminist scholarship and changing views about the importance and relevance of research directed toward understanding the gendered lives of girls and women (Henderson & Shaw, 2006).

Debates have also occurred among feminist scholars. While early feminist researchers directed their attention to the critique of existing knowledge, their work quickly became linked to the importance of understanding women's experiences, of hearing women's voices, and of revealing the difficulties and challenges of women's everyday lives. This was seen to be important in terms of changing the conditions of women's lives. In addition, women's unique standpoint was valued in terms of its potential for enhanced and more nuanced understandings of social reality (Harding, 2007; Smith, 1990). As feminist research progressed, though, more attention was paid to the diversity of women's lives and the problems of essentialization or of assuming a commonality of experience among women. That is, it became evident that "one size does not fit all" (Henderson, 1994b).

More recently, new theoretical approaches have developed within the field of feminist studies, and new ideas have been borrowed and adapted from other disciplines too, such as sociology, critical studies, and cultural studies. New epistemological approaches have also emerged, leading to a variety of opinions about how feminist research should be conducted, and debates about whether or not there is a unique feminist method (Harding, 1987; Hesse-Biber & Piatelli, 2007). Even the naming of this field of research has become controversial, with debates about whether it should be called "feminist studies," "women's studies," or "gender studies." In addition, differences of opinion exist about the relationship between this area of scholarship and the developing field of "men's studies" (Henderson & Shaw, 2006). A further complication relates to the issue of the activist nature of feminist scholarship because different theoretical perspectives have different implications for social change (Gannon & Davies, 2007).

In this chapter, we trace some of these developments and debates within feminist research, paying particular attention to the approaches that have had the greatest impact on research within the leisure studies field. We argue that there are differences among feminist researchers in terms of their theoretical and epistemological approaches. These differences are reflected in the degree to which researchers focus on *individual* lives and lived experiences, *social contexts* and *interactional* dimensions, and/or gendered *social structures* and *structured relations* of power. Nevertheless, while we recognize that these differences can lead to tensions and contestations, we also see value in the variety of approaches that exist to study leisure, women, and gender. This diversity of perspectives is evidence of the growth and development of feminist research. New insights and new understandings have led to new questions and new directions, which contribute in different ways to our grasp of the complex ways in which gender permeates society. Attention to different feminist perspectives and approaches also alerts us to issues of global diversity and the variety of ways in which we can work towards social change and social justice worldwide.

DIVERSE FEMINIST THEORIES INFORMING RESEARCH ON LEISURE, WOMEN, AND GENDER

Feminist theory informing research on leisure, women, and gender has been categorized in various ways (Henderson & Shaw, 2006; Hesse-Biber, 2007; Tong, 2009). While each theory focuses on girls/women and/or gender in research and practice, they vary in *what* they see as the core reason(s) for gender inequality, *if* gender inequality is the sole focus, and *how* best to address or change such inequality.

The Beginnings: Liberal and Care-Focused Feminisms

In the first era of feminist research, feminist researchers within various disciplines (sociology, psychology, history, philosophy, education) and fields (law, medicine, language) offered critiques of the extant androcentric research and sought to alter who produced knowledge, the focus of research, and how it was produced. One of the earliest forms of feminist thought to do this was *liberal feminism,* with its central focus on the importance and autonomy of the individual and the natural equality and freedom of all human beings. Liberal feminism, paralleling theories of individual rights (Tong, 2009), argues that rights and opportunities should be equally available for women and men. Hence, liberal feminists often work to eradicate oppressive gender roles and change socialization practices through the elimination of legislation and social conventions that limit girls' and women's opportunities. This is evident in the causes liberal feminists champion, such as voting rights, women's right to own property, right to divorce, equal educational access, freedom of expression, and equal employment opportunities. As a result, legislation and education are tools frequently used by liberal feminists (Paule-Koba, on Title IX in the United States, this volume). In addition, many liberal feminists believe changing patterns of socialization, as well as attitudes, are needed to overcome patriarchy. Other feminists would argue that those strategies alone are not enough to bring about the large-scale social changes needed to achieve the goals of feminism. At the same time, societies where economic and political structures and practices have emphasized economic and social equality (e.g., Marxist, socialist) have often fallen short when it comes to the rights of women. Hence, liberal feminists' emphasis on rights of the individual continues to be seen as relevant by many.

Still, others would argue that by emphasizing individual rights, a dichotomy and antagonism is established between autonomy and nurturing, between individual freedom and relations with others, and between independence and community (Tong, 2009; Tuana & Tong, 1994). The worry is that an emphasis on rights will result in a devaluation of nurturing and caring. According to Tong (2009), it is this concern that frames what she calls *care-focused feminism.* Within this category, the work of Carol Gilligan (1982) and Nel Noddings (1984, 2002) suggests that an *ethic of care* held by many women is preferable to an ethic of rights, because of women's predilection to seek ways to comprehend the needs, desires, and motivations of others. That is, in an ethic of care the moral concepts of rights and duties are replaced with responsibility, bonding, and sharing. As noted by Tong (2009), from the perspective of care-focused feminism, "(m)orality is not about affirming others' needs through the process of denying one's own interests. Rather, morality is about affirming one's own interests through the process of affirming others' needs" (p. 169). This suggests particular social policy and/or legislative change. For example, in some societies, extending the benefits of public pension programs (e.g., Social Security in the United States) to women who are full-time mothers and homemakers, and paid maternity leave, might be legislation supported by this perspective.

An important criticism of both liberal and care-focused feminist approaches has been their lack of attention to structured relations of power. *Radical feminists* (e.g., Firestone, 1970; Daly, 1978) were perhaps the first to draw attention to the notion of systemic male power and the need to critique patriarchy and androcentrism. They revealed ways in which gendered power structures invade, oppress, and disempower women in all areas of their lives, and they argued that equity legislation does little to break down these pervasive relations of power. This raised questions such as, is it enough to expect equality of *opportunity?* Is equality of opportunity even possible without addressing equality of *conditions* in a fundamentally patriarchal society?

Another critique of early feminist thinking relates to the notion of difference. That is, how and in what ways are structured inequalities faced by different women differently? How do feminists reconcile the fact that women who have benefitted from equity legislation have tended to be middle-class white women? By raising the problem of essentialization, or assumptions about the universality of female oppression and commonality of female experience, this critique challenged feminists to think about the extent to which women's lives are shaped by more than gender. That is, while early feminist research certainly generated new knowledge of women's lives and experiences, it also tended to both *essentialize,* what Bordieu (2001) refers to as the "biologicization of the social" (p. 3), and dichotomize gender while ignoring the many other dimensions along which power is distinguished. Gender differences were generalized with little attention given to the importance of race, class, age, sexual orientation, and cultural context. Yet at the same time that essentialism is criticized, Hesse-Biber (2007) notes that some feminist researchers have called for what Spivak (1994) terms "strategic essentialism." She and others (e.g., Bordo, 1990) see this strategy as necessary if feminists are to advance their political agenda—and if women are to look past differences in nationality, race, sexual orientation, age, and social class and work together on issues of mutual concern (e.g., paid work, reproductive rights). Similarly, Bhavnani (2007) emphasizes the need to look for *interconnections* among women to empower women's lives. Still, it is out of concerns for the lack of attention to differences among women that Marxist and socialist feminist approaches, as well as global and multicultural critiques, emerged.

Centering Structure: Marxist and Socialist Feminisms

Marxist and *socialist feminists* were increasingly seen to provide an answer to this critique of essentialism, since both approaches purport that it is classism (capitalism) rather than sexism (patriarchy) that is at the root of women's oppression. However, socialist feminists take this argument further and have increasingly looked at the intersections of class and sex, race/ethnicity, and sexual orientation in their theorizing and research (Tong, 2009). Arising in the 1970s in the UK, Europe, and North America in response to Marxist and radical feminist perspectives, socialist feminism combines the Marxist belief in the importance of class analysis of power with acknowledgment of the radical feminist belief that patriarchy is a critical contributor to women's oppression (Cole, 1994). The key to addressing power and oppression is seen to rest in patriarchy, racism, capitalism, and structured power relations. For example, this approach identifies the exploitation of women and men as wage laborers, but it also points out the importance of recognizing that the oppression of women is also due to their roles in the patriarchal sexual hierarchy, specifically their roles as mother, domestic laborer, and consumer. Socialist feminism also recognizes how racial oppression relates to class exploitation and sexual oppression (Tuana & Tong, 1994).

Within socialist-feminist thinking, the focus is on the relationship between the material conditions of societies and the social structures and ideologies that are a part of them. They pay attention to structures and relationships within social institutions such as religion, education, the economy, sport/leisure, and the family. People are seen as social beings who exist as part of larger social institutions, not just as individuals with abstract rights. Thus, attention is paid to what is good for people as part of a community, not just what is good for the individual. Equality, cooperation, sharing, and political commitment are valued, as well as freedom from sexual stereotyping, and freedom from personal possessiveness (Jaggar,

1983). Stress is placed on the greater struggle of women of color, ethnic minority groups, and disadvantaged economic classes in gaining equal opportunity. Unlike Marxism, there is no assumption that a classless society will eliminate male privilege nor that economic oppression is secondary to women's oppression. While the significance of the class system is acknowledged, women's oppression is seen to relate to a variety of systemic relations of power, including, but not limited to, the political, social, and economic structures associated with capitalism (Tong, 2009).

Within a socialist-feminist perspective, the belief is that for oppression to be eliminated, human reproductive labor, as well as productive labor, has to be reorganized. Jaggar (1995) suggested that this reorganization has to address issues of reproductive freedom, childcare, adequate family support, compulsory heterosexuality, and mandatory motherhood as promoted by male-dominated systems. Indeed, much feminist research on women and leisure in the 1980s in the UK, Australia, and North America emphasized issues of motherhood and the ethic of care, in seeking to understand women's leisure and relative inequality (or "leisure lack"). These issues continue to be central to understanding gendered leisure, as evidenced by a number of chapters in this text (Hilbrecht; Scraton & Watson; Sullivan, this volume).

Yet, moving beyond Marxist feminism also has its drawbacks. For example, Marxist feminists' focus on the conflict experienced by women around paid and unpaid work is still an important concern in most if not all women's lives, but this issue may be receiving less attention in recent years in leisure studies. Marxist feminism points to the commonality of "women's work" regardless of age, race, class or religion. Thus, women's work is seen to include not only the production of goods but also the production and reproduction of human beings within the family. This becomes the standpoint from which many women could interpret reality. Marxist feminists' insistence that women's reproductive work is also "real work" elevates the gender struggle between men and women to an equally crucial human struggle on par with class struggles. Men's historic control of reproduction as the initiators (i.e., with or without consent) and/or by claiming the child as their private property is challenged. Reproductive technologies have helped women to resist men's control over their bodies. However, struggles over the work (both paid and unpaid) and reproductive practices of women continue to be intense within countries around the world, as women's bodies and women's rights continue to be central to many political, religious, and social agendas today.

Moving Forward: Intersectionality, Multicultural Feminisms, and Global Perspectives

In contrast to liberal and care-focused feminist perspectives that essentialize *woman* and Marxist perspectives that center on class, there is a group of intersectional, multicultural, and global/postcolonial feminist perspectives that challenge feminist thinkers to recognize differences *among* women that emerge from the fact that not all women are "created or constructed equal" (Tong, 2009). A recognition of women's differences followed from socialist feminist approaches that raised awareness of the need to focus on the interconnections of gender not only with class, but with other structures and practices of privileging and oppression as well. In the process of doing feminist research, the categories that were initially the focus of the research (e.g., gender) were often inadequate (Wylie, 2007). That is, in seeking to understand gender, feminist researchers frequently found that racism or classism was what they most, or also, needed to understand to explore an issue initially framed in terms of gender. Hence, feminist researchers were faced with the challenge of how to "theorize difference without losing the analytic force of gender analysis" (Raey, 2007, p. 606). This required new theoretical frameworks or approaches where differences were not seen as cumulative but contextual, not as marginal but constitutive. This also required the recognition that identities or subjectivities are relational and multiple, enduring but fluid, more important in some contexts than others but always present.

Intersectionality is one perspective/approach that arose out of these realizations. According to Dill, McLaughlin, and Nieves (2007), "Intersectionality is grounded in feminist theory, asserting that people live multiple, layered identities and can simultaneously experience oppression and privilege" (p. 629). This perspective evolved from the writing of women of color, women whose lives were at once shaped not only by gender, but by multiple systems of power. Identity studies, globalization/transnationalism, and queer/sexualities studies are areas of scholarship that also critique and organize around processes of intersectionality. Research framed by this perspective examines not only individual experiences but also how cultural, economic, and ideological structures produce and reproduce group identities. Interdisciplinary approaches to research are required and working for social justice is a commitment, often making the work of interdisciplinary scholars "problematic" for universities that are organized in (sub-)disciplinary ways and with reward structures that value publications more than social action (Dill et al., 2007).

Similarly, *multicultural feminism* arose in response to, and as a critique of, a unitary or predominant focus on gender differences in feminist theorizing and research. That is, in much of the earlier feminist work, sexism and/or classism was given as *the* reason(s) for women's oppression. What was ignored in this work was how and why racism, ethnocentrism, ableism, heterosexism, and ageism were more or equally important contributors to some women's marginalization. The exclusive emphasis on gender and sexism as the roots of women's disadvantaged status was likely a consequence of both the relatively privileged position of feminist theorists and researchers and "their desire to prove that women are men's full equals"; however, in so doing they ended up stressing "women's sameness to each other as well as women's sameness to men" (Tong, 2009, p. 204). According to Spelman (1998), these feminists "failed to realize that is it possible to oppress people both by ignoring their differences and by denying their similarities" (Tong, 2009, p. 204).

In reaction to this assumption of commonality and sameness among women, multicultural feminists seek to explore and highlight differences among women and to develop a feminism inclusive and resonant of the lives and experiences of women who are not white, middle-class, young, and heterosexual. They also tend to focus on women's diversity within any particular nation. In terms of leisure, specifically, the work of some multicultural feminists (e.g., in the United States, that of Collins, 1990; hooks, 1990) provides valuable insights into how popular culture shapes ideologies and discourses of race and gender. This perspective also presents distinct challenges to feminists who seek to acknowledge the diversity of women's experience. For example, it illuminates the potentially problematic use of the term "women of color." In the context of the United States, specifically, in what sense is this word representative and inclusive of women who are African American, Latina American, Asian American, and Native American? Are these categories even "accurate" (Shinew & Stodolska, this volume)? Does such terminology actually serve to "other," marginalize, and/or "exoticize" these women? That is, does such language continue to center women of non-color, are they still the reference point? Further, the work and thinking of multicultural feminists raise questions about the category of race itself. That is, how "colored" or "non-colored" does one have to look to be considered one race or another? While a woman may appear "white" or "of color" phenotypically, that does not mean she is "white" or "of color" genotypically (Tong, 2009). Neither is it any indication for whether a woman thinks of herself as a woman of color or as a woman of non-color. Further, multicultural feminists assert that the meaning of skin color, hair texture, and other "bodily markings" of race is fluid and contextual. For example, what it means to be white in the United States may be very different than what it means to be white in the United Kingdom, South Africa, or Japan. What it means to be a person of color and a person of non-color today in the United States is very different than what it meant 100 years ago. That is, race and ethnicity are socially constructed and deconstruct-ed—which is not to say that race is unimportant or insignificant (Tong, 2009). Indeed, "race matters" (West, 1994), as it is a practice and process of perceiving, relating, and being, now largely taken for granted, particularly by those advantaged by its categories (Alcoff, 2006). Hence, multicultural feminists challenge us to critically reflect on what it means to be white or a woman of non-color as well as on what it means to be a woman of color, *and* also to critically consider the many cultures or identities of difference in addition to gender and race (e.g., age, class, ableism, sexual orientation) that shape women's lives.

It is with such issues, specifically when they involve women from so-called "First World" and "Third World" nations, that *global* and *postcolonial feminists* are also concerned. That is, global and postcolonial feminists focus on how women experience their identity and status as a woman *differently* depending on global power relations—that is, if they are members of a nation that dominates other nations economically, politically, and culturally (so-called First World or minority-population nations), or members of a nation that is dominated by others in these ways (so-called Third World or majority-population nations) (Tong, 2009). While recognizing that all women are disadvantaged as women, a particular interest within these ap-proaches is with the status and identity of women of Third World nations, nations that are disadvantaged economically, politically, and culturally in the processes and practices of colonialization and globalization. Hence, issues of sexuality and reproduction that are often the gender concerns of more privileged First World women are not the primary focus of Third World feminists; rather, economic and political issues are, though such feminists also see these issues as inseparable. Further, according to global/postcolonial feminists, the world is an interconnected place where the op-pression and/or privileging of women (and men) in one part of the world affects the conditions of women's (and men's) lives in other parts of the world. Oppression is a globally interactive and interconnecting practice.

The political and religious struggle over girls' access to schooling in Afghanistan and Iraq that has come to light in the beginning of the twenty-first century is an example of the interconnectedness of economic, political, and reproductive concerns resulting from First World and Third World political and ideological conflicts. In addition, research has clearly shown that women's sense of what it means to be a "woman" may well be exclusive. It incorporates notions of difference and "otherness" based on country of origin and ethnicity that allows for a disjunction between an espousal of feminist principles on the one hand and a woman's everyday interactions with other women on the hand (e.g., see Vassiliadou, 2004).

Still, because of the belief that Third World women's oppression is often greater *as members of Third World nations* than as women, some do not accept the label *feminist*. Further, for some the concern is not just the oppression of women but that of an entire people, female *and* male (Walker, 1983, in Tong, 2009). In addition, global/postcolonial feminism asks us to think differently about how political, economic, and cultural structures and practices are produced, shifting the focus from nations and governments to multinational corporations, media conglomerates, and religious movements (Kitch, 2007)—practices that are often related to leisure.

Thus, central to intersectional, multicultural, and global/postcolonial feminist thought is that no woman is free until all women are free and that women cannot work together as equals until they recognize and attend to their differences. These perspectives are compelling, highlighting the shortcomings of other feminist traditions. They also provide distinct challenges to feminist theorizing and research in their call for more complex, nuanced, and inclusive renderings of gender relations, femininity, and womanhood. Further, they challenge women advantaged by race, class, culture, and/or nationhood to recognize how their "gains" as women may well come from the continued oppression of "other" women and men; that is, to recognize the interconnections of global and local processes (Kitch, 2007)—or *glocalization* (Giulianotti & Robertson, 2006). At the same time, global and postcolonial feminists struggle with issues of "ethical relativism" or the idea that there is no cultural absolutism (Tong, 2009). So, for example, do First World feminists have "the right" to impose their notions of gender equality on Third World women (and men); do they have to respect gender practices and beliefs—even those that are exploitative and oppressive—as an expression of cultural difference? Leisure and recreation are spaces, places, and experiences through which imperialism, globalization, glocalization, and post-colonization have been, and continue to be, enacted (see, for example, Kay; Shinew & Stodolska; Tirone & Gahagan, this volume). Questions about these practices in relation to issues of gender equality need to be explored. However, such questions are only further complicated—and made more interesting—by the "postmodern turn" discussed next.

Influences from Other Disciplines: Social Constructionism, Postmodernism, and Poststructuralism

As suggested by the discussion thus far, a central dilemma raised as a result of the debates and contestations among feminist researchers relates to a question of structure versus agency. This issue has been the focus of a long-standing debate in sociology and in other disciplines (e.g., see Giddens, 1984). For feminist researchers in the leisure field, it raises the question of how much they should pay attention to individual lives and the experiences and actions of individual women, versus the extent to which they should focus on structured relations of power within society, including structural aspects of sexism, classism, racism, heterosexism, ageism, etc. Does attention to individual lives neglect societal power structures? On the other hand, does a structural focus, whether related to gender, class, and/or other forms of power, tend to ignore the issue of agency?

One of the theoretical approaches that has been "borrowed" from other disciplines (in this case from sociology) and adapted by some feminist leisure researchers is *social constructionism*. Early proponents of social constructionism (e.g., Berger & Luckmann, 1966) argued that all meaningful human activity is constructed through dialogue, discourse, and social practices. That is, that there is no reality and no meaning associated with objects or behaviors until that meaning is collectively developed. At first glance, this way of thinking would not seem to be a good fit with feminist critique and feminist action because of its relativist stance and its tendency to see all constructed meanings as equally valid or "legitimate." Yet, critical constructionists, including feminists, have come to see this approach as a way to bridge the divide between an individualistic and a structuralist orientation to research (e.g., Burr, 2003). For example, critical constructionists draw on the work of Foucault and others that link discourse not only with disciplinary power and social control, but also to personal power and agency. For some feminists, then, critical constructionism is a framework for interrogating dominant discourses and ideologies through analysis of the ways in which discourses or ideologies, such as those associated with femininity, "the family," or sexuality, are socially constructed and reproduced (e.g., Wodak & Meyer, 2001; see also Shaw, 2010; and Harrington, this volume). Moreover, this approach allows for analysis not only of how these dominant ideologies are reinforced, but also how they are negotiated and reconstructed through individual and collective action. The social action focus of this approach, therefore, relates to ways in which embedded discriminatory and disempowering beliefs and actions can be challenged at the individual or group level, and relatively less attention is paid to legislative change. Dominant discourses related to patriarchy, classism, and other structures of power are examined in terms of the processes that lead to the reinforcement of those power relations and also the ways in which discourses can also be challenged and resisted through alternate social practices.

Feminist constructionism is also a vehicle through which men's power and dominant ideologies of masculinity can be explored and challenged. The notion of social constructionism is one that does not essentialize femininity or masculinity, and it sees value in research on men's lives and men's experiences as well as women's. Not only are men a part of the process of the social construction of meaning, but individual men connect in different ways to dominant ideologies of masculinity, and they vary in terms of their access to male power (for example, differences are evident between men based on race, ethnicity, sexuality, and/or age) (Hibbins, this volume). In this way, critical constructionism can provide a link between "women's studies" and "men's studies," through looking at differences among men and the potential for change in the social practices and actions of men as well as women. Nevertheless, critical constructionism is similar to a number of other feminist approaches in terms of the struggle with notions of multiple oppressions and with how best to incorporate difference and diversity into research, theory, and practice.

Postmodernism and *poststructuralism* have also had an impact on feminist theorizing and feminist research. Arising in the 1980s, primarily within philosophy, cultural studies, and linguistics, these perspectives presented a new critique and challenge to scholars throughout the humanities and social sciences. Postmodernists' rejection of "meta-narratives" and grand theories challenged some of the fundamental goals of modernist thinking, while poststructuralists' denial of the idea of structured or systemic relations of power had major implications for sociological theorizing. Societies were seen to be diffuse, contingent, fragmented, and not subject to macro-level or even micro-level "certainties." Consistent with these ideas, existing epistemological and methodological ideas and approaches were also criticized and seen to be of little value both by postmodernists and poststructuralists.

For feminist researchers, with their commitment to understanding power and oppression and to advocating for social change, postmodernism and poststructuralism represent a particular challenge, and an "uneasy" relationship has developed between these new perspectives and feminism (Gannon & Davies, 2007). Poststructuralism, in particular, seemed to invalidate concepts such as patriarchy, dominant ideology, and hegemonic femininity and masculinity (Henderson & Shaw, 2006). Moreover, the relativist stance of poststructuralism and postmodernism was seen to be either apolitical or politically conservative (Gannon & Davies, 2007). Postmodernism also typically denies collectivist thinking, thereby preventing the possibility of collectivist action (Aitchison, 2003). In 1994, Scraton argued that postmodernist ideas were ushering in a new post-feminist era and an end to the "politics of emancipation." And in 2003, Aitchison suggested that the effect of poststructuralism on feminist leisure research, at least in the United Kingdom, could be observed in the decline of feminist contributions to the literature in the 1990s, after the clear progress that had been made in the previous decade.

Nevertheless, the sometimes vitriolic debate about postmodernism and poststructuralism has moderated in recent years. Some feminist scholars, including Patti Lather and Judith Butler, have embraced these perspectives, combining them with a moderated critical approach (Gannon & Davies, 2007) that incorporates a more contingent and limited take on notions of power, freedom, and agency compared to "mainstream" feminism. Other feminist researchers, both in leisure studies and in other fields, have talked about the contributions that postmodernism and poststructuralism can make to gender scholarship through providing new insights and new pathways to understanding and theorizing.

One of the contributions that the "post-isms" are seen to make to feminist research is the idea of multiple realities, multiple subjectivities, and multiple identities (Henderson & Shaw, 2006), an idea consistent with the perspective of intersectionality. That is, the critique of collective experience leads to greater sensitivity towards the many different meanings of "femininity" and "masculinity" and how these notions are enacted, performed, and communicated (Harrington, this volume). This, in turn, directs greater attention to issues of diversity and difference. Second, poststructuralist notions of the diffusion of power (based primarily on Foucault's work) place emphasis on personal power and multiple ways of accessing power. Despite the challenge this might represent to ideas of structured power and oppression, this approach is valued for its optimism and its recognition of the many ways in which agency, contestation, and resistance can be facilitated (Wearing, 1998). Third, the postmodernist focus on culture and cultural codes, including a wide variety of cultural representations, discourses, and forms of language, further reinforces the need to center attention on issues of cultural difference and diversity. The "situatedness" of thought, experience, and emotion (Gannon & Davies, 2007) reinforces the importance of taking context and place into account, not only within particular societies and cultural groupings, but also globally. Indeed, this notion is at the center of postcolonial and global feminist challenges to liberal, care-focused, Marxist, and socialist thinking. In addition, the critique of existing epistemologies has led to opportunities for new forms of research, particularly deconstructionism, discourse and text analysis, narrative analysis, autoethnography, and performative research. Within feminist leisure studies, the influence of postmodernism and poststructuralism can be seen in Wearing's (1998) work on multiple leisure identities, Green's (1998) study of women's friendships, empowerment and resistance, and Aitchison's work (e.g., 1999b) on tourism, space, place, sexuality, and power.

Postmodernism and poststructuralism, then, can be seen to have provided some new ways of thinking about research and leisure, more specifically, about feminist leisure research. Despite the uneasy relationship with feminism, Gannon and Davies (2007) argue that critical postmodernism and critical poststructuralism open up "new futures" for feminist researchers. A question remains, though, about whether or not these new ideas of the 1980s and 1990s create an inevitable gap or divide among feminist researchers that weakens the feminist agenda. That is, can the "postmodern turn" be reconciled with other approaches to feminist research in ways that are mutually respectful and beneficial and that strengthen feminist goals related to equity and social justice? If so, how can this be accomplished?

Doing Feminist Leisure Research

Changes in our ways of thinking about women, gender, and leisure have occurred in ways both evolutionary, building on what has come before, and revolutionary, marking a schism with previous thinking, or a paradigm shift. That is, like the many women of the matryoshka, feminist approaches to leisure research may be seen as a whole *and* as distinct and separate.

In our discussion of a number of feminist approaches, we have indicated their "wholeness" as well as their distinctiveness. We have also suggested the types of questions that those using a given approach might ask about women, gender, and leisure. Whether one starts from the perspective of liberal feminism and its focus on gender equality in leisure opportunities, multicultural feminism and its concern with the recognition of differences among women in leisure, critical constructionism and the negotiation of agency/empowerment and structure/disempowerment in leisure, or postmodernism and its assumption of leisure as a performative space for multiple and fluid identities, some of the tensions and debates, as well as the rich and layered complexity of gendered lives and leisure, are illustrated. Hence, it is probably most useful to think of these approaches or perspectives as heuristic devices, strategies or ways to shift the lens or turn the kaleidoscope, and in so doing, to get different insights. Still, it is difficult to separate ways of knowing from one's values and beliefs—and from the political, economic, and social consequences of those values and beliefs. For these reasons, there are often lively debates among those doing feminist leisure research using these different approaches; these debates, however, ultimately add to the research we do on, the understandings we have of, and the social action we take for girls, women, and their leisure.

Summary

Hesse-Biber (2007) classifies feminist research by what she calls "critical moments" that are defined by the "dialogues surrounding issues of epistemology, methodology, and method" (p. 4). In this conceptualization, during the first moment, feminist researchers sought to challenge the androcentric bias of research and "correct" this bias by adding women to research samples and asking questions to highlight how women's experiences differed from those of men. Henderson (1994b) refers to this as the "add women and stir" approach and notes that while it brought attention to the lives of girls and women, gender was an afterthought in which particular renderings of men and masculinity were still centered as the norm and gender was essentialized.

In reaction to this "biologicalization of the social" (Bordieu, 2001), a variety of theoretical approaches emerged, leading to a period of contestation and critique and, at times, to divisions between feminist researchers. During this second significant moment or turn, the dialectic of structure versus agency was often centered. Feminist researchers were faced with competing notions of empowerment and oppression in women's lives, and they were grappling with ways to recognize the relational and/or socially constructed notions of gender and the contradictions of gender as subject to both reproduction and transformation. A body of leisure research, informed by these various perspectives has developed, though, as evidenced by the chapters in this volume.

The imperative of globalization can be seen as a third critical moment in feminist research. Multinational corporations, media conglomerates, and religious movements are seen to be superseding governments and nation-states in shaping discourses and practices of power and inequality. The meshing of the global and local, or the notion of glocalization, acknowledges the fluidity of power and the intersections of structure and agency. Global and postcolonial feminists focus on how women experience their identity and status as a woman differently depending on global power relations (e.g., see chapter by Kay, this volume). Hence, they ask us to think about oppression as a globally interactive and interconnecting practice that is, at the same time, both about *and* more than gender (e.g., the low-wage labor of Third World women and men that is required by much First World tourism and the sexual exploitation of Third World women and men in this tourism). Leisure research from this perspective is more likely to be found in the United Kingdom, Europe, and Australia than in the United States. As yet, relatively little feminist leisure research has come from the "majority world," or the "Global South," but hopefully this will change as the third critical moment in feminist research progresses.

In sum, as noted by Vassiliadou (2004), "although feminism is a general theory of the oppression of women by men, it is a highly contradictory one" (p. 56). The different feminist theories/approaches to research just described, and the tensions and contestations that exist among them, provide evidence of this claim. Indeed, one of the challenges feminists face is whether and how to accommodate the variety of foci and concerns of feminist work. This book is intended to offer at least an initial response to that challenge. In providing a discussion of the feminist theories and thinking that have had the greatest impact in studying leisure, women, and gender, this chapter provides a context for the presentations of research in the chapters that follow. The subsequent sections bring together *some* of the diversity of research on leisure, women, and gender. By doing so, we hope to illustrate the many valuable but different contributions that feminist researchers have made employing a variety of theoretical, epistemological, and methodological approaches. In the last section of the book, we identify themes and meanings—both within and across the sections exploring the personal, social, and cultural-political lives of girls and women, and their leisure and recreation—that emerge from our reading of our colleagues' research. To us, this valuation of diversity within feminist research is consistent with the notion of matryoshka, and the many selves and many voices that have contributed and continue to contribute to feminist scholarship on leisure, women, and gender. In addition, we build on the insights of this book's contributors, including some of the tensions and gaps that currently exist, and we discuss possible ways for moving forward in terms of future research on leisure, women, and gender.

References

Aitchison, C. C. (1999b). New cultural geographies: the spatiality of leisure, gender, and sexuality. *Leisure Studies, 18*(1), 19–39.

Aitchison, C. C. (2003). *Gender and leisure: Social and cultural perspectives.* London, UK: Routledge.

Alcoff, L. M. (2006). *Visible identities: Race, gender, and the self.* New York, NY: Oxford University Press.

Berger, P., & Luckmann, T. (1966). *The social construction of reality: A treatise in the sociology of knowledge.* New York, NY: Doubleday.

Bhavnani, K. K. (2007). Interconnections and configurations: Toward a global feminist ethnography. In S. N. Hesse-Biber (Ed.), *Handbook of feminist research: Theory and praxis* (pp. 639–650). Thousand Oaks, CA: Sage.

Bordieu, P. (2001). *Masculine domination.* Palo Alto, CA: Stanford University Press.

Bordo, S. (1990). Feminism, post-modernism, and gender-skepticism. In L. Nicholson (Ed.), *Feminism/Postmodernism* (pp. 133–156). London, UK: Routledge.

Brah, A., & Phoenix, A. (2004). Ain't I a woman? Revisiting intersectionality. *Journal of International Women's Studies, 5*(3), 75–86.

Burr, V. (2003). *Social constructionism* (2nd ed.). East Sussex, UK: Routledge.

Cole, C. L. (1994). Resisting the canon: Feminist cultural studies, sport, and technologies of the body. In S. Birrell & C. L. Cole (Eds.), *Women, sport and culture* (pp. 5–29). Champaign, IL: Human Kinetics.

Collins, P. H. (1990). *Black feminist thought: Knowledge, consciousness, and the politics of empowerment*. New York, NY: Routledge.

Daly, M. (1978). *Gyn/Ecology: The metaethics of radical feminism*. Boston, MA: Beacon.

Dill, B. T., McLaughlin, A. E., & Nieves, A. D. (2007). Future directions of feminist research: Intersectionality. In S. N. Hesse-Biber (Ed.), *Handbook of feminist research: Theory and praxis* (pp. 629–637). Thousand Oaks, CA: Sage.

Firestone, S. (1970). *The dialectic of sex*. New York, NY: Bantam.

Gannon, S., & Davies, B. (2007). Postmodern, poststructural, and critical theories. In S. N. Hesse-Biber (Ed.), *Handbook of feminist research: Theory and praxis* (pp. 71–106). Thousand Oaks, CA: Sage.

Giddens, A. (1984). *The construction of society: Outline of a theory of structuration*. Cambridge, UK: Polity.

Gilligan, C. (1982). *In a different voice*. Cambridge, MA: Harvard University Press.

Giulianotti, R., & Robertson, R. (2006). Glocalization, globalization, and migration: The case of Scottish football players in North America. *International Sociology, 21*(2), 171–198.

Green, E. (1998). "Women doing friendship": An analysis of women's leisure as a site of identity construction, empowerment and resistance. *Leisure Studies, 17*(3), 171–185.

Harding, S. (Ed.) (1987). *Feminism and methodology*. Bloomington, IN: Indiana University Press.

Harding, S. (2007). Feminist standpoints. In S. N. Hesse-Biber (Ed.), *Handbook of feminist research: Theory and praxis* (pp. 45–70). Thousand Oaks, CA: Sage.

Henderson, K. A. (1994b). Perspectives on analyzing gender, women, and leisure. *Journal of Leisure Research, 26*, 119–137.

Henderson, K. A., & Shaw, S. M. (2006). Leisure and gender: Challenges and opportunities for feminist research. In C. Rojek, S. M. Shaw, & A. J. Veal (Eds.), *A handbook of leisure studies* (pp. 216–230). Basingstoke, UK: Palgrave Macmillan.

Hesse-Biber, S. N. (2007). Feminist research: Exploring the interconnections of epistemology, methodology, and method. In S. N. Hesse-Biber (Ed.), *Handbook of feminist research: Theory and praxis* (pp. 1–26). Thousand Oaks, CA: Sage.

Hesse-Biber, S. N., & Piatelli, D. (2007). From theory to method and back again: The synergistic praxis of theory and method. In S. N. Hesse-Biber (Ed.), *Handbook of feminist research: Theory and praxis* (pp. 143–154). Thousand Oaks, CA: Sage.

hooks, b. (1990). *Feminism is for everybody: Passionate politics*. Cambridge, MA: South End.

Jaggar, A. M. (1983). *Feminist politics and human nature*. Totowa, NJ: Rowman & Allanheld.

Jaggar, A. M. (1995). The politics of socialist feminism. In N. Tuana & R. Tong (Eds.), Feminism and philosophy: Essential readings in theory, reinterpretation, and application (pp. 299–324). Boulder, CO: Westview Press, Inc.

Kitch, S. L. (2007). Feminist interdisciplinary approaches to knowledge building. In S. N. Hesse-Biber (Ed.), *Handbook of feminist research: Theory and praxis* (pp. 123–139). Thousand Oaks, CA: Sage.

Mendez, J. B., & Wolf, D. L. (2007). Feminizing global research/globalizing feminist research. In S. N. Hesse-Biber (Ed.), *Handbook of feminist research: Theory and praxis* (pp. 651–662). Thousand Oaks, CA: Sage.

Mies, M. (2007). A global feminist perspective on research. In S. N. Hesse-Biber (Ed.), *Handbook of feminist research: Theory and praxis* (pp. 663–668). Thousand Oaks, CA: Sage.

Noddings, N. (1984). *Caring: A feminine approach to ethics and moral education.* Berkeley, CA: University of California Press.

Noddings, N. (2002). *Starting at home: Caring and social policy.* Berkeley, CA: University of California Press.

Raey, D. (2007). Future directions in difference research: Recognizing and responding to difference. In S. N. Hesse-Biber (Ed.), *Handbook of feminist research: Theory and praxis* (pp. 605–612). Thousand Oaks, CA: Sage.

Scraton, S. (1994). The changing world of women and leisure: Feminism, "postfeminism" and leisure. *Leisure Studies, 13*(4), 249–261.

Shaw, S. M. (2010). Diversity and ideology: Changes in Canadian family life and implications for leisure. *World Leisure Journal, 52*(1), 4–13.

Smith, D. E. (1990). *The conceptual practices of power: A feminist sociology.* Boston, MA: Northeastern University Press.

Spelman, E. V. (1998). *Inessential woman: Problems of exclusion in feminist thought.* Boston, MA: Beacon.

Spivak, G. C. (1994). Can the subaltern speak? In P. Williams & L. Chrismen (Eds.), *Colonial discourse and post-colonial theory: A reader* (pp. 66–111). New York, NY: Columbia University Press.

Tong, R. (2009). *Feminist thought* (3rd ed.). Boulder, CO: Westview.

Tuana, N., & Tong, R. (Eds.) (1994). *Feminist philosophy: Essential readings in theory, reinterpretation, and application.* Boulder, CO: Westview.

Vassiliadou, M. (2004). Women's constructions of women: On entering the front door. *Journal of International Women's Studies, 5*(3), 53–67.

Walker, A. (1983). *In search of our mothers' gardens.* New York, NY: Harcourt Brace Jovanovich.

Wearing, B. (1998). *Leisure and feminist theory.* Thousand Oaks, CA: Sage.

West, C. (1994). *Race matters*. New York, NY: Vintage.

Wodak, R., & Meyer, M. (Eds.) (2001). *Methods of critical discourse analysis*. London, UK: Sage.

Wylie, A. (2007). The feminism question in science: What does it mean to "do social science as a feminist"? In S. N. Hesse-Biber (Ed.), *Handbook of feminist research: Theory and praxis* (pp. 567–577). Thousand Oaks, CA: Sage.

Section 2
Personal Lives

Chapter 6
Introduction:
Expanding Opportunities for Leisure

Valeria J. Freysinger, Susan M. Shaw, Karla A. Henderson, and M. Deborah Bialeschki

The Russian doll represents the many facets of women's lives. One of those is their personal lives. This focus suggests a social psychological approach, based on individual actions, activities, experiences, and psychological states. Individual experiences and practices, however, are only partially understood if separated from broader contexts. For feminists, research on individual lives requires attention to the gendered nature of those lives, including the gendered nature of leisure activities and contexts, and the need to interpret findings in terms of the wider sociocultural and ideological environment. Moreover, important differences exist among individuals in terms of leisure experiences, accessibility, and outcomes.

Although women share some commonalities simply because they are women in a patriarchal society, leisure experiences are not necessarily the same for all women, just as leisure is not the same for all men. Social class, cultural background, marital and familial situation, employment status and type of occupation, and other factors affect the availability of leisure, the manner and circumstances in which leisure is experienced, and the benefits that accrue from leisure involvement. Thus, diversity and difference among women and the different ways in which they experience patriarchy needs to be constantly acknowledged and incorporated into our understandings of gendered lives.

The social-psychological study of leisure has typically been associated with particular types of experience, such as freedom, enjoyment, relaxation, self-expression, affiliation, and escape from the everyday routine world. Leisure has also been described in terms of activities and constraints on participation. While these notions can help us to understand women's leisure, they also need to be challenged and interrogated. Leisure can be an elusive experience, and may be especially so for many women and other traditionally disadvantaged groups. Further, leisure does not necessarily occur only in clearly demarcated blocks of time, in particular settings, or during particular activities. Leisure may be glimpsed in brief, fleeting moments or may be associated with social interactions in different settings. For example, leisure can be experienced in intermittent moments such as brief, warm interactions with others or moments of quiet reflection or raucous humor. In addition, many activities traditionally thought of as leisure, such as time with children and other family members, are not necessarily experienced that way by women because of their caregiving and other gendered responsibilities. Further, the experiences of particular activities can vary depending on specific circumstances and contexts. However, considerable evidence suggests that leisure is a meaningful concept in women's lives, and those leisure activities and experiences can make significant contributions to their sense of self and their overall life quality.

In this section of the book, these ideas about individual leisure and the gendered nature of women's leisure are further explored. Specific leisure activities, contexts, and experiences are discussed within a critical framework that challenges simplistic notions of choice and self-determination and recognizes the complexity of women's and men's lives. In addition, the importance of leisure for women's sense of self and the importance of entitlement, empowerment, and resistance are discussed. Thus, couched in a framework of personal lives and elements of gendered leisure and gendered constraints, the central themes of this section relate to *leisure activities, leisure contexts, leisure experiences*, and *personal identity*, as well as *entitlement, empowerment*, and *resistance*.

LEISURE ACTIVITIES

The chapters about individual lives focus on a range of leisure activities. These include sports for girls and women (Schmalz and Bialeschki), sports for older adults (Dionigi), women motorcycle-riders (Roster), leisure in sororities (Berbary), women's friendships (Hutchison), and solo traveling (Gibson, Jordan, & Berdychevsky). Both *traditionally female* activities (e.g., sororities) as well as nontraditional activities (e.g., motorcycling, traveling alone) are included, which suggests opportunities for some degree of personal choice. At the same time, Samdahl's chapter and discussion in many of the chapters (Schmalz and Berbary), alert readers to the ways activity choices are constrained by ideologies of gender as well as socially constructed notions of gender-appropriate leisure activities. Ideological factors can also lead to *constraints* indicating culturally approved forms of leisure. For example, women may be constrained into aerobics because of a strongly felt need to lose weight or to remain slim that arises from cultural beliefs about the ideal female body image (Frederick & Shaw, 1995). Shannon (this volume) further discusses the female ideal of thinness and the role that parents play relative to body image and leisure for their daughters. Thus, what seems on the surface to be an individually chosen leisure activity may not be experienced as leisure for some participants or may have aspects of constraint and obligation. An individual's freedom of choice clearly is a complex question whether pertaining to leisure or to other life experiences.

Many of the activities discussed in this section of the book focus on ordinary, everyday life, and these activities generally make up the bulk of women's leisure. Nevertheless, less frequent leisure, such as solo travel and solo vacations, may be particularly important as escapes from gendered responsibilities and notions of freedom and autonomy. These responsibilities, and especially family caregiving responsibilities, often limit women's opportunities for personal leisure in their everyday lives (see Hilbrecht's chapter).

Constraints can also be seen to limit participation in *serious*, or highly involved, forms of leisure. The concept of serious leisure is a popular and controversial idea that has emerged from the work of Stebbins (1992). While the binary division of serious versus *casual* is problematic, and leisure activities may represent more of a continuum than a dichotomy (Shen & Yarnal, 2010), this conceptualization may also be useful for understanding some aspects of gendered leisure. When activities require a considerable commitment of time and/or money, such as the activities of amateur musicians, marathon runners, or mountain climbers, they are often male-dominated activities. Many women may feel they do not have the resources, either temporally or financially, to commit themselves to such activities in that sense of serious leisure. Thus, they may seek less involving activities that fit better with their home and interpersonal responsibilities. Motorcycling (see Roster), as well as competitive sports (Dionigi) and solo traveling (Gibson, Jordan, & Berdychevsky), however, can be seen as forms of serious leisure, and thus, may provide a different kind of leisure experience for women compared to *everyday* activities.

Johnson's chapter on gay men's leisure reminds readers that not only women's leisure is gendered. This chapter also highlights the additional constraints on leisure related to heterosexism and homophobia, and the importance of acceptance and companionship in leisure. Questions of diversity again arise along with the need to avoid simplistic and dichotomous concepts of leisure, gender, and gendered constraints.

LEISURE CONTEXTS

Leisure activities cannot be separated from leisure contexts. This interrelationship is particularly evident in the discussions of friendships in leisure

(Hutchinson) and leisure activities, which are based primarily on social interactions and social connections (Berbary and Johnson). Leisure can be a means to develop friendships and social support. In addition, other aspects of the social context (e.g., physical setting or environment, temporal aspects, and gendered expectations of others in the setting) also influence the leisure activity and leisure experience. Leisure space, for example, is important insofar as whether it is *safe space* or not is important, particularly for gay and lesbian youth and for other groups who experience marginalization (Johnson and Bialeschki). Safe spaces are needed for leisure to occur. Further, Roster emphasizes that leisure may be a way to enlarge a woman's personal space. These contexts can also be seen as *containers* (Henderson et al., 1989) that help to define the activity as leisure or not. Although leisure can occur in almost any context, certain containers are more likely to be seen by observers and participants as leisure.

Leisure contexts can also be explored related to constraints. Some contexts allow for greater degree of self-expression, while others can be limiting relative to social expectations and notions of appropriate behaviors. For example, the social environment of sororities is explored by Berbary regarding the ways traditional views of appropriate femininity dominate and influence leisure. Likewise, Hilbrecht's chapter suggests that the family leisure environment may constrain women's leisure experience in a different way due to dominant assumptions about mothers' roles. It should be noted, too, that leisure contexts can also influence beliefs and expectations about gender. Although gendered ideologies can constrain leisure participation and leisure experience, the social context within which leisure occurs can also influence the ways in which gendered ideologies are perpetuated and/or challenged.

LEISURE EXPERIENCES AND PERSONAL IDENTITY

A number of dimensions of leisure relate to the notion of leisure as positive experience. Women and men actively seek enjoyable and intrinsically motivating activities as well as emotional involvement. They may simply be relishing intrinsic aspects of enjoyment (Roster), or they may also be experiencing the enjoyment of escape from everyday work, responsibilities, and routines. This notion of escape also relates to the idea of leisure as self-determined activity. Despite criticisms of a simplistic notion of leisure as *freedom of choice* and recognition of the many gendered constraints on women's leisure, some sense of increased choice and decreased obligation may remain an important aspect of leisure for women, especially if leisure experiences can be seen to lie somewhere along a continuum from choice to constraint. Increased choice may simply mean the opportunity to relax and to take time for self as opposed to worrying about others. In addition, however, choice may also suggest greater opportunities for autonomous leisure activities selected because of the activity itself or the social context. Elements of autonomy can be found in the discussion in some of the chapters, such as Gibson et al.'s discussion of tourism activities, Roster's research with women motorcycle riders, and Dionigi's chapter on older female athletes.

A source of enjoyable leisure for many people, and perhaps especially for women, is affiliation or relationality. Despite the work associated with parenting and family activities, mothers may highly value leisure activities with family. Family interactions can be important sources of enjoyment and satisfaction (Hilbrecht). Leisure as affiliation, however, is not limited to interactions with family members. Connections and interactions with friends, work colleagues, and neighbors are also central to the leisure lives of many women. Hutchinson illustrates the value of female friendships as leisure in her chapter. Berbary also illustrates some of the affiliative aspects of leisure and their personal meanings among sorority sisters. Parry's analysis goes beyond the idea of enjoyment and positive experience to show how friendships in leisure contribute in many ways to women's health. Thus, although interactions in leisure can have negative aspects (Schmalz), the positive experiences of friendships and relationality are highly valued.

Another positive dimension of leisure may include activities that express, construct, and reconstruct an individual's sense of self and identity. Personal identity benefits could include presenting and thinking of oneself in a positive way because of a particular leisure involvement and feeling good about that self-presentation. Leisure may provide more opportunities for personal identity development compared to many work and family contexts. The increased opportunities for choice and for autonomous action, as discussed above, may also have implications for identity development. Dionigi discusses this link between autonomous leisure and self-identity in her chapter. A strong sense of identity, self-expression, and self-esteem can also be found among women who become highly involved in autonomous leisure, as is the case among many female motorcycle riders (Roster) as well as some solo women travelers (Gibson et al.). Further, personal identity may be particularly important for women and men in stigmatized groups. Johnson's chapter reveals the importance for gay men of various leisure spaces such as bars and rodeos. These spaces allow gay men to develop and solidify a positive sense of masculinity and identity despite living in a homophobic and patriarchal society.

ENTITLEMENT, EMPOWERMENT, AND RESISTANCE

The notion of a strong sense of personal identity for women and other disempowered groups leads directly to notions of entitlement, empowerment, and resistance. Not surprisingly, considerable attention is given to these interrelated concepts in the chapters on gendered lives. This attention reflects both an awareness of the pervasiveness of gender and gender-based inequities as well as the potential for leisure as an avenue for social change and social justice.

Entitlement can be defined as the individual's belief that she or he has a personal right to leisure and can take advantage of leisure opportunities. This sense of entitlement is reflected in this gendered lives section. Dionigi, for example, illustrates how older women feel entitled to participate in elite sports, and how their high levels of involvement reflect and influence their sense of entitlement. Women who are involved in other highly involving activities, such as motorcycle riding and solo traveling, can also be seen to reflect a sense of entitlement linked to self-expression and self-esteem. Further, feeling entitled to leisure can be an enabler, which opens up opportunities and encourages and facilitates independent and autonomous leisure. A sense of entitlement does not mean that constraints and constraining social messages about appropriate gendered behavior do not exist. Samdahl, for example, warns readers of the profound repercussions of socialization into narrowly perceived gendered roles, and the difficulty of changing perceptions and attitudes. Nevertheless, a sense of entitlement to leisure is an important step representing support for the idea of leisure as a personal right and a determination to put this idea into practice.

Linked to the idea of entitlement is the notion of empowerment. Many of the authors in this section discuss empowerment as an important aspect of women's lives that can result from their leisure involvement. A sense of empowerment in leisure can spill over into other aspects of women's and men's lives, including their personal and work lives. This empowerment assists people to exercise greater control over negative and disempowering situations. Thus, they may be more able to challenge the status quo. A range of leisure opportunities can provide this sense of empowerment, especially from highly involving and self-determined leisure (Dionigi and Roster) and leisure that assists in the development of positive and supportive social groups and social connections (Hutchinson). Further, Parry draws direct linkages between leisure, empowerment, and health. Thus, the benefits of empowerment enable women, as well as men, to take control over their own health and thereby to improve their health, well-being, and quality of life.

Close connections also exist between empowerment and resistance. "Resistance" refers to questioning, challenging, and seeking to change processes and circumstances that are disempowering. The connections between leisure and resistance have been explored in the literature (e.g., Shaw, 2001), and leisure has been described as an important site for women's resistance because of its relative freedom and associated opportunities for both individual and collective acts of resistance.

One form of resistance is challenging constraints on women's time and women's leisure. This focus means challenging narrowly constructed views of appropriate forms of leisure activity for girls and women. For example, when a woman takes up a nontraditional activity, such as riding a motorcycle or going on a vacation alone, she presents herself as strong, independent and/or athletic. Thus, her actions challenge the traditional view of femininity whether she deliberately seeks to make such a challenge or not. Her actions may influence and encourage others. The same case can be made for men who engage in activities that are nontraditional for *men*. Nevertheless, expectations about women's responsibilities for caregiving of children and/or older, dependent adults can also be resisted through individual women's determination to challenge such expectations and to insist on their right to some personal time and personal leisure. In addition, women and girls who challenge stereotypes and *constraints into* activities such as aerobics and fitness designed for weight loss can also be seen to be resisting narrow and constraining conceptualizations of the ideal female body (e.g., see Frederick & Shaw, 1995).

The notion of resistance through leisure also addresses the broader question of ideology (discussed in more detail in section 4 of this book). Ideological systems that devalue women and other disadvantaged groups (e.g., based on race, class, age, ability/disability, and/or sexual orientation) are constantly constructed, negotiated, and reconstructed. Thus, actions including leisure practices that challenge and resist aspects of these ideological systems can be part of that process of reconstruction. Such practices, whether they are resisting women's assumed responsibilities for childcare or expectations about men's but not women's right to personal leisure, contribute to ideological and social change. They challenge the idea that ideological systems are fair, just, and inevitable.

CONCLUDING PERSPECTIVES

This introduction and the contributions in this section suggest that leisure is an important aspect of women's lives, but one that reflects the gendered patriarchal nature of society. The nature of women's leisure activity has been discussed using examples from the chapters. Distinctions exist between everyday and special leisure activities, as do distinctions between highly involving activities and casual leisure. Including references to the range of leisure activities that women and girls participate in was not possible, but some of the specific examples included sports, physical activity, friendships, tourism, and family life. The examples provide a brief, if limited, illustration of the breadth of leisure as it is understood, embodied, and performed by individuals. Other areas of women's lives such as outdoor and nature-based recreation, religion, volunteering, media, and education were not used as examples but may be salient activities. The aspects of personal identity, entitlement, empowerment, and resistance, however, apply in similar ways, regardless of the activity.

The importance of understanding the social, physical, spatial, and environmental contexts of women's leisure is also stressed, and we argue that these containers help to determine the quality of experience and some of the benefits of leisure. Social contexts and opportunities for friendship are seen to be particularly important. The notion of leisure as freedom of choice is critiqued, although the degree of choice, self-determination, enjoyment, and escape from everyday life and everyday responsibilities are all indicated as important aspects of the leisure experience for women. Moreover, positive leisure experiences and contexts, and particularly autonomous or self-determined leisure, are described as contributing to a sense of personal identity.

Entitlement, empowerment, and resistance are also discussed specifically regarding their importance for understanding the leisure of women and other disadvantaged groups. A sense of entitlement to women is conceptualized as a leisure-enabler that facilitates opportunities and participation. This idea is linked to empowerment, which can further facilitate positive change in women's lives in general as well as in their leisure. Broader societal change is also addressed through the notion of resistance, and the argument is made that various types of leisure practice can be seen as acts of personal and/or collective resistance that challenge dominant ideologies of gender, femininity, and masculinity.

As noted at the beginning of this introductory chapter, separating out the individual from the social and cultural contexts can never be fully realized and focusing on the individual tells only part of the story. Thus, although the individual as the center of the Russian doll is pivotal, individual lives can only be understood when seen in relation to the layers surrounding the individual and when taking into account the gendered nature of individual life. At the same time, understanding contexts and gendered relations requires an exploration of how individuals make sense/meaning of their lives. Sections 3 and 4 provide additional insights into how gender shapes leisure-lives, how leisure provides a context for the performance of gender, and how individual leisure relates to broader societal, cultural, and political aspects of social life.

REFERENCES

Frederick, C. J., & Shaw, S. M. (1995). Body image as a leisure constraint: Examining the experience of aerobic exercise classes for young women. *Leisure Sciences, 1*(2), 57–73.

Henderson, K. A., Bialeschki, M. D., Shaw, S. M., & Freysinger, V. J. (1989). *A leisure of one's own: A feminist perspective on women's leisure.* State College, PA: Venture Publishing, Inc.

Shaw, S. M. (2001). Conceptualizing resistance: Women's leisure as political practice. *Journal of Leisure Research, 33*(2), 186–201.

Shen, X. S., & Yarnal, C. (2010). Blowing open the serious leisure-casual leisure dichotomy: What's in there? *Leisure Sciences, 32*(2), 162–179.

Stebbins, R. A. (1992). *Amateurs, professionals and serious leisure.* Kingston, ON: McGill-Queen's University Press.

Chapter 7
A Look Backward and Forward: Women's Participation in Physically Active Recreation and the Homophobic Response

Valeria J. Freysinger, Susan M. Shaw, Karla A. Henderson, and M. Deborah Bialeschki

> Leisure and the cultivation of human capacities are inextricably interdependent.
> —Margaret Mead, in *Redbook*, 1963

Throughout history, the ways women found leisure were as varied as the women themselves. Leisure was often an outgrowth of a household task, a part of social encounters, a function of family interactions, part of a broader social movement, or a concept of time attached to class status, as previously noted. In this chapter, a history of the recreation activity participation of women is presented. As discussed in earlier chapters, one way leisure has been conceptualized is as an individual's perception or experience of activity. Hence, whether activities that have traditionally been seen as recreation *actually were* experienced as leisure by women is unknown. Still, these activities and women's participation in them have often been categorized as their leisure. This categorization has had an influence on their lives, including how they perceived themselves, how they were perceived by others, and how we have come to think about gender. The history presented here is a *select* history in that it is primarily a history of the recreation participation of white, middle- and upper-class women in the United States, and of these women's sport, physical, and outdoor recreation participation. In this discussion, the concerns and interests that contributed to increasing opportunities for girls and women to participate in such activities are also presented. Further, how girls' and women's participation in physically active leisure, particularly sport, continues to be contested terrain is illustrated through an examination of the discourse of heterosexism and its resultant homophobia.

Women's Participation in Sport, Physical, and Outdoor Recreation

In the United States, one of the first shifts in women's transition from home-based leisure to public leisure was through spectatorship at male sporting events. Although women were not directly involved in the activity while spectating, they were given a connection to these activities (Gerber, Felshin, Berlin, & Wyrick, 1974). Women in the audience were thought to make male sport more respectable in that the male athletes would more likely behave like *gentlemen* if *ladies* were present. Thus, *ladies' stands* were erected for horse racing, baseball, and other male athletic meets. This early solicitation of women as spectators was supported by society at large. It got some white middle- and upper-middle-class women, whose lives were often restricted to hearth and home, outdoors and provided them with social contact. However, it also helped teach them that their chief role in sports was to provide applause and to *support* males' athletic endeavors (Gerber et al., 1974).

From spectating, a few women began to challenge the passivity of females and began to engage in physical activities and sports. An article in *The Journal of Health* in 1831 encouraged women to engage in restricted calisthenics such as making circles with their arms, jumping rope, and playing badminton (Calisthenics, 1831). At this same time, young, unmarried frontier women began to demonstrate outstanding riding skills (i.e., sidesaddle) and attended shooting matches where women also sewed and exchanged stories (Welch & Lerch, 1981). Yet, in 1837 Donald Walker's book, *Exercise for Ladies*, warned women against horseback riding as it would *deform* the lower part of their bodies. Still, in 1856, Catherine Beecher published the first fitness manual for women (History of Women in Sports Timeline, n.d.). In the United States and Canada, the *hygiene movement* of the later 1800s and early 1900s also promoted women's participation in moderate physical activity in order to improve their physical and mental fitness (Ehrenreich & English, 1973). In the United States, this concern for women's health was very much a response to the increasing racial and ethnic diversity of its population, due to waves of immigration from non-Northern/Western European countries and the migration of former African American slaves from the South to the industrializing cities of the North. *Race purity* and *eugenics* were ideologies that informed the early fitness movements in the United States and elsewhere. Fears of disease, and the belief ethnic and racial minorities and the poor were the source or cause of many diseases, led to the persecution of some groups. For example, Mary Malone, who immigrated to the United States from Ireland in 1884 and came to be known as *Typhoid Mary*, was one of a number of known healthy carriers of typhoid who worked as a cook for wealthy families, and through this work, infected others. She was also the only female and the only one who was Irish—*and* the only one who, once caught, was quarantined in a clinic until her death (Leavitt, 1997). At the same time, the hygiene movement and others, perhaps unintentionally, helped increase opportunities for a broader spectrum of girls and women to be physically active. In the process, these movements changed thinking about notions of feminine and masculine *nature.*

Another primary purpose of early physical recreation for women was to provide the opportunity for a respectable social encounter between men and women. In the Victorian era of puritanical sexual morality, recreation provided a common ground for mixed-sex activities. Thus, most early recreational physical activity was conducted in a mixed setting (Gerber et al., 1974). Croquet was one of the first social sports adopted by American white women and was firmly established by the time the Civil War ended in the late 1860s (Welch & Lerch, 1981).

Sports for upper-class women gained in popularity in the early 1900s in the United States. These female participants had the leisure time and the finances to belong to clubs with appropriate facilities. They entered into a leisure culture of conspicuous consumption that also included dining, bathing, and drinking at the nation's most exclusive resorts and clubs (Cahn, 1994). For many of these women, sport became a liberating and adventurous pastime that allowed them to display their wealth and strengthen elite social ties. For example, women who first played tennis during the late 1800s had to be wealthy enough to join the clubs as well as have access to the needed equipment.

A consequence of wealthy women's involvement in these activities was that they became socially acceptable pastimes and to be seen as consistent with the refinement expected of *proper ladies.* The notion that refined women played refined games protected elite sportswomen from violating the boundary between proper womanhood and *vulgar* women of other classes (Cahn, 1994). Thus, individual sports such as tennis and golf became associated with upper-class status and were acceptable competitive activities for young women, while team activities, such as basketball and softball, were associated with men from lower classes and were viewed less favorably for women.

Many of the early recreation activities for women in the early twentieth century were outdoor-oriented. Indoor recreation facilities had not yet been constructed on any large scale. Being outside was now considered healthy for women. Some of the popular outdoor activities were horseback riding, swimming/bathing, ice and roller skating, biking, and sleigh/carriage riding (Gerber et al., 1974). During this time of initial growth in women's outdoor recreation, most of the accepted activities were those endeavors that did not interfere drastically with the perception of the *ideal woman*. Activity that emphasized beauty and aesthetic appeal reflected the transcendent female image and was acceptable. This attitude affected not only the choice of outdoor activities, but the style in which they were played: "Croquet, archery, bowling, tennis, and golf were the primary sports, though a few women played baseball, rowed, and participated in track and field competitively. . . . sports were chosen which could be performed without acquiring an indelicate sweat" (Gerber et al., 1974, p. 4).

One of the most popular outdoor activities that encouraged the growth of female sport enthusiasts was bicycle riding. Where roads and nerve permitted, the old high bicycle gained its advocates. The invention of the velocipede and tricycle allowed even more women to bike. In 1887, the advent of the safety bicycle (i.e., a bicycle that was chain-driven with wheels of equal size) and development of pneumatic rubber tires opened new worlds of physical activity to women (Paxson, 1974). To accommodate ladies' need for modesty, a drop frame was designed. Women could also purchase a folded screen that attached to the front of the bicycle to keep the feet and ankles from view when mounting or riding the bicycle (Welch & Lerch, 1981). By 1898, the League of American Wheelmen had over 100,000 female and male dues-paying members, and it seemed that white women, in particular, had taken a great step toward equal treatment by freely participating with the men. Indeed, according to suffragist Elizabeth Cady Stanton (1896), "Bicycling [has done] more to emancipate women than anything else in the world. I stand and rejoice every time I see a woman ride on a wheel. It gives women a feeling of freedom and self-reliance" (History of Women in Sports Timeline, n.d.).

Athletic clubs were often formed during this early period of recreation growth, and they also gave more affluent, white women the opportunity to participate. These clubs offered facilities as well as organized competitions. One of the first clubs in North America was the Ladies' Club of the Staten Island Cricket and Baseball Club, started in 1877 with the chief activity for women being tennis (Gerber et al., 1974, p. 29). Bowling also became an upper-class activity for both women and men, with clubs for women in large cities (Welch & Lerch, 1981). Prominent society women formed the Chicago Women's Athletic Club in 1903 as a lavish setting for exercise and leisure with a gymnasium, a swimming pool, bowling alleys, fencing rooms, a Turkish bath, and sitting and dining rooms (Knobe, 1905).

Some recreation opportunities were also available to young working-class women. For example, the YWCA ran a summer camp program in 1874 at Asbury Park, New Jersey, that provided these women with "pleasant respite from their jobs" (Welch & Lerch, 1981, p. 226). By 1916, thousands of women were enrolled in gymnasium classes and swim programs. These programs, however, were mostly racially segregated until the Civil Rights movement of the 1960s.

The male members of the recreation and sport clubs, however, almost always exerted control over what was acceptable in women's participation. For example, in February of 1889, Madison Square Garden hosted its first women's bicycle competition. The first-place woman won $1,634 by pedaling 624 miles ("Women on Bicycles," 1889). Women's racing was brought to an end, however, as a result of social pressure, by the American Wheelmen's Bicycling Club, which did not approve of contests among females.

Up until the twentieth century, most recreational activities for women were not team sports. Only when the colleges began to develop programs of physical activities for women did team sports develop. Colleges had clubs for sports that paralleled those in the general society. College clubs had competitions for females only, however, and in some cases male spectators were not welcome. For example, the first intercollegiate women's basketball game was between Berkeley and Stanford on April 4, 1896. Only women were allowed to observe the game because it was not considered proper for men to see women sweating from vigorous effort (Welch & Lerch, 1981).

In the early decades of the twentieth century, it was more important for women to look well than to win. People, especially men, wanted women first and foremost to have a neat, attractive appearance. Disagreeable expression, uncouth language, yelling, screaming, or any form of "masculine behavior" was seen to detract from the aesthetic feature of the game. For example, in 1906, it was a rule at one college that no girl who persisted in careless dress could play in any match or game (Gerber et al., 1974).

Even though the aesthetic received the most attention, many white women continued to increase their participation in organized physical pursuits during the next several decades. The belief that girls and women had the right to participate in sports in and out of school and that school sports should not be limited to just boys' programs continued to grow (Cozens & Stumpf, 1974). A 1901 issue of *Cosmopolitan* indicated that open-air athletics for girls were very popular that year. Among the sports mentioned were skating, tobogganing, rowing, tennis, golf, lacrosse, swimming, riding, cycling, and certain track and field events (Cozens & Stumpf, 1974).

During the 1920s, recreational activities also gained a place of prominence for women in the African American community. Track and field, basketball, baseball, and tennis gained a foothold as acceptable sports for girls. Athletic events became community social events that enhanced racial pride and neighborhood identity as the girls played for spectators in churches, recreation centers, or gymnasiums that seated more than 3,000 fans (Cahn, 1994). Attitudes toward the body and concepts of femininity developed in African American communities that allowed women to be strong and athletic (Welsh-Asante, 1993, 1994). Beauty, personality, and athleticism were not considered by many to be mutually exclusive qualities in African American women (Gissendanner, 1994).

As in other areas of women's lives, progress was frequently followed by periods of backlash and retrenchment. By the end of the 1920s, a wariness and suppressed hostility in gender relations was felt in women's sports. Assertive female athletes posed a challenge to men and masculinity. As more girls and women moved into community-based recreation programs, they invaded the previously exclusive male domain and claimed strength, speed, and power as a right of womanhood (Cahn, 1994). The media persistently constructed athletic competition among women as an antagonistic battle between the sexes that threatened men's rule over sport. Such media constructions continued into the 1970s in the United States and culminated in the *Battle of the Sexes*, a tennis match between active professional tennis star, Billie Jean King, and former world-ranked number 1 professional tennis player, Bobby Riggs. Riggs, who boasted of his "superior male attributes," was soundly beaten by King 6–4, 6–3, 6–3. According to a front-page article in the *New York Times*, with her "crushing . . . rout . . . Mrs. Billie Jean King struck a proud blow for herself and women around the world" (Amdur, 1973, p. 1).

Women's sport participation represented a threat to traditional gender roles and to the patriarchy in general. Sporting ability was hardly compatible with women's traditional subordinate role and posed a serious threat to the myth of female frailty (Lenskyj, 1986). The desire to engage in physical recreation activities led to the belief that participation in such activities brought out unladylike behavior and masculine appearance, particularly in white women. Since women were believed to be unable to bear prolonged mental and physical strain, games and sports were modified for women, and they were encouraged to cultivate good form rather than establish records (Welch & Lerch, 1981).

In addition, women had always been portrayed as needing protection, and by participating in certain activities, some women were demanding that this perception be changed. The adventures of women explorers document that in some cases women were successful in overcoming the stereotypes and the view that their actions were aberrations from the norm (Olds, 1986). For example, Mary Schaffer and Mary Adams explored many areas in the Canadian Rockies at the beginning of the twentieth century. They lamented that only men had the privileges of seeing the unexplored country and decided they should also be able to see this country. They said, "We can starve as well as they, the muskeg will be no softer for us than for them; the ground will be no harder to sleep upon, the waters no deeper to swim, nor the bath colder if we fall" (Schaffer, 1911, pp. 4–5).

After the Progressive Era (1890s–1920s) in the United States came several decades of conservatism concerning women's recreation involvement. The vote had been won, but many women's rights issues were still unsolved. Male supremacist values tended to be fostered by the post-World War I economic depression, fears about racial/ethnic *contamination* and the decline of the White (i.e., Anglo) race, the growing influence of anti-feminist Freudians, the "Red Scare" (which swept the United States and Canada after World War I and targeted such women as Jane Addams, Carrie Chapman, and organizations such as the Women's Christian Temperance Union and the Young Women's Christian Association), and the growth of authoritarianism in governments.

ADDRESSING GIRLS' AND WOMEN'S RECREATION NEEDS

Conservative attitudes influenced women's leisure and sport experiences. For example, many of the women who were teaching physical education or planning organized recreation programs for girls and women accepted the philosophy that they should *not* follow the male model. For girls and women, the emphasis was supposed to be on the joy of playing rather than on winning championships. Unlike the men's programs, women leaders did not want to neglect anyone to train the elite. They did not want sport and recreation activities professionalized. They wanted to avoid excessive publicity about women athletes and sporting events. Female physical educators and recreation programmers did not want to see women exploited like men (Bowers, 1934).

An alternate approach for girls and women grew. On one hand, the approach was conservative because protection of girls continued to be the focus. On the other hand, the approach was radical because it was antithetical to the traditional sporting values of competition, elitism, and winning at all costs. Some physical education teachers and recreation leaders also promoted leadership by women who were more experienced, sympathetic, tactful, and capable of meeting the individual needs and interests of girls and women (Bowers, 1934).

Most physical educators and recreation programmers during the 1930s emphasized that recreation and leisure could be a means for emphasizing altruism. Physical recreation with a de-emphasis on competition provided an outlet for the perceived urge for females to care for and help somebody or something. It helped girls and women find joy in altruistic service. By focusing on group welfare, girls and women could participate in sports and avoid developing into self-centered women who were unhappy and unpopular (Bowers, 1934). The image of the *ideal woman* remained, even though it was slightly less restrictive than it had been previously.

Many communities organized Girls Recreation Councils to promote more and better recreation for girls and women. These councils were organized by physical education and recreation professionals from organizations such as the Girl Scouts, Campfire, Girl Reserves, city recreation departments, YWCAs, YWHAs, settlement houses, Girls' Friendly, and Girls and Boys Clubs, as well as industry (e.g., the Kellogg Company). Often the councils worked with Mothers' Clubs that helped by developing play areas; employing women leaders on playgrounds; and helping pass laws, ordinances, and bonds to further recreation opportunities (Bowers, 1934).

Addressing girls and women's recreational interests and needs often set the stage for contradictions and tensions between notions of ideal femininity and the abilities and skills that were required and engendered by participation in such activity, particularly sport. In sport and other physically active leisure, girls and women were allowed a new freedom to express all dimensions of self and the opportunity to gain pleasure in bodily strength and skill. However, the acceptability of these expressions often came with parameters. This can perhaps be seen most clearly with girls' and women's participation in sport where the ideology of heterosexism is centered and homophobia is pervasive.

HETEROSEXISM, HOMOPHOBIA, AND WOMEN'S PHYSICALLY ACTIVE LEISURE

As women's culture moved from the homosocial world of intense women's friendships of the nineteenth century that were, at least in part, a response to a highly sex-segregated society, to the heterosocial world of the early decades of the twentieth century, the public nervously struggled with the lack of clarity around masculinity and femininity, especially in sport. The strong link between sport and masculinity made the arena of physical recreation ripe for accusations of lesbianism for women who engaged in activities such as team sports. This was particularly the case if those sports required physical contact and the use of one's body to physically dominate, overpower, or coerce others (Metheny, 1973). Some sports advocates tried to assert that athleticism could be feminine (e.g., gymnastics), and the gracefulness and body type required by such sports were seen as "proof" of heterosexuality. However, this strategy did little to diminish the lesbian *stigma* of other sports. The construction of gender as *dualistic*, the construction of sport as a masculine practice and expression, and the traditional view of what was feminine all had a powerful, often discouraging, influence on girls' and women's participation. Stepping beyond dominant gender ideologies and discourses often resulted in being labeled masculine or a *tomboy* at the least, and lesbian and deviant at the extreme. Of course, this accusation only held power because heterosexism was centered as normal and hence, was threatening to many women who did not want the stigma to interfere with their lives. Thus, homophobic attitudes and the fear of being accused of being masculine and not heterosexual deterred some girls and women from physically active pursuits.

Leaders of women's sports unwittingly contributed to the homophobic climate when they oriented their programs toward the new feminine heterosexual ideal athlete (Cahn, 1994). For example, when girls began to play in the All-American Girls Baseball League in 1943 (the league made famous by the movie, *A League of Their Own*), they wore skirts and make-up while playing and took part in charm classes to ensure that their femininity on and off the field was not questioned (Lesko, 2005). These practices, however, only resulted in instilling society's fear and loathing of lesbians into the practice and imagery of sport and as a result, privileged heterosexuality and condemned lesbianism. Thus, the lesbian athlete became the negative symbol of female social and sexual independence, the mark of unacceptable womanhood. She came to represent the line not to be crossed or risk falling into the despised category of *mannish women*.

From the tensions between the stereotypical views of femininity and a woman's desire to pursue what were considered unfeminine leisure interests arose the *female apologetic*. These apologetic women, both heterosexual and homosexual, avoided being labeled deviant by trying to remain feminine and yet excel in nontraditional leisure pursuits such as sports and outdoor activities. The apologetic was seen when women attributed their success to luck and not skill, when they dressed and presented themselves in overtly feminine ways, and when they treated their own achievements as trivial.

The conflict between women's involvement in physical recreation and conventional notions of femininity continues today. Blatant attempts have been made to reassure the public that women in sports, particularly exceptional athletes, are "normal" women. This can be seen, for example, in various women's professional sports (e.g., women's professional basketball and soccer) and their promotion of, and media attention given to, those female athletes who have a boyfriend, are married, and/or have children. Further, women continue to be *heterosexualized* and represented as sport *for* men in sporting discourses (e.g., the swimsuit issue of *Sports Illustrated*).

Nevertheless, physical recreation activities have created a space for some women to explore unconventional gender and sexual identities (Peper, 1994). Athletically inclined lesbians did find possibilities for self-expression and a social life through sport. Even though public condemnation was an ever-present reality, many lesbians constructed an alternative set of affirmative meanings and experiences from within the culture of sport. They found the athletic life to be compatible with coming to terms with homosexual desires as well as providing a collective process to forge community ties with other lesbians. Given the danger of open declarations, however, lesbians in sport communicated their presence primarily through action, style, and unspoken understandings. They often followed a code of "play it, don't say it" in a way that ensured their survival in a hostile culture, yet preserved social spaces that offered a degree of comfort and freedom (Cahn, 1994; Kivel & Johnson, this volume).

This strategy of concealment and secrecy provided a degree of protection but also kept lesbianism underground. While rumors existed, the reality of a gay sport culture was never revealed. The silence never permitted lesbian athletes to speak to the wider public. Although the rumors were present, the reality was ignored. Thus, the silence, innuendo, rumor, and outright discrimination perpetuated fear and ignorance (Griffin, 1993; Peper, 1994) and the old fears about the relationship between masculinity and sport linger, as do the cultural fears about physically strong, sexually independent women. Nelson (1995) stated in her book, *The Stronger Women Get, the More Men Love Football*, that female athletes have had a long tradition of dissociating themselves from feminism. Many have tried to send reassuring signals that they are not feminist, not dykes, not aggressive, and not muscular. It has been a survival strategy that is only slowly changing.

Gay, lesbian, bisexual, transgender, and queer (GLBTQ) issues are in the news. While polls indicate growing public acceptance (particularly by younger people) for diversity in lifestyles, laws and policies such as those related to gay marriage and civil unions and other equality granting measures continue to struggle for support. Nevertheless, youth continue to identify publicly as GLBTQ at younger ages. Lesbian and gay couples establish domestic partnerships and create lives together that often include children. GLBTQ individuals are found in every job, in every segment of the population, and make fundamental positive contributions to the fabric of society. They have also sought to add meaning to their lives through leisure experiences and have sought opportunities to build leisure support systems (e.g., Gay Games, gay rodeos, gay bands) that contribute to the quality of their lives.

CONCLUSION

From the 1930s to the 1950s, women continued to make small gains in their *public leisure activities*. Much of women's leisure was still centered within the home and was a function of family and role expectations. With the social tumult of the 1960s and 1970s, recreation and leisure for women received visibility as an issue of freedom and equality.

Gains in recreation activity for women in North America were reflective of societal changes in attitudes brought by continued social reforms based on the revived feminist and equal rights' movement, the Civil Rights movement of the 1960s, and the increased social awareness and commitment to change of the 1970s that demonstrated a renewed sensitivity to fairness and discrimination. Consciousness was raised and strength in sisterhood was evident (Bailey, 1993).

Sport was a most visible example of how the contemporary women's movement related directly to girls' and women's leisure. For women in sport, emerging societal attitudes toward justice meant that they could approach athletic resources and opportunities from a political perspective (Cahn, 1994), as evidenced in the United States with the passage of Title IX in 1972. Women were encouraged to take up sport and fitness activities as pleasurable recreation in response to the increased positive perceptions about physical freedom, bodily pleasure, and leisure.

Yet, beneath the surface, an undercurrent of resistance and backlash is present (Paule-Koba, this volume). Homophobia is part of that backlash. It is a discourse that is given power by the extent to which heterosexuality is normalized. The homophobic response to girls' and women's interest and skill in physically active recreation and sport, particularly those activities that are seen as *innately* masculine, constructs such interest and skill as deviant. Sport and many other forms of recreation still manage to be maintained as bulwarks of male privilege and as subtle forms of male domination. Feminist activists continue to weather the anti-feminist backlash waged by conservatives of the *New Right*. Today, women involved in recreation activities are facing the barriers to their involvement with a greater sense of entitlement supported by the inroads made by feminism. They are energized by personal power and enjoyment attained through their own participation. This sense of entitlement and determination carries the stamp of recent history and provides hope for a future in which adequate leisure, athletic pleasures, and personal power are available to all women.

References

Amdur, N. (1973, September 20). Mrs. King Defeats Riggs, 6–4, 6–3, 6–3, amid a circus atmosphere. *New York Times*, p. 1. Retrieved from http://www.nytimes.com

Bailey, N. (1993). Women's sport and the feminist movements: Building bridges. In G. Cohen (Ed.), *Women in sport: Issues and controversies* (pp. 297–304). Newbury Park, CA: Sage.

Bowers, E. (1934). *Recreation for girls and women.* New York, NY: A. S. Barnes.

Cahn, S. K. (1994). *Coming on strong: Gender and sexuality in twentieth-century women's sport.* New York, NY: Free Press.

Calisthenics. (1831). *The Journal of Health, 2,* 191–193.

Cozens, F., & Stumpf, F. (1974). The role of the school in the sports life of America. In G. Sage (Ed.), *Sport and American society* (2nd ed.). Reading, MA: Addison-Wesley.

Ehrenreich, B., & English, D. (1973). *Complaints and disorders: The sexual politics of sickness.* New York, NY: Feminist Press.

History of women in sports timeline. Retrieved from http://www.northnet.org/stlawrenceaauw/timeline.htm

Gerber, E., Felshin, J., Berlin, P., & Wyrick, W. (Eds.) (1974). *The American woman in sport.* Reading, MA: Addison-Wesley.

Gissendanner, C. H. (1994). African-American women and competitive sport, 1920–1960. In S. Birrell & C. Cole (Eds.), *Sportswomen and culture* (pp. 81–92). Champaign, IL: Human Kinetics.

Griffin, P. (1993). Homophobia in women's sports: The fear that divides us. In G. Cohen (Ed.), *Women in sport: Issues and controversies* (pp. 193–203). Newbury Park, CA: Sage.

Knobe, B. D. (1905). Chicago women's athletic club. *Harper's Bazaar, 39,* 539–546.

Leavitt, J. W. (1997). *Typhoid Mary: Captive to the public's health*. Boston, MA: Beacon.

Lenskyj, H. (1986). *Out of Bounds: Women, sport, and sexuality*. Toronto, ON: Women's Press.

Lesko, J. (2005). *League history*. Retrieved from http://www.aagpbl.org/league/history.cfm

Metheny, E. (1973). Symbolic forms of movement: The feminine image in sports. In M. Hard (Ed.), *Sport in the socio-cultural process* (pp. 277–290). Dubuque, IA: William C. Brown.

Nelson, M. B. (1995). *The stronger women get, the more men love football: Sexism and the American culture of sports*. New York, NY: Harcourt Brace.

Olds, E. (1986). *Women of the four winds*. Boston, MA: Houghton Mifflin.

Paxson, F. (1974). The rise of sport. In G. Sage (Ed.), *Sport and American Society* (2nd ed.). Reading, MA: Addison-Wesley.

Peper, K. (1994). Female athlete=lesbian: A myth constructed from gender role expectations and lesbiphobia. In R. J. Ringer (Ed.), *Queer words, queer images: Communication and the construction of homosexuality* (pp. 193–208). New York, NY: New York University Press.

Schaffer, M. T. S. (1911). *Old Indian trails of the Canadian Rockies*. New York, NY: Knickerbocker Press.

Welch, P., & Lerch, H. (1981). *History of American physical education and sport*. Springfield, IL: Charles C. Thomas.

Welsh-Asante, K. (Ed.) (1993). *The African aesthetic: Keeper of the traditions*. New York, NY: Greenwood.

Welsh-Asante, K. (1994). Images of women in African dance. *Sage: A Scholarly Journal on Black Women, 8*(2), 16–19.

Women on bicycles. (1889, February 12 and February 17). *New York Times*, p. 2.

Chapter 8
Women, Gender, and Leisure Constraints

Diane M. Samdahl

I grew up the youngest of five children. I watched my two older sisters play with dolls and talk about boys while my two older brothers rode bikes, built a tree house, and went fishing with my father. My brothers' lives were inherently more interesting than my sisters' but I was seldom allowed to join them. *I'm too young,* I thought to myself, drawing on the explanation I'd heard repeatedly whenever they went off without me. One weekend when I was about four, my dad was going to take my brothers fishing. I begged to join them but my father said no. When they returned that evening they had a string of fish and fun stories about their long day on the lake. As I listened to them talk I had a sudden flash of insight—it wasn't my age that kept me home (after all, one brother was only two years older than me). Rather, my dad wouldn't take me fishing because girls couldn't pee over the side of the boat! Without knowing it, I had created my first understanding of gendered leisure constraints.

Of course, being able to pee over the side of the boat had nothing to do with my brothers getting to go fishing. They also learned to hunt, had access to my dad's toolbox and scrap lumber, and went carp fishing with a spear they manufactured from a bamboo pole and a knife. At times, giving in to my pleading, my mother would force my brothers to let me climb into the tree house or take a turn at bat, but those victories were always hollow. Over time I came to understand that I would always be an outsider to my brothers' world of fun and games, not because I was younger but because I was a girl.

When I was four and wanted to go fishing, my life was clearly constrained by gender. To be more precise, my life was constrained by a gendered belief that fishing wasn't appropriate for girls, which my father unquestionably upheld and enforced. But I see now that my brothers, too, were socialized into cultural expectations about how they should act as boys. Gender socialization, it seems, was shaping us all.

My story is undoubtedly different than yours. I grew up in the newly emerging suburbs of the 1950s. But though our stories might differ, we all came to understand at a young age that there were broad cultural expectations for how boys and girls should act. Encountering those expectations might have initially felt restrictive but over time we each reached our own understandings and solutions—we became boys and girls, and eventually men and women, against that backdrop of a cultural discourse that defines gender.

That is the simple explanation about how individuals learn to embrace gender-appropriate attitudes and behaviors. We literally *become* boys and girls as we engage in that process of socialization, of learned differentiation. However, though socialization might describe how boys and girls learn to be different, it does little to soothe that four-year-old girl inside of me who wanted to go fishing. Even at that young age, I could see that my brothers had privileges that were not available to me, and that their actions and options were often more desirable than mine. And though I saw and resented many of the constraints that I encountered, my brothers moved easily into the boyhood that was opening for them. If gender socialization was simply a process whereby infants are molded into girls and boys, why was that process significantly more painful for me than for my brothers?

Today, 50 years later, I can honestly say that I no longer want to go fishing—but that in itself raises some interesting reflections. Did I succumb so thoroughly to my father's gendered expectations that I gave up not only my frustration but also my very *desire* to go fishing? Did I move from having a father who restricted me to having an internalized constraint that I began to carry inside of me? But wait! Am I really constrained because I don't go fishing today? I don't even *want* to fish! Leisure constraints seem more complex than they appeared when I was four years old and my father said "no."

EARLY RESEARCH ON LEISURE CONSTRAINTS AND CONSTRAINT NEGOTIATION

Research on leisure constraints, referred to in the early years as *barriers* to leisure, emerged in the 1980s with evidence that personal and situational factors affected people's access to desired leisure activities. The most obvious dimensions were characteristics like socioeconomic status, age, and disability (cf. Buchanan & Allen, 1985; Henderson, Bedini, Hecht, & Schuler, 1995; Jackson, 1988; McGuire, Dottavio, & O'Leary, 1986; Searle & Jackson, 1985). People expressed frustration that constraints caused by characteristics like these kept them from being able to engage in something they wanted to do. Much of that early research confirmed that people saw those factors as barriers that blocked leisure engagement.

A seminal article that gave shape to this body of work was published by Crawford, Jackson, and Godbey (1991). The article proposed a hierarchical model of leisure constraints that negatively impact participation. Constraints were categorized using terminology that is still employed today. According to this model, desired leisure activities might be impeded by *intra*personal constraints (e.g., low self-confidence), *inter*personal constraints (e.g., demands imposed by family), or structural constraints (e.g., lack of money or time). These constraints were purportedly hierarchical, in that the intrapersonal or interpersonal constraints had to be resolved before structural constraints had any impact. This hierarchical model presented a template that was embraced by researchers who uncovered leisure constraints for widely diverse populations, including people with developmental disabilities, adolescents contemplating new leisure activities, and people who had recently immigrated into the country (cf. Hawkins, Peng, Hsieh, & Eklund, 1999; Raymore, Godbey, & Crawford, 1994; Stodolska, 2000). The utility of the leisure constraints model was solidified as researchers used the language of constraints to explain factors that impact leisure engagement.

Early in this research, however, something else began to emerge. Kay and Jackson (1991) and Shaw, Bonen, and McCabe (1991) were among the first to report that people often circumvented possible barriers to engage in leisure activities who might otherwise have been constrained. Researchers followed up with studies about the *negotiation* of leisure constraints by examining the creativity and resourcefulness that people demonstrated when surmounting potential barriers to their leisure (cf. Henderson, Bedini, Hecht, & Schuler, 1995; Jackson, Crawford, & Godbey, 1993; Jackson & Rucks, 1995; Nadirova & Jackson, 2000). People saved money, modified plans, used adaptive recreation equipment, and found other ways to get around leisure constraints. Leisure constraints were not necessarily barriers to participation.

Samdahl (2005; see also Samdahl & Jekubovich, 1997) reflected on the irony that arose when researchers unilaterally applied the concepts of leisure constraints and constraint negotiation to understandings of leisure. Some people undoubtedly face real constraints that might be insurmountable, but the leisure-constraints model was being applied too widely. Researchers proclaimed that people who do not participate in a leisure activity must have encountered leisure constraints, while people who did participate in that activity must have successfully negotiated their constraints. Leisure constraints seemed to explain everything and, therefore, nothing.

Examining Gendered Leisure Constraints

Interest in women's leisure began to coalesce during the 1990s. Stemming from a broader critique that social science research had often overlooked women's lives, feminist leisure researchers pointed out that basic conceptualizations of leisure were based on ideas about work and free time that described men's lives but were woefully inadequate when applied to women's lives (e.g., Wearing & Wearing, 1988). For example, a mother who remains out of the workforce to raise her children cannot easily delineate between work and free time, and her recreation activities are often infused with fun and enjoyment but also parental responsibilities and obligations. How do stereotypical definitions of leisure apply to her?

The concurrent rise of these two lines of research—leisure constraints and an interest in studying women—led to a natural convergence. Perhaps the terminology made the leisure constraints model so attractive to early feminist leisure researchers. The leisure constraints model provided an effective framework for talking about women's leisure, and the idea of leisure-constraint negotiation captured the resourcefulness and ingenuity of women who overcame constraints and participated in activities that posed gender-based risks or sanctions.

In summarizing leisure-constraints research, Shaw (1994) pointed out that researchers repeatedly concluded that women perceived more constraints than men did in their leisure. Women had greater constraints on time and money, more familial commitments, and were socialized into an *ethic of care* that made them more willing to sacrifice personal desires for the sake of others. The idea of leisure constraints helped highlight factors that diminished women's access to leisure.

In addition to noting comparative differences in leisure constraints for women and men, researchers also examined the impact of constraints on women's leisure behaviors and experiences. This research addressed issues such as constraints on women's comfort in the outdoors, perceptions of safety and danger at night, and body image as a leisure constraint (cf. Bialeschki & Henderson, 1988; Frederick & Shaw, 1995; Jackson & Henderson, 1995; James, 2000). If the leisure constraints model painted a deficient image of women by amplifying their constraints and limitations, discussions of leisure-constraint negotiation provided a balance by showing how women responded with innovation and resourcefulness. Actions such as forming women-only groups or learning self-defense were strategies that helped women overcome leisure constraints. Research on leisure-constraint negotiation showed that women were not just passive victims of inequity.

In addition to facing constraints in their ability to access leisure, women often found that leisure was a site for the reproduction of constraining gender roles and expectations. Whereas men might be guided towards contact sports, women were encouraged to participate in athletic activities that showcased graceful movement of their bodies (e.g., gymnastics, swimming, aerobics). Other activities like dating, dancing, and family leisure accentuated the gender differences between men and women. Shaw (1994) warned that leisure is not gender-neutral: "The types of activities into which women and men are channeled, and the nature of certain types of free time activities, function to perpetuate gender stereotypes and gender-based inequities" (p. 12). Rather than enhancing individual freedom, women's leisure often reinforces the structured power relationships within society.

Henderson (1996) cautioned against overgeneralizing with assumptions that *all* women face similar leisure constraints. Race, ethnicity, parental status, age, and other factors shape the lives and experiences of women. Likewise, Henderson emphasized the need to examine men's leisure with that same sensitivity to variation in lifestyles and experiences. A growing body of literature on leisure for lesbians and gay men added another dimension to this discussion, as did research on women in other cultures. The term *constraints* seemed to become woefully inadequate in relation to the larger issues of sexism, patriarchy, and homophobia. The leisure-constraints model, with its implicit focus on barriers to participation, had become too narrow for the new questions about gender that were gaining attention.

WHAT REALLY CONSTRAINS PEOPLE?

Many researchers in gender studies draw upon the work of Michel Foucault, a French philosopher whose writings explored ways that power and inequity are interwoven into the fabric of life. According to Foucault (1977), people become complicit in their own imprisonment as they internalize the *normality* of societal rules and prescriptions that control behavior. These expectations are framed in the cultural discourse learned while growing up—that internalized voice that tells how to act (or how *not* to act) as a girl, a student, an adult, or an African American, for example. Internalizing this cultural discourse is a parsimonious way to maintain social order that creates an invisible form of control whereby people monitor themselves without need for external force. Under normal circumstances, children acquiesce to their parents, secretaries take a back seat to the work of their bosses, and teachers are happy with modest salaries, regardless of whether children are stronger than their parents, secretaries do much of the work for their bosses, and teachers have advanced degrees. These cultural discourses not only tell people *how* to act, they establish a belief system that makes people *want* to act in the prescribed manner and be satisfied with the results. These hegemonic systems carry the *genetic code* of a society, establishing order and normality while preserving status and inequity.

Cultural discourse and the implicit power hierarchy are typically invisible, buried within the cultural values that hold society together. Children, immigrants, and others who are transitioning into a culture might temporarily *see* discourse within patterns and codes of interaction, but that insight often disappears once people become fully acculturated. For example, gender inequity was visible when I was 4 years old and watched my brothers receive unearned privilege but by the time I was 10 it was no longer a concern. The inequity had not disappeared; it had simply become invisible to me.

Effective socialization requires people to accept the constraints and restraints that culture places on their behavior, not just through tolerance, but by embracing the opportunities and expectations the imposed social order makes available to them. This outcome was apparent in Tsai's (2006) study of women in contemporary Taiwan. Although modernized in many respects, Taiwan is still influenced by Confucian beliefs that idealize women as passive and subservient. Even women with modern careers remained devoted to home duties and filial responsibilities, and they acquiesced to patriarchal control outside the workplace. However, they expressed little frustration or dissatisfaction and said they had never thought about whether leisure should be more available to them. The absence of freedom in the Western sense was not problematic, and many of these women were satisfied and fulfilled with their lives. In a similar study in Turkey, contemporary Muslim women navigated between discourses of Islamic traditions and modern Western culture (Koca, Henderson, Asci, & Bulgu, 2009). Their ability to negotiate that web of opportunity was largely influenced by the extent of patriarchal control over their lives.

Cultural discourse becomes constraining when it creates conflicting or contradictory expectations. Stalp (2006) revealed this in a study of women quilters. Quilting is a stereotypical female activity that resides within a broader discourse of homemaking. However, quilting also requires time and space in ways that conflict with other obligations in the household. To engage in quilting, these women had to negotiate and redefine what it meant to be a homemaker and let go of some familial obligations in order to take up others.

Although quilters had to negotiate competing demands that reside within the same discourse of homemaking, the need for negotiation might also arise when competing discourses make contradictory demands on an individual. The study of romantic love by Herridge, Shaw, and Mannell

(2003) is a good example. Young women in heterosexual relationships placed high priority on spending leisure time with their boyfriends. This time together was rewarding, but it reduced their ability to spend time alone or with family and friends. By emphasizing how a romantic relationship should become the center of a woman's life, the ideology of romantic love displaced other sources of pleasure that had been important to these women.

Sometimes women negotiate the juncture of competing discourses in a direct fashion, such as in Auster's (2001) study of women motorcycle riders. Operating a motorcycle is a stereotypically masculine act that is a nontraditional leisure activity for women in the United States. In addition to societal values that define motorcycling as unfeminine, women motorcyclists face potential disapproval from parents and peers and might be unwelcome within existing groups of motorcyclists. In Auster's study, women motorcyclists were strongly aware of this social stigma, especially during their first year as motorcyclists. However, after operating a motorcycle for a year, most of these women were able to shrug off any message that motorcycling was inappropriate. They had, in essence, (re)negotiated the gender discourse that defined motorcycling as unfeminine.

Women themselves often perpetuate a constraining discourse of motherhood by feeling guilty, or making other mothers feel guilty, when taking time for themselves (Miller & Brown, 2005; Thomsson, 1999). This fear of appearing selfish if, as a mother, a woman is not willing to put family members' interests before her own is an example of how gender discourse becomes internalized and re-emerges as that inner voice telling us what we should or should not do. What happens, however, when women are unable to live up to internalized expectations? For example, the media posits an unrealistic ideology of the female body, and most adolescent girls and women are unable to live up to that feminine ideal. The ensuing body dissatisfaction spurs embarrassment and self-consciousness that often impacts women's leisure (Frederick & Shaw, 1995; James, 2000; Lietchy, Freeman, & Zabriskie, 2006; Sullivan, this volume). This dissatisfaction remains a persistent constraint unless women let go of that ideal and accept a realistic image of how their bodies should look.

An extreme example comes from a study of women who suffered brain injuries that seriously impacted their ability to return to normal routines (Samdahl, Jacobson, & Hutchinson, 2001). Before their injuries, these women had resided comfortably within the cultural expectations of what a wife and mother should be. Things like cooking for family gatherings and organizing their children's sporting events had been engaging and rewarding, but after their brain injuries these women retained mental deficits that made those activities impossible. However, those mental deficits also made it difficult to envision any other way to live their lives. These women faced ongoing frustration and despair because they were unable to return to the role of family homemaker or find a satisfying alternative. The brain injuries created physical and cognitive impairment, but the real constraint became their inability to renegotiate the cultural gender discourse that had defined and shaped their lives before their brain injuries.

In each of these examples, women's leisure was impacted by the discourse that defined cultural expectations for women. The women in Taiwan were comfortably situated within their cultural discourse and did not challenge it. Thus, the question about whether or not they were constrained was complicated by differing cultural perspectives about what women should desire in their lives. Imposing an *absolute* judgment that Taiwanese women are constrained is problematic and reflects a Western perspective. In contrast, the Muslim women in Turkey had begun to embrace a Western ideology that conflicted with their Islamic traditions. They were often torn between competing discourses of traditional fidelity and self-expressive freedom.

The studies of women quilters and romantic love illustrate how gender discourse creates similar conflicts for women in the contemporary United States. The ideologies that tell women how to be a homemaker or how to be in love create widespread expectations that impose constraints in other aspects of women's lives. However, when that conflict becomes visible, as it did for the women who operated motorcycles, a newly negotiated meaning was possible, essentially creating a new gender discourse that redefined motorcycling as appropriate for women. Women who are unable to fulfill their internalized expectations engage in mostly unsuccessful behaviors, as evidenced in James's (2000) study of adolescent girls who attempted to reduce their embarrassment at the swimming pool. The women with brain injuries were the most constrained because they were unable to engage in the requisite processes of renegotiating what their lives could be.

In these examples, *gender itself* was a constraint that had to be negotiated. This process is more dynamic than overcoming a barrier to participate in a desired leisure activity. In effect, negotiating gender discourse entails an examination of what it *means* to be a woman, exposing and challenging the values that shape cultural opportunities and expectations. Other studies that highlight the negotiation of gender come from research on gay men and lesbians who reside outside the normative expectations of heterosexuality (cf. Bialeschki & Pearce, 1997; Jacobson & Samdahl, 1998; Johnson, 2005; Kivel & Johnson, this volume). Gender negotiation can be absent, intentional, or possibly unavoidable, depending upon the ways individuals are situated in relation to gender norms and expectations.

In conjunction with the purpose of this chapter, the discussion has focused on gender as a constraint. However, Shogan (2002) noted that Foucault saw constraints as both restrictive *and* freeing. The rules of a game, for example, delineate what is acceptable and what is forbidden within that game and shape a potentially chaotic environment into a venue where temporal norms open opportunities for action and engagement. Likewise, the codes that define gender impose restrictions that keep women away from what society sees as socially inappropriate activities and venues but may open up rewarding opportunities in family and relational leisure. Shogun cautioned that the removal of all gender proscriptions would produce a vacuum in which leisure becomes impossible. With that understanding, we might think about gender as a factor that may simultaneously enrich and constrain women's leisure.

RE-ENVISIONING CONSTRAINTS AND CONSTRAINT NEGOTIATION

The concept of leisure-constraint negotiation, when first introduced, added a dynamic quality to leisure-constraint research by highlighting the resourcefulness of people who found ways to participate in activities in spite of potential constraints. When applied to women's leisure, leisure-constraint negotiation contested the image of women as helpless victims of discrimination and emphasized, instead, how women can be active agents who creatively respond to inequity. However, as research questions became more complex, so too did the need for complex integrated answers.

Constraints do not exist in isolation from other aspects of people's lives, as evidenced in the ramifications of quilting, riding a motorcycle, or falling in love. It is too simplistic to think of negotiation in reference to overcoming one constraint at a time. A more complete understanding requires envisioning a complex world where people live at the intersection of multiple and often competing discourses. Constraint negotiation, therefore, entails a balancing act whereby people acquiesce to some aspects of one cultural discourse while rejecting or redefining aspects of other cultural discourses.

This clustering of constraints was discussed early in constraints research (Jackson, 1993) in an attempt to "focus attention on how people encounter, experience, and respond to an array of constraints that influence their leisure behavior" (p. 130). Jackson reported socioeconomic and activity-based patterns among people who encountered similar constellations of constraints. This aggregate perspective, however, was largely ignored until more recent calls for studying "constraints in context" (Henderson & Hickerson, 2007; Shaw & Henderson, 2005). Skowron, Stodolska, and

Shinew (2008) proposed an ecological model that encompasses multiple dimensions including sociocultural and environmental factors that influence leisure.

Most models of leisure-constraint negotiation focus on individual adaptability (e.g., Crawford et al., 1991; Hubbard & Mannell, 2001; Schneider & Wilhelm Stanis, 2007). However, the social contexts that facilitate (or block) the negotiation of leisure constraints are gaining attention. Auster (2001, 2008) spoke about the value of an *enriched* environment whereby supportive family and friends enable women to overcome the constraining effects of traditional gender socialization. Similar findings have been reported in studies of mothers, girls in outdoor settings, and women of color (cf. Brown, Brown, Miller, & Hansen, 2001; Culp, 1998; Henderson & Ainsworth, 2003; Little, 2002). Interacting with people who validate alternative forms of gender expression appears to facilitate girls' and women's ability to engage in recreation activities that have typically been viewed as unfeminine. This affirms the need to look at the broader social context when understanding leisure-constraint negotiation.

The ecological model presented by Skowron et al. (2008) drew attention to the physical and political environment as well as personal and social influences on women's leisure. Their study of Latina women's engagement in physical activity highlighted sociocultural constraints such as the physical nature of their jobs, cultural expectations about family roles and obligations, and the lack of culturally sensitive childcare. However, physical factors in the environment also restricted these women's leisure, including lack of transportation, weather, and fear of dogs roaming loose in the neighborhood. These factors created a network of constraints that must be simultaneously encountered and negotiated (Shinew & Stodolska, this volume).

Environmental factors were also apparent in a study of Iranian women's leisure (Arab-Moghaddam, Henderson, & Sheikholeslami, 2007). Iranian women were not as likely to identify personal constraints that emerge in Western research on women's leisure (e.g., lack of time, skills, or money). More important in their view was the lack of a community infrastructure that acknowledged and supported the leisure needs of Iranian women. This included perceived lack of concern by the government for women's issues such as health and safety in public places. A similar finding was reported by Hunter and Whitson (1991), who studied the development of a community skating facility in a small Canadian town, pitting local men's interest in hockey against women's need for sidewalks that would facilitate movement around neighborhoods.

Shaw and Henderson (2005) spoke about the importance of examining social structures that impact women's leisure opportunities. Physical and social environments encourage some forms of leisure engagement while discouraging others. The development (or lack of development) of sites and resources that address women's needs is part of a broader political discourse that shapes communities. The history of focusing on constraints and constraint negotiation as a personal act in which individuals engage on their own is too restrictive to capture the array of factors that constrain and facilitate people's leisure.

WHAT NEXT?

Samdahl (2005) raised yet another concern about the way leisure-constraint negotiation has been studied. When a canoeist negotiates the rapids, the river remains the same but the canoeist successfully meets that challenge. Likewise when a lesbian passes as straight, society's homophobic attitudes remain the same even though woman has learned to negotiate her social world to reduce strife. When two countries negotiate a treaty, however, *both* sides must compromise as they seek a mutually acceptable solution. Leisure researchers have studied constraint negotiation like the canoeist on the rapids or a lesbian who passes as straight, by focusing on strategies of personal adaptation. To view negotiation in this manner ultimately leaves the world (e.g., the river, the homophobic society) unchanged. What would research look like—and what impact might it have—if researchers sought to understand negotiation as a process that changed the obstacles themselves rather than simply the ways by which people avoid them?

To understand this form of negotiation takes us directly into the study of gender *relations* and the established structures of power that reside in our gendered lives. Constraints are not randomly or equitably distributed throughout society, nor are the resources that people need to overcome those constraints. When negotiation is examined as an interaction between people, or between individuals and the cultural discourses that shape their lives, the hidden rules that affect those interactions may become visible. Gender relations at their core frame a set of relationships that empower men more than women.

Unless the embedded values and power inequities inherent in culturally defined gender expectations are confronted, how and why leisure is gendered will be overlooked. Many of the gender constraints addressed throughout this chapter have fallen disproportionately upon women. Why, for example, can men ride motorcycles without the stigma that women motorcycle operators encounter? Why do men express less fear in the outdoors than women experience? Why weren't my brothers as frustrated as I was when we were learning gender-appropriate behaviors in our childhoods? Further, why is the public display of heterosexual relationships more appropriate than same-sex relationships—for both sexes?

Henderson (1991a) professed her hope that a feminist analysis of constraints on women's leisure would produce a model of critique, correction, and transformation. The critique has been well-documented in the literature. The correction and transformation, however, cannot occur until leisure constraints are viewed as the result of systemic inequity that is gender relations. To negotiate—truly *negotiate*—those factors, women must no longer be complicit in the power relationships that constrain them. Resistance can lead to a renegotiated order where power and opportunity are distributed more equitably.

During the past two decades, research on women's leisure has come a long way. Constraints must be viewed not as simple factors that inhibit participation but as networks of sociocultural beliefs that shape expectations and opportunities. The constructed nature of gender needs to be dismantled and reassembled into a discourse that resists the patriarchal heritage. It is necessary to re-envision what it *means* to be a woman or a man.

This challenge must be undertaken on multiple levels. It no longer is sufficient to study how individuals overcome constraints on their own; focusing only on individuals ignores the cultural factors that placed constraints in their paths in the first place. Researchers must embrace critical, sociological perspectives that expose the institutionalized power relations that reside in gender discourse. Though this task is big, change can and does occur on a personal level. By envisioning the dismantling of women's leisure constraints, a space is created where new gender discourse can emerge.

In that new leisure space, girls and women will find encouragement and support when they want to try activities that have traditionally been viewed as unfeminine. Family responsibilities will be openly negotiated so all members of the family are supported in their leisure endeavors. Communities will install sidewalks and public transportation to meet the needs of women. Architects and landscapers will design communities with attention to the safety concerns of women. Employers will commit to pay equity for women and create jobs with flexible work hours. Affordable daycare will be universally available. Television and advertisements and all forms of media will display images that challenge and disrupt traditional gender expectations, and children will be empowered to follow their interests without constraints that are shaped only by gender. In that new leisure space, four-year-old girls will be invited to go fishing with their brothers. That is how we begin to dismantle women's leisure constraints.

REFERENCES

Arab-Moghaddam, N., Henderson, K. A., & Sheikholeslami, R. (2007). Women's leisure and constraints to participation: Iranian perspectives. *Journal of Leisure Research, 39*, 109–126.

Auster, C. J. (2001). Transcending potential antecedent leisure constraints: The case of women motorcycle operators. *Journal of Leisure Research, 33*, 272–298.

Auster, C. J. (2008). The effect of cohort on women's sport participation: An intergenerational study of collegiate women ice hockey players. *Journal of Leisure Research, 40*, 312–337.

Bialeschki, M. D., & Henderson, K. A. (1988). Constraints to trail use. *Journal of Park and Recreation Administration, 6*, 20–28.

Bialeschki, M. D., & Pearce, K. D. (1997). "I don't want a lifestyle—I want a life": The effect of role negotiations on the leisure of lesbian mothers. *Journal of Leisure Research, 29*, 113–131.

Brown, P. R., Brown, W. J., Miller, Y. D., & Hansen, V. (2001). Perceived constraints and social support for active leisure among mothers with young children. *Leisure Sciences, 23*, 131–144.

Buchanan, T., & Allen, L. (1985). Barriers to recreation participation in later life cycle stages. *Therapeutic Recreation Journal, 19*, 39–50.

Crawford, D. W., Jackson, E. L., & Godbey, G. (1991). A hierarchical model of leisure constraints. *Leisure Sciences, 13*(4), 309–320.

Culp, R. H. (1998). Adolescent girls and outdoor recreation: A case study examining constraints and effective programming. *Journal of Leisure Research, 30*, 356–379.

Foucault, M. (1977). *Discipline and punish: The birth of the prison.* (A. Sheridan, Trans.). New York, NY: Pantheon.

Frederick, C. J., & Shaw, S. M. (1995). Body image as a leisure constraint: Examining the experience of aerobic classes for young women. *Leisure Sciences, 17*, 57–73.

Hawkins, B. A., Peng, J., Hsieh, C. M., Eklund, S. J. (1999). Leisure constraints: a replication and extension of construct development. *Leisure Sciences, 21*, 179–192.

Henderson, K. A. (1991a). The contribution of feminism to an understanding of leisure constraints. *Journal of Leisure Research, 23*, 363–377.

Henderson, K. A. (1996). One size doesn't fit all: The meanings of women's leisure. *Journal of Leisure Research, 28*, 139–154.

Henderson, K. A., & Ainsworth, B. E. (2003). A synthesis of perceptions about physical activity among older African-American and American-Indian women. *American Journal of Public Health, 93*, 313–317.

Henderson, K., Bedini, L., Hecht, L., & Schuler, R. (1995). Women with physical disabilities and the negotiation of leisure constraints. *Leisure Studies, 14*, 17–31.

Henderson, K. A., & Hickerson, B. (2007). Women and leisure: Premises and performances uncovered in an integrative review. *Journal of Leisure Research, 39*, 591–610.

Herridge, K. L., Shaw, S. M., & Mannell, R. C. (2003). An exploration of women's leisure within heterosexual romantic relationships. *Journal of Leisure Research, 35*, 274–291.

Hubbard, J., & Mannell, R. C. (2001). Testing competing models of the leisure constraint negotiation process in a corporate employee recreation setting. *Leisure Sciences, 23*, 145–163.

Hunter, P. L., & Whitson, D. J. (1991). Women, leisure, and familism: relationships and isolation in small town Canada. *Leisure Studies, 10*, 219–233.

Jackson, E. L. (1988). Leisure constraints: A survey of past research. *Leisure Sciences, 10*, 203–215.

Jackson, E. L. (1993). Recognizing patterns of leisure constraints: Results from alternative analyses. *Journal of Leisure Research, 25*, 129–149.

Jackson, E. L., Crawford, D., & Godbey, G. (1993). The negotiation of leisure constraints. *Leisure Sciences, 15*, 1–11.

Jackson, E. L., & Henderson, K. A. (1995). Gender-based analysis of leisure constraints. *Leisure Sciences, 17,* 31–51.

Jackson, E. L., & Rucks, V. C. (1995). Negotiation of leisure constraints by junior-high and high-school students: An exploratory study. *Journal of Leisure Research, 27,* 85–105.

Jacobson, S., & Samdahl, D. M. (1998). Leisure in the lives of old lesbians: Experiences with and responses to discrimination. *Journal of Leisure Research, 30,* 233–255.

James, K. (2000). "You can feel them looking at you": The experiences of adolescent girls at swimming pools. *Journal of Leisure Research, 32,* 262–280.

Johnson, C. W. (2005). "The first step is the two-step": Hegemonic masculinity and dancing in a country-western gay bar. *International Journal of Qualitative Studies in Education, 18*(4), 445–464.

Kay, T. A., & Jackson, G. (1991). Leisure despite constraint: The impact of leisure constraints on leisure participation. *Journal of Leisure Research, 23,* 301–313.

Koca, C., Henderson, K. A., Asci, F. H., & Bulgu, N. (2009). Constraints to leisure-time physical activity and negotiation strategies in Turkish women. *Journal of Leisure Research, 41,* 225–251.

Lietchy, T., Freeman, P. A., & Zabriskie, R. B. (2006). Body image and beliefs about appearance: Constraints on the leisure of college-age and middle-age women. *Leisure Sciences, 28,* 311–330.

Little, D. E. (2002). Women and adventure recreation: Reconstructing leisure constraints and adventure experiences to negotiate continuing participation. *Journal of Leisure Research, 34,* 157–177.

McGuire, F. A., Dottavio, D., & O'Leary, J. T. (1986). Constraints to participation in outdoor recreation across the life span: A nationwide study of limitors and prohibitors. *The Gerontologist, 26,* 538–544.

Miller, Y. D., & Brown, W. J. (2005). Determinants of active leisure for women with young children—an "ethic of care" prevails. *Leisure Sciences, 27,* 405–420.

Nadirova, A., & Jackson, E. L. (2000). Alternative criterion variables against which to assess the impacts of constraints to leisure. *Journal of Leisure Research, 32*, 396–405.

Raymore, L. A., Godbey, G. C., & Crawford, D. W. (1994). Self-esteem, gender, and socioeconomic status: Their relation to perceptions of constraint on leisure among adolescents. *Journal of Leisure Research, 26*, 99–118.

Samdahl, D. M. (2005). Making room for "silly debate": Critical reflections on leisure constraints research. In E. L. Jackson (Ed.), *Constraints to leisure* (pp. 337–349). State College, PA: Venture Publishing, Inc.

Samdahl, D. M., Jacobson, S., & Hutchinson, S. (2001). When gender is problematic: Leisure and gender negotiation for marginalized women. In J. White & S. Clough-Todd (Eds.), *Women's leisure experiences: Ages, stages and roles* (pp. 139–146). UK: Leisure Studies Association.

Samdahl, D. M., & Jekubovich, N. J. (1997). A critique of leisure constraints: Comparative analyses and understandings. *Journal of Leisure Research, 29*(4), 430–452.

Schneider, I. E., & Wilhelm Stanis, S. A. (2007). Coping: An alternative conceptualization for constraint negotiation and accommodation. *Leisure Sciences, 29*, 391–401.

Searle, M. S., & Jackson, E. L. (1985). Socioeconomic variations in perceived barriers to recreation among would-be participants. *Leisure Sciences, 7*, 227–249.

Shaw, S. M. (1994). Gender, leisure, and constraint: Towards a framework for the analysis of women's leisure. *Journal of Leisure Research, 26*, 8–22.

Shaw, S. M., Bonen, A., & McCabe, J. F. (1991). Do more constraints mean less leisure? Examining the relationship between constraints and participation. *Journal of Leisure Research, 23*, 286–300.

Shaw, S. M., & Henderson, K. A. (2005). Gender analysis and leisure: An uneasy alliance. In E. L. Jackson (Ed.), *Constraints to leisure* (pp. 23–34). State College, PA: Venture Publishing, Inc.

Shogan, D. (2002). Characterizing constraints of leisure: A Foucaultian analysis of leisure constraints. *Leisure Studies, 21*, 37–38.

Skowron, M. A., Stodolska, M., & Shinew, K. J. (2008). Determinants of leisure time physical activity participation among Latina women. *Leisure Sciences, 30*, 429–447.

Stalp, M. C. (2006). Negotiating time and space for serious leisure: Quilting in the modern U.S. home. *Journal of Leisure Research, 38*, 104–132.

Stodolska, M. (2000). Changes in leisure participation patterns after immigration. *Leisure Sciences, 22*, 39–63.

Thomsson, H. (1999). Yes, I used to exercise, but . . . A feminist study of exercise in the life of Swedish women. *Journal of Leisure Research, 31*, 35–56.

Tsai, C. L. (2006). The influence of Confucianism on women's leisure in Taiwan. *Leisure Studies, 25*, 469–476.

Wearing, B., & Wearing, S. (1988). "All in a day's leisure": Gender and the concept of leisure. *Leisure Studies, 7*, 111–123.

CHAPTER 9
GIRLS, GENDER, AND RECREATIONAL SPORTS

DOROTHY L. SCHMALZ

Recreational sports can play a powerful role in girls' development. In my research, I have seen the relationship girls can have with sports and how participation can empower them to embrace who they are as developing young women. The focus of this chapter is on what I (and others) have found about the beneficial outcomes that sport participation affords girls and the effects of social stereotypes of gender in sport participation. Given the results of the extant research, I also propose directions for gender and recreational sport research in the future.

BACKGROUND INFLUENCES

As suggested by theories of development, children's growth is influenced in part by others in their immediate environment, such as family. However, even though the women in my family provided strong, independent, and athletic role models, I never considered myself to be athletic. I did not participate in sports, competitively or recreationally, as a girl. In my teens, I did attend a residential summer camp, which I now recognize was pivotal in my becoming who I am. Both of my grandmothers were active in sports. My paternal grandmother played basketball, and my maternal grandmother was often on the golf course or participating in some physical activity with her friends. My grandmothers' activity was exceptional because they were born in 1900 and 1910, respectively, when girls and women were discouraged from participating in sports and physical activity and few opportunities existed for them.

Although my grandmothers were positive role models, my mothers' influence was what I believe led me to pursue the career I now have. Golf was my mother's most frequent activity, and had the greatest impression on me. My brother and I spent many afternoons at the swimming pool while she played 18 holes of golf at the country club to which we belonged. She was among the best female players at the club, and she gave most of the top male players a competitive game. She knew the strategies of the game, the rules, and the biomechanics better than most club members, and was a rule judge for the United States Golf Association. Quantities of golf clubs, bags, balls, and shoes were stacked and organized in our garage and basement throughout my childhood. She seemed confident, strong, and empowered. What struck me as a child and influenced my interest in girls' and women's participation in recreational sports as a researcher, was that despite my mother's extensive ability, knowledge, involvement, and passion for the game, club rules denied her the right to vote, affording her with no voice in how the golf program operated for no reason other than that she was a woman.

My mother was not one to sit quietly and let rules be rules. She did what she could to fight the status quo, but the women's movement had not yet achieved the success with gender equality that many women enjoy now. Her efforts to earn voting rights for women in the club were unsuccessful. I often heard her express frustration at the exclusiveness of the standard and her disagreement with the decisions that were made by the men on the board, some of whom did not even play golf.

My mother died the fall that I started my Master's degree in recreation and leisure studies. I believe her experiences at the golf course and in recreational sports throughout her life were a direct influence on my research agenda. Though she was special, her story is common. For generations, women have experienced prejudice and discrimination simply because they were not men. As discussed in the introductory chapter of this book, social stereotypes and gender inequalities have persisted in social domains including sport and physical activity. Characteristics such as competitiveness and aggressiveness have been seen as defining masculinity. However, participation in traditionally masculine activities and occupations can be empowering for women when they have the opportunities to participate and effect change.

Beneficial Outcomes of Girls' Recreational Sport Participation

Participation in recreational sports yields psychological benefits for children and adolescents of both sexes. Some of the benefits are increased levels of self-esteem and self-confidence, enhanced body image and identity development, and reduced rates of depression (Biddle, Whitehead, O'Donovan, & Nevill, 2005). Much of the research about children's experiences of recreational sport has been cross-sectional in design and therefore limited in its applicability and the ability to predict the direction of the relationships (e.g., does participation result in higher psychological well-being or does higher psychological well-being influence participation—or are both true?).

Nevertheless, to gain insight into how and why some of these benefits occur, my colleagues and I conducted a longitudinal study to explore the links between girls' participation in recreational sports and their self-esteem (Schmalz, Deane, Birch, & Davison, 2007). Our longitudinal sample consisted of 9-year-old girls who were subsequently tested at 11 and 13 years. One of the most interesting findings was that participation seemed to positively influence self-esteem, but the reverse was not true. Another finding from our study was that participation in recreational sports at age 9 had a greater positive effect on self-esteem at age 11 than participation at age 11 had on self-esteem at age 13. We speculated this result may be reflective of the view that younger children are socially afforded more latitude to participate in activities regardless of gender. As they approach adolescence, pressures to conform to social norms of gender and appropriate behavior become more prominent. Thus, as the girls got older, their participation in recreational sports may have put them at risk of stigma and thus their self-esteem was no longer positively affected by such participation.

Our findings are consistent with other research that has found that sport-participation rates among girls decrease significantly as girls approach puberty. Theories regarding this pattern suggest that a lack of access and availability as well as social perceptions about the gender appropriateness of girls' participation are responsible for the decrease. The desire or perceived pressure to conform to social expectations of femininity that girls experience may play out in a tendency to drop out of sport participation at this age. Yet, no measures had been developed to assess what girls themselves are experiencing, and what they think may be influencing their attrition from sports.

My colleagues and I collaborated to develop the Girls Disinclination from Activity Scale (G-DAS) (Davison, Schmalz, & Downs, 2010) as a tool to assess the experiences of girls that might contribute to their attrition from sport. The scale consists of five subscales of constructs that could explain girls' disengagement from physical activity and sport as they move into the teenage years: (a) competence, (b) appearance, (c) perceived exertion, (d) identity, and (e) availability. Respondents are asked to indicate the degree to which each item reflects why they do not like sport and physical activity. To test the reliability and validity of the scale, a sample of 98 girls completed the questionnaire at age 13, and then again at age 15. At each age, girls also wore an accelerometer for seven days as a means of correlating their scores from the G-DAS with an objective measure of their physical activity. All five of the subscales were negatively correlated with girls' physical activity as measured by the accelerometer (e.g., girls who had lower levels of perceived competence or higher concern for appearance had lower physical activity). Perceived competence had the greatest effect on girls' disengagement from participation. We anticipate that information from studies using this scale will provide recreation and leisure programmers with insights into how they might frame sport environments for girls to keep them involved and allow them to reap the beneficial outcomes sports may provide.

Other research suggests that adequate support is also an important element in facilitating a positive environment for girls' sport participation. In a study of boys and girls aged 11 through 13 years, we explored how children who were at risk of inactivity might benefit from support from people in their environments (Davison & Schmalz, 2006). Results indicated that girls and overweight children were more likely to show a disinclination for participation in sport, yet support from family and friends was a link to keeping these children involved.

In addition to support from significant others (Davison & Schmalz, 2006), we have found that the structure of the environment in which girls participate in sports can facilitate self-empowerment and confidence as well as other positive developmental outcomes. In a study of a girls' residential summer camp, we investigated how a free-choice program affects girls' involvement and interest in various sports (Schmalz, Kerstetter, & Kleiber, 2010). The environment of the camp was unique in that it provided a balance of support and structure; that is, it provided an environment in which girls felt safe and were encouraged to self-select activities and establish personal-achievement goals. Our results indicated that girls experienced positive changes in sense of self in addition to other positive developmental traits such as an increased ability for goal setting, time management, and problem solving.

The potential beneficial outcomes of children's sport participation are not new to social scientists. However, as noted in the introductory chapter of this book, gender stereotypes around appropriate free-time activity such as recreational sports continue. Because of the psychological benefits afforded to girls through sport participation, it is important to explore how gender stereotypes affect their participation.

GENDER STEREOTYPES IN RECREATIONAL SPORTS

Legislation, such as Title IX of the Educational Amendments Act of 1972 in the United States, has made inroads in reducing the persistent gender inequalities that exist in sport and physical activity programs. However, notions of *appropriate* and *inappropriate* gendered activity participation are still influential for individuals of all ages, including young children.

Children as young as two years old are aware of and practice gender roles (Boyle, Marshall, & Robeson, 2003). Although improvements in access and availability of sports for girls and women in the last 30 years is evident, perceptions of *boys'* sports and *girls'* sports persists. Metheny (1965) pioneered investigations into gender stereotypes of appropriate and inappropriate sport participation for women and men. She concluded many years ago that sports in which girls and boys were expected and encouraged to participate paralleled qualities reflective of personality traits associated with gender. So-called feminine sports (e.g., dance, figure skating, gymnastics) are typically those that are seen as aesthetically pleasing and lacking in face-to-face competition or overt physical aggression while so-called masculine sports (e.g., football, wrestling, basketball) are generally physically aggressive and competitive, involving a high degree of face-to-face and bodily contact.

Many women today have earned recognition and are celebrated athletes in sports such as basketball, soccer, and ice hockey, sports that Metheny's (1965) research categorized as masculine. Riemer and Visio (2003) revisited Metheny's classifications to assess their validity in the twenty-first century. Their findings indicated that although more sports fell into the *gender neutral* category than Metheny's original results indicated, social stereotypes of feminine and masculine sports persisted. Gymnastics and aerobics continue to be considered feminine sports and football and wrestling remain masculine sports.

Studies exploring perceptions of gender stereotypes in sport are useful for ascertaining what progress has been made regarding gender equity. The degree to which individuals "let" stereotypes affect their behavior has also been measured using the stigma-consciousness construct (Pinel, 1999, 2002). A stigma is a negative attribute that is assigned to individuals who are members of stereotyped groups (Jones et al., 1984). People differ in the extent to which stigmas influence their interests and behavior. Some people may not let stereotypes associated with (in)appropriate sports affect their interest in and pursuit of such activities, while others will curb their behavior to avoid being stigmatized.

My research has explored gender stereotypes in sport, and examined how individuals' level of gender-stigma consciousness might affect their perceived competence or participation in sports and physical activities. Overall, the findings suggested that gender stereotypes do not affect girls' participation as much as they do boys' (Schmalz & Kerstetter, 2006; see also, Trussell, this volume). Specifically, in a study of 8- through 10-year-old children, we explored the relationship of stigma consciousness and sport participation in so-called masculine and feminine sports. The study population identified three sports as stereotypically feminine (i.e., ballet, dance, gymnastics) and two sports as stereotypically masculine (i.e., football, wrestling). These results differed slightly from what Riemer and Visio (2003) found, but included far fewer gender-stereotyped sports than the list that Metheny (1965) originally published. We also found girls were more likely to participate in sports identified as masculine than boys were to participate in sports identified as feminine. This finding may reflect changes in social perspectives that have benefited girls more than boys. Interestingly, the results also indicated that boys *and* girls who had high levels of stigma consciousness of gender stereotypes in sports were less likely to participate in feminine sports than to participate in masculine sports. This can be explained by the fact that stereotypical masculine qualities are given greater value in current society than stereotypical feminine qualities, and many women believe they will gain greater respect by achieving in traditionally masculine fields (Liben, Bigler, & Krogh, 2001). Our finding that girls and boys who had high stigma consciousness preferred masculine sports may well support the view that feminine traits and behaviors remain devalued and should be avoided.

In another study of the effects of gender stereotypes on children's sport participation, we took children's stigma consciousness to the next level by examining how consciousness of gender stereotypes might affect childrens' recreational rather than competitive sport participation (Schmalz, Kerstetter, & Anderson, 2008). The findings from this study also showed that boys' sport participation was more negatively affected by stigma consciousness of gender stereotypes than was girls'. Specifically, boys who had higher levels of gender-stigma consciousness were less likely to participate in sports at the competitive level than boys with low levels of gender-stigma consciousness. Stigma consciousness of gender did not affect girls' participation, recreationally or competitively. We considered that this finding may be due to the social pressure put on boys to play sports in the United States, where sport is seen as a context for practicing/displaying a particular masculinity (Johnson, this volume). Boys who fear that they are not competitive or athletic enough might withdraw from sports for fear of failing to make the grade.

While the findings in these studies could be linked to the types of sports and activities made available to the children, they also offer a social commentary. In today's society, girls who pursue so-called masculine activities are at less risk for gender stigma than boys who pursue so-called feminine activities, and in fact, these girls may experience enhanced status as a result of participation in masculine-identified activities. Any indication of femininity or inability to perform successfully in sports for boys may raise questions about their masculinity because sport is a practice of masculinity in many cultures. Girls and women appear to experience greater social latitude in sports than boys and men. Our studies however, did not include social-psychological measures of self or the psychological benefits children gain from sports participation.

To gain greater insight into how children's self-perceptions may be affected by gender stereotypes of sports, we explored how children's physical self-descriptions differed depending on the gender type of sport (i.e., masculine vs. feminine) in which they participate (Schmalz & Davison, 2006). Physical self-description is a multidimensional construct proposing that individuals possess self-descriptions regarding their coordination, flexibility, physical activity, body fat, sports competence, global physical self, physical appearance, strength, and endurance (Marsh, 1994). We proposed that because stereotypes in sports have the power to affect children's participation interest (Schmalz & Kerstetter, 2006), the stereotypes might also affect their physical self-descriptions. Specifically, we wondered if children who participate in *cross-gendered* (i.e., gender-inappropriate sports) might have higher self-descriptions and overall sense of self than children who participate in gender-appropriate sports. The premise of the hypothesis was that when children go against the norm, they will need more confidence to pursue their activities in the face of social stigma (Messner, 2002). Children who conform to social expectations, whether they be about gender or other identities, do not bring attention to themselves or their behavior. We speculated that the hypothesis may be more apparent for boys because girls more commonly participate in what are seen as boys' sports than boys in girls' sports (Schmalz & Kerstetter, 2006). The results partially supported our hypothesis. Boys and girls who participated in gender-typed and cross-gendered sport types had more positive physical self-descriptions across several dimensions than boys and girls who participated only in gender-typed sports. This suggests that the relationship between sport and gender is complex and nuanced, requiring *both-and* rather than *either-or* thinking.

DIRECTIONS FOR THE FUTURE

The results of the studies in which I have been involved supported the notion that gender stereotypes in sports persist. However, the results indicated that boys are more bound by social stereotypes than girls. Although this news may be good for girls' participation, it raises concerns about how gender stereotypes affect boys' sport participation. Despite the progress some girls have enjoyed by pursuing traditionally masculine activities, our research suggests that little advancement has been made in the valuation of gender traits associated with femininity. In all of the studies discussed, few boys participated in traditionally girls' sports. In interviews that were conducted as part of the studies, boys clearly avoided association with what they considered girls' sports for fear that they would be considered too "girlie." The power of gender stereotypes in affecting children's sport participation remains alarming. Despite the progress made, many children and adolescents of both sexes continue to be denied the beneficial outcomes that participation in recreational sport provides. The results of these studies support the perspective that research should make the study of men's experiences in recreational sport as much a priority as women's experiences have been in recent years.

Research on gender stereotypes and instruments measuring their effects need refinement in future studies. Individuals are apt to deny that stereotypes affect their behavior, since admitting to them may suggest the undesirable characteristics of conformity and lack of individuality. Yet stereotypes infiltrate ways of thinking at early ages, leading to beliefs that the way things are done (e.g., boys wear blue, girls wear pink) is inherent, rather than socially constructed (Link & Phelan, 2001). Subsequently, the influence of stereotypes becomes subtle and must be measured in a way that taps internalization of prejudices rather than an explicit awareness of social stereotypes.

Lastly, differences based on race and ethnicity have received little attention in gender-stereotype research. For example, African American women and European American women have different perceptions of body image (Story, French, Resnick, & Blum, 1995). Less is known about how girls and women of minority races participate in sports and physical activity, or how stereotypes of race may influence behavior (Howard, Shinew, & Stodolska, this volume).

Progress has undeniably been made regarding girls' opportunities to participate in recreational sport. Although my mother was unable to benefit, the country club where she played golf changed their bylaws a few years ago to allow women to hold voting memberships. She would be pleased at the change and would be optimistic about the directions for the future. As a college professor, I have the good fortune of working with young people every day. The perspectives they bring to the classroom of what defines a socially appropriate role for girls and women in society and sport are encouraging and reflective of the progress that has been made. However, gender stereotypes in sport persist and can have detrimental effects on boys' and girls' rates, frequencies, and types of participation. We owe it to the women and men responsible for the progress we enjoy to continue to work toward reducing stereotypes of appropriate behavior for both sexes and toward the goal of mutual respect and appreciation.

REFERENCES

Biddle, S. J. H., Whitehead, S. H., O'Donovan, T. M., & Nevill, M. E. (2005). Correlates of participation in physical activity for adolescent girls: A systematic review of recent literature. *Journal of Physical Activity and Health, 2*, 423–434.

Boyle, D. E., Marshall, N. L., Robeson, W. W. (2003). Gender at play. *American Behavioral Scientist, 46*, 1326–1345.

Davison, K. K., & Schmalz, D. L. (2006, March). Youth at risk of physical inactivity may benefit more from activity-related support than youth not at risk. *International Journal of Behavioral Nutrition and Physical Activity, 3*, Article 5. Retrieved from http://www.ijbnpa.org.

Davison, K. K., Schmalz, D. L., & Downs, D. S. (2010). Hop, skip … no! Explaining adolescent girls' disinclination for physical activity. *Annals of Behavioral Medicine, 39*(3), 290–302.

Jones, E. E., Farina, A., Hastorf, A. H., Markus, H., Miller, D. T., & Scott, R. A. (1984). *Social stigma: The psychology of marked relationships*. New York, NY: W. H. Freeman.

Liben, L. S., Bigler, R. S., & Krogh, H. R. (2001). Pink and blue collar jobs: Children's judgments of job status and job aspirations in relation to sex of worker. *Journal of Experimental Child Psychology, 79*, 346–363.

Link, B. G., & Phelan, J. C. (2001). Conceptualizing stigma. *Annual Review of Sociology, 27*, 363–385.

Marsh, H. W. (1994). The importance of being important: Theoretical models of relations between specific and global components of physical self-concept. *Journal of Sport and Exercise Psychology, 16*, 306–325.

Messner, M. A. (2002). *Taking the field: Women, men and sports* (vol. 4). Minneapolis, MN: University of Minnesota Press.

Metheny, E. (1965). *Connotations of movement in sport and dance*. Dubuque, IA: William C. Brown.

Pinel, E. (1999). Stigma consciousness: The psychological legacy of social stereotypes. *Journal of Personality and Social Psychology, 76*, 114–128.

Pinel, E. (2002). Stigma consciousness in intergroup contexts. *Journal of Experimental Social Psychology, 38,* 178–185.

Riemer, B. A., & Visio, M. E. (2003). Gender-typing of sports: An investigation of Metheny's classification. *Research Quarterly for Exercise and Sport, 74,* 193–204.

Schmalz, D. L., & Davison, K. K. (2006). Differences in physical self-concept among adolescents who participate in gender-typed, cross-gendered, and gender-neutral sports. *Journal of Sport Behavior, 29,* 335–352.

Schmalz, D. L., Deane, G. D., Birch, L. L., & Davison, K. K. (2007). A longitudinal assessment of the links between participation in physical activity and self-esteem among girls from age 9 through 13. *Journal of Adolescent Health, 41,* 559–565.

Schmalz, D. L., & Kerstetter, D. L. (2006). Girlie girls and manly men: Children's stigma consciousness of gender in sports and physical activities. *Journal of Leisure Research, 38,* 536–557.

Schmalz, D. L., Kerstetter, D. L., & Anderson, D. M. (2008). Stigma consciousness as a predictor of children's participation in recreational vs. competitive sports. *Journal of Sport Behavior, 31,* 276–297.

Schmalz, D. L., Kerstetter, D. L., & Kleiber, D. A. (2011). An evaluation of developmental outcomes at a free-choice-oriented girls' summer camp. *Journal of Outdoor Recreation, Education, and Leadership, 3*(1), 53–69.

Story, M., French, S. A., Resnick, M. D., & Blum, R. W. (1995). Ethnic/racial and socioeconomic differences in dieting behaviors and body-image perceptions in adolescents. *International Journal of Eating Disorders, 18,* 173–179.

Chapter 10

"Mom, there are certain activities fat girls shouldn't do.": Considering the Leisure Experiences of Overweight Girls and the Role of Parents

Charlene S. Shannon

Kayla is 10 years old and lives with her single mother and younger brother. Although her mother describes her as very outgoing, Kayla spends a lot of her free time drawing, watching television, and doing arts and crafts projects. When her mother can provide the opportunities, she likes to go for walks, ride her bike, and participate in drama. She also loves swimming. She describes herself as "happy most of the time." Her weight, however, is a concern. She has a Body Mass Index (BMI) of 32.8, which is greater than the 95th percentile for her age and gender and categorizes her as obese. Kayla has experienced being teased and called names at school because of her weight. She also gets frustrated that she can't move as quickly as her friends, and gets out of breath and tired quickly when playing active games with them. Both her physician and her mother are concerned about what Kayla's life may be like if her weight is not managed.

Kayla is not unique in facing challenges with her weight. The rates of childhood overweight and obesity are alarming in North America. In the United States in 2005–2006, 30% of children between the ages of 2 and 19 years were overweight (i.e., they had a BMI [body mass index] of $\geq$ 85th percentile) and almost 16% were obese (i.e., BMI $\geq$ the 95th percentile) (Ogden, Carroll, & Flegal, 2008). Recent Canadian statistics indicate that in 2004, 26% of children aged 2 to 17 years were overweight, and 8% were obese (Shields, 2005). Although the statistics indicate a greater percentage of boys are overweight or obese compared to girls, a significant number of girls are affected by their weight status.

The health and social-psychological consequences of childhood obesity are well documented. Childhood obesity has been linked to increased risk of cardiovascular disease and type 2 diabetes, hypertension, sleep disturbances, and respiration difficulties (Dietz, 1998). Overweight and obese girls are at greater risk of developing breast and reproductive-system cancers and experiencing hormonal disturbances that can negatively affect their reproductive functions and cause infertility (Lash & Armstrong, 2009). Weight-based stigma is a psychosocial consequence of childhood obesity that can cause poor body image, body dissatisfaction, low self-esteem, depression and anxiety (Friedman, 2005), and social marginalization (Strauss & Pollack, 2003). Weight-based teasing and social marginalization are more prevalent in overweight girls than overweight boys (Tang-Péronard & Heitmann, 2008). This difference may be due, in part, to the socio-cultural feminine ideal of thinness (Davison, Markey, & Birch, 2003).

Lifestyles that are dominated by sedentary pursuits and involve little participation in physical activity have been linked with childhood obesity (Hills, King, & Armstrong, 2007). Analyses of children's free time use indicate that children are not active enough to maintain and promote health (Eaton et al., 2006). Girls' participation in physical activity has consistently been found as lower than boys and declines as girls move through adolescence (Bélanger, Gray-Donald, O'Loughlin, Paradis, & Hanley, 2009; Schmalz, this volume) making girls more vulnerable to obesity and its associated physical and psychosocial consequences. Recommendations based on this research suggest limits be placed on screen time and other sedentary pursuits and that physical-activity levels, preferably participation in moderate to vigorous activity, be increased (e.g., Laurson et al., 2008). However, such recommendations fail to appreciate the complexities of leisure behavior and the role that parents play in their children's free-time use. The purpose of this chapter is to discuss factors that influence how girls who are overweight spend their free time. This discussion is based on my ongoing research with parents of overweight girls who are participating in a community-based Lifestyle Management Program, which is described next.

RESEARCH WITH OVERWEIGHT GIRLS AND THEIR PARENTS

Family-based intervention programs have been established because of the long-term effects of childhood obesity (e.g., Dalton & Kitzmann, 2008). I have been involved with the pediatric Lifestyle Management Program (LMP), which was established at the University of New Brunswick in 2004 to help families with overweight or obese children make lifestyle changes to facilitate improved health. The inclusion of a leisure-education component was unique to the LMP compared with other intervention programs. I have served as a leisure educator working alongside pediatric nurses and dieticians to deliver the LMP. Initially, I met with both parents and their child during one-on-one leisure-education sessions. However, the program structure changed based on emerging research on family-based pediatric obesity intervention programs (e.g., Golley, Magarey, Baur, Steinbeck, & Daniels, 2007). Since September 2007, either my graduate students or I have met exclusively with parents for one-on-one sessions.

Semi-structured interviews were conducted with parents (22 mothers, 2 fathers) prior to beginning the LMP and after their participation. Case notes recording interactions with parents during leisure-education sessions provided new data. The repeated interaction enhanced my understanding and interpretation of interview data. Finally, children completed pencil-and-paper activities to explore their leisure interests, barriers, sources of leisure enjoyment and satisfaction, and perceived competence in leisure pursuits. During sessions, these exercises were reviewed and discussed with either the parent or the parent-child pair, and the discussions were recorded in case notes (Shannon, 2008).

Discussions were focused on physically active leisure, since a main goal of the LMP was to increase children's activity levels to promote health. Through those conversations, much was learned about the girls' non-active leisure pursuits and their experiences with all forms of free-time activity (e.g., active, passive, structured, unstructured). Time constraints and support from parents, peers, and teachers have been found to be key reasons girls who are overweight or obese are not engaged in active pursuits (Neumark-Sztainer, Story, Hannan, Tharp, & Rex, 2003). My conversations with the girls and/or their parents in the LMP revealed that aspects of girls' leisure experiences were influential as well.

Perceived Competence and Leisure Satisfaction

The girls completed one exercise asking them to list activities they were good at. A large number of passive pursuits were identified, such as reading, doing crafts, sewing, playing board games, singing, playing musical instruments, writing stories, baking, and "talking" on MSN. These activities were also the ones that parents, during their initial interviews, indicated their daughters engaged in most frequently. Many girls listed physically active pursuits, including dancing, bike riding, horseback riding, swimming, basketball, skating, and tae kwon do. However, they did not engage in these activities as regularly as the passive pursuits, in part, because they were not home-based and were more dependent on parental involvement (e.g., transport to a program).

The activities that the girls were good at produced valued outcomes and were considered satisfying. Michaela "loved" doing crafts because they were "fun." When 12-year-old Amy had a bad day at school, she explained that making jewelry helped "me feel better about [herself]." Tina, age 11, explained reading gave her the chance to learn new things and use her imagination. Ella, age 9, enjoyed practicing the piano because she was "always trying to learn a harder song."

Physical activity was not satisfying for many of the girls because they had not acquired a level of skill to comfortably participate with others. Some girls avoided participating in certain activities because they perceived their skill level to be less than their peers' skill level, as noted by this mother:

> Bronwyn [age 8] gets invited to go swimming or to [national park] to go hiking, but she never wants to go and I think there's some anxiety there about . . . like, she can't keep up on walks and she's not a deep-end swimmer so she doesn't want to go.

When the girls were asked to list leisure activities at which they wanted to improve, all identified at least one physically active leisure pursuit. The motivation for improvement was most often related to enhancing their enjoyment in activities with their peers. For example, Laura's mother was surprised her daughter (age 10) wrote that she wanted to improve at skating. Her mother thought she was a "pretty good" skater. Laura's response was, "But mom, I'm not as good as my friends." She believed skating with her friends would be "less stressful and more fun" if she were better at it.

Body Image and Leisure Participation

Body-image issues can cause girls to feel uncomfortable while participating in activities (James, 2000). Most parents reported their daughters were not self-conscious about their bodies or how they looked in their clothes unless they had been teased about their weight. Weight-based teasing did not necessarily lead girls to cease their participation, especially in activities they were passionate about. However, it did affect enjoyment while participating. "Depending on who's at the lake, you know, some of the kids tease her, and she doesn't stop swimming I think because she loves it, but she'll say she didn't have as much fun," reported the mother of 6-year-old Yolanda.

The adolescent girls I spoke with were no longer experiencing weight-based teasing, but were concerned about what others were *thinking* about their bodies. Ashley, 13, started going to the local recreation complex with her father. They walked on the treadmill in the cardio room, or played badminton or basketball in the gymnasium. Ashley said she was uncomfortable exercising in front of others. Her perceptions of what others were thinking about her dominated her thoughts and detracted from her enjoyment: "Why is the fat girl in here?" "She's going to break the treadmill." "She shouldn't be here." Although no negative comments were made to her directly, her thoughts were linked to her sense of entitlement, in spite of being overweight, to participate in active leisure. Leah echoed this perception in discussing her concerns about "looking silly" while engaged in physical activity: "Mom, there are certain activities fat girls shouldn't do." Her ideas of what was appropriate and what was not were based on the portrayal of girls who were overweight in television and movies. She interpreted media representations as messages or instructions on how to behave as a girl who was overweight.

Although boys can access sports such as football in which being "heavy" is an asset, one mother observed, "there isn't an equivalent activity for the heavy girl." As a result, these girls seemed to struggle to understand the role of physically active leisure in their lives in a society focused on girls and women being thin and that does not portray girls who are overweight enjoying or succeeding in active leisure pursuits.

Structured Opportunities

Parents who wanted to increase their daughters' participation in physical activity searched for activities that would develop skill or allow their daughters to participate comfortably at their existing skill level. Locating beginner-level programs, especially in smaller communities, in which girls aged 10 years and older would be able to participate with other girls their age was difficult. Older girls who felt marginalized because of their overweight status explained that learning to swim, skate, or dance with 6-year-olds was not appealing. The girls all expressed how much they valued the relational aspects (e.g., socializing, making friends) of leisure and indicated this opportunity would not be present if they had to participate with much younger children.

Girls interested in trying less common activities such as martial arts, racquet sports (e.g., tennis, squash), and wall climbing were able to do these activities with their friends or other youth their age. Children, it seems, are not expected to take up or master these activities at an early age and instructional opportunities existed for a wider age range.

Some of the girls were interested in non-competitive sport participation. When Leah and I talked about her interest in volleyball and the idea of playing lunch-time intramurals at school, she explained, "I like volleyball, but I don't like the pressure of competition." No opportunities for non-competitive sport participation existed in Leah's community. Ava, 14, was interested in swimming regularly with her friends. She tried out for her high school swim team and did not make it. Her mother was frustrated:

> I understand they have limits on how many swimmers can compete, but she wasn't interested ... doesn't care about competing, just swimming a couple of times a week with her friends and improving. I talked to the coach about letting her practice with

the team, but he said—not an option. I don't get that—there is room for her in the pool.

The organized recreation and sport opportunities within schools and the community did not appear to support girls in getting or being active with their friends or other girls. Without the chance to develop or improve their skills in active leisure pursuits, girls did not have the opportunity to increase their competence in active pursuits. Therefore, sport or active leisure participation was experienced as less satisfying.

THE ROLE OF PARENTS

The family environment is a modifiable factor that contributes to childhood obesity (Timperio et al., 2008). While the girls' experiences with particular physically active and passive activities affected their interests and choices related to their free time, their parents were also influential.

Parents as Co-Participants

The literature indicates that parents participating in active leisure with their children are a key influence on physical activity levels (Heitzler, Martin, Duke, & Huhman, 2006). Fathers' physical activity levels have been found to have a greater influence on girls' levels of physical activity than mothers' (Davison, Cutting, & Birch, 2003). Other research, however, has suggested that because mothers tend to spend more leisure time with their children, especially when they are younger, mothers have more opportunities to be co-participants and therefore, to influence their daughters' activity levels (Spurrier, Magarey, Golley, Curnow, & Sawyer, 2008).

In my research, I asked parents about active and passive leisure activities in which they participated with their children. Parent-child leisure tended to be sedentary in nature with only occasional physical activity participation. Girls watched television and movies, played board games, worked on craft projects, went out for dinner, and attended church with parents. Mothers and daughters sometimes participated in separate leisure activities while in the same room, "We do have leisure together in the evening. She'll color and watch television and I curl up and read my book," reported mother of 6-year-old Nikki.

Mothers who were overweight or obese described poor health (i.e., knee or back problems, cardiovascular disease, diabetes) as limiting their ability to be co-participants. Michaela's mother said, "Exploring in a park is out. We can't keep up with her and obviously she can't be off in the woods on her own. I can't bike ride with her because it hurts my knees." For other mothers, lack of motivation, energy, and time stopped them from engaging in physically active leisure with their children. All but two mothers were engaged in paid employment outside the home and were primarily responsible for household and childcare tasks. These mothers understood their child's need to be active but to be a co-participant was difficult. Yolanda's mother described not having energy at the end of the day for physical activity with her daughter. Kelly explained that "with four girls who have very individual interests, finding the time to organize and do something physically active with them regularly or even just with Katherine [age 10] is nearly impossible."

Once girls reach adolescence, mothers' willingness and availability to co-participate may no longer be a significant influence on their daughters' physically active leisure. Ava and Leah said their mothers regularly invited them to go swimming, walking, or bike riding, but the girls were not interested in their mothers' activities or participating in leisure with their mothers. This finding supports that during adolescence, girls engage in more leisure with their friends than family, and friends are more influential in their leisure choices (Salvy et al., 2008). However, girls who feel they cannot participate at the same level as their peers are not able to locate age-appropriate opportunities for activity skill development, and/or are dealing with body image concerns, participating in active leisure with friends instead of parents is not an easy substitution.

Parents as Facilitators

Parents facilitate children's leisure participation by enrolling children in activities, transporting them, observing participation, and providing encouragement (Shannon, 2006; Anderson, Trussell, this volume). Mothers often support their daughters by enrolling them in and transporting them to activities (Davison, Cutting, & Birch, 2003). Mothers have also been identified as a key influence in whether their daughters start and continue physical activity (Griffith et al., 2007).

Community resources (e.g., facilities, recreation opportunities) and parents' resources (e.g., money, time) affected what mothers were able to facilitate for their daughters in my study. Daughters' negative experiences in particular activities (e.g., peer victimization) were sometimes a barrier for parents' facilitation of continued participation. Even when opportunities existed for their interested daughters, some mothers made decisions not to support or facilitate participation because of their concern to protect their daughters' self-esteem. One mother, Susan, did not support her 10-year-old daughter, Sarah, in trying out for cheerleading. Susan told Sarah that the logistics—the schedule and transportation—were the issue. What Susan shared with me, however, was different. "I knew Sarah wouldn't make it.

You see what the girls on the squad look like and you've seen what she looks like … you don't want her to get rejected." Sarah's mother perceived it was appearance, rather than skill, that would influence whether Sarah made the squad. Sarah may not have been making the link between her body shape or weight and those of the girls who were participating, and may not yet have been aware of societal stereotypes related to the image of cheerleaders. Her mother's awareness of and sensitivity to the social constructions of cheerleading and childhood obesity affected Sarah's opportunity to attempt or engage in this activity.

Some mothers had concerns about their daughters' potential success in an activity because of the impact of their weight on physical ability or performance. Katherine was interested in gymnastics. Her mother was worried that if she enrolled Katherine in gymnastics, her self-esteem would be affected because "you need to be petite to be a good gymnast and Katherine is not a petite girl." Bronwyn asked her mother about joining skating. Her mother was apprehensive: "Because of her weight, balance would be a problem and she probably doesn't have the ankle strength to hold up that weight. Another thing she'd fail at? Not good for the self-esteem."

Parents as Role Models

Participating in leisure with children is one way parents can model behaviors. How parents spend leisure time separate from their children can also send messages about how certain behaviors are valued (Shannon, 2006). Mothers, in particular, can be important role models for their daughters and influence the leisure-related attitudes and values they develop and carry into adulthood (Shannon & Shaw, 2008). Daughters attend to what their parents are doing. Girls who perceive that their parents are physically active tend to be more active throughout adolescence than girls who perceive their parents as sedentary (Madsen, McCulloch, & Crawford, 2009). Clearly, an important link exists between parents' behaviors and their daughters' well-being.

When interviewed, parents were asked about their own leisure behaviors. Only five of the mothers were regularly physically active. They tended to be active during their lunch hours, before their children were up in the morning, or after their children were in bed. Their behaviors were not visible to their daughters, and mothers rarely talked to their daughters about the active leisure in which they engaged. "I'm not sure if she knows that I go to the gym at lunch. I never talk about it." Other mothers only modeled passive leisure behaviors. "When she goes to do her homework, I turn on the TV and when she comes down before bed, she'd probably see me on the computer—e-mail, looking for recipes, online shopping, that kind of thing." Daughters who are not able to accurately assess their parents' leisure behaviors or who observe their parents as primarily sedentary, may not perceive that physically active leisure is important.

Most mothers who were not active were concerned about the messages their behavior was sending but were reluctant role models. "I guess I am a role model whether I want to be or not, because she is watching what I do. Of course she is. But I don't really want her following in my footsteps or doing what I do." These mothers expressed needing help to develop strategies for managing their roles and their time as a first step toward engaging in physically active leisure.

Research continues to emerge on the influence of mothers on their children's physical activity levels and the importance of serving as explicit role models (Griffith et al., 2007). Given this, engaging in physically active leisure may be one more task mothers perceive they must do, not necessarily for themselves, but to meet the needs of their children.

CONCLUSIONS

Awareness that their daughters may experience negative physical, social, and psychological consequences if they do not conform to a certain ideal body image places pressure on mothers, as role models and primary caregivers of their children, to find ways to help their daughters achieve a healthy weight. At the same time, mothers often feel compelled to try to mitigate any negative consequences of their daughters' weight status. Mothers may feel guilty or responsible and assume the blame if their children are not physically healthy and happy. However, putting sole responsibility for daughters' weight on mothers disregards the larger social and structural issues related to girls, physical activity, and leisure. At the same time, when mothers prevent daughters from participating in activities of interest for fear daughters may have negative experiences, opportunities are not only restricted, but daughters may be left feeling that their leisure interests, and perhaps attempts to be involved in active pursuits, are not supported. Being a *good mother* in North America today is a complex and demanding practice (Frisby and Harrington, this volume). The message that mothers often get is to put children and their well-being first. Perhaps nowhere is this seen more clearly today than in the public discourse around the so-called *obesity epidemic*. However, those messages that exhort mothers to engage in physically active leisure only as part of their roles as mothers may well perpetuate the understanding that mothers' personal leisure is related to the needs of her children (i.e., as co-participants or examples) and that active leisure is not something for mothers and daughters both to enjoy for the pleasure it can bring and/or for personal well-being.

FUTURE RESEARCH

The interrelationships between parents' roles in their daughters' leisure and the leisure experiences of girls who are overweight are complex. Although parents' roles are influential, girls also have the opportunity to make choices about what they do. Researchers need to move beyond measuring what girls are doing (e.g., rates of participation in physical activity) and seek to understand why girls who are overweight choose activities and derive satisfaction from the activities (primarily sedentary) that they do. Research could help address what needs are being met through activity for girls and their parents, what meanings girls associate with the physically active and sedentary activities in which they engage, and what qualities of leisure experiences produce feelings of enjoyment and satisfaction.

The dominant discourses on childhood obesity often point to parents as responsible for their child's weight status, and most parents with whom I interacted felt the blame. The broader social and cultural factors that influence children's free-time use and parents' roles as co-participants, facilitators, and role models cannot be ignored. Interesting questions might relate to the characteristics of programs and/or spaces in which girls, both overweight and not, feel comfortable participating. Another area for future inquiry is how the built environment within a community, as well as the opportunities available for leisure, interacts with parental roles as leisure facilitators.

Finally, research needs to explore how leisure participation can address weight criticism and body dissatisfaction among girls, including those who are overweight. Knowledge related to how recreation leaders and coaches in youth-serving organizations can help girls develop a healthy sense of self and an interest in participating in active leisure is needed. Understanding what recreation and sport program structures, formats, and services will best support girls at various ages to comfortably participate in health-promoting leisure pursuits is also important. The goal of all these efforts should be to facilitate the development of physically and mentally healthy girls who can carry these attitudes and behaviors into adult life.

NOTE

Graduate Student Leisure Educators: Kate Morrison (from January 2006 until April 2008), Tara Werner (since September 2006); Sarah Wagner (since September 2008).

REFERENCES

Bélanger, M., Gray-Donald, K., O'Loughlin, J., Paradis, G., & Hanley. J. (2009). When adolescents drop the ball: Sustainability of physical activity in youth. *American Journal of Preventive Medicine, 37*(1), 41–49.

Dalton, W. T., & Kitzmann, K. M. (2008). Broadening parental involvement in family-based interventions for pediatric overweight: Implications from family systems and child health. *Family and Community Health, 31*(4), 259–268.

Davison, K. K., Cutting, T. M., & Birch, L. L. (2003). Parents' activity-related parenting practices predict girls' physical activity. *Medicine and Science in Sports and Exercise, 35*(9), 1589–1595.

Davison, K. K., Markey, C. N., & Birch, L. L. (2003). A longitudinal examination of patterns in girls' weight concerns and body dissatisfaction from ages 5 to 9 years. *International Journal of Eating Disorders, 33*(3), 320–332.

Dietz, W. H. (1998). Health consequence of obesity in youth: Childhood predictors of adult disease. *Pediatrics, 102*(Suppl), 18–25.

Eaton, D. K., Kann, L., Kinchen, S., Ross, J., Hawkins, J., Harris, W. A., Lowry, R., McManus, T., Chyen, D., Shanklin, S., Lim, C., Grunbaum, J. A., & Weschler, H. (2006). Youth risk behavior surveillance—United States, 2005. *Journal of School Health, 76*(7), 353–372.

Friedman, K. E. (2005). Weight stigmatization and ideological beliefs: Relation to psychological functioning in obese adults. *Obesity Research, 13*, 907–916.

Golley, R. K., Magarey, A. M., Baur, L. A., Steinbeck, K. S., & Daniels, L. A. (2007). Twelve-month effectiveness of a parent-led, family-focused weight-management program for prepubertal children: a randomized, controlled trial. *Pediatrics, 119*(3), 517–525.

Griffith, J. R., Clasey, J. L., King, J. T., Gantz, S., Kryscio, R. J., & Bada, H. S. (2007). Roles of parents in determining children's physical activity. *World Journal of Pediatrics, 3*, 265–270.

Heitzler, C. D., Martin, S. L., Duke, J., & Huhman, M. (2006). Correlates of physical activity in a national sample of children aged 9–13 years. *Preventive Medicine, 42,* 254–260.

Hills, A. P., King, N. A., & Armstrong, T. P. (2007). The contribution of physical activity and sedentary behaviours to the growth and development of children and adolescents: implications for overweight and obesity. *Sports Medicine, 37*(6), 1–12.

James, K. (2000). "You can feel them looking at you": The experiences of adolescent girls at swimming pools. *Journal of Leisure Research, 32,* 262–280.

Lash, M., & Armstrong, A. (2009). Impact of obesity on women's health. *Fertility and Sterility, 91*(5), 1712–1716.

Laurson, K. R., Eisenmann, J. C., Welk, G. J., Wickel, E. E., Gentile, D. A., & Walsh, D. A. (2008). Combined influence of physical activity and screen-time recommendation on childhood overweight. *Journal of Pediatrics, 153*(2), 209–214.

Madsen, K., McCulloch, C. E., & Crawford, P. B. (2009). Parent modeling: Perceptions of parents' physical activity predict girls' activity throughout adolescence. *Journal of Pediatrics, 154*(2), 278–283.

Neumark-Sztainer, D., Story, M., Hannan, P. J., Tharp, T., & Rex, J. (2003). Factors associated with changes in physical activity: A cohort study of inactive adolescent girls. *Archives of Pediatrics and Adolescent Medicine, 157,* 803–810.

Ogden, C. L., Carroll, M. D., & Flegal, K. M. (2008). High body mass index for age among US children and adolescents, 2003–2006. *Journal of the American Medical Association, 299*(20), 2401–2405.

Salvy, S-J., Wojslawowicz Bowker, J., Roemmich, J. N., Romero, N., Kieffer, E., Paluch, R., & Epstein, L. H. (2008). Peer influence on children's physical activity: An experience sampling study. *Journal of Pediatric Psychology, 33,* 39–49.

Shannon, C. S. (2006). Parents' messages about the role of extracurricular and unstructured leisure activities: Adolescents' perceptions. *Journal of Leisure Research, 38,* 398–420.

Shannon, C. S. (2008). Constraining overweight children's leisure: Understanding the role of parents. *Proceedings of the 12th Canadian Congress on Leisure Research* (pp. 401–404). Montreal, QC.

Shannon, C. S., & Shaw, S. M. (2008). Mothers and daughters: Teaching and learning about leisure. *Leisure Sciences, 30,* 1–16.

Shields, M. (2005). Measured obesity: Overweight Canadian children and adolescents. In: *Nutrition: Findings from the Canadian Community Health Survey.* Ottawa: Statistics Canada, Cat no 82-620-MWE2005001.

Spurrier, N. J., Magarey, A. A., Golley, R., Curnow, F., & Sawyer, M. G. (2008). Relationships between the home environment and physical activity and dietary patterns of preschool children: A cross-sectional study. *International Journal of Behavioral Nutrition and Physical Activity, 5,* 31.

Strauss, R. S., & Pollack, H. A. (2003). Social marginalization of overweight children. *Archives of Pediatrics and Adolescent Medicine, 157,* 746–752.

Tang-Péronard, J. L., & Heitmann, B. L. (2008). Stigmatization of obese children and adolescents, the importance of gender. *Obesity Review, 9*(6), 522–534.

Timperio, A., Salmon, J., Ball, K., Baur, L. A., Telford, A., Jackson, M., Salmon, L., & Crawford, D. (2008). Family physical activity and sedentary environments and weight change in children. *International Journal of Pediatric Obesity, 3*(3), 160–167.

CHAPTER 11
SORORITY SPACES: DISCIPLINE OF GENDERED REPUTATION IN PUBLIC LEISURE

LISBETH A. BERBARY

FADE IN:
AUGUST: CRESCENT AVE - MID-AFTERNOON - DAY OF RUSH

The camera zooms in on the roofs of the houses lining the long forested street. The roofs are wide and black, the first feel we get for the large Southern antebellum houses that set the Greek feel of the Crescent area. The camera then moves to focus in on the Zeta Chi sorority house. The house has bright white wood siding, a black roof, and eight windows facing the street, each divided into nine smaller windows by black moulding and each framed by impressive black shutters. The flatness of the roof is broken up by three triangular windows, and the front stoop is covered by a triangular roof held up by four large white columns, all adding to the impressiveness of the large antebellum house. Most importantly, above the stoop on the triangular roof-front hang three, two-feet-high, black, cast-iron Greek letters that read ZXX (Zeta Chi Chi), the formal name for the Zeta Chi sorority.
(Ethnographic screenplay, Berbary, 2008)

Part of a larger system termed "Greek Life," sororities are initiatory, women-centered social organizations for undergraduate students that are juxtaposed against fraternities, the male-centered organizations that are the founding organizations of the Greek system. Fraternities and sororities were first nationally recognized in the 1800s and have a long history in the United States. Although black, Jewish, and interest-based fraternities and sororities have joined the scene, traditional Greek organizations have historically been grounded in an elite, white, Christian, and heteronormative discourse. In the Southern United States, this discourse is particularly apparent and reinforced by Southern culture, which has been geographically shaped by a history of plantations, slavery, war, the *Bible Belt*, and images of the southern belle, southern gentlemen, and southern hospitality (Scott, 1984; St. Pierre, 1995).

Fraternities and sororities have gained a particularly impressive following in many southern U.S. universities specifically because the Greek system's values generally mimic those of the larger culture of the South. Current members often have had siblings, parents, grandparents, and even great-grandparents that have also been members of Greek organizations. Having had a relative in a fraternity or sorority makes one a *legacy* and often can increase the chance of being offered a *bid for membership* upon completion of the rigorous recruitment process. Potential members are reviewed during this process based on letters of recommendation, photographs, interviews, academic transcripts, proof of interests, self-presentation, and casual conversations with current members.

Those individuals accepted into the members-only subculture find themselves consumed by a world of leisure events and social obligations such as extravagant parent weekends, date nights, dances, bar crawls, intramural sport teams, tailgating events, pageants, carnivals, homecoming activities, haunted houses, cause-walks, and fraternity house parties. These leisure events are part of an elaborate social networking system that strives to encourage mingling within the Greek system and takes on philanthropic purposes by involving members in student leadership positions around fundraising and community development. This extensive leisure repertoire forms the foundation of Greek life and membership, making sororities rich sites for leisure research.

ETHNOGRAPHIC LEISURE RESEARCH

I was never a member of a sorority. Therefore, my entrance into Zeta Chi, a traditional Southern sorority from which I gained permission to conduct my 10-month ethnographic study, was also my introduction to sororities and sorority life. As a 28-year-old from Buffalo, New York, I had only watched sorority life from afar. My first taste of Southern sorority women came during a football game where I found myself in sweatpants among a sea of short-skirt, high-heel-clad sorority women. My eyes were quickly opened to the complex discursive expectations for gendered behavior (i.e., those behaviors that individuals are expected to *perform* in order to maintain that which is considered by the subculture to be appropriately female and/or male) that are found within sororities and within the spaces where sorority leisure activities played out.

Sororities can illuminate how individuals are disciplined to perform specific gendered behaviors, because they are a narrowly defined, gendered system that is set up within the larger Greek-life culture. Within the Greek system, discursive expectations for femininity are constructed by the juxtaposition of the masculine fraternity culture—a culture that demands a specifically feminine sorority culture to maintain its heteronormative status. These expectations for gender performance are even more strongly disciplined within Southern sororities. The narrowly defined expectations of gender in southern culture based on the "Southern Belle" and "Southern Gentlemen" are reinforced and magnified, resulting in extreme expectations of *hyper-masculinity* in southern fraternities. Such gender expectations are then further reinforced and magnified in southern sororities as sorority women construct themselves as the *other*, or the counterpart, to that hyper-masculinity.

These intense expectations of gender take place in all spheres of Greek life, but are particularly apparent in their public leisure spaces. Gendered behaviors within sororities are so disciplined both to maintain a level of femininity that supports expectations put forth by fraternity culture, *and* to construct a good reputation for the sorority relative to other local sororities. Public leisure spaces take on significance because a reputation is more susceptible to tarnish in public spaces where other sororities, fraternities, and the general public can observe behavior and make judgments. Therefore, those expectations of femininity that are promoted within the sorority become more important for members to uphold in spaces where public attention can quickly shape perceptions of the entire sorority. Hence, the perception of leisure spaces as *free* spaces for individual expression and freedom is challenged. Instead, within sororities, leisure spaces, where individual gendered performances are watched, judged, and restricted, often become discursively disciplined.

Ethnographic Screenplay

To illustrate the ways that sorority women's gendered behaviors are disciplined within public leisure spaces, I use the results of my ethnographic study with Zeta Chi. Zeta Chi was a traditional sorority with over 150 members ranging from freshmen to seniors who were mostly white, middle class, Christian, heterosexual women between the ages of 18 and 24. Zeta Chi was located at "USouthern," a pseudonym for a large university situated in an active college town in the southeastern region of the United States. This research began in July 2007 and continued until May 2008, with data collected in multiple sorority leisure spaces such as dances, flag-football games, bars, dinner parties, parents' weekends, pageants, and carnivals.

Data were collected specifically through participant observations, in-depth interviews, artifact collection, and informal interviews centered on the notions of culture, discipline of gendered expectations within that culture (or social pressures used to maintain appropriate gender roles), and individual acceptance of or resistance to those gendered expectations.

Data were analyzed using poststructural and feminist theories. During the analysis, themes that grew out of repetition within the data were also identified. However, rather than follow a conventional analysis to reduce data into discrete stagnant groups, representative of some almost positivistic notion of *the real*, my poststructuralist analyses were focused on showing the complexity of the data. I highlighted the overlapping, contradictory, and contingent nature of themes in motion that were often experienced simultaneously within complicated lived experiences.

I explored dialogic creative options for representation of my data because of its complexity. Recognizing the need for a literary form that allowed for movement through settings, descriptive storytelling, the use of quotations, and the integration of my own voice, I chose to construct a pseudo-screenplay to represent the gendered lives of sorority women in this context. This ethnographic screenplay is composed of quotes and passages taken directly from transcripts and field notes and rearranged into a script that conveys insight into each major theme—culture, discipline, and the acceptance or resistance of discipline. My intent was not to create a screenplay for production, but to use, as Kohn (2000) stated, the "epistemologically diverse, unanchored, free flowing, floating, and authorless" possibilities of a screenplay to represent my data (p. 489). The following presents portions of this screenplay and offers interpretations of the meanings as they relate to young women and leisure.

Public Reputation and Discipline

Upon my entrance into Zeta Chi culture, the sorority women of Zeta Chi clearly appeared to be disciplined to "act like ladies" to maintain hyper-femininity within visible public leisure spaces—where reputations about femininity could be easily tarnished, especially since most members often wore their Zeta Chi apparel and therefore were easily identified as sorority members. A negative reputation would not only hurt the individual, but would affect the entire sorority, causing a loss of new potential members and a decrease in social events with the top fraternities.

CUT TO:
METZGER'S DOWNTOWN BAR - DATE NIGHT - 9:45 PM

Summer arrives with her clique. They search the crowd for people they recognize. She sees Yarah and waves to her, spots some of her pledge-class friends, grabs her roommates, and makes her way to them with dates following behind. On the way over, Summer grabs her date, Brooks, to take a picture with the hired photographer who walks around snapping photos. Though she doesn't seem overly excited as the picture is snapped, she puts on a picture-perfect grin. She grabs hold of her roommate as they continue walking across the room.

Summer

I don't recognize half of these people. They must be new Zeta Chi.

Roommate C

Yeah, I only recognize a few of them. I think that girl is Yarah's little sister. See, she has a ZXX necklace.

Roommate C points to Margaret, who has by this time been drinking for more than an hour straight. She is hanging all over a boy nicknamed Pinky and seems to be having some trouble standing up straight. She looks up at Pinky, but her eyes don't seem to focus.

Summer

Wow, it looks like she's been drinking a little too much.

Roommate C

Yeah, she is sloppy drunk. She can't even walk. That is like taking it to a whole different level. Totally unladylike. She obviously hasn't learned our ways yet.

Margaret and Pinky begin kissing.

Summer

Whoa, she is like making out with that kid in the middle of the dance floor.

Roommate S

Wow, I mean it happens to everyone at some point but there is definitely a difference between like, kind of, randomly making out for a short period in the corner and that — making out in the middle of everything.

Roommate C

It doesn't happen to me.
That's really gross.

Roommate S

Yeah, Yarah needs to take care of her.

Summer

I hope she knows that guy. Though he doesn't seem too with it either.

Roommate C

Yeah, well, it's one thing if he's falling down and acting stupid, but it is different if a new Zeta Chi does it. She'll get a reputation quick.

Compliance with expectations for individual behavior was not left up to chance within Zeta Chi. Instead, disciplinary structures disseminated expectations and maintained fulfillment of *ladylike* behavior. All new members of Zeta Chi were immediately taught the expectations for gendered performance through New Member Meetings. These meetings, run by current members, disseminated rules related to public gendered performance such as no dancing on tables or bars, no smoking while in your car if marked with Zeta Chi letters, and no unladylike behaviors (e.g., swearing, making out, drunkenness) when wearing Zeta Chi apparel. Many of my participants agreed that "acting like a lady" was of utmost importance, and you should act in the way you were raised. They assumed that to be respectful, modest, appropriate, gracious, tasteful, and reserved. The women noted that these notions of femininity and their desire to "act like a lady" were grounded in those expectations that had been passed down and reinforced within their southern Christian upbringing.

CUT TO:
USOUTHERN FRESHMAN DORM ROOM

Inside of a USouthern dorm room we find Margaret, a newly pledged Zeta Chi sorority member, pouring newly purchased eyeliner, mascara, blush, and lip gloss from a Macy's bag onto her desk top. She seems exasperated as she moves from the desk to the mirror to her closet and back again, picking up dresses, holding them up to herself, and then throwing them on the bed. She has spent the last half hour sorting through dresses as she attempts to get dressed for one of her first Zeta Chi social events. Her Roommate, M, a high school friend who decided not to rush a sorority, sits on her own bed looking on in disbelief.

Margaret
Do you think it's too short?

Margaret makes a face as though she is very uncomfortable.

Roommate M
Well, I mean Margaret, isn't that the point? Isn't the point of these things to be a little sexy, have a little fun?

Roommate M pulls out clear nail polish and begins doing her nails.

Margaret
No, they told us it's very important how we look and act in public.

Roommate M

That doesn't mean you can't look sexy and have a little fun, does it?

Margaret

Well, they specifically told us not to publicly draw attention to ourselves. Like nothing too revealing, no dancing on tables, no taking pictures with alcohol if we are under 21 . . .

Roommate M

Man, that's a lot to worry about. Who told you that? What do you mean *they* tell you?

Margaret

We have to go to these things at Zeta Chi called New Member Meetings and we have to go through like a certain number of hours for the first six weeks of school. We like learn about like Zeta Chi morals and stuff. That's where I've been going on Wednesday nights.

Roommate M

And they tell you exactly how to act when you are in public?

Margaret

You make it sound horrible. I mean it's not like "you have to do this or else," it's more like they just tell us to act in a ladylike manner that would portray or I guess embody the ideals that Zeta Chi has set forth.

Roommate M

Well what happens if you don't act ladylike?

Margaret

Well if you really are out of control, like wearing a miniskirt, dancing drunk on a table, then you get sent to Standards, which is like the Zeta Chi "court" and they just talk to you and like give you a punishment.

Her roommate is shocked and answers with her usual sarcasm.

Roommate M

Oh, right. That doesn't sound horrible. What was I thinking?

Although new member meetings disseminated such overt expectations, both overt and covert discipline within the subculture maintained these expectations among Zeta Chi women. Overt discipline came in the form of "Standards," a ruling body run by elected upperclassmen that acted similar to a court system. Every week, Standards would organize to reprimand and give out punishments (e.g., forced exclusion from future social events) to women who had committed public offenses of inappropriateness. The most common offenses were those warned against in new member meetings concerning public gendered appearance and behavior that could potentially create negative press for Zeta Chi. Most members who were brought into Standards accepted their punishment with the recognition that the reputation of the group was more important than their individuality.

CUT TO:
UNOFFICIAL OFF-CAMPUS ZETA CHI APARTMENT - DATE NIGHT

The camera scans the crowded downtown streets and eventually focuses on the old, brown, four-story building that is Summer and Christine's apartment. A roommate's long-time boyfriend is sitting in the living room watching football on TV, drinking a beer. He is dressed in black pants, a tie, and black suit coat. We hear voices coming from the front of the apartment and the camera leaves the man behind, following the voices to where we find Summer and her two roommates getting ready for date night.

Summer
I feel like I'm stuffed in this dress. I can barely breathe.

She begins to adjust the dress in the mirror, pulling it up and re-organizing her breasts.

Summer
My boobs are everywhere. I even have them in the back. Wait till I have to sit down, I'll probably explode.

Roommate S chuckles, recognizing that Summer has a good sense of humor about her size.

Roommate S
Better watch those boobs. How soon you forget your Rush debacle!

Roommate S says half joking, remembering that someone tattled on Summer for having a dress that was too revealing.

Summer
You know I really can't help it. What, do you want me to wear? A sack?

Roommate C
Maybe you better. At least pull it up a bit. You don't want people to think you're trashy or that you're asking for it.

Roommate C isn't joking. Summer is a little surprised and offended. She feels the need to defend herself.

Summer

It's not like I act slutty. The problem is like a combo of dressing and behavior. Everyone knows I'm a dead end. I don't sleep around like some people.

Summer reminds herself that Roommate C is waiting until marriage to have sex and so everything seems trashy to her. She quickly tries to forget the comment.

Roommate S

Yeah seriously, the best part about that whole thing was that we all know the girl-who-called-you-out's reputation. Talk about sleeping around.

Roommate C

For real, it's a joke she is talking to people about being more ladylike. She's had oral sex with half of the Jewish Fraternity.

Roommate S

I know. Talk about being a slut. She doesn't need a dress to make herself look slutty. Not that you look slutty.

Looking to Summer.

Summer

Oh thanks, I feel better.

Roommate C

Yeah maybe someone needs to tell that girl oral sex with half of a fraternity doesn't make you a good girl. A lot more people are having sex than should be and outside of relationships. I'm kind of, just 'cause of my upbringing, I'm just appalled at people.

Summer

Yeah, my friend told me they call her "cum dumpster #2."

Roommate C

I wonder who's cum dumpster #1?

Roommate S

Gross. Maybe someone should tell her, "Hey, don't be a whore, that's not ladylike!"

I also found a powerful covert system of discipline that was taking place within the sorority, particularly at public leisure events. This was the discipline of *girl talk*—the rumors, discussions, and confrontations that occurred among the women reinforcing the boundaries of appropriateness through joking, name-calling, opinion-gathering, trash-talking, complimenting, and complaining. This covert system did not have the explicit rules and dissemination processes that comprised the more overt system of discipline. Instead, it was comprised of a slow process of socialization in which women began to unconsciously adopt the expectations and boundaries of ladylike appearance and behavior as noted through each other's reactions. Members disciplined themselves based on how friends reacted to the behaviors and appearances of others. They accepted or imitated some gender performances while making fun of, negatively commenting on, or covering up others. Although sorority participants sometimes were aware of their complicity within the more overt systems of discipline, they were mostly unaware of the more covert discipline and considered the intense group- and self-surveillance of sexuality, appearance, drinking, and general behavior to be natural aspects of being a woman and therefore incontestable.

Public Safety and Discipline

I originally thought that new member meetings, Standards, and girl talk, which were coordinated to uphold such narrowly defined notions of femininity, were strictly to earn and maintain a ladylike reputation for Zeta Chi. However, as I became more involved with participants, I came to understand that there was an underlying concern for public safety that drove the disproportionate focus and strong disciplinary talk around sexual behaviors and drinking. Many of these behaviors were not only strongly disciplined because they could earn Zeta Chi a bad reputation, but also because such public behavior left the women of Zeta Chi open to the male gaze and desire, therefore creating greater possibility for personal harm. The discipline regarding these women's behaviors and appearances clearly was meant to ensure *girl safety* in a highly heteronormative Greek university environment. Whereas discipline within Zeta Chi always seemed restrictive, this same discipline was productive, as it was used to protect the women.

CUT TO:
METZGER'S DOWNTOWN BAR - DATE NIGHT - 9:45 PM

The camera focuses in on a familiar downtown bar, where sorority women are entering the front door and walking up a staircase. At the top of the stairs, IDs are checked and those who are of age are given plastic bracelets to indicate their status at the bar. The music is blaring. The dark, semi-small space feels crowded, loud, and sweaty.

Margaret—a freshman Zeta Chi—and her date arrive at the front door. Margaret uses a fake ID that her sorority big sister Yarah gave her to get her in over age. She is successful and after receiving her bracelet, Margaret and her date walk into the loud, dark, hot space. Margaret quickly scans the crowd for familiar faces and meets eyes with Yarah, her sorority big sister, who calls her and her date over. Margaret grabs her date and pushes through the crowd trying to make her way to Yarah and her friends, who are in the middle of the room dancing around their dates.

Yarah
Hey you two! Margaret, you look gorgeous.

The two girls hug. Margaret's nerves calm down now that she has Yarah's approval.

Margaret
Thanks, I love your dress.

Yarah
Hey, let's go get you a drink.

Margaret
What about my date?

Yarah
Find out what he wants to drink and we'll go get it.

Margaret whispers in her date's ear to find out what he wants to drink while Yarah turns back to joke with her friends. Margaret taps Yarah on the shoulder and the two head over to the bar.

Yarah
So how is it going? Do you like him?

Margaret
Yeah, he is nice. But I don't necessarily trust him. Before we went out to dinner he apparently was "pre-gaming" and was like pounding beers.

Yarah
I kind of think that is just something that boys do. Like girls may just have a drink or two to have a head start, but guys want to already be drunk so they like pound the beers.

The girls make their way to the bar and Yarah orders the drinks. While the bartender makes the cocktails, Yarah keeps a close eye on everything that goes into them. After a few minutes, they pay for their drinks and begin to try making their way back to their dates.

Yarah
Hey, hold your cup from the top as we walk back. Like this . . .

Yarah grabs her beer-filled cup from the top so that the palm of her hand covers the opening as they walk back through the crowd with their drinks.

Margaret
Why?

Yarah
You don't want to get roofied, do you? Girls get roofied all the time. Someone just slips something into your drink and you don't even know it.

Margaret
Really?

Yarah
Yeah, but don't worry. I'm watching out for you. I'll teach you the ropes. Just remember not to trust anyone too quickly and always take care of your friends. If you ever see one of them too drunk, get them home and quick before some guy does . . . you can't trust college guys. They only want one thing.

I first started to piece together the covert ways that girl safety influenced the expectations of ladylikeness within Zeta Chi when a woman I was interviewing told me the safe way to carry my glass through the bar crowd. She and all of her friends made sure to watch their drink as it was poured and carried it so that their palm protected the opening because she had known friends who had been "roofied," or drugged, at bars. Once her story alerted me to issues of safety, I realized that I had stories that covertly were about girl safety rather than just expectations of ladylikeness. These stories included discussion about buddy systems, not walking home alone, taking care of drunk women to avoid male predators, fending off men, only dating men you know, not accepting drinks in bars, going to the bathroom together at bars, and in the most extreme cases, avoiding rape. Many of the expectations of ladylike behavior worked to reinforce feminine decency to protect women from potential emotional, physical, and sexual harm by men. These issues of safety gave me a new perspective on restrictive expectations of girl talk and the rules of Standards. Rather than being restrictive only because of expectations about ladylikeness and reputation, they were also restrictive to protect the women from those discourses of masculinity that expected masculine sexuality, power, and action, and simultaneously constructed women as weak and passive sexual objects.

Within the Greek system, expectations of masculinity seemed to be as proscribed as those of femininity within Zeta Chi. These expectations upheld the notion that men were innately different from women. Many participants accepted this whole-heartedly and assumed not only innate difference but also an inability to change *innate male behaviors,* including those behaviors that could cause harm to women or force women to restrict their own behaviors in fear of negative male attention. My participants often discussed differences between men and women. They stated that because of innate differences, men were only concerned with sex—not relationships, were free to act how they please, could drink and act dumb without consequences, and could sleep with as many women as they liked, gaining the reputation of stud rather than whore. Most accepted these innate and incontestable differences. Even when I asked one woman why she felt she had to change her behavior rather than ask men to change theirs, she responded with "that's just the way things are." From the women's perceptions of men, there was no comparable *gentlemanlike* behavioral expectations within the fraternity culture that surrounded Zeta Chi.

FOCUSING ON DISCOURSE IN LEISURE SPACES

Although leisure spaces are often perceived as spaces for the expression of individual choice and freedom, they can be sites for the production and re-production of power relations that discipline individuals' gendered behaviors (Aitchison, 1999b; Scraton & Watson, 1998; Wearing, 1998). Sorority leisure spaces clearly illuminate the ways power relations can restrict individual behavior, specifically regarding discourses of gender that constitute individuals as appropriate *female* or *male* subjects. Whether upholding heteronormative expectations of a narrowly defined gender discourse, or working to protect against an aggressive male gaze, the women of Zeta Chi found themselves in a "punishable, punishing universality" (Foucault, 1977, p. 178) in public leisure spaces.

Even in strictly disciplined leisure spaces, however, the productive component of power simultaneously created potential for resistance. Resistances did occur, although they were local and fleeting. For some women, these resistances exposed *incontestable expectations of gender* as contestable. A few women began to see how they were disciplined and started to re-constitute themselves as something other than what had always been expected. Many of the women who did resist often existed on the edges of the sorority, or ended up de-sistering or being dismissed by the sorority itself due to unladylike behaviors. Yet, their small resistances created cracks in the discursive foundation and provided insight into or illuminated the discipline and resistance of dominant discourse within leisure spaces. Even in strictly disciplined leisure spaces, women were able to penetrate boundaries, signify new meanings, and create spaces for alternative possibilities.

These relationships between leisure spaces, power, cultural discourse, discipline, and resistance highlight the gendered nature of leisure spaces and force the consideration of how such spaces both reflect and affect the ways in which individuals perform gender (Massey, 1994). This awareness allows people to begin considering not only how discursive expectations constitute gendered individuals within space, but also how to potentially reorganize the space, reconstitute selves, and challenge dominant discourse to resist such expectations. Rather than only ask, "How do individuals experience leisure?" we should ask questions such as: What discourses of gender exist within this leisure space? How are expectations of these gendered discourses disseminated and disciplined? How can we construct leisure spaces that promote resistance and re-creation of discursive expectations? Questions such as these help to illuminate the ways that leisure spaces not only affect individuals' behaviors, but also are themselves part of a discursive system that disseminates and disciplines behaviors. That is, even asking such questions helps to shape identities and performances of gender within leisure spaces. To gain a more complete understanding of women's leisure, a move from focusing solely on the individual to focusing on specific leisure spaces *and* the relationships between that space, individuals, discursive discipline, and cultural discourse is necessary. Through a more in-depth understanding of space, power relations, and gender, a contextualized understanding of women's leisure experiences can continue to emerge.

References

Aitchison, C. C. (1999b). New cultural geographies: The spatiality of leisure, gender, and sexuality. *Leisure Studies, 18*(1), 19–39.

Berbary, L. A. (2008). *Subject to sorority: Women's negotiations of competing discourses of femininity.* (Unpublished doctoral dissertation). University of Georgia, Athens.

Foucault, M. (1977). *Discipline and punish: The birth of the prison.* (A. Sheridan, Trans.). New York, NY: Random House.

Kohn, N. (2000). The screenplay as postmodern literary exemplar: Authorial distraction, disappearance, dissolution. *Qualitative Inquiry,* 6(4), 489–511.

Massey, D. (1994). *Space, place, and gender.* Minneapolis, MN: University of Minnesota Press.

Scott, A. F. (1984). *The southern lady: From pedestal to politics 1830–1930.* Charlottesville, VA: University Press of Virginia.

Scraton, S., & Watson, B. (1998). Gendered cities: Women and public leisure space in the postmodern city. *Leisure Studies, 17*(2), 123–137.

St. Pierre, E. A. (1995). Arts of existence: The construction of subjectivity in older, White southern women. (Unpublished doctoral dissertation). The Ohio State University, Columbus.

Wearing, B. (1998). *Feminism and leisure theory.* Thousand Oaks, CA: Sage.

Chapter 12
Older Women and Competitive Sports: Resistance and Empowerment through Leisure

Rylee A. Dionigi

Today's older women grew up during a time that did not actively encourage girls to compete in sport. Traditionally, many girls were not even given the opportunity to learn or practice the skills required for sport performance (Hayles, 2005). Gender stereotypes position women and girls as housewives and/or caregivers, not competitive athletes! Dominant discourses of femininity in the past have defined women as relatively weak, passive, and incompetent (Young, 1990). Consequently, physically demanding competitive sports were believed to be dangerous for the female body. Historically, exercise was only considered appropriate for girls or women if the activities were passive or therapeutic in nature (Hargreaves, 1994; Vertinsky, 1995; Historical Perspectives chapter, this volume).

Similarly, sport was thought to be inappropriate and risky for older people. Older adults were discouraged from participating in strenuous activity for fear that it would place too many demands on their aging bodies (Grant, 2001; Vertinsky, 1995, 1998). Dominant discourses of aging emphasized decline, frailty, dependency, and disengagement in later life (O'Brien Cousins & Vertinsky, 1999; Wearing 1995). Older people generally were expected to slow down and take a well-earned rest (Grant, 2001). Sport was traditionally promoted to and organized for young people, especially males, and based on a model of performance and power (Coakley, 2007). Therefore, dominant sport *power and performance* discourses promoted masculinity, winning, strength, aggression, youthfulness, and performance enhancement (Coakley, 2007; Tinning, 1997). Hence, competition and athleticism were not considered appropriate for older adults or women.

Although sport is now encouraged for people of all ages, genders, and abilities, these stereotypical understandings of women, older age, and competitive sport are embedded in Western culture. These orthodoxies affect public access to sport and an individual's decision to play. These stereotypes have also shaped the way people think about sport and how it *should* be played among different groups such as older people and women. For instance, *pleasure and participation* discourses are typically used to describe, legitimate, and promote sports participation in later life (Coakley, 2007; Tinning, 1997). This model emphasizes joy, inclusion, fair play, cooperation, pleasurable movement experiences, and friendly participation through sport. When older women compete in sport to win or push their bodies to the limit, such competitive practices seem to contradict the pleasure-and-participation philosophy. Yet many older women from around the world choose to train for and regularly compete at Masters, Veteran's and/or Senior's tournaments in *physically demanding* sports not typically associated with older women, such as track and field, swimming, cycling, weightlifting, triathlons, marathons, tennis, badminton, hockey, basketball, netball, and softball.

By choosing activities that go against the *cultural grain*, these older women are using leisure as a site for resistance regardless of their intent or reasons for participation. Resistance can be individual and/or collective, intentional or unintentional, and has the potential for personal empowerment and/or collective social change (Shaw, 2001, 2006). However, by resisting traditional stereotypes tied to aging and gender, older women who compete in sport are also involved in reinforcing, internalizing, or conforming to other dominant cultural values and ideologies often tied to youthfulness and/or competition (Dionigi, 2008). Nevertheless, the potential for personal empowerment is possible when older women use their bodies in sporting activities, win medals in events that were previously inaccessible to them, maintain friendships through sport, and travel distances to compete. They have the opportunity to experience great joy and pride in their achievements and develop an identity as a sportsperson.

Therefore, the purpose of this chapter is to examine older women's participation in physically demanding competitive sports as a potential leisure context for resistance, conformity, and personal empowerment. I draw on qualitative data from older female Masters Games competitors and interpret their talk and actions within a framework of research on women's resistance through sport and leisure (e.g., Hargreaves, 1994; Shaw, 2001) and leisure as a site for resistance to ageism (Wearing, 1995). I became interested in this topic because I am a young, white, middle-class woman who has played sports since childhood. I endeavor to maintain participation in sports for as long as I am able and continue to enjoy it. I witnessed my grandmother play sports into her 80s, and it was her determination, resilience, and spirit that inspired me to learn more about the individual and cultural meanings of sports participation in later life. In this chapter, I take the perspective that personal and cultural practices and understandings of sport and leisure are linked to power relations, as discussed earlier in this text (see section 1, chapter 5). Therefore, I make the assumption that although older women are influenced by social norms and practices, they are also active agents who participate in the construction and reconstruction of their identities and social worlds.

THE EXPERIENCES OF OLDER WOMEN IN SPORT

I observed and interviewed 70 older women (aged 55–82 years) who competed in individual and/or teams sports at the 2001 8th Australian Masters Games (AMG). These data are taken from a larger study that explored the experiences, motives, and actions of older male and female Masters athletes (Dionigi, 2008). Stage 1 of data collection involved observations of the participants competing and socializing at the AMG, as well as on-site, short, semi-structured interviews with 55 older women during the event. The women were interviewed face-to-face for approximately 10–30 minutes about their exercise history, why they competed in sport, the place sports participation had in their lives, and what they gained from their participation. Stage 2 of data collection involved in-depth interviews ranging from 50–150 minutes each, with 15 older women about their meanings and experiences of sports participation five months after they competed in the AMG.

The majority of women were Australian, but a few participants were from New Zealand. They were white and primarily from middle-class backgrounds. Participants were married, widowed, or single, and lived independently in their own homes or retirement villages. Approximately one third of the women had participated in sports from a young age. Another third restarted sports participation later in life after a break (e.g., due to family or work commitments), and the remaining third began participating after the age of 50. At the time of data collection, these women were regularly training for and competing in sports such as track and field, half-marathon, cross-country running, triathlon, cycling, squash, tennis, badminton, field hockey, netball, and basketball at Masters or Veterans events ranging from local to national competitions.

My analysis here focuses on two key themes that emerged from this research because they demonstrate how resistance, conformity, and empowerment were evidenced among older female athletes: *competing to win* and *"I'm out here and I can do this."*

Competing to Win

Many older women said that when they participated in sports they "try to win," and/or aim to achieve a "personal best." They were competitive. These findings challenge traditional images and ideologies of femininity and aging as decline discourses, which position older women as not suited to athletic competition. Consequently, several participants expressed feelings of guilt, embarrassment, or avoidance about being competitive because they recognized that it was not considered appropriate behavior. For instance, a 60-year-old swimmer said:

> It should be for fun, but I take it too serious . . . Oh, it's just me. I'm just competitive and I feel really guilty [giggles] because a lot of these people are just here for fun and that's what it should be. It's supposed to be fun, but I can't make it [just for] fun.

Some women said that they were not competitive, and then displayed competitive behavior when I watched them perform. Many considered their age and ability as the main reasons why they did not (and should not) take competing in sport or winning seriously. They said that they were "past it," and should acknowledge that they are "too old" to be competitive. One 76-year-old swimmer and tennis player described these dominant discourses or stereotypes of aging:

> I think it comes, mainly because of age and aspiration. I think when you're young, you want to be the best, that means a lot, or to win . . . but, in the latter years, as long as you're enjoying it. I mean you still like to win the game of tennis, but it's not paramount . . . but then, I suppose I'm competitive in [tennis], to a degree.

This woman initially drew on pleasure-and-participation discourses that typically frame sport for older people to make sense of her sporting experiences. By the end of her statement, however, she acknowledged that she was somewhat competitive and enjoyed winning, which aligns with the power-and-performance model of sport.

Most women invested in some aspects of the power-and-performance discourse, but through their participation they rejected the win-at-all-costs and aggressive practices that this model promotes. For example, a 60-year-old squash player said:

> I am [a competitive person] when I play, but I'm not aggressively competitive, but I like to win, but . . . I don't do it at-all-costs . . . If I lose that's the end of it . . . I don't brood over it and I don't make excuses.

In a sense, these women appeared to be apologetic about their reasons for enjoying competition and winning. Then again, they were out there competing in physically demanding sports and they defined themselves as competitive.

In contrast, many older women were unapologetic and candid in discussing the importance of performance and competition. A 76-year-old tennis player said that she had a "doggedness to win" when she was younger and such eagerness remained with her now. She explained, "You're out there to outwit your opposition, and if you can do it by powerful play, or clever play, or just good luck [laughs], that's what you do." An 82-year-old track and field athlete, who competed in her first competitive long-distance run at 60 years of age said, "I suppose it's just the competitiveness in me is why I do it anyway. . . . I suppose my nature makes me keep pushing." Regardless of when they began competing, as many older women identified themselves as competitive as not, and they felt they were expressing this identity through their continued involvement in sports. They spoke about joy in winning medals and breaking records, and they reported appreciating the recognition and status that accompanied competition. Many medal-winners proudly wore their medals throughout the Games, even at the nightly social activities.

I saw many older women adopt tactics such as using state-of-the-art sporting equipment and wearing sports apparel to enhance their performance and chances of athletic success at the AMG. Such practices are usually associated with elite or youth sports (Hayles, 2005, p. 115). In particular, cyclists wore Lycra outfits and clip-in shoes, and track and field athletes wore spiked shoes and used starting blocks for sprints. Many women indicated that they constantly monitored their performance levels in comparison to their previous standards, and/or in comparison to others of the same or significantly younger age. Some participants said that they kept detailed accounts of their times, competition rankings, or past performances.

These findings highlight that discourses and practices of competition were pervasive in shaping the meanings of participation in sports, regardless of age or gender. The talk and actions of many older female athletes reinforced as well as disrupted the power-and-performance sport model, challenged the aging-as-decline discourse and stereotypical notions of femininity, and partially resisted aspects underlying pleasure-and-participation sport discourses. It appeared that these individuals were shifting the definition of what it means to be an older woman as well as an older athlete, at the personal and collective levels.

On one hand, their investment in the power-and-performance model, and the practices it promotes, reinforced the value of competition, youthfulness, masculinity, and strength embedded in sport. Therefore, collectively their behavior did not represent a fundamental challenge to hegemonic masculinity tied to sport. Rather, Masters sports gave these older women the opportunity to conform to those discourses and practices. The women did reject aspects of this model, such as the use of aggression and the win-at-all-cost mentality. This finding has also emerged in research on younger women's participation in traditionally male-dominated sports. Theberge (2000) found that female ice hockey players invested in the mainstream ideologies of the men's game through their expressions of strength, power, domination, speed, and physical aggression. However, they also demonstrated grace, finesse, and emotion on the ice, which opposed the masculine power-and-performance model of competitive sports. Similarly, a study by Guthrie and Castelnuovo (1992) of elite female bodybuilders explored how this context encouraged both resistance and compliance to dominant gender ideologies.

On the other hand, the older women in my research challenged the boundaries of the acceptable subjects of these power-and-performance discourses and practices by proving that older women can be competitive and strong. They were showing that Masters sports are not only about pleasure and participation but also serious competition. By investing in performance discourses that emphasized strength, youthfulness, determination, and power, these women were attempting to (re)define aging. They were demonstrating resistance by claiming their right to compete in a traditionally male-dominated, youth-oriented activity, which can be personally empowering (Shaw, 2006).

"I'm Out Here and I Can Do This"

The ability to compete in physically demanding, competitive sports signified to these female athletes, as well as spectators, that they were unlike the stereotypical older woman. Many of my study participants seemed to acknowledge that their sporting practices challenged age and gender norms. They expressed feelings of pride and personal empowerment when discussing this differentiation. A 73-year-old triathlete, for example, commented:

> A man that works at the retirement village, where I now live, he said, "I wish the rest of the residents were like you," because I ride a bike and I swim and I run. I don't worry about trivial things, which happens very often when people get very old and they worry about things that don't really matter. I'm too busy to worry about that.

And a 73-year-old runner and swimmer noted:

> It's sort of a feeling of *power* [she squints her eyes and really emphasizes this word] alright, when my grandsons can go to school and say, "My grandma runs half-marathons" and everybody else

says, "Oh no, my grandma's in a nursing home," you know, and so, that's good [she stands straight, puffs her chest out and appears proud] and I like that kind of feeling.

These statements suggest that resistance to the dominant beliefs about older age can be interpreted as a form of power in and of itself (Shaw, 2001). By investing in the competitive ideologies and practices of mainstream sport, these women were expressing a powerful, youthful, vital, and active image that challenged the dominant passive, disabled, and dependent image of older people.

Several women also acknowledged that they were resisting gender norms and expectations. For example, a 66-year-old athlete described the reaction when her husband told her to do something that she would enjoy: "I think he thought I was going to join a knitting club or cooking club or something [grins], but I joined athletics [track and field] and life has never been the same since." A 60-year-old hockey player explained how sport helped her break away from stereotypical gender roles: "I was known as either my husband's wife or a mother . . . but only was it on the hockey field that I got my own identity." These perceptions are consistent with Shaw's (1994) contention that when leisure is interpreted "as a situation of choice, control, and self-determination . . . women's participation in activities, especially nontraditional activities, can be seen to challenge restrictive social roles" (p. 9).

Not only did these women feel empowered through resisting gender and aging stereotypes, they also experienced joy and satisfaction in realizing that they had the physical and mental ability to achieve in vigorous competitive physical activity. One participant, a 59-year-old hockey player, said, "It's personal pride to think, Ok. I'm out here and I can do this!" Likewise, a 73-year-old woman who ran in her first half-marathon at age 67 explained, "Well, it is just satisfying to know you can run a half-marathon or swim 1,500 meters, which I do, and that makes you feel as though you are actually still here." Moreover, I watched a lady compete in the 80–85 years women's triple jump, which involved her making a short sprint down the track (in spiked shoes), hopping on one leg, leaping forward on the other, then jumping and landing on both feet into the sand pit. She broke the world record for her age group. The ability to use one's body in such a powerful, natural, and effective way was liberating for these individuals, especially when dominant beliefs about the aging female body assume that it is not capable of such extreme activity (Hargreaves, 1994; Vertinsky, 1995).

Therefore, in addition to challenging dominant views of aging and femininity, these women were resisting, pushing, and monitoring the physically aging female body. At a personal level, managing and adapting to aging bodies helps provide older people with "a sense of self-worth, identity, and empowerment" (Grant, 2001, p. 795). The women in my research were (re)positioning themselves as strong, independent, and resilient in spite of an aging body. Evidently, "sport and fitness activities can be liberating for women because they defy the cultural stereotype of women as passive and weak" (Henderson, Bialeschki, Shaw, & Freysinger, 1989, p. 105).

At the collective level, the growing number of older women participating in atypical activities such as Masters and Veterans competitions is actively redefining the conservative view that only passive exercise and gentle movements are appropriate for older women (Hargreaves, 1994). Their actions also challenged broader ageist discourses. As supported by Wearing (1995), "When applied to older persons, leisure emphasizes what a person *can* do rather than what they are no longer physically capable of doing. Therefore it has distinct possibilities for resistance to ageism" (p. 272). Hargreaves argued that the accomplishments of older women in Masters events have transformed the belief that sport for the elderly is fundamentally therapeutic to a view of later life as a time for "positive health and autonomy" (p. 268). Although my data provides further empirical support for Hargreaves's argument, more research on the experiences of older female sports participants is needed.

Concluding Thoughts: What's Next?

Rigorous theoretical and empirical research into competitive sport as a context for resistance and empowerment for older women is rare. The multiple and conflicting discourses of sport, aging, and gender circulating in society make understanding how these notions intersect with the personal lives of women important. My analysis shows that although the talk and actions of these individuals provided alternatives to the dominant understandings of what it means to be an older woman or athlete, they simultaneously reinforced the value Western society places on being competitive and youthful. In one sense, this outcome may work to reproduce the undesirability of old age and has the potential to perpetuate hegemonic masculinity in sport. More importantly, however, the stories of these older female athletes can lead to a change in attitude toward the capabilities and expectations of older women.

Given the focus on white, middle-class, Australian women in my study, further research needs to explore the experiences of women from different cultural and socioeconomic backgrounds to determine the factors affecting their participation in sport. Also, future research should take a life-history approach to compare the stories of women who began sport later in life and women who have always played sport, with a focus on issues of identity management and socialization into sport. Exploring the differences between women involved in individual sports and in team sports, as well as between those who are members of a Masters sporting club and those who are not, will help to determine the value of social support among older women in this context.

Although my research reveals that participation in sports can be an empowering experience for older women, recognizing that many older women do not have the means, ability, or desire to compete in sports is vital. Competitive sport is just one type of leisure activity that can have powerful and contradictory personal and broader outcomes for older women. Therefore, examining the experiences of older women who do not compete in sports and determining the varied ways in which resistance is played out in their lives through other forms of leisure is equally important.

REFERENCES

Coakley, J. J. (2007). *Sport in society: Issues and controversies* (9th ed.). New York, NY: McGraw-Hill.

Dionigi, R. A. (2008). *Competing for life: Older people, sport, and ageing.* Saarbrüecken, Germany: Verlag Dr. Müller.

Grant, B. C. (2001). "You're never too old": Beliefs about physical activity and playing sport in later life. *Ageing and Society, 21,* 777–798.

Guthrie, S. R., & Castelnuovo, S. (1992). Elite women bodybuilders: Models of resistance or compliance? *Play and Culture, 5,* 401–408.

Hargreaves, J. (1994). *Sporting females: Critical issues in the history and sociology of women's sports.* London, UK: Routledge.

Hayles, C. (2005). *Governmentality and sport in later life.* (Unpublished doctoral dissertation). University of Queensland, Australia.

Henderson, K. A., Bialeschki, M. D., Shaw, S. M., & Freysinger, V. (1989). *A leisure of one's own: A feminist perspective on women's leisure.* State College, PA: Venture Publishing, Inc.

O'Brien Cousins, S., & Vertinsky, P. (1999). Ageing, gender, and physical activity. In P. White & K. Young (Eds.), *Sport and gender in Canada* (pp. 129–152). Don Mills, ON: Oxford University Press.

Shaw, S. M. (1994). Gender, leisure, and constraint: Towards a framework for the analysis of women's leisure. *Journal of Leisure Research, 26,* 8–22.

Shaw, S. M. (2001). Conceptualizing resistance: Women's leisure as political practice. *Journal of Leisure Research, 33,* 186–201.

Shaw, S. M. (2006). Resistance. In C. Rojek, S. M. Shaw, & A. J. Veal (Eds.), *A handbook of leisure studies* (pp. 533–545). New York, NY: Palgrave Macmillan.

Tinning, R. (1997). Performance and participation discourses in human movement: Towards a socially critical physical education. In J. Fernandez-Balboa (Ed.), *Critical postmodernism in human movement, physical education, and sport* (pp. 99–119). New York, NY: SUNY Press.

Theberge, N. (2000). *Higher goals: Women's ice hockey and the politics of gender.* New York, NY: SUNY Press.

Vertinsky, P. (1995). Stereotypes of aging women and exercise: A historical perspective. *Journal of Aging and Physical Activity, 3,* 223–237.

Vertinsky, P. (1998). Aging bodies, aging sport historians, and the choreographing of sport history. *Sport History Review, 29,* 18–20.

Wearing, B. (1995). Leisure and resistance in an ageing society. *Leisure Studies, 14,* 263–279.

Young, I. M. (1990). Throwing like a girl: a phenomenology of feminine body comportment, motility, and spatiality. In *Throwing like a girl and other essays in feminist philosophy and social theory* (pp. 141–159). Bloomington, IN: Indiana University Press.

CHAPTER 13
TIME USE IN DAILY LIFE: WOMEN, FAMILIES, AND LEISURE

MARGO HILBRECHT

In the summer of 2009, an article targeting employed mothers appeared in the Toronto *Globe and Mail*. It began: "Not enough time for the kids? Hmm, let's see, 168 hours in a week . . . 56 for sleeping . . . 50 hours for work and commute . . . which leaves 62 hours for chores and kids. So, what's the problem?" (Barton, 2009, p. L1). The author reported that another journalist, Laura Vanderkam, a married mother of one preschool child, analyzed data from the American Time Use Survey and concluded that an average mother fritters away many of her spare hours. Vanderkam advised women to focus on using their time purposely, to plan activities, and to use leisure time *well*.

Barton's article comments generated a flurry of angry letters and website postings. Most readers clearly did not share Vanderkam's (Barton, 2009) privileged lifestyle, which included a cleaning service, a husband who did laundry and shared cooking, and a child with no sleep issues and still too young for a tightly packed schedule of extracurricular activities. Her experiences did not resonate with most mothers who could not afford or chose not to hire a domestic worker, whose partner did not share household chores, or single parents with a substantially heavier workload.

Not only did Vanderkam (Barton, 2009) overlook dimensions of social class related to time use, she also ignored completely how fathers spend time. By doing so, she neatly reinforced and situated responsibility for home and family as the sole domain of mothers. Leisure was deemed valuable only if it was planned and purposive. Otherwise the time was "frittered" away. Nothing suggested that leisure could be found in everyday moments. One reader resisted with:

> Even I find it necessary to have some down time . . . It's simply not healthy or normal to spend all of your time on a treadmill, like a rat on a wheel. It is during downtime that our thoughts are freed up so that we have the opportunity to simply enjoy the moment either with ourselves or with our children. (*The Globe and Mail*, 2009)

Vanderkam's (Barton, 2009) view that the heightened levels of time pressure and lack of leisure time reported by mothers is an outcome of poor time-management skills does not consider broader sociocultural forces that shape women's allocation and understanding of time. As a mother of three, my time is interwoven with the needs and expectations of family members, although both the amount of time and timing of activities have changed over the years. From babies' unpredictable schedules to children's school routines, and now seasonal adjustments related to their university holidays and demands of summer jobs, I continue to feel the pull away from my own activities and interests and the push toward accommodating responsibilities of family life. My chapter explores the time use of women with families, and how interpersonal, institutional and cultural factors influence time for leisure and other important activities.

THINKING ABOUT TIME

Time is a complex phenomenon. How people think about time is guided by shared cultural understandings and bounded by artificial constructs such as weekends or weekdays and other schedules and routines. While going about daily activities, people live in the present but may be focused on past experiences or future commitments. Time can be objectively quantified in hours and days, but it is also subjectively experienced as rushed or relaxed, passing quickly or dragging by slowly. As Daly (2001) observed, "Time oscillates between standardized units and a qualitatively uneven experience" (p. 8). Thus, time can be challenging to conceptualize and research.

When studying time, the most common approach has been to treat time as a neutral commodity easily subdivided into fixed units of hours or minutes with activities linked together in sequential fashion (Knights, 2006). Some people refer to this approach as a *masculine* experience of time, also known as linear, monochronic, or industrial time. Conversely, *feminine* experiences of time are grounded in recurring rhythms and activity patterns, task-based instead of clock-based, and embedded in process and meaning instead of decontextualized (Davies, 1990). This dualistic approach to conceptualizing time has been challenged, since gender is a multidimensional construct and experiences of time vary according to self-identity and social positioning. Odih (1999) preferred the notion of *relational* time as a way of understanding how men and women shape their behavior to reflect gendered expectations of others. Fathers' time is more likely to be autonomous and individual, while mothers' time is more likely to be collective, shared, and linked to the claims or needs of other family members due to the cyclical nature of family life and routine household activities (Knights, 2006). Because of the pressure on mothers to be constantly available to children, time for personal leisure is often unpredictable and/or fragmented, which makes planning or pursuing activities outside the home difficult (Bryson, 2007). Common sayings such as "A woman's time is never her own" reflect the relational aspects of time, particularly for women with families. Contrast this saying to The Rolling Stones song, "Time Is on My Side," and one can better appreciate gender differences associated with experiences of time.

Considering these differences, it is perhaps not surprising that Vanderkam's (Barton, 2009) article generated a lively discussion. By taking a linear, objective approach to time management, women's lived experiences were incompletely depicted. These experiences include the clock-based time of the workplace, the cyclical and collective nature of household time, and the intersection between these temporal realities. Finding time for leisure may be especially challenging, and women's leisure may not fit neatly into activity categories most often used in traditional research methods. Still, a quantitative focus on hours and minutes remains one of the most pervasive methods of investigating and understanding time use. This approach is worth examining related to leisure opportunities.

STUDYING TIME USE

Time-use research began almost a century ago as a method of understanding living conditions of the working class. The goal was to influence policy development to improve workers' quality of life (Szalai, 1973). Although less suited to capturing subjective aspects such as how people feel about the way they spend their time (Gershuny, 2004), time diaries show the influence of factors such as gender, income, employment status, and life-cycle stage on people's lives. By examining the full range of human activity, groups may be identified relative to advantage or disadvantage regarding time for leisure, employment, caregiving, and health-related activities such as physical activity and sleep. This research allows group comparisons to be made and outcomes distinguished from individual experience. As Oakley (2005) summarized, "Only large-scale comparative data can determine to what extent the situations of men and women are structurally differentiated" (p. 249). Consequently, studying time-use remains useful in informing policy development to foster social equality.

Time-diary research is well established in developed or Western nations with a similar shared cultural understanding of time. Participants record their main activities during a specific time frame (usually one day) along with where and with whom the activities take place. The total time for all activities during a 24-hour period must sum to 1,440 minutes. Therefore, when more time is spent on one activity, time available for other pursuits decreases. All activities are categorized according to a schema designed by the researcher. Leisure is defined as *free time* and includes activities unrelated to other domains necessary for meeting economic, household, or biological needs. This definition allows for consistency in longitudinal and comparative studies, but it ignores respondents' perceptions of how an activity is experienced. For example, walking the family dog is usually categorized as unpaid domestic labor. Different individuals, however, may experience it as leisure, caregiving, or even as a type of personal care for those in need of exercise who under other circumstances might prefer just to let the dog out in the back yard.

Some patterns are highly gendered and consistent cross-nationally. With few exceptions, multinational time-use data indicate that compared to fathers, mothers with children living at home spend less time working for pay, have less time for leisure, and spend more time on caregiving and unpaid domestic labor such as cooking, cleaning, and laundry. Fathers, on the other hand, devote more time to employment and have greater amounts of leisure (e.g., see Bianchi & Raley, 2005; Bianchi, Robinson, & Milkie, 2006; Craig, 2006b; Fast & Frederick, 2004; Gershuny, 2000; Hilbrecht, 2009; Jacobs & Gerson, 2004; Sayer, 2005; Stalker, 2006). Some changes are evident in longitudinal data. Women's employment time has increased from previous generations with a corresponding decrease in time for leisure (Marshall, 2006). Both mothers and fathers spend more time caring for children than in the past (Sayer, 2005), although gender remains an important predictor of the type of care (Craig, 2006b). For fathers, most of the increase is in more pleasurable caregiving activities such as playing, reading, and talking to children. Mothers disproportionately perform the work-like physical care (Craig, 2007). The gender gap in housework has also narrowed, although likely the result of women doing less domestic work rather than men doing substantially more (Bittman, 1998; Craig, 2006a).

In dual-earner households, men's and women's combined workload of paid and unpaid labor is similar, but the distribution of time spent on various tasks shows a strong gender asymmetry (Bittman & Wajcman, 2000). These patterns are linked to social norms and expectations that assign mothers primary responsibility for home and family and emphasize the provider role among fathers. Even among married or cohabiting couples *without* children, employed women still spend more time on housework than men (Marshall, 2006). Therefore, in a heterosexual relationship, women's greater domestic workload may be part of *doing gender* (West & Zimmerman, 1987; Harrington, this volume). Responsibility for these tasks is deeply embedded as part of a gendered self-identity and then reproduced and reinforced through everyday interaction and routines.

Some explanations have been advanced regarding why gender differences persist despite high levels of maternal workforce participation and a public discourse of equality. Hochschild and Machung (1989) referred to the *stalled revolution*, where women's work is devalued compared to men's, resulting in an ongoing rationalization of her unequal share of housework. Others have suggested *lagged adaptation*, according to which the adjustment in household behaviors may take years, or even generations to catch up to cultural expectations (Gershuny, Godwin, & Jones, 1994). Sullivan (2004) believes behavioral change occurs slowly and that it may take decades for gender ideologies to shift. She cited the results of multinational longitudinal time-use studies to show that meaningful change has occurred, albeit slowly, in both employment and domestic spheres for men and women in Western nations.

Whether attributable to lagged adaptation, a stalled revolution, or simply a slow rate of change, gender differences in time use affect women's leisure opportunities. Moreover, similar patterns of gendered time use are evident among adolescents who usually do not have many household responsibilities. In a study of Ontario high school students, this difference was especially notable on weekends when time was more discretionary and not structured by school routines. On Sundays, 12- to 14-year-old boys reported on average one hour and 27 minutes *more* free time than girls. Boys spent more time on computer games and physically active leisure, while girls devoted significantly more time to household chores, homework, and personal care (Hilbrecht, Zuzanek, & Mannell, 2008). Some negotiation of domestic responsibilities may occur within families, but power dynamics are such that parents, and not their teenagers, generally assign and enforce household chores. Therefore, although most Canadians support the idea of gender equality, patterns of time use indicate that from a young age, boys are privileged with respect to leisure and girls are disadvantaged by a heavier domestic workload.

Quantity of time is only one dimension of temporal experiences. Time-use studies can also be structured to address the quality of time by including relational factors and considering the impact of previous, concurrent, and subsequent activities. By examining the last period of leisure in the day, for example, Sullivan (1997) determined that married mothers with young children in the United Kingdom more often combined leisure with other activities and were significantly more likely than men to have their leisure interrupted by childcare or domestic work. Similarly, Mattingly and Bianchi (2003) reported a "triple burden" (p. 1022) for women in the United States. Compared to men, they had less leisure time, and a weaker relationship between leisure time and reduced levels of time pressure. In addition, leisure was *contaminated* more often by concurrent activities such as childcare or housework, as opposed to *pure* leisure in which there is either no secondary activity or the secondary activity is also leisure. Bittman and Wajcman (2000) reported similar findings for women in Australia and also noted that women's leisure was more often fragmented throughout the day. They suggested that fragmentation not only affected quality of leisure but also contributed to women's heightened levels of time pressure.

Childcare time is relevant to discussions of leisure for two reasons. First, it can displace time for leisure and second, it has both work-like and leisurely qualities, depending on the type of activity and perceptions of the person performing it (Craig, 2006c). Childcare activities show gender specialization, which is most apparent when children are young. Rather than relieving mothers of some of the more routine aspects of physical care, Bittman and Wajcman (2000) found that fathers with children less than two years old spent one third of their caregiving time playing with children. Women spent more time during the week on childcare (30 hours compared to 8 hours for men) and devoted a greater proportion to physical care such as bathing, dressing, and feeding. Less than one sixth of mothers' time involved playing with children. This finding supports qualitative studies where fathers view time with children as an opportunity for play, whereas mothers more often experience it as caregiving (e.g., Such, 2006).

Childcare also highlights a limitation of using time diaries to study leisure. Without collecting data on affective experiences, determining whether time with children is experienced as childcare, family leisure, or *contaminated* adult leisure cannot be conclusive. Leisure can be associated with any type of activity and varies individually. Perceptions may change depending on the circumstances (Shaw, 1985b). For example, a mother and child riding bicycles together may experience this as an enjoyable family leisure activity. If, however, the mother would have preferred a longer and more physically intense ride but no one else could care for her child, the presence of the child may constrain or *contaminate* the mother's leisure experience. Alternatively, the same bike ride may be viewed as childcare if she is taking her child to school, using bicycles for transportation. Over two decades ago, Deem (1986) found that for women, conventional definitions of leisure such as those used by time-use researchers were lacking, because *malestream* definitions of leisure as time or activity did not resonate with their experiences. Still today, for mothers, leisure is often integrated with other aspects of daily life and not necessarily seen as a separate activity. For mothers, leisure is viewed as time free from childcare responsibilities or time just for themselves (Green, Hebron, & Woodward, 1987; Harrington, 2001; Kay, 2001).

Since mothers' time is so circumscribed by caregiving, an experiential view of leisure seems appropriate. This subjective notion, however, is challenging to incorporate into time-use studies. By treating all episodes of leisure time as equally free or enjoyable, time diaries cannot address the relative importance of an activity. They are effective at demonstrating inequality as measured in absolute minutes but cannot convey the symbolic meaning of a particular event or activity. Quantity and quality do not always equate. Consequently, qualitative studies that explore perceptions and meanings associated with leisure time in greater depth have contributed substantially to understanding how women experience, value, negotiate, and prioritize time for self, family, and others.

SOCIAL CONTEXTS AND TEMPORAL REALITIES FOR WOMEN WITH FAMILIES

Mothers' time is closely linked to the needs of others (even the unborn—see chapter by Sullivan, this volume). Thus, adhering to the advice of work–life balance experts who advocate that women *take control* of time is difficult. Family life can be unpredictable, so mothers' time allocation changes in response to the needs and demands of family members as well as external events and organizations. Therefore, studies that consider interpersonal relationships, institutional policies, and sociocultural dimensions of women's multiple roles broaden the discussion of time, gender, and leisure.

An important consideration is the cultural context of motherhood in Western societies. *Intensive motherhood* has become a dominant approach for middle-class women. Raising children is more expert-guided, labor-intensive, and emotionally absorbing than in previous generations (Hays, 1996). Despite the contributions of fathers to nurturing and caring for their children (Kay, 2009a), by and large mothers remain the primary caregivers and are held morally accountable for children's optimal growth and development by strong sociohistorical traditions of maternal care (Risman, 2004). The tendency toward a *concerted cultivation* approach to child-rearing (Lareau, 2003), where children's abilities and talents are actively monitored and fostered through purposive leisure activities (Shaw & Dawson, 2001), means that much time is spent (usually by mothers) organizing, scheduling, and transporting children to various engagements (Shaw, 2008). In addition, by linking parental involvement in homework and other school-related activities to children's academic achievement, the education system has increased parents' workloads. Women are more likely than men to take on these responsibilities, which results in decreased leisure time for mothers during the school year (Hilbrecht, 2009). Many women are part of the *sandwich generation* too and have eldercare responsibilities that may be time-consuming, as well as physically, financially, and emotionally exhausting.

Employment commitments also structure time in ways that can either conflict with or enrich other life domains. Approximately 73% of mothers in Canada with children less than 16 years old are workforce participants (Statistics Canada, 2007). The highest rates are for women aged 25 to 44 years, coinciding with the time they are most likely to be raising families (Statistics Canada, 2009). Work hours often are long or scheduled during hours incompatible with family life, leaving little time for leisure or presenting barriers to leisure activities and programs designed to complement a traditional weekday schedule. In addition, maintaining friendships, which have been shown to enhance women's emotional well-being and subjective quality of life, may be difficult (Lewis, Rapoport, & Gambles, 2003; Parris, Vickers, & Wilkes, 2008).

Both Clough (2001) and Harrington (2001) highlighted the importance of social relationships in shaping leisure experiences and in privileging types of leisure time. In a study of female academics, Clough identified four types of leisure linked to time including family, partner, work colleagues, and time for self. Each was characterized by different experiences, purposes, and meanings. Personal leisure was highly valued but also the most likely to be delayed or cancelled if other demands arose. In addition, the role of partners was emphasized since spouses or ex-spouses were gatekeepers who could either block or facilitate women's leisure. Using both family-activity diaries and in-depth interviews, Harrington (2001) explored gender differences in the context of family leisure in Australia. A predominant theme that emerged for mothers was the importance of creating an *oasis*, or time away from obligatory household and workplace tasks. Consistent with Clough's (2001) research and the intensive motherhood discourse, women were more likely to put aside personal leisure and privilege children's and family leisure time. In addition, Harrington identified a purposive component to partner leisure as a way to maintain or strengthen the marital bond. While experiences of couple leisure may be affected by the state of the relationship, parents seemed overwhelmingly positive in their assessments of couple leisure, whereas with family leisure, mothers expressed contradictory feelings.

For many women, family leisure is synonymous with family time. Although a full discussion of family leisure is beyond the scope of this chapter (Bedini; Frisby; Harrington; Kay; Scraton & Watson; and Trussel, this volume, for a further discussion), it is an important aspect of family life and linked to notions of good parenting and active involvement in children's lives (Shaw, 2008). Family leisure is somewhat unique in that both the purpose and outcome of spending time together is social interaction. Therefore, the quality of time is not necessarily related to the quantity, and the outcome not readily measurable (Brannen, 2002). Family activities are often selected with children's interests and developmental needs in mind and mothers usually orchestrate these events. Consequently, it is not surprising that this type of leisure time is viewed as a parental responsibility and sometimes experienced as work-like (Shaw & Dawson, 2001). Family leisure, therefore, is "not 'leisure' for parents in the taken-for-granted sense of freedom of choice or unobligated time" (Shaw, 2008, p. 10). Despite outcomes that may fall short of anticipated ideals, family leisure is still valued as an important opportunity to spend time together, impart family values, and develop a sense of shared identity.

Insights from qualitative studies of family leisure have contributed to research on women's caregiving time and policy support for maternal employment. Craig and Mullan (2010) compared four countries with different work–family policies and attitudes toward maternal care—USA, Australia, Denmark, and France—to see how these differences affected time with children, paying special attention to family leisure. Of particular interest were family meals, watching television together, and leisure activities taking place outside the home. Leisure time spent in non-home settings, such as going on picnics or other outings together, was deemed especially important for parent-child relationships. These activities are considered more developmentally beneficial than passive activities like watching television because there is usually a greater focus on parent–child interaction, sharing new experiences, and strengthening family bonds. Although mothers in countries with less support for maternal employment spent more time overall with children, the amount of mother–child leisure time was remarkably similar cross-nationally. In Australia and the USA, where there is an active debate (and much anxiety) regarding substitute care, mothers spent *less* time on non-home leisure than in Denmark and France, where there is a national childcare policy and higher rates of maternal labor force participation. Craig and Mullan demonstrated that policy support for maternal employment had little effect on family leisure time. Indeed, non-home leisure, which can be viewed as high quality time with children, was higher in countries supporting women's employment.

DIRECTIONS FOR FUTURE RESEARCH

Although quantitative and qualitative approaches have been discussed separately, both are necessary in informing research design to advance an understanding of women's time use and leisure. Time-diary studies are the most common, and a very useful, method of exploring time allocation, but other research methods may be better to capture meanings and processes associated with negotiating, prioritizing, and preserving leisure time.

For women, one of the main drawbacks of time-use research is the tendency to ignore or diminish the constraining aspects of childcare (Budig & Folbre, 2004). Researcher-imposed definitions of leisure and other activities may create a distorted view of how time is experienced. Additionally, a dominant focus on the individual rather than households obscures the influence of other family members on parents' time. Some studies address these issues, but it is less common in nationally representative data sets. Collecting *affect information* with time diaries, such as feelings of enjoyment and perceptions of choice, would allow a better understanding of temporal conditions conducive to women's leisure.

Specific population subgroups that have been largely overlooked should be included in future studies. For instance, immigrant women's time use has not been well researched in comparison to the general population, either for those recently arrived or in a later stage of acculturation. Their experiences of time, family, and leisure may differ from the dominant culture. Similarly, in Canada, time use of aboriginal women may provide insight into their experiences of motherhood and leisure. Time-diary data is not collected for the Territories, which makes time-use patterns of indigenous women who mainly reside in northern Canada largely invisible in General Social Surveys. Women's time use in blended families as stepparents and among lesbian partners also may reveal different patterns and experiences. The challenges of parenting a child with severe disabilities can drastically change women's time allocation and access to leisure. Research on this topic is beginning to emerge in the United Kingdom (e.g., Thomas, Carter, Hunt, Hurley, & Robertson, 2009) and has potential to influence social policy. Furthermore, dimensions of social class and poverty have only been addressed in a limited way.

Time for women's friendships has been somewhat overlooked due to the emphasis on time for family and/or self in leisure research, but these friendships are important to well-being (Hutchinson, this volume). Moreover, time spent volunteering should be investigated, since women are often encouraged or expected to *give* their time to schools and children's activities as a form of leisure. Recent research suggests that outcomes from volunteering may be less beneficial to mothers than informal socializing with friends (Kroll, 2009).

To understand women's time use, considering the ways in which annual and seasonal rhythms are linked to opportunities for leisure would be illuminating. Women are largely responsible for the planning and celebration of religious and secular holidays as well as family events such as birthdays and other festivities. *The Christmas Imperative* (Bella, 1992) is one example of how women's time has been studied related to broader cultural rhythms and role expectations, but more research needs to be conducted and in different cultural settings.

The findings presented in this chapter highlight how the time use of women with families differs from men's not only in its allocation but also in the importance of social roles and relationships to the experience of leisure time. Gender differences in role expectations guided by sociocultural and institutional norms may limit women's time for leisure. Therefore, time-management strategies that fail to consider these factors are largely ineffective in generating more time for leisure. Addressing inequalities in other domains at the interpersonal, institutional, and policy levels will be more valuable in promoting social change.

REFERENCES

Barton, A. (2009, August 3). Not enough time for the kids? *The Globe and Mail*, pp. L1, L2.

Bella, L. (1992). *The Christmas imperative: Leisure, family, and women's work.* Halifax, NS: Fernwood.

Bianchi, S. M., & Raley, S. B. (2005). Time allocation in families. In S. M. Bianchi, L. M. Casper, & R. B. King (Eds.), *Work, family, health, and well-being* (pp. 21–42). Mahwah, NJ: Lawrence Erlbaum.

Bianchi, S. M., Robinson, J. P., & Milkie, M. A. (2006). *The changing rhythms of American family life.* New York, NY: Russell Sage Foundation.

Bittman, M. (1998). Changing family responsibilities: The role of social attitudes, markets and the state. *Family Matters, 50,* 31–37.

Bittman, M., & Wajcman, J. (2000). The rush hour: The character of leisure time and gender equity. *Social Forces, 79*(1), 165–189.

Brannen, J. (2002, October 25). The work-family lives of women: Autonomy or illusion? Paper presented to the *Gender Institute Seminar,* London School of Economics. Retrieved from http://www.lse.ac.uk/collections/worklife/Brannenpaper.pdf

Bryson, V. (2007). *Gender and the politics of time: Feminist theory and contemporary debates.* Bristol, UK: Policy Press.

Budig, M. J., & Folbre, N. (2004). Activity, proximity or responsibility? Measuring parental childcare time. In N. Folbre & M. Bittman (Eds.), *Family time: The social organization of care* (pp. 51–68). London, UK: Routledge.

Clough, S. (2001). A juggling act: Women balancing work, family, and leisure. In S. Clough & J. White (Eds.), *Women's leisure experiences: Ages, stages, and roles* (Vol. 70, pp. 129–138). Eastbourne, UK: Leisure Studies Association.

Craig, L. (2006a). Does father care mean fathers share? A comparison of how mothers and fathers in intact families spend time with children. *Gender & Society, 20*(2), 259–281.

Craig, L. (2006b). Children and the revolution: A time-diary analysis of the impact of motherhood on daily workload. *Journal of Sociology, 42*(2), 125–143.

Craig, L. (2006c). Parental education, time in paid work and time with children. *British Journal of Sociology, 57*, 553–575.

Craig, L. (2007). *Contemporary motherhood: The impact of children on adult time.* Hampshire, UK: Ashgate.

Craig, L., & Mullan, K. (2012). Shared parent-child leisure time in four countries. *Leisure Studies, 31*(2), 211–229.

Daly, K. (Ed.) (2001). *Minding the time in family experience: Emerging perspectives and issues.* Oxford, UK: Elsevier Science.

Davies, K. (1990). *Women, time, and the weaving of the strands of everyday life.* Aldershot, UK: Avebury.

Deem, R. (1986). *All work and no play? The sociology of women and leisure.* Milton Keynes, UK: Open University Press.

Fast, J., & Frederick, J. (2004). *The time of our lives: Juggling work and leisure over the life cycle 1998, No. 4.* (Cat. No. 89-584-MIE). Ottawa, ON: Minister of Industry.

Gershuny, J. (2000). *Changing times: Work and leisure in postindustrial society.* Oxford, UK: Oxford University Press.

Gershuny, J. (2004). Costs and benefits of time sampling methodologies. *Social Indicators Research, 67*(1–2), 247–252.

Gershuny, J., Godwin, M., & Jones, S. (1994). The domestic labour revolution: A process of lagged adaptation. In M. Anderson, F. Bechhofer, & J. Gershuny (Eds.), *The social and political economy of the household* (pp. 151–197). Oxford, UK: Oxford University Press.

Globe and Mail, The. (2009, August 3). Globe life/family/relationships comments. Retrieved from http://www.theglobeandmail.com/life/family-and-relationships/sorry-moms-168-hours-a-week-is-plenty-of-time/article1239478/

Green, E., Hebron, S., & Woodward, D. (1987). *Leisure and gender: A study of Sheffield women's leisure experiences.* Sheffield, UK: The Sports Council and Economic & Social Research Council.

Harrington, M. (2001). Gendered time: Leisure in family life. In K. Daly (Ed.), *Minding the time in family experience: Emerging perspectives and issues* (pp. 343–382). Oxford, UK: Elsevier Science.

Hays, S. (1996). *The cultural contradictions of motherhood.* New Haven, CT: Yale University Press.

Hilbrecht, M. (2009). *Living in real time: Parents, work, gender, and well-being.* Germany: Verlag VDM.

Hilbrecht, M., Zuzanek, J., & Mannell, R. C. (2008). Time use, time pressure, and gendered behaviour in adolescence. *Sex Roles, 58*(5–6), 342–357.

Hochschild, A., & Machung, A. (1989). *The second shift: Working parents and the revolution at home.* New York, NY: Viking.

Jacobs, J. A., & Gerson, K. (2004). *The time divide: Work, family, and gender inequality.* Cambridge, MA: Harvard University Press.

Kay, T. A. (2001). New women, same old leisure: The upholding of gender stereotypes and leisure disadvantage in contemporary dual-earner households. In S. Clough & J. White (Eds.), *Women's leisure experiences: Ages, stages, and roles* (Vol. 70, pp. 113–128). Eastbourne, UK: Leisure Studies Association.

Kay, T. A. (Ed.) (2009a). *Fathering through sport and leisure*. New York, NY: Routledge.

Knights, D. (2006). Passing the time in pastimes, professionalism, and politics: Reflecting on the ethics and epistemology of time studies. *Time & Society, 15*(2–3), 251–274.

Kroll, C. (2009). The motherhood penalty in civic engagement: Examining social capital and subjective well-being by gender and parental status. *Social Science Research Network,* Social Science Electronic Publishing. Retrieved from http://papers.ssrn.com

Lareau, A. (2003). *Unequal childhoods: Class, race, and family life*. Berkeley, CA: University of California Press.

Lewis, S., Rapoport, R., & Gambles, R. (2003). Reflections on the integration of paid work and the rest of life. *Journal of Managerial Psychology, 18*(8), 824–841.

Marshall, K. (2006). Converging gender roles. *Perspectives on labour and income, 7*(7), 5–17. (Statistics Canada Cat. no. 75-001-XIE).

Mattingly, M. J., & Bianchi, S. M. (2003). Gender differences in the quantity and quality of free time: The U.S. experience. *Social Forces, 81*(3), 999–1030.

Oakley, A. (2005). *The Ann Oakley reader: Gender, women, and social science*. Bristol, UK: Policy Press.

Odih, P. (1999). Gendered time in the age of reconstruction. *Time and Society, 8*(1), 9–38.

Parris, M. A., Vickers, M. H., & Wilkes, L. (2008). Friendships under strain: The work-personal life integration of middle managers. *Community, Work, & Family, 11*(4), 405–418.

Risman, B. J. (2004). Gender as a social structure: Theory wrestling with activism. *Gender & Society, 18*(4), 429–450.

Sayer, L. C. (2005). Gender, time, and inequality: Trends in women's and men's paid work, unpaid work, and free time. *Social Forces, 84*(1), 285–303.

Shaw, S. M. (1985b). The meaning of leisure in everyday life. *Leisure Sciences, 7*(1), 1–24.

Shaw, S. M. (2008). Family leisure and changing ideologies of parenthood. *Sociology Compass, 2*(2), 1–16.

Shaw, S. M., & Dawson, D. J. (2001). Purposive leisure: Examining parental discourses on family activities. *Leisure Sciences, 23*(4), 217–231.

Stalker, G. (2006). Gender convergence and life-course differentiation in the Canadian use of time. *Loisir Et Societe/Society and Leisure, 29*(2), 159–192.

Statistics Canada. (2007). *Women in Canada: Work chapter updates.* (Cat. no. 89F0133XIE). Ottawa, ON: Minister of Industry.

Statistics Canada. (2009). Labour force and participation rates by sex and age group. Retrieved from http://www40.statcan.gc.ca/l01/cst01/labor05-eng.htm

Such, E. (2006). Leisure and fatherhood in dual-earner families. *Leisure Studies, 25*(2), 185–199.

Sullivan, O. (1997). Time waits for no (wo)man: An investigation of the gendered experience of domestic time. *Sociology, 31*(2), 221–239.

Sullivan, O. (2004). Changing gender practices within the household: A theoretical perspective. *Gender & Society, 18*(2), 207–222.

Szalai, A. (1973). *Use of time: Daily activities of urban and suburban populations in twelve countries.* The Hague: Mouton.

Thomas, M., Carter, B., Hunt, A., Hurley, M., & Robertson, S. (2009, September). *Trapped at home?* Paper presented to the 31st Conference of the International Association of Time Use Research, Lueneburg, Germany.

West, C., & Zimmerman, D. (1987). Doing gender. *Gender & Society, 1*(1), 125–151.

CHAPTER 14
WOMEN'S TRANSCENDENTAL EXPERIENCES WITH MOTORCYCLING

CATHERINE A. ROSTER

Somewhere on a desert highway
She rides a Harley-Davidson
Her long blonde hair flyin' in the wind
She's been runnin' half her life
The chrome and steel she rides
Collidin' with the very air she breathes
The air she breathes.
　　　　　—From "Unknown Legend" by Neil Young

The contemporary definition of leisure as a personal experience based on individual freedom of choice has been expanded to include its importance in forming a self-identity and enhancing personal well-being. A greater appreciation of leisure as a self-directed opportunity with personal and social consequences for individuals has resulted in discourse about the role of facilitators and the sociocultural context surrounding women's self-directed leisure pursuits.

Researchers, myself included, have explored how self-directed leisure experiences can create a sense of empowerment (e.g., Freysinger & Flannery, 1992; Henderson & Bialeschki, 1991; Roster, 2007; Shaw, 2001). How empowerment arises from women's leisure choices, the depth and breadth of their leisure experiences has received relatively little attention. There is much yet to learn about the relationship between empowerment and leisure's role in women's lives, especially leisure experiences that are personally challenging, resist gender and sociocultural stereotypes, and present opportunities to enrich the emotional, physical, and social well-being of women participants.

Neil Young's song lyrics depict a female motorcyclist whose ride through a desert highway with the wind blowing through her hair manifests an exhilarating experience that signifies personal freedom and inner strength from commanding a machine bigger than she. However, unconventional leisure choices can place women on a collision course with societal expectations that dictate appropriate ways for women to express self-identity. Underlying tensions arise from dichotomies such as strength versus weakness, masculinity versus femininity, and entitlement versus fear. Perhaps somewhere in this tension-filled space empowerment emerges.

I draw upon my research with female motorcyclists as well as the work of other scholars in this chapter to describe *transcendental leisure experiences* and illustrate how these experiences foster empowerment. I define "transcendental leisure experiences" as engagement in self-demanding and self-directed activities that challenge individual, gender, and sociocultural boundaries. My desire to understand why female motorcyclists engaged in this risky, male-dominated leisure activity gave me entrée into the lives of many courageous women whose stories revealed deeper insights into the challenges and rewards of empowerment. Some of these women had conquered amazing odds to engage in a leisure activity that enriched their life. Others had only begun to embark on a quest they hoped would afford them a greater sense of well-being. For all these women, motorcycling became a transcendental experience that gave them a renewed sense of self and purpose to their everyday lives.

MOTORCYCLING AS A TRANSCENDENTAL LEISURE EXPERIENCE FOR WOMEN

Leisure scholars have recognized that some leisure experiences are more personally meaningful, demanding, or challenging than others. For instance, researchers have evoked the term *self-determined* or *autonomous leisure* (Freysinger & Flannery, 1992; Samuel, 1992) to describe activities that foster self-expression and promote a determination to do something for oneself. The term *highly involving leisure* describes the psychological and emotional attachment that individuals attach to certain leisure activities (Havitz & Dimanche, 1990). Stebbins (1982) coined the term *serious leisure* to define leisure pursuits that require special skills, knowledge, and experience. What seems to be missing from these conceptualizations is an appreciation for how the meaning behind participation in activities instills feelings of empowerment by virtue of transcending individual, gender, and sociocultural boundaries. By engaging in these activities, participants embrace the opportunity to express themselves in boundary-stretching ways that can ultimately shift a society's perceptions about what pursuits—such as motorcycling—are appropriate and for whom.

Motorcycling is still a largely male-dominated leisure pursuit, but women now account for over 10% of motorcycle owners in the United

States and nearly one quarter of all riders (Motorcycle Industry Council, 2009). My research revealed that female motorcyclists view their participation as a vehicle for self-expression and an opportunity to enhance their physical, emotional, spiritual, and social well-being. Riding motorcycles was not the easiest route to these benefits, but it was the path these women chose because it was an exciting and challenging leisure activity. Furthermore, female motorcyclists seemed to gravitate to motorcycling for self-expression *because of*, rather than despite, the challenges they were sure to experience.

Modern-day female motorcyclists seem to embrace the spirit of rebelliousness and independence that has characterized people involved with motorcycling, yet they also have rejected negative sociocultural stereotypes that associate motorcycling with the violent *machismo* subculture of biker gangs (Ferrar, 2000; Wolf, 1991). The emotional high women get from engaging in this physically dangerous but thrilling activity appears similar to male participants. However, women's emotions may be made more intense by knowing they are experiencing benefits that come from participation in an activity that represents boundary-stretching challenges and opportunities. Motorcycling is boundary-stretching in at least three ways for women: a) it is an existential experience, in the sense that it provides the self with an undiluted freedom to express itself in new, uncharted territories; b) it represents significant personal effort, skill attainment, commitment, and goal-striving, which can contradict self-limiting preconceptions women harbor about their capabilities; and c) it represents a challenge to sociocultural stereotypes and gender barriers that dictate socially appropriate ways for members of a society to express self-identity through leisure pursuits.

My research, which included personal interviews, focus groups, and e-mail survey responses from 163 female motorcyclists located in a southwestern region of the United States indicated that the central motivation behind women's participation in motorcycling was a quest to experience "freedom." Nearly 43% of all female motorcyclists stated that the most appealing aspect of motorcycling was that it provided a sense of freedom from the routine, mundane demands of their everyday lives. The appeal of freedom proved to be significantly more important than other factors in attracting women to the sport such as fun/recreation (32%), tangible or intangible properties associated with the product itself (14%), and opportunities for excitement/adventure (7%). Focus group participants described riding as a "thrill," "a sacred time just for them," and an experience that left them feeling "alive," "exhilarated," and more deeply focused and highly connected with nature and their inner selves (Roster, 2007). The existential meanings participants derive from motorcycling have been documented by other scholars. For instance, Schouten and McAlexander (1995) used an in-depth ethnographic analysis of the biker subculture and concluded that motorcycling represents "a sanctuary in which to experience temporary self-transformation" (p. 50).

My focus groups revealed that freedom can be interpreted in multiple ways. For some women, freedom came from *combating personal fears and situational obstacles* that had prevented them from engaging in motorcycling, despite their desire to do so. Concerns included time away from family, financial costs, and effort required to achieve skills and knowledge needed to ensure a sense of self-efficacy. Confronting these issues seemed critical toward enabling them to participate safely and responsibly. For others, participation in motorcycling represented a *coming out* of sorts that represented a cry for freedom of self-expression from constricting social norms, cultural stereotypes, and stifling expectations of important others including family members. Ultimately, freedom appeared to represent the sense of empowerment women gained from claiming leisure space, engaging in a personally challenging quest to attain skills that enhanced their feelings of self-efficacy and self-confidence, and by asserting self-identity through engagement in nontraditional gender recreation. Consequently, motorcycling women enlarged their personal space by garnering supporters and ushering in entirely new social networks ready and willing to support their quest.

THE INFLUENCE OF GENDERED AND COLLECTIVE GROUP IDENTITIES ON WOMEN'S PARTICIPATION IN MOTORCYCLING

Women of all races, sexual orientations, ages, economic levels, and cultural backgrounds participate in motorcycling. Despite their diversities, the women riders in my research generally were united by shared feelings of freedom and release (from pressures associated with their everyday lives) that they experience when commanding a motorcycle. Women also were united by a collective understanding of what it takes to be a female participant in this challenging male-dominated recreational leisure activity. Green (1998) suggested that leisure experiences can provide an outlet for women to fortify personal identity through sharing experiences that unite them in resisting social stereotypes associated with gender boundaries. Likewise, Auster (2001) noted the vital role that female mentors play in providing social support to newcomers who wish to participate in male-dominated motorcycling.

Thus, motorcycling appears to be an intensely personal experience that takes place within a broader social community of riders united by their affiliation with the sport. Marketing scholars have documented the close-knit social networks and camaraderie among bikers, especially those who share a strong bond with the Harley-Davidson brand (McAlexander, Schouten, & Koenig, 2002; Schouten & McAlexander, 1995). Women now represent a growing subculture within the Harley ranks (Koons, 2006)—a sisterhood of sorts that coexists alongside the brotherhood that has predominated the biker community.

A central theme that emerged from my investigation of female motorcyclists was that of *girl power* (Roster, 2007). Scholars have illustrated how empowerment can arise from collective group actions and social support networks (Auster, 2001; Freysinger & Flannery, 1992; Gibson et al., this volume; Shaw, 2001). Girl power seemed to embrace a concept that extends beyond the benefits of group affiliation and female mentorship networks. By banding together, these women riders sought to put a new face on the sport of motorcycling designed to increase its accessibility and attractiveness to other women. Many women felt like pioneers forging a path for other women to follow. These female motorcyclists relished opportunities to demonstrate their collective power and display positive gender role models. For example, the women I interviewed valued all-girl rides to benefit causes important to women, such as collecting money for breast cancer or delivering school supplies to children (Roster, 2007). Women have also capitalized on their growing market influence to pressure Harley-Davidson to expand women's fashions and produce bikes tailored to women riders' needs (Koons, 2006).

Female bikers drew strength from banding together to exercise girl power and relished their collective displays of empowerment. Privately, however, such open displays were not without costs. The motorcycle subculture has been notorious for its denigration of women who participate in the sport. Historically, men who command powerful Harley motorcycles have demonstrated the ultimate essence of machismo by riding with a sexily clad female clutching him from the backside of the bike (Brownmiller, 1984; Wolf, 1991). Further, the image of motorcyclists in general has been tarnished by associations with violent outlaw gangs, like the Hell's Angels. Female motorcyclists expressed concerns about reactions from others rooted in sociocultural stereotypes associated with the biker culture that has portrayed female participants as either promiscuous or dykes. Some women admitted that alone they felt vulnerable, especially when faced with negative reactions and safety concerns expressed by those close to them.

These negative reactions and concerns played on their fears and concerns about participation. Some women perceived their enjoyment of this particular form of leisure conflicted with other life roles and attitudes of important others. Professional women worried if others would view them as reckless or deviant. Mothers and caregivers worried about the contradiction between being there for their children and engaging in a risky activity that could endanger their lives. As sisters, daughters, and wives, women worried about the attitudes of prominent male figures in their lives, even though these same males were often the ones who introduced them to the activity. Women sometimes feared telling protective males that their desire to participate had gone beyond riding on the back of a motorcycle to commanding it themselves. In some cases, these tensions were so great that women either denied their desires or hid their active participation in motorcycling from important others who might take a dim view of their engagement. When tensions were present, empowerment was experienced collectively, but it was compromised at an individual level until women reconciled these tensions.

My findings suggested that empowerment can be experienced at either an individual or group level, but that the sustainability of personal empowerment required some combination of individual fortitude and social support to resolve the tensions. Furthermore, empowering leisure experiences seemed to become transcendental when individuals successfully conquered obstacles and inspired and nurtured opportunities for others.

NEW FRONTIERS FOR NONTRADITIONAL GENDER LEISURE RESEARCH

Researchers have shown that self-determined leisure choices that require considerable effort and perseverance, especially those that contest or resist gender, social, or cultural ideologies, can lead to a sense of empowerment (e.g., Henderson & Bialeschki, 1991; Hollander, 2002; Raisborough, 2007; Roster, 2007; Shaw, 2001). Leisure researchers agree that leisure is defined and experienced at an individual level (Shaw, 1985b), but it is enacted within a broader contextual background that includes social and cultural gender expectations that dictate what leisure activities are appropriate for whom within members of a society (Henderson, Bialeschki, Shaw, & Freysinger, 1996). What is *not* well understood is how individual feelings of empowerment that arise from participation in boundary-stretching leisure activities can reshape how gender is constructed among members of a society. Individual success stories, fortified by the collective support of women who have resisted social stereotypes and are willing to mentor others, may well create transformational shifts in gendered leisure boundaries.

The metaphor of the matryoshka, the female Russian stacking doll, aptly captures the many facets of self that represent the totality of influences that impact women's everyday lives. Contradictions among personal, social, and cultural tiers surrounding women's leisure choices can temper the sense of empowerment women gain from participation in boundary-stretching activities. As a result, women may compartmentalize opposing facets of their lives in an effort to strike a balance between accommodation and resistance toward gender expectations. In the short term, compartmentalization may represent a viable compromise that enables women to embrace challenges while avoiding these dilemmas in their lives.

However, in the long term, women who do not feel free to embrace their choices both privately and publicly may deny themselves the full benefits of empowerment associated with living a self-directed life. What is needed is an integrated view of self-directed leisure (such as motorcycling) that recognizes boundary-challenging individual choices take place within social and cultural contexts. Future discourses should acknowledge that empowerment takes place in stages, as women resolve these tensions in life spaces and achieve a balance of life. Women who achieve this personal plateau may become ambassadors for change, dispelling myths about some people's inability to participate in certain leisure activities and creating inroads that lead to broader inclusion.

What leisure activities are appropriate and for whom is tied to sociocultural meanings of masculinity and femininity that are internalized by members of a society and perpetuated at a macro-level by popular culture and media. Gender boundaries can shift through the actions of women who embrace leisure opportunities that defy these boundaries. The women in my research studies embraced the positive attributes of strength, independence, freedom, adventure, and power that were associated with the masculine biker culture, but rejected stereotypes that suggested women riders were passive, sexually promiscuous, drug addicts, or rebellious members of society. Future research should explore how gender boundaries are perpetuated and confronted by nontraditional participants, whether male or female. For instance, males who are drawn to ballet, ice-skating, cooking, quilting, or other stereotypical feminine forms of leisure no doubt experience similar personal challenges and realize feelings of empowerment similar to women who choose masculine leisure outlets. As gender lines blur, an understanding of issues surrounding social-cultural forces that accompany these choices must become more inclusive to include the lived experiences of both males and females who cross gender boundaries through leisure to develop a fuller appreciation of the meaning and impact these choices have on individuals' lives.

Although some traditionally male-dominated leisure subcultures are becoming more inclusive, like motorcycling or golf, new participants can find themselves confronted by social dynamics that may be equally or even more formidable than the challenges surrounding their opportunity to participate in the first place. Researchers could explore the challenges facing new entrants into leisure communities who do not represent traditional stereotypes of participants. These issues warrant further investigation from researchers who are interested in nontraditional gender leisure research.

CONCLUDING PERSPECTIVES

Leisure experiences that represent boundary-stretching opportunities can be transcendental on many levels. The experience itself often transports the self into new uncharted territories. At a micro-level, transcendental leisure choices defy preconceived personal limitations and contest boundaries imposed by societal and cultural expectations. At a macro-level, the collective force of nontraditional participants can create powerful shifts in societal and gender boundaries that restrict leisure choices for members of a society.

Framing these types of leisure experiences as transcendental, as opposed to more commonly used terms like serious leisure, self-determined leisure, or highly involving leisure, offers benefits that could lead to a more holistic view of the meaning of leisure experiences in everyday life. First, it places the focus on experience, outcomes, and benefits. Neither the activity nor the skills needed to participate make an experience transcendental for an individual. Most important is the individual's experience of confronting boundaries and addressing challenges. Second, leisure pursuits can be transcendental without demanding high levels of involvement, or even successful attempts at participation. Third, transcendental leisure experiences can place constraints within a broader perspective that considers individual, gender-related, and sociocultural barriers. Last, individual and collective sources of empowerment can significantly alter society's views of gender-appropriate leisure pursuits.

The growing insurgence of female motorcycle riders reflects the changing face of motorcycling in the United States as a leisure activity. Once the symbol of rebellious male youth, the rising costs of owning a motorcycle and especially a Harley-Davidson motorcycle have shifted demand to older and more affluent consumers. Concurrently, women's economic and social power is rising to some extent. These economic and societal shifts have opened up new leisure avenues to women, including leisure activities like golf and motorcycling that have traditionally been all-male clubs. By tapping into their collective strengths and nurturing new participants, women can exercise girl power to challenge gender-related obstacles that have prevented their full and equal participation in male-dominated leisure activities. Ultimately, their collective influences can help shape societal perceptions of women who choose to participate in male-dominated activities and expand leisure opportunities for all women.

REFERENCES

Auster, C. J. (2001). Transcending potential antecedent leisure constraints: The case of women motorcycle operators. *Journal of Leisure Research, 33,* 272–298.

Brownmiller, S. (1984). *Femininity.* Toronto, ON: Random House.

Ferrar, A. (2000). *Hear me roar: Women, motorcycles, and the rapture of the road.* North Conway, NH: Whitehorse.

Freysinger, V. J., & Flannery, D. (1992). Women's leisure: Affiliation, self-determination, empowerment, and resistance? *Loisir et Société, 15,* 303–321.

Green, E. (1998). "Women doing friendship": An analysis of women's leisure as a site of identity construction, empowerment, and resistance. *Leisure Studies, 17*(3), 171–185.

Havitz, M. E., & Dimanche, F. (1990). Propositions for testing the involvement construct in recreational and tourism contexts. *Leisure Sciences, 12,* 179–195.

Henderson, K. A., & Bialeschki, M. D. (1991). A sense of entitlement to leisure as constraint and empowerment for women. *Leisure Sciences, 13,* 51-65.

Henderson, K. A., Bialeschki, M. D., Shaw, S. M., & Freysinger, V. J. (1996). *Both gains and gaps: Feminist perspectives on women's leisure.* State College, PA: Venture Publishing, Inc.

Hollander, J. A. (2002). Resisting vulnerability: The social reconstruction of gender in interaction. *Social Problems, 49,* 474–496.

Koons, C. (2006, February 22). Harley-Davidson markets to women. *The Wall Street Journal,* p. 1.

McAlexander, J. H., Schouten, J. W., & Koenig, H. F. (2002). Building brand community. *Journal of Marketing, 66,* 38–54.

Motorcycle Industry Council. (2009). Motorcycling in America goes mainstream says 2008 motorcycle industry council ownership survey. Retrieved from http://www.reuters.com

Raisborough, J. (2007). Women's leisure and auto/biography: Empowerment and resistance in the garden. *Journal of Leisure Research, 39*, 459–476.

Roster, C. A. (2007). "Girl power" and participation in macho recreation: The case of female Harley riders. *Leisure Sciences, 29*, 443–461.

Samuel, N. (1992). L'aspiration des femmes a l'autonomie: Loisir familial et loisir personnel. *Loisir et Société/Society and Leisure, 15*, 343–354.

Schouten, J. W., & McAlexander, J. H. (1995). Subcultures of consumption: An ethnography of the new bikers. *Journal of Consumer Research, 22*, 43–61.

Shaw, S. M. (1985b). The meaning of leisure in everyday life. *Leisure Sciences, 7*(1), 1–24.

Shaw, S. M. (2001). Conceptualizing resistance: Women's leisure as political practice. *Journal of Leisure Research, 33*(2), 186–201.

Stebbins, R. A. (1982). Serious leisure: A conceptual statement. *Pacific Sociological Review, 25*, 251–272.

Wolf, D. R. (1991). *The rebels: A brotherhood of outlaw bikers.* Toronto, ON: University of Toronto Press.

Young, N. (1992). *Unknown legend* [Song lyrics]. Retrieved from http://www.musicbabylon.com

Chapter 15
A Reader's Reflections on Women's Friendships

Susan L. Hutchinson

"A few years back, when I finally got smart enough to go to a therapist, she asked me how I had held it together all these years. It didn't take long to come up with an answer. 'That's easy. I belong to a book club.'"
(Angry Housewives Eating Bon Bons, p. 9)

Angry Housewives Eating Bon Bons (Landvik, 2005) was one of the first books our book group read. The book begins with a snowstorm. In the midst of the storm, a frazzled young mother watched aghast as four hoodlums started a snowball fight with some children on the street. When she yelled at them they called back: "Oh, good, you've come out to play!" (p. 34). The hoodlums end up being four other young women who also live on Freesia Court. *Angry Housewives* tells a story of their friendships and lives through membership in a book club. Though a fictional account, the meanings of leisure and friendships described throughout the book resonated with my own experiences. Being part of a book group has provided a lens to reflect on the interconnections between leisure, friendships, and gender relations in my own and other women's lives.

As my book group members and I discussed this book and others, we asked ourselves questions that leisure scholars might also ask when critically examining the relationships between leisure and friendships in women's lives. Why are women's friendships important? What do they mean to women? As a group we continue to be drawn to books about women's lives, in part to try to better understand our own lives. Although I bring a personal lens as a book club member to reflect on women's friendships in this chapter, I also bring a scholarly interest. A body of literature exists on friendships in sociology, but this chapter focuses specifically on research that has examined friendships in relation to women's leisure. I begin by considering ways our book group and leisure scholars have viewed what it means to be a friend and how friendships happen in leisure contexts.

Being and Becoming Friends

Two women in my book group have lived in the same area for their entire lives. The rest of us are "come-from-aways" who, whether by choice or obligation, have left our pasts, families, and friends to build new lives elsewhere. *Angry Housewives* was one of the first books we read as a group. We were envious of the women of Freesia Court who had shared four decades of their lives together. We admitted that trying to maintain old friendships and cultivate new ones is difficult when also trying to be a *good* mother, partner, and daughter as well as worker and community member. We appreciated what it meant for the women of Freesia Court to come slowly to trust each other with the painful parts of their lives and what it also meant for them to come to be accepted just for who they were. We recognized we are more privileged than many other women. We are all reasonably financially secure (e.g., we can buy our book for next month's book group meeting if it isn't available at the library—and can afford to host a gathering with food and wine), educated, and none of our kids are "troublemakers." We are able to leave the care of our families to others, at least for a few hours, while together.

At our last book group meeting, I asked the women what it meant to them to be part of the book group and about their friendships more generally. They all said taking time for themselves *is* important. They also saw differences among us in terms of how we spend time with friends. These differences seem to be cultural and age-related. The women who are younger or who were raised in more liberal cultures seem to have different views from those of us who are older or perhaps more traditional in our views. Although eating, drinking, and having fun are essential parts of the book group, as they may be for other all-women's social gatherings, we have some "productive" purpose for gathering each month. One woman said it was the "investment of effort" that made the book group special for her. Would we feel the same about getting together to just have fun? While some women said invitations to gather for coffee or dinner outings are regular occurrences in their neighborhoods, the book group provides a socially acceptable outlet for those of us who said we would feel "too guilty" to leave our families to get together in an evening "just for fun."

We talked about what it means to be a friend and the ways we made friends and stayed friends. We agreed that "true friendship" meant "being there" when needed both emotionally and practically. Making efforts to stay connected was highly valued and having common interests, values, and shared experiences were also mentioned. For some "being there" meant being visible on Facebook or calling to touch base on a regular basis. For others, more instrumental forms of reciprocity were valued, such as offers to drive children to sporting events. Although pre-existing friendships existed between several of the group members, there was heartfelt agreement that the book group represents, as one woman said, a "sisterhood"—perhaps because of the opinions, values, and intimacies we have shared over the months of discussing our books. As an example, when discussing *The Next Thing on My List* (Smolinski, 2008), we made a list of 10 things we wanted to do in our lives before our next milestone birthday (e.g., before turning 40). These lists were a lens into our personal lives and private selves.

How typical are our experiences compared with other women? Are women's friendships different from men's? Within our book group, we argued that men's and women's friendships are different. Although the men and women we knew enjoyed spending time together in shared activities, we believed women to be more "emotional" in both the tone and content of their talk. This perspective, however, was not fully supported in the literature: "Although men emphasize activity and women emphasize talk in accounts of their friendships, their friendship *behaviors* are more similar than different" (Walker, 1995, p. 275; emphasis in original). Nevertheless, in studying men's and women's friendships, Walker did note that men would use more humor than women to deal with "intimate interactions" (p. 293).

Another defining feature of friendships, according to Walker (1995), is class. Walker found marked differences between the friendships of middle-class compared to working-class participants in her study. Working-class friends spent more time together than middle-class friends and often met informally in friends' homes or public spaces (e.g., bars or playgrounds). Much of the talk centered on "everyday work and family activities" (p. 282). Middle-class friends tended to meet less frequently and gatherings tended to be more organized or pre-arranged (e.g., a planned dinner). This difference was attributed to busier schedules and less free time available. High levels of interdependence and reciprocity were typical of the friendships of working-class women, who relied on each other for loans and shared services such as childcare, as compared to middle-class women who sought individuality and "celebrated shared leisure and the existence of large networks of interesting friends" (p. 273). For the most part, the friendships between women within my book group parallel those of Walker's middle-class respondents.

WOMEN'S FRIENDSHIPS AS CONTEXTS FOR REPRODUCTION AND RESISTANCE

"The research areas of leisure and friendship can be bridged by the concepts of personal agency, identity, and subjectivity: key concepts for understanding the process of becoming gendered." (Green, 1998, p. 172)

What do women learn through their friendships? How to be a good woman? How to recognize or even confront societal injustices? Writing about the interconnections between women's talk, leisure, and friendships, Green (1998) argued:

> Women's talk, an essential ingredient of women's friendships, accomplishes more than meets the eye; it includes discourses of belonging and similarity which enable women to "mirror" traditional aspects of femininity such as caring and vulnerability, whilst at the same time allowing for contradictory or counter discourses of difference. (p. 183)

Although reproduction and resistance seem important aspects of women's friendships, I wonder if one is more prominent than the other at different life stages. These life-stage differences were made visible to me when I compared my two all-women's social groups: my book group (the women are mostly in their late 30s and 40s) and a group of women who play Bunko. Bunko is a dice game with 12 women who rotate in pairs of winners and losers between tables. With a couple of exceptions, most of the Bunko women are in their mid-20s and 30s. Both groups meet once a month, and eating and drinking are large parts of the activities.

In the book group, we have created a safe environment to express ourselves but, as one woman mentioned, we also value differences. We try to be provocative, to choose books which challenge our own views. Discussions about the books sometimes lead to challenging each others' assumptions of the ways things are or should be. The books (and wine) are "levers," as one group member described, to explore dimensions of ourselves and our world that are typically not accessible in everyday conversations. While we will make time to support each other in the face of a crisis (e.g., failed relationship) or to celebrate a significant life event (e.g., new job), for the most part we have agreed that the book group is an escape from everyday family life.

The contrasts between these groups were striking to me when I reflected on one Bunko evening. Whereas the book group seems to engender empowerment, the Bunko group was a veritable wealth of lessons reinforcing traditional gender-related social norms. I listened as the young women talked about strategies for shaving body hair on a daily basis (because that's what their husbands' liked) and then talking about the pros and cons of body waxing, bras, and underwear for maximizing sexual appeal. The talk then shifted to parenting strategies and comparisons of their children's teachers and performance in school. With laughter, food, and alcohol, it was nonetheless clear much was to be learned about being a good woman and mother from this group.

Regardless of the context, leisure's potential for identity development and expression is evident. In leisure, most people yearn to belong *and* to be seen as individuals (Kleiber, 1999). Both leisure and friendships are also contexts for learning how to conform to or resist traditional gender-stereotyped roles and images (Green, 1998; Green, Hebron, & Woodward, 1990). Hey (1997) and other leisure scholars (e.g., Wearing, 1992) have argued that for girls, a significant part of identity development relates to learning how *to be a woman*. It seems that friendships continue to be contexts for the social construction of gendered identities into young adulthood as well. While earlier writing by feminist leisure scholars focused on gender-related constraints women encountered in their leisure (Green et al., 1990; Shaw, 1994), there has been a shift to consider ways in which women's leisure contexts can also be vehicles for self-empowerment (e.g., Green, 1998; Wearing, 1992, 1995). Women's leisure can provide opportunities to exercise choice and personal power at the same time as experiencing freedom from caring responsibilities. Our book group members felt that although time away from domestic caring responsibilities was key, expressing caring for each other in small ways *was* an essential part of the book group (see also Piercy & Cheek, 2004, who have written about women's quilting groups as contexts for *tending and befriending* between different generations of women).

WOMEN'S FRIENDSHIPS AS A SELF-CARE RESOURCE

"Long-term friendships with other women in groups or as individuals can provide stability and a 'linking thread' through personal and situational change." (Green, 1998, p. 182)

Evidence is compelling that leisure-based friendships do help women maintain their health and well-being, in addition to contributing to their development as women. Nimrod (2008) reviewed research on the relationships between social networks and dimensions of psychological well-being in later life and identified a myriad of benefits, including increased coping efficacy, hope, and optimism, as well as strengthened sense of personal control and self-worth. In most cases, leisure-based friendships were viewed as a source of support or a context for people to experience a sense of belonging and feeling cared for, which can help people feel more capable of managing stress in their lives. However, as I and other leisure researchers have cautioned (e.g., Hutchinson & Kleiber, 2005; Warner-Smith & Brown, 2002), not all friendships are beneficial. Being socially excluded or unable to engage in previously valued shared activities may exacerbate distress (Parry, this volume).

Glover and Parry (2008) examined the experiences of friendship of women who had experienced infertility. Their findings reflected losses and gains in friendships. For example, they found that the women's previous friends who already had children "lacked empathy". . . and "could not grasp the 'emotional pain' and 'personal stress' associated with infertility" (p. 215). New friendships also became an additional source of distress when the women compared themselves to others (e.g., when a new friend became pregnant). Some child-centered leisure-based social situations the women felt obligated to attend (e.g., baby showers) also created stress. At the same time, Glover and Parry found that the women experienced benefits as a result of their new friendships with others who were also experiencing infertility. These gains included experiences of mutual aid (e.g., emotional support as well as information), which helped the women *get by* as they coped with the stresses of infertility. "Getting by" implies both coping with the distress of the situation as well as finding opportunities to experience a shared social identity and a sense they could be themselves in the company of others who accepted them for who they were.

Although many women may initially come together because of a shared leisure interest, a leisure-based social group can also evolve into a context for shared support, as is true in our book group. When we first started meeting, discussions about the book (or wines) dominated. Over time, an unspoken understanding evolved that we are there for each other. If one group member is struggling, less time may be spent on discussing the book and more on giving her the time and space to share her story. When we talked about what our book group meant to us, many said that the advice and words of support given in times of stress provided not only affirmation that "I'm okay" individually and collectively, but also encouragement that we *are* capable of dealing with life. On a personal note, knowing others believe in me is a powerful force to help me also believe in myself.

These personal experiences mirror what also seems to be true for other women's leisure-based groups. Aday, Kehoe, and Farney (2006) wrote about the importance of participation in seniors' center activities for older women living alone. The women in their study developed new supportive friendships that sometimes extended beyond the senior center. The women attributed these friendships and activities to helping them improve their outlook on life, reduce a sense of loneliness, cope better, and feel more independent. The friendships helped the women maintain a positive social identity in the face of other role losses due to divorce, widowhood, or retirement, and they helped the women cope with life's challenges.

Such suggestions also resonate with women's descriptions of their experiences within the Red Hat Society (Hutchinson, Yarnal, Stafford-Son, & Kerstetter, 2008). The Red Hat Society is a social organization for women over 50 years in which the women dress in flamboyant purple costumes with red hats to attend social gatherings (for more description, see Son, Kerstetter, Yarnal, & Baker, 2007; Yarnal, 2006; Yarnal, Chick, & Kerstetter, 2008). In response to an online survey, many Red Hatters wrote about the importance of membership for helping them cope with stressful life circumstances such as caring for an ailing spouse, their own health concerns, becoming widowed, moving, or retirement. The support provided led them to use words like "loved" and "accepted" to describe what membership in the group meant to them. One example of the significance of the group for social support was expressed:

> Originally we formed the group to keep in touch with our friends and have some fun; however, the purpose changed somewhat when a couple of our members faced life-threatening illnesses. We became a strong support network that was there for those who needed it. As a result, our bond of friendship is stronger, as is our appreciation for the passage of time. (Hutchinson et al., 2008, pp. 988–989)

Being able to spend time together in a shared activity without having to talk about problems was valued as much as the opportunities to talk and share together. The chance to experience positive emotions and to escape problems, even temporarily, can be a powerful salve.

LEISURE-BASED SOCIAL GROUPS: WHAT MATTERS FOR FOSTERING WOMEN'S FRIENDSHIPS?

As a final point of reflection, I wondered what occurs to transform a social group of women joined for a shared leisure interest into one that becomes an essential source of support. From my perspective, four aspects seem to matter for deepening women's friendships in and through leisure contexts. First, regular and sustained contact with each other (i.e., being together) is an important ingredient. I find that when I miss a book group gathering I feel "out of the loop" when we meet again the next month. Second, for friendships to deepen, a social space for women is needed to provide and receive support. Recognizing and maintaining these *norms of reciprocity* allow women to feel they are needed while also knowing they can rely on friends when necessary. A colleague of mine noted that the flexibility of the group to accommodate different ways of being present is another element of leisure-based social groups. She commented that as someone who is shy, she does not have a high level of comfort in social situations. For her, being able to be present in her own way (i.e., watching and listening rather than having to talk) is essential to feeling comfortable and accepted. A final essential ingredient is having fun together.

Citing the works of Coates (1996) and Hey (1997), Green (1998) suggested that women's talk in all-women's leisure spaces is a collaborative process (i.e., talk-as-play), which promotes mutual self-disclosure and laughter. "The main goal of talk-as-play is not the exchange of information but the construction and maintenance of friendship through enjoyment of *how* things are said, as well as what is being said" (Green, 1998, p. 179; emphasis in original). Shared experiences of enjoyment can cultivate a shared social identity, history, and memories, which seem important to fostering a sense of belonging within a leisure-based social group and a deepening sense of intimacy within friendships.

WHERE TO GO FROM HERE?
RESEARCHING WOMEN'S FRIENDSHIPS AND LEISURE

Sociability and companionship are the hallmarks of friendships for most people regardless of gender, ethnicity, age, or class. A friend is someone for whom one has warm feelings, someone to talk to, someone with whom to share activities, and someone who is "always there when you need them" (Walker, 1995, p. 274). Despite this common perspective, the differences between men and women, and between different groups or cohorts of women, merit further exploration, particularly if viewed from a feminist or gender-relations perspective. Some leisure scholars have highlighted the gendered nature of leisure spaces with men's leisure and, by extension, friendships mostly occurring in public spaces such as bars and women's leisure in the home (e.g., Green, 1998).

Will leisure contexts and friendships continue to be spaces in which gender relations are reproduced or will younger (and older) cohorts experience greater freedom for self-determined engagement? My own hunch is that social norms of acceptable gendered behavior have changed significantly for the young women I see in my classes and at restaurants and bars. The same may be true for older women who may have the financial freedom and health to engage in more adventurous or demanding activities with friends than our mothers may have had.

Of personal interest to me is to further examine how and why women maintain ongoing friendships across life stages and transitions. Is there change or continuity in women's friendships as women live different parts of their lives? What happens to women's friendships when women (or others) move away, form partnerships, have children, care for aging parents, get married or divorced, bury loved ones, or experience diminished physical or cognitive abilities? Anecdotally, I have stories of women, like my aunt, who have met with the same group of women once a month for lunch for over 50 years until the last of their group members had passed away, even after one member had moved into a care facility. This group was a small but defining feature of their lives as women and friends. Much can be learned from women who have successfully maintained friendships across decades, like my aunt and the *Angry Housewives* of Freesia Court (Landvik, 2005).

ACKNOWLEDGMENT

I would like to thank all the wonderful women of my book group for sharing their thoughts about friendships and for being my friends: Christine, Barb, Tanja, Lisa, Anne, Sandy, Kim, and Kathleen. I don't want to imagine what life would be like without the book group—and their friendship.

REFERENCES

Aday, R. H., Kehoe, G. C., & Farney, L. A. (2006). Impact of senior center friendships on aging women who live alone. *Journal of Women and Aging, 18*(1), 57–73.

Coates, J. (1996). *Women talk.* Oxford, UK: Blackwell.

Glover, T. D., & Parry, D. C. (2008). Friendships developed subsequent to a stressful life event: The interplay of leisure, social capital, and health. *Journal of Leisure Research, 40*(7), 208–230.

Green, E. (1998). "Women doing friendship": An analysis of women's leisure as a site of identity construction, empowerment, and resistance. *Leisure Studies, 17*(3), 171–185.

Green, E., Hebron, S., & Woodward, D. (1990). *Women's leisure, what leisure?* London, UK: Macmillan.

Hey, V. (1997). *The company she keeps: An ethnography of girls' friendships.* London, UK: Open University Press.

Hutchinson, S. L., & Kleiber, D. A. (2005). Leisure, constraints, and negative life events: Paradox and possibilities. In E. Jackson (Ed.), *Constraints to leisure* (pp. 137–149). State College, PA: Venture Publishing, Inc.

Hutchinson, S. L., Yarnal, C. M., Stafford-Son, J., & Kerstetter, D. (2008). Beyond fun and friendship: The Red Hat Society as a coping resource for older women. *Ageing & Society, 28*(7), 979–999.

Kleiber, D. A. (1999). *Leisure experience and human development: A dialectical approach.* New York, NY: Basic.

Landvik, L. (2005). *Angry housewives eating bon bons.* New York, NY: Random House.

Nimrod, G. (2008). Time for old friends and grandchildren? Post-retirement get-togethers and life satisfaction. *Leisure/Loisir, 32*(1), 21–46.

Piercy, K. W., & Cheek, C. (2004). Tending and befriending: The intertwined relationships of quilters. *Journal of Women & Aging, 16*(1/2), 17–33.

Shaw, S. M. (1994). Gender, leisure, and constraint: Towards a framework for the analysis of women's leisure. *Journal of Leisure Research, 26*, 8–22.

Smolinski, J. (2008). *The next thing on my list.* New York, NY: Crown.

Son, J., Kerstetter, D., Yarnal, C., & Baker, B. (2007). Promoting older women's health and well-being through leisure environments: What we have learned from the Red Hat Society. *Journal of Women & Aging, 19*(4), 16–32.

Walker, K. (1995). "Always there for me": Friendship patterns and expectations among middle- and working-class men and women. *Sociological Forum, 10*(2), 273–296.

Warner-Smith, P., & Brown, P. (2002). "The town dictates what I do": The leisure, health, and well-being of women in a small Australian country town. *Leisure Studies, 21*, 39–56.

Wearing, B. (1992). Beyond the ideology of motherhood: Leisure as resistance. *Australian and New Zealand Journal of Sociology, 26*, 35–58.

Wearing, B. (1995). Leisure and resistance in an ageing society. *Leisure Studies, 14*, 263–279.

Yarnal, C. (2006). The Red Hat Society: Exploring the role of play, liminality, and communitas in older women's lives. *Journal of Women and Aging, 18*(3), 51–73.

Yarnal, C. M., Chick, G., & Kerstetter, D. (2008). "I did not have time to play growing up . . . So this is my play time. It's the best thing I have ever done for myself": What is play to older women? *Leisure Sciences, 30,* 235–252.

CHAPTER 16
WOMEN'S MENTAL HEALTH AND THE POWER OF LEISURE

DIANA C. PARRY

Mentally I have really struggled with all the things going on in my life. My son has a brain tumor. My husband and I both have breast cancer. Since we are both sick and unable to work, we lost our house, all of our savings, and most of our friends in the process. Plus, I have fought cancer once before in my life. Years ago when our son was two, I was diagnosed with ovarian cancer. I knew then that I had to fight so I could be around to mother my son. I could not bear the thought of my son growing up without his mother. But this time, when I heard breast cancer from the doctor, it was different. I did not feel like I could fight. I just couldn't cope with what was happening in my life. I couldn't fight cancer again in my life while simultaneously watching my son and husband battle the disease. My doctor said to me, "You're going to have to go on anti-depressants because physically, emotionally you can't cope with all this." I didn't want to take the medication because I was worried about how it would interact with all the cancer medication. But I knew I had to do something or I literally would not survive. Since I started dragon boat racing, though, I have not had to take anything. No anti-depressants. I get out there and I physically beat the water, I get out all my negative emotions and it just brings all the natural little endorphins forward. So it fights actual depression.

Sitting across from Sarah (not her real name) during our interview exploring the links between women's experiences with breast cancer survivorship and dragon boat racing (a woman-centered, community-based leisure pursuit focused on life after medical treatment for breast cancer that involves 18 to 20 women paddling together to propel a 40- to 60-foot craft along a race course of 500 to 650 meters long) I was struck by the powerful link between leisure and mental health. Sarah had been suicidal and placed on anti-depressants, yet she was sitting across from me smiling, without medications, and discussing her passion for dragon boat racing and its contribution to *life* after breast cancer. Sarah was not alone. Many of the women I interviewed told me stories of low moments in their lives and how dragon boat racing pulled them out of the depths of despair and provided a new path. Upon reflection I realized all my research projects about women (e.g., menopause, infertility, pregnancy, motherhood) raised and dealt with issues connected to mental health. This realization highlighted the social relevance and importance of this dimension of health. I use the word *dimension* intentionally to reflect the distinct social shift away from traditional conceptualizations of health based upon a medical model and narrowly focused on physical well-being (Stewart, Parry, & Glover, 2008). Alternative discourses around health are taking shape and capture dimensions of well-being. These multidimensional views of health resist the separation of mind, body, and spirit, but do not necessarily preclude a biomedical perspective. A multidimensional conceptualization redefines health as the ability to live life fully—with vitality and meaning (Insel & Roth, 2006).

Health is, at least in part, determined by decisions about living one's life including making leisure choices. Insel and Roth (2006) identified social, spiritual, intellectual, environmental, physical, and mental dimensions of health. Although all dimensions of health interact with and impact overall wellness, they are often unpacked so that they might be explored in-depth to understand how each contributes to overall health (Wiersma & Parry, 2010). In this chapter, I explore the mental dimension of health, including the links between mental health and leisure choices, pursuits, and experiences.

CONCEPTUALIZING MENTAL HEALTH

The focus of some dimensions of health, such as physical well-being, is self-explanatory. In contrast, mental health requires clarification and definition. Part of the ambiguity surrounding this dimension is that other terms such as *psychosocial health* or *emotional health* are often used interchangeably with mental health. All three overlap. Each set of terms, however, means something slightly different and therefore, warrants clarification (Wiersma & Parry, 2010). "Psychosocial health" is the broadest term, as it encompasses intellectual, social, spiritual, and emotional dimensions of health (Donatelle, Davis, Munroe, & Munroe, 1998). "Emotional health" refers

> to the feeling component and to the ability to express emotions when appropriate and to control inappropriate expressions of emotion. Feelings of self-esteem, self-confidence, self-efficacy,

trust, love, and many other emotional reactions and responses are all part of emotional health. (Donatelle et al., 1998, p. 4)

Mental health, as conceptualized by the World Health Organization (2001), is based upon subjective well-being and includes aspects of self-efficacy, autonomy, competence, and actualization of one's intellectual and emotional potential. Mental health includes the realization of one's abilities, the capacity to cope with daily stressors, participate in fulfilling relationships with others, work productively and fruitfully, and contribute to community life. With respect to women's mental health, Murphy (2004) explains that mental health "refers not simply to the absence of symptoms or problems, but to the presence in a woman of *well-being* and *growth* and the ability of a woman to solve problems in a reality-based way" (p. 227, original emphasis). In short, mental health reflects a zest for life and is foundational to well-being.

MENTAL HEALTH AS A GENDERED CONCEPT

Barnes and Bowl (2001) asserted that mental health must be understood as a *gendered concept*. The gendered nature of mental health becomes evident in the historical role that medical science in general, and psychiatry in particular, have played in understanding women's mental health (Morrow, 2007). Morrow (2007) noted that women have "historically been understood as located on the irrational or nature side of the nature/culture binary, [so] it is not surprising that in Western thinking, women more than men have come to be understood as mentally unstable" (p. 356). This view of women stems in part from the historical link between women's mental health and their anatomy or reproductive capabilities. The thinking was that simply being a woman could make one susceptible to mental illness. Women who did not adhere to traditional gender roles were often viewed as mentally unstable (Ripa, 1990), as were lesbians (Blackbridge & Gilhooly, 1985). Rummery's (2004) research revealed how women who were abused by male partners were often labeled as mentally ill (and thus the men were not to blame). Morrow's historical analysis of mental health as a gendered concept led her to conclude that the predominance of men in medical science combined with sexist beliefs led to viewing women as mentally unstable and more prone to mental illness.

Men and women report equal rates of mental illness or poor mental health. Gender differences do arise, however, in "the types of diagnoses, the development and course of mental illness, treatment practices, and in the access and utilization of mental health services" (Morrow, 2007, p. 357). According to Murphy (2004), women comprise the main clients for mental health services worldwide. For example, within North America, women comprise 60–75% of mental health clients and Canadian women receive more prescriptions for all drugs than Canadian men, but this is most evident in psychotropic (e.g., mood-altering) drugs. Women have higher rates of medical consultations than men and consistently report higher levels of distress, anxiety, and depression leading to more professional treatments (Murphy, 2004). While these statistics are staggering, Morrow (2007) argued that the differences between men's and women's mental health experiences provide a rationale for involving women in mechanisms to address mental health disparities and engage women in strategies to improve mental health. One strategy is leisure choices, pursuits, and experiences.

LEISURE'S ROLES IN MENTAL HEALTH

My research on women's health has taught me that leisure choices, activities, and experiences play a powerful role in mental health. I conceptualize leisure as pursuits that are intrinsically motivated with a level of perceived freedom (Mannell & Kleiber, 1997). The roles of leisure in women's mental health can be explained by what I call the *sphere of sociability*, *survival strategies*, and *preventing identity theft*.

The Sphere of Sociability

The concept and contributions of the sphere of sociability to mental health became evident to me in my research with women who had experienced infertility. Many participants in my study discussed a need to form new friendships with others who had also experienced infertility. Their previous friends lacked empathy and a *true* understanding of the pain of infertility. Feeling isolated and alone, the women sought others with a shared experience of infertility. The new friendships grew within leisure-oriented social contexts such as shopping, dining out, visiting antique shows, and walking on a track. Leisure spaces were casual, unpretentious, and engaging, buttressing an effective socialization process for the women dealing with infertility. The friendships developed in leisure contexts led to byproducts. These byproducts are conceptualized as *social capital*, including norms of reciprocity, obligation, and sanctions. *Norms of reciprocity* refer to the cooperative interchange of favors or privileges that are standard between friends or within a social network (Putnam, 2000). They were demonstrated in my study when friends shared different information with each other about infertility treatments. *Obligation* refers to the act of binding oneself to a social tie, which was illustrated by participants who felt obligated to attend baby showers of friends who were previously infertile. Finally, *sanctions* refer to penalties that act to ensure compliance or group conformity (Halpern, 2005). The social consequences of not attending the baby shower, for instance, drove some women to participate in activities that were detrimental to their own well-being, such as binge eating. These forms of social capital are all crucial to an individual's mental health, but in different ways, as illustrated by the three forms of action social capital may facilitate: (a) getting by, (b) getting ahead, and (c) getting left behind (Glover & Parry, 2008).

The first form of action, *getting by*, refers to emotional support, which helps individuals maintain their mental well-being. My research participants noted how their new friends were available to them to talk through their infertility problems, encourage them between treatments, and offer a shoulder to cry on when treatments failed (Glover & Parry, 2008). Friendships were credited with helping women see themselves through the trying experiences of infertility and come to closure with the outcomes. The women reported their friendships as contexts where they felt supported and enabled to cope with the experience of infertility.

The second form of action, *getting ahead*, is tied to the material dimension of friendship, which gives friends access to information and resources. Acquiring valuable information from friends is one of the most common and important byproducts of friendship. Women in my study described sharing their treatment experiences, notes about doctors, and tips or advice they received regarding infertility (Glover & Parry, 2008). When the women received information themselves, they felt empowered and in greater control of their situations. Participants tried new treatments, were referred to new specialists, and tested different strategies to address their infertility. Although access to resources and information did not necessarily mean curing their infertility, the information helped them to come to some sense of closure with their experiences and to feel in control of their experience.

The third form of action, *getting left behind*, recognizes the harm friendships can have on an individual's mental health. Its inclusion in this discussion provides a more balanced perspective related to leisure and health because it acknowledges the ill effects friendships can create for individuals. Obstructive action can represent a setback. For example, women who remained infertile felt compelled to support friends who conceived or adopted children, even though such support made them feel uncomfortable themselves. The activities that generated stress or negative emotions in the participants were often child-centered activities such as birthday parties and toy shopping. These leisure-like events reminded the research participants of their own childlessness, which seemed to create negative self-appraisals and emotions. Nevertheless, the social norms and sanctions embedded in their friendships compelled these women to continue to support their friends even when stressful for themselves.

Leisure friendships are important because they offer mental and empathetic support to individuals (see also, Hutchinson, this volume). Green (1998), for example, noted friendships are important contexts in which women review their lives and use humor to undermine sexist imagery. Taken together, my findings indicate the contribution and drawbacks of the sphere of sociability for women's mental health. Through their connections with others who shared a similar identity, women gained emotional support and access to resources they might not otherwise have accessed. Yet, social networks may also be a context in which some women experience negative thoughts, emotions, and feelings. Thus, leisure can bring women together, contributing to their mental health by providing emotional support and access to resources, and it can also be a context in which women experience negative emotions rather than buffer them.

Survival Strategies

I learned about the power of leisure to transform mental health states and act as a survival strategy throughout negative life events or transitional life experiences while studying women's experiences with menopause. When I entered my Master's program, my mother was going through menopause and having a difficult time emotionally. Leisure choices, experiences, and activities helped her negotiate this challenging time, and I wanted to explore the roles of leisure for other menopausal women (Parry & Shaw, 1999).

Menopause occurs at the time in a woman's life when coincidental changes also may be taking place, such as the sickness or death of a parent, children leaving home, or personal health problems. In addition, around midlife, women often personally confront the problem of ageism and must deal with societal expectations and attitudes regarding acceptable behavior for older women (Freysinger, Alessio, & Mehdizadeh, 1993). These midlife experiences can have dramatic effects and may cause women to reexamine their total life situations, including their work, relationships, and family obligations as well as their reactions to socially imposed gender-role expectations (Greer, 1991; Moran & Keating, 1992). Although the outcome of such reevaluations may be positive, the process of self-examination and change is often complex and difficult (Moran & Keating, 1992).

Given the challenges women face at midlife, menopause can be a complex physiological and psychological experience. Stressful life events are associated with increased ill health (Coleman & Iso-Ahola, 1993), and these events, combined with hormonal changes, may make women more vulnerable to the negative symptoms of menopause (Greene, 1990). The importance of everyday life events and their impact upon the experience of menopause also mean that positive daily activities have the potential to exert a beneficial influence and help improve the health and well-being of women. At least some leisure is usually a daily pursuit.

The women in my study found physically active leisure enhanced their mental health through providing a feeling of physical and emotional well-being (Parry & Shaw, 1999). In addition, some leisure activities provided women with a sense of familiarity based on the security of familiar activities and routines. That is, leisure provided some continuity, which was deemed important because of the other changes the women were facing in their lives. The women gained comfort from the knowledge that at least one aspect of their lives remained unchanged, and this sense of continuity seemed to help the women face the other challenges in their lives. Other leisure practices allowed women to develop new interests, to focus on themselves, and to improve their attitudes toward self. The women reported they were taking care of their own needs during their leisure, thereby demonstrating a sense of entitlement. Finding an appropriate balance among leisure continuity, new interests, and leisure for self helped women negotiate their journey through the transitional years of menopause and midlife.

Other examples of research also demonstrate the ways leisure can act as a survival strategy during negative or transitional life experiences by contributing to women's mental well-being. For example, Shannon and Shaw (2005) studied the ways a breast cancer diagnosis can alter a woman's experience of leisure and choice of leisure pursuits. Shannon and Shaw found the women in their study described leisure as an important coping strategy for negative emotions that resulted from a breast cancer diagnosis and/or treatment including anxiety, stress, fear, anger, guilt, and feelings of uselessness. The women became aware of the therapeutic benefits of leisure pursuits such as gardening, journal writing, and walking, which they described as vital to maintaining good mental health throughout their breast cancer experience. The findings of these studies demonstrate how mental health can be transformed through leisure and act as a survival strategy during challenging times in life.

Preventing Identity Theft

One of the ways that women's mental health can be negatively influenced is through socialization into female gender roles. Morrow (2007) noted that psychosocial explanations of women's mental health examine the ways that women are more susceptible to poorer mental health because of their socialization into the roles of wife and mother. These roles hold inferior social status and relegate a disproportionate burden of family caregiving to women. Women usually are socialized to put the needs, wants, and desires of family members ahead of their own, which can result in a lack of personal identity for women and a selfless focus on others. Researchers have demonstrated that an ethic of care and lack of entitlement serve as leisure constraints for women (e.g., Bialeschki & Michener, 1994; Currie, 2004; Miller & Brown, 2005; Sullivan, this volume). Yet other researchers have demonstrated leisure as a context in which women resist socialized gendered roles and ideologies to maintain their sense of self and identity (Dionigi, this volume; Roster, this volume; Shaw, 2001). In her work with first-time mothers, Wearing (1990a) examined the importance of leisure to women's sanity and mental health. Leisure was a context in which first-time mothers resisted the selflessness demanded of them by motherhood by refusing to do housework and cook, co-opting others (e.g., husbands, family members, and other women with children) to help with childcare, and prioritizing a need for self-space.

Issues of identity were raised by participants in my study of breast cancer survivors involved in dragon boat racing. Many of the women I interviewed discussed feeling a loss of identity upon completion of medical treatment for breast cancer (Parry, 2007). While undergoing treatment for breast cancer, they took on the identity of *cancer patient*. When the treatment ended, that identity no longer fit, and many women discussed a need to develop a new identity. Part of what made the development of new identity challenging was that the women had changed as a result of their breast cancer. Their previous identity no longer fit. Many participants specifically discussed how they no longer wanted to put the needs, wants, and desires of others before themselves. They had developed a new appreciation for their own health, broadly defined, through their experiences with breast cancer. Both sentiments are summarized below:

> When I was diagnosed with breast cancer, I let go of my whole life to focus on getting better. I let go of my role as a mother, wife, and employee because I could no longer fulfill those responsibilities in the same capacity. I let go and [presumed] a new identity: cancer patient. Upon completion of my chemo treatments, I discovered that my previous life no longer existed. I felt my life had been shattered. I tried to pick up some pieces from my previous life, but found I couldn't continue where I left off. I had changed. Things that I accepted before the disease, I wouldn't accept because I did not want to settle any more. For example, in my previous life I tried to juggle everything including the kids, my husband, my job. There had been a major imbalance because my needs had come last. My new outlook made me realize that life was too short and too precious to live like that again. I no longer wanted to sacrifice today to save for tomorrow. Consequently, I

found myself without an identity. I did not feel comfortable in my own skin and was shocked to find myself left with a void. I had to build a new life that suited the new me. Dragon boat racing helped tremendously. It became part of my new identity. The women I met through dragon boat racing understood my new mindset. The four hours a week I spent dragon boating was a reprieve for me. The women made me feel normal and helped me realize I could cope with what my life had to offer. They gave me the reassurance and strength to carry on with life and create a new identity.

This quotation demonstrates the powerful role leisure can play in women's sense of identity, by encouraging feelings of self-efficacy, competence, autonomy, and the ability to participate in fulfilling relationships with others. All are foundational to mental health.

FUTURE DIRECTIONS

I focused this chapter on the links between women's mental health and their leisure choices, pursuits, and experiences. The discussion has highlighted the benefits and drawbacks of social leisure contexts to women's mental health, the roles leisure plays in helping women survive negative life events and transitional times in life, and the ways that leisure can contribute to a woman's sense of identity. These insights contribute to an understanding of the complex relationship between leisure and mental health, and they also raise areas for future study.

A focus on women's mental health from a leisure perspective is most important. An *explicit* research focus on critical connections between gender, leisure, and mental health is crucial, as is indicated in the few research projects that have already taken up this challenge. For example, Fullagar (2008) studied the link between leisure and women dealing with depression. Leisure was a source of depression for the women in this study, as they often felt responsible for caring for others and not entitled to their own leisure. However, leisure also played a pivotal role in the women's recovery as their choices, pursuits, and experiences enabled them to let go of negative self-evaluations and enhance their mental health. Through their recovery, the women recognized leisure as a source of *emotion play* including lightness, letting go, relaxation, and enjoyment. Recovery from depression was linked to deliberately seeking a voice and a space for themselves through their leisure pursuits. Leisure, therefore, provided opportunities for women to feel their way through recovery from depression by rethinking the impossible demands placed upon them and identifying ways to care about and for themselves, not just others. Fullagar's research represents a direction for future research, as it addresses the complexity of mental health, as well as leisure (Fullagar, this volume). More studies are needed with an explicit focus on mental health (or illness) and leisure.

Diversity among women (i.e., Aboriginal, racialized, and immigrant women) from a mental health and leisure perspective has been little explored and demands attention in future leisure research as well. One notable exception is Pondé and Santana's (2000) research with women from a low socioeconomic bracket in Brazil. Pondé and Santana surveyed 552 women about their occupational history, work conditions, leisure pursuits, and psychological states. About half the women who participated in leisure pursuits reported lower levels of anxiety and fewer symptoms of depression. Although the women did not indicate that they engaged in leisure to address mental health, they, nonetheless, reaped the benefit of enhanced mental well-being. Poverty and social inequality are key factors in mental health, and disproportionally affect women (Morrow, 2007). The degree to which leisure intersects with social differences such as race, ethnicity, socioeconomic status, sexual orientation, and gender identity is not known, though these intersections are receiving increasing attention, as a number of chapters in this volume illustrate. How leisure choices, experiences, and pursuits impact the development of mental health problems and their progression (and how such choices contribute to or alleviate these health effects) requires greater exploration (Morrow, 2007).

Lastly, feminist involvement in women's mental health is critical (Rummery, 2004). The gendered nature of mental health; gender differences in types of mental health diagnosis, treatments, and experiences; and the disproportionate number of women who are impacted by poor mental health speak to the need for a feminist critique of practices that might be damaging to women (Burstow, 2005). Leisure researchers seem particularly well equipped to take on this role, given the strong body of feminist literature that exists and continues to grow (Henderson, 2000; Shaw, 2001; Wearing, 1990a). I hope this chapter encourages some of those researchers and perhaps you, the reader, to take up this challenge and contribute to this timely and socially relevant area of research.

REFERENCES

Barnes, M., & Bowl, R. (2001). *Taking over the asylum: Empowerment and mental health.* Basingstoke, Hampshire, UK: Palgrave.

Bialeschki, M. D., & Michener, S. (1994). Re-entering leisure: Transition within the role of motherhood. *Journal of Leisure Research, 26*(1), 57–74.

Blackbridge, P., & Gilhooly, S. (1985). *Still sane*. Vancouver, BC: Press Gang.

Burstow, B. (2005). Feminist antipsychiatry praxis—Women and the movement(s). In W. Chan, D. Chunn, & R. Menzies (Eds.), *Women, madness, and the law: A feminist reader* (pp. 245–258). London, UK: Glasshouse.

Coleman, D., & Iso-Ahola, S. (1993). Leisure and health: The role of social support and self-determination. *Journal of Leisure Research, 25*, 111–128.

Currie, J. (2004). Motherhood, stress, and the exercise experience: Freedom or constraint? *Leisure Studies, 23*(3), 225–242.

Donatelle, R. J., Davis, L. G., Munroe, A. J., & Munroe, A. (1998). *Health: The basics* (Canadian edition). Scarborough, ON: Prentice Hall Allyn Canada.

Freysinger, V., Alessio, H., & Mehdizadeh, S. (1993). Longitudinal study of time changes and gender differences. *Activities, Adaptation, and Aging, 17*(4), 25–42.

Fullagar, S. (2008). Leisure practices as counter-depressants: Emotion-work and emotion-play within women's recovery from depression. *Leisure Sciences, 30* (1), 1–18.

Glover, T. D., & Parry, D. C. (2008). Friendships developed subsequent to a stressful life event: Links with leisure, social capital, and health. *Journal of Leisure Research, 40*(2), 208–240.

Green, E. (1998). "Women doing friendship": An analysis of women's leisure as a site of identity construction, empowerment, and resistance. *Leisure Studies, 17*, 171–185.

Greene, J. (1990). Psychosocial influences and life events at the time of menopause. In R. Formanek (Ed.), *The meanings of menopause: Historical, medical, and clinical perspectives* (pp. 79–115). Hillsdale, NJ: The Analytic Press.

Greer, G. (1991). *The change: Women, aging, and the menopause*. London, UK: Hamish.

Halpern, D. (2005). *Social capital.* Cambridge, UK: Polity.

Henderson, K. A. (2000). False dichotomies, intellectual diversity, and the "either/or" world: Leisure research in transition. *Journal of Leisure Research, 32*(1), 49–53.

Insel, P. M., & Roth, W. T. (2006). *Core concepts in health.* New York, NY: McGraw Hill.

Mannell, R. C., & Kleiber, D. A. (1997). *A social psychology of leisure.* State College, PA: Venture Publishing, Inc.

Miller, Y. D., & Brown, W. J. (2005). Determinants of active leisure for women with young children—An "ethic of care" prevails. *Leisure Sciences, 27*, 405–420.

Moran, J., & Keating, N. (1992). Making sense out of feeling different: The experience of menopause. *Canadian Women's Studies, 12*(2), 17–20.

Morrow, M. (2007). Women's voices matter: Creating women-centred mental health policy. In M. Morrow, O. Hankisvsky, & C. Varcoe (Eds.), *Women's health in Canada* (pp. 355–379). Toronto, ON: University of Toronto Press.

Murphy, M. (2004). Women and mental health. In N. Worcester & M. H. Whatley (Eds.), *Women's health: Readings on social, economic, and political issues* (pp. 227–232). Dubuque, IA: Kendall/Hunt.

Parry, D. C. (2007). There is *life* after breast cancer: Nine vignettes exploring dragon boat racing for breast cancer survivors. *Leisure Sciences, 29*(1), 53–69.

Parry, D. C., & Shaw, S. M. (1999). The role of leisure in a woman's experience of menopause and mid-life. *Leisure Sciences, 21*(3), 205–218.

Pondé, M. P., & Santana, V. S. (2000). Participation in leisure activities: Is it a protective factor for women's mental health? *Journal of Leisure Research, 32*(4), 457–472.

Putnam, R. D. (2000). *Bowling alone: The collapse and revival of American community.* New York, NY: Simon & Schuster.

Ripa, Y. (1990). *Women and madness: The incarceration of women in nineteenth-century France.* Cambridge, UK: Polity.

Rummery, F. (2004). Mad women or mad society: Towards a feminist practice with women survivors of child sexual assault. In N. Worcester & M. H. Whatley (Eds.), *Women's health: Readings on social, economic, and political issues* (pp. 233–238). Dubuque, IA: Kendall/Hunt.

Shannon, C. S., & Shaw, S. M. (2005). "If the dishes don't get done today, they'll get done tomorrow": A breast cancer experience as a catalyst for changes to women's leisure. *Journal of Leisure Research, 37*(2), 195–215.

Shaw, S. M. (2001). Conceptualizing resistance: Women's leisure as political practice. *Journal of Leisure Research, 33*(2), 186–201.

Stewart, W., Parry, D. C., & Glover, T. D. (2008). Writing leisure: Challenges to dominant discourse. *Journal of Leisure Research, 40*(3), 360–384.

Wearing, B. (1990a). Beyond the ideology of motherhood: Leisure as resistance. *Australian and New Zealand Journal of Sociology, 26*(1), 36–58.

Wiersma, E., & Parry, D. C. (2010). Leisure and emotional health: Public health perspectives. In L. Payne, B. Ainsworth, & G. Godbey (Eds.), *Leisure, health, and wellness* (pp. 61–69). State College, PA: Venture Publishing, Inc.

World Health Organization. (2001). *The world health report 2001—Mental health: New understanding, new hope.* Retrieved from http://www.who.int/whr/2001/chapter1/en/print.html

CHAPTER 17
WOMEN AND TOURISM

HEATHER J. GIBSON, FIONA JORDAN, AND LIZA BERDYCHEVSKY

Many people regard travel as an integral part of their leisure and work lives. Flying from A to B, hopping on and off a train, taking a road trip, and setting sail on a cruise offer the promise of excitement and escape from daily routines. Tourism, however, is not only an industry that enables travel—it is a social phenomenon influenced by sociostructural and cultural forces. When exploring the social and cultural aspects of tourism, the extent to which all touristic experiences are shaped by issues such as socioeconomic factors, disability, race, and age become apparent. For example, gender is associated with tourism as an industry and as an experience. Consider the women smiling invitingly from holiday brochures and advertisements, the largely invisible women who clean hotel rooms, the local women encountered in the markets and shops, the mothers on vacation entertaining and taking care of their children, the woman eating in a hotel restaurant by herself, or the groups of older women laughing and hurrying back to join their tour bus. All of these scenarios are common in the world of tourism every day. Yet, little is known about the experiences of these women. Our interest in understanding more about these diverse lived experiences has informed our research and thinking about women and tourism.

THE JOURNEY BEGINS . . .

We began our journey into the world of women and tourism as Master's students on three separate continents and time periods. Heather transferred her interest in women and sport in the late 1980s into a gender approach to tourist roles over the life course in a United States context (Gibson, 1989; 1994; Gibson & Yiannakis, 2002). Fiona, from a management background, examined the gendered and sexualized culture of UK tourism organizations in the mid-1990s (Jordan, 1997). Liza investigated the sexual behavior of the Israeli female tourists in the later part of the first decade of the twenty-first century (Berdychevsky, 2009; Berdychevsky, Poria, & Uriely, 2010). When our (Heather and Fiona) work on solo travelers began in the 1990s, little research had been done in this area, aside from the important edited collection by Kinnaird and Hall (1994) and the special edition of *Annals of Tourism Research* edited by Margaret Swain (1995). By contrast, in the field of leisure research, several significant feminist projects had identified that women had less leisure time than men. In addition, women's access to, and experiences of, everyday leisure were often more constrained. These studies led us to question whether women's experiences of leisure travel were likely to be similarly constrained.

The idea for the solo women travelers project was conceived following Fiona's 1997 presentation of a study in which she investigated the lack of provision among British travel companies for women wishing to take a solo holiday (Jordan, 1998). Fiona had just begun her Ph.D. thesis exploring whether holidays were really sites of freedom and escape for women traveling alone or were regulated by the same gendered social expectations that feminist scholars had identified as constraining other aspects of women's leisure. Heather had just finished interviewing both men and women in their retirement years about their travel experiences (Gibson, 2002) and was intrigued by one particular traveler's tale about both the joys and tribulations of traveling solo. The design of our research was also shaped by a shared curiosity to understand why women of our acquaintance who were educated, financially solvent, and confident in most areas of their lives still balked at the prospect of traveling alone. We chose to focus our study on women's solo travel and to explore the constraints and barriers they encountered in undertaking this form of leisure.

We enlisted over 70 female volunteers from Gloucestershire in the United Kingdom and Gainesville, Florida in the United States and interviewed them about their experiences of traveling solo. In our early work, informed by a social-feminist theoretical framework and social conceptions of tourism, we used a leisure constraints model (Crawford, Jackson, & Godbey, 1991) to ascertain whether the constraints inherent in women's everyday lives influenced their solo travel behavior. However, we found in analyzing the interview data that ideas of solo travel as a constrained form of leisure were too narrow to explain the richness of the women's stories. For theoretical inspiration, we turned to new perspectives on gender, leisure, and tourism offered by scholars such as Aitchison (1999a; 1999b) and Wearing (Wearing & Wearing, 1996; Wearing, 1998). Using *new cultural geographies*, researchers were exploring the gender power relations inherent in the creation and consumption of leisure and tourism and conceptualizing space and place as fluid and contested (Aitchison,

2001). Examining the sociospatial dimensions of tourism provided us with unique insights to help understand the experiences of female travelers.

At the same time, British, American, and Australian women in the leisure research community were beginning to incorporate poststructuralist perspectives into their work. Foucault's (1976, 1977) thinking on social surveillance and self-surveillance and on power relations as unstable and negotiable were of particular interest to us. Many women in our study felt uncomfortable being observed as unaccompanied women, particularly when dining alone. Some talked about being sexually harassed or how fears of being hassled led them to avoid certain holiday spaces and places at different times. These themes resonated strongly with Foucault's notions of the power of the collective gaze to influence self-surveillance and behaviors in social contexts and to render spaces more or less inclusive for those using them. We began to theorize women's experiences of solo travel related to the sexualization of tourism spaces and the significance of surveillance in influencing travel behaviors (Jordan, 2008; Jordan & Gibson, 2005).

Despite the difficulties encountered when traveling alone, the women in this study of solo travel saw a potential journey of self-discovery, and holidays as a site of resistance and empowerment. Stories about breaking out of the strictures of a tour group, resisting the surveillant gaze of male residents encountered in different countries, and feeling empowerment from the travels permeated the interview data. For us as experienced international travelers, the idea that individual female tourists had power to resist many of the potentially constraining gendered spaces they encountered reflected our own experiences as well. Tourism spaces as sites of resistance, therefore, offered a new and more positive lens for viewing women's experiences of solo travel.

Our study initially focused on the experiences of women in their late 20s and older, which reflected our ages and life stages at the time of embarking on the research. The third author, Liza, provided insight into an aspect of younger women's tourist behavior that our interviews did not cover. In contrast to other work, where the issue of sexual behavior on holiday was not a theme in the women's stories, Liza used the travels of Israeli women to specifically explore the differences between their sexual behaviors in a tourism context (i.e., *liminoid space* characterized by anonymity and timelessness outside everyday social conventions) compared to their everyday lives.

Liza's research about Israeli women suggested a typology of women's sexual behavior based on type of tourist experience (e.g., rest and relaxation, city break, backpacking trip, and business trip) and the nature of the relationship in which sexual activity took place (e.g., with regular or with casual partner). Within the context of backpacking vacations, for example, casual sex was described by women as an integral part of this experience (Berdychevsky et al., 2010). The women saw sex as an additional adventure in what was already regarded as an extreme form of liminoid space. Thus, they regarded sexual adventures that might elicit social discomfort and concern at home as a source of excitement, self-investigation, and in certain cases even fulfillment in the backpacking context.

With an interest in gender and tourism spanning over 20 years among us, seeing how much and the ways in which this body of knowledge has grown is encouraging. Yet we are somewhat disappointed that the research has not expanded as much as we hoped during this time. When we started out, we sought to apply new theoretical concepts in the context of an empirical study and to challenge the positivist methodological hegemony that characterized much tourism scholarship at that time. More importantly, we wanted to highlight the significance of feminist and poststructuralist thinking in providing ways to conceptualize women's diverse experiences of tourism. These perspectives are valuable in contributing to understanding the tourism experiences of women related to a wider body of knowledge about leisure behavior.

WOMEN AND TOURISM SCHOLARSHIP IN THE TWENTY-FIRST CENTURY

The literature about women as tourists was scarce when we began researching solo women travelers. Heather wrote a chapter reviewing and critiquing the literature on women and tourism from three perspectives: women as consumers (i.e., tourists), women as producers (i.e., workers in the tourism industry), and theoretical perspectives (Gibson, 2001). Since that chapter was written, scholars have added new dimensions to understanding the relationships between women and tourism. In the remainder of this chapter, we focus on the following aspects: a) women's employment in the tourism industry, b) sex tourism and romance tourism, and c) women's experiences of tourism (e.g., motivations, constraints, benefits).

Women's Work? Women's Employment in Tourism

Studies of women's employment in tourism in the past decade have reflected debates in the wider realm of the gendered nature of work, including such topics as the *glass ceiling*, double standards, unequal pay, and sexual harassment in the workplace (e.g., Iverson, 2000; Poulston, 2008). The research has revealed that male hospitality and tourism employees earn between 7% and 20% more than their female counterparts in Norway (Thrane, 2008), Spain (Muñoz-Bullón, 2009) and the United Kingdom (Burgess,

2000). In addition, men tend to occupy jobs with higher responsibilities and status. Although some progression by women into higher status, higher-paying jobs has occurred, barriers (e.g., occupational segregation and traditional attitudes towards women's progression) still exist (Ng & Pine, 2003). Thus, women in the tourism industry and hospitality services face disadvantages and relatively little progress seems made on these issues since Jordan's 1997 study.

Studies of the role of women in other tourism enterprises show that tourism development can have both beneficial and detrimental effects. Hemingway (2004) suggested that women in tourism locales are central in representing the cultural identity of the host community with roles such as house caretakers and custodians of a society's culture. For local women, particularly in developing countries, tourism can bring vital employment opportunities, economic freedom, and independence (e.g., Davis, 2007). Thus, Ghodsee (2003) claimed that tourism is "a valuable tool for promoting women's economic well-being" (p. 465). Yet, Marshall (2001), in a study of Grand Manan (an eastern Canadian island), found that although tourism can create possibilities for women regarding independence and supplementary income, it cannot reconfigure the basic structure of gender relations of a society frequently rooted in tradition and religious values.

Marshall (2001) observed that tourism is both positive and negative for local women. Tourism may simultaneously offer the promise of more local empowerment *as well as* foster exploitation and commodification of the local population and of the host female population, specifically. For example, McKenzie Gentry (2007) emphasized the opportunities afforded to Belizean women from tourism-based employment while describing impediments like the reinforcement of traditional gender roles in the "housewifization of labor" (p. 477) and gender-based segregation in the tourism industry.

Thus, the employment of women in the tourism industry continues to be a mixed blessing. In attempting to explain the experiences for these women, scholars emphasize that any analysis must consider factors including the type of tourism in a locality (McKenzie Gentry, 2007), structural conditions (i.e., ethnicity, nationality and cultural capital) that shape women's employment in the tourism industry (Vandegrift, 2008), and state and corporate initiatives that might affect tourism's impact on local women (Hemingway, 2004). Perhaps somewhat optimistically, Hemingway suggested that the negative outcomes of tourism development for local women could be reduced by changes in the law and the introduction of corporate codes of conduct designed to develop the concept of responsible tourism. These initiatives may help, but the gendered nature of societies is still the genesis of the largely negative employment-based conditions women experience as tourism workers. Arguably, nothing exemplifies the continued exploitation and commodification of women like the realm of sex tourism that has continued to grow.

Sun, Sea, Sand, and Sex Tourism

Studies on the complex phenomenon of sex tourism in different geographical locations have been added to the literature in the past decade (e.g., Clift & Carter, 2000). Taking a lead from Oppermann (1999), Ryan and Hall (2001), as well as McKercher and Bauer (2003) argued that differentiating between *sex tourism* and *sex in tourism* is essential. They offered multidimensional models of the relationships between tourism and sex based on factors such as the nature of the sexual encounter (e.g., voluntary/exploited, commercial/noncommercial, enhancing/degrading for self-identity), the tourism industry's role in facilitating the sexual encounter, the importance of sex as a motivation for tourists, and so forth. Such models have been criticized by Jeffreys (1999), who suggested that the term *prostitution tourism* might be more apt. Moreover, these models appear to overlook ambiguities in the sex and tourism relationship, such as the issues of romance, mutual involvement, and possible expectations of migration and marriage on the part of local residents (Cabezas, 2004). For example, in a study of sexual relationships between tourists and locals in the Dominican Republic, Herold, Garcia, and DeMoya (2001) found that one of the goals for some of the local males, called *beach boys*, was to be invited back to North America and Europe by their tourist "girlfriends."

Cabezas (2004) and Piscitelli (2007) described types of sex workers who may not recognize themselves as such. In the context of Cuba and the Dominican Republic, Cabezas pointed out that the double standards of appropriate sexual behavior for men and women result in definitions of male sex workers as "national heroes . . . conquering the bodies of foreign invaders" and their female counterparts as "deviants and a detriment to society" (p. 1008). Similarly, the gendered distinction sometimes made between sex tourism (i.e., male tourists engaging in sexual relations) and romance tourism (i.e., female tourists engaging in sexual relations) has been the subject of some debate (Aston, 2008).

Herold et al. (2001) conceptualized romance and sex tourism as the two ends of a continuum of motivations rather than as distinct categories. Their findings revealed that more of the female tourists were located toward the romance end and more of the male tourists toward the sex end of the continuum. The prevailing assumption was epitomized by Pruitt and LaFont (1995), who suggested that female tourists are motivated by a search for romance and companionship. Belliveau (2006) claimed that sex during tourism offers an opportunity for women to recover from failed relationships and to satisfy unfulfilled sexual desire. Thomas (2005) also found that for the women in her study, expectations of "having a wild time" or "fun" (p. 574) on holiday in Tenerife were closely linked to male attention.

These sentiments could be equally true for men. Sánchez Taylor (2001) problematized the distinction between male sex tourism and female romance tourism. She argued that: (a) sexual-economic exchanges are not always straightforward and male tourists, as well as local women, might not necessarily perceive themselves as prostitute-users and prostitutes; (b) female tourists, as well as male tourists, can be sexually predatory and hostile; (c) this distinction reproduces essentialist understandings of female and male sexuality where men benefit from sexual access to women's bodies; and (d) claiming that tourist women having sex with local men are not sex tourists downplays the significance of racialized and economic power. Yet, she also recognized that by virtue of being male, the beach boys are not as vulnerable to violence from their female tourist sexual partners, to police harassment, or to legal prosecution as their female sex worker counterparts. Jeffreys (2003), however, criticized the tendency to include women within the ranks of sex tourists. She argued that "careful attention to the power relations, context, meanings and effects of the behaviors of male and female tourists who engage in sexual relations with local people, makes it clear that the differences are profound" (p. 223).

Sisters are Doing it for Themselves: Women's Experiences of Tourism

Of course, not all female tourism experiences revolve around sexual behavior, although the sexualization of tourism more generally can have a profound effect on touristic encounters. Women-centered research in tourism has continued to develop over the last decade. In particular, studies have added to knowledge about the experiences of female travelers in different countries such as the study by Berdychevsky et al. (2010) of Israeli female backpackers, Chiang and Jogaratnam's (2006) study of the motivations of American women to travel alone, Heimtun's (2007a) study of the role of travel in the lives of single midlife women in Norway, and Wilson's study of Australian female travelers overcoming constraints (Wilson & Little, 2005). A core theme in the studies of women's travel is that women's tourist experiences differ from men's due to the gendered nature of society. Elsrud (2001) indicated that while male and female budget travelers abound and women travelers seem to be accorded more freedom to travel, they frequently confront the continued social construction of such travel as a male domain. Thus, the continued need for gender-sensitive research exists.

Studies during this time period have adopted various theoretical perspectives. Pennington-Gray and Kerstetter (2001) used a benefits-sought framework to understand the travel of university-educated women. They identified benefits-sought dimensions such as rest/relaxation, cultural experiences, socializing, and family time and linked them to different types of female travelers. Small (2005) found that women in their 40s seemed to be searching for freedom from their roles as women and mothers on their vacations. Nonetheless, she found that total freedom was not possible for these women, as they mentioned having to negotiate their motherhood roles to find a leisure space for themselves while traveling. Thus, while some women were willing to resist the ethic of care, Gustafson (2006) revealed that Swedish women's work-related travel remained adversely affected by the presence of young children, an experience not shared by men. Likewise, Jennings's (2005) study of women's experiences of long-term ocean cruising showed that some of these women reluctantly engaged in this lifestyle out of a sense of commitment to their partners. One big complaint about the cruising lifestyle was that they still felt obligated to fulfill domestic roles while on board the boat. Thus, women may experience a sense of freedom within the tourism realm, but the influence of gender in the context of family roles is still significant.

Research on solo women's travel appears to demonstrate some escape from nurturing roles. Chiang and Jogaratnam (2006) investigated the motivations of female solo travelers, finding five motivational dimensions: the desire to experience, escape, relax, socialize, and develop self-esteem. Obenour (2005) studied the journey for female backpackers and found that the women felt a sense of emancipation by overcoming the constraints they faced from traveling solo. Similarly, in studying midlife single women in Norway, Heimtun (2007a) highlighted the significance of social identities in the context of women's travel. Obenour suggested whatever situation the women encountered while on the road, traveling solo helped them to engage in the existential authenticity of self-making through the independence afforded by this travel style (Roster, this volume). However, gendered realities are never far away.

Despite the evidence of resistance and empowerment of women in some of these studies, Wilson and Little (2005, 2008) identified four categories of constraints that impacted solo women travelers: sociocultural, personal, practical, and spatial. Further, Wilson and Little (2008) explored Valentine's (1989) concept of the *geography of fear* in the context of female solo international travel. For their solo female travelers, the geography of fear manifested itself through perceptions of them by others, susceptibility to vulnerability, a sense of restricted access, and a feeling of conspicuousness. We also found evidence of the geography of fear among the solo women travelers in our study (Jordan & Gibson, 2005) and noted how theoretical perspectives can result in different interpretations. In using a poststructural analysis, we found that although the women were aware of the *surveillance of the gaze*, they often resisted the gaze, which led Jordan and Aitchison (2008) to recommend the idea of the "mutual gaze" to better reflect the fluidity of the power relations being negotiated.

WHERE TO NEXT?

In line with the ideas of Aitchison (2001) and Wearing (1998), we believe that poststructural theorizing may provide some promising avenues for future research into this topic. We do not advocate conceptualizations of a society without structure but rather see value in the notion of power relations as fluid and negotiable, allowing for individuals potentially to resist constraints in leisure and tourism. Moreover, within a poststructural feminist perspective, acts of resistance may result in empowerment. For us, the stories women told us about their travels epitomized these theoretical tenets. Many women advocated the power of solo travel to change their lives and those of others. We often hear from solo women travelers that simply seeing the stories of other solo female travelers published in the academic literature or newspapers gave them more confidence and legitimized their choice to travel alone. We are saddened to think that although many of these women in the twenty-first century have more choices than their Victorian counterparts, they tell us that they are still perceived as an oddity and foolhardy for confronting the pervasive geography of fear (Valentine, 1989). Therefore, an ongoing commitment to advance understandings of women's experiences of travel is needed.

We also believe that additional conceptualizing of the cultural dimensions of gender and tourism would be of value. In particular, the extent to which the interplay of structure and cultures and the *social-cultural nexus* of tourism (Aitchison, 2003) serve to create the spaces of tourism as gendered and sexualized could assist in understanding more about the experiences of different people. Greater recognition of the diversity of touristic experiences opens up the possibility of further researching issues such as the role of travel in the leisure lives of older women, women with disabilities, women from minority ethnic groups, and women on family vacations. Following recent work in *Leisure Studies* (e.g., Kay, 2006b), this focus on researching individual tourists also allows for more exploration of men's tourism experiences as young adults, fathers, grandfathers, and workers.

In addition to drawing on leisure studies for theoretical inspiration, new thinking in tourism studies provides potentially valuable avenues for conceptualizing gender and tourism. Exploring links between tourism roles as performed (Edensor, 2000) and Foucault's ideas on the power of surveillance may enable exploration of the ways such performances serve to create particular spaces as more or less inclusive for different tourists. The growing interest in tourism and embodiment (Jordan, 2007; Small, 2007) may also help us to understand how issues such as body image and physical appearance impact the tourist experiences of men and women. The developing mobilities paradigm offers theoretical perspectives to help blur the boundaries between tourism and everyday leisure in a way that broadens conceptualizations of women's touristic experiences. As Sheller and Urry (2006) explain, this work seeks to "highlight that many different mobilities inform tourism, shape the places where tourism is performed, and drive the making and unmaking of tourist destinations" (p. 1). Combining such perspectives with further feminist analyses of tourism provides the opportunity to develop our understandings of the multifaceted influences of gender on tourism and we are optimistic that the journey will be an exciting one.

REFERENCES

Aitchison, C. C. (1999a). Heritage and nationalism: gender and the performance of power. In D. Crouch (Ed.), *Leisure/Tourism geographies: Practices and geographical knowledge* (pp. 59–73). London, UK: Routledge.

Aitchison, C. C. (1999b). New cultural geographies: The spatiality of leisure, gender, and sexuality. *Leisure Studies, 18*(1), 19–39.

Aitchison, C. C. (2001). Theorizing other discourses of tourism, gender, and culture: Can the subaltern speak (in tourism)? *Tourist Studies, 1*(2), 133–147.

Aitchison, C. C. (2003). *Gender and leisure: Social and cultural perspectives.* London, UK: Routledge.

Aston, E. (2008). A fair trade?: Staging female sex tourism in "sugar mummies" and "trade." *Contemporary Theatre Review, 18*(2), 180–192.

Belliveau, J. (2006). *Romance on the road: Traveling women who love foreign men.* Baltimore, MD: Beau Monde.

Berdychevsky, L. (2009). *Sex in the city vs. sex in another city: Women's sexual behavior during their tourist experiences.* Unpublished master's thesis. Ben-Gurion University of the Negev, Beer Sheva, Israel.

Berdychevsky, L., Poria, Y., & Uriely, N. (2010). Casual sex and the back-packing experience: The case of Israeli women. In N. Carr & Y. Poria (Eds.), *Sex and the sexual during people's leisure and tourism experiences* (pp. 105–118). Cambridge, UK: Cambridge Scholars.

Burgess, C. (2000). Hotel accounts—Do men get the best jobs? *Hospitality Management, 19*(4), 345–352.

Cabezas, A. L. (2004). Between love and money: Sex, tourism, and citizen-ship in Cuba and the Dominican Republic. *Journal of Women in Culture and Society, 29*(4), 987–1015.

Chiang, C., & Jogaratnam, G. (2006). Why do women travel solo for pur-poses of leisure? *Journal of Vacation Marketing, 12*(1), 59–70.

Clift, S., & Carter, S. (Eds.) (2000). *Tourism and sex: Culture, commerce, and coercion.* London, UK: Pinter.

Crawford, D., Jackson, E., & Godbey, G. (1991). A hierarchical model of leisure constraints. *Leisure Sciences, 13*(4), 309–320.

Davis, C. V. (2007). Can developing women produce primitive art? And other questions of value, meaning, and identity in the circulation of Janakpur art. *Tourist Studies, 7*(2), 193–223.

Edensor, T. (2000). Staging tourism: tourists as performers. *Annals of Tourism Research, 27*(2), 322–344.

Elsrud, T. (2001). Risk creation in traveling: Backpacker adventure narra-tion. *Annals of Tourism Research, 28*(3), 597–617.

Foucault, M. (1976). *The history of sexuality: An introduction* (Vol. 1). New York, NY: Pantheon.

Foucault, M. (1977). *Discipline and punish: The birth of the prison.* London, UK: A. Lang.

Ghodsee, K. (2003). State support in the market: Women and tourism employment in post-socialist Bulgaria. *International Journal of Politics, Culture and Society, 16*(3), 465–482.

Gibson, H. (1989). *Tourist roles: Stability and change over the life cycle.* (Unpublished master's thesis). The University of Connecticut, Storrs, USA.

Gibson, H. (1994). *Some predictors of tourist role preference for men and women over the adult life course.* (Unpublished doctoral dissertation). The University of Connecticut, Storrs, USA.

Gibson, H. (2001). Gender in tourism: Theoretical perspectives. In Y. Apostolopoulos, S. Sönmez, & D. J. Timothy (Eds.), *Women as producers and consumers of tourism in developing regions* (pp. 19–43). Westport, CT: Praeger.

Gibson, H. (2002). Busy travelers: Leisure-travel patterns and meanings in later life. *World Leisure, 44*(2), 11–20.

Gibson, H., & Yiannakis, A. (2002). Tourist roles: Needs and the life course. *Annals of Tourism Research, 29*(2), 358–383.

Gustafson, P. (2006). Work-related travel, gender, and family obligations. *Work, Employment and Society, 20*(3), 513–530.

Heimtun, B. (2007a). Depathologizing the tourist syndrome: Tourism as social capital production, *Tourist Studies,* 7(3), 271–293.

Hemingway, S. (2004). The impact of tourism on the human rights of women in South East Asia. *International Journal of Human Rights, 8*(3), 275–304.

Herold, E., Garcia, R., & DeMoya, T. (2001). Female tourists and beach boys: Romance or sex tourism? *Annals of Tourism Research, 28*(4), 978–997.

Iverson, K. (2000). The paradox of the contented female manager: An empirical investigation of gender differences in pay expectation in the hospitality industry. *Hospitality Management, 19*(1), 33–51.

Jeffreys, S. (1999). Globalizing sexual exploitation: Sex tourism and the traffic in women. *Leisure Studies, 18*(3), 179–196.

Jeffreys, S. (2003). Sex tourism: Do women do it too? *Leisure Studies, 22*(3), 223–238.

Jennings, G. R. (2005). Caught in the irons: One of the lived experiences of long-term ocean cruising women. *Tourism Review International, 9*(2), 177–193.

Jordan, F. (1997). An occupational hazard? Sex segregation in tourism employment, *Tourism Management, 18*(8), 525–534.

Jordan, F. (1998). Shirley Valentine, where are you? Tourism provision for mid-life women travelling alone. In C. Aitchison & F. Jordan (Eds.), *Gender, space and identity: Leisure, culture and commerce* (pp. 69–88). Eastbourne, UK: LSA Publications.

Jordan, F. (2007). Life's a beach and then we diet: Critical discourses of tourism and the body. In A. Pritchard, N. Morgan, I. Ateljevic, & C. Harris (Eds.), *Tourism and embodiment: Critical issues of gender, sexuality and the body* (pp. 92–106). Wallingford, UK: CAB International.

Jordan, F. (2008). Performing Tourism: Exploring the productive consumption of tourism in enclavic spaces. *International Journal of Tourism Research, 10*(4), 293–304.

Jordan, F., & Aitchison, C. C. (2008). Tourism and the sexualisation of the gaze: Solo female tourists' experiences of gendered power, surveillance and embodiment. *Leisure Studies, 27*(3), 329–349.

Jordan, F., & Gibson, H. (2005). We're not stupid . . . but we'll not stay home either: Experiences of solo women travellers. *Tourism Review International, 9*(2), 195–212.

Kay, T. A. (2006b). Where's dad? Fatherhood in leisure studies. *Leisure Studies, 25*(2), 133–152.

Kinnaird, V., & Hall, D. (1994). *Tourism: A gender analysis*. New York, NY: John Wiley & Sons.

Marshall, J. (2001). Women and strangers: Issues of marginalization in seasonal tourism. *Tourism Geographies, 3*(2), 165–186.

McKenzie Gentry, K. (2007). Belizean women and tourism work: Opportunity or impediment? *Annals of Tourism Research, 34*(2), 477–496.

McKercher, B., & Bauer, T. G. (2003). Conceptual framework of the nexus between tourism, romance, and sex. In T. G. Bauer & B. Mckercher (Eds.), *Sex and tourism: Journeys of romance, love, and lust* (pp. 3–18). New York, NY: Haworth Hospitality.

Muñoz-Bullón, F. (2009). The gap between male and female pay in the Spanish tourism industry. *Tourism Management, 30*(5), 638–649.

Ng, C. W., & Pine, R. (2003). Women and men in hotel management in Hong Kong: Perceptions of gender and career development issues. *Hospitality Management, 22*(1), 85–102.

Obenour, W. L. (2005). The "journeys" of independence for female backpackers. *Tourism Review International, 9*(2), 213–227.

Oppermann, M. (1999). Sex tourism. *Annals of Tourism Research, 26*(2), 251–266.

Pennington-Gray, L. A., & Kerstetter, D. L. (2001). What do university-educated women want from their pleasure travel experiences? *Journal of Travel Research, 40*(1), 49–56.

Piscitelli, A. (2007). Shifting boundaries: Sex and money in the North-East of Brazil. *Sexualities, 10*(4), 489–500.

Poulston, J. (2008). Metamorphosis in hospitality: A tradition of sexual harassment. *International Journal of Hospitality Management, 27*(2), 232–240.

Pruitt, D., & LaFont, S. (1995). For love and money: Romance tourism in Jamaica. *Annals of Tourism Research, 22*(2), 422–440.

Ryan, C., & Hall, C. M. (2001). *Sex tourism: Marginal people and liminalities.* London, UK: Routledge.

Sánchez Taylor, J. (2001). Dollars are a girl's best friend? Female tourists' sexual behaviour in the Caribbean. *Sociology, 35*(3), 749–764.

Sheller, M., & Urry, J. (2006). The new mobilities paradigm. *Environment and Planning, 38*(2), 207–226.

Small, J. (2005). Women's holidays: Disruption of the holiday myth. *Tourism Review International, 9*(2), 139–154.

Small, J. (2007). The emergence of the body in holiday accounts of women and girls. In A. Pritchard, N. Morgan, I. Ateljevic, & C. Harris (Eds.), *Tourism and embodiment: Critical issues of gender, sexuality and the body* (pp. 73–91). Wallingford, UK: CAB International.

Swain, M. B. (1995). Gender in tourism. *Annals of Tourism Research, 22*(2), 247–266.

Thomas, M. (2005). "What happens in Tenerife stays in Tenerife": Understanding women's sexual behaviour on holiday. *Culture, Health & Sexuality, 7*(6), 571–584.

Thrane, C. (2008). Earnings differentiation in the tourism industry: Gender, human capital and socio-demographic effects. *Tourism Management, 29*(3), 514–524.

Valentine, G. (1989). The geography of women's fear. *Area, 21*(4), 385–390.

Vandegrift, D. (2008). "This isn't paradise—I work here": Global restructuring, the tourism industry, and women workers in Caribbean Costa Rica. *Gender & Society, 22*(6), 778–798.

Wearing, B. (1998). *Leisure and feminist theory.* Thousand Oaks, CA: Sage.

Wearing, B., & Wearing, S. (1996). Refocusing the tourist experience: The flâneur and the choraster. *Leisure Studies, 15*(4), 229–243.

Wilson, E., & Little, D. E. (2005). A "relative escape"? The impact of constraints on women who travel solo. *Tourism Review International, 9*(2), 155–175.

Wilson, E., & Little, D. E. (2008). The solo female travel experience: Exploring the "geography of women's fear." *Current Issues in Tourism, 11*(2), 167–186.

CHAPTER 18
FEMINIST MASCULINITIES: INQUIRIES INTO LEISURE, GENDER, AND SEXUAL IDENTITY

COREY W. JOHNSON

I stand in front of the mirror and dry myself off. I lather my face's overnight growth with Edge super-sensitive shaving cream and scrape it away with swipes of my Gillette Mach Three super razor. I spray Nioxin bio-nutrient cleanser into my recently washed hair and scalp to "keep the hair I have, and encourage the growth of new hair" and then—perhaps defeating the purpose of the Nioxin—I work in a healthy dose of styling gel with my fingertips, molding and sculpting until I am happy with the way each section of my hair is shaped. Finally, I swab deodorant under each arm to prevent perspiration or underarm odor.

Looking at myself in the mirror, I sigh as I consider my clothing options. The oppressive summer days of the South are already upon us. Though it is cool this morning, the forecast calls for highs in the upper-90s. I look at my trousers stacked on the shelf of my closet, torn between a pair of khaki shorts to beat the summer heat, or my faded denim blue jeans—more characteristic of the event. My faded denim blue jeans win and I pull them up over my black Calvin Klein boxer briefs. Wearing my usual boxer shorts is out of the question—they bunch up and make these jeans too tight.

I go in search of my favorite T-shirt, not just any T-shirt, but one that will fit the events of the day: old, rugged, one color, simple, and without flare. I also want it to fit snugly, to emphasize my broad shoulders and chest in contrast to my thin waist. I find the right one buried in the bottom of a dresser drawer between an old concert model and a button-down polo. It's a white and green ringer T-shirt bought at the Gap more than three years ago. I slide it onto my damp torso and stuff the ends into what room is left in the jeans. Then I crouch down into the bottom of my closet and pull out my brown hiking boots, which seem practical for walking around in the dust and dirt at the rodeo. However, they are not perfect. No, perfect would be a pair of cowboy boots. I look in the mirror. I am certainly no cowboy, but I won't stand out. I look kinda butch, I think to myself. Besides, I am not actually going to ride the bulls.

Once we take our seats at the gay rodeo, all is forgiven. Alex's eyes shine in amazement. Cowboys are everywhere and it is safe to assume that all are gay! I think I even see a bit of drool slip down Alex's mouth as he says, "I have never seen gay cowboys before—except in porn. They are damn hot!" Turning to my friend Nicholas, a fellow academic, I half-jokingly ask, "Doesn't your boyfriend's objectification of these men bother you?" Nicholas responds, "What boyfriend?" and we laugh. Attempting to be more serious, I offer a bit of preliminary analysis explaining how, in general, I think cowboys or cowboy imagery is an easy masculine image to replicate because we have all experienced its iconography in movies and television. Cowboy imagery has been sustained as an acceptable masculine image.

"Meaning they don't actually have to be a cowboy to look like one?" Nicholas asks.

"Exactly," I say, noting that many of the people dressed in cowboy attire I have encountered have probably never even ridden a horse. However, here at the rodeo, the cowboys seem to be more "authentic."

Like many scholars, my education has afforded me the opportunity to engage with layered theories that both confirm and challenge the ways I know and understand the world. At the center of my scholarship is the interplay between my situated self as a gay man, my interests in masculinity and sexual identity in leisure, and my goals as an advocate for social justice. Understanding these intersections and their tensions helps me know more about myself as a researcher, and ultimately the topics of focus in this chapter—my musings on masculinity, scholarship on gay bars and media consumption, and recommendations for future research.

A MAN FINDING HIS HOME IN FEMINISM

I remember sitting at a large conference table in my first graduate research seminar reading Henderson (1991b), who challenged researchers to discover the passions and curiosities that motivate them to pursue research. Unsure of my abilities but determined to try, I began to search for a line of scholarly inquiry that would not only inspire my intellectual curiosity but also change the lives of those disadvantaged in society.

You would think that living as a gay man in a heterosexual world, I would have readily seen the opportunities to locate social injustice and oppression. However, at first, injustice and oppression were unrecognizable to me. Growing up in a small rural town in Ohio, I felt the sting of derogatory comments like *faggot* and *queer*, and I had often feared for my safety.

I failed, however, to see the relationship between those experiences and leisure. Instead, I viewed leisure as a context that provided for the development of my own positive gay identity. As extolled in most foundational texts, leisure for me included establishing social relationships, allowing creative self-expression, boosting self-esteem, and increasing my knowledge of shared cultural practices and history. Because initially I perceived leisure to be a positive experience, I failed to recognize that many people, marginalized because of their gender, race, ability, or sexual identity, did not participate in leisure because they did not fit the *typical* participant profile, or felt that they were treated differently, were denied access, or feared for their safety. My recognition of this dynamic and sometimes oppressive nature of leisure for gay men and lesbians was illuminated while reading *Breaking the Surface*, the autobiography of Greg Louganis (Louganis & Marcus, 1995). Louganis talked about the potential consequences he faced attempting to balance his gender, sexuality, and leisure:

> So after more than ten years of classes and performances and competitions, I gave up acrobatics, gymnastics, and dance. I'd hoped to compete in gymnastics at the Olympics one day, but now that dream was gone. At twelve years old, I decided that I would kill myself. I went into my parents' medicine cabinet and took a bunch of different pills, mostly aspirin and Ex-Lax. Then I took a razor blade out of the cabinet and started playing with it over my wrist. I started to bleed, but I didn't go deep enough to cut any veins or arteries…. I never told my parents about the suicide attempt, and they didn't notice the missing medicine or the scratches on my wrists. Afterward, I was even more angry and depressed, because I didn't see any way out. (pp. 40–41)

My emerging consciousness of gay and lesbian experiences like those faced by Louganis encouraged me to think about leisure differently, more critically. Through projects like my Master's thesis (Johnson, 1998) and its subsequent publication (Johnson, 2000), I slowly began to think about how issues of masculinity and sexual identity were important, yet unacknowledged and understudied in leisure studies.

I began to understand leisure as a cultural site where people learn about social roles, which are constantly influenced by the values and fundamentals of the dominant culture, as well as personal beliefs, past experiences, and future goals. Although I believe that individual expression, personal growth, and creativity are often fostered in leisure, leisure can also be used to promote and enforce mainstream discourses and ideals. I began to see how leisure might be used as a form of social control to keep individuals and/or groups of individuals in a state of inequality. I thought if scholars understood more about leisure and its inescapable ties to masculinity and sexual identity, those oppressed by the androcentric/heterosexist ideologies validated as *normal* in leisure could be liberated.

Feminist theory opened up spaces for this type of work. Feminism provided a theoretical lens, a political position, and a substantive body of literature for the selection and situation of problems in leisure (see section 1, chapter 5 of this volume). Although feminist theory does not clearly stipulate rules for research, investigation, or interpretation, it encourages an exploration of all aspects of social life that contribute to inequality and oppression, including the study of men.

Therefore, I am a feminist who believes that studying men is a necessary step toward reaching the goals of feminism. According to Kimmel (1996b, 2009), feminism has changed the expectations and experiences of women to include those spheres of life that have traditionally been restricted and regulated by men. Those changes have impacted, influenced, and challenged men in a variety of ways. Feminist men have responded most directly and favorably to these feminist critiques and have used the resources of feminist thinking to begin a critique of the patriarchal social structures of masculinity. Hence, some of the theoretical perspectives of feminism shifted to include the lives of men.

However, men cannot appropriate the use of feminism for the study of gender (and masculinity) without consideration of the issues surrounding their privileged subjectivity as men. We must ensure that we are not responsible for creating and recreating androcentric biases, reinforcing male privilege, and/or erasing the important position of women in the creation and dissemination of new knowledge. Despite the challenges I face as a man doing feminist work, I am encouraged by feminists who desire men's participation. Harding (1991/1993) wrote:

> Men who want to be part of the solution rather than only the problem for feminism can promote the understanding produced by women feminists. They can criticize the sexism and androcentrism of male colleagues and of male thinkers, writers, and public figures. They can move material resources to women and to feminists. . . . What better alternative could there be for moving toward more democratic societies than . . . [for men] to join [women] and reinvent ourselves as "other"? (p. 161–162)

Uncovering (My Fragile) Masculinity

One Sunday afternoon in early April, a friend asked if I wanted to accompany him and some friends to the park for a picnic. As we settled in for a day in the sun, I removed my shoes and socks and cringed in embarrassment and disbelief. I had attended an AIDS benefit the night before that encouraged men and women to dress in costume and "play with" their gender identity. In the spirit of the event, I had painted my toenails hot pink. Without polish remover or the desire to take a trip to the drugstore, opting for time with friends on a beautiful spring day, I was now standing in the park with hot pink toenails shining in the cool green grass. My masculinity was now open to attack. Despite my attempt to muster some form of gender transgressivity, I felt feminine in front of my friends who upon noticing my pink toenails, began to revel in their masculine identities. I tried to get over it, but eventually put my shoes and socks back on in an effort to avoid the marks of femininity, which friends would constantly remind me of throughout the day. I did not wish to deal with that label of inferiority based entirely on having bright pink toenails in the wrong place at the wrong time.

For as long as I can remember I have been cognizant of the essentialized notion of what it is supposed to mean to be a man—most men do. I have not always been successful in my performance of it—most men aren't. Despite success or failure at presenting acceptable performances of manhood, a persuasive and often subversive set of cultural norms exist as part of mainstream discourse to inform and guide behavior. Connell (1995) described *masculinity* as those practices in which men (and sometimes women) engage male social gender roles, with the effects being expressed through the body, personality, and culture. Culture, then, serves as both a cause and effect of masculine behavior. In Western society, a masculinity has taken shape that secures and maintains dominance. Masculine power is balanced by the general symbolism of difference, whereby masculinity is valued over femininity. While masculinity is grounded in difference, it is not a static characteristic or personal identity trait. Masculinity, instead, is a fluid construct organized within social relations that ultimately changes those relations, such as in the contexts described above. According to Connell, masculinity is not just an object of knowledge but the interplay between the agency of the individual and the structure of social institutions.

Situating investigations specifically within culture and cultural practices is important as scholars approach the study of masculinity. By placing masculinity in a historical moment and cultural context, researchers examine how at that moment, in that culture, the framework of patriarchy emphasizes the control of emotions and denial of alternatives to heterosexuality around the construction of masculinity. As Humphries (1985) suggested, researchers "cannot take seriously the staple references to masculinity and instead develop our own images of how we want to be" (p. 77). Although masculinity could be performed in many ways, men often feel obligated consciously or unconsciously to perform masculinity in *hegemonic* ways—or ways that are dependent upon the current cultural climate and expressive of dominant ideological norms of masculinity.

Hegemonic Masculinity

Most people would agree that some socially constructed characteristics of masculinity are valued more than others. The value of those characteristics is often based on their relationship to dominant ideological discourses. *Hegemonic masculinity* is the configuration of male gender practices that serves to legitimize patriarchy and heterosexuality, which guarantees the dominant position of men and heterosexuals and the subordination of women and non-heterosexuals. Connell (1995) used terms such as *hegemonic masculinity* and *marginalized masculinities* to describe structures of practice constructed in social situations. Hegemonic masculinity fosters access to power for those who are heterosexual and male. Therefore, hegemonic masculinity is a powerful tool used to secure and maintain the current social order. Consequently, hegemonic masculinity is an elaborate performance of social authority. It is not easy to challenge openly. Men who eventually choose to separate from hegemonic masculinity choose to confront a dilemma of difference. Who would dare challenge and forgo such authority?

Resisting Hegemonic Masculinity

Despite the ways in which many men reinforce hegemonic masculinity, many men also openly challenge hegemonic masculinity. As Connell (1995) suggested, to understand gender means constantly going beyond gender into the realms of public culture that exist in peer groups, schools, workplaces, sports organizations, and the media. Within these institutions, how conventional definitions of masculinity are sustained and also how they are resisted can be examined.

Connell (1995) wrote that "Renunciation means giving up everyday masculine privileges and styles of interaction and also has important consequences for sexuality and emotional expression" (p. 131). Despite its usefulness, Connell indicated that renunciation could also cause a temporary loss of gender identity, resulting in the mockery of men by other men, increasing men's internalized sexism.

In addition to renunciation, men can use several other strategies to negotiate hegemonic masculinity including the enactment of hypermasculinity. To resist the stigma of effeminacy, men sometimes adopt hypermasculine qualities (Messner, 1997). This super-macho style is a celebration of hegemonic masculinity and permits men to distance themselves from the stigma associated with being effeminate and/or homosexual (Humphries, 1985). Men might over-conform and/or succumb to hypermasculinity in several ways. Butch attire, large muscles, and testosterone-induced images vividly articulate ideals of manhood (Levine, 1998). Consequently, hyper-masculine men become an idealized sexual image connected with symbolic power and strength. These sexualized images are perpetuated in stories, and more importantly in mass media related to jocks, military men, con-struction workers, and cowboys. Some parody may exist in men's adoption of hypermasculine styles, as they undoubtedly are making a cultural shift away from femininity (Connell, 1995).

MY SCHOLARSHIP ON MASCULINITY AND SEXUAL IDENTITY

With these presuppositions in mind, I have focused my line of inquiry on masculinity and sexual identity primarily in two areas: gay bars and media consumption.

Gay Bars

The gay bar has been an important space for gay men and lesbians since the gay liberation movement began, ignited by the riots that occurred outside the Stonewall bar in New York City at the end of the 1960s. Since the Stonewall riots, and perhaps even before the riots, the gay bar served as a pivotal site for gay male social life, providing a cultural environment where release and enjoyment can occur away from the heterosexualized locations of everyday life.

Although gay men have become more visible and have created ad-ditional and alternative spaces and places for their leisure, the gay bar remains a central social institution and leisure context for many gay men. For example, in my early research on leisure in the lives of gay and lesbian young adults, I reported that gay bars often served as:

> an emotional shelter where anti-hegemonic mores are not seen as sick or perverse but valuable and positive, providing a symbolic space and place for the discovery and being of a gay/lesbian identity in leisure. A gay/lesbian/homosexual space offers a perspective from which to see, create, and imagine an alternate reality. (Johnson, 2000, p. 17)

My intent is not to imply that the gay bar is a leisure context for all gay men, nor to speak about gay bars as monolithic sites that are always positive. In my review of the literature and personal experience, gay bars often focus on specific clientele, offer an array of types of entertainment, and may stratify themselves according to social identity categories such as gender and race. In addition, the size of the gay community, the geographic location of the bar, and access to alternative opportunities also heavily influence the culture of a gay bar. No matter what combination of characteristics stratify the clientele, the gay bar frequently serves as a leisure context and is a suitable site for examining the ways gay men construct, reinforce, resist, and transform meanings of masculinity.

Some of the most popular gay bars emphasize hypermasculinity or macho images. While all gay bars have examples of masculinity, those gay bars that celebrate hypermasculinity and machismo have interested me most. What I can speculate from research is that although gay men in hypermasculine bars sometimes celebrate and reinforce hegemonic heterosexual masculine ideologies, they also seem to openly challenge and/or create a new gendered meaning in these bars where they perceive freedom from heterosexual ideologies. Therefore, I chose to examine masculinity in a country-western gay bar.

The country-western culture for gay men has a certain novelty. Because country-western culture is grounded in heteronormative ideologies and gay men are perceived as the antithesis of those ideologies, individuals (both gay and straight) often find it hard to believe that country-western gay bars even exists. Further, people are struck by how much they tend to resemble heterosexual country-western bars they have been to before, despite the majority of the clientele being made up of gay men and lesbians.

After spending two years as an ethnographer in one country-western gay bar site, I was better able to identify social practices gay men used to actively negotiate their meanings of masculinity. Gay men in my study were active and creative agents who constructed their own subject position related to the social practices and cultural discourses in the bar. By examining these social practices and cultural discourses, I discerned how the gay men engaged in a negotiation process that included both acquiescence and opposition to heteromasculine ideologies. Interrogating the ways gay men in the bar simultaneously reinforced and challenged hegemonic masculinity helps to understand how the idealized (hetero)sexual messages connected to symbolic power, strength, and self-worth position gay men. Gay men serve as both the victims and benefactors of a patriarchal society, which maintains the perceived superiority of men. I identified three social practices used to negotiate the double bind of gay masculinity in that context. Each included aspects of resistance and/or reinforcement related to heterosexual masculinity: a) dancing the two-step (Johnson, 2005), b) dressing as a cowboy or regular guy (Johnson, 2008), and c) socially distancing themselves from women (Johnson & Samdahl, 2005).

Masculinity and Media

The products of popular and media culture not only exist to provide pleasure in the context of leisure—they also have the capacity to impart information about gendered and sexual identities through the transmission of cultural values and social norms. To be more critical of these meaning-making products, I have begun to scrutinize how these products convey normative social expectations and how those expectations continue to reinforce power relations and encourage domination and marginalization, building on the extant research into this topic.

For instance, scholars have examined the relationship between gay male identity and media. For the most part, their research describes the influence of media texts on the sexual-identity development of masculinity in gay men and how gay male identity affects the creation of new media. Much of the media is characterized as delaying or reversing the course of gay male identity development. For example, Carnaghi and Maass (2007) found that gay men "acquire a rich repertoire of disparaging terms" (p. 148) about their own cohort by internalizing the heterosexist stereotypes presented in the mass media. In addition to attitudes suggestive of inter-nalized homophobia, several researchers examined the ways in which het-eronormativity is replicated by the images of gay men in the media. Phillips (2006), for example, described the tendency of mass media to portray gay men as effeminate, which positions them as inferior to heterosexual men and ultimately might cause "negative psychological consequences, like poor self-esteem and negative self-judgments" (p. 407).

Male participants of various sexual orientations viewed stereotypi-cally effeminate gay men more negatively than stereotypically masculine gay men in a study by Glick and colleagues (2007). The authors credited the award-winning motion picture *Brokeback Mountain* for popularizing the images of hegemonic masculine gay men as more acceptable than those who are more feminine. Glick et al. theorized that the less masculine-acting the gay man, the more likely he was to be *Othered* not only due to his at-traction to men, but also due to a seeming resemblance to women. In other words, such men violate the gender norms of sexual identity. Exceptions in reality shows such as *Queer Eye for the Straight Guy* present five gay men as experts in stereotypically feminine endeavors such as fashion, decorat-ing, and cuisine (Pullen, 2007). However, these gay men are summoned to help heterosexual men (who are portrayed as inept at the aforementioned skills) pursue relationships with discerning women. Although the show has been marked as progressive, gay males in *Queer Eye* are portrayed as at the service of heterosexuals: males and females in pursuit of heteronormative relationships. Thereby, according to Pullen, homosexual desire is disavowed.

Given that young men consume large quantities of media, my line of inquiry has focused specifically on how media consumption influences the ways in which young men construct their identities through a media socialization process. Consistent with participatory-action research, collective-memory work was the technique used to allow men to recall, examine, and analyze their earliest media memories and experiences within a broader cultural context. I sought how their individual experiences linked to collective, shared experiences of similar and/or different men in society (Haug, 1992). What I found is that men drew distinct differences between their individual understandings of self *and* the social pressures of gender and sexual identity socialization as they wrote, analyzed, and interpreted their media memories. This process gave participants an opportunity to engage in social science research that solidified and challenged their own hegemonic thinking related to what it means to men (Kivel & Johnson, 2009), white men and men of color (Johnson, Richmond, & Kivel, 2008), and gay and straight men (Johnson & Dunlap, 2009).

MAPPING NEW DIRECTIONS

More scholarship on masculinity and sexual identity in leisure studies must occur. More researchers must to do it! However, the complex tensions raised in examining masculinity and sexual identity over the past 12 years have changed how I think about emancipation for men, women, and sexual minorities as well as sexual majorities. I believe in striving for equality and first-class citizenship rights for all people through institutional policies and/or the effective training of leisure service professionals. However, considering the tensions and additional questions raised in my scholarship, I believe researchers are often just managing shifts in discourses that create a *virtual equality* (Vaid, 1995). I believe to escape the confining and oppressive structures of gender and sexual identity, both intellectual and political mobility—grounded firmly in the communities where people live—are needed so that hegemony (and power) are situated and understood as contextual and contingent.

This intellectual and political mobility can be entered into leisure studies, and leisure in general, through conceptualizations inspired by *Queer*. The concept of Queer helps explore and interrogate the discourses where, in contexts like gay bars and media, gender and sexual identity are simultaneously produced in, and most importantly produced by, leisure. As a form of identity (i.e., Queer), a system of thinking (i.e., queer theory), and a means of action (i.e., queering), queer subverts the privilege, entitlement, and status obtained through hegemonic masculinity and heterosexuality, and questions how those behaviors function to maintain dominance. Queer moves beyond the limits of difference offered by the masculine/feminine binary and categories of sexual identity (e.g., straight, gay, lesbian), and instead interrogates their existence. Queer attempts to become more transgressive and socially transformative, forcing the consideration of social responsibility and perhaps, the audacity of socially constructed categories.

* * *

As the dust settles around us at the rodeo, the announcer calls participants over for the Wild Drag Race. As Nicholas and I continue our discusssion, our eyes wander with each man that passes, but our conversation never skips a beat. Finally, one man brings our conversation to a halt. Silence spreads over us and all our heads turn sharply to the left as Alex says, "Uh, um, well . . . who gives a damn why they dress that way as long as they keep doing it!" The cowboy passing seems to hear Alex or feels our stares and he turns his head over his shoulder and tips his wide brim tan cowboy hat in our direction offering a sly smile. He knows we are watching and laughs to himself. This man, dressed like many of the rodeo participants, is in a dusty pair of worn cowboy boots halfway covered by his worn Wrangler blue jeans that pull tight around his legs and rear. Despite the heat, his shirt is long sleeved and plaid, tucked at the waist. On his back is a white square piece of paper with the number 16 in black letters pinned to the shoulders. Although I missed it the first time he passed, when he passes by again I confirm what I already know: an unneeded, shiny silver belt buckle rests on the front of his stomach, somewhere between his belly-button and his bulging crotch. Once again he catches us staring (and Alex drooling). This time he stares back. Alex smiles and says, "We sure have come a long way from Brokeback Mountain." I smile and understand that indeed my two lines of research inquiry are more connected than I had ever imagined.

REFERENCES

Carnaghi, A., & Maass, A. (2007). In-group and out-group perspectives in the use of derogatory group labels: Gay versus fag. *Journal of Language and Social Psychology, 26*(2), 142–156.

Connell, R. W. (1995). *Masculinities.* Cambridge, UK: Polity.

Glick, P., Gangl, C., Gibb, S., Klumpner, S., & Weinberg, E. (2007). Defensive reactions to masculinity threat: More negative affect toward effeminate (but not masculine) gay men. *Sex Roles, 57*(1), 55–59.

Harding, S. (1991/1993). Reinventing ourselves as other: More new agents of history and knowledge. In L. S. Kauffman (Ed.), *American feminist thought at century's end: A reader* (pp. 140–164). Cambridge, MA: Blackwell.

Haug, F. (1992). Feminist writing: Working with women's experiences. *Feminist Review, 42* (Autumn), 16–32.

Henderson, K. A. (1991b). *Dimensions of choice: A qualitative approach to recreation, parks, and leisure research.* State College, PA: Venture Publishing, Inc.

Humphries, M. (1985). Gay machismo. In A. Metcalf & M. Humphries (Eds.), *The sexuality of men* (pp. 70–85). London, UK: Pluto Press.

Johnson, C. W. (1998). *Living the game of hide and seek: Leisure in the lives of gay and lesbian young adults.* (Unpublished master's thesis). University of North Carolina, Chapel Hill, NC.

Johnson, C. W. (2000). Living the game of hide and seek: Leisure in the lives of gay and lesbian young adults. *Leisure, 24*(3/4), 255–278.

Johnson, C. W. (2005). "The first step is the two-step": Gay men's negotiation strategies of a traditionally gendered dance. *International Journal of Qualitative Studies in Education, 18*(4), 445–464.

Johnson, C. W. (2008). "Don't call him a cowboy": Masculinity, cowboy drag, and a costume change. *Journal of Leisure Research, 40*(3), 385–403.

Johnson, C. W., & Dunlap, R. J. (2009, October). Collective memories of men's sexual identities and media consumption. *Abstracts from the 2009 Leisure Research Symposium.* Asburn, VA: National Recreation and Park Association.

Johnson, C. W., Richmond, L., & Kivel, B. (2008). "What a man ought to be, he is far from": Exploring collective meanings of masculinity & race in media. *Leisure/Losir, 32*(2), 1–28.

Johnson, C. W., & Samdahl, D. M. (2005). "The night they took over": Gay men's reaction to lesbian night in a country-western gay bar. *Leisure Sciences, 27*(4), 331–348.

Kimmel, M. S. (1996b). Baseball and the reconstitution of American masculinity. In M. A. Messner & D. F. Sabo (Eds.), *Sport, men, and the gender order: Critical feminist perspectives* (pp. 55–66). Champaign, IL: Human Kinetics Books.

Kimmel, M. S. (2008). *Guyland: The perilous world where boys become men.* New York, NY: Harper.

Kivel, B., & Johnson, C. W. (2009). Consuming media, making men: Using collective memory work to understand leisure and the construction of masculinity. *Journal of Leisure Research, 41*(1), 105–129.

Levine, M. P. (1998). *Gay macho: The life and death of the homosexual clone.* New York, NY: New York University Press.

Louganis, G., & Marcus, E. (1995). *Breaking the surface* (1st ed.). New York, NY: Random House.

Messner, M. A. (1997). *Politics of masculinities: Men in movements.* Thousand Oaks, CA: Sage.

Phillips, D. A. (2006). Masculinity, male development, gender, and identity: Modern and postmodern meanings. *Issues in Mental Health Nursing, 27*(4), 403–423.

Pullen, C. (2007). *Documenting gay men: Identity and performance in reality television and documentary film.* Jefferson, NC: McFarland.

Vaid, U. (1995). *Virtual equality: The mainstreaming of gay and lesbian liberation.* New York, NY: Anchor.

SECTION 3
LIVES IN SOCIAL CONTEXTS

Chapter 19
Introduction: Social Identities, Relations, and Practices

Valeria J. Freysinger, Susan M. Shaw, Karla A. Henderson, and M. Deborah Bialeschki

The chapters of section 2 illustrated some of the many activities that girls and women think of as recreation and leisure; the outcomes of those experiences; and the gendered opportunities for, and constraints to, their leisure. These discussions reveal the ways in which "personal lives" are enacted in, and cannot be separated from, social contexts. The chapters in section 3 further examine some of those contexts, most specifically family and work. They provide insight into how social contexts interact with what might be called social identities (i.e., identities associated with age, gender, race, ethnicity, able-bodiedness, and/or social class), and how these identities are shaped and performed in leisure. Further, the chapters illuminate the consequences of leisure (or its lack) for girls' and women's well-being and development across the course of life.

This section is roughly organized around the discourse of chronological age and development. There is both continuity and change in how we engage with friends/peers, family, and paid work as we move across life. There is also consistency, as well as change, in meanings and practices of gender, race, ethnicity, social class, and able-bodiedness as we age, because we are historically situated biological, psychological, and sociocultural beings. Thus, the chapters in this section help to reveal how recreation and leisure are contexts for these social practices and processes.

The Discourse of Chronological Age and Development

In many societies, chronological age (or years since birth) is one way to "structure" or think about individuals' lives, and the continuity and change they experience as they move from childhood through later adulthood. Chronological age is seen as a useful way to conceptualize individuals' lives, because it is believed to be an indication of several issues that are socially meaningful across a variety of cultures, though cultures differ as well in the meanings they make of age. In general, age is thought to be an indication of an individual's capabilities and capacities or maturation (physical, cognitive, emotional, and social). Because of maturation, chronological age is also the basis for assigning or allowing individuals certain rights and privileges in many cultures (e.g., the right to legally drive or consume alcohol or to collect one's pension without penalty). Further, because of our age we are expected by familiar others, and society in general, to have the capacity to perform various social "roles" and responsibilities. Finally, chronological age identifies our year of birth (or birth cohort), indicating the era or historical period through which we have lived, the social and cultural changes and historical events we have experienced as a consequence, and at what age we experienced them.

Some of these ways of thinking about leisure, age, and development are both illustrated *and* complicated by the research presented in the chapters in this section. For example, in order to participate in a sport, a child must have the physical potential to develop the necessary sport-specific skills, the cognitive maturity to understand the rules of the game, the emotional capacity to deal with winning and losing, and the social maturity to constructively interact with teammates and coaches. However, how we determine if and when children have those capacities is not as straightforward as it may seem, as Anderson's chapter on the sport participation of girls with disabilities illustrates. Another example relates to parents' involvement in children's play and recreation and the social expectations for such involvement. Trussell explored this enactment of parenthood in her research and found how sport participation is a gendered practice for both children and their parents. Similarly, an increasingly common "role" for mid-life and older women is caregiving for aging parents, spouse or partner, and/or other family members. Bedini's research provides important insights into how this gendered undertaking alters the experience and significance of leisure for these women.

The relationship between age and leisure has been conceptualized as *derivative, adjustive, generative,* and *maladaptive* (Kleiber, 1999). For example, Sullivan's chapter on the leisure of first-time mothers and Trussell's research on mother's and father's involvement in children's youth sport participation illustrate, among other things, the derivative nature of leisure—changes in leisure as an outcome of becoming and being a parent. The adjustive potential of leisure is addressed in Howard's chapter on African American women's experience of work. Howard contends that leisure might well be a way for these women who experience both racism and sexism in their daily lives in the academy, to cope with negative work and renew/enhance their sense of self and well-being. The participation of girls with disabilities in sport, as explored by Anderson, provides evidence of the generative potential of leisure, since not only did these girls experience growth and development as *girls* and as *female athletes* through their participation, but their parents and peers also developed a different perspective on ability as they learned about the athletic potential of these girls, despite their disabilities. Recreation and leisure as contexts of identity development are also discussed by Tirone and Gahagan. Their qualitative, longitudinal research highlights the implications of this process for the health of adolescents and young adults who are the children of first-generation Indian and Pakistani immigrants to Canada. However, their research further indicates one way that leisure may be maladaptive or an impediment to women's health and development: that is, when leisure is a space/place and practice of sexism and/or racism.

Childhood, adolescence, young and middle adulthood, later life, identity development, family, parenthood, paid work, grandparenthood, and caregiving are often seen as some of the "normative" stages and practices of the life course. However, developmental and life-course perspectives typically frame the social contexts of girls' and women's lives within a particular lens—a lens that rarely captures gender, able-bodiedness, race, ethnicity, class, and sexual orientation and how these factors intersect with each other and with age. This lens, then, cannot fully account for the fluidity of identities. It does not acknowledge relations of power, is not activist in orientation, and rarely incorporates feminist insights.

At the same time, feminist approaches to leisure research, while increasingly cognizant of the diversity of women's experiences, pay relatively little attention to age in general and later life, specifically. A number of chapters in this section of the book, though, bring together insights from feminist thinking and developmental perspectives. For example, in their chapter Tirone and Gahagan describe how Canadian Indian and Pakistani youth respond differently to racism as young adults compared to when they were adolescents. Was such change in sense of self and others due to maturation (an "internal" process) or life experiences ("external" forces)? Perhaps, as noted by the authors, an explanation can be found in "both/and" rather than "either/or" thinking. That is, age and aging are also social constructed and culturally and historically situated. We construct categories of difference—and (in)equality—when we decide that years since birth are meaningful in specific ways, with the social significance we make of those years and associated bodily and psychological changes and with our social and cultural practices that change across history and shape individuals' experiences of aging from birth 'til death. Women at ages 22, 47, and 71 have both common experiences as women and different experiences because of their ages.

Collectively, then, the chapters in this section challenge us to conduct more nuanced research, research that employs "both/and" rather than "either/or" thinking. As represented by the matryoshka, women's lives are complex and this complexity requires us to de-center the personal and incorporate the social and cultural.

DE-CENTERING THE PERSONAL AND CENTERING THE SOCIAL

What is often missing from life-course and developmental, as well as feminist, approaches to leisure is addressed in the research and thinking presented in the chapters in this book. While the chapters in this section illustrate some of the meanings of chronological age and how it is one way to understand girls' and women's recreation and leisure, the chapters also clearly present the possibilities for what a critical, activist, and feminist lens or approach to understanding the social contexts of leisure, women, and gender across life might look like. As noted above, these chapters explore and illuminate the complexity of social lives. They illustrate that leisure is a space/place/practice where gender, race, class, (dis)ability, age, and sexual orientation are always enacted and sometimes resisted and transformed.

Further, these chapters provide ample evidence that women are "pulled" in many different directions, facing multiple and often competing demands and responsibilities in their lives as daughters, mothers, grandmothers, friends, spouses, lovers, sisters, and community members. They also show just how and why it is too simplistic to think of leisure as freedom of the individual (as if the individual exists separate from society, culture, and history) and as necessarily "positive" or "beneficial" (as if leisure exists separately from relations of power). That is, these chapters "positively complicate" our understandings of leisure, women, and gender. Specifically, the chapters illustrate that the social contexts of girls' and women's lives powerfully shape their leisure and challenge us to think more critically about our notions of family leisure, work and leisure, and leisure and health/coping.

For example, Sullivan's chapter on the leisure of new mothers indicates that some life changes can be so overwhelming and "identity bending" that there is no space for leisure to be a way to cope with new responsibilities and expectations, that is, for leisure to be *adjustive*. In fact, even thinking about leisure may be distressing, as it presents a reminder of what used to be and no longer is—a self that has been lost. Sullivan found that "the shock" of new motherhood did not wait until the birth of the baby. Rather, she heard from these women that they "had not been in touch with much of 'their leisure' since becoming pregnant" (see p. 306). Even the best prepared were caught off-guard by the changes that becoming a mother brought—changes related to one's sense of one's body, a lack of time for self and feelings of guilt when it was taken, exhaustion, and a disconnect with husbands or male partners. All of these changes constrained the possibility of leisure, even for the women in Sullivan's study who were relatively well-educated and living in economically stable, two-parent households. Given the many possibilities and expectations about girls' and women's lives in societies where the battle for "equal rights" is believed by many to be over, Sullivan contends that to experience motherhood is to experience a "contradiction between being a mother and being a woman in today's society" (see p. 298).

Harrington's chapter provides further insight into why this is so. Based on her critical reading of the literature on family leisure, and her research on class, gender, identity, and leisure in Australian families, Harrington discusses family as a space within which gender and class are enacted, and leisure as a space within which family and gender are performed. Rather than thinking about family as a set of relationships and roles, a system, or a "social institution," Harrington suggests that we think of family as "performative space"—that is, a space where we do "family things." We call many of those "family things" we do leisure. It is not too far of a stretch to think about leisure as a space for "practicing" and "displaying" to others "our family," and that those practices and performances are gendered and classed. As noted by Harrington, "(f)rom this perspective, family leisure consists of sets of activities that show to relevant others that you are a 'good' (or 'bad' or 'indifferent') mother or father to the children you are raising. This conceptualization also helps us understand why parents talk about themselves as a 'sporting family,' an 'active family,' or indeed a 'stay-at-home family'" (see p. 327). Harrington implores us not to idealize or romanticize family leisure and shows us how doing so ignores the gendered, and potentially oppressive, experiences and practices of family. At the same time, it renders some families "healthy" and others "dysfunctional," and these consequences cannot be separated from classism and racism. She provides us with a perspective that allows us to think about family leisure differently; an approach that recognizes the individual in context and that there is pleasure and meaning, as well as oppression and constraint, in family leisure.

The possibility of both pleasure and constraint in family leisure is also evident in Trussell's chapter on the gendered enactment of family leisure. In her research, Trussell has explored organized youth sport and how it may serve to reinforce, resist, and/or transform dominant gender ideologies within families and the larger society. As Trussell notes, despite legislation and policy in many countries intended to create equality in children's physical activity and sport participation, boys' participation continues to exceed that of girls'. In part this is due to parental support (or lack thereof), especially when it comes to children's participation in types of sport that challenge traditional gender ideologies. Similarly, research indicates that *how* parents support their children's youth sport participation is often gendered as well. Yet, the sports in which children participate *and/or* the ways their parents are involved *may* be an opportunity to resist and transform dominant notions of gender. For example, in her research on rural Canadian parents' and children's participation in organized sport, Trussell found that girls playing ice hockey was increasingly acceptable, though it entailed some adjustments in the process. Further, some mothers reported tensions between the more egalitarian attitudes that they believed characterized their families and the more traditional gender ideologies of sport and the larger community. At the same time, Trussell suggested that the idea of equality was clearer for the young women in the study than the young men (Schmalz, this volume). In terms of parental involvement, Trussell found that while the "public face" of youth sport organizations was increasingly one of egalitarianism, dads continued to perform the more visible and central roles in children's youth sport (e.g., coach, trainer) and moms the more supportive roles (e.g., team manager, fundraising). Trussell concludes that in North America and elsewhere today, "active" and "sporting" families are highly valued and seen as an indication of concerned and responsible parenting (see also Coakley, 2009; Harrington, this volume). Still her and others' research indicates that parenting, the caring and raising of children, continues to be a "mother-led dance" (Dyck & Daly, 2009).

A number of other chapters in this section also illustrate the centrality of caregiving to women's lives, the satisfactions and stress it may engender, and the potential role leisure might play in coping and in women's mental and physical health. Bedini explores family caregiving and caregivers' leisure. She proposes that caregiving should be seen as a new "life stage," like marriage and parenthood, work and retirement. Bedini traces the history of research and policy related to caregiving generally, and caregiving and leisure, specifically. The fact that it took as long as it did for researchers and policymakers in the United States to recognize family caregiving and the constraints and challenges it brings to those (predominantly women) providing the care for family members (aging spouse, parents) speaks volumes about women's continuing status as "second-class" citizens, the undervaluation of their family work, and the relatively low status of older people in many Western societies. This is especially so when the degree to which family caregiving puts the caregiver (particularly female caregivers) at risk for poor health and earlier mortality is recognized. Bedini and colleagues' initial research in this area showed that while family caregivers valued their leisure, the time and energy caregiving required of them left them with little leisure—personal or otherwise. They also found that until the end of the twentieth century, discussions about caregiver stress often ignored the potential role of leisure in mitigating such stress. Further, recreation agencies and professionals were most times excluded from any conversations about how to best address this problem. Bedini's subsequent research with family caregivers has highlighted the complexity of their perceptions of leisure. However, Bedini concludes that what we know about caregiving in North America, particularly about leisure and caregiving, is primarily about white women's experiences. Her recognition of this fact highlights our limited understanding of the intersections of gender and race in the context of family caregiving and leisure.

How and why race and ethnicity distinguish the family context of women's lives and leisure is discussed by Shinew and Stodolska, who have explored the relationships between ethnicity, race, gender, immigration status, and leisure, and most recently the leisure-time physical activity (LTPA) of Latina women in the United States. Their interest in this topic stems from several concerns including the reported health disparities between non-Hispanic Whites and Latinos and the relatively low LTPA participation on the part of Latina women regardless of their education, occupation, or marital status. Both their research and the research of others identify several distinct values of Latino culture that shape gendered experiences of family: collectivism, *familismo*, *personalisimo*, and *marianismo/machismo*. These values emphasize the group/family/community as opposed to the individual, personal as opposed to institutional relationships, and "traditional" gender relationships. They powerfully shape Latina women's time for and feelings of entitlement to LTPA or personal leisure. At the same time, how the Latina women in Chicago who Shinew and Stodolska studied think about physical activity—the meanings they make of and purposes they see for physical activity—are also influenced by the reality of their limited discretionary income, paid work, family, neighborhoods, community agencies, and the attitudes of many in the United States towards Latinos. That is, it is not only ethnicity and economic-marginality perspectives (Floyd, 1998) that help to explain Latina women's experiences of leisure. Issues of discrimination and feelings of (un)welcomeness (Phillips, 2000) must be considered, too.

Howard also explicitly addresses the intersections of gender and race in her chapter, specifically in relation to women's employment and health. As a graduate student in Health Promotion, Howard was troubled by the research on leisure-time physical activity and health that equated race and social class, and by how the statistics that "documented" the poorer health status of African American women shaped public discourse on race and health. The resourcefulness and resilience of black women in facing and responding to material and immaterial disadvantage in adaptive ways was absent in this discourse. Hence, she undertook research on the work experiences of African American women who were university professors, a relatively privileged group in terms of education, occupation, and income. She gained rich (and disturbing) insights into just how racism and sexism "work" in the "post-Civil Rights" United States and how these women "cope with" such discrimination. Her research clearly illustrates the limitations of "functionalist" analyses of the work-leisure and health-leisure relationship and the advantages of using black feminist theory (e.g., Collins, 2000a). Howard found that the African American women in her study struggled with, negotiated, were exhausted by, resisted, contested, and worked to change and transform their racist and sexist workplaces. Her research provides "some insight into the particular stress that racism and sexism impose." Hence, Howard's chapter suggests that research on leisure, stress, and coping/health would benefit from employing a black feminist approach that recognizes "the unique constraints and challenges that confront those facing a lifetime of structural disadvantages" (see p. 365).

Scraton and Watson, whose research has also centered the tensions between and the intersection of individual experiences and collective power relations, present their work on older people, family, and leisure in the United Kingdom in their chapter, and again the significance of caregiving in women's lives is highlighted. Their initial work on this topic was with older white women but subsequently included the leisure of people diverse in class, gender, ethnicity, and age. This work has revealed the degree to which grandparenting specifically, and family generally, are important contexts of older individuals' leisure. Importantly, their approach has incorporated a critical social analysis of aging that challenges the dominant discourse of aging as deficiency or loss. Scraton and Watson examined leisure not only in terms of how the ethic of care continued to construct a gendered discourse around grandmotherhood and domestic work but also at grandfatherhood and leisure. In this work on the leisure lives of older people, Scraton and Watson have found family and leisure experiences in old age (including grandparenting) continue to be gendered regardless of material differences of class and ethnicity. At the same time they have found that older women evidence both agency and resistance through leisure, indicating "the potential of using a 'leisure' lens on the lives of older people in order to challenge the dominant pathological view of ageing and the stereotypical view of older people as passive 'victims' of age, culture, ethnicity, and gender" (see p. 387). The resourcefulness of older women, their ability to cope with and adapt to changing life circumstances and to create meaningful and pleasurable experiences in the things they were still able to do, often in the face of material constraints, is a significant finding of their research and parallels the agency of African American women discussed by Howard.

CONCLUSION

The chapters in this section illustrate girls' and women's gendered experiences of leisure and recreation across the course of life. They also illuminate the diverse *and* shared experiences of gender, of being girls and women, at different points in the life course. Further, they demonstrate some of the many ways to study, think about, and understand the social contexts of girls' and women's lives and leisure. These include studying leisure in relation to specific types of activity participation (i.e., sport), family practices (i.e., parenting and grandparenting), and work experiences (including both paid and unpaid labor). Finally, these chapters demonstrate the importance of examining how gender intersects with able-bodiedness, social class, race, and/or ethnicity across the course of life—as well as the challenges of such research. For example, Shinew and Stodolska note that a major challenge in researching Latina women's leisure is defining "Latino." Racial identifications are both problematic and meaningful and this needs to be addressed in our research (Freysinger & Harris, 2006; West, 1994).

As much as these chapters tell us about how gender and its intersections with other social identities shape women's leisure, they also inform us about how gender, age, race, social class, and/or able-bodiedness "work" or are enacted in leisure. Further, as discussed by Harrington, leisure is a space/place where family and gendered and classed parenting are performed. That is, these chapters challenge us to think in more complex and nuanced ways about leisure. Thinking of leisure only as an "independent" (its effect on health, for example) or "dependent" (e.g., how age changes leisure participation) variable ignores leisure as social and cultural practices that are historically situated. The next section provides further evidence for this conceptualization of leisure and the important insights such a perspective can provide us as we seek to more fully understand leisure, women, and gender.

REFERENCES

Coakley, J. (2009). The good father: Parental expectations and youth sports. In T. A. Kay (Ed.), *Fathering through sport and leisure* (pp. 40–50). New York, NY: Routledge.

Collins, P. H. (2000a). *Black feminist thought: Knowledge, consciousness, and the politics of empowerment* (2nd ed.). New York, NY: Routledge.

Dyck, V., & Daly, K. (2009). Rising to the challenge: Fathers' role in the negotiation of couple time. In T. A. Kay (Ed.), *Fathering through sport and leisure* (pp. 183–199). New York, NY: Routledge.

Floyd, M. (1998). Getting beyond marginality and ethnicity: The challenge for race and ethnic studies in leisure research. *Journal of Leisure Research, 30*(1), 3–22.

Freysinger, V. J., & Harris, O. (2006). Race and leisure. In C. Rojek, S. M. Shaw, & A. J. Veal (Eds.), *A handbook of leisure studies*. London, UK: Palgrave MacMillan.

Kleiber, D. (1999). *Leisure experiences and human development: A dialectical approach*. New York, NY: Basic.

Philipp, S. F. (2000). Race and the pursuit of happiness. *Journal of Leisure Research, 32*(1), 121–124.

West, C. (1994). *Race matters*. New York, NY: Vintage.

CHAPTER 20
"YES, I'M A GIRL . . . AND I HAVE A DISABILITY . . . BUT I'M ALSO AN ATHLETE!": GETTING OFF THE SIDELINES WITH DISABILITY SPORT

DENISE M. ANDERSON

> "Equal opportunity to participate in sport, whether for the purpose of leisure and recreation, health promotion, or high performance, is the right of every woman, regardless of race, color, language, religion, creed, sexual orientation, age, marital status, disability, political belief or affiliation, national or social origin." (Brighton Declaration on Women and Sport, 1994)

I was, am, and always will consider myself to be, an athlete. While I do not currently engage in competitive sport, my ties to sport and physical activity remain an integral part of who I am. Both organized and informal sport and recreation pursuits provided me with outlets that in my youth and young adulthood I identified as places filled with camaraderie and good times. They allowed me entrée into something special, something that gave my life that extra meaning. As an adult, I reflect on that time and recognize the outcomes as much more than they initially appeared: self-esteem, leadership abilities, relatedness, self-efficacy, independence, health—the list could go on. Of course, I also believed that these experiences were available to everyone who sought them, either on a school team (in rural Illinois that was the only option) or in pickup games with neighbors or classmates on the playground. Not everyone may make the high school team, but, I reasoned, everyone can run around the block or sign up for a recreational summer swim team—or so I thought. What I explore in this chapter illuminates my faulty thinking as a high school student. Specifically, the chapter presents what I have learned over the years in my teaching, research, and practice about the sport and other physically active recreation participation of girls with disabilities. The first step in this discussion is a second look at the research that I have conducted on girls with disabilities and their participation in sport and physically active recreation. Specifically, the first section of the chapter looks at the meanings of sport and activity participation held by the girls who I interviewed, all but two of whom had been born with a congenital physical disability such as spina bifida or osteogenesis imperfecta (brittle bone disease). The two who did not have a congenital disability were twins who were conjoined at the waist at birth and when surgically separated, were left "amputees" in that each only had one leg. In the next section of the chapter, I describe the constraints that still impact the sport and physical-activity participation of girls and women with disabilities (despite equal opportunity legislation in the United States, such as the American with Disabilities Act), outlining specific constraints that were identified by the girls in my research, including the lack of relevant role models. Because my research was not specifically limited to addressing the *formal sport* participation of girls with disabilities, much of it has as a central focus the differences in girls' experiences based on whether their participation was limited to informal sport and physical activity or included formal participation on sport teams. Finally, the chapter ends with a critical look at what I envision to be the next steps for researchers and practitioners alike in continuing to address the role that physical activity and sport can and should be playing in the lives of girls (and women) with disabilities.

Meanings of Participation in Sport and Physically Active Recreation

The benefits of engagement in sport and informal physical activity are well documented. In short, participation can lead to greater psychological, mental, and emotional functioning, as a number of other chapters in the volume illustrate (e.g., see Bedini; Frisby; Fullagar; Hutchinson; Parry; Shannon; and Tirone & Gahagan, this volume). However, what does physical activity specifically mean to adolescent girls with physical disabilities? In the research that I have conducted with these girls, they have identified a number of meanings of, as well as constraints to, engagement in physical activity (Anderson, Bedini, & Moreland, 2005; Bedini & Anderson, 2005). First, physical activity allows girls with disabilities the chance to simply get out and move, and they recognize the inherent benefit of that. Girls with disabilities feel that active recreation is important because of the health benefits, both physical and psychological, of movement. Perhaps more important though is the freedom it provides; a freedom that can serve as an equalizer, leveling different playing fields, not just athletic ones, between those with and without disabilities.

Freedom, seen by many in North America as an inherent quality of participation in what is identified as leisure, is recognized by girls with disabilities as freedom *from* their disability (freedom to forget), freedom *to* have fun, as well as freedom *to* gain independence. They appreciate the fact that physically active recreation programs provide them with opportunities away from home and help them "minimize" their disabilities. That is, if they are not confined to individualized, home-bound activities, they become more like girls without disabilities, thus making the disability a smaller piece of who they are and what they are about. Thus, organized physical activity may provide them with a sense of empowerment, the place where they can "feel like others." Participation provides them with a freedom that other activities do not in that it allows them to transcend their disability. While some may anticipate that the girls would be further reminded of their "limitations" in a physically demanding activity, in my research I have found the opportunity to participate in sports and other physically active leisure allowed them a space in which they could forget they were different from others. The girls saw themselves as "athletes," not as "wheelchair athletes," but simply "athletes." This was even more apparent for the girls who had the opportunity to participate on a high-school swim team, where obviously a wheelchair would not be used (Anderson et al., 2005; Anderson, Wozencroft, & Bedini, 2008). Participation in physically active leisure may also provide a context for them to enter into what Csikszentmihalyi (1997) has identified as a state of flow, losing self-consciousness as they become immersed in the activity. Furthermore, the girls reported that their engagement in physical activity allowed *others* to transform their image of people with disabilities (Anderson et al., 2008). Unfortunately, these same girls have also indicated that there are not many opportunities for them to engage in physically active recreation outside the realm of home or physical therapy.

CONSTRAINTS TO PARTICIPATION IN SPORT AND PHYSICALLY ACTIVE RECREATION

As outlined and illustrated elsewhere in this book, girls and women have always faced constraints to participation in leisure that are gender-bound. Girls' physical activity rates continue to lag behind boys due to gender stereotypes, homophobia, parents' perceptions of safety, and lack of community programming (French & Hainsworth, 2001; Kolkka & Williams, 1997). My research indicates that other barriers include lack of affordable and accessible recreation facilities, low social support, and a simple lack of anticipated enjoyment for activities that are offered. Girls in my study also report having fewer active role models to whom they can look when charting their own path, either toward or away from an active lifestyle, whether it be in organized sport or informal physical activity.

Smith and colleagues (Smith, Austin, Kennedy, Lee, & Hutchinson, 2005) have suggested that there are three general categories of barriers that prevent people with disabilities, regardless of gender, from participating in leisure: intrinsic barriers (e.g., participant's lack of knowledge, health problems), environmental barriers (e.g., architectural impediments, others' attitudes), and communication barriers (e.g., language barriers for non-English speaking participants, staff without basic sign language skills). For girls with disabilities specifically, the barriers intensify as they experience stereotypes tied not only to their sex but also their disability, misperceptions related to their abilities as girls and as girls with a disability, particularly a "visible" disability. In addition to these and other stigmas associated with being a girl with a disability, lack of social support and structural constraints related to accessibility and affordability may also constrain participation. Inadequate staffing of programs is a very real hurdle both to program availability as well as to program satisfaction. Researchers have referred to some of this lack of opportunity as "barriers of omission" where a specific barrier may not be present but the needs of a group are not being met (Smith et al., 2005). For example, despite the passage of the Americans with Disabilities Act (ADA) and Title IX in the United States, in my research I have found that girls with disabilities continue to report lack of opportunities as a significant barrier to their participation in sport and other physically active recreation (Anderson et al., 2005; Anderson et al., 2008; Bedini & Anderson, 2005). In addition to a lack of staffing, in some instances a mandate to provide programs for the majority may leave out the minority, particularly if that programming is seen as inherently difficult to provide and budgets are tight.

I have found that girls with disabilities also identify a lack of role models as a constraint to their physical activity participation. This constraint no doubt serves as a double-edged sword in that lack of opportunities likely leads to fewer role models over time, and fewer role models means fewer people fighting for increased opportunities. Even when opportunities may present themselves, girls report that their participation is influenced by stigma. That is, they report being stared at and being seen as helpless, which may lead to their being the recipient of overprotection when they do have the opportunity to participate in activities such as water skiing or wheelchair basketball. In the United States, Title IX has been in existence for over 40 years, and yet gender disparities in sport participation still exist for able-bodied women. Extant research indicates the "double whammy" of being both female and having a disability lends itself to even less participation, as these girls and women must negotiate intersecting constraints (Deegan, 1985; Henderson & King, 1998).

Whether by choice or necessity, girls with disabilities often find themselves engaged in activities that may more accurately be classified as *informal participation*, participation that occurs around the home or neighborhood rather than the formal participation of league play; disability sport competitions on local, state, regional, or national levels; or community-based recreation programs. Regardless of the reasons behind the types of participation in which girls with disabilities are more likely to be engaged, my research has found that there is a difference in the experiences tied to the participation, at least with regard to physically active recreation.

THE IMPORTANCE OF TYPE OF SPORT AND PHYSICAL ACTIVITY PARTICIPATION

In trying to more clearly understand the impact that sport and physical activity can have on girls with disabilities, my research has also tried to determine if there are any discernible differences between the experiences of girls who participate in *formal* or *organized* sport (e.g., wheelchair basketball, wheelchair track and field, swim team) and girls whose primary physical activity participation might be classified as *informal* (e.g., catch in the backyard, shooting hoops in the driveway) (Bedini & Anderson, 2005). Striking differences between the two groups were related to social support. For example, the two groups of girls differed in terms of how various social groups including parents, family friends, personal friends, peers, and role models showed (or did not show) support for their participation in sport *as well as* their place in the larger world. As a metaphor for life in that larger world, sport is often seen as a context for life lessons related to such things as disappointment, coping, stress, and leadership, but it is also a context for friendship, support, teamwork, and social integration. Therefore, the context it provides for facilitating social support for girls with disabilities has implications beyond the playing arena. Yet, what this support looks like, and the impact it has, appears to differ dependent upon the structure of the activity.

Both formal and informal recreation activities undoubtedly provide opportunities for increased socialization and social support. This participation also has the potential to facilitate social support beyond sport. However, this benefit of participation appears to be more diverse and far-reaching for those involved in formal activities, starting with opportunities to interact with role models. As mentioned earlier, role models can be an important piece of the puzzle in engaging girls with disabilities in physical activity. This was supported in one of our studies, in that we found that girls with disabilities whose participation was limited to informal pursuits had difficulty naming any role models who they felt had influenced their participation in sport and leisure. In fact, most had none. Conversely, those participating in formal physical activity programs such as disability/wheelchair sport pointed to camp counselors, older adults and coaches, and high-level disability sport athletes (Paralympians) as role models (Anderson,

2009; Anderson et al., 2008). These role models seemed to serve the dual purpose of both introducing the girls to sport and providing encouragement for continued participation that would ultimately lead to greater skill development and commitment to sport and physical activity. That is, girls with experience in formal activities reported receiving greater social support to engage in physical activity than girls who did not participate in such activity. Beyond role models, these girls' parents, peers, and others would attend competitions and vocally support the girls' continued participation in the activity. Because formal sport lends itself to formal support through scheduled events, it was easier for participants in formal activities to identify various social supports who they felt valued their participation in the activities. However, those who were not engaged in formal activities reported experiencing skepticism from others, that is, doubts that they could do anything physical, or they noted that those around them were overprotective. In other words, the social support of those around them was focused on disability rather than ability.

Girls with disabilities who participated in formal physical activities and sport differed in other important ways as well. Likely there is little more important to an adolescent girl than "fitting in." While this can be hard for any teenager, it is doubly so for the teenage girl with a disability. However, I have found that those who are active in formal activities are more likely than those who are not involved in such activity to identify themselves as "normal" (Anderson et al., 2008). Because these girls had formal membership in an activity that paralleled that of their non-disabled peers at school (high school sport), they saw themselves as more like those without disabilities. That is, while those engaged in informal activities felt camaraderie with others *with disabilities*, those in formal disability sport programs felt more like girls, female athletes, whom others would classify as "normal." This was especially true in the sport of swimming, where many of them swam on both their disability sport team as well as their high school team where a wheelchair was not part of the sport experience.

Differences between formal and informal participants were also seen with regard to the goals that the girls held, harkening back to the "larger world" impact of participation I identified earlier. Past work has found that people who participate in disability sport often see potential for success in all areas of life, not just sport (Blauwet, 2005). This certainly appeared to be the case for the adolescent girls who participated in organized sport in my research: they had plans related to college and career, as well as higher levels of sport competition (Anderson, 2009). While it is impossible to know whether their sport participation was the direct impetus for these goals, or if girls who participated in disability sport were already different in important ways, many of the girls felt that their sport participation had given them the confidence to believe leaving home for college was possible, or that they could achieve goals that others may have originally doubted they were capable of achieving. Again, while informal participation had its benefits, those benefits were more focused on the more immediate aim of increased physical functioning.

In sum, it appears that when girls with disabilities have the opportunity to engage in formal sport and other organized physical activity programs, the perceived benefits include the opportunity and ability to move beyond the status of someone with a disability. Further, these girls were also more likely to indicate that their physical activity participation provided social opportunities, fun, sport-skill growth, and the opportunity to be challenged to improve sports skills, not only basic physical skills. And while the girls differed in degree of disability, with some using prosthetics or walkers rather than wheelchairs outside of competition, these findings were true regardless of type or degree of disability. In contrast, those engaged in informal activities were more likely to talk about benefits in terms of the therapeutic aspects of the activity.

These differences in experiences should not be interpreted as meaning that informal participation is a "waste of time" or that these girls were less motivated. For some girls, informal participation was simply all that was available to them within their community, or their parents were unaware of other opportunities or unable to make the time commitment inherent in formal wheelchair sport programs (due to a lack of programs, I found that many parents would drive their daughters up to two hours one way for practice at least once a week to participate). Engagement in physical activity, whether formal or informal, produced some degree of benefit for all of these girls. However, it appears that formal participation allowed the girls access to a larger social world that participation in informal physical activity simply did not, and perhaps could not.

DIRECTIONS FOR FUTURE RESEARCH AND PRACTICE

Despite the stereotypes and stigma, the reality is that girls with disabilities are more similar to their able-bodied counterparts than different. For example, identity formation is an important developmental milestone for all adolescent girls (Erikson, 1968). While their disabilities are inevitably an integral part of their personas, there is little doubt that girls with disabilities do not want it to serve as the sole identifier of who they are, just as an able-bodied girl would likely want to be seen as multifaceted, as embodying multiple identities. Despite ever-present barriers, my scholarship, and that of others, indicates that leisure may offer opportunities for adolescent girls with disabilities to develop their identities along the same lines as all other youth. Kelly (1983) summed up the importance of leisure to identity development when he stated,

> The significance of leisure in human development, and especially in the formation of personal and social identities, precludes any definition of leisure as residual. Whatever else it may be, leisure is not leftover time. . . . There is always the possibility that leisure can be a central determinative of other aspects of life and a major element in the process of our self-definition and development. (p. 116)

Kelly's words are consistent with what a number of contributors to this volume have noted: defining leisure as free time is insufficient. I believe that Kleiber (1999), who has also outlined the importance of leisure to identity development, would agree. Girls with disabilities who participate in sport and physically active recreation are describing self-defining and developmental experiences when they speak about their leisure, not merely free time or activities. The meanings and outcomes they attribute to participation exemplify leisure as experience, experience that lends itself to a framework of participation that may facilitate identity development. In fact, leisure has long been seen as contributing (whether positively or not) to one's personal and social identity. This may be particularly so during adolescence, the time period in which identity development comes to the fore (Erikson, 1968). However, as Kleiber pointed out, the freedom to choose a leisure activity is an inherent characteristic of a leisure experience, yet freedom implies that there are a multitude of opportunities from which to choose. It is hard to have freedom to choose when choice is limited to one activity. A person should have access to multiple leisure opportunities to explore interests and to find activities that are in line with her values, as well as an opportunity to reinforce those interests. Research suggests that for girls with disabilities, such is possible if support is present. Sport is just one form of physical activity, yet it is one that is a socially accepted and revered activity, one that likely provides an outlet for social identity that would be deemed "normal," something that many girls with disabilities in my research had identified as something they desired. While my research findings certainly suggest that participation in disability sport can contribute to the development of an athletic identity, continued research is needed to examine this phenomenon, taking into consideration the considerable variability among girls with different degrees of disability, support, and experience. In addition, it also needs to take into consideration other identities that may be developed or influenced through this participation beyond that of an athlete.

Out of necessity, the girls in my study who participated in disability sport had someone, an athlete or a coach, who introduced them to the sport, and it appeared that specific role models helped the girls' interest in sport participation grow. Their interest was also reinforced when they shared the value that they placed on their health, independence, and fun and identified these values as motivators for participation in sport and physical activity. However, as Kleiber (1999) has noted, feedback and comfort with an activity is also necessary for a leisure activity to impact identity development. This is where social support for participation is key and likely why these girls indicated that support and feedback from multiple sources, including role models, were important in that they cemented their commitment to participation. They are comfortable participating in the sport because they are playing with others who "get" what it is like to have a disability but more important perhaps is that they are comfortable identifying as an athlete outside their world of disability sport as well because able-bodied peers "get" what sports are, regardless of the context. However, what remains to be explored are the additional social constructs that can impact not only their comfort level but also their experiences in sport and the world beyond sport, including school and other social environments. For example, while the girls in my studies provided a glimpse into their perceptions of reactions and support from their able-bodied peers, it would be beneficial to talk to these peers to gain a greater understanding of their perceptions of the girls' participation in sport. How does their understanding of the girls' participation ultimately translate into an understanding of other commonalities that may be held beyond sport participation? What are the short- and long-term ramifications of this understanding for both the individuals involved as well as the societal perspective of people with disabilities and their abilities? If an understanding of the commonalities inherent in all forms of sport can be achieved, then the examination can move toward exploring how sport-related issues such as race, socioeconomic status, sexuality, and gender apply to people with disabilities, much as they have already been studied for able-bodied athletes. Often these variables limit access; how might they further contribute to the limited access that people with disabilities currently experience and is such experience of such barriers different than it is for able-bodied athletes?

A continued emphasis on the voice of the participant, particularly the female participant, is key to better understanding the experiences they have in leisure. As pointed out in several other chapters, much of the enlightening research about women, gender, and leisure has come from qualitative approaches that allow researchers access to the female voice. My own research has utilized *standpoint theory,* which specifically acknowledges that obtaining the standpoint of the people who are in the subordinate position within society is necessary to understand those groups. It may also be important to focus on the voices of the advocates for those groups, including parents. In a side conversation I had with a mother of a girl who was interviewed for one of my studies, the mother explained that for her daughter's participation to be a reality, "you can't go the extra mile; you have to go an extra 1,000 miles." This comment was made in response to the great deal of effort that has to be put into facilitating participation in disability sport due to lack of accessibility to "easily accessible" community programs. Often, there is simply not a critical mass for a wheelchair sport team; other times, agencies simply do not put forth the effort to program for this group. Regardless of the reason, as an important social support structure, the parents could provide further insight into how to advance this movement.

Practitioners can certainly take center stage with regard to issues of access and advocacy, although some issues are "bigger" than just the leisure field. Often, our society as a whole continues to turn a blind eye to enhancing opportunities for people with disabilities. Too many people feel that the ADA has done its job and that discrimination in the provision of a multitude of services no longer exists. The ADA has helped ensure basic services for people with disabilities, but it should be clear that able-bodied individuals would be considerably disappointed and disgruntled if that was all that was provided for them. Without a larger effort both within and beyond the field of leisure services, all people with disabilities, not just adolescent girls, will continue to experience a lack of opportunities in too many sectors. However, if access can be more clearly understood and facilitated, in this case for adolescent girls, the social support that practitioners may provide, or at least facilitate, can undoubtedly have an impact on their overall development as they enter into the developmental stage of identity development. If the girls' social worlds are limited by either themselves or those around them, there are certain identities that remain inaccessible.

The benefits of participation in active leisure for girls with disabilities, whether through sport or other physical activity, seem to be far-reaching. However, information gathered during the 2006 Winter Paralympics by the Women's Sports Foundation (Zurn, Lopiano, & Snyder, 2006) revealed that only 20.9% of participants were women, despite an equal number of events open to men and women, leading them to give the Paralympics a grade of D+ for female participation. During the 2004 Summer Paralympics in Athens, less than 33% of the 3,806 participants were women, compared to 44% for the Olympics, despite the fact that of the 43 million Americans and 650 million people worldwide who have documented disabilities, half are women (Bender, 2006). While these statistics are for elite levels of sport participation, the participants of tomorrow are the girls with disabilities of today.

Media coverage of participation in events such as the Paralympics is disheartening, serves as an additional barrier to participation, and impedes access to role models. Similar to the situation that able-bodied female athletes face, female athletes with disabilities see little media coverage in competition, thereby limiting the exposure that younger females may have to role models who would encourage them to pick up a ball, "run" a race, or play catch with their friends. Continued emphasis on increasing recognition for the accomplishments of all women and researching how to facilitate those accomplishments should be a goal of all stakeholders who look to continue the advancement of opportunities for girls and women in leisure. If people can "see" it being done, more will know it can be done.

Finally, it is important to remember that, as with able-bodied adolescent girls, not all girls with disabilities are going to be interested in the same types of activities. We cannot afford to assume that they will be so "grateful" for any opportunity that they will be willing to engage in just any activity. For the benefits of active participation to be realized, the elements of interest and enjoyment (i.e., intrinsic motivation) are critical and need continued research. Therefore, work that examines recreation activities for girls with disabilities beyond traditional sport or physical activity can teach us a great deal about how to better provide active leisure experiences for all girls and women. After all, in the end it really isn't whether you win or lose the game, or even how you play the game, but that you get the chance to play the game, whatever game you choose.

REFERENCES

Anderson, D. M. (2009). Adolescent girls' involvement in disability sport: Implications for identity development. *Journal of Sport and Social Issues, 33*(4), 427–449.

Anderson, D. M., Bedini, L. A., & Moreland, L. (2005). Getting all girls into the game: Physically active recreation for girls with disabilities. *Journal of Park and Recreation Administration, 23*(4), 78–103.

Anderson, D. M., Wozencroft, A., & Bedini, L. A. (2008). Adolescent girls' involvement in disability sport: A comparison of social support mechanisms. *Journal of Leisure Research, 40*(2), 183–207.

Bedini, L. A., & Anderson, D. M. (2005). I'm nice, I'm smart, I like karate: Recreation of girls with physical disabilities. *Therapeutic Recreation Journal, 39*(2), 114–130.

Bender, K. (2006, August 11). Disabled women push barriers in sports. *Women's eNews*. Retrieved from http://www.womensenews.org/article. cfm/dyn/aid/2858

Blauwet, C. (2005). Promoting the health and human rights of individuals with a disability through the Paralympic movement. Retrieved from http://www.toolkitsportdevelopment.org

Brighton Declaration on Women and Sports. (1994). Retrieved from www. sportsbiz.bz/womensportinternational/conferences/brighton_declaration.htm

Csikszentmihalyi, M. (1997). Finding flow: The psychology of engagement with everyday life. New York, NY: Basic Books.

Deegan, M. J. (1985). Multiple minority groups: A case study of physically disabled women. In M. J. Deegan & N. A. Brooks (Eds.), *Women and disability: The double handicap* (pp. 37–55). New Brunswick, NJ: Transaction.

Erikson, E. H. (1968). *Identity: Youth and crisis*. New York, NY: W. W. Norton.

French, D., & Hainsworth, J. (2001). "There aren't any buses and the swimming pool is always cold!": Obstacles and opportunities in the provision of sport for disabled people. *Managing Leisure, 6*, 35–49.

Henderson, K. A., & King, K. (1998). Recreation programming for adolescent girls: Rationale and foundations. *Journal of Park and Recreation Administration, 17*(2), 28–41.

Kelly, J. R. (1983). *Leisure identities and interactions*. Boston, MA: George Allen & Unwin.

Kleiber, D. A. (1999). *Leisure experiences and human development*. New York, NY: Basic.

Kolkka, T., & Williams, T. (1997). Gender and disability sport participation: Setting a sociological research agenda. *Adapted Physical Activity Quarterly, 14*(1), 8–23.

Smith, R. W., Austin, D. R., Kennedy, D. W., Lee, Y., & Hutchinson, P. (2005). *Inclusive and special recreation: Opportunities for persons with disabilities* (5th ed.). New York, NY: McGraw-Hill.

Zurn, L., Lopiano, D., & Snyder, M. (2006). *Women in the 2006 Olympic and Paralympic Winter Games: An analysis of participation, leadership, and media coverage.* East Meadow, NY: Women's Sports Foundation.

CHAPTER 21
INTERSECTIONS OF ETHNICITY AND GENDER IN THE LEISURE AND HEALTH OF ETHNIC MINORITY WOMEN AND YOUNG ADULTS

SUSAN TIRONE AND JACQUELINE GAHAGAN

This chapter draws together ideas from two scholars whose research and teaching focus on leisure and health promotion—and how those ideas are shaped by the intersections of ethnicity/race and gender. We came to our interest in leisure and health promotion in the contexts of ethnicity/race and gender through various research projects, as well as professional practice. Our chapter focuses first on the findings of Susan's research into the leisure of ethnic minority women and young adults. We then discuss how understanding the complexity of ethnicity/race, gender, and leisure has implications for understanding the health status of many ethnic/racial minorities. The chapter concludes with questions for future research on women, gender, and leisure.

LEISURE OF ETHNIC MINORITY WOMEN AND YOUNG ADULTS

In the 1990s, Susan studied leisure in the lives of women from the South Asian countries of India and Pakistan who were immigrants to Canada (Tirone, 1997; Tirone & Shaw, 1997). All of the women were mothers whose children attended school in Canada at the time of the interviews. They spoke about their lives in terms of what gave them a sense of fulfillment, satisfaction, enjoyment, and relaxation—ways that most other Canadians think about leisure. However, Susan found that the women valued their relationships with immediate and extended family members above other endeavors such as their jobs, careers, and leisure. These women discussed their perceptions of leisure in the context of Canadian society and how Canadian leisure impacted their lives and the lives of their children. They were perplexed when discussing the leisure of their non-Indian/Pakistani Canadian women friends because from their perspective, leisure in the Canadian context was used for self-gratification, often excluding other family members. The participants in the study expressed concern that leisure promoted individualism and had the potential to disrupt the traditional interconnectedness of their South Asian family. They expressed tremendous concern that their children, who were being raised in Canada, might adapt Canadian values associated with leisure, and that this might cause the younger generation to drift away from the highly prized "joint-family" activities and values that characterized their lives and culture. In fact, some of the women described "Canadian leisure" as selfish because of the focus on individualism it promoted (Tirone & Shaw, 1997).

This study left Susan wondering about the children of immigrants to Canada from non-Western cultures and how their leisure interests might differ from those of their parents, given that they were being raised in a culture that thought about or defined leisure in terms of individualism, freedom from familial obligation, and personal choice. That question resulted in a subsequent longitudinal study of teenage and young adult Canadians whose parents were immigrants from South Asia (Tirone & Pedlar, 2000, 2005). In this qualitative study conducted in three phases over a 10-year period, a number of questions were explored, but its primary focus was on the leisure experiences of this group of young people. What Susan learned in this study extended far beyond the ways leisure is usually thought about and studied. It also suggested how and why leisure is important to personal health and is both an experience of the individual and much more than that. The study began as an exploration of leisure for children of immigrants whose parents identified strongly with the traditional cultural practices of South Asia. The intention was to explore how leisure was experienced by this group of second-generation Canadians, considering that they lived and experienced the traditions of average Canadians as well as those of their parents and extended family. The study did not intend to focus on racism, but issues of discrimination arose in the first phase of the study as participants talked about some of the barriers they encountered in their leisure. In subsequent phases of the study, questions were asked about their experiences of race and racism and how these had changed over the years. Several findings from the longitudinal study illustrate these contentions.

How Ethnicity/Race and Racism "Work"

The findings over a 10-year period indicated that race/ethnicity was central to these individuals' experiences of leisure, and that their discourses around racism and discrimination changed with age. In the first phase of the study, the participants were, on average, 18 years of age, and they all spoke about times when they had encountered hurtful and overtly racist incidents. These incidents often occurred at school as well as in leisure and in recreation settings. Several of the participants clearly identified the incidents as racist and discriminatory (Tirone, 1999/2000). For some participants, these incidents affected their leisure, inhibiting their enjoyment of some public programs and activities such as sport, physical activity, and playground activities. For example, one person described a summer sports program she attended at a local park when she was in primary school. She recalled being the object of hurtful name calling due to her skin color and that these incidents were not addressed by the program leaders. Hence, she became reluctant to attend summer recreation programs. Only in a few cases were the participants able to recall that an adult leader, coach, or teacher intervened to help them and the other children address these incidents. This meant that many of them were required to defend themselves and deflect emotionally hurtful situations without adult advocates. However, in phases two and three of the study, when study participants were 23 and 28 years of age, respectively, they were less inclined to label hurtful incidents as racist or discriminatory. As young adults, they explained that if they objected to an incident, calling it racist or declaring they had experienced discrimination, people were offended and were reluctant to discuss the incident. That is, the participants found that if they framed these incidents as something less offensive *to those perpetrating the incident*, they were more likely to be able to engage those who offended them in discussions about the outcome of an offensive verbal or physical act. One participant who lived and worked in the United States at the time of the third phase of the study explained that she believed it was best to be what she called "proactive" in addressing discrimination; that is, she thought it was best to educate the people around her about social injustice experienced by minorities rather than confronting them over offensive behavior:

> Especially in America, I found myself talking more and more about my culture and where I come from and what we believe in. And hearing a lot of experiences from the African American society here, especially in (name of state) especially in (large city in the United States) and listening to the things that they've been through and the life that is set out for them, the privileges that they do and don't get, I think, open dialogue is definitely a huge thing. And, we all need to be more sensitive, and we all need to be more educated and we all need to accept people, you know, on the inside and not pass judgment on the outside. And until we do that, I think that we will always have a problem with racism and you know it's a really, really unfortunate thing, because we as humans are better than that and we just need to grow up.

However, racism and offensive behaviors were an everyday reality, and some study participants spoke about how they were not always able to address incidents when they occurred. Sometimes the participants began to doubt their own behavior or to feel insecure about their appearance. For example in the second phase of the study a participant who is a practicing Sikh said:

> I explain to people certain things you know, like, when I was a little kid I couldn't cut my hair so I explained to them I'm not allowed to cut my hair. It's against my religion and stuff like that. You can't expect, I mean, I sometimes get annoyed but I don't really get mad when people don't understand, 'cause I mean, how would they? They've had no exposure.

Later in the same interview she said,

> Sometimes *I don't know how to read things right.* I mean, it could be many things. It could be that I'm a minority, it could be something totally, it could be my personality or something, you know. Once in a while, and this is mostly old people, senior citizens, you know, *you don't know if it is your own paranoia.* It's really hard to tell. But they'll just give you this really dirty look or something, you know. If you come into a restaurant or something, and then part of you thinks is it just because they're racist, you know. Or is it something else? It's really hard to tell. I mean, who knows what it is? (Emphasis added)

These reflections tell us much about how race and racism "work"—that those who are the targets of racism must worry about offending those who, knowingly or not, perpetrate it; must "second guess" or doubt themselves, their perceptions and feelings, and decide if they are "overreacting." To live one's life without ever having to negotiate these kinds of daily stressors is a tremendous privilege, and those who enjoy this privilege are rarely aware of having it.

When discrimination and racism result in self-doubt and self-consciousness, people are known to withdraw from places where these incidents occurred; avoiding restaurants and other leisure venues where they may experience "dirty looks." Therefore, racism and discrimination may lead people to withdraw from activities and places where they would otherwise experience leisure that has the potential to contribute to health and personal well-being. All participants who were part of the last phase of the study tried to find ways to address issues that "may be discriminatory" by softening the way they approach those whose behaviors are offensive. These "soft" approaches aim to ensure that conversations remain relatively friendly and non-offensive for their dominant group peers. But clearly, racism undermines the confidence of people in minority groups and prevents them from participating in community activities, including leisure activities that may have a profound effect on a sense of health and well-being. In avoiding labeling racism and discrimination, we may or may not be able to address the behaviors and conditions that negatively impact minority groups and prevent them from enjoyment of leisure. But it should not be up to those who experience racism to do all the work of "anti-racism." It should be the work of those who are privileged or advantaged by their race as well, including those who are recreation and leisure services professionals.

Another significant consideration arising from this longitudinal study that helps us understand leisure as a site where cultural tensions between dominant cultural practices and those of more socially marginalized groups are played out is the notion of *situatedness*. Essentially, this concept refers to the practice whereby those who identify with minority ethnic and racial groups while living within dominant cultural communities and societies act or behave in certain ways in order to negotiate their multiple identities; specifically, how they may look and behave differently in their leisure when they interact with their peers, versus when they interact with dominant group others. Some researchers describe the lives of minority group members as individuals who are living between or outside of several different sets of cultural practices and beliefs (Anderson, 1999; Novak, 1971; Waters, 1990). Perceptions held by both dominant and minority group members related to those who appear to be "outside" of the dominant culture may prevent the meaningful inclusion of minority groups in some forms of leisure. Leisure occurring within ethnic communities may allow minority group members to celebrate and affirm their cultural identity, though it may also serve to further distinguish and to possibly marginalize them (Gramann & Allison, 1999).

Concepts such as *biculturalism* and *bicultural identity formation* are helpful for conceptualizing leisure of ethnic minorities who live in cultural contexts such as Canada or the United States, where dominant groups are white, English-speaking, Euro-Caucasians. That is, minority ethnic young people (and individuals of all ages) may feel compelled to act differently depending on the cultural setting. For example, some may adopt different clothing styles, different language and patterns of speech, different body language, and different activities, including leisure, in different settings. In so doing, they develop an identity rooted in two or more sets of cultural beliefs and traditions (Hebert, 2001). The results of the longitudinal study we are reporting here indicated that study participants experienced cultural traditions and leisure rooted in two or more cultures and their enjoyment of their diverse leisure remained salient throughout the 10 years of the study.

For example, study participants valued the time they had for family dinners and celebrations that involved Indian music, dance, and food. Some enjoyed wearing traditional clothing and friendships with peers who shared their religious and cultural traditions. They also enjoyed participating in the leisure that is typically enjoyed by non-Indian/Pakistani Canadian teens and young adults—attending popular cultural events, such as concerts, plays, and community events. Adding to the diversity of their leisure the participants explained a tremendous interest in the leisure and cultural traditions of friends from other minority ethnic groups. They gave many examples of their friendship groups that gathered for dinners where the food reflected the cultures of a variety of ethnic traditions and participation in festivals and other "traditional" cultural practices that were neither South Asian nor Canadian. Such engagements reflected the participants' interest in diverse leisure and little in the way of constraints—perhaps due to their preferences for leisure that did not prioritize only one set of cultural traditions.

A third issue arising from our discussions of the findings of Susan's longitudinal study is related to the complexity of life resulting from the intersection of ethnicity/race and gender in the lives of this group. Complexity was evident in how individuals had to negotiate and navigate between and within cultures for leisure, and how racism was often a factor that inhibited or at least changed the character of their enjoyment of public leisure places. Added to this for the young women were the expectations they faced relative to their roles as young women in families that prioritized some clearly defined gender-based roles for women. For example, most of the participants, both female and male, reported that their parents would prefer them to marry South Asian partners. The women also noted the expectation that they would participate in the care of the parents, both their own and those of their husband, if and when that became necessary. At the same time, the young women in the study were just as likely as their male peers to report being supported and encouraged by their parents to seek advanced education and careers. One woman said:

> I would say being a woman in IT [information technology] is rare enough; that has its own disadvantages. A lot of the time because you're a woman, people view you as inferior and not capable to do a job. *But I wouldn't say there is an ethnic portion to it at all.* . . . Yeah, heritage-wise, no, not really. I mean I pretty much set out a goal for myself and will do whatever I can to accomplish it. And, uh, I think as a woman, it's a little bit more intense to prove yourself in a predominantly male environment. But I think once you do prove yourself, a lot of people just lighten up and understand that oh, yeah, she is for real and she does know what she's talking about. (Emphasis added)

The circumstances of the one young woman who openly identified as lesbian illustrated the complexity of the intersections of race/ethnicity, gender, and sexuality. She explained:

> It's pretty taboo to be gay in Indian society, let alone be female and be in that situation. I've tried to bring it up to my parents several times, to which they shunned anybody like that, and, uh, pretty much said it's a hideous lifestyle and no one should live like that.

Perhaps not surprisingly, most participants in this study experienced complicated negotiations with their families, their ethnic communities, and the dominant groups with which they interacted in order to pursue the work, education, family life, and leisure they preferred. Many spoke of the strategies they used to adhere to the traditional practices they held dear, while finding ways to be included in the communities where they lived. Issues they encountered in relation to race/ethnicity and gender were constant reminders of how pervasive dominant group norms are in North American society. For example, in North America, we may assume that minority groups will strive to fit into social groups by adopting the practices and leisure of their dominant group peers and assimilating into the dominant group by discarding traditional cultural practices. However, one participant in this study commented on the importance of sustaining one's participation in the traditions that are important parts of her identity and ethnic group membership:

> We have all kinds of nationalities and races that I associate with. And none of us would ever stand for anyone being put down, or anyone experiencing racism. Umm, I think that a lot of that has to do with just being in this cultural mosaic, and being able to experience your culture and other people's culture freely. Instead of this "melting pot" that, you know, sucks the life out of everybody and makes them all robotic almost.

This person elaborated further when she described the diversity within her friendship group. She believed that people are genuinely interested in new experiences and so she makes a point of extending invitations to cultural events to her friends and colleagues:

> I like to educate people here about it because they don't normally get that opportunity. And when they hear about the things that you do, the events and activities, the weddings and festivals or whatever, you know, they're always like, "oh, can I come to the next one you go to, 'cause I want to experience it," or whatever. Or at least try the food or something, you know. And it's nice

to hear that, 'cause it's nice to know that, something that you do that is completely yours and belongs to your culture or religion, is fascinating to somebody else who really wants to experience the things that you experience, 'cause it's completely different from what they're used to.

PROMOTING DIVERSITY IN LEISURE

While countries like Canada recruit immigrants from many different countries and cultures, we have not yet found ways for all immigrants to be included and feel welcome. A number of studies have found the health of many immigrants is compromised in the years following immigration and settlement, and many health conditions they encounter are preventable (e.g., see Fullugar, this volume; Pottie, Ortiz, & tur Kuile, 2007). This indicates the need to ensure leisure and other health-promotion efforts address the challenges to good health faced by ethnic minority immigrant populations living in Canada. Given the extant research on the potentially positive relationship between leisure and health (through stress coping), and the results of Susan's longitudinal study, clearly one of these challenges is ethnic discrimination or racism. If such experiences prevent individuals from engaging in public leisure spaces, or if their leisure participation results in incidents of racism, the implications for their health are profound. We see the importance of reframing issues of difference within the conceptual framework of *determinants of health* (Public Health Agency of Canada, 2001) in an effort to attend to the complex interplay of these factors on health, broadly defined. We also argue for the need to reframe leisure and health promotion as unique but overlapping fields. Such a perspective may allow us to take a more robust, cross-sectoral approach to addressing the health and social needs of diverse populations and to more fully address health and social inequalities through, for example, research, policy, and programming reforms that speak to the needs of more diverse populations in Canada. These new approaches need to address leisure as an important determinant of health.

We wonder how experiences of gender, race/ethnicity, sexual orientation, and other intersecting identities of difference and disadvantage in many societies may be reframed in light of the potential for leisure to contribute to health and well-being. Many studies of leisure and racial or ethnic minority groups discuss, describe, and reflect upon the ways in which some people who identify with those groups experience different leisure, and reasons for those differences (e.g., see Arai & Kivel, 2009; Floyd, 2007; Giles, this volume; Howard, this volume; Hutchison, 1987; Shinew & Stodolska, this volume; Stodolska, 2000). From these and many other studies we have learned a great deal about unique activities, preferences, and constraints encountered by minority ethnic and racial groups in their leisure. Susan's exploratory studies into the leisure *experiences* of young people who identify as ethnic and racial minority community members has found that, in some cases, they see their leisure as *multidimensional*. That is, some of their leisure occurs within the dominant culture and therefore resembles the same leisure practices of their dominant group peers, while at other times it occurs within their ethnic communities or families and is enhanced by the traditional cultural practices of their parents and ancestors (Tirone & Pedlar, 2005). As ethnic minority group members celebrate leisure characterized by traditional cultural practices, it remains unclear why such leisure cannot include participation of dominant group members whose leisure would then be enhanced by that involvement. The results of Susan's studies indicate that dominant groups are genuinely interested in diverse leisure. Further, we wonder if participation in ethnic-specific activities might serve as the catalyst for dialogue about ethnic and racial difference, and whether the changing discourses about racism and discrimination might facilitate acceptance and inclusion of diverse groups of people in societies in North America.

Another significant consideration in understanding persistent tensions between dominant cultural practices and those of more socially marginalized groups is the notion of located or situated identities of ethnic minority youth (Hebert, 2001; Howard, 2000). As noted previously, this concept refers to times when people who identify with minority ethnic and racial groups while living within dominant cultural communities and societies look and behave differently in their leisure, depending on the context in which leisure occurs. It appears that concepts such as biculturalism and bicultural identity formation might be a helpful way to conceptualize the diversity of leisure that characterizes some ethnic minorities who live in cultures such as Canada or the United States. Their leisure often reflects tremendous variety and diversity, and future research should explore and expand upon those multifaceted experiences.

Different expressions of leisure in varying settings or times can create conflict between young people and their parents when the parents view leisure as disruptive to family cohesion and a sense of health and well-being. For example, some of young people in the longitudinal study said their parents referred to them as "coconuts"—brown on the outside and white on the inside—suggesting a bicultural response to bridging various cultural traditions and beliefs. Biculturalism plays out as situatedness and is very evident in the leisure of minority ethnic groups, as discussed above. The complex and the dynamic nature of leisure, gender, family, and biculturalism/multiculturalism will be an important subject for researchers to explore in the years to come, as North American populations become increasingly diverse.

Our research findings and professional practice experiences also suggest several questions that we believe need to be considered in future scholarship on women, gender, leisure, and health promotion. First, as noted by others in this text, it is not enough to focus on gender as a stand-alone social construct or determinant of health in seeking to understand, and advocate for, girls' and women's recreation and leisure. Rather, the intersectionality of experiences of race/ethnicity, as well as immigrant status, must also be considered for the many reasons highlighted above.

Second, Susan's longitudinal study suggests that how race/ethnicity and incidents of racism are thought about in the context of leisure shift with age. Few studies have documented this shift and no longitudinal studies that we know of have explored whether this is true of individuals' experiences of gender and sexism as well. If and how recreation and leisure are contexts for, and practices of, social inequality (as well as equality) may change with age. That is because as those who are subject to discrimination age, how they think about their experiences of racism changes. Perhaps this is a "survival" and "health maintenance" strategy that allows one to "manage" the stress of disadvantage, whether that disadvantage is based in race/ethnicity, gender, sexual orientation, class, age, or some combination. Research on "leisure as coping" needs to consider more than gender, class, or racial *differences* as key singular determinants of health in this coping strategy. Leisure *as* a practice of social (in)equality must be explored, as this may help explain any group differences in pursuing/using leisure to cope with stress as well as promoting one's health status.

REFERENCES

Anderson, M. (1999). Children in-between: Constructing identities in the bicultural family. *Journal of the Royal Anthropological Institute, 5*(1), 13–26.

Arai, S., & Kivel, B. D. (2009). Critical race theory and social justice perspectives on whiteness, difference(s) and (anti)racism: A fourth wave of race research in Leisure Studies. *Journal of Leisure Research, 41*(4), 459–470.

Floyd, M. F. (2007). Research on race and ethnicity in leisure: Anticipating the fourth wave. *Leisure/Loisir, 31*(1), 245–254.

Gramann, J. H. & Allison, M. T. (1999). Ethnicity, race and leisure. In E. J. Jackson & T. L. Burton (Eds.), *Leisure studies: Prospects for the twenty-first century* (pp. 283–297). State College, PA: Venture Publishing, Inc.

Hebert, Y. (2001). Identity, diversity, and education: A critical review of the literature. *Canadian Ethnic Studies/ Études ethniques au Canada, 33*(3), 155–185.

Howard, J. A. (2000). Social psychology of identities. *Annual Review of Sociology, 26*, 367–393.

Hutchison, R. (1987). Ethnicity and urban recreation: Whites, Blacks and Hispanics in Chicago's public parks. *Journal of Leisure Research, 19*, 205–222.

Novak, M. (1971). *The rise of the unmeltable ethnics.* New York, NY: Harper and Brothers.

Pottie, K, Ortiz, L., & tur Kuile, A. (2007). Here's a thought . . . Preparing for diversity: Improving preventive health care for immigrants. *Our Diverse Cities, 4*, 59–63.

Public Health Agency of Canada. (2001). *Determinants of health: What makes Canadians healthy or unhealthy?* Ottawa: Public Health Agency of Canada. Retrieved from http://www.phac-aspc.gc.ca/ph-sp/determinants/index-eng.php

Stodolska, M. (2000). Changes in leisure patterns after immigration. *Leisure Sciences, 22*, 39–63.

Tirone, S. (1997). Leisure, ethnic diversity and disability: The lives of South Asian Canadians. *Journal of Leisurability, 24*(3), 23–37.

Tirone, S. (1999/2000). Racism, indifference and the leisure experiences of South Asian Canadian teens. *Leisure/Loisir, 24*(1), 89–114.

Tirone, S., & Pedlar, A. (2000). Understanding the leisure experiences of a minority ethnic group: south Asian teens and young adults in Canada. *Loisir et societe/Society and leisure, 23*(1), 145–169.

Tirone, S., & Pedlar, A. (2005). Leisure, place, and diversity: The experience of ethnic minority young adults. *Canadian Ethnic Studies, 37*(2), 32–48.

Tirone, S., & Shaw, S. M. (1997). At the centre of their lives: Indo Canadian women, their families, and leisure. *Journal of Leisure Research, 29*, 225–244.

Waters, M. C. (1990). *Ethnic options: Choosing identities in America.* Berkeley, CA: University of California Press.

Chapter 22
Becoming a Mother: Where Does Leisure Fit?

Anne-Marie Sullivan

Introduction

As I write this, I am on my third journey of motherhood and finally feel that I have a pretty good handle on being pregnant, having a baby, and bringing that baby into my world. In 2003, however, when I learned that I was pregnant with my first child, I was not so certain. I did all the things that a woman is "supposed" to do during pregnancy: visit my doctor regularly, eat well, get lots of sleep, avoid certain foods, activities, and environmental hazards, and read as many pregnancy books as I could in those nine months. So why then, when this beautiful little girl came into my world, did I feel so completely unprepared and overwhelmed? When I described some of my feelings to my mom friends, they all gave the same response: "That's completely normal so don't worry about it." I needed more than a brush-off. I really began to wonder, is it really normal? Why is it that so much of what we focus on during pregnancy is just that, pregnancy? What about life beyond the bump? What happens when you leave the hospital with this tiny human being who is completely dependent on you for everything? I distinctly remember stepping into the elevator with Emma in her infant carrier, thinking "I am too young to be doing this." The reality of the situation, however, was that I was in fact quite a bit older than a number of the teen mothers I saw on the unit in the days I was there. Surely, if a 16-year-old can sort it out, I would be okay. The scary part was that in many ways I was not really okay. I had lost a sense of myself and I was unsure of how to cope with this new part of my identity: a mother. Hence, I set out to explore whether other women walked into pregnancy, labor, and "life with a baby" in ways similar to myself and were then "shocked" when they discovered that their expectations did not in many ways resemble the reality that life with a baby was.

The purpose of this chapter, then, is to share the stories of seven women as they embarked on the journey of motherhood. The primary goal of the research was to explore how pregnancy and early mothering impact leisure engagement and what this impact means to leisure as coping. I begin by examining what motherhood looks like in the twenty-first century, including concepts of "intensive mothering" (Hays, 1996), and "mother-work" (Porter, 2008). From there, I present some of the findings from my own work in the area of mothering (Sullivan, 2008). To begin, I talk about the women's experiences with pregnancy and then look at their experiences with the baby. To conclude, I present what I believe are a number of pressing issues that may direct future research in this area that will help inform our understanding of women, gender, and leisure.

Motherhood in Twenty-first Century North America

Having children is a major life event, and most will agree that a child changes all aspects of life. Recently, parenting, and in particular, mothering, has become a multifaceted, high-stress, demanding role with ever-increasing responsibilities, in what Shaw & Hilbrecht (2008) refer to as an "age of anxiety" (Warner, 2005). The majority of women are likely to experience motherhood as a contradiction between being a mother and being a woman in today's society. Becoming a mother likely changes a woman more than almost any other life change.

Hays (1996) described the challenges of modern motherhood, identifying it as "intensive mothering," where women must strive to do it all. Women are charged with being primary caregivers to children while maintaining careers. This means large amounts of money, time, and effort are devoted to child rearing. In today's economy, to be able to provide for children as expected, both parents in many families must be employed. Parents are encouraged to have their children involved in any number of outside activities, including swimming, dance lessons, hockey, and music, all of which have high monetary and time commitments. If "good parenting" involves these commitments (as Harrington discusses in her chapter), then parents, and mothers in particular, are now required to do a lot in the course of a day.

A similar view of mothering has been identified as "motherwork" (Porter, 2008). From this perspective, mothering is "active, it is work to preserve, grow, and train a baby into adulthood, work that depends on the mother being aware of her practices and thinking and planning how best to carry out her work" (p. 133). Inherent to this understanding of mothering is the notion of blame. Women are often blamed for failings of their children, with "bad mothering" often cited as the root cause of "bad children." Motherwork, unfortunately, remains undervalued in our society, yet women are expected to figure out how to best engage in active mothering with little reward.

In this "age of anxiety" (Warner, 2005), women are expected to be everything for everyone. Parents, mothers in particular, are seen as ultimately responsible for all aspects of child rearing. Gone is the notion that "it takes a village to raise a child." Mothers are responsible for seeing their children to adulthood in every way, and if anything goes wrong along that journey, Mom will be held responsible. In addition to being primarily responsible for child rearing, women are also encouraged to maintain employment outside the home in a workforce that does little to accommodate the demands placed on women in the home. Few employers offer flexibility in scheduling, and many women feel that they hit a brick wall in terms of career advancement once they have children. How then do women balance these two demanding roles in a society that does not bend to allow these two roles to mesh in any way?

LEISURE AS COPING

Leisure scholars have suggested that leisure can act as a buffer against adverse effects of stress on mental and physical health (Coleman & Iso-Ahola, 1993). Further, leisure can help people cope with various types of stress experienced in daily life as well as life changes (Coleman, 1993; Coleman & Iso-Ahola, 1993; Iso-Ahola & Park, 1996). Iwasaki and Mannell (2000) identified leisure coping strategies and leisure coping beliefs as two important dimensions in the potential of using leisure to "manage" stress. They defined "leisure coping beliefs" as "people's generalized beliefs that their leisure helps them cope with stress" (p. 165), while "leisure coping strategies" is defined as those leisure practices or methods that people actually employ to manage stress. For example, Iwasaki and Mannell found that by providing companionship, leisure allowed an opportunity for stress to be shared with others. When necessary, leisure also provided an escape from stress, leaving the individual rejuvenated and better prepared to deal with stress. Finally, leisure has been found to decrease negative moods and increase positive feelings. Whether leisure is intentionally chosen to deal with stress, or diminished stress is a byproduct of activity participation, the ultimate outcome is a reduction in stress.

The value of leisure in coping with particular life circumstances has also been studied in relation to a number of varying life circumstances. Klitzing (2003, 2004) reported that leisure was an important coping strategy for women living in a homeless shelter. Iwasaki (2003) examined the role leisure played in helping police officers and emergency personnel cope with stress and the resulting impact on health. Kleiber and his colleagues (2002) explored leisure as a resource in coping with negative life events, such as the loss of a loved one, injury, or the loss of employment (Kleiber, Hutchinson, & Williams, 2002). Hutchinson and colleagues took the examination of injury one step further and studied the daily coping techniques, including leisure, of people following a traumatic injury or onset of a chronic illness (Hutchinson, Loy, Kleiber, & Dattilo, 2003).

All of these researchers have found similar results. Leisure is a potential coping strategy and as such, is invaluable to people living with disabilities and illness, as well as people dealing with major negative life events (see also, Parry, this volume). This research also shows that leisure is equally important in coping with minor stresses experienced in daily life. Little attention, however, had been paid to how new mothers cope with stress, whether leisure may assist in their coping, or how it may do so. Hence, I undertook the study of first-time mothers described next.

THE STUDY: FIRST-TIME MOTHERS

In my study, I explored the experiences of seven women as they embarked on the journey of motherhood for the first time. More specifically, I examined how women coped with the stress of becoming a mother. The women were Euro-Canadian, between 29 and 34 years of age, in a committed relationship (defined as living with the father of the baby), and pregnant with their first child. While no attempt was made to recruit women with specific educational backgrounds, all but one had university degrees. Two of these women were in Ph.D. programs, one was a lawyer, one a librarian at a university, two were employed as primary school teachers, and the final woman was a chef who had trained but not at the university level. All but one of the couples were legally married and had planned the baby. The non-married couple had been living together for four years and had not planned the pregnancy, but both were committed to the new direction of their lives.[1]

Each of the women was interviewed twice, once during her pregnancy and again within the first 12 months of her child's life. In the first interview, women were asked to talk generally about their lives before pregnancy and the changes—for example, emotional or physical—they were experiencing with being pregnant. Specifically, women were asked whether pregnancy had impacted leisure involvement and to describe how this looked from their perspective. In the second interview, women were invited to talk about life since the arrival of a baby. The primary focus was on the impact of a baby on her life in general and how she was coping.[2]

Anticipating Motherhood

I invited women who were pregnant with their first child to talk to me openly about their pregnancies and their thoughts and feelings regarding first-time motherhood. To link the study to my area of interest in the research world, I focused quite a bit on the impact of pregnancy on leisure engagement. I wondered about purposefully using leisure as a coping strategy during those early days of motherhood. I wanted to get a sense of how the women saw leisure fitting in their lives upon the arrival of a baby. I wanted to know what, if any, impact pregnancy had on leisure participation. All the women in the study were in their last trimester of their pregnancies and all were still well enough to be working. Even though the women continued to work with little to no modifications in their positions, all found their leisure had been dramatically impacted in a number of ways throughout their pregnancies. They commented that some of the changes were by choice and some were imposed on them by others.

A number of women reported that one of the first changes they noted in leisure participation was related to alcohol consumption. All the women indicated this was a personal choice for the well-being of the baby. Melanie commented, "Well, the first thing to go was my wine and I miss that. I mean, I know that it is important and obviously I am ok with that but still I do miss it. I used to get together with my girlfriends and drink lots of wine (laughs), and now I can't do that. So girls' night is just not the same." Anna mentioned, "I don't go to happy hour with people from work anymore. I used to go on Friday evenings for a few drinks, but it's not the same if I can't have a drink." It is not uncommon for women to conceal pregnancies until they feel ready to share the news with people in their lives. For the women in the study, part of the cover-up meant hiding changes in leisure patterns. Lucy indicated, "I stopped going to dinner with friends for the first while because I was afraid they would suspect that I was pregnant because I wasn't having a drink. Um, it's not that I am a heavy drinker but I would normally have wine with my meal, and if I didn't they might ask me. My husband and I decided not to tell people until we were past the first 12 weeks."

A second area that was significantly impacted by pregnancy was the physical realm of leisure engagement. Lucy indicated that she has always been physically active, swimming, running, and going to a gym regularly throughout the week. Once pregnant, however, that changed: ". . . and then all of a sudden you don't have the energy and you're just trying to get through the day, get through work, get home and put your feet up, and then all of a sudden you notice that you are just not doing anything anymore." Melanie, too, was physically active before pregnancy: "I was a regular gym goer and I can't even tell you the last time I went to the gym. For the first two months, I continued to go at lunch time but since then all that's totally gone. The fatigue has been a huge issue for me, and even though I sleep through the night, I find that I have to sit down a lot during the day and I have to nap sometime in the evening." So, fatigue clearly had an impact on physical activity for these women.

For one woman, her husband was the primary reason for her reduced physical activity. "We used to hike and canoe and talk long walks but now, well, I think he thinks that I am not capable of anything anymore. It's like he's scared of me, um, not scared of me, but scared that something will happen if I keep doing things. I mean, I feel fine, but he doesn't get it, so he doesn't want to go with me anymore." Other women expressed similar sentiments regarding the cautions they received from other friends and family members.

Even more passive activities changed as a result of pregnancy. Lucy loved to read but "This has been a change during pregnancy because it's all been baby, baby, baby. I try to pull out a regular book, and I find I can't get through it because *What to Expect* is there. Any number of articles that I have seem more relevant to what I should be doing and what I should be reading." An avid piano player, Lucy shared, "Um, even my piano playing has changed, it's probably increased but just because I know she can hear it and that's something I want her to enjoy, but now I am playing for her, not me really."

Overall, women expressed a number of changes related to leisure participation and meaning stemming from pregnancy; however, all the women believed that life and leisure would return more to normal once that baby came. They acknowledged that life would be different with a baby but all commented on ways that a baby would fit into their current leisure patterns. Melanie commented, "I guess just assuming that hopefully once my body is back to normal, the baby will not really have any impact on things thinking leisure-wise, like our ability to go do things we want to do, you know, we'll just kind of say let's pack the baby up and go right along with us doing whatever we want." Anna assumed her situation would look similar to her friends with children: "I have girlfriends to look at who have kids and it really seems like not much has really changed from before they had babies, so I guess it will be the same for me." The postnatal interviews I conducted provide some insight into whether and to what extent this was so.

Early Mothering

Given that I was curious to understand the transition from pregnancy to motherhood, I followed up with all the women in their early mothering days. To allow the women some time to adjust to motherhood, I waited until the babies were all between 6 and 12 months old. During the second interview, women were asked to talk about life with a baby. Specifically, I was interested in hearing how their experience compared to what they had anticipated and how they were doing with re-engaging in meaningful leisure.

Shifting Leisure

For the women in this study, life with a baby was not as they had predicted in the first interview. When reminded of her response to leisure with a baby, Melanie quickly replied, "Yeah, I had no idea what I was in for. When I was here last time, I really believed that life would go back to normal. I lied. There is no such thing as *normal* anymore. I thought that I would be out doing all kinds of things with the baby, and even though she is a great baby, I don't have it in me to deal with the packing up and all the stuff that has to happen just to get out the door." Melanie went on to explain that she had actually cancelled her gym membership because it was evident she was not going to be able to use it while her daughter was still an infant. Melanie also voiced a number of concerns related to her body image and felt that the baby only partially explained her lack of return to physical activities; she was still struggling to lose weight from pregnancy and felt this too was an issue impacting a number of leisure areas, including physical activities, socializing, and intimacy with her husband. Other women echoed Melanie's words, citing lack of time and energy, changes in relationships, body image, and feelings of guilt related to "self" leisure.

Fatigue levels impacted leisure engagement during pregnancy, and women still cited fatigue as a barrier to leisure since their baby's birth. In fact, many women felt more tired since the baby came home than during pregnancy. Lucy noted, "I mean I was tired while I was pregnant but I could nap, and overall I took things easy. Sometimes I still nap while [baby] is napping but there seems to be so much to do and I just can't get it all done, so I try to use lots of her nap times to get stuff done." Anna was not expecting night-waking to have as large an impact as it did, indicating that she had pulled all-nighters during university and assumed it would be the same this time around. She had not accounted for being woken from slumber as often as she was. She did note that this was improving as the baby was getting older, but she still felt quite tired a lot of the time.

Anna commented as the first of her friends to have a baby: "None of them have a baby, so they don't really understand the process involved in going for coffee. They drop over sometimes, but they are still working and I am just around, and feel like I don't really have the energy in the evenings and the baby's schedule is busy in the evening. I feel like I am missing out on things with my friends." Sophia was surprised by the change in her relationship with her husband, "I mean it's just not the same, he works and I am here all the time and when he comes home he wants to just relax and do nothing and I am itching to do anything. He doesn't get it. And he doesn't know how to help. I mean we are not really in tune with each other anymore. I know that I am more focused on the baby but still I want to be with him, too. It's a lot harder than I imagined."

Many of the women stated that they understood that a certain amount of weight gain was inevitable during pregnancy. All the women in this study saw themselves of normal weight pre-pregnancy and all indicated that their pregnancy weight gain was within normal ranges. However, some of the women were still struggling to lose weight gained during pregnancy, and others commented that even though they were back at their pre-pregnancy weight, their bodies were not the same anymore. They had not expected to feel unhappy with their bodies and looked for ways to accept the changes. Mary commented, "It's just crazy, I mean I keep telling myself that my body is amazing for growing this baby and still feeding him, but, um, I guess I just can't convince myself that I am okay with my body. I do really want to be but I am not. And to tell the truth, it prevents me from doing some things I used to do. I don't feel okay in my own body yet." The women in this study all engaged in various forms of physical activity as part of health, as well as keeping a certain appearance, so they were not yet back in that mental space. While they acknowledged that they "needed" to return to physical activity to regain that appearance, they were lacking motivation because of body image issues.

A final reason given for reduced leisure involvement was related to feelings of guilt. Sophia stated, ". . . and at times I want to do something and I plan for it but then I can't follow through with leaving because I will miss [the baby] and then I feel guilty. [My husband] encourages me to do things for myself so the guilt is really self-induced." Mary, too, had difficulty leaving the baby to do things for herself, so she looked for opportunities where she could include her son. She attended community-based play groups, and while this met some of her own needs, she did not really know these women, and socializing with them was not the same as spending time with her own friends, where the focus was on herself rather than her son.

Leisure as Coping

When I started this research, I was interested in examining how women used leisure to cope with pregnancy and early mothering. What I learned from the women in my study was that they were not really using or experiencing leisure as a coping strategy. From the literature, we know that leisure has provided many different groups with coping abilities, but the women here did not appear to see leisure as coping. Leisure is often defined as involving "perceived freedom" and "intrinsic motivation" (Mannell & Kleiber, 1997), yet the women in the study felt that the changes to their leisure during pregnancy were motivated by external influences, and they no longer experienced freedom in their choices. So while some of what they experienced may still have "looked like" leisure, they did not necessarily define or experience it as leisure because of how the changes were prompted.

Once the baby came along, the women did not engage in much activity that they defined as "self leisure." They selected activities focusing on the baby, and while they did meet some leisure needs through these opportunities, many of their personal leisure needs went unmet. Clearly, the women in this study were still not convinced at the time of the second interview that they had achieved a satisfactory balance between being a woman and a mother. At the same time, those mothers whose child was closer to one year were starting to see "the light at the end of the tunnel" and talked about starting to return to some meaningful "self leisure" engagement.

DIRECTIONS FOR PRACTICE AND FUTURE RESEARCH

Previous research indicates that becoming a parent results in a significant change in sense of self and is likely one of the most profound transitions life has to offer (Miller, 2005). This contention was supported in my study of new mothers. The women in this study felt unprepared for the magnitude of this transition and were uncertain as to how to begin to move beyond the initial shock. They experienced a loss of self and were unsure how to go about regaining self.

Overall, while pregnancy and parenting are often viewed as a "natural" part of human life, it is not something that can be fully understood until it has been experienced. Further, it is important for professionals involved in prenatal care to seek ways of better preparing women and men for the changes that this transition brings. The women in this study had a number of advantages in that they were all in committed relationships, were receiving prenatal care, were active participants in that care, and were all well-educated with relatively stable household incomes. This is not always the case, and if these women who felt they were prepared discovered that they were not, it is imperative that we seek to better understand this process for those who do not have the resources these women had.

The findings suggest that during pregnancy and the first year of motherhood, women reported only minimal participation in personal leisure. As previously noted, leisure has been found to be an important element of coping, yet these women had not been in touch with much of "their leisure" since becoming pregnant. The women were still struggling to sort out their new identities as mothers, suggesting that women experiencing motherhood for the first time may benefit from leisure education with an emphasis of self in leisure, leisure awareness, and leisure resources for their new self. While there are any number of playgroups offered by most community recreation centers, it may be that these require a little more structure both for moms to be able to avail themselves of such opportunities and to remind them to take care of their own needs as well as their babies' needs. At the same time, leisure service professionals should advocate for policies (e.g., workplace policies) that support parents and their needs (Fullagar and Hilbrecht, this volume).

Further examination is needed to better understand the changing relationships—including a mother's relationship with her "previous self"—in a woman's life that result from mothering. Further, these women were not prepared for the changes to their significant relationships, particularly with their husbands. Given the research that claims the importance of couple and family leisure in maintaining family cohesiveness (Orthner & Mancini, 1991; Zabriskie & McCormick, 2001), it is imperative that we examine how to foster these relationships as the family grows.

Many claim that motherhood is a "natural" part of being a woman. Becoming a mother, however, is a major transitional life event (and one that holds cultural significance, as discussed by Harrington in her chapter, this volume). Women often must move from a relatively comfortable, known reality to the unknown reality of parenting (Barba & Selder, 1995). Such transition requires shifts in personal goals, responsibilities, relationships, and personal identity, as well as confronting and figuring out how to negotiate the ideologies of motherhood that all societies and cultures impose. The idea of "becoming a mother" is not simply the act of giving birth; it is acknowledging and accepting all the life changes that come with the responsibility of a child (Mercer, 2004). Becoming a mother is a permanent change, and once a woman adds "mother" to her life identities, she is forever changed. As leisure scholars, it is imperative that we continue to examine the process of family-making and how this process impacts women and their continued ability to engage in meaningful personal leisure. Further, it is important that we also reconsider our notions of leisure as coping to accommodate the complex and nuanced experiences and practices of leisure.

My study examined a small, and rather homogeneous, group of women. Without purposefully looking for women similar to myself, that is exactly what I found: late 20s, white, middle-class, university-educated, married women. Clearly, additional work needs to focus on how those of diverse social class standing, race/ethnicity, sexual orientation, family practices and structures, and historical moments experience, and are allowed to enact, mothering. Women today are expected to "do it all" in this world of "perfect madness" (Warner, 2005). How then do they do it and maintain a sense of harmony among all the roles a mother in today's world must occupy? Mother, educator, model, wife, employee, taxi driver, and woman? We need to seek answers to these questions so we may better prepare women for motherhood, so that she may be better equipped, and have the personal and social resources needed, to raise healthy children. Further, we need to focus on educating social institutions about parenting as a part of social life, not just family life, so that policies may be developed that support the responsibility of parenting and practices of family life.

REFERENCES

Barba, E., & Selder, F. (1995). Life transitions theory. *Nursing Leadership Forum, 1*, 4–11.

Coleman, D. (1993). Leisure based social support, leisure dispositions, and health. *Journal of Leisure Research, 25*, 350–361.

Coleman, D., & Iso-Ahola, S. E. (1993). Leisure and health: The role of social support and self-determination. *Journal of Leisure Research, 25*, 111–128.

Hays, S. (1996). *The cultural contradictions of motherhood.* New Haven, CT: Yale University Press.

Hutchinson, S. L., Loy, D. P., Kleiber, D. A., & Dattilo, J. (2003). Leisure as a coping resource: Variations in coping with traumatic injury and illness. *Leisure Sciences, 25*(2–3), 143–161.

Iso-Ahola, S. E., & Park, C. J. (1996). Leisure-related social support and self-determination as buffers of stress-illness relationship. *Journal of Leisure Research, 28*, 169–187.

Iwasaki, Y. (2003). Examining rival models of leisure coping mechanisms. *Leisure Sciences, 25*, 183–206.

Iwasaki, Y., & Mannell, R. C. (2000). Hierarchal dimensions of leisure stress coping. *Leisure Sciences, 22,* 163–181.

Kleiber, D. A., Hutchinson, S. L., & Williams, R. (2002). Leisure as a resource in transcending negative life events: Self-protection, self-restoration, and personal transformation. *Leisure Sciences, 24,* 219–235.

Klitzing, S. W. (2003). Coping with chronic stress: Leisure and women who are homeless. *Leisure Sciences, 25,* 163–181.

Klitzing, S. W. (2004). Women living in a homeless shelter: Stress, coping and leisure. *Journal of Leisure Research, 36,* 483–512.

Mannell, R. C., & Kleiber, D. A. (1997). *A social psychology of leisure.* State College, PA: Venture Publishing, Inc.

Mercer, R. T. (2004). Becoming a mother versus maternal role attainment. *Journal of Nursing Scholarship, 36,* 226–232.

Miller, T. (2005). *Making sense of motherhood: A narrative approach.* Cambridge, UK: Cambridge University Press.

Orthner, D. K., & Mancini, J. A. (1991). Benefits of leisure for family bonding. In B. L. Driver, P. J. Brown, & G. L. Peterson (Eds.), *Benefits of leisure* (pp. 215–301). State College, PA: Venture Publishing, Inc.

Porter, M. (2008). *Transformative power in motherwork.* Newcastle, UK: Cambridge Scholars.

Shaw, S. M., & Hilbrecht, M. (2008). *"It could be your fault": Parental responsibilities for children's health and children's leisure in the age of anxiety.* 12th Canadian Congress on Leisure Research, Montreal, QC.

Sullivan, A. M. (2008). *Becoming a mother: Exploring women's coping strategies.* Presented at the 12th Canadian Congress on Leisure Research, Montreal, QC.

Warner, J. (2005). *Perfect madness: Motherhood in the age of anxiety.* New York, NY: Riverhead.

Zabriskie, R., & McCormick, B. (2001). The influences of family leisure patterns on perceptions of family functioning. *Family Relations: Interdisciplinary Journal of Applied Family Studies, 50*(3), 66–74.

ACKNOWLEDGMENTS

I would like to thank the women who so willingly shared their personal stories. Without their honesty and openness with a number of personal topics, this study could not have happened. I would also like to thank Memorial University of Newfoundland for providing funding to support this research.

FOOTNOTES

[1] It is important to note that the criteria used to select potential participants were determined in order to avoid additional elements that may be a source of stress for women during pregnancy. Women had to be over the age of 19 (age of majority in Newfoundland) and under 35 (age where additional prenatal screening becomes part of prenatal care) and they had to be in a committed relationship (living with the baby's father). As well, this was to be her first pregnancy (in at least the second half of the pregnancy), and she was to be receiving prenatal care. Fortunately, all of the women who participated in the first interview had successful pregnancies and deliveries and were available to participate in the second interview.

[2] At the start of the first interviews, all of the women asked me whether I was a mother. When asked whether it mattered if I was a mother, all indicated that it did, that there was some information they would not want to share with a non-mother. Subsequently, the interviews were conversational in nature and mutual disclosure resulted in the rich data this study generated.

CHAPTER 23
YOUTH SPORT: VISIBLE DADS, HIDDEN MOMS, AND GENDERED CHILDREN

DAWN TRUSSELL

Kathy glances at the family calendar with a fretful look—green for her daughter's dance program, red for her son's hockey practices, and black for her work schedule. If she hurries, she can drop off her daughter at the dance studio and her son at the arena just in the nick of time. She has 10 minutes to change out of her work clothes, pack the kids' equipment, and be on the road. Her daughter is old enough to make grilled cheese sandwiches for herself and her younger brother. "Hurry up, we need to get going!" she yells to her children. She grabs a pickle from the fridge, glances over to the sink, mumbles to herself "the dishes can wait," and heads out the door.

Organized youth sport was an instrumental part of my childhood. I have many wonderful memories of being on the ball diamond, playing with my friends, looking up at the bleachers at my mother, and beaming with pride at my father, who was the umpire. Yet, it was not until my first research project that I began to reflect upon and understand the extent that youth sport shaped not only my life, but also that of my family. In my first project, I explored the family leisure of rural-dwelling Canadians, and organized youth sport quickly emerged as a major experience and practice of their leisure activities (Trussell, 2005; Trussell & Shaw, 2007, 2009). Just as striking was the extent to which such leisure was gendered. In particular, mothers expressed a considerable amount of fatigue and strain as they tried to negotiate the physical and emotional demands related to their children's sport participation.

Certainly, the extant research indicates that gender remains a significant issue in children's physical activity and organized sport participation. Participation rates for young females have increased dramatically over the past two generations (Coakley & Donnelly, 2009; Sabo, 2009). Yet, young male participation rates continue to be higher than those of young females, even with policy and legislation aimed at equality in Canada, the United States, and other Westernized cultures (see for example, Coakley & Donnelly, 2009; Fairclough, Boddy, Hackett, & Stratton, 2009; Raudsepp & Viira, 2000; Sabo, 2009; Trussell & McTeer, 2007; Vilhjalmsson & Kristjansdottir, 2003).

In part, gender differences in organized youth sport are influenced by parental support. Traditional gender ideals that reinforce the notion that sport participation is more important for sons than it is for daughters (Lareau, 2002) and that sons have a higher athletic ability than daughters (Fredricks & Eccles, 2005) may be evident. Yet, research has also shown that daughters are more active when they receive encouragement from their parents, and particularly when family members are active participants themselves (Casey, Eime, Payne, & Harvey, 2009). Sport, as a masculine domain, also provides the opportunity to enhance the father–daughter relationship, but in a "nuanced and complex way. They [daughters] enjoy the attention and camaraderie, but often feel pressured to train, compete, and achieve in ways that please their fathers (and not necessarily themselves)" (Willms, 2009, p. 142).

The *type* of sport participation may also be influenced by cultural ideologies reinforcing the belief that sons should participate in "masculine" sports, while daughters should participate in "feminine" sports. That is, organized youth sport may provide an important context where sons are taught traditional ideals of masculinity, what it means to be a man (Messner, 2001), and the significance of male bonding and male space (Kay, 2009b)—whereas daughters are taught to be "ladies as well as athletes" (Coakley, 2009, p. 44). However, Coakley also points out "some fathers make concerted efforts to choose or organize for their children sports programs that emphasize gender equity" (p. 45). Thus, understanding the reinforcement or potential resistance of traditional gender ideologies within the family unit is particularly important as the "family is a primary socializing agent where gender roles are learned" (Shakib & Dunbar, 2004, p. 275) and may have long-term implications for sport participation patterns.

Parental responsibilities related to the facilitation of children's participation in sport may also have important implications for gender research. Although sport is widely assumed to be a central context for fathering (Marsiglio, Roy, & Fox, 2005), little research has investigated the important role of mothers in children's sport practices. Notable exceptions are Thompson (1999) and Chafetz and Kotarba's (1999) research on the gender differentiation of parent responsibilities and expectations in the facilitation of children's sport participation. These authors challenge the widespread "perception that it is fathers rather than mothers who are predominantly involved in their children's sport" (Harrington, 2009, p. 58).

The various ways mothers and fathers provide support for children's participation in organized sport may reproduce and validate traditional definitions of femininity and masculinity—that is, practices of "doing gender" (West & Zimmerman, 1987). While fathers are more involved in the public aspects of children's sport participation (coach, manager, game strategizing, and playing/practicing with the child), mothers are more involved in what is referred to as the "domestic" responsibilities (Chafetz & Kotarba, 1999; Thompson, 1999). Mothers are charged with the responsibility of facilitating the physical and emotional labor of children's sport participation. Tasks such as laundering uniforms, washing water bottles, preparing meals, and chauffeuring children to and from activities are often done by mothers. Further, the time demands required to support their children's sport participation may become all-consuming, with parents feeling powerless to make changes to the existing sport structure (Anderson & Doherty, 2005; Kay, 2000c).

Given these gendered parental responsibilities and gendered rates of participation for boys and girls, organized youth sport is clearly an important context for understanding the (re)production—and possible transformation—of gender ideologies. In this chapter, I illustrate the connection between organized youth sport, and changing cultural ideals and practices associated with gender and parenting. I examine data from a qualitative study that explored the lives of seven families (7 mothers, 6 fathers, and 19 children—9 boys and 10 girls) from a small community in Canada to understand divergent experiences and meanings of organized youth sport for mothers, fathers, and children.

One of the central research questions for the study sought to understand the connections between family life (interactions, values, and relationships) and achieving and/or resisting sociocultural expectations associated with parenting and/or gender ideologies (see Harrington, this volume). For this chapter, I pay particular attention to how organized youth sport may reinforce, resist, and/or transform dominant gender ideologies within families, as well as broader gender relations. Three main themes include the gendered nature of parents' private and public youth sport involvement; ideological equality, cultural reality, and boys' sport participation; and broadening perspectives of femininity and girls' sport participation.

In the next section, I discuss the gendered nature of the physical and emotional work that is required to support children's sport participation. I illustrate how mothers' and fathers' responsibilities related to supporting organized youth sport could reproduce and validate traditional definitions of femininity and masculinity. Yet, at the same time, these roles can also be a context of resistance to traditional gender discourses. The following sections outline the gender ideals that shape young males' and females' type of sport participation. Societal and other pressures on families related to cultural values associated with gender are also discussed in detail. The concluding section situates the findings in light of relevant literature and raises future questions for leisure research and practice.

The Gendered Nature of Parents' Private and Public Youth Sport Involvement

The parents in this study talked about the work related to facilitating children's sport participation. Similar to Chafetz and Kotarba (1999) and Thompson (1999), the sense of time stress and fatigue because of their hectic schedules was particularly evident for the mothers who were the "managers" of their children's lives. They would often be the one who orchestrated the family's schedules, coordinated the decision-making process of what activities the children would participate in, completed the registration responsibilities, and chauffeured the children to and from practices. The husbands would assist them in this role; however, the inequality of the distribution of work was not generally recognized by fathers, mothers, or children.

The respective roles that the mothers and fathers held within the sport organizations also revealed the gendered politics of organized youth sport. Many of the parents initially spoke of a sense of equality in the organizational roles (e.g., opportunities to serve on the board of directors). For example, one mother said: "I would say it's probably about 50/50. Where I think a few years ago it was more dads" (Mother, family #4). Indeed, applying a gendered analysis to parents' organizational responsibilities revealed a sense of change and women's increasingly public roles. The mothers' increased participation in these leadership roles may be partly related to the new opportunities for their daughters to participate in sport. For the girls' hockey league, for example, the girls and the mothers talked about league rules that required a female in the dressing room:

> My mom . . . she's my trainer. She usually opens the door and helps us get dressed because in Atom girls' hockey, the boys [meaning her coaches] aren't allowed to come in the dressing room while the girls are getting dressed. (Middle child, female, age 11, family #7).

> With the girls' team there has to be a female. Like you can have all male coaching staff but the trainer has to be female. (Mother, family #4)

Yet, this analysis also demonstrated the reproduction of sport as a traditionally masculine domain, with men at the visible, central roles that tended to be more widely recognized, and women in the hidden, peripheral roles. It appeared women's traditional responsibilities for planning and organization within the family unit had extended into the public domain and the organization of the children's sport leagues (e.g., team manager, board of directors). This was particularly evident in local leagues and traditionally feminine sports (i.e., there was no discussion of any fathers who volunteered their time to support their daughters' figure-skating organization). In contrast, the fathers' organizational responsibilities tended to be in more visible and central positions (e.g., coach, trainer), in traditionally masculine sports, that were more widely recognized. Moreover, although both mothers and fathers talked about the importance of fundraising and the high costs of children's sport participation, it tended to be the mothers who talked about the work (planning and organizing) of fundraising activities.

At times, the family unit revealed conflicting gender values that did not align with the sport organization, yet they felt powerless to initiate change. That is, when families that typically embodied egalitarian principles in their household were confronted with gender inequity in the sport organization, they would simply avoid confrontation. For example, although one mother did not agree with the assigned roles that she thought reflected and reinforced traditional gender ideology (specifically, very few women in leadership roles in the highly competitive leagues) she would not try to initiate change. As she explained: "I allow it to carry on even though I feel differently" [Interview starts to feel awkward with calculated responses.] (Mother, family #2).

The children's interviews revealed that they recognized both parents' involvement and contributions. However, it was the fathers' more visible roles that were often told with enthusiasm and pride. The way that more highly regarded, visible, leadership roles filled by fathers compared to the less visible leadership roles that were typically the mothers' responsibility was best exemplified by one child who said: "Well, my dad does the timekeeping; he's really good at it! He does the announcing and he has the stereo for the music. I've heard some really good comments about him." When asked if his mom was involved at all, he replied, "I guess she does the 50-50 draws" (Male, age 14, family #2). Thus, embedded in the children's discourse was the gendered nature of the parents' leadership roles. Further, these gendered practices had implications for the children's perceptions of the value and importance of their parents' varying responsibilities.

Maintaining the Masculine Ideal and Boys' Sport Participation

The influence and underlying pressures put forth by family members, other children, and society at large related to cultural values of gender-appropriate activities also shaped the children's decisions for their sport involvement. On the surface, it appeared that children could choose any sport activity they wanted. It was also evident, though, that stigma and stereotyping influenced their decisions for their sport involvement at a deeper level. All participants were asked an open-ended question about girls and boys playing nontraditional sports (i.e., girls playing hockey and boys figure-skating). For the majority of mothers, fathers, and children, their initial response indicated a perception of "fairness" and "equality" for both girls and boys and their right to play any sport they may choose.

However, the cultural reality for young boys was that they were quite limited in their sport decisions, and gender stereotypes still shaped their sport involvement. These gender stereotypes were particularly evident in the fathers' interviews, though it seemed that some tried to balance their concerns by recognizing the physical skill of girls. For example, some mothers who did not have any sons responded that it was socially acceptable for young boys to become a figure-skater, and these mothers expressed the belief that boys should have the opportunity to pursue this option if they were interested. Yet, the majority of the fathers, both with sons and without, did not respond directly to the question of equal opportunity as it related to young boys. Instead, their response alluded to the difficulties that boys who figure-skated might encounter. For example, one father without sons said: "It might be a little tougher for a boy that's figure-skated. [Why?]. Figure-skating . . . it's not quite boyish or manly. But the way the girls can skate on my daughter's team that figure-skate too, every boy should take figure-skating. They're just amazing skaters!" (Father, family #7).

The children's perspectives on boys' opportunities to participate in nontraditional sports were somewhat reflective of their own personal experiences and what they saw in the larger sporting community. For example, many of the female figure-skaters believed that boys should have the opportunity to figure-skate and made reference to the *one* boy who was a member of their club. As a young figure-skater explained:

> Guys can figure-skate because I remember when I was in level six I think, there was a boy. [Was there?] Yeah, so it's whether they enjoy it or they're not scared to do it. [Why would they be scared to do it?] Because they'd be embarrassed because usually there's only girls in figure-skating and he was like the only guy. (Youngest child, female, age 10, family #6)

In contrast, the young male participants were hesitant to say that boys should have the opportunity to play any sport, including nontraditional activities such as figure-skating. At this point, the interviews would become somewhat strained and uncomfortable. As one male child stated: "I wish I could say the same things as what I said for the girl answer, but well, I don't know. It would be kind of weird if like . . . I don't know any guys who figure-skate so . . ." (Oldest child, male, age 15, family #6).

The struggle for boys to participate in nontraditional (i.e., "feminine") sports was influenced by the potential negative repercussions within their peer groups. As one young girl expressed it: "Yeah, I think that anyone should be able to do anything. It's just they . . . they have to like believe and don't listen to their friends saying: 'Oh that's a girl's sport.'" (Youngest child, female, age 10, family #4) Additionally, a male child revealed what would happen within his peer group if one of his friends decided to figure-skate: "He'd take a beating that's for sure. But if he really wanted to do it then you know, good for him. Shouldn't let us lippin' him off I guess you would say . . . shouldn't stop him from doing what he wants to do." (Oldest child, male, age 15, family #6)

BROADENING PERSPECTIVES OF FEMININITY AND GIRLS' SPORT PARTICIPATION

The idea for equality was clearer for the young women in this study as all but one of them played ice hockey—a sport that has "traditionally" been male. The participants' responses also indicated the concept of equal opportunity for the young women. As one father explained, he believed his daughters could do anything they wanted: "I think it's fairly wide open for them to pick and choose what they want to do" (Father, family #7). This sentiment was echoed by a young male who had no sisters. He stated that girls should have the opportunity to play hockey: "If they want to play they can play. There's no issue, like why they can't play" (Oldest child, male, age 16, family #3). Indeed, 6 out of the 10 girls who were interviewed for this study simultaneously enjoyed the opportunity to play both hockey and figure-skating, at some point in their lives.

Moreover, it became clear that there was a sense of broadening perspectives about femininity. Many of the participants, and particularly the mothers, talked about changing perspectives as it related to their daughters' participation in hockey. For some women, their own beliefs were transformed, and for others, there was an awareness of a broader societal shift. They perceived that young women could now enjoy some of the previously exclusive masculine activities. As one mother explained: "Girls can definitely play hockey. It's really come a long way. I think things are changing.

I think you find more and more girls doing that. It was never a girl's sport for me back then. It didn't make sense" (Mother, family #6).

Yet, it was clear, too, that the sense of change experienced by the mothers varied. For example, most women felt that their own families embodied an egalitarian lens towards their sons' and daughters' sport participation, whereas broader society still valued men's sport more than women's sport:

> I think girls are very much accepted [in their community sport]. I'm not sure that the view of society is quite the same. You listen to different people involved in sports, and I still think the attraction in hockey is male hockey. Women's hockey really hasn't got the same kind of pull. I think there's wonderful female athletic people out there, but I'm not sure society views it the same. (Mother, family #2)

Another mother, who had three daughters and was involved in the initial startup of girls' hockey in the community, indicated that poor opinions of girls' hockey were evident locally. As she explained:

> You always have the parents and . . . it's mostly male. They don't think that the girls' is as good and there will always be those people. We have one mom—two out of three boys played triple A boys' hockey—and she came to the year-end tournament and we won in triple overtime. Beat a team we've never beat before all year and my daughter scored after triple overtime and she goes, "I don't know why people don't come and watch girls' hockey, it's such good hockey!" And it is good hockey, but there's still that stereotype that its *girls'* hockey. (Mother, family #7)

Yet, several of the fathers who had daughters that played hockey expressed the ideal of equal opportunity for the young women's participation in a traditionally masculine sport. Unlike the mothers, they did not sense diverse opinions connected to the quality of girls' hockey and their respective abilities on any level. For example, one of the fathers whose wife was cited above indicated that: "From a society standpoint, I don't believe that there's any discrimination at all" (Father, family #2). Another father noted the changes that occurred since the onset of girls' hockey. When asked if there were "gender-appropriate" sports for girls, he responded: "No, I don't think so. Not anymore. I think that has really changed in the last, even five or eight years. Girls' hockey is really . . . the last couple of years has become really popular" (Father, family #6).

DISCUSSION AND FUTURE ISSUES

This study indicated the significance of organized youth sport in reinforcing, resisting, and/or transforming dominant gender ideologies within families, as well as broader gender relations. It also revealed the contradictions and complexity of children and parents' sport involvement. That is, embedded in the participants' discourse was the struggle they experienced in reconciling a sense of fairness and rights of the individual, with the social reality of the gendered nature of sport. These conflicting ideals of "ideological equality" versus "cultural reality" were exemplified in the children's sport decision-making process as well as the parental responsibilities.

Underlying pressures by family members, other children, and broader society, as they related to cultural values of gender-appropriate activities, shaped the children's decisions for their sport involvement. Although on the surface it appeared that children could choose any sport activity they wanted, it was also evident that stigma and stereotyping influenced their decisions for sport involvement at a deeper level. The notion of ideological equality versus cultural reality revealed deeply entrenched opposition to changing ideals of gender-appropriate activities, and it was particularly apparent for the young boys (Schmalz, this volume).

In contrast, the young women's sport decisions were less controlled with broadening perspectives of femininity. At the same time, this may also further represent and reinforce broader cultural values related to the inferiority of women and their sporting practices (i.e., it's okay for girls to play boys' sports and this may even be a "step up" whereas for boys to play "girls' sport" is a "step down"). For that reason, boys who decide to participate in "inferior" girls' sports will encounter greater stigma and stereotypes. Thus, consistent with previous research on resistance (Shaw, 2001), the findings indicated that the process of challenging traditional gender-appropriate activities was not linear but complicated and contradictory and simultaneously contained both reproductive and resistant aspects.

The process of "undoing gender" (Deutsch, 2007) or resisting gender (Shaw, 2001) was also contradictory with respect to the mothers' and fathers' involvement in sport organizations. Many parents talked in terms of gender equity and equal organizational contributions. Indeed there was evidence that mothers are currently more involved than in previous years, and this was emphasized in the positive context of gender equality. In some ways this may be seen as progress, since earlier research by Thompson (1999) and others revealed women's extensive support roles in hidden activities, such as laundry, care of equipment, and food preparation, while the fathers dominated the higher status organizational positions.

In this study, though, the women's involvement in higher profile organizational roles was often an extension of their *hidden* domestic roles. While a few of the mothers had become coaches or team trainers, almost all of the mothers continued to occupy hidden leadership positions such as serving on the board of directors or being the team manager. The fathers' more visible public positions such as the coach or scorekeeper provided them with more public recognition and status within the community, as well as within the private context of the family unit. This was evidenced by many of the children who spoke with pride and excitement of their fathers' roles and contributions, while the mothers' roles received less recognition. Thus, it could be argued that although women's roles in the public sphere of sport have increased, they have increased in the context of the hidden and invisible positions (similar to the private sphere), and their workload has in fact intensified compared to earlier years. "Doing gender" (West & Zimmerman, 1987) in providing support for children's participation in organized youth sport can be seen to reproduce and validate traditional definitions of femininity and masculinity.

In sum, this study illustrates the complexity of the connections between youth sport participation (and organizational responsibilities) and the contradictory processes of negotiation, construction, and reconstruction of gender ideologies. Further, by revealing the connection of organized youth sport to changing gender ideologies, this study calls attention to the transformation of cultural values and future issues that should be examined. For example, why are there broadening perspectives of femininity in youth sport, while the masculine ideal remains relatively constant and unwavering? Moreover, are these perspectives really broadening or just shifting and reconstructing gender (and inequality) in more nuanced or subtle ways? As Willms (2009) questioned, does girls' participation within the hyper-masculine domain of sport "represent growth and change or reconstitute old systems of dominance in a new context?" (p. 128). Examination of the context of the participants' responses (i.e., "calculated words" and uncomfortable body language) may also reveal much about how gender "works" and is "done" (West & Zimmerman, 1987). Questions linked to these perspectives and their intersection with social differences of class, race, ethnicity, sexuality, and disability may provide important insights of how gender relations are (re)constructed.

Future research might also examine the nature of gender construction through the experiences of mothers who grew up when new ideas about girls' participation in "male" sports were developing. Will their lives continue to reflect women's hidden work and the concept of "doing gender" much like their mothers, or will they exhibit new perspectives and new practices that challenge sports organizations and assumptions about volunteer roles?

The answers to these and other questions will not only tell us much about women and leisure but leisure as a context for the construction of gender as well.

REFERENCES

Anderson, J., & Doherty, W. (2005). Democratic community initiatives: The case of overscheduled children. *Family Relations, 54*, 654–665.

Casey, M., Eime, R., Payne, W., & Harvey, J. (2009). Using a socioecological approach to examine participation in sport and physical activity among rural adolescent girls. *Qualitative Health Research, 19*(7), 881–893.

Chafetz, J., & Kotarba, J. (1999). Little league mothers and the reproduction of gender. In J. Coakley & P. Connelly (Eds.), *Inside sports* (pp. 46–54). New York, NY: Routledge.

Coakley, J. (2009). The good father: Parental expectations and youth sports. In T. A. Kay (Ed.), *Fathering through sport and leisure* (pp. 40–50). New York, NY: Routledge.

Coakley, J., & Donnelly, P. (2009). *Sports in society: Issues and controversies.* Toronto, ON: McGraw-Hill Ryerson.

Deutsch, F. (2007). Undoing gender. *Gender & Society, 21*(1), 106–127

Fairclough, S., Boddy, L., Hackett, A., & Stratton, G. (2009). Associations between children's socioeconomic status, weight status, and sex, with screen-based sedentary behaviours and sport participation. *International Journal of Pediatric Obesity, 4*, 299–305.

Fredricks, J. A., & Eccles, J. S. (2005). Family socialization, gender, and sport motivation and involvement. *Journal of Sport & Exercise Psychology, 27*, 3–31.

Harrington, M. (2009). Sport mad, good dads: Australian fathering through leisure and sport practices. In T. A. Kay (Ed.), *Fathering through sport and leisure* (pp. 51–72). New York, NY: Routledge.

Kay, T. A. (2000c). Sporting excellence: A family affair? *European Physical Education Review, 6*(2), 151–169.

Kay, T. A. (2009b). Fathers and sons. Being "Father Angel." In T. A. Kay (Ed.), *Fathering through sport and leisure* (pp. 106–123). New York, NY: Routledge.

Lareau, A. (2002). Invisible inequality: Social class and childrearing in Black families and White families. *American Sociological Review, 67*(5), 747–776.

Marsiglio, W., Roy, K., & Fox, G. (2005). Situated fathering: A spatially sensitive and social approach. In W. Marsiglio, K. Roy, & G. Fox (Eds.), *Situated fathering: A focus on physical and social spaces* (pp. 3–26). Lanham, MD: Rowman & Littlefield.

Messner, M. A. (2001). Boyhood, organized sports, and the construction of masculinities. In M. S. Kimmel & M. A. Messner (Eds.), *Men's lives* (5th ed.) (pp. 88–99) Needham Heights, MA: Allyn & Bacon.

Raudsepp, L., & Viira, R. (2000). Sociocultural correlates of physical activity in adolescents. *Pediatric Exercise Science, 12*, 51–60.

Sabo, D. (2009). The gender gap in youth sports: Too many urban girls are being left behind. *The Journal of Physical Education, Recreation & Dance, 80*(8), 35–40.

Shakib, S., & Dunbar, M. D. (2004). How high school athletes talk about maternal and paternal sporting experiences: Identifying modifiable social processes for gender equity physical activity interventions. *International Review for the Sociology of Sport, 39*, 275–299.

Shaw, S. M. (2001). Conceptualizing resistance: Women's leisure as political practice. *Journal of Leisure Research, 33*(2), 186–201.

Thompson, S. (1999). *Mother's taxi: Sport and women's labour.* New York, NY: State University of New York Press.

Trussell, D. (2005). *Family leisure in the rural context: Women's experiences of life on the family farm* (Unpublished master's thesis), University of Waterloo, ON.

Trussell, D., & McTeer, W. (2007). Children's sport participation in Canada: Is it a level playing field? *International Journal of Canadian Studies, 35*, 113–132.

Trussell, D., & Shaw, S. (2007). "Daddy's gone and he'll be back in October": Farm women's experiences of family leisure. *Journal of Leisure Research, 39*(2), 366–387.

Trussell, D., & Shaw, S. (2009). Changing family life in the rural context: Women's perspectives of family leisure on the farm. *Leisure Sciences, 31*(5), 434–449.

Vilhjalmsson, R., & Kristjansdottir, G. (2003). Gender differences in physical activity in older children and adolescents: The central role of organized sport. *Social Science & Medicine, 56*, 363–374.

West, C., & Zimmerman, D. (1987). Doing gender. *Gender & Society, 1*(1), 125–151.

Willms, N. (2009). Fathers and daughters. Negotiating gendered relationships in sport. In T. A. Kay (Ed.), *Fathering through sport and leisure* (pp. 124–144). New York, NY: Routledge.

ACKNOWLEDGMENTS

The author extends her gratitude to Dr. Susan Shaw for her earlier guidance on this study, the seven families who opened their homes and shared their perspectives and experiences, and the Social Sciences and Humanities Research Council of Canada (Doctoral Fellowship) and Sport Canada (Sport Participation Research Initiative) for their financial support.

Chapter 24
Families, Gender, Social Class, and Leisure

Maureen Harrington

Introduction:
A Lesson about Leisure

Going to university was not part of the plan when I was growing up in a working-class family in London, Ontario, Canada. My immigrant parents always said get as much education as you can, but university was for "other" children, those whose parents could afford it, like the owner of the construction company my dad worked for. On weekends, I would sometimes go with Dad to the building site in north London's Sherwood Forest where he earned extra money building his boss's new Tudor-style mansion. Once the house was up, Dad spent many weekends over several months doing all the finishing carpentry inside the house to the boss's wife's exacting standards. But he enjoyed his craft and during his breaks, Dad liked to tell his boss's wife stories over coffee and biscuits and make her laugh. One Saturday when we were driving into Sherwood Forest, I spotted a little girl riding a Shetland pony in a field near the boss's house and asked my dad who she was. He told me matter-of-factly she would have to be the daughter of a rich man who, instead of going to war, had stayed home to make money. I knew that my dad had gone to World War II with the Essex Scottish Canadian Regiment, and was taken prisoner of war from the beach at Dieppe. Working men fight wars and rich men make money; children in rich families ride ponies and children in working families play around construction sites while their father earns extra needed cash. I was six years old, and this was the beginning of class consciousness for me.

As it turned out I did go to university, thanks to the Ontario Student Loans scheme, and I went on to earn a Ph.D. in Sociology, thanks to a Canada Council doctoral fellowship. Reflecting back, I can see how this childhood memory set me on my intellectual journey. In my doctoral studies, I specialized in social class and stratification theories and sociology of work and occupations. Along the way, I also encountered feminist theory and scholarship, and my research career over the last two decades has largely been spent asking questions about women's (and men's) work, leisure, and family lives. This brings me to what I can contribute to this volume, my reading of the literature on family leisure and my research on class, gender, identity, and leisure in Australian families.

FAMILY LEISURE

For many years, leisure-studies research on family leisure had not progressed much beyond looking at family leisure as a vehicle for family interaction and bonding, particularly for the married couple (e.g., Couchman, 1982; Hill, 1988; Holman & Epperson, 1984; Orthner, 1975; Orthner & Mancini, 1980, 1991). Gradually over the last 20 years, there has been a surge of interest in expanding the empirical base and developing more complex theoretical explanations of family leisure experience. Shaw (1992b) took us to task for holding up a rosy picture of family leisure, leaving its negative aspects unexamined while the concept itself had become reified. Moreover, in spite of years of feminist research on women's leisure, with notable exceptions like Bella (1989, 1992), as a field we failed to recognise gender inequality at the heart of the meaning and practice of family leisure. Freysinger (1997) implored researchers to move forward from simply descriptive empirical research, work on clearing up inconsistencies in measurement, and arrive at a deeper and richer theory about family leisure.

Although "family leisure" was not a concept they used, socialist-feminist researchers concerned with material conditions and hegemonic masculinity that shapes gender relations in the United Kingdom have indirectly contributed to our understanding of gendered family leisure (Deem, 1986; Green, Hebron, & Woodward, 1990; Wimbush & Talbot, 1988). Meanwhile, liberal feminist researchers in North America used symbolic interactionism to theorize about subjective experiences and meanings of leisure within families, although this work too tends to focus on the married couple (see Bella, 1989; 1992; Henderson, Bialeschki, Shaw, & Freysinger 1996; Samdahl, 1988; Samdahl & Jekubovich 1997; Shaw, 1985a). This advanced family leisure research, but the emphasis on individual agency in symbolic interactionism ignored the influence of social structure on family life and leisure (Wearing, 1998). Shaw (1997) and Wearing (1998) introduced a feminist poststructuralist power analysis to inform this area, through their reading of the work of Foucault (1982). Wearing constructs leisure as "personal space" where the subjectivities of men, women, and children can resist, challenge, and subvert what she considers hegemonic masculinity and inferiorized femininity. However, some may argue that Wearing's work underplays the dynamic nature of social relationships, romanticizes "agency" and overemphasizes an individualized notion of leisure.

Nonetheless, the concept of leisure as space may be extended to thinking about family leisure as "performative space," including the notion of temporality that is captured in narratives and memories of family times. That is, rather than treating "family" as a form, it can be analyzed as "a distinctive social configuration that is continually brought into being through people's activities, interactions, and interpretations, situated within powerful discourses of family life" (DeVault, 2000, p. 487). Family is enacted in manifold social settings where individuals "constitute certain actions and activities as 'family' practices" (Finch, 2007, p. 66) and see themselves and can be seen by others as doing "family things." The ensuing narratives and memories of doing family things become markers of self-identity and family identity over time. Conceptualizing family leisure as performative space could include the spatial dimensions of sites of leisure practices (e.g., middle-class families taking their children through the zoo as DeVault [2000] observed, and Hallman, Mary, and Benbow [2007] illustrate), and the *interstices* that intervene between leisure spaces, for example, the drive to and from a child's sport activity.

This idea of family leisure as performative space is consistent with Morgan's (1996) concept of "family" as a set of activities that people "do" rather than a social institution or structure that people belong to or "are." These family practices "are often little fragments of daily life . . . part of the normal, taken-for-granted existence" of members, and the significance of these practices "derives from their location in wider systems of meaning" (Morgan, 1996, p. 190, cited in Finch, 2007, p. 66). Finch argues that family practices are inherently social in that they are not only "done" but "displayed," as their meaning "has to be both conveyed to and understood by relevant others . . . to be effective as constituting 'family' practices" (p. 66). From this perspective, family leisure consists of sets of activities that show to relevant others that you are a "good" (or "bad" or "indifferent") mother or father to the children you are raising. This conceptualization also helps us understand why parents talk about themselves as a "sporting family," an "active family," or indeed a "stay-at-home family."

All families engage in a myriad of family leisure practices that they "do" that "display" their meaning to others, even those practices members may wish were unseen (like tantrums and tears). When Shaw (1997) called for a more critical research agenda on family leisure, she was aware that the blanket positive view of family leisure failed to recognise its inherent contradictions in practice and meaning, and the propensity for family leisure to become idealized. She urged us to deconstruct the concept of "family leisure," detach it from a normalized formation of happy families, and determine whether it has inclusive application across a diversity of family forms and structures. Shaw (1992a, 1997) sensitized us to consider not just the benefits but also the "conflictual or negative outcomes" of family leisure (1997, p. 100), such as "constraints on individual leisure or family stress or conflict" (1997, p. 104). This was an important advance in theorizing family leisure, but her later work with Don Dawson (Shaw & Dawson, 2001) set a new course of research. Their concept of "purposive leisure" has been taken up by other researchers, including some with a less critical perspective on families and leisure.

Family Leisure as Purposive Leisure

The term "purposive leisure" was first used by Shaw and Dawson (2001) in their qualitative study of leisure in 31 families in Ontario, Canada, to refer to the meanings parents attach to shared family leisure activity. Family leisure was highly valued by the parents in their study and showed "a strong sense of purpose" (p. 223) in its accomplishment. Parents described their resolve and effort to organize and facilitate family leisure activities for the good of their children. Shaw and Dawson explained that family leisure seemed to be "purposive" to the achievement of two broad and complementary parental goals. In the short term, parents saw engaging in family leisure as a way of enhancing the family as a cohesive, communicative, and bonded unit, to give its members "a sense of family" and "memories of having good times together" (p. 224). Over the longer term, parents wanted to provide their children with opportunities to develop healthy lifestyle patterns and to learn values that parents hoped would serve them throughout life (see also Shaw & Dawson, 1998). Shared family leisure offered opportunities for children to learn values and life lessons "through doing and seeing rather than being told what to do" (Shaw & Dawson, 2001, p. 226). Trussell's chapter in this volume also makes the same point with daughters playing ice hockey, learning new perspectives on femininity through their mothers' organizational involvement in their sport.

As noted above, some have taken up the notion of purposive leisure in their research on family leisure but done so from a less critical perspective. For example, Zabriskie and colleagues (Zabriskie & McCormick, 2003; Agate, Zabriskie, Agate, & Poff, 2009) have proposed a "Core and Balance Model of Family Leisure Functioning." This model built on Kelly's (Kelly, 1999) theoretical ideas of "core plus balance" leisure styles and Iso-Ahola's (1984) observation that individuals use leisure to meet their needs for stability and change. This model has been operationalized through the development a number of quantitative measures of family and leisure (e.g., family leisure satisfaction, family leisure involvement, family life satisfaction). Much of the research using these instruments has been based in Klein and White's (1996) interpretation of family systems theory. However, Klein and White caution that "systems" is only a heuristic device and "the family" can be reified if you forget that with this approach you are just looking at a family *as a system*, not that the family *is a system* (p. 175). Hence, to assert that "family systems purposively facilitate family leisure activities . . . to increase family functioning" (Zabriskie & McCormick, 2003, p. 167), assumes the family *is* a system, something that is antithetical to Shaw and Dawson's (2001) conceptualization of family and White and Klein's (2002) warning that "systems are heuristics, not real things" (p. 123).

Such a family systems perspective, while providing one lens on family leisure, does not acknowledge or account for the contradictions and conflict between and among members engaged in family leisure—nor its idealization both by subjects themselves and those doing the research. For example, Palmer and colleagues (2007) apply the concept of "purposive leisure" to family volunteering on service expeditions where parents take their children to lesser developed countries "to show gratitude for the numerous blessings they had been given" (p. 447). Families who go on service expeditions, entailing both service and sacrifice, I would argue, see themselves and are seen by others as doing "good works" that "continue to define and influence the entire identity of the family for many years to come" (Palmer et al., 2007, p. 438). To me this illustrates the concept of family leisure as performative space. While the core-and-balance model may be intuitively attractive to some, when examined from a more critical perspective, it can be shown that it does not illuminate discernable differences—arising, for example, out of gender, social class, culture—in family practices and meanings that I and others have found.

Elizabeth Such (2006), for example, argues that in spite of gendered differences in the experience of family leisure for mothers and fathers, their discourse of family leisure "shows remarkable similarity . . . it is considered a duty that is purposive in terms of promoting family togetherness and bonding" (p. 189). In their study based on unobtrusive observations in public zoos, Hallman et al. (2007) explain that "family trips to the zoo are redolent with purpose and meaning" (p. 885). Being there together and taking photographs of family members in that setting are "activities that constitute and reflect the emotional work of creating and maintaining positive family functioning" (p. 873). Purposive leisure is meaningful for parents as a way of being, doing or "practicing" family both at home and in public space (see also DeVault, 2000), which aligns with the concept of family leisure as performative space. Trussell's chapter on parental involvement with adolescent children's organized youth sport involvement also illustrates this, but also the gendered reality of such performances, at least in the context of youth sport.

Nevertheless, many researchers recognize that "family leisure" is partially an ideological construct (e.g., Shaw & Dawson, 2003; Hallman et al., 2007). As Hallman and colleagues explain, "beliefs [about an ideology of togetherness] shape behavior and can set into motion actions indicative of how conscious and deliberate a particular family is about spending time together" (p. 873), which also links to the earlier discussion of family leisure as performative space. Idealizations, or what Daly (2003) refers to as "the *implicit* theories that families live by" (p. 171; emphasis in the original), inform everyday practices within families including shared leisure. Families "draw meaning from the cultural matrix of which they are a part and express meanings about the kind of family they wish to appear" (p. 774). This presents challenges for researchers interviewing family members about family leisure because ideological notions of how families *ought to* behave are implicit in what members say constitute their family leisure practices. Parents are going to gloss over any negative aspects of family leisure and accentuate the positive, hence presenting their leisure practice as an idealized offering to the researcher. Moreover, family leisure experiences may differ in both relevance and quality among different family members, particularly by gender and generation, and this aspect of family leisure practice may also be concealed by idealization (Harrington, 2001; Larson, Gillman & Richards, 1997; Shaw, 1992b).

Shaw and Dawson (2003) have taken up this problem of the disjuncture between idealized family leisure and the reality of lived family life: they ask how do "parental ideals about the values and benefits of family activities [match] up to the reality of the experience of family leisure" (p. 183)? Juxtaposing parents' expectations for family leisure with the experience itself enhances our knowledge of what family leisure means for families and how it is actually experienced as part of family life. However, we still need to ask how age, gender, class, ethnicity, religion, and other cultural processes may mediate both the meaning and experience of family leisure for members of any given family. Parents value family leisure or "purposive leisure" because it is a site for transmitting values, interests, and a sense of family which they hope will guide their children into their adult and future family lives. This concept of family leisure is valuable in giving us a way of understanding parents' intentions; however, we must also bear in mind that the purposes or intentions of various family members for leisure may arise from their different *subject positions*, may conflict with one another, or be at cross-purposes.

I think it is important to draw attention to the performative character of purposive leisure. From this point of view, *status-positioning leisure* can be seen as a performance of family life within our pluralist performative culture (Rojek, 2000). Understanding purposive leisure from the subject positions of mothers and fathers attunes us to the complex gender relationships that inform "family leisure." Readers are asked to consider whether there are gendered differences in how mothers and fathers accomplish purposive leisure. My position is that masculine and feminine identities as fathers and mothers in any specific family are performative, negotiated through interaction, and socially constructed vis-à-vis one another. It is through their gendered identities and implicit theories they live by (Daly, 2003) that parents create the performative space of family leisure. Firstly, mothers and fathers may emphasize distinct but complementary goals for family leisure. Secondly, the gendered acts mothers and fathers perform may bring about particular kinds of family leisure; these may be related to how their family identity is "forged and experienced" through class, religion, or other cultural processes (Dowling, 2009, p. 834). I illustrate these theoretical points using examples from my research on Australian families.

FAMILY LEISURE STUDY OF AUSTRALIAN FAMILIES

Twenty-eight two-parent families living in Brisbane, Queensland, Australia were involved in a study that replicated the Ontario, Canada, study by Sue Shaw and Don Dawson (1998, 2001, 2003). The families were selected from responses to newspaper advertisements and personal contacts through a local community sport club. The research design used a purposive sampling technique with specific criteria: at least one child 10 years or older who would be willing to be interviewed and family income falling into one of two categories (above $25,000 or below $24,999 as an imperfect proxy for "class"). The first criteria allowed me to view family leisure from children's as well as parents' perspectives and also gave the sample some homogeneity in terms of family life stage. Children in these families ranged in age from 8 months old to 24 years, with two to seven children in each family. Seventeen of the families had incomes ranging from $25,000 to $60,000 per year and 11 had incomes in the narrower range of $20,000 to $24,999. Along with parents' education and occupation, these income categories were used to identify families as being either "low-income" or "middle-income" (the preferred terminology in Australia). The "middle-income" families had an average of 1.9 children per family, and the "lower-income" families averaged 3.6 children. Altogether there were 56 parents and 72 children, for a total of 128 individuals in the study.

The families completed a seven-day Family Activities Diary in which they recorded all activities they considered leisure or free-time, involving one or more family members, where they did this, and who else was involved. The diary was primarily used to contextualize one-to-one interviews with each parent and at least one child that were analyzed qualitatively. The interview canvassed each family member's favorite and least favorite leisure activities and those of other members of their family; what they did as a family that they considered leisure; and for parents, why was this important to them, what some of the benefits of their family leisure activities were, and whether they could they describe times when these benefits were not achieved.

Findings from the Family Leisure Study

As found in Shaw and Dawson's Ontario study, parents in this study said they value family leisure for creating occasions in which family members could communicate and bond with each other. Moreover, family leisure is also valued for teaching and instilling what parents hope will be lifelong values. It seems that parents in Queensland, like those in Ontario and elsewhere, engage in purposive leisure. However, analysis of the transcript data from my study suggests that mothers and fathers tend to emphasize different aspects of purposive leisure with their children.

Parents' Gendered Approaches to Purposive Leisure

In the context of family leisure, gender identity is most visible when parents attach a particular meaning to their role in the family. For example, one mother said, "seeing my family together and enjoying each others' company [makes me feel] like I have fulfilled a purpose of the day . . . it feels as though it's my job to bring us together to do those things." She mentions family drives as a special time for her not only because she likes doing it but also because her husband "usually takes care of [their 18-month-old boy] more. So that gives me time as well. Like he will push him around in the pram and he will take over the role of what I usually do when he's not there" (Mother, middle-income family #27). The interviews with both parents in this family indicate this is a blended family, with an 11-year-old boy from her previous marriage having had some difficulties getting along with her new husband, and both agree that shared family leisure helped them bond. She notes that her husband now "seems to make a more conscious effort to make sure he's around to do those things," and he says family leisure is very important because "if you can't bond with your children like at play time as such or your regular leisure time, then you'll never get to know each other" (Father, middle-income family #27). This family is one where gender roles seem most traditional, particularly when the wife says, laughingly, "I do all the bloody housework!"

While the father discussed above appreciates the value of family leisure for bonding with his new stepson, it was mothers who most often focused on the importance of family leisure for bonding and communication, or the emotional aspects of family life. Many of the fathers tended to focus on family leisure as occasions in which they are able to teach their children skills and knowledge. As an illustration, excerpts from the individual interviews with the mother and father in Family #8 (lower-income) and Family #20 (middle-income) show gender differences in valuing family leisure within the same family. Mother #8 says "we get together and hopefully bring home that we are a family to encourage and support each other," and Mother #20 explains that family leisure is important because it gives "the feeling of being a close-knit family unit. And getting on with each other and enjoying each other's company." Both of these mothers also said they hoped children were learning values about being sociable from family leisure. Compare their responses to their spouses: Father #8 (lower-income) explains, "[The most important family activity was to] fix [son's] bike. I had to fix his bike. He was there and he helped me. It was important because it is something that [my son] wanted and he really loves his bike. He's always popping tires, and I'm always having to fix his tires." For Father #20 (middle-income), family leisure entails playing and supporting sport: "Yeah I enjoy [coaching cricket] and also enjoy [doing] something that [son] and [daughter] do. So it's something I can do with them. Oh, actually [youngest son] does it too now. So, it's something we can do with the three kids. So, the family sort of does it together. Yeah. And [my wife] gets involved on weekends as well with . . . that." It is worth noting that in her interview, his wife specifically mentioned that her least favorite leisure activity was cricket.

Mothers also expressed the wish that family leisure would forge long-lasting bonds among its members so the family will not drift apart, as this mother of three young teenage children from a middle-income family implies: "Building common interests so that later on you can go back to those interests and there is a tie . . . have closer ties with them as you are away from your kids so much that they are growing up so quickly that you really need to grab hold of the moment as much as you can" (Mother, family #7). Her husband picks up on the same theme but again emphasizes teaching more instrumental values rather than bonds per se: "it is becoming harder and harder [to create the family unit], and as they get older they tend to get further apart. So hopefully, all the stuff you tried to teach them in the earlier years will stay with them now" (Father, family #7).

Leisure is one of the crucial sites in which mothers and fathers create their subjective identities as parents, both as they are positioned in relation to social institutions, discourses, and practices of parenthood and by the choices they exercise, that both reaffirm dominant parenting discourses and practices and resist them. Practitioners can learn much about how parents see themselves as "good parents" through family leisure. Knowing that mothers and fathers have different ways of engaging in purposive leisure can help practitioners understand what it is about the family that parents want their children to carry with them into their future lives.

Kinds of Purposive Leisure, Gender, and Social Class

The second theme from my Australian family leisure study is how lower- and middle-income parents may be deliberately pursuing different goals for their children, for example, values they wish to inculcate, skills they want to transmit, or attitudes towards others. This theme is a little more tenuous in this research, because unlike gender identity, which is relatively stable and a source of many family practices (e.g., mothers make salads and fathers cook meat at an Australian family barbecue), it is less easy to argue that family leisure practices arise out of class identity as opposed to other layers of identity experienced within families. For example, a few of the lower-income families (but none of the middle-income families) in this study are members of evangelical Christian faiths, and family leisure revolves around the church community. It raises a critical question whether the family leisure activities they do (e.g., Bible study, playing in the Salvation Army band, painting scenery for church pageants) derive from their faith, expressing a religious rather than a class identity. Or, it may be that belonging to religious groups compensates parents in low-income families who lack many cultural and material resources by offering "social sites that offer opportunities for social participation . . . a religious message that makes sense of everyday life, and a strong commitment to a moral code of decent family-centered living" (Wilcox & Bartkowski, 2005, p. 314, cited in Harrington, 2009, p. 70) not readily available to other low-income families.

With this caveat, I think there is still a case to be made that middle-income and lower-income parents may have different trajectories in mind for their children's futures. Purposive leisure as used here is similar to classed parenting practices analyzed by Lareau (2000, 2002, 2003) in her work on families in the United States. She argues that middle- and working-class parents perceive the nature of childhood and position themselves in their children's lives differently in order to equip them either for scholastic and occupational achievement and success by training them to "take on the world," or for constraint and lower horizons by "not straying away from the family." A few examples from my study illustrate both gender and class identities. The first two excerpts illustrate both the male emphasis on teaching instrumental skills (particularly in the area of sport) and middle-class values of discipline, achievement, and confidence. Asked about the importance of family leisure, Father #3 (middle-income family) states:

> Definitely. That's reflected in our involvement in the tennis club, and although we haven't been directly involved in [son's] karate we have always been there to take him. We're there to offer support. Karate is a different sport. It's something that I can't relate to, as I have never done karate, but I have played tennis so it is easier to relate to. . . . Basically, it gives them a discipline. [Our daughter] doesn't worry about losing a match and is confident in her own abilities and feels that she will get there one day.

Father #6 (middle-income family) is more explicit about "father's role" to teach his children sport skills, while also alluding to the middle-class values of self-confidence and success:

> [The most important leisure activity with another family member was] with [11-year-old daughter] when we were doing soccer skills because she was just signing up for soccer . . . so I was teaching her a lot of stuff. The fact that she actually learned something. . . . As we played, she got better and better, so she became more confident. It possibly showed a relating of my father role. . . . The values that you have to work hard to succeed and that success can link very much with the ego . . . sport has been important for that.

In contrast, the transcripts from some interviews show family leisure discourses that emphasize not the individual achievement orientation associated with the middle class, but a working-class desire for family togetherness and sense of security in an uncertain world. Consider how Mother #12 (lower-income family) explains why she encouraged her daughter to drop out of gymnastics:

> I just think it's important for all of us to do a lot of things together as a family. Another thing about gym is that [our daughter] went off for three hours at a time on her own. She quite often didn't have tea [dinner] with the family. And I really resented that because I like to do a lot of things as a family. But I felt . . . jealous. I think that they're taking my child away for three hours and I want her back. Well, I think that's their childhood memories. They're going to be the family together, doing things together. Rather than, "I went to gym, I don't know what the rest of the family did when I was a child." I don't like the way certain sports split the family up.

Of course this may be an idealization, turning what might simply be a lack of money to continue with the child's sport into a moralized choice for making family memories. But less ambiguous about the lived experience of lower-income families is the final excerpt, in which a father explains the values he wants to impart to his children through family leisure:

> I hope that I've got through to the kids that vandalism is senseless. The values that you don't touch other people's property and steal from anyone. You don't be unkind or fight and hope they will be well adjusted in terms of playing with other kids. There is never a fight in the street, and they are good kids in the street and they get on like a house on fire. (Father, lower-income family #17)

These examples highlight both gendered differences in terms of which parent is concerned about bonding and who is more interested (or equipped) to teach particular values, skills, and knowledge. They also tentatively suggest class differences in what is valued (i.e., individual achievement versus keeping safe) and what values are being taught. These examples are offered to suggest that we may get a more nuanced understanding of purposive leisure if we understand the gender and class identities constructed in families by their everyday practices, including family leisure.

Future Directions

I have argued for considering purposive leisure as performative space in which mothers and fathers practice gendered parenthood and that leads to a few questions for further research. Do mothers and fathers engage in creating a sense of family, pass on values, and teach their children about healthy lifestyles in ways born out of their own gendered upbringing, leisure repertoires, and embodied experience? It would be interesting to find out if this holds for some families more than others. For example, a small-scale but in-depth qualitative study of affluent families might reveal a number of contradictions in family leisure. They may perform family life by engaging in status positioning commodity-intensive leisure, or family practices may be less important than other social practices. Anecdotal evidence suggests affluent families do less together as a family in daily life than middle- or low-income families, with children otherwise occupied in structured activities across sport, music, dance, language lessons, etc., and ferried around by paid help. Parents may have crowded professional lives and consciously sacrifice purposive leisure for material comfort. Whether they mirror their own gendered upbringing or personal leisure repertoire in their children's lives would need to be seen. Affluence as a result of social mobility may result in a different display of family leisure practices than those parents who were also raised in affluence.

Another area for further exploration derives from my interest in whether parents more generally inculcate values through purposive leisure as a performance of gendered parenthood. While my small study suggests this is so, further research is needed that asks parents in similar social circumstances to address what they want for their children's future, what values they try to convey to their children, and how family leisure contributes to this purpose. Do parents' identities as mothers and fathers play a part in how they "do" family leisure, or does personal preference, constraint on choices, or convenience play a part? Further questions might arise from an analysis that takes into account more directly a family's position in the labor market. Does class mediate the meaning and experience of family leisure for its members? Does class identity have enough currency in contemporary families to also shape parents' notions of what they *ought* to do or what is *possible* to do for family leisure? Finally, the question of religion in forming family identity and the role of religious social networks, meanings, and activities as purposive leisure would also be an interesting study. Just as Palmer and colleagues' (2007) study of families on service expeditions could be looked at as performative space, so too could other family activities organized through religious organizations, like family summer camps, pilgrimages, or indeed church-based social activities. This field is rich with research opportunities once nuance and difference in purposive leisure as performative space are centered in the design of the research.

REFERENCES

Agate, J. R., Zabriskie, R. B., Agate, S. T., & Poff, R. (2009). Family leisure satisfaction and satisfaction with family life. *Journal of Leisure Research, 41*(2), 205–223.

Bella, L. (1989). Women and leisure: Beyond androcentrism. In E. L. Jackson & T. L. Burton (Eds.), *Understanding leisure and recreation: Mapping the past, charting the future* (pp. 151–179). State College, PA: Venture Publishing, Inc.

Bella, L. (1992). *The Christmas imperative: Leisure, family, and women's work.* Halifax, NS: Fernwood.

Couchman, R. (1982). Family recreation: A new dynamic in family life. *Leisurability, 9*(4), 4–8.

Daly, K. J. (2003). Family theory versus the theories families live by. *Journal of Marriage and the Family, 65*, 771–784.

Deem, R. (1986). *All work and no play? The Sociology of Women and Leisure.* Milton Keyes, UK: Open University Press.

DeVault, M. L. (2000). Producing family time: Practices of leisure activity beyond the home. *Qualitative Sociology, 23*(4), 485–503.

Dowling, R. (2009). Geographies of identity: Landscapes of class. *Progress in Human Geography, 33*(6), 833–839.

Finch, J. (2007). Displaying families. *Sociology, 41*(1), 65–81.

Foucault, M. (1982). The subject and power, In H. Dreyfus & P. Rabinow (Eds.), *Michel Foucault: Beyond structuralism and hermeneutics* (pp. 208–220). Brighton, NY: Harvester.

Freysinger, V. J. (1997). Redefining family, redefining leisure: Progress made and challenges ahead in research on leisure and families. Introduction to special issue. *Journal of Leisure Research, 29*(1), 1–4.

Green, E., Hebron, S., & Woodward, E. (1990). *Women's leisure, what leisure?* Basingstoke, Hampshire, UK: Macmillan.

Hallman, B. C., Mary, S., & Benbow, P. (2007). Family leisure, family photography and zoos: Exploring the emotional geographies of families. *Social & Cultural Geography, 8*(6), 871–888.

Harrington, M. A. (2001). Gendered time: Leisure in family life. In K. J. Daly (Ed.), *Minding the time in family experience: Emerging perspectives and issues* (pp. 343–382). Oxford, UK: Elsevier Science.

Harrington, M. (2009). Sport mad, good dads: Australian fathering through leisure and sport practices. In T. A. Kay (Ed.), *Fathering through sport and leisure* (pp. 51–70). London, UK: Routledge.

Henderson, K. A., Bialeschki, M. D., Shaw, S., & Freysinger, V. J. (1996). *Both gains and gaps: Feminist perspectives on women's leisure.* State College, PA: Venture Publishing, Inc.

Hill, M. S. (1988). Marital stability and spouses shared time. *Journal of Family Issues, 9,* 427–451.

Holman, T. B., & Epperson, A. (1984). Family and leisure: A review of the literature with research recommendations. *Journal of Leisure Research, 16,* 277–294.

Iso-Ahola, S. E. (1984). Social psychological foundations of leisure and resultant implications for leisure counselling. In E. T. Dowd (Ed.), *Leisure counseling: Concepts and applications* (pp. 97–125). Springfield, IL: Charles C. Thomas.

Kelly, J. R. (1999). Leisure behaviors and styles: Social, cultural, and economic factors. In E. L. Jackson & T. L. Burton (Eds.), *Leisure Studies: Prospects for the Twenty-First Century* (pp. 135–150). State College, PA: Venture Publishing, Inc.

Klein, D. M., & White, J. M. (1996). *Family theories; An introduction.* Thousand Oaks, CA: Sage.

Lareau, A. (2000). My wife can tell me who I know: Methodological and conceptual problems in studying fathers. *Qualitative Sociology, 23*(4), 407–433.

Lareau, A. (2002). Invisible inequality: Social class and childrearing in Black families and White families. *American Sociological Review, 67,* 747–776.

Lareau, A. (2003). *Unequal childhoods: Class, race and family life.* Berkeley, CA: University of California Press.

Larson, R. W., Gillman, S. A., & Richards, M. H. (1997). Divergent experiences of family leisure: Fathers, mothers, and young adolescents. *Journal of Leisure Research, 29*(1), 78–97.

Morgan, D. H. J. (1996). *Family connections.* Cambridge, UK: Polity.

Orthner, D.K. (1975). Leisure activity patterns and marital satisfaction over the marital career. *Journal of Marriage and the Family, 37,* 91–103.

Orthner, D.K., & Mancini, J. A. (1980). Leisure behavior and group dynamics: The case of the family. In S. E. Iso-Ahola (Ed.), *Social psychological perspectives on leisure and recreation* (pp. 307–328). Springfield, IL: Charles C. Thomas.

Orthner, D. K., & Mancini, J. A. (1991). Benefits of leisure for family bonding. In B. L. Driver, P. J. Brown, & G. L. Peterson (Eds.), *Benefits of leisure* (pp. 289–301). State College, PA: Venture Publishing, Inc.

Palmer, A. A., Freeman, P. A., & Zabriskie, R. B. (2007). Family deepening: A qualitative inquiry into the experience of families who participate in service expeditions. *Journal of Leisure Research, 39*(3), 438–458.

Rojek, C. (2000). *Leisure and culture.* London, UK: Macmillan.

Samdahl, D. M. (1988). A symbolic interactionist model of leisure: Theory and empirical support. *Leisure Sciences, 10*(1), 27–39.

Samdahl, D. M., & Jekubovich, N. J. (1997). A critique of leisure constraints: Comparative analyses and understandings. *Journal of Leisure Research, 29*(4), 430–452.

Shaw, S. M. (1985a). Gender and leisure: An examination of women's and men's everyday experience and perception of family time. *Journal of Leisure Research, 17*(4), 266–282.

Shaw, S. M. (1992a). Research update: Family leisure and leisure services. *Parks and Recreation, 27*(12), 13–16.

Shaw, S. M. (1992b). Dereifying family leisure: An examination of women's and men's everyday experiences and perceptions of family time. *Leisure Sciences, 14*(3), 271–286.

Shaw, S. M. (1997). Controversies and contradictions in family leisure: An analysis of conflicting paradigms. *Journal of Leisure Research, 29*(1), 98–112.

Shaw, S. M., & Dawson, D. J. (1998). *Active family lifestyles: Motivations, benefits, constraints and participation,* Ottawa, ON: Canadian Fitness and Lifestyle Research Institute.

Shaw, S. M., & Dawson, D. J. (2001). Purposive leisure: Examining parental discourses on family activities. *Leisure Sciences, 23*(4), 217–231.

Shaw, S. M., & Dawson, D. J. (2003). Contradictory aspects of family leisure: Idealization versus experience. *Leisure/Loisir, 28*(3–4), 179–201.

Such, E. (2006). Leisure and fatherhood in dual-earner families. *Leisure Studies, 25*(2), 185–199.

Wearing, B. (1998). *Leisure and feminist theory.* Thousand Oaks, CA: Sage.

White, J. M., & Klein, D. M. (2002). *Family theories: An introduction* (2nd ed.). Thousand Oaks, CA: Sage.

Wilcox, W. B., & Bartkowski, J. P. (2005). Devoted dads: Religion, class and fatherhood. In W. Marsiglio, K. Roy, & G. L. Fox (Eds.), *Situated fathering: A focus on physical and social spaces* (pp. 299–320). New York, NY: Rowman and Littlefield.

Wimbush. E., & Talbot, M. (1988). *Relative freedoms: Women and leisure.* Milton Keyes, UK: Open University Press.

Zabriskie, R. B. (2000). *An examination of family and leisure behaviour among families with middle school aged children.* (Unpublished doctoral dissertation). Indiana University, Bloomington, IN.

Zabriskie, R. B., & McCormick, B. P. (2003). Parent and child perspectives of family leisure involvement and satisfaction with family life. *Journal of Leisure Research, 35*(2), 163–189.

CHAPTER 25

LATINA WOMEN'S FAMILY ROLES: WHAT IMPACT DO THEY HAVE ON THEIR PHYSICAL ACTIVITY PARTICIPATION?

KIMBERLY J. SHINEW AND MONIKA STODOLSKA

We have spent several years researching diversity-related topics in the United States. Some of our research projects have explored the relationships between ethnicity, race, gender, immigration status, and leisure. Recently, much of our research has focused on the leisure behavior of Latinos. Part of our motivation to research this particular sub-population is their growing presence in our society. For instance, in recent years many U.S. cities have witnessed a sharp increase in the Latino population. Due to U.S. immigration policies and relatively high fertility rates, the numbers of Latinos are expected to increase from 15.1% of the total population in 2007 to 17.7% by the year 2015 (U.S. Census Bureau, 2009). The increasing population of Latinos has been noticed by many recreation service providers in our state who frequently look to us, as researchers, for advice on how to serve their diverse clients. For instance, some of the leisure service providers in Chicago suburbs have commented that the percentage of Latinos in their communities has jumped from under 10% just 10 years ago to over 40% today.

We are hearing that serving the recreational and leisure needs of this sub-population has created many challenges for these leisure service providers. One reason for this may be because Latinos' leisure participation patterns, including participation in leisure time physical activity (LTPA), often differ from those of the mainstream population (e.g., Crespo, 2000; Gobster, 2002). In general, we know that Latinos tend to gravitate toward non-organized, informal leisure activities and spend most of their leisure time with family members and other Latinos in fairly sedentary pastimes. According to the National Center for Health Statistics (NCHS) (2006), Latinos' rates of involvement in LTPA are much lower when compared to non-Hispanic Whites. Although differences in leisure participation patterns between non-Hispanic Whites and Latinos are typically accepted as part of cultural diversity, the lack of participation in LTPA among members of this group can have serious negative consequences for their physical and mental health. According to NCHS (2006), Latinos are one of the most sedentary segments of the U.S. population. Moreover, regular LTPA tends to be even less prevalent among Latina women than men, regardless of their education, occupation, or marital status (American Heart Association, 2009).

The purpose of this chapter is to examine the physical activity patterns of Latina women. More specifically, we will examine Latina women's roles in their families and how this impacts their physical activity participation. We will begin by briefly examining Latino culture and women's place in it. We will then summarize what we have learned through our and others' research about Latinas' LTPA patterns including their perceptions of physical activity, and we will highlight some of their most common constraints. Finally, we will conclude by identifying some directions for future research in this area.

LATINO CULTURE

Identifying a succinct conceptualization of the Latino culture is difficult given the heterogeneity within this population in the United States and around the world. The category "Latinos," adopted by the U.S. Census in 2000, has its origin in the 1970 Census that identified Hispanics (a preferred term at that time) as Spanish speakers and persons belonging to a household where Spanish was spoken, persons with Spanish heritage by birth location, and persons who self-identify with Spanish ancestry or descent (Gibson & Jung, 2002). People of Latino ethnicity could be of one or more races (e.g., White, African American, Native American, Asian, Mulato, Mestizo, or Zambo). Despite its wide usage, the term "Latino" is highly debated. Latin America is made up of around 20 nations that have different histories, traditions, constitutions, and backgrounds. Moreover, Latinos in the United States include people of diverse immigration histories with various levels of attachment to their cultural heritage. Tann (2005) noted that given "the intra-ethnic diversity of the population, coupled with numerous factors related to length of time since immigration, naturalization status, degree of acculturation, and individual variability" (p. 137), conceptualizing a concise picture is difficult. However, despite the large degree of ethnic diversity within the Latino population, Tann contended that some level of shared ethnic identity among Latinos does seem to exist due to certain common cultural values and language similarities.

One primary characteristic of the Latino culture that contributes to this unique identity is its collectivist nature; that is, Latinos place a higher value on the family and larger community than they do on the individual

(Triandis, 1989). Central beliefs of collectivist cultures include the valuing of interpersonal relationships and the interaction between the individual, family, and the environment (Gloria, Ruiz, & Castillo, 2003; Triandis & Suh, 2002). Also central to Latino culture is *familismo*—a strong attachment to families that has been found to significantly condition their leisure behavior (Keefe & Padilla, 1987; Shaull & Gramann, 1998). Attachment to extended kinship networks tends to persist even after several generations in the United States (Shaull & Gramann, 1998), although kinship networks are often redefined following immigration (Acevedo, 2009). Families are broadly inclusive, close-knit, and seen as the primary source of financial and emotional support. The nuclear family in the Latino culture often includes the immediate family, grandparents, aunts, uncles, cousins, and members of the community unrelated by blood but close to the family. Hence, multigenerational Latino households are common (Purnell & Paulanka, 2003). In Latino families, important decisions tend to be made by the whole family, not the individual. Latino culture also demands that respect (*respeto*) be shown to elders and authority figures. While valuing family and interpersonal relationships, Latinos also place importance on individuals as opposed to institutions (*personalismo*) and tend to trust and cooperate with those they know personally rather than people affiliated with impersonal, formal structures.

Research indicates that despite the often large households with aunts, grandmothers, and mothers (which might imply several helping hands) residing in one household, many Latina women feel a great sense of personal obligation to their families and feel guilty when they spend time on themselves and away from their caregiving duties. Clearly, this is not just an issue that affects Latina women but rather is common among women of various races and ethnicities (Henderson & Bialeschki, 1991). This feeling of guilt and ethic of care seems to influence the leisure patterns of many Latina women. Patriarchal gender relations have often been associated with Latino families, where men serve as the financial providers for their families, while married women are primarily responsible for the care of children and operation of the domestic sphere (Hondagneu-Sotelo, 1992). Many Latina women experience cultural pressures to sacrifice their personal lives for their families and to never put their own needs ahead of those of the others (*marianismo*) (Gil & Vazquez, 1996). Research, however, also shows that not all Latino and Latino-American families are characterized by this type of patriarchy (*machismo*) (Klein, 1995), and that changes relative to the contributions to the family economy (i.e., paid employment) lead to more egalitarian gender relations among some Latino immigrants in the United States (Acevedo, 2009; Hondagneu-Sotelo, 1992).

Latinas' Physical Activity Patterns

Much of our research as it relates to Latina women has focused on leisure time physical activity (LTPA) and physical activity (PA) in general. Our findings have added to an expanding literature base that has significantly increased in recent years. As mentioned, most of this research has shown that Latinos have higher rates of physical *in*activity than Whites across age categories. Moreover, whereas physical activity tends to decrease with age for most populations, Latino Americans are relatively inactive even in their childhood and adolescence (Crespo, 2000; Jamieson et al., 2005). However, Crespo (2000) also suggested the differences between LTPA participation rates among Latinos and members of other ethnic groups might be attributed to the fact that Latinos are overrepresented in highly physically demanding jobs, which in turn may limit their desire and ability to participate in LTPA. Studies on physical activity that focus solely on activity taking place in leisure time might underestimate their overall levels of activity participation.

This issue may be particularly relevant for Latina women, who consider activities not done during leisure, but in the context of the house or family care (e.g., general cleaning, vacuuming, carrying small children, caring for older adults) and walking (to the bus, at work, to a grocery store) as physical activity. Perceptions and understandings of the role of PA differ between Latinas and women from other groups. For instance, studies have shown that Latina women's perception of PA is broader than exercise and involves "doing something, moving around, walking, dancing, lifting boxes, carrying babies" or "not having certain time for exercising but rather doing those daily activities that must be done" (Tortolero, Masse, Fulton, & Torres, 1999, p. 137). Latinas in this study also seemed to make a distinction between PA and sport, in that although they had positive attitudes toward PA, they perceived sport as an activity reserved for children and men. Berg, Cromwell, and Arnett's (2002) study showed that Mexican American women considered LTPA to be a prescriptive therapy for a specific illness, rather than a means of health promotion or disease prevention. The women were motivated to participate primarily for its role in restoring health (improving sleep, making them stronger physically, and giving them more energy) and by a strong commitment to their families. For example, some women were motivated to participate in LTPA to share experiences with their children, to increase bonds among family members, and to enhance their ability to do things for their family. Given the social nature of walking, it is not surprising that numerous studies have found that walking is the most frequent LTPA among Latina women and other racial/ethnic minority members (Ainsworth, Keenan, Strogatz, Garrett, & James, 1991; Bild et al., 1993; Clark, 1999; Gobster, 2002).

In one of our research projects with Latina women between the ages of 18 and 66, we distinguished between moderate LTPA, vigorous LTPA, and walking. Findings indicated that less than half of women had engaged in vigorous or moderate LTPA during the last seven days, 41% and 42%, respectively. In other words, more than half of the women had not participated in vigorous *or* moderate LTPA in the past week, which is not uncommon for women in general. However, about 77% of women indicated that in a usual week they walked for at least 10 minutes while at work, for recreation, for exercise, to get to and from places, or for any other reason (Skowron, Stodolska, & Shinew, 2009). We also asked the women if they exercised, where they usually did so and found that the most common location was the home (Davitt, Stodolska, & Shinew, 2009). Further, due to previous findings that work environments may influence leisure activities (e.g., see Crespo, 2000), we asked the Latina women about the type of work they performed. Almost 25% of the women indicated their work was "mostly walking" and another 38.1% described their work as "mostly standing."

In summary, although there is a great deal of heterogeneity within the Latino population, there does seem to be some level of shared ethnic identity. Part of this identity for Latinas is a great sense of obligation to their family, and this can impact their willingness to spend time on their own during their leisure time. Moreover, their idea of physical activity is rather comprehensive and can include household chores and child-rearing activities.

COMMON CONSTRAINTS TO LTPA AMONG LATINAS

The literature that explores constraints of Latinas to participation in LTPA has grown in recent years. In addition to exploring activity participation, many studies on LTPA among Latina women have also identified constraints related to minority status (e.g., lack of money and lack of access to transportation) and cultural differences. For instance, in terms of culture, lack of exposure to LTPA, absence of role models, specific gender role expectations, language problems (both English not being their native language and others not understanding Spanish), lack of culturally sensitive childcare facilities, culturally inappropriate facilities and programs, absence of people from their own minority group who use the area and facilities, and lack of self-confidence or self-efficacy have all been shown to affect participation in LTPA among many Latinas. Similarly, family responsibilities that are known to constrain physical activity among the non-Latina population might be especially pronounced among Latina women who tend to have larger families (Sternfeld et al., 1999; Tortolero et al., 1999).

Evenson, Sarmiento, Macon, Tawney, and Ammerman (2002) reported that Latinas' LTPA was also constrained by their lack of driver's licenses and, thus, their dependence on others for transportation, the lack of public transportation where they lived, lack of sidewalks and parks close to home, lack of money, safety issues, and fear of unattended dogs. Furthermore, their study identified a number of barriers related to gender and sociocultural issues, including cultural upbringing in the home country that did not involve structured exercise and sport, placing the needs of their husbands, children, and households before their own, and lack of time due to household responsibilities. Issues such as lack of support from their husbands, lack of culturally sensitive childcare, language barriers, and isolation in the community were also mentioned.

Social support as both a constraint to and facilitator of LTPA participation among Latina women has been examined (Eyler et al., 1999; Tortolero et al., 1999; Wilcox et al., 2000). Actions such as driving people to exercise classes, telling others about community exercise programs, asking friends about their progress in an exercise program, or providing encouragement or reinforcement for participation in exercise may facilitate LTPA. Eyler et al. (1999) established that Latina women had higher social support for PA than other minority women, and that women with high levels of social support were less likely to be sedentary than women with low levels of social support. Additionally, results of Wilcox and colleague's (2000) study showed that lower social support for exercise from family and friends, greater perceived barriers to exercise, and not frequently seeing others exercise in the neighborhood were all related to sedentary behavior among an ethnically diverse rural sample. Ransdell and Wells (1998) argued that minority women, including Latinas, might be less informed about the role of PA in the etiology of chronic disease and that they may have less flexibility in their working hours. Moreover, they may participate in more physically demanding occupations, have more household responsibilities, and be more constrained by the lack of money to join health clubs, buy exercise equipment, or consult with fitness/health professionals. While much has been done in the last decade to raise awareness of the benefits of exercise among Latina women, their busy schedules and disadvantaged socioeconomic position still act as important constraints on their leisure-time physical activity participation.

In our survey research on constraints (Skowron et al., 2008), we asked the women, "How much does each of the following factors limit your participation in physical activity?" Latina women mentioned lack of childcare, lack of time, and not being able to afford to go to fitness/recreation facilities as the three most important barriers affecting their LTPA. Fear of unattended dogs and bad weather were also mentioned as important constraints, as was rarely seeing other Latino people exercise. In a follow-up study that included interviews with Latina women, the main constraints reported were connected to their family roles and to the necessity of childcare in particular. Many of the women noted that Latino communities put pressure on the role of mother and wife, and "this leaves very little, if any, time for exercise." Most interviewees did not have family members who lived in their neighborhood who could take care of their children, and they did not feel comfortable leaving their children with non-family members.

Due to the transitory nature of some of the neighborhoods in which Latinos live, issues of safety and fear of crime have surfaced as important constraints in some of our research (Stodolska, Acevedo, & Shinew, 2009; Stodolska & Shinew, 2009). These concerns have been expressed primarily in relation to park use but exist in other contexts as well. The problem of gang activity, in particular, was often raised by the participants in a focus group study we conducted with Latino Americans residing in Chicago. Some of the parks in their neighborhood were considered "gang territory" and were often subject to territorial fights among competing gangs. Participants commented, however, that gangs were not only present in the parks, but that they "hijacked" the entire neighborhood and made it unsafe to play, walk, or bike on the street. This issue is particularly relevant to Latina women, who indicated fearing not only for their children's safety but for their own. One participant noted that presence of gangs made jogging in the park very unpleasant. Another Latina woman commented that she made sure to watch her children closely while they were playing and often drove to a different neighborhood to go for walks. She further commented that she only allowed her children to play inside her house, in her fenced backyard while she watched them, or at a family member's or close friend's house. Her comments were echoed by all other female participants who had young children. While the desire to protect one's children from crime is certainly typical of all parents, regardless of their ethnicity or race, it may be that Latina women are likely to be particularly sensitive about such issues as they are socialized to be protective of their children and to be responsible for the welfare of their families. Furthermore, most of the women who participated in the study were living in neighborhoods with high crime and thus needed to be even more vigilant about watching their children.

Another constraint that has surfaced in our research is undocumented status (Stodolska & Shinew, 2009). Lack of legal status inhibits some Latinas' ability to deal with the crime issues in their neighborhoods and use community leisure services to their full extent. Some of the participants in our study commented that those Latinos who reside in the United States illegally are reluctant to go to authorities regarding gang-related issues in their parks because they do not want to bring attention to themselves. They are also reluctant to register for recreational programs, because they do not want their name and address to be part of a permanent record. Fear of deportation is a real concern that can impact their overall LTPA patterns.

Findings of our study with Latinos in Chicago revealed a number of other constraints related to LTPA (Stodolska & Shinew, 2010). For instance, the women were concerned that communities in which many Latinos reside lack access to natural environments suitable for LTPA and the ones that are available are former brown fields with serious environmental problems. Disadvantaged socioeconomic situations prevent many Latina women from moving to neighborhoods with quality natural environments suitable for recreation. Jogging trails full of potholes, dilapidated playground equipment, trash, lack of water fountains, and unsanitary restrooms dissuaded women from using parks. Latina women mentioned not being able to afford to buy or to rent recreation equipment. However, some of the women also believed that staff of some parks did not trust Latinos enough to offer recreation equipment rentals. Lack of English fluency also seemed to hinder Latinas' ability to take advantage of opportunities for LTPA available in the community. One of the women interviewed in our study explained that she was afraid to enter the local recreation center, as she did not speak English, while others believed that the Anglo staff intentionally failed to distribute information in Spanish to give preference to children of white, Anglo residents. Racial tensions related to the different racial background of other park users, staff of recreation centers, and even police officers were also mentioned by focus group participants as negatively affecting their participation in LTPA. Latina interviewees recounted experiencing discriminatory acts in parks, recreation centers, playgrounds, and swimming pools. One of the young Latina mothers described an incident where a fight broke out between African American and Latina women watching their children at a playground. Another female interviewee mentioned that sometimes she witnessed Latino children being prevented from using the local swimming pool when African American attendants were on duty.

Clearly, our research and that of others on Latinas' constraints indicates that there are several issues that can make leisure participation difficult. Some of these constraints are related to social class, and others are related to gender and cultural differences. Taken together, it is evident that constraints are common and negotiation strategies must be employed by Latinas wishing to participate in physical activity or other leisure activities.

FINAL THOUGHTS ON FUTURE RESEARCH

Understanding the leisure behavior of Latinos is an important area of inquiry that has evolved over time. As we noted in the introduction, while physical activity is only one type of leisure-time activity, it is one of increasing interest because of its relation to physical and mental health. Further, while we have explored this form of leisure to better understand the leisure of the growing Latino population in the United States and provide advice to leisure service providers, this research also tells us much about how ethnicity is experienced and how it "works" or is "done" in the context of leisure. In addition, we have learned is that it is not enough to consider gender alone. Race, ethnicity, and social class must also be considered.

Further, although progress has been made, there is more to learn. Research questions are complex, given the heterogeneity of the population. As noted by Tann (2005), the intra-ethnic diversity of the population, coupled with numerous factors related to length of time since immigration, naturalization status, degree of acculturation, and socioeconomic status all influence the leisure behavior of this population. For instance, we know little of the effect of acculturation and the length of time spent in the United States on LTPA among Latina women. Do Latina girls who were born or who grew up in the United States and who were educated in mainstream American schools feel more entitled to leisure than their immigrant mothers? Moreover, anecdotal evidence suggests that involvement in LTPA among middle- and upper-class women in Mexico and some other Latin American countries is significantly higher than among their lower-class counterparts (thus, mirroring trends observable among the mainstream American population). However, since the majority of studies on Latinos' LTPA focused on the working-class population in the United States, trends among middle- and upper-class Latina American women might have gone unnoticed. Thus, first of all, we need to urge caution about generalizing findings obtained on a select segment of the Latino population to all Latino Americans. Second, additional research is needed that would examine social-class variations in LTPA participation among Latina women in the United States. It would be interesting if cross-group comparisons were conducted holding social class constant (e.g., Floyd, Shinew, McGuire, & Noe, 1994) and if research examined changes in LTPA patterns among Latina women who immigrate to the United States and experience changes in their social-class membership (upwards or downwards mobility).

As Latinos go from a "minority" population to a "majority" population in certain areas of the United States, their leisure behavior is likely to be profoundly impacted. Current problems such as language barrier and lack of culturally sensitive programs could become less of a concern. Additionally, as Latina women become more involved in work outside the home, their roles in the family may change. As Latina women make more of a contribution to the overall family income, this may lead to more egalitarian gender relations within Latino families (Acevedo, 2009). Will this reduce Latina women's ethic of care or increase their sense of entitlement to leisure? Will they be more willing to allow others to care for their children? Another potential research question is how multiracial/multiethnic identities may change "Latinos." We recognize there is already considerable intra-ethnic diversity, but as intermarriage between races/ethnicities becomes more common, what type of impact will this have on their culture (including gendered family practices) and leisure? There is no doubt we live in an extraordinarily complex and ever-changing society. It is our responsibility to identify, understand, and appreciate theses changes and incorporate them into our research. Understanding leisure as it relates to the richness that racial and ethnic diversity brings to community life is an exciting and worthwhile endeavor that deserves further investigation.

REFERENCES

Acevedo, J. C. (2009). *A cross-cultural study of leisure among Mexicans in the state of Guerrero, Mexico and Mexican immigrants in the United States.* (Unpublished master's thesis). University of Illinois, Urbana-Champaign.

Ainsworth, B., Keenan, N., Strogatz, D., Garrett, J., & James, S. (1991). Physical activity and hypertension in Black adults: The Pitt County study. *American Journal of Public Health, 81,* 1477–1479.

American Heart Association. (2009). Heart disease and stroke statistics. Retrieved from http://circ.ahajournals.org/cgi/reprint/CIRCULATI ONAHA.108.191261

Berg, J. A., Cromwell, S. L., & Arnett, M. (2002). Physical activity: Perspectives of Mexican American and Anglo American midlife women. *Health Care for Women International, 23,* 894–904.

Bild, D., Jacobs, D. J., Sidey, S., Haskell, W., Anderssen, N., & Oberman, A. (1993). Physical activity in young Black and White women. The CARDIA study. *Annals of Epidemiology, 3,* 636–644.

Clark, D. O. (1999). Identifying psychological, physiological, and environmental barriers and facilitators to exercise among older low income adults. *Journal of Clinical Geropsychology, 5*, 51–62.

Crespo, C. J. (2000). Encouraging physical activity in minorities. *The Physical and Sportsmedicine, 28*, 36–51.

Davitt, B., Stodolska, M., & Shinew, K. J. (2009, October). *Determinants of physical activity participation among Latino visitors to outdoor recreation areas*. Poster presented at the NRPA Leisure Research Symposium, Salt Lake City, UT.

Evenson, K. R., Sarmiento, O. L., Macon, M. L., Tawney, K., & Ammerman, A. S. (2002). Environmental, policy, and cultural factors related to physical activity among Latina immigrants. *Women & Health, 36*, 43–57.

Eyler, A. A., Brownnson, R. C., Donatelle, R. J., King, A. C., Brown, D., & Sallis, J. (1999). Physical activity social support and middle- and older-aged minority women: Results from a U.S. survey. *Social Science and Medicine, 49*, 781–789.

Floyd, M. F., Shinew, K. J., McGuire, F. A., Noe, F. P. (1994). Race, class awareness, and leisure activity preferences: Marginality and ethnicity revisited. *Journal of Leisure Research, 26*, 158–173.

Gibson, C., & Jung, K. (2002). Historical census statistics on population totals by race, 1790 to 1990, and by Hispanic origin, 1970 to 1990, for the United States, regions, divisions, and states. *Working Paper Series No. 56*. Retrieved from http://www.census.gov/population/www/documentation/twps0056/twps0056.html

Gil, R. M., & Vazquez, C. I. (1996). *The Maria paradox: How Latinas can merge old world traditions with new world self-esteem*. New York, NY: G. P. Putnam & Sons.

Gloria, A. M., Ruiz, E. L., & Castillo, E. M. (2003). Counseling and psycho-therapy with Latino and Latina clients. In T. B. Smith (Ed.), *Affirming diversity in counseling and psychology* (pp. 167–189). Boston, MA: Pearson.

Gobster, P. H. (2002). Managing urban parks for a racially and ethnically diverse clientele. *Leisure Sciences, 24*, 143–159.

Henderson, K. A., & Bialeschki, M. D. (1991). A sense of entitlement to leisure as constraint and empowerment for women. *Leisure Sciences, 13*, 51–65.

Hondagneu-Sotelo, P. (1992). Overcoming patriarchal constraints: The reconstruction of gender relations among Mexican immigrant women and men. *Gender and Society, 6*, 393–415.

Jamieson, K. M., Araki, K., Chung, Y. C., Kwon, S. Y., Riggioni, L., & Musalem, V. A. (2005). Mujeres (In)Activas: An exploratory study of physical activity among adolescent Latinas. *Women in Sport and Physical Activity Journal, 14*, 95–105.

Keefe, S. E., & Padilla, A. M. (1987). *Chicano ethnicity*. Albuquerque, NM: University of New Mexico Press.

Klein, A. M. (1995). Tender machos: Masculine contrasts in the Mexican baseball league. *Sociology of Sport Journal, 12*, 370–388.

National Center for Health Statistics (NCHS). (2006). *Health United States, 2006*. U.S. Department of Health and Human Services, Centers for Disease Control and Prevention. Retrieved from http://www.cdc.gov/nchs/data/hus/hus06.pdf#027

Purnell, L. D., & Paulanka, B. J. (2003). *Transcultural health care: A culturally competent approach* (2nd ed.). Philadelphia, PA: F. A. Davis.

Ransdell, L. B., & Wells, C. L. (1998). Physical activity in urban, White, African-American and Mexican-American women. *Medicine and Science in Sport and Exercise, 30*, 1608–1615.

Shaull, S. L., & Gramann, J. H. (1998). The effect of cultural assimilation on the importance of family-related and nature-related recreation among Hispanic Americans. *Journal of Leisure Research, 30*, 47–63.

Skowron, M. A., Stodolska, M., & Shinew, K. J. (2008). Determinants of leisure time physical activity participation among Latina women. *Leisure Sciences, 30*, 429–447.

Sternfeld, B., Ainsworth, B. E., & Quesenberry, C. P. (1999). Physical activity patterns in a diverse population of women. *Preventive Medicine, 28*, 313–323.

Stodolska, M., Acevedo, J. C., & Shinew, K. J. (2009). Gang of Chicago: Perceptions of crime and its effect on the recreation behaviour of Latino residents in urban communities. *Leisure Sciences, 31*, 466–482.

Stodolska, M., & Shinew, K. J. (2009). *La Calidad de Vida dentro de La Villita:* An investigation of factors affecting quality of life of Latino residents of an urban immigrant gateway community. *Journal of Immigrant and Refugee Studies, 7*, 267–289.

Stodolska, M., & Shinew, K. J. (2010). Environmental constraints on leisure time physical activity among Latino urban residents. *Qualitative Research in Sport and Exercise, 2*, 313–335.

Tann, S. E. (2005). Implications for quality of life research on Latino populations. *Journal of Transcultural Nursing, 16*, 136–141.

Tortolero, S., Masse, L., Fulton, J., & Torres, I. (1999). Assessing physical activity among minority women: Focus group results. *Women's Health Issues, 9*, 135–142.

Triandis, H. D. (1989). Cross-cultural studies of individualism and collectivism. *Nebraska Symposium on Motivation, 37*, 41–133.

Triandis, H. D., & Suh, E. M. (2002). Cultural influences on personality. *Annual Review of Psychology, 53*, 133–160.

U.S. Census Bureau. (2009). Population: Estimates and projections by age, sex, race/ethnicity. Retrieved from http://www.census.gov

Wilcox, S., Castro, C., King, A., Housemann, R., & Brownson, R. (2000). Determinants of leisure time physical activity in rural compared to urban older and ethnically diverse women in the United States. *Journal of Epidemiology and Community Health, 54*, 667–672.

CHAPTER 26
LET YOUR SOUL GLOW:
THE INTERSECTIONS OF RACE,
GENDER, HEALTH, AND LEISURE

SHEWANEE HOWARD

In my student and professional experiences, I admired black women who were working with and researching the same issues and topics that interested me. These were black women who were teaching about health and well-being in public schools and higher education. These were black women teaching and talking about black women's experiences in the world. Topics related to black women's identity, body image, and the realities of race and gender—topics that were central to my life experiences—predominated. It was not until my doctoral work, however, that I met a black woman who had been writing and researching about some of the same issues I was thinking about. During my years as an undergraduate and Master's student, researching black women was not *discouraged* by my professors, but many did not seem to have an understanding of how the experiences of black women might be different from those of other women. Other professors would say, "Maybe you should consider working with someone else who has more experience in that specialized area." I never thought that talking about me and other black women was a *specialized area*. I felt comfort and security in—and that there was a glaring need for—writing of black women.

This belief emerged from the research I read for undergraduate and Master's classes in the 1990s related to health, exercise and fitness, and sport and physical activity participation. This research often cited socioeconomic and gender differences in many indicators of quality of life, equated any racial differences with socioeconomic status, and painted a picture of disadvantage and marginalization. However, in reading that research, I was left with questions about whether racial and ethnic differences could be reduced to socioeconomic differences, and just how race and ethnicity were a part of the picture of group differences in physical activity and health. In attempting to answer these particular questions, I could not escape the idea that race and ethnicity meant much more than I had ever considered and I started asking, *what are the meanings of race and ethnicity, and of health?*

I returned to graduate school to pursue my doctorate in educational leadership and answer questions about the intersections of race, gender, age, social class, and health. This was an intellectual journey to explore new strategies to help "my community" of students, faculty, family, and friends learn what it means to be healthy; to learn that "health is a personal journey and not a destination" but also to learn that it is a journey embedded in society, culture, and history. In my dissertation research, I sought to bring together my interests in health promotion, well-being, and social (in)equality, by giving voice to black women in higher education, a group of individuals who are advantaged by their educational and occupational achievements at the same time they must negotiate constraints to health and well-being because of racism and sexism in the United States.

Currently, as a junior faculty member in the higher-education community, I am constantly developing questions, and searching for answers to those questions, that are most pertinent to my students *and* my research. These questions have to do with race, gender, social class, and health. With any course I teach, I attempt to center a critical sociocultural perspective that allows me to explore with my students what practices and experiences shape the lives of historically disadvantaged groups. That is, whether the course is concerned with psychoactive drugs or human sexuality, I engage students in discussions and debates that will allow them to think in more critical ways about health and the many discourses surrounding health today in the United States and abroad (e.g., the discourse of lifestyle and "healthy leisure choices").

The more I read, the more questions I have about the health status of black women in North America. I cannot separate myself from the research. I am a black woman in the United States whose family has a history of diabetes and stroke. I have a full-time job and value the time and leisure I have with family and friends. As I thought about what I wanted to say in this chapter, the entwinement of self and research subject became apparent. There was no denying that I could *not* separate myself from my research, nor did I want to. Hence, after some initial trepidation when invited to contribute this chapter, I came to welcome the opportunity to speak about my understandings of race, gender, and health in the United States in relation to women, gender, and leisure. This discussion is based in both lived and research experiences and thus, like many other chapters in this book, is a story of a personal and scholarly journey.

WHAT WE "KNOW" ABOUT THE HEALTH OF BLACK WOMEN IN THE UNITED STATES

While many Americans at the beginning of the twenty-first century suffer from a host of acute and chronic conditions, including cardiovascular disease, cancer, and stroke, black women are particularly vulnerable to heart disease. It is the leading cause of death for black women in the United States (Eberhardt, Ingram, & Makuc, 2001). "The higher mortality rates of heart disease in black women seem to be the result of a higher proportion of black women exhibiting the risk factors for increased mortality—cigarette smoking, hypertension, diabetes, high blood cholesterol, inadequate physical activity, and obesity" (Society for Women's Health Research, n.d.). Smoking and high blood pressure and cholesterol are also risk factors for cancer and obesity. "In 2005, African American women were 10% less likely [than Whites] to have been diagnosed with breast cancer; however, they were 34% more likely to die from breast cancer, as compared to non-Hispanic white women" (Office of Minority Health, 2008). Further, from 2003–2006, 30.7% of non-Hispanic black women over the age of 18, compared to 26.6% of non-Hispanic white women, were overweight but not obese. The Centers for Disease Control and Prevention (CDC) stated that "In 2004, African Americans had the highest age-adjusted all-causes death rate of all races/ethnicities. In addition, African Americans had the highest age-adjusted death rate for heart disease, cancer, diabetes, and HIV/AIDS" (Office of Minority Health, 2008).

That is, black women in the United States are disproportionately affected by a host of diseases when compared to other populations. We need to recognize and critically reflect on these statistics, because they are at least part of the context, the public discourse, for how black women—including the black women in higher education in my study—think about and experience themselves as women, as black women, and their health and lifestyle choices (or leisure). But what do these statistics *not* tell us about black women? Another discourse that is often missing from the discussion is recognition of black women's ability to juggle multiple social roles and threats to good health, all the while finding the strength to overcome discrimination. While disease may challenge the physical health of black women, resiliency is the crux of black women's negotiations of the complexity of race and gender. According to Jones and Shorter-Gooden (2004), black women are constantly "shifting" to accommodate race, class, and gender differences in the United States. Whether it is through their behaviors or voices, black women are constantly changing roles in society to adjust to visible, invisible, internal, and external stimuli. In answer to the question, *how do black women cope with racism and sexism?*, these researchers found that a "central way that many black women respond to racial and gender bias: They fight back. . . . These women are often well practiced at battling myths, scanning, denying, seeking support, and retreating to their own community. But they're no longer content to simply suppress negative emotions. They're motivated to put an end to the prejudicial demands, pressures, and pulls that kindle the feelings of anxiety, sadness, anger, and shame. They're ready to take on the task of educating and challenging others, to do everything they can to make the world a better, more just place" (Jones & Shorter-Gooden, 2004, p. 87).

Hence, the focus of my research and teaching is not just about broadening concepts of health to be inclusive of race and gender. Rather it is about shifting discourses of health from blaming the victim to understanding *victimization*—the social conditions, cultural practices, and institutional structures that construct advantage and disadvantage and make it nearly impossible for too many black women to participate in the kinds of health behaviors that we are exhorted to participate in today in the United States—including participating in leisure activity *for* our health and well-being. Writing and reading about diseases and chronic health problems that disproportionately affect black women requires a deliberate effort to examine how race and ethnicity, poverty, discrimination, self-image, employment, and access to and the availability of resources construct black women's opportunities to experience optimal health and leisure. I undertook such a project in my qualitative study of black women in higher education, and it is to this research that I now turn.

THE LIVED EXPERIENCES OF BLACK WOMEN IN HIGHER EDUCATION

My research has involved examining the ways in which black female faculty negotiate and navigate their bodies in the academy, more specifically, the challenges they experience in the classroom in relation to their embodied selves (i.e., their raced and gendered subjectivities) (Howard, 2007). Such an examination required a framework that was sensitive to understanding the lived experiences of black women and black feminist thought offered such awareness. According to Collins (2000b), "Two interlocking components characterize this standpoint. First, black women's political and economic status provides them with a distinctive set of experiences that offers a different view of material reality than that available to other groups . . . Second, these experiences stimulate a distinctive black feminist consciousness concerning that material reality" (p. 184). That is, subordinated groups like black women experience the world differently than privileged groups and therefore their realities will be different. Tenets of black feminist thought include understanding the lived experiences of black women; valuing speaking and listening; creating an ethic of care and treasuring individual expression; holding researchers accountable for what constitutes knowledge; and acknowledging black women as constructors of knowledge (Collins, 2000a). In using this theoretical framework, the experiences of black women in academe were not only valued, but validated and nurtured, and the intersectionality of race, gender, and class was allowed.

Based on previous research, I undertook my study with the assumption that black women in higher education are in a contested terrain. My research provides rich description of just how and why this is so. The women in my study indicated that they experienced a number of challenges in being faculty in higher education in predominately white universities, including a lack of support from colleagues, disrespectful behavior from university personnel, a questioning of their intellectual ability by students and faculty, and the lack of acknowledgment or valuing of their scholarly and research abilities and interests (Howard, 2007). For example, a black female psychologist/assistant professor explained the daily challenges working at a predominately white university:

> Today is my last day of work. I feel like the Elephant Man up in this joint. You ever seen that movie? It's a story about a horribly deformed man that's treated like crap although he is intelligent. He just decides to remain silent because people look at him crazy anyway. Well, that's me. I ain't saying jack no more. They don't think I know sh*t anyway. "What's a Negro doing with a degree anyway?" "She must be some freak of nature." "Look, she talks." "Let's second guess everything she says and always get a second opinion." Sorry, I'm just venting. I just saw the Elephant Man movie the other day and just related to it too much! My job is cool. I just can't let the little stuff get to me. . . . Man, my white co-workers don't have a clue . . . . "What's wrong? Aren't you having a good day?" (Howard, 2007, p. 42)

This statement speaks truth to the experience of race and how racism works. The participant believed that her doctoral degree and years of experience counseling college students were disregarded by her white colleagues. She was tired of her intellect being questioned and resolved not to speak because she believed that her voice, expertise, and opinions were not valued by her colleagues or institution. She struggled with negotiating her identity in a space that did not appear to value raced and gendered perspectives. As I spoke to more black women about their experiences in the academy, it became evident that this was a shared or collective experience for many of them. When another black female professor was asked, "What does it feel like teaching at a predominantly white university," she responded with the following statement:

> (It's) what I imagine it would be like to be on a battlefield. Where you have some victories, you have some defeats, but you're always fighting one battle or the other. Whether it is a battle that is strictly dealing with pedagogy or whether it is the kind of underlying battle of race and gender, it is always there. It is never finished. You know there may be times when you are sort of coasting along, and things are going well, but I am *not* saying it is like being at war. But I *am* saying it is like being on a battlefield. (p. 50)

How are black women to approach a career/workplace where every day there is at least the potential for a challenge to their right to be there? These particular dynamics make the academy a difficult space to navigate. Black female faculty members also spoke of confronting stereotypical images of black women in the classroom and how this experience conveyed to them that their presence was not always valued. A black female professor had the following to say when she was asked what it feels like being a black female professor:

> Being a black female professor in the classroom is like a tight rope act. It's a tremendous balancing act. You are at once trying to figure out how to compartmentalize things. You're constantly trying to, I feel like I am constantly trying to be aware of myself while I am aware of the students and I'm aware of my identity so that I'm kind of dealing automatically with what I know the stereotypes are for them. So, if I know already that they might be dealing with this stereotype of the aggressive, black woman, I am constantly trying not to be that ... because most things are not overtly handed to you like on a racist platter. Usually, the issues I deal with are not handed to me in an obvious way, they are subversive. . . . You just feel like you could be toppled over at any time. (p. 62)

The idea of having to "perform" one's identity may be particularly resonant when considering the experiences of black women in higher education. This study participant entered the classroom aware that many of her students would perceive her in terms of particular stereotypical images of black women in the United States (i.e., black women as verbally aggressive, controlling, and antagonistic—the antithesis of hegemonic notions of femininity *and* intellectuality). As a professor in 2006, this individual had to be concerned that in managing her classroom and having high expectations of students, she may be perceived as being "aggressive" or as *Sapphire*, a stereotypical image of black women (Jewell, 1993).

In addition to having to negotiate stereotypical notions of black women, even as faculty in university classrooms, the black women interviewed also talked candidly about not having the luxury or ability to separate race, gender, class, and age from daily interactions with colleagues and students. These women spoke about the ways in which black men and white women have an advantage to "pick/choose" which oppression to address. One participant articulated the conflation of social class with raced and gendered notions of black female professors:

> As soon as I come in and write [name] on the board, already instant division. My god, she's black, she's a woman, she's got a doctorate, so not only is she one of those go-off-on-you black girls and she's got nice shoes. She's got a cushy job. She doesn't know what's going on with me. Its complex . . . the way I speak indicates to them that I'm not from here. The way I dress indicates that I'm not from here. The way I wear my hair. You know all that kind of stuff. So as soon as I start to outline those things and tell them about myself and what I do, never let them find out that I've been somewhere. I have a lot of students who have been places, a vast majority of them haven't. So that becomes an issue I think . . . an intimidation at times. (p. 68)

This study participant had developed an understanding of the culture of her students. She was aware that many of them came from working-class backgrounds and that many of them were the first in their family to attend college. She recognized that her status as an educated, middle-class black woman likely conflicted with images they had of black women before they entered the classroom. However, because of her compassion for her students, and her commitment to social change, she consciously employed teaching strategies to dispel myths about black women.

In my research, the classroom was experienced as a space for black female faculty to resist racist, classist, and sexist notions of black women. They did not want their students to develop "colorblindness" or "genderblindness." Rather they wanted their students to see and hear a black woman in the front of the classroom because they rarely see a black woman in this role. Activism and outreach are some of the ways these women spoke about combating discrimination in the classroom and beyond. One participant illustrates the consciousness she aspires her students to develop:

> I'm not going in there trying to dismantle my gender either because I mean, unlike some people, I do want them to see a black woman there. I'm not interested in them not seeing that I'm a black woman, because I don't believe in this sort of blindness that some people want a blank slate there. Color blindness, gender

blindness. No, I think I want them, I really do want them to be constantly aware of the fact that I'm a black woman in front of them because they haven't had one (Howard, 2007, p. 62).

Hence, despite challenges in the classroom, black female faculty members used this same space to address social injustices. As I noted in an earlier reporting of this work, "They embrace the challenges by continuing to work, write, teach, and inspire students to become activists as well. Seeing the classroom as agency is also seeing the classroom as change. They believe that they have the fire within to ignite the change in the world that they want to see in the future. For them, their activism begins in the classroom" (Howard, 2007, p. 80).

IMPLICATIONS FOR FUTURE RESEARCH ON WOMEN, GENDER, AND LEISURE

In the face of the sometimes "unwelcoming" practice of higher education, the black women faculty in my research found ways to negotiate the raced and gendered images that are inscribed on them, their bodies and their intellects, and to construct a space that supported their interests and causes. However, such "successes" did not come without costs, one of those costs being the stress that racism and sexism in the workplace engender (Harrell, Hall, & Taliaferro, 2003; Williams, 1997). Black women faculty spoke about managing stress that the academy can bring. Costs such as stress have implications for health (i.e., hypertension and other stress-related diseases and illnesses) and so influence people's participation in leisure. Keeping in mind the lived experiences of being black and female that require black women to "shift" how they present themselves in the world provides some insight into the particular stress that racism and sexism impose. Two decades ago, Allen and Chin-Sang (1990) contended that "the exclusion of aging black women from leisure studies has contributed to misrepresentation of their lives as well as distortion of our understandings of leisure experience as people age" (p. 734). While research in leisure studies has become more inclusive of the diversity of individuals who comprise any given society, as noted elsewhere in this book (e.g., see chapters by Anderson, Frisby, Fullagar, Harrington, Kay, Kivel & Johnson, Scraton & Watson, Shinew & Stodolska), we have only begun to scratch the surface of diversity and difference in our explorations of women, gender, and leisure. Further, while research into the role leisure may play in negotiating, buffering, and coping with stress has been undertaken (Coleman & Iso-Ahola, 1993; Hutchinson, Loy, Kleiber, & Dattilo, 2003; Iwasaki & Mannell, 2000), future research in this area should perhaps consider if and how "all stress is not equal" and the unique constraints and challenges that confront those facing a lifetime of structural disadvantages.

This leads to my second recommendation for future research: the need to consider sociocultural contexts and health discourses related to leisure. For example, popular (and much scholarly) discourse centers *lifestyle choices* as the cause of many of the poor health conditions that plague black women in the United States (Helfrich Jones, Granger, Short, & Taylor, 2004; Pereira et al., 2005; Parra-Medina, Wilcox, Salinas, Addy, Fore, Poston, et al., 2011). Poor diet, physical inactivity, high stress, lack of adequate sleep, and tobacco and alcohol consumption are behaviors that are purported to put many black women (and others) at risk for disease and disability. However, we need to question and shift this discourse of "lifestyle" and "choice." We need to think about lifestyle and choice in the context of how racism, sexism, classism, and ageism work. The reality is that many people, specifically women, and especially black women, too many of whom work minimum-wage jobs, maintain the responsibilities of family, and provide support to loved ones on a daily basis, often do so at the expense of their personal health. Still, experiences of race and gender cross lines of social class.

My third recommendation for future research on women, gender, and leisure is to examine in new ways the leisure–work relationship. Much early research on leisure was based in studies of work (paid employment) that were framed by functionalist sociological perspectives. These studies examined the impact of work hours and type on hours and type of leisure. As has been clearly shown in the research on women, leisure, and work since that time, such understandings of the leisure–work relationship are quite incomplete. Further, my research on the experiences of black female faculty suggests that unless we ask questions about *experiences* of work related to race, gender, and class, we are likely to "miss" the complexity of the leisure–work relationship. Having a "bad day at work" or finding one's workplace constraining and overwhelming, and thus having little energy for or interest in leisure, may mean quite different things to individuals whose position in society varies by race or gender. There is a need to study the intersectionality of race, gender, work, and leisure—and to consider individual experiences in context.

As discussed in earlier chapters in this book, the potential of leisure is that it allows individuals to express emotions, relax, revitalize the mind and body, and to build relationships and connect with others. Black women experience challenges regardless of their social class that require a consciousness about how they must "shift" in various spaces to be allowed to occupy or be a part of those spaces. Stressful environments and the inability to "properly manage" stress can be detrimental to the health of black women. Instead of assuming that people should have the capability to manage stress through healthy lifestyle and leisure choices, a critical approach that considers the practices and experiences of race, gender, and class is needed. Only by understanding the nuance and complexities of these practices and experiences can we start to bridge the gap between theory and practice, mind and body, and constraints and opportunity.

REFERENCES

Allen, K., & Chin-Sang, V. (1990). A lifetime of work: The context and meanings of leisure for aging Black women. *The Gerontologist, 30*(6), 734–740.

Coleman, D., & Iso-Ahola, S. E. (1993). Leisure and health: The role of social support and self-determination. *Journal of Leisure Research, 25*, 111–128.

Collins, P. H. (2000a). *Black feminist thought: Knowledge, consciousness, and the politics of empowerment* (2nd ed.). New York, NY: Routledge.

Collins, P. H. (2000b). The social construction of Black feminist thought. In J. James & T. D. Sharpley-Whiting (Eds.), *The Black feminist reader* (pp. 183–207). Malden, MA: Wiley-Blackwell.

Eberhardt, M., Ingram, D., & Makuc, D. (2001). *Health, United States, 2001, with urban and rural health chartbook*. Hyattsville, MD: National Center For Health Statistics.

Harrell, J., Hall, S., & Taliaferro, J. (2003). Physiological responses to racism and discrimination: An assessment of the evidence. *American Journal of Public Health, 93*(2), 243–248.

Helfrich Jones, M. L., Granger, B. B., Short, L. M., & Taylor, M. C. (2004). A new response to heart disease in women. *Nursing Management, 35*(7), 19–25. Retrieved from Health Source: Nursing/Academic Edition database.

Howard, S. D. (2007). *Standing on the auction block: Teaching through the Black female body*. (Doctoral dissertation). Miami University. Retrieved from Ohiolink Digital Dissertations (OCLC 170714139).

Hutchinson, S. L., Loy, D. P., Kleiber, D. A., & Dattilo, J. (2003). Leisure as a coping resource: Variations in coping with traumatic injury and illness. *Leisure Sciences, 25*(2–3), 143–161.

Iwasaki, Y., & Mannell, R. C. (2000). Hierarchical dimensions of leisure stress coping. *Leisure Sciences, 22*, 163–181.

Jewell, K. S. (1993). *From mammy to Miss America and beyond: Cultural images and the shaping of U.S. social policy.* New York, NY: Routledge.

Jones, C., & Shorter-Gooden, K. (2004). *Shifting: The double lives of Black women in America.* New York, NY: Harper Perennial.

Office of Minority Health (OMH). (2008, February). *Highlights in minority health and health disparities: African American history month.* Centers for Disease Control and Prevention. Retrieved from http://www.cdc.gov/omhd/Highlights/2008/HFeb08.htm

Osteoporosis: Bone density variations between Black and White women may be due to lifestyle factors. (2006, January). *Health & Medicine Week*, 1218. Retrieved from ProQuest Health Management. (Document ID: 976378991).

Parra-Medina, D., Wilcox, S., Salinas, J., Addy, C., Fore, E., Poston, M., & Wilcox, D. K. (2011). Results of the Heart Healthy and Ethnically Relevant Lifestyle Trial: A cardiovascular risk reduction intervention for African American women attending community health centers. *American Journal of Public Health, 101*(10), 1914–1921.

Pereira, M. A., Kartashov, A. I., Ebbeling, C. B., Van Horn, L., Slattery, M., Jacobs, D., & Ludwig, D. (2005). Fast-food habits, weight gain, and insulin resistance (the CARDIA study): 15-year prospective analysis. *Lancet, 365*(9453), 36–42.

Society for Women's Health Research. (n.d.). *What do African American women suffer from?* Retrieved from http://www.goafrican.com/african-american-store/african-american-health-care-02/

Williams, D. (1997). Race and health: Basic questions, emerging directions. *Annals of Epidemiology, 7*(5), 322–333.

CHAPTER 27
LEISURE OF FAMILY CAREGIVERS

LEANDRA A. BEDINI

This chapter presents the journey I have taken in studying family caregivers' leisure. It is impossible to study this topic without also gaining insight into women, gender, and leisure. How and why this is so will become clear as I discuss my research journey. I first describe how beginning with a simple literature review, I confirmed and elaborated my hunch that informal family caregivers were not able to pursue their leisure the way they wanted. I then describe how not only my study, but also those of others in and outside of the field of leisure, provided insights into unique defining characteristics of caregivers and their perceptions of their leisure. I continue sharing what it is known about caregivers' burdens, leisure, and health, especially that of female caregivers, and briefly discuss considerations for applying what we know on micro- as well as macro-levels. I end with considerations about what directions future study and discussion regarding caregiver leisure should take.

MY JOURNEY STUDYING FAMILY CAREGIVERS' LEISURE

I did not actually become a full-fledged caregiver myself until the early 2000s, but as early as 1990, I was noticing that research about older adults always focused on how to involve frail older adults in leisure activities, or how to run activity programs in long-term care. It struck me that no one was acknowledging the person who many times was providing the care to these frail individuals—the family caregiver. Certainly, I thought, their leisure had to be compromised in some way. So, I engaged my graduate assistant at that time to help me look into the literature and identify what was being written about family caregivers and their leisure (Bedini & Bilbro, 1991). We examined 25 journal articles, book chapters, and research papers on the topic. We were not surprised to find that the majority of them identified lack of leisure as a contributing factor to what is called "caregiver burden" (Zarit, Reever, & Bach-Peterson, 1980). Studies showed how caregivers reported giving up leisure activities because of lack of time and energy, and, in many cases, feeling socially isolated. This research also noted that family caregivers' leisure activities (e.g., playing cards, reading, hobbies, vacations, physical activity, friends) were how they coped with their stress and burden. This review of the literature made it clear to us that family caregivers (a) enjoyed and valued their leisure, (b) often had to reduce or abandon it altogether because of the inability to "do it all," and (c) experienced negative effects from the loss of leisure in terms of reducing opportunities for "me time," exercise, and socialization. The "surprise" of this literature review for me was that although the majority of the articles expressed serious concern with the loss of leisure for caregivers, in the rec-ommendations for how to deal with caregiver burden, every community service imaginable was listed (healthcare, transportation, housing, mental health counseling)—except recreation programs. So, I saw a gap in the discourse around caregiver burden and turned my attention to addressing the leisure needs of family caregivers.

As I examined the literature further over the next decade, I noted how many of the articles that recognized the link between caregiver stress and abandonment of leisure pursuits were written by professionals other than those in the recreation field specifically. Further, the majority of these studies focused on some aspect of the caregivers' lives other than leisure, though some acknowledged the caregivers' loss of leisure. Slowly, over the next decade or so, recreation professionals (mostly those who worked with people with disabilities) began to write on the topic of caregiving and lei-sure. Leisure scholars (e. g., Dunn & Strain, 2001; Dupuis & Smale, 2000; Keller & Hughes, 1991; Rogers, 2001; Voelkl, 1998) examined specific, small groups of family caregivers in relation to their perceptions and ex-periences of leisure. In 1998, the National Family Caregivers Association conducted a national study in which family caregivers reported loss of leisure as one of the top three consequences of being a family caregiver. This strong "endorsement" from the caregivers themselves provided a powerful argument that leisure was, indeed, important and lacking for this population.

Although I now had adopted the "lofty mission" of bringing fam-ily caregivers to the forefront of leisure research, I also pursued parallel research interests in other disenfranchised groups. Karla Henderson and colleagues' book *A Leisure of One's Own: A Feminist Perspective on Women's Leisure* (Henderson, Bialeschki, Shaw, & Freysinger, 1989) helped me to identify that there were sub-groups of women within the larger circle of women who were disenfranchised. For example, in my work with people with disabilities, I noted that many women were constrained in their leisure not only because of their gender, but also because of their disabilities. As a result, Henderson and I began a collaboration that examined the leisure of women with disabilities, finding a new and insightful world of experiences and perspectives that greatly informed my future research, not only for this population, but also for women who were caregivers (e.g., Bedini & Henderson, 1993/94; Bedini & Henderson, 1994; Henderson & Bedini, 1995; Henderson & Bedini, 1997; Henderson, Bedini, & Hecht, 1994; Henderson, Bedini, Hecht, & Shuler, 1995).

The work I did with women with disabilities greatly informed my work with family caregivers, understanding the effect of ethic of care, perceived gender roles, life/work balance, and constraints to leisure. In the mid-1990s, using the conceptual foundation of *ethic of care*, Guinan and I interviewed 16 women who were family caregivers about their sense of entitlement to leisure (Bedini & Guinan, 1996a, 1996b). The interviews were incredibly rich and detailed. If we learned nothing else, we learned that these women had a strong "need" to share their experiences. We also found that for some of these women, "merely" going out for lunch to meet with our interviewer was seen as not only respite but also leisure. This was the first time I truly understood the sense of loss these women felt for social interaction, spontaneity, freedom, and all the other aspects of what is often considered a healthy leisure lifestyle.

The participants were easily grouped into four categories, differentiated by what we called *entitlement to leisure*: resistors (did not need leisure), resenters (wanted it, missed it, and were resentful they could not get it), consolidators (merged their leisure with their caregiving), and rechargers (sought exercise opportunities to "charge up" for caregiving efforts). These categories seemed to reinforce the concept that not all women, as well as not all caregivers, perceived their role and potential consequences to their leisure the same way. Phoenix and I (Bedini & Phoenix, 2004) subsequently used the words of the women in this study to create questions for a questionnaire for a larger female-family-caregivers study. We were able to accomplish three major goals through this larger study. First, the results of the study provided a fairly good demographic and conceptual profile representing close to 500 female family caregivers. Second, we were able to provide specific information about the lives of these women with regard to their perceptions of leisure in their lives. Finally, we were able to confirm the four categories of "entitlement to leisure" constructed in the earlier qualitative study. Further, as we found in the qualitative interview study, the majority of the women in our survey study were resentful about giving up their leisure, saw leisure as unobligated time, and clearly valued their leisure, but they felt they had difficulty accessing it (Bedini & Phoenix, 2004).

As noted earlier, it was unequivocally clear that these women wanted to share their stories and seek out advice from anyone who might have suggestions for balancing all of the responsibilities that came with the caregiver role. Of the more than 500 questionnaires received, just over 200 of them included comments or notations unrelated to the actual questions of the study, but directly related to being a caregiver. These "additional" data were presented in many ways: written in the margins or back of the survey, post-it notes, handwritten and typed letters, and even samples of writings and booklets written by the caregiver. Roy-Farrug and I (Bedini & Roy-Farrug, 2004) analyzed these data utilizing a research technique called "margin analysis," which is a form of content analysis designed to examine seemingly "stray data" that might accompany a survey. These data illustrated loss, guilt, and resentment, as well as the women's great need to share their experiences.

Conducting these studies on women also inadvertently raised my awareness of how the research process can affect study participants. From the qualitative and quantitative data, we learned about their appreciation that someone out there was listening to them. We heard how the interview itself was considered leisure because it gave them a legitimate excuse to leave the house and caregiver responsibilities. Study participation also helped some individuals realize that they might benefit from working with a mental health professional if they were to continue giving care to a loved one. This finding suggested the potential therapeutic value of the interview process in research. That is, at least some of the women in our studies found benefit not only in being interviewed and being able to write about their lives, but also in being able to see their need for support and help. These processes of data collection, particularly with marginalized groups whose voices are little sought or heard, may be especially powerful (Bedini & Henderson, 1995/6).

As just noted, we have begun to understand potential differences in the sense of entitlement to leisure among female caregivers. For the most part, however, we are finding that it is not as much the sociodemographics, per se, that set one group from another; rather, it is the attitude/socialization toward the importance of leisure in their lives that appears to separate these groups (e.g., Bedini & Gladwell, 2009; Bedini & Guinan, 1996a). As I began to understand caregivers' leisure, as well as how they differed in sense of entitlement to leisure, I noted that one of the particular losses that family caregivers often reported was pleasure travel. Examining this leisure loss through qualitative interviews, Gladwell and I focused on learning about the barriers that prevent caregivers from fulfilling travel experiences (Bedini & Gladwell, 2006; Gladwell & Bedini, 2004). Subsequently, in a survey study we confirmed that loss of travel was significant to this population more generally and identified five barriers to leisure travel experienced by family caregivers: Environmental, Personal, Service Provision, Financial, and Shared Leisure. The last barrier of *Shared Leisure* provided specific indications that the bond of partnership between spousal caregivers and their mates is strong, affecting caregivers' desire to travel. In this case, we expected gender differences based on traditional role assumptions (i.e., wife would not travel without husband), but found that the loss of the partner's ability to travel negatively affected both partners' desire to pursue travel, regardless of gender of the caregiver (Bedini & Gladwell, 2009). The leisure experience of travel, then, was seen as something meaningful only if shared with their chosen travel companion. For these individuals travel entailed much more than the trip.

CAREGIVING, CAREGIVERS' HEALTH, AND LEISURE

Research clearly shows that caregivers' health is negatively affected by caregiver burden. According to a study by the National Alliance for Caregiving and the American Association of Retired Persons (NAC/AARP, 2009), 23% of those caring for more than five years describe their health as poor to fair. Studies also show that caregivers are less able to cope with the burden of caregiving than non-caregivers (e.g., Mannell, Salmoni, & Martin, 2002; Ory et al., 1999). For example, studies have shown that caregiving can negatively affect one's perceived stress, immune system, and cortisol levels (Kim & Knight, 2008; Mills et al., 2004). In addition, compromises to the immune system can last up to three years after caregiving ends (i.e., Kiecolt-Glaser & Glaser, 2002). In fact, some studies note an earlier mortality rate for individuals who experience caregiver stress (Schulz & Beach, 1999).

It is important to note that health risks for female caregivers, in particular, are significant. In 1999, The Commonwealth Fund surveyed women, comparing those who were caregivers with non-caregiver women (Collins et al., 1999). They found that female caregivers rated their own health as fair or poor, had one or more chronic health condition, exhibited depressive symptoms, were twice as likely in the past year not to get needed medical care, and had difficulty getting medical care. Other research shows that increased coronary heart disease (CHD) is also a concern for those female caregivers who spend nine or more hours a week caring for a spouse who is ill or disabled (Lee, Colditz, Berkman, & Kawachi, 2003). Most recently, NAC/AARP (2009) identified that women (20%) are more likely than men (12%) to experience declining health due to caregiving. Within the caregiver category, female caregivers also experience more emotional and physical health consequences than male caregivers (e.g., Amirkhanyan & Wolf, 2006; Navaie-Waliser, Spriggs, & Feldman, 2002; Yee & Schulz, 2000).

In light of these realities, my recent research has focused on the relationship between leisure and caregiver health and well-being. In a recent study, Gladwell and I examined three "areas" of leisure (*participation, satisfaction with time for leisure,* and *satisfaction with the quality of the leisure experience*) in relation to male and female caregivers' perceived stress and quality of life. We found that the variable *satisfaction with the quality of leisure experience* reduced perceived stress that, in turn, increased quality of life (Bedini, Gladwell, & Dudley, 2009). We also found a similar pattern whereby *satisfaction with the quality of leisure experience* decreased perceived stress, which increased the self-reported health of family caregivers (Bedini, Gladwell, Dudley, & Clancey, 2011). That is, a caregiver's quality of life and self-reported health were both increased by reducing perceived stress that was a result of the caregiver being satisfied with the quality of his or her leisure experiences.

Overall, these results suggest that meaningfulness within a leisure experience might be the key to decreased stress and increased quality of life, as well as perceptions of health, for this population. These results can have important implications for recreation programmers who might need to move beyond provision of "cookie cutter" activities for this particular population and move to more individualized programs to address their *satisfaction with the quality* of their leisure experiences. It is interesting to note as well that results indicated that caregiving women reported higher qualities of life than caregiving men. In addition, leisure's effect in reducing perceived stress was somewhat stronger for the female than for the male caregivers. These last results raise very interesting questions about the power, and gendered experience, of leisure in stress reduction, especially for those who are caregiving.

Issues in Applying What We Know

The focus of my research agenda has recently shifted from seeking to understand caregivers' perceptions and experiences of leisure to understanding how to design leisure interventions to support/enhance caregivers' well-being. It is my hope that this line of inquiry can provide the foundation for applied research projects, test different leisure designs in the community, and lead to the development of models for leisure interventions.

I began almost 20 years ago "knowing" that leisure education was the solution to reducing stress and increasing coping skills in family caregivers. As my research progressed, I soon came to believe that this was not the case. Family caregivers rarely seek out help with their leisure. In my research, I have also found that caregivers are very cramped for time and overwhelmed with fatigue, guilt, and worry; hence, why should I expect that they would seek out a leisure education program for themselves? Most importantly, however, I have come to understand that many caregivers are unlikely to accept suggestions for improving their health, unless those suggestions come from someone they see as important (e.g., doctor, elder, religious figure). For some, research suggests that this may well be a gendered issue, based in the *ethic of care* that frames femininity in our (and many other) culture(s). Family caregivers, particularly female caregivers, often compromise their own health in deference to the health of their care-recipient. Given these realities, I came to feel that proposals from a recreation professional would likely have little clout.

Now, however, after many years of learning more about the behaviors and attitudes of this population, the additional medical benefits of leisure, and the social and cultural discourses they must negotiate, I am back to thinking that leisure education is necessary, but perhaps for an audience broader than the caregiver alone. Leisure education has the potential to empower service providers, policymakers, and members of the medical community to provide infrastructure for family caregivers to access leisure. It is clear that caregivers remain overlooked by medical, social, and political systems with regard to support that will enable them to access and enjoy their leisure. *Caregiving in the U.S.* reports that 43% of caregivers feel they do not have a choice about becoming a caregiver. At the same time, studies show that about 70% of working caregivers make changes, ranging from going in late to completely quitting their jobs, to accommodate their caregiving responsibilities (NAC/AARP, 2009). Not surprisingly then, recent estimates place the value of informal caregiving in the United States at approximately $316 billion. These statistics give an indication of how far we have to go for sociopolitical support of family caregivers who will only be increasing in number as the baby boomers age. In turn, support from larger community systems will contribute to removing barriers that impede their pursuit of satisfying and meaningful leisure experiences.

Finally, leisure-education programs that do address the caregiver alone are warranted to help meet the intrinsic leisure needs of caregivers. As suggested by the four categories of caregivers discussed above (resistors, resenters, consolidators, and rechargers), women often struggle to maintain any sense of entitlement to leisure. Similar to Bialeschki and Michener's (1994) study that found that mothers often "shelve" their leisure, family caregivers seem to have a similar pattern of postponing their personal leisure enjoyment in deference to their caregiving responsibilities. The feminist approaches to research presented in chapter 3 would likely provide diverse explanations as to why caregivers postpone leisure. These and other questions for future research are addressed next.

QUESTIONS FOR FUTURE STUDY ON FAMILY CAREGIVERS AND LEISURE

The prevalence of caregivers in the United States is growing. Of the over 45 million caregivers in the United States, women still make up the majority (over 63%). Women are also more likely than men to take on more of a burden and care longer than male caregivers (e.g., Navaie-Waliser et al., 2002). While these numerical differences are significant, my research on the lives and leisure of family caregivers indicates that experiences and consequences of caregiving are gendered in other important ways as well. This research, as well as that of others, suggests a number of directions for future research.

One of the primary challenges of researching as well as serving family caregivers lies in the difficulty in finding them—and, furthermore, in finding a representative group of these individuals. For example, the member lists of most large caregiver organizations in the United States that might provide access to caregivers (e.g., National Family Caregivers Association, National Alliance of Caregiving) are comprised primarily of individuals who are Caucasian/White. Caregivers of color are greatly underrepresented as members in these organizations. A number of reasons for this racial disparity have been proffered. First, it may be that individuals in various cultures do not necessarily identify, or think of themselves, as a family caregiver. We need to better understand how diverse racial groups, for example, African Americans, Asian Americans, and Latino Americans, think about (and experience) family caregiving. Is it expected and accepted as a family responsibility and not seen as a distinct "life stage" or "role" in their lives? Researchers like White-Means (1993), as well as Dilworth-Anderson and colleagues (2002, 2004), have studied cultural as well as racial differences in family caregivers (see Scraton & Watson, this volume). This research has examined cultural and traditional contexts of providing care to family members as well as the importance of religious affiliation for African American caregivers. It is important to note, however, that studies focusing on racial and ethnic differences in family caregiving with specific attention to issues of leisure are few and far between.

Since the majority of caregivers are female, less is known about male caregivers. One study that focused on male caregivers in the United States to understand their leisure found that while men's approach to caregiving often differs from that of female caregivers, their response to caregiver stress is similar. For example, male caregivers who reported fewer leisure opportunities also demonstrated poorer emotional and physical health (Shanks-McElroy & Strobino, 2001). While this study provides much-needed insight into the lived experiences of male caregivers and their leisure, more needs to be learned. For example, are there differences among men who care for spouses versus parents? Are men who are married and/or parents different from single and/or childless male caregivers? In addition, while there may be fewer differences among men with regard to caregiving stress, there are still differences in their approaches and uses of leisure that differentiate them from women as family caregivers.

I believe that one of the most important tasks in these areas of research would be to design longitudinal work to follow these caregivers throughout their entire experience as well as years after they cease caregiving responsibilities. With health research suggesting effects lasting well past the end of caregiving, following individuals' interest in and pursuit of leisure in relation to their health is warranted.

Finally, I strongly believe that caregiving should be considered a stage of life. To date, few texts on aging even mention family caregiving, much less acknowledge it as a life stage. With the aging of the baby boomers in the United States, it can be expected that more family members will be called upon to care for their family members. Little government support in the United States contributes to the potential increase in numbers of family members caring for one another. With that said, we identify marriage and parenthood as life stages, although not everyone experiences either or both of these. Retirement is often identified as a life stage; however, many individuals do not work (or have no choice but to continue to work) and so cannot retire. Therefore, there is little argument that a facet of life that currently affects over 20% of the U.S. population and stands to grow exponentially should be considered as a common experience in individuals' lifespan.

In summary, I believe we have come a long way in identifying a "hidden" population, many of whom are women, who need to be understood, and empowered on how to find, access, and pursue their rights to leisure. There is also a lot of work to do, however, to get the medical, social, and political communities to identify and become active in connecting caregivers with healthy leisure options. The problems are more clearly identified today than in the past, and there are more individuals within and outside of the research arenas who are taking notice. But, unless this knowledge is applied, we will not progress. With the rapid aging of populations worldwide, this is the prime time for societies to take note.

REFERENCES

Amirkhanyan, A. A., & Wolf, D. A. (2006). Parent care and the stress process: Findings from panel data. *Journal of Gerontology, 61B*(5), S248–S255.

Bedini, L. A. & Bilbro, C. W. (1991). Caregivers, the hidden victims: Easing caregiver burden through recreation and leisure services. *Annual in Therapeutic Recreation, 2*, 49–54.

Bedini, L. A. & Gladwell, N. J. (2006). Barriers to leisure travel of family caregivers: A preliminary examination. *Topics in Geriatric Rehabilitation, 22*(4), 322–333.

Bedini, L. A., Gladwell, N. J. (2009). Ambiguous loss and shared leisure barriers of family caregivers. *American Journal of Recreation Therapy, 8*(2), 23–30.

Bedini, L. A., Gladwell, N. J., & Dudley, W. N. (2009, October). *Meditation analysis of leisure, stress, and quality-of-life in family caregivers.* Proceedings of Symposium on Leisure Research, NRPA, Salt Lake City, UT.

Bedini, L. A., Gladwell, N. J., Dudley, W. N., & Clancey, E. J. (2011). Mediation analysis of leisure, perceived stress, and quality of life in family caregivers. *Journal of Leisure Research, 43*(2), 153–175.

Bedini, L. A., & Guinan, D. M. (1995, October). *Motherhood revisited?: Recurrent roles of family caregivers and the relationship to leisure.* Paper presented at the Leisure Research Symposium, National Recreation and Parks Association, San Antonio, TX.

Bedini, L. A., & Guinan, D. M. (1996a). "If I could just be selfish . . .": Caregivers' perceptions of their entitlement to leisure. *Leisure Sciences, 18*, 227–239.

Bedini, L. A., & Guinan, D. M. (1996b). The leisure of caregivers of older adults: Implications for CTRS's in non-traditional settings. *Therapeutic Recreation Journal, 30*, 274–288.

Bedini, L. A., & Henderson, K. A. (1993/94). Interdependence, social support, and leisure: Describing the experience of women with physical disabilities. *Annual in Therapeutic Recreation, 4*, 96–107.

Bedini, L. A., & Henderson, K. A. (1994). Women with disabilities and the challenges to leisure service providers. *Journal of Parks and Recreation Administration, 12*(1), 17–34.

Bedini, L. A., & Henderson, K. A. (1995/96). The therapeutic value of the interviewing process in research. *Annual in Therapeutic Recreation, 6*, 55–63.

Bedini, L. A., & Phoenix, T. L. (2004). Perceptions of leisure by family caregivers: A profile. *Therapeutic Recreation Journal, 38*, 366–382.

Bedini, L. A., & Roy-Farrug, A. (2004, October). *You didn't ask but . . .": An analysis of unsolicited survey comments about the leisure of female family caregivers.* Paper presented at the American Therapeutic Recreation Association Annual Conference, Kansas City, MO.

Bialeschki, M. D., & Michener, S. (1994). Re-entering leisure: Transition within the role of motherhood. *Journal of Leisure Research, 26*, 57–74.

Collins, K. S., Schole, C., Joseph, S., Ducker, L., Simantov, E., & Yellowitz, M. (1999). *Health concerns across women's lifespan.* Commonwealth Fund 1998: Summary of Women's Health.

Dilworth-Anderson, P., & Williams, S. W. (2004). Recruitment strategies for longitudinal African-American caregiving research: The family caregiving project. *Journal of Aging and Health, 16*, 137S–156S.

Dilworth-Anderson, P., Williams, I. C., & Gibson, B. (2002). Issues of race, ethnicity, and culture in caregiving research: A twenty-year review (1980–2000). *The Gerontologist, 42*, 237–272.

Dunn, N. J., & Strain, L. A. (2001). Caregivers at risk?: Changes in leisure participation. *Journal of Leisure Research, 33*(1), 32–56.

Dupuis, S. L., & Smale, B. J. A. (2000). Bittersweet journeys: Meanings of leisure in the institution-based caregiving context. *Journal of Leisure Research, 32*(3), 303–340.

Gladwell, N. J., & Bedini, L. A. (2004). Regaining lost leisure: The leisure travel of family caregivers. *Tourism Management, 25*, 685–693.

Henderson, K. A., & Bedini, L. A. (1995). "I have a soul that dances like Tina Turner, but a body that can't.": Physical activity and women with mobility impairments. *Research Quarterly for Exercise and Sport, 66*(2), 151–161.

Henderson, K. A., & Bedini, L. A. (1997). Woman, leisure, and double whammies: Empowerment and constraints. *Journal of Leisurability, 24*(1), 36–46.

Henderson, K. A., & Bedini, L. A., & Hecht, L. (1994). "Not just a wheelchair, not just a woman": Self-identity and leisure. *Therapeutic Recreation Journal, 28*(2), 73–86.

Henderson, K. A., Bedini, L. A., Hecht, L., & Shuler, R. (1995). Women with physical disabilities and the negotiation of leisure constraints. *Leisure Studies, 14*, 17–31.

Henderson, K., Bialeschki, M. D., Shaw, S. M., & Freysinger, V. J. (1996). *Both gains and gaps: Feminist perspectives on women's leisure.* State College, PA: Venture Publishing, Inc.

Keller, M. J., & Hughes, S. (1991). The role of leisure education with family caregivers of persons with Alzheimer's disease and related disorders. *Annual in Therapeutic Recreation, 2*(2), 1–7.

Kiecolt-Glaser, J. K., & Glaser, R. (2002). Depression and immune function: Central pathways to morbidity and mortality. *Journal of Psychosomatic Research, 53*(4), 873–876.

Kim, J., & Knight, B. G. (2008). Effects of caregiver status, coping styles, and social support on the physical health of Korean American caregivers. *The Gerontologist, 48*(3), 287–299.

Lee, S. L., Colditz, G. A., Berkman, L. F., & Kawachi, I. (2003). Caregiving and risk of coronary heart disease in U.S. women: A prospective study. *American Journal of Preventive Medicine, 24*(2), 113–119.

Mannell, R. C., Salmoni, A. W., & Martin, L. (2002). Older adults caring for older adults: Physically active leisure lifestyles as a coping resource for the health of caregivers. *Loisir et Societe/Society and Leisure, 25,* 397–420.

Mills, P. J., Adler, M. S., Dimsdale, J. E., Perez, C. J., Ziegler, M. G., Ancoli-Isreal, S., et al. (2004). Vulnerable caregivers of Alzheimer disease patients have a deficit in adrenergic receptor sensitivity and density. *American Journal of Geriatric Psychiatry, 12,* 281–286.

National Alliance for Caregiving and American Association of Retired Persons (NAC/AARP). (2009). *Caregiving in the U.S.* Bethesda, MD.

National Family Caregivers Association. (1998). *Family caregiving demands recognition: Caregiving across the lifecycle.* Milwaukee, WI: Author.

Navaie-Waliser, M., Feldman, P. H., Gould, D. A., Levine, C. L., Kuerbis A. N., & Donelan, K. (2002). When the caregiver needs care: The plight of vulnerable caregivers. *American Journal of Public Health, 92*(3), 409–413.

Navaie-Waliser, M., Spriggs, A. & Feldman, P. H. (2002). Informal caregiving: Differential experiences by gender. *Medical Care, 40,* 1249–1259.

Ory, M. G., Hoffman, R. R., Yee, J. L., Tennstedt, S., & Schulz, R. (1999). Prevalence and impact of caregiving: A detailed comparison between dementia and non-dementia caregivers. *The Gerontologist, 39,* 177–185.

Rogers, N. B. (2001). Family obligation, caregiving, and loss of leisure: The experiences of three caregivers. *Activities, Adaptation & Aging, 24*(2), 35–49.

Schulz, R., & Beach, S. R. (1999). Caregiving as a risk factor for mortality. *Journal of American Medical Association, 282*(23), 2215–2219.

Shanks-McElroy, H. A., & Strobino, J. (2001). Male caregivers of spouses with Alzheimer's disease: Risk factors and health status. *American Journal of Alzheimer's Disease and Other Dementias, 16,* 167–175.

Voelkl, J. E. (1998). The shared activities of older adults with dementia and their caregivers. *Therapeutic Recreation Journal, 32* (3), 231–239.

White-Means, S. I. (1993). Informal home care for frail Black elderly. *Journal of Applied Gerontology, 12*(1), 18–33.

Yee, J. L., & Schulz, R. (2000). Gender differences in psychiatric morbidity among family caregivers: A review and analysis. *The Gerontologist, 40,* 147–164.

Zarit, S. H., Reever, K. E., Bach-Peterson, J. (1980). Relatives of the impaired elderly: Correlates of feelings of burden. *The Gerontologist, 20,* 649–655.

Chapter 28
Older Age, Family, and Leisure

Sheila Scraton and Beccy Watson

Our research journey over the past couple of decades has taken us through many diverse theoretical and empirical landscapes, although the focus on feminist analysis and gender has remained a constant companion. For both of us, the importance of feminist praxis, the relationship between theory and practice, is fundamental to our academic approach, and our research reflects our concern to further understand women's lives, in order to make a difference through knowledge and its application to education, policy, and practice.

In this chapter, we concentrate specifically on our work on older people, family, and leisure that has been an important strand throughout our feminist research journey. It is also a journey that we have made together, part of our commitment to collective work and our belief that we grow and learn as researchers from each other. Our differences have helped us to look outwards as well and, we hope, grow, as we work in the fluid and dynamic area of feminist analysis and gender relations. Although nearly two decades separate us in age, we both began our research in leisure studies through an exploration of gender inequalities and a concern to understand and challenge gender oppression and unequal power relations. Our roots in the United Kingdom (UK) are in social and cultural analysis, and we have benefited not only from colleagues working in leisure and sport studies, but also critical work in sociology, women's studies, and cultural studies. Sheila's research journey has been a little longer, and it flourished in the 1980s and early 1990s when women's leisure began to receive critical attention. Beccy began her research in the 1990s, and together we have travelled through the landscapes of socialist feminism, radical feminism, black feminism, poststructuralism, and, more recently, the debates around intersectionality and the complex power dynamics of gender, race, ethnicity, class, and age (see chapter 3 for a further discussion of these approaches).

Rich material collected and analyzed during the 1980s and 1990s on women, gender, and leisure emphasized the significance of leisure not only as a site for the reproduction of inequalities, but also as a space and place for resistance and the transformation of gender relations (Green, Hebron, & Woodward, 1990; Henderson, Bialeschki, Shaw, & Freysinger, 1996; Shaw, 2001). The theoretical and lived experiences of the tensions between and across individual experiences (micro) and collective power relations (macro), shared inequalities and diversity/difference, and the complexities of multiple axes of power have driven our research agendas. We focus here specifically on older women who have received little attention in studies of leisure and, indeed, have been largely ignored in broader feminist social analysis in the United Kingdom until relatively recently (Arber, Davidson, & Ginn, 2004; Davidson, Warren, & Maynard, 2005). As we will discuss below, we began with a study of older white women and then, recognizing the ethnocentricity of our research agenda, focused on our increasingly complex multiethnic society, exploring the leisure lives of older people across gender, ethnicity, and age. It became apparent from our empirical data that the family and the under-researched area of grandparenting were significant aspects of the leisure lives of these older people. An added dimension has been Sheila becoming a grandparent herself! As with much feminist research, our experiences and consciousness play a large part in driving our research agendas. As Beccy's children reach adulthood and Sheila's children begin their own families, it seems appropriate and pertinent to reflect back on our research over the past 20 years that has explored the complexities of older age, family, and leisure.

OLDER AGE, FAMILY, AND LEISURE

Critical feminist work of the 1980s and 1990s emphasized the gendered constraints many women face within the household due to the social expectations of femininity and motherhood (Green et al., 1990; Kay, 1998, 2000b; Shaw, 1992, 1997). At the end of the twentieth century, there was work exploring women's leisure in "nontraditional" family forms, for example, lone parenthood (Watson, 1999) and leisure as a potential site for resistance and autonomy (Green, 1998; Wearing, 1998). However, as discussed above, older women have been largely absent from these studies. Early research on older people and leisure tended to focus on white men, particularly within the context of retirement (Long & Wimbush, 1985), relying on functional definitions of leisure and the "problems" of disengagement from paid work.

More recently there has been a growth within the United Kingdom of critical social analyses of aging that have challenged the dominant discourse of gerontology, with its focus on aging as deficiency. This critical approach has influenced our thinking, as it focuses on older people as active citizens, while emphasizing the continuing impact of class and gender relations (Arber et al., 2004; Cook, Maltby, & Warren, 2005; Davidson et al., 2005). However, even within this work, it has been acknowledged that there is little known about the lives of older women from minority ethnic groups.

Initially in our research into older age and leisure we focused specifically on white women, gender, and class, exploring leisure as a potential site of agency in the context of pervasive inequalities, for example, in living in lower-income households. However, increasingly we were cognizant of the need to include ethnicity in our focus and analysis. Wray's work represents one of the first studies comparing the experiences of older women from different ethnic groups living in the United Kingdom (Wray, 2003). Her examination of agency, ethnicity, and culture makes a valuable contribution to debates on older women's leisure, although leisure in her research is an emerging context rather than a central focus.

As our research developed to include a wider group of diverse older women, we began to look at the role of the family and gender relations in different ways. Although evidence had suggested that an ethic of care faced by women in older age continues to reproduce a gendered discourse around grandmotherhood and domestic labor (Arber & Ginn, 1991, 1995), Wearing had begun to look at grandparenting as a part of leisure. Here she traces positive sources of pleasure and identity and also some of the complexities surrounding cultural expectations of mothers becoming grandmothers (Wearing, 1990a). It was apparent that there was little developed analysis of fatherhood and leisure, although this has now been remedied somewhat by the special edition of *Leisure Studies* in April 2006, edited by Kay, and her recently published edited collection (Kay, 2009a). However, there was no work looking specifically at grandfatherhood, which led to a further project focusing on grandfatherhood and leisure (Scraton & Holland, 2006). This research drew on literature from sociology, gerontology, and social policy, although as Clarke and Roberts (2004) recognized, "there is almost no research in Britain which considered the experience of becoming and being a grandparent from the point of view of the older people themselves" (p. 189).

Using our empirical studies, we now move on to highlight some of the findings that we suggest have contributed to the debates about older age, family, and leisure over the years.

Our Studies

We are drawing on three empirical studies separately conducted over a period of approximately 15 years in a large northern city in the United Kingdom.

- Older white working-class women (Scraton, Bramham, & Watson, 1996; Scraton & Watson, 1998);

- Older South Asian women (Scraton & Watson, 2008; Watson & Scraton, 2001);

- Older men (white, African Caribbean, South Asian) (Scraton & Holland, 2006).

These projects involved qualitative research using in-depth interviews plus observations and active participation in community settings, where appropriate. The studies raise various methodological issues including, for example, our position as white researchers (Watson & Scraton, 2001), use of interpreters, and so on, and these are addressed in some of our previous publications. While our studies do not provide any generalizable information, they do identify some important issues that we discuss next.

Persistent Inequalities

Our data clearly suggest that gendered discourse still determines experiences of family and leisure into old age. Growing old was and remains a gendered process. This was obvious across different religions, ethnicities, and classes. There were considerable differences in the sizes of households, with the working-class, white women all living alone (mostly widowed), apart from one whose husband was still alive. In contrast, the majority of the older South Asian women and men lived in extended intergenerational family settings. Many of the women described a clear division of domestic labor and family-caring responsibilities. Our research seemed to confirm continuities of gender relations for this generation of women, although for the white women, most of whom were living alone, isolation rather than responsibility for others was more of a problem. The women living in extended families still retained a responsibility for caring and domestic labor, although those who lived with their married sons had handed over many domestic duties to their daughters-in-law, thus passing on this gendered division of labor to the next generation of women. Grandparenting also involved this clear gendered division of labor and ethic of care. Many of our male participants appeared reluctant to be directly involved in a caring role with their grandchildren, while at the same time expressing affection for them. There was a tension, in that many of the grandfathers seemed unable or unwilling to break the pattern of caring and activity set with their own children. The family remained a feminized sphere for many of the men that was outside or peripheral to their masculine identities. For example, to have any contact with grandchildren was largely dependent on the presence of a wife or partner who retained a responsibility for organizing contact and providing care and support.

Discourses of gender around domestic labor and caring responsibilities have implications for *access* to leisure and, also, the *experiences* of leisure for both older women and men. It was interesting to listen to the differences in the older women's and men's expectations and perceptions of leisure and recognize that, for these older people, a gendered division of labor *and* leisure persists into the twenty-first century. For example, our research across all our studies on older women and men from different ethnic backgrounds found that the family remains a place of obligation and duty for most older women and relatively few men. Gendered constraints within the family, relating to housework and childcare were very similar to those identified in earlier studies on women and leisure (Green et al., 1990). Yet even within these constraints, the older women showed remarkable agency and resistance, carving out their own moments of leisure and pleasure. A significant aspect of our research has been exploring the potential of using a "leisure" lens on the lives of older people in order to challenge the dominant pathological view of aging and the stereotypical view of older people as passive "victims" of age, culture, ethnicity, and gender.

Leisure Spaces, Resistances, and Identities

Wearing (1998) reminds us that "leisure emphasizes what a person can do rather than what she or he cannot, and the importance of an individual's choice of leisure experience" (p. 276). A striking theme across all our research has been the resilience and resourcefulness shown by the older women. Often faced with a range of material constraints, all older women appeared to carve out spaces (both emotional and physical) with family and friends who were important in their lives. What came over strongly was the ability of the older women to cope with new and changing personal circumstances and to use their family and social networks to find pleasure in the things that they could still do. "Passive" leisure around the family emerged as highly significant as the women talked about the joys and pleasures of memory, nostalgia, and reminiscence about their children, partners, and homes. While this was apparent for all the women, there were differences in notions of belonging, with the older white women talking about changes in their local area/community, and the South Asian women reflecting on the significance of belonging, albeit in different spatial contexts. For example, they spoke of maintaining contacts by phone and e-mail with family members in different countries.

The family home is a leisure space that can bridge both the personal and the social and involve leisure as *being* as well as *doing*. For all the women in our research regardless of ethnicity, family and home provided the space for reminiscence and reflection as well as for doing specific leisure activities such as sewing, reading, and watching television. A key area that emerged in our specific study of South Asian women related to leisure as both "being" and "doing," and centered on the significance of religion and faith, intricately tied to family. Prayer is about personal space, for some more of an obligation, but often a very real source of satisfaction, calm, and pleasure for many of the women. It was also about social space often experienced through shared prayers in the family home or in a community or religious setting. In our research with older South Asian women, participants identified with Muslim and Sikh religions and ethnicities. Although their experiences of religion and faith were articulated and experienced differently, there was seemingly a sense of belonging that religion brought to the women's lives. This was similar for the older white women we had researched earlier who created a sense of "family" or community through their attachment to a local church that provided a focus and social space for their leisure. Other than the recognition of the decline of religion as a feature of leisure amongst the dominant white majority in the United Kingdom (Rojek, 2000), there has been very little work within leisure studies that examines the relationships between religion, faith, and leisure. Our research suggests that religion can be an important space of leisure that is personal, intimate and social, and is often shared with family and/or friends. It was also evident that spaces associated with religion, churches, church halls, temples, and community centers are important social contexts and sites for leisure, regardless of personal religious affiliation. Without further research, it is difficult to know whether this is an age, gender, or cultural phenomenon, although it would appear that age and gender are significant for church attendance within the Christian faith in the United Kingdom. This is certainly an area worthy of further investigation.

Grandparenting as Leisure

Grandmotherhood did not always emerge as a significant aspect of the lives of the older white women. This may have been because they were a slightly older age group and, as indicated above, were mainly living alone. Some did talk about visiting their children and families, but none stressed their role as grandmother; they did not talk as explicitly about being a grandmother in the same ways that many South Asian women did. However, the South Asian women who talked a lot about their children and grandchildren often were living in extended families. They talked about grandmothering in terms of domestic or caring support in a number of examples, yet overwhelmingly the main response appeared to be one of pleasure gained from grandchildren. The home was often described as a women's space, inhabited by their children, then daughters-in-law, and grandchildren. Evidently, there were differences in levels of responsibility and caregiving for grandchildren, depending, for example, on whether both parents were working, the ages of children, and so on. We return to changing households and working patterns in final sections of the chapter.

The project on grandfatherhood (Scraton & Holland, 2006) developed out of our increasing awareness to explore issues of gender and age across different ethnicities. What became immediately clear on talking to the men were the tensions, ambivalences, and complexities of grandfatherhood. Although there have been shifts in gendered notions of parenting and childcare, the men in the study seemed unable or unwilling to break the gendered pattern of childcare set with their own children. Consequently, many of the men were missing the opportunity to develop close and mutually beneficial relationships with their grandchildren. The pictures of grandfatherhood suggested limited self-esteem, identity, or personal enrichment associated with their grandfathering role. This is in contrast to our, and others, limited research findings on the role of grandmotherhood (Kornhaber, 1996; Wearing, 1990a). Not all the men seemed happy with this situation, and often talked with a tinge of sadness about lost opportunities to develop a closer bond with their grandchildren. They seemed to feel it was an inevitability and outside their control.

Interesting methodological issues were raised around researching grandfatherhood. Men often appeared less comfortable in engaging in in-depth conversations about their emotions or subjective feelings in relation to grandfathering, made more problematic by gender and ethnic differences between researched and researchers. Consequently, it was difficult to explore the notion of leisure in relation to families and parenting; there is perhaps a need to rethink our research methods and methodologies (Scraton, Watson, & Long, 2003). Men have featured more in research on aging that is focused around transitions into retirement from paid employment and so on, and clearly, further work is required to examine their caring roles in older age.

Whether through choice or not, the gendered division of labor and care in grandparenting did allow for more separate individual leisure time for many of the men in the study. As in early studies of gender and leisure, leisure for most of the men was conceptualized as a sphere separate from areas of obligation. Although not taking direct responsibility for grandparenting, the men clearly saw grandparenthood as an obligation and more akin to work with leisure as their free time and space. It was striking, for instance, that none of the men mentioned fathering or grandfathering as a part of their leisure. Meanwhile, the research suggested that there are cultural differences around notions of choice, duty, and responsibility. For the Indian Sikh respondents in particular, grandfathering, although defined by the men as obligation and duty, was articulated more positively in relation to the family. For these men, the identity of grandfatherhood was tied to important familial relationships and denoted an identity as a respected elder in the community. This remained highly gendered, as there was little evidence that their grandfathering involved direct care and responsibility, although there was clear evidence that it did provide a sense of pleasure and satisfaction. As with all the research discussed in this chapter, there are consistencies across ethnicity, age, and gender as well as differences and ambiguities. However, this preliminary research does suggest that grandparenting as a leisure space remains a highly gendered space.

Continuing the Journey

Throughout our journey through leisure, age, gender, and ethnicity, we have certainly begun to discover more about the lives of different older women and men. These older people have grown up in a world highly differentiated by gender (as well as ethnicity, race, class). What we feel our research offers to the growing critical research on older people in the United Kingdom is our view of their lives through a leisure lens. Our critical approach to leisure keeps the challenging issues of freedom and constraint and structure and agency within leisure at the forefront of our work. Our empirical studies inform analyses of leisure that move debates beyond dichotomous explanations. For us, and some other leisure researchers (for example, Wearing, 1998), conceptualizing leisure as personal space is highly significant, particularly as we seek to examine a diverse range of experiences across parenting and grandparenting. Wearing (1998) emphasizes leisure as a positive source of satisfaction and the (potential) enlargement of the self; we remain interested in space as personal *and* social across a variety of leisure contexts. This approach retains a focus on social positioning as well as "everyday" individual experiences, thus emphasizing difference that goes beyond plurality and diversity (Brah & Phoenix, 2004). This allows us to explore the "messy" borderlands between materialist accounts and poststructuralist analysis and across inequalities and difference. That is, there is much work (still) to be done that engages critically with difference and diversity for older people (Bedini, this volume). As with most research, our findings have generated more questions, both empirical and theoretical, and we close our chapter by pointing towards some new directions that need exploration.

Shifting Gender Relations in the Family?

There is considerable work on the new politics of masculinity that explores the challenge to dominant forms of masculinity and inequitable gender relations (Ashe, 2007; Connell, 2005). However, there is also recent work that suggests that the domestic division of labor remains very much intact, with unequal gender relations continuing to impact women's lives (Crompton, Brockmann, & Lyonette, 2005). Questions relating to shifting and more fluid gender relations need to guide future leisure research within families with older members and in increasingly complex and changing family forms. The relationships among family, leisure, and older people in community or private-care homes would also provide an interesting and important context. Different spatial contexts and living arrangements for older people and their linkages to leisure are crucial topics for further investigation.

"Young" Grandparenting and Work-Family-Leisure Balance

Related to the above is the increasing number of "young" grandparents, who themselves have many leisure and ongoing work interests. It has been stated that the "new 60s" are the "old 40s" in terms of age. As the post-war generation reaches retirement and older age, it will be important to look at their experiences of leisure, family, and grandparenting. The "over 55s" are identified as a growing leisure market with notions of the "grey pound" and "SKI-ers" (Spending the Kids' Inheritance) dispelling the myth that older people simply "stay in and grow old." It will be interesting to research the implications of grandparenthood *on* leisure, as well *as* leisure, for older "active" women and men as their families have their own families and may also have expectations of support and childcare.

Mixed-Race/Mixed-Heritage Families and Grandparenting

It has been stated that the "mixed" population is the third largest ethnic category in the United Kingdom, with predictions that by the census in 2020 it will have become the single largest minority group (Sims, 2007). Our research has tried to capture pictures of different older people in the United Kingdom by focusing on different ethnicities and religions.

However, our research has been carried out in specific communities, and it will be important to begin to explore leisure of older people with mixed-race grandchildren and the experiences of mixed-race peoples as they age. In the United Kingdom context for example, there is no work on the experiences of mixed-race British African Caribbean families and diverse, "established" minority ethnic communities in relation to their leisure.

Rediscovering Class, Family, and Gender

We increasingly feel that questions of class need to be revisited in future research projects. Although class is often missed from social analyses of inequalities and is largely ignored in recent studies of leisure, it remains a key determining feature, together with gender, ethnicity, and age, of leisure experiences and opportunities (see also chapters by Frisby and Harrington, this volume). As more middle-class women are retiring with pensions from full-time careers and with economic independence, the gap between women from different class locations will potentially become greater as they reach old age. We need more studies that look at the impact of economic disadvantages including long-term unemployment, limited or no home ownership, lack of pension and how these intersect with gender, ethnicity, and other social relations in old age.

Theorizing and Researching Intersectionality

As we have journeyed through feminism and research on gender it has become increasingly obvious to us that feminist leisure studies needs to engage more fully with debates around intersectionality and multiplicity (Aitchison, this volume). Our data have highlighted the lived experiences of being older, working-class, gendered, racialized, and from different ethnicities and faiths. We have only begun to touch on these complex debates, but they are crucial for our theoretical understanding and have major implications for our methodologies (Flintoff, Fitzgerald, & Scraton, 2008; Scraton & Watson, 2008). As the research on diversity and difference across and within older populations demonstrates, it is important to have empirical studies that deal with the complex analytical task of understanding multiple and intersecting identities and inequalities (Grabham, Cooper, Krishnades, & Herman, 2009). There are "invisible" communities among older people, including couples in civil partnerships and those of diverse sexuality, that are underrepresented and under-researched. There are also increasing numbers of women who choose to live alone and/or do not have children. Dominant discourse based upon gerontological approaches of aging that center on diminished health also poses questions around disability; at the same time, the aging and old age of disabled people are largely ignored.

In summary, our research journey has taken us along many pathways looking at the intersections of gender, age, class, and ethnicity. As suggested above, there is much work to do to ensure that the journey is continued and that we learn and understand more about discourses of aging and growing old and the multiple and complex roles leisure plays within these.

REFERENCES

Arber, S., Davidson, K., & Ginn, J. (2004). *Gender and ageing: Changing roles and relationships.* London, UK: Open University Press.

Arber, S., & Ginn, J. (1991). *Gender and later life: A sociological analysis of resources and constraints.* London, UK: Sage.

Arber, S., & Ginn, J. (1995). Gender differences in the relationship between paid employment and informal care. *Work, Employment, and Society, 9*(3), 445–471.

Ashe, F. (2007). *The new politics of masculinity.* London, UK: Routledge.

Brah, A., & Phoenix, A. (2004). Ain't I a woman? Revisiting intersectionality. *Journal of International Women's Studies, 5*(3), 75–86.

Clarke, L., & Roberts, C. (2004). The meaning of grandparenthood and its contribution to the quality of life of older people. In A. Walker & C. H. Hennessey (Eds.), *Growing older: Quality of life in old age* (pp. 188–209). London: Open University Press.

Connell, R. W. (2005). *Masculinities.* Cambridge, UK: Polity.

Cook, J., Maltby, T., & Warren, L. (2005). A participatory approach to older women's quality of life. In A. Walker (Ed.), *Understanding quality of life in old age* (pp. 23–37). Maidenhead, UK: Open University Press.

Crompton, R. Brockmann, M., & Lyonette, C. (2005). Attitudes to women's employment and the domestic division of labour. *Work, Employment and Society, 19*(2), 213–233.

Davidson, K., Warren, L., & Maynard, M. (2005). Social involvement: Aspects of gender and ethnicity. In A. Walker (Ed.), *Understanding quality of life in old age* (pp. 64–84). Maidenhead, UK: Open University Press.

Flintoff, A., Fitzgerald, H., & Scraton, S. (2008). The challenges of intersectionality: Researching difference in physical education. *International Studies in the Sociology of Education, 18*(2), 73–85.

Grabham, E., Cooper, P., Krishnades, J., & Herman, D. (2009). *Intersectionality and beyond*. London, UK: Routledge.

Green, E. (1998). "Women doing friendship": An analysis of women's leisure as a site of identity construction, empowerment and resistance. *Leisure Studies, 17*(3), 171–185.

Green, E., Hebron, S., & Woodward, D. (1990). *Women's leisure, what leisure?* London, UK: Macmillan.

Henderson, K. A., Bialeschki, M. D., Shaw, S. M., & Freysinger, V. J. (1996). *Both gains and gaps: Feminist perspectives on women's leisure.* State College, PA: Venture Publishing, Inc.

Kay, T. A. (1998). Having it all or doing it all? The construction of women's lifestyles in time-crunched households. *Leisure and Society, 21(*2), 435–454.

Kay, T. A. (2000b). Leisure, gender and family: The influence of social policy. *Leisure Studies, 19*(4), 247–265.

Kay, T. A. (Ed.) (2006). Fathering through leisure (Special Issue). *Leisure Studies, 25*(2).

Kay, T. A. (2009a). *Fathering through sport and leisure*. London, UK: Routledge.

Kornhaber, A. (1996). *Contemporary grandparenting*. London, UK: Sage.

Long, J., & Wimbush, E. (1985). *Continuity and change: Leisure around retirement*. London, UK: SC/ESRC.

Rojek, C. (2000). *Leisure and culture*. Basingstoke, UK: MacMillan.

Scraton, S., Bramham, P., & Watson, B. (1996). Staying in and going out: Elderly women, leisure and the postmodern city. In S. Scraton (Ed.), *Leisure, time and space: Meanings and values in people's lives* (pp. 101–120). LSA Publication, No. 57.

Scraton, S., & Holland, S. (2006). Grandfatherhood and leisure. *Leisure Studies, 25*(2), 233–250.

Scraton, S., & Watson, B. (1998). Gendered identities: Women and public leisure space in the "postmodern" city. *Leisure Studies, 17*(2), 123–137.

Scraton, S. & Watson, B. (2008, May). *Intersectionality and leisure: Examining the dilemmas of difference.* Presented at the 12th Canadian Congress on Leisure Research, Montreal, Quebec.

Scraton, S., Watson, B., & Long, J. (2003, September). *Ageing and serious leisure: Exploring gender, ethnicity and class in lived retirement.* Presented at the European Sociological Association International Conference, Universidad de Murcia, Spain.

Shaw, S. M. (1992). Dereifying family leisure: An examination of women's and men's everyday experiences and perceptions of family time. *Leisure Sciences, 14*(4), 271–286.

Shaw, S. M. (1997). Controversies and contradictions in family leisure: An analysis of conflicting paradigms. *Journal of Leisure Research, 29*(1), 98–112.

Shaw, S. M. (2001). Conceptualizing resistance: Women's leisure as political practice. *Journal of Leisure Research, 33*(2), 186–200.

Sims, J. M. (2007). *Mixed heritage, identity, policy and practice.* London, UK: Runneymede Trust.

Watson, B. (1999). *Motherwork–Motherleisure: Analysing young mothers' leisure lifestyles in the context of difference.* (Unpublished doctoral dissertation). Leeds Metropolitan University.

Watson, B., & Scraton, S. (2001). Confronting whiteness? Researching the leisure lives of South Asian mothers. *Journal of Gender Studies, 10*(3), 265–277.

Wearing, B. (1998). *Leisure and feminist theory*. London, UK: Sage.

Wearing, B. (1990a). Beyond the ideology of motherhood: Leisure as resistance. *Australian and New Zealand Journal of Sociology, 26*(1), 36–58.

Wray, S. (2003). Women growing older: Agency, ethnicity and culture. *Sociology, 37*(3), 511–527.

SECTION 4
BEYOND THE (INTER) PERSONAL

Chapter 29
Introduction: Power, Culture, and Politics

Valeria J. Freysinger, Susan M. Shaw, Karla A. Henderson, and M. Deborah Bialeschki

In this section of the book, leisure and the gendered nature of leisure are firmly located in the broader cultural and societal context. Attention is paid to the linkages between individual and relational leisure practices and the broader social, political, economic, and ideological environments in which these practices occur. This focus can be seen to represent the outer layers of the matryoshka, with increased consideration of macro- rather than micro-issues. The notion of power as a social structure is central to this perspective, providing a theoretical basis for understanding patriarchy and the relationships between gendered power structures and gendered lives. Attention to culture is also of particular significance, because power and power relations are never static or absolute but influence and are influenced by cultural beliefs, values, and taken-for-granted assumptions. Thus, the concept of culture alerts us to the many and diverse ways in which leisure may be connected to gendered relations of power. Further, both power and cultural diversity are closely linked to the idea of politics, political action, and the political nature of leisure practice. Gender-based inequities in leisure reflect broader political systems, and challenges to these systemic inequities are clearly a form of political practice.

Power:
Relations of Power and Intersectionality

Many chapters in this volume have discussed women's unequal access to leisure, including access to leisure time, as well as access to sport and other leisure activities. Discussions of family leisure and family caregiving in other chapters also reveal the heavy workload that women face and their resultant lack of personal leisure. In this section, too, there is evidence of historic, unequal opportunities for girls and women in organized sport in the United States (Paule-Koba, this volume) and major constraints on sports opportunities for girls in India (Kay, this volume). All of these examples can be seen to reflect structured relations of power, and thus patriarchy at work. This structuralist perspective has traditionally been based on the assumption that societal structures are independent of individual desires, motives, or actions (e.g., Smelser, 1988). In other words, it is a person's social location (e.g., being male or female, wealthy or poor), not behaviors, that determines his or her relationship to existing structures of power and the various ways in which power can be expected to privilege and benefit or oppress and constrain. Thus, this deterministic perspective is sometimes seen to be incompatible with constructionist approaches such as West and Zimmerman's (1987) notion of "doing gender."

Nevertheless, some of the more recent feminist theorizing has focused on ways of incorporating and integrating structuralist and constructionist perspectives. Risman (2004), for example, has argued persuasively for the conceptualization of gender as a social structure. In part, she bases this argument on the tenacity of gender stratification in families (Risman, 1998). Yet, at the same time, Risman (2004), like others (e.g., Connell, 2005), has adopted a more "integrative approach" that treats gender as a "socially constructed stratification system." This approach recognizes that while beliefs about gender are contested and challenged through interactional processes, dominant ideologies remain powerful and continue to reinforce and reproduce gender as a social structure.

These dual notions of the social construction of gender alongside structured relations of gendered power are evident in many of the chapters in this section. For example, in Delamere and Dixon's discussion of the "male world" of digital game play, it is clear that opportunities were still available for female players to contest traditional notions of femininity. Nevertheless, the social processes involved were complex and contradictory, involving reproduction as well as resistance, and disempowerment as well as empowerment.

Frisby's chapter on women, poverty, and leisure access also addresses power, inequity, and exclusion. Her chapter raises the important issue of intersectionality and the need to be aware of differences among women in terms of power and access to resources. The intersection of different, structured dimensions of power, such as class, race, colonization, disability/ability, and age are evident in the feminization of poverty in Canada (and elsewhere) and lead to marked inequities in access to leisure. Thus, to ignore intersectionality is to mask these differences and to fail to adequately address the complexities of structured relations of power and the existence of multiple oppressions.

In their chapter on homophobia and heterosexism, Kivel and Johnson focus on another form of discrimination and oppression and another dimension of structured relations of power. Their powerful autobiographical insights, as well as their research with youth and young adults, reveal the many difficulties of living in a homophobic society. The challenges of finding and negotiating leisure opportunities, spaces, and contexts in a heterosexist world have been given relatively little attention in the leisure literature to date. Yet the persistence of oppressive homophobia in many parts of the world makes this, as with the issue of poverty, a pressing area of feminist concern.

Fullagar's chapter also opens up new avenues for feminist researchers. Her research links women's leisure not only to health and well-being, but also to problems associated with the nature of health policies in Australia. Fullagar's analysis is framed within a structuralist understanding of gender relations, at the intersections of sexism, classism, heterosexism, and racism. Yet, she also incorporates poststructuralist ideas such as "truth regimes" and "moralism." She critiques the new health policies, which emphasize healthy living and exercise interventions. These policies, she argues, fail to address issues of social class, power, and exclusion. Thus they fail to recognize the life situations of women who do not fit within the dominant white, middle-class discourse of health, physical activity, and leisure. Further, Fullagar's focus on healthcare as a social institution shows the value of research that links leisure to other components of social life, and the ways in which notions of power and intersectionality can usefully be applied to this broader focus of analysis.

CULTURE:
A DIVERSITY OF CONTEXTS AND VOICES

The notion of intersectionality of axes of power, as well as the discussion of leisure's relationship to other social institutions, introduces complexity to the study of gender and gender relations. The concept of culture adds considerably to this complexity. It requires us to think more broadly about not only "leisure in society" (Coalter, 1999), but "leisure in *societies*," to become acutely aware of diversity and difference, and to consciously incorporate this awareness into our research.

Intersectionality alerts researchers to issues of race, class, sexual preference, age, and (to some extent) disability/ability. Yet, according to Hesse-Biber (2007), it was not until the first decade of the twenty-first century that feminist scholars expanded their focus to think more deeply about culture and "cultural placement." In the past, Western feminist researchers have been criticized for their ethnocentrism and their tendency to universalize concepts such as patriarchy (Kandiyoti, 1999). However, patriarchy may have different meanings, different roots, different expressions, and dramatically different implications for women's lives depending on the cultural and geographic context. Issues such as imperialism, colonialism, national identity, and global context (or location) have, to date, been given insufficient attention.

The notion of culture directs attention to the wide diversity of contexts and voices that need to be taken into consideration. It suggests the need for more in-depth exploration of the many different components which define a particular cultural context (such as specific beliefs, practices; values; geographies; ethnicities; identities; languages; histories; and political, educational, and economic systems). Moreover, a variety of subcultures can also exist within a wider cultural context, such as particular sports cultures, ethnic cultures, or academic cultures, which can be identified within the broader cultural landscape of any one particular society.

For feminist researchers, especially for those who are sympathetic to an integrated constructionist/structuralist approach, culture represents the basis on which gender and other relations of power are constructed and reconstructed. These include constructions of ideologies of masculinity and femininity and diverging beliefs and assumptions about appropriate behaviors, dress codes, work roles, family roles, etc., for women, men, girls, and boys. These beliefs and practices vary considerably between different cultural settings, and between different historical eras. The cultural context also influences the possibilities of particular forms of challenge and contestation, including the availability of alternate and resistant discourses. Thus, taking account of culture means attending to multiple, new, and evolving layers of meaning, experience, and practice. More specifically, for leisure researchers, the concept of culture suggests a wide variety of ways in which leisure practices and beliefs might contribute to cultural constructions of patriarchy and gendered relations of power and/or challenge and contest existing inequities.

The complexities of researching leisure and culture are particularly evident in the chapters by Giles, Paule-Koba, Hibbins, and Kay. Giles's ethnographic research on the Dene Games in northern Canada reveals not only the clash between dominant white perspectives and aboriginal perspectives on women's sport participation, but also different voices among Dene women with regard to cultural practices and beliefs. This, Giles argues, calls for a reexamination of feminist theory and feminist practice. While white Canadian feminists may advocate for gender equity in the Dene Games in terms of equal participation, Dene women themselves may conceptualize equity in different ways. According to Giles, a postcolonial and postmodern framework that incorporates a nuanced understanding of gender and development is needed both for understanding the cultural context of the Dene Games, and for enhancing cultural sensitivity towards women, equity, and sport participation within that context.

Paule-Koba's research adds a different type of complexity by addressing the subculture of competitive sports at the college and university level in the United States. Within this subculture, few would openly challenge the concept of gender equity in sports. In practice, however, equity legislation (Title IX) is undermined in a variety of ways. For example, the practice of "blaming the victim" is evident in the discourse surrounding the Title IX legislation. Within this discourse, the outcome of the moving towards equal opportunities for women in sport becomes seen, instead, as a process which denies opportunities to men. According to Paule-Koba, this reflects the "naturalization" of the superiority of men's sport and the devaluation of women's sport. Systemic discrimination is not recognized within this perspective and legislative attempts at equity are seen, instead, as a form of reverse discrimination. Delamere and Dixon, by contrast, pay attention to a very different type of sub-culture—that of the world of digital game play. Their research reveals overt sexism within game-playing cultures. Yet, at the same time, the women and girls who participated in their studies talked about played digital games as engaging, as fun, and as an activity linked to entitlement and empowerment.

Hibbins's chapter addresses the question of sexual and gender identities, as well as the issue of migration. These are issues of increasing importance in the new global economy and the globalized marketplace. Hibbins's research allows us to hear the voices of Chinese and Taiwanese immigrants to Australia. The tenuous position of these new immigrants is reflected in their disempowerment through racialization and marginalization and their position as "other" in the broader Australian cultural context. New immigrants face a variety of challenges, including job insecurity and discomfort with respect to the "macho" and sexualized dominant white culture. Yet, at the same time, they are privileged in their patriarchal positions within their Chinese or Taiwanese families. The clash of cultures (East/West or majority/minority) is evident here as well as the contradictory and complex implications for men as well as women in terms of gender, leisure, and gendered relations of power. As travel and immigration become increasingly common, these intersections of power and culture, as well as different forms of gendered culture clearly require greater attention. Further, with its focus on male migrants, Hibbins's research (as well as Johnson's research, this volume) represents a minority of studies within the leisure and gender field that have focused on men, male cultures, and the gendered nature of men's leisure.

Despite the need for much improved understanding of the global cultures, global geographies, and their relationship to gender and leisure, we have only just begun to scratch the surface of these issues. Kay's chapter brings this gap and the "missing populations" to our attention. She takes us through her personal journey and her personal experiences of working in non-Western locations and/or cultural contexts. For example, she reflects on her research with young Muslim women in the United Kingdom, as well as her research with young women in Delhi, India. We need, she argues, to think globally and to extend our research on cultural diversity within and between the wide diversity of cultural groups that exist across the globe. Further, we need to better understand the role that sport and other forms of leisure play in these diverse settings. Kay's work with multinational research teams represents a relatively new and innovative way for moving forward with this type of research. Her chapter, as well as other chapters in this and earlier sections of the book, bring to our attention how different ideologies and practices are constructed in diverse settings. Together these chapters suggest a diversity of ways in which leisure practices reflect and reproduce dominant ideologies and relations of power, as well as the ways in which ideologies and power structures are resisted and contested in different cultural contexts.

Politics:
The Many Possibilities for Action

The focus on power, intersectionality, and culture in the chapters in this section lead inevitably to issues of politics and political change. These issues include not only questions relating to "formal politics," such as government policy, but also to informal political and social activism at local and community levels. Like the notion of cultural diversity, there are many layers and possibilities associated with the political nature of gender and leisure research. Some of the authors of chapters in this section draw a direct link between their research and "formal" politics; that is, between their research agenda and government or state laws and policies. Paule-Koba's chapter directly addresses a United States federal law (Title IX) that is designed to prohibit gender discrimination in educational institutions. This law has been controversial since its inception in 1972, primarily due to the "blame the victim" approach among some critics that the law provides sports opportunities for women at the expense of men. Paule-Koba's analysis, however, challenges this approach. Based on research with male college students and athletic coaches, she sheds light on the ways in which women's sports continue to be devalued and the ways in which traditional gender ideologies are perpetuated. Thus, her research illustrates the contradictory outcomes of this particular piece of pro-equity legislation. Giles's research on women's participation in the Dene Games reveals comparable, yet different, outcomes of what was deemed to be pro-equity government policy in Canada. Her chapter reveals the danger of imposing Western ideas and policies related to gender equity on groups with different cultural practices and beliefs. This suggests, also, that feminist researchers interested in policies and policy implementation need to be constantly reflective and willing to reexamine concepts and approaches that may not necessarily be appropriate in different sociocultural contexts.

Fullagar's chapter on the gendered politics of health does not look at specific government policies, but rather at the new directions in health promotion that have become dominant in Australia and in other parts of the world. The notion of "lifestyle diseases" and the focus on physical activity and the prevention of obesity reflect, she argues, a new era of "healthism"— an ideology that is problematic for feminist leisure scholars who are particularly cognizant of the importance of choice and self-determination. Fullagar's research, as well as that of Giles and Paule-Koba, stresses the need for feminist scholars to remain critical and vigilant, challenging new policy directions and taking little for granted. Even when new laws and policies appear to be benign or even positive in nature, close attention is needed to examine the implications of new initiatives in terms of their potential negative as well as positive implications for women's leisure. To date, there has been relatively little attention from feminist leisure scholars to government legislation and government policy. However, these three studies of government policies and programs indicate that there might be a wide variety of ways in which formal politics may influence women's lives and gender relations more broadly, as well as women's access to and enjoyment of leisure.

Critiquing and challenging government policy, though, is only one way in which feminist research is political. In fact, all of the chapters in this section address power and politics, and the connection between politics and leisure. Kivel and Johnson advocate for activist scholarship. The strong activist underpinning of their work is clear in terms of addressing homophobia and heterosexism. Understanding how these systems of oppression and hatred operate, and how they are perpetuated is an important step towards finding solutions, such as creating support programs, "safe zones," and programs for educators. Frisby's community-based research is also explicitly activist, and her research team has been highly successful in terms of including a wide range of different community partners and influencing policy development. Further, her research, as well as Kay's research in different parts of the world, also clearly had a major effect on the lives of the women and girls who participated in their studies.

A number of feminist researchers have directed attention to the potential for leisure and leisure practice to challenge dominant ideologies of gender and hegemonic notions of femininity and masculinity (e.g., Dionigi, this volume; Freysinger & Flannery, 1992; Shaw, 2001 and 2006; Wearing, 1998). This form of political action is clearly evident in Delamere and Dixon's research, with its focus on the many ways in which gender is expressed and constructed through digital game play. Players' strategic negotiations of gender reveal not only the culture and sociopolitical implications of gaming, but also the possibilities for resistance and empowerment. The potential for game play to influence the way in which people "think, learn, play, and understand the world" is discussed by the authors.

Hibbins's chapter highlights some of the political dimensions of migration, particularly for men. Migration and acculturation, he argues, challenges notions of hegemonic masculinity and may also influence behavior in the domestic sphere, such as the division of household labor. In addition, while Kay's work places emphasis on the need for deep understanding of different cultures, ideologies, and practices on a global level, Hibbins's work also includes the notion of "transnational leisure spaces," where there is interaction among people from a variety of cultural backgrounds. These dynamic leisure spaces may well play an increasingly important and political role in terms of the intersection of sexuality, ethnicity, and gender.

Concluding Thoughts

As can be seen from this brief overview of the chapters in this section, much of the research on power, culture, and politics within feminist leisure scholarship is relatively recent. New ideas are emerging and new trails are being blazed. The need for research that addresses these broad, societal, cultural, and political questions is evident. Power, power relations, and politics are central to understanding the gendered nature of leisure, and the paucity of gender and leisure outside the white, Western world clearly needs to be rectified. Yet, venturing into these areas of research is complex and challenging in a number of ways.

First, macro-level research presents a dilemma related to the ongoing debate about structure versus agency (e.g., see Giddens, 1984, and chapter 3 in this volume). To the extent that structured power relations (sexism, heterosexism, racism, classism, etc.) exist, and are perpetuated and reinforced, there would seem to be little opportunity for fundamental change. On the other hand, notions of individual or personal power in the postmodern world might appear to deny the notion of patriarchal, heterosexist, and racist society. Thus, researchers need to be sensitive to this debate, and consider the implications of their research in terms of agency and structure.

Second, research in different cultural contexts raises other dilemmas, such as the limitations of conducting research as an "outsider." That is, how significant is the issue of standpoint and shared experience between the researcher and the researched? Are critical theorizing and self-reflexivity sufficient? Gender may be a particularly difficult concept to navigate across cultural divides. Can different methodological approaches, such as participatory research or ethnography, help in terms of connection and understanding, as well as empowerment for those involved in the study?

Third, the notion of social changes through research is also complex. One issue is whether more attention needs to be paid to policy change, and whether this should be addressed at the national or state level, or at the community level, or both? Further, should the focus be on developing laws and policies that promote equity in terms of leisure, sport, and/or health and well-being? Or, is the primary job of the researcher in this field to critique laws and policies in terms of their outcomes and/or their ideological underpinnings? Alternatively, should more attention be paid to social change through personal power, resistance, and activism, and, if so, how should this be done?

It is evident that there are many layers and complexities associated with research on power, culture, and politics as they relate to leisure, women, and gender. Research in this area represents a wide range and diversity of concerns and issues. This section provides a brief glimpse into some of the research that has been conducted to date. Clearly more research is needed, and all of these chapters provide ideas for possible future research directions.

REFERENCES

Coalter, F. (1999). Leisure sciences and leisure studies: The challenge of meaning. In E. L. Jackson & T. L. Burton (Eds.), *Leisure studies: Prospects for the twenty-first century* (pp. 507–522). State College, PA: Venture Publishing, Inc.

Connell, R. W. (2005). *Masculinities* (2nd ed.). Berkeley, CA: University of California Press.

Freysinger, V. J., & Flannery, D. (1992). Women's leisure: Affiliation, self-determination, empowerment, and resistance? *Loisir et Societe/Society and Leisure, 15*(1), 303–322.

Giddens, A. (1984). *The constitution of society: Outline of a theory of structuration*. Cambridge, UK: Polity.

Hesse-Biber, S. N. (2007). Feminist research: Exploring the interconnections of epistemology, methodology, and method. In S. N. Hesse-Biber (Ed.), *Handbook of feminist research: Theory and praxis* (pp. 1–26). Thousand Oaks, CA: Sage.

Kandiyoti, D. (1999). Islam and patriarchy: A comparative perspective. In S. Hesse-Biber, C. Gilmartin, & R. Lydenberg (Eds.), *Feminist approaches to theory and methodology: An interdisciplinary reader* (pp. 236–256). Bloomington, IN: Indiana University Press.

Risman, B. J. (1998). *Gender vertigo: American families in transition.* New Haven, CT: Yale University Press.

Risman, B. J. (2004). Gender as a social structure: Theory wrestling with activism. *Gender & Society, 18*(4), 429–450.

Shaw, S. M. (2001). Conceptualizing resistance: Women's leisure as political practice. *Journal of Leisure Research, 33*(2), 186–201.

Shaw, S. M. (2006). Resistance. In C. Rojek, S. M. Shaw, and A. J. Veal (Eds.), *Handbook of leisure studies* (pp. 533–545). London, UK: Palgrave MacMillan.

Smelser, N. J. (1988). Social structure. In N. J. Smelser (Ed.), *Handbook of sociology* (pp. 103–129). Beverly Hills, CA: Sage.

Wearing, B. (1998). *Leisure and feminist theory.* London, UK: Sage.

West, C., & Zimmerman, D. (1987). Doing gender. *Gender & Society, 1*(1), 125–151.

CHAPTER 30
THE POLITICS OF TAKING ACTION: WOMEN, POVERTY, AND LEISURE-ACCESS POLICY

WENDY FRISBY

CAUTIONARY TALES FROM THE FIELD

The *cautionary tales from the field* that will be the focus of this chapter deal with my critical reflections on attempts to "take action" based on research done with diverse women living below the poverty line within the context of local Canadian leisure-access policy reform. My story is based on three community-based research projects that were conducted over the last 15 years using a feminist participatory action research (FPAR) approach (Reid & Frisby, 2008).[1] All three projects involved working with diverse women living on low income in Canada, various community partners, and my academic colleagues, to increase the women's access to recreation offered at community centers operated by local governments. In all cases, being able to participate in community recreation programs was an issue women identified as being important to the quality of their lives by reducing their social isolation, a lived reality that they tied to their poor physical and mental health due to living in conditions of constant material deprivation. Most saw having access as a right of citizenship, because local taxed-funded recreation programs in Canada have historically been available for all (Frisby, Alexander, & Taylor, 2010). However, living situations combined with community-center policies and practices often create significant barriers to participation (Tirone, 2003–2004).

Taking action was enmeshed in all three projects described below and took on many different forms—some actions were large, some were small, some were realized, some were thwarted, and some remain hopes for the future (Reid, Tom, & Frisby, 2006). Policy change, particularly in terms of what is known as "leisure access policy" (which provides subsidies for citizens on low income), was an aim in all of these projects. This was complicated, however, because not all the women on low income saw this as a priority. Indeed some were understandably cynical about and suspicious of government policy reform because of how public policy was adversely affecting their lives (Gurstein, Pulkingham, & Vilches, 2011). In addition, even though we had committed representatives from local government involved in our projects, they were working at the community level and often had little input or control over policymaking in their recreation departments. As a result, these representatives were often disillusioned about making change on the policy level and most just wanted to keep working on the front line to try to make things better for the community members with whom they came in daily contact.

Nonetheless, given the humiliating and privacy invading nature of most leisure access policies in Canada (Taylor & Frisby, 2010), this policy issue was identified by women in each FPAR project as a major hindrance to their inclusion. Because I am privileged and have never lived in poverty, I was largely unaware that in most Canadian cities, people on low incomes have to prove that they are poor by providing their financial records to recreation staff, in order to receive a subsidy that still makes participation in community recreation unaffordable (Taylor & Frisby, 2010). This is because after paying for basic living necessities such as housing and food, people living in poverty have little or no discretionary income for leisure (Tirone, 2003–2004). Yet due to the rise of neoliberalism in local government, where a business-oriented approach is increasingly adopted, user fees are now commonly charged for recreation programs that were at one time covered by tax-based dollars (Frisby et al., 2010). As a result, policy change has remained on the agenda as an important action item to increase recreation participation and reduce social isolation. Before I go into my three tales from the field in more depth, I would first like to describe the context and provide a brief note on the FPAR methodology used in each project.

POVERTY AND POLITICAL SHIFTS IN MUNICIPAL RECREATION

In Canada, one in five families live below the poverty line, which means that more than 70% of household income goes toward the basic necessities of food, clothing, and shelter. The intersections of poverty in relation to gender, colonial histories, age, racism, and (dis)ability become apparent when we learn who is most likely to live in poverty. In Canada, these include over 50% of households headed by single mothers, 48% of the Aboriginal population, 43% of recent immigrants, 15% of persons with disabilities, and twice as many women as men over 65 years of age (National Council of Welfare, 2004).

In 2009, the United Nations and the Organization for Economic Cooperation and Development gave Canada a "D" grade in social performance due to rising poverty rates, ranking it 15th out of 17 developed countries, just ahead of the United States, which was ranked in 16th place (Lafleur, 2009). The feminization of poverty globally is apparent, as the United Nation estimates that two out of every three poor adults in the world are women. Furthermore, the UN estimates that women do two-thirds of the world's paid and unpaid work, yet only receive 10% of the world's income (Lorber, 2005). This is due to a number of factors including patriarchy (where women's lives and contributions are devalued), the gendered division of domestic responsibilities, racialization, unequal access to education and higher-paying jobs, and unequal pay for work of equal value (Frisby, Maguire, & Reid, 2009).

Another contextual factor I would like to point out is that the site of all three FPAR projects was municipal recreation departments. The reason for this is that along with schools, taxed-based community centers remain one of the few spaces where democratic and equitable recreation participation is supposed to take place. Historically, these departments were tied to a social welfare ideology and targeted low-income urban youth, especially males, to prevent them from being idle and to prepare them for employment and war (Frisby et al., 2010). However, with the rise of neoliberalism in local government (Brodie, 2005), many of these centers now operate more from a market-driven approach tied to values of efficiency, cost recovery, and political accountability. The consequence of this is that the target market has shifted to middle-income earners, so they are in essence using tax dollars to target the same consumer markets as the private sector (Thibault, Kikulis, & Frisby, 2004). Offering recreation programs to the poor becomes a low or non-priority in this scenario, even though there were examples of front-line staff involved in our projects who resisted the shift to neoliberalism and continued to advocate for citizens living in impoverished conditions (Frisby & Millar, 2002).

A METHODOLOGICAL NOTE

I would now like to very briefly describe what I mean by feminist participatory action research (or FPAR for short). Drawing on a framework developed by Bryant (2002), a key feature of our approach to FPAR is collaborative knowledge production that honors: 1) experiential knowledge (e.g., from the women who know first hand what it is like to live in poverty), 2) instrumental knowledge (e.g., from the community partners who have knowledge about resources, power, and decision-making structures in the community), and 3) academic knowledge (e.g., from the researchers who can bring theories and methodologies to help investigate social problems and policy-change processes). While not all three projects were full FPAR, all had at least some of the key dimensions that we have written about elsewhere (see Reid & Frisby, 2008) which are briefly summarized below. Within FPAR:

1. Centering gender and women's diverse experiences in the analysis is central, in part, because earlier participatory action research tended to focus on men's economic activities (Brydon-Miller, Maguire, & McIntyre, 2004). In addition, we know that women and girls participate less in organized recreation (Henderson, Bialeschki, Shaw, & Freysinger, 1996), and the majority of the world's population who live in poverty are girls and women (Lorber, 2005).

2. Considering how gender intersects with other axes of oppression—including, but not limited to, race, class, sexuality, ability, and birth nation—is critical to contemplating the implications of research and taking action to influence policy (Davis, 2008).

3. Using participatory research processes are central, and I would like to give you an example to illustrate. As I mentioned previously, a problem that spanned young lone mothers, recent immigrant women, older women, and women with disabilities living in poverty in our projects was "social isolation." Given my privileged social location, I had not anticipated that this would be a central problem when I began this work several years ago. Nor was it talked about much in the literature that more typically linked biomedical disease states to low socio-economic status. Social isolation makes lots of sense when you think about the consequences of living in constant material deprivation. A person living on or below the poverty line cannot participate in our consumer-oriented society the way members of other social classes do. Few people on low income want to be identified as being poor because of all the harmful social stigmas attached, so becoming isolated is a common occurrence (Reid, 2004). The key point is that if we had not engaged in participatory research processes at the start, we might have tried to study a social issue that was less relevant than social isolation to the women's daily lives. We continue to find ways to engage with those living in poverty in all phases of the research, including determining the appropriate research questions, deciding on the data collection methods, analyzing the data, and communicating the results (Frisby, 2006; Frisby, Reid, Millar, & Hoeber, 2005).

4. Issues of representation are also crucial to FPAR, as we must continually ask how we adequately represent meanings when we are working across complicated and shifting identities and axes of power. This was most apparent in our most recent project when we were working with recent immigrant Chinese women who spoke primarily Mandarin and Cantonese. My colleagues and I have just written a chapter on this issue, where we argue that while the challenges of making meaning across differences in language, race, culture, and class appear daunting, we eschew the very problematic alternative that would mean we engage only in research with people most like ourselves (Creese, Huang, Frisby, & Ngene-Kambere, 2011). Using art, journal writing, small-group discussions, interviews, and panel presentations to policymakers are some of the ways that we have tried to more adequately represent the women's voices.

5. Being reflexive means thinking critically about the knowledge claims being made and the power imbalances inherent to the research. This requires researchers to turn the gaze on themselves and not just on those they are collaborating with. As an older, white, middle-class, heterosexual mother and academic who was born in Canada, I need to think very carefully about my multiple positions of privilege and how it influences the research, relationships, the knowledge claims made, and the possibilities for taking action (Frisby, 2006).

6. An action component is the final dimension of our FPAR framework (Reid & Frisby, 2008). We have found few details about this dimension in the leisure literature, hence the leisure-access policy focus of this chapter. I will now provide more information on what policy change entailed in the three FPAR projects.

TALE #1:
UNANTICIPATED POLICY CHANGE (KWAP)

The first project I was involved in, the Kamloops Women's Action Project (or KWAP for short), happened by chance. I got a phone call from a public health nurse in the city of Kamloops in the province of British Columbia, Canada, who was working on a provincially funded project known as "Healthy Communities." She was working with a group of young single mothers living on low incomes, and when she asked them what would make their community healthier, they said having access to community recreation. The mothers were angered by a new hockey arena that was being built and receiving lots of media attention, because they knew they and their children would never to able to afford to go skating in it or play expensive sports like hockey, ringette, or figure skating. The public health nurse wanted research done that would capture the experiences of the single mothers to lobby for policy change and more free programs.

At the time, I had just begun reading about participatory action research and thought it might be appropriate given the Kamloops context, although I was worried because I had no training or experience with the methodology, and I was a white, middle-class academic interloper into the community. Nonetheless, I flew to Kamloops on a regular basis and engaged in a participatory approach, mostly by trial and error, with the public health nurse, the single mothers, four women from the First Nations (Aboriginal) Band, and several community partners (see Figure 1). A number of actions occurred, such as offering low-cost parallel programs for the mothers while their children were engaging in various recreation activities.

One of the more sustainable actions took place at the end of the KWAP project when a community partner suggested that we share our results with the city council. I simply saw this as a way of communicating the results and was not yet deeply thinking about what it might mean in terms of policy change. Because we had been operating from a collaborative approach, we decided that each party should be heard at the council meeting. Some of the single mothers told their stories of social isolation and the role community recreation could play in reducing it for themselves and their families. The recreation staff said they wanted a change in leisure-access policy so that more programs were offered for free. They also wanted

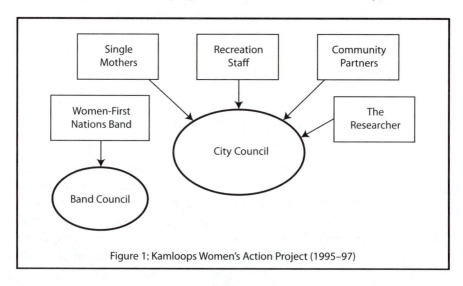

Figure 1: Kamloops Women's Action Project (1995–97)

responsibility for low-income citizens written into their job descriptions, which are typically organized around direct program provision by activity type or age group, thus serving to keep the poverty issue invisible. The community partners included the public health unit, social services, the YWCA, and the women's center. They said they had not thought of referring their clients to municipal recreation programs, but now saw the important role it could play in breaking social isolation, promoting health, and other social outcomes. The First Nations (Aboriginal) women did not want to talk to city council and instead decided to speak to their band council. The researcher (i.e., me) provided data on the benefits and barriers to participation based on interviews and surveys conducted with single mothers in the Kamloops area.

In the end, somewhat radical and quick policy change did occur, as more programs were offered for free to avoid the humiliating practice of having to prove poverty in order to get a subsidy that is still inadequate. Staff also had responsibility for low-income citizens built into their job descriptions, and parallel parent/child programs continued to be offered. In addition, new partnerships were formed between organizations that rarely had direct contact with one another. This was vitally important, since it was the community partners who had relationships with people on low income and could encourage them to attend recreation programs.

The policy insights we learned from KWAP were that unintended actions may have the most impact. It was hearing from multiple stakeholders that heightened the possibilities for policy change. The women telling their stories clearly had an impact, the community partners put political pressure on council to make changes, the staff had ideas on how to organize things differently, and the research added legitimacy. We now think that each story told affected a different member of city council in different ways, and it resulted in many programs being offered for free, the co-programming of activities for mothers and their children in adjacent rooms, and the addition of a focus on "income level" (rather than activities or age groups) to some staff members' job descriptions. Yet, while policy change did occur, engaging in reflexivity reminds us that many other isolated people remained largely unaware of the policy changes made and the public recreation opportunities available. As a result, reform is always ongoing.

Based on this local effort, another action strategy we used to influence policy was the development a workbook entitled *Leisure Access: Enhancing Recreation Opportunities for Those Living in Poverty* (Frisby & Fenton, 1998). We sent this free workbook to the Canadian Parks and Recreation Association and its provincial affiliates and asked them to make it available to municipalities. It is also available free for downloading on the Leisure Information Network (LIN) in Ottawa, Canada. The benefits of this approach are that it makes the work accessible beyond the usual academic outlets, thus broadening knowledge translation. The limitation is that people on low income are the least likely to have the computer technology that would make it possible for them to locate these types of resources (Gurstein, 2007). While the impact of the workbook has not been evaluated in a systematic way, as discussed next, it did lead directly to Tale #2.

TALE #2:
LACK OF SUSTAINABILITY AND POLITICAL RISKS IN TAKING ACTION (WOAW)

The second FPAR project—Women Organizing Activities for Women (or WOAW for short)—evolved when Jennifer Fenton and I were invited to conduct a workshop on leisure access by a leisure-access staff person who had run across the workbook from project #1. His municipality was desperately trying to look like they were promoting gender equity because they were facing a legal suit from a parent who claimed his daughter did not have equal access to gymnastics facilities and coaching. The staff person was genuinely interested in doing something for those living on low income, and he mobilized several community partners who in turn encouraged over 80 women to attend our leisure-access workshop. The women varied considerably in terms of age, ethnicity, health status, ability, and sexuality, but shared the circumstance of living on low income. Participants worked on the worksheets contained in the workbook that encouraged them to contemplate the benefits and barriers of recreation participation and action steps to promote the inclusion of low-income populations. An outcome was that a community-based organization was formed, and over the next five years, WOAW members organized over 1,000 free or low-cost programs for low-income people in the community (Frisby, Reid, & Ponic, 2007; Reid, 2004). Shortly after WOAW formed, we worked together to write a successful research grant, which was challenging because although the women knew the most about their lived experiences, literacy was an issue and the norms and requirements of academic grants were understandably baffling to most. WOAW eventually received a provincial award from Promotion Plus (an organization in British Columbia, Canada, that promotes physical activity for girls and women) for its efforts to promote inclusion for low-income women and their families.

It was the municipal recreation staff involved in WOAW who instigated change to their city's leisure-access policy. Upon request, each resident now receives a voucher each year entitling them to a certain number of free programs. This contrasts with the individualized "prove poverty" policy model that had existed previously (Taylor & Frisby, 2010). Other

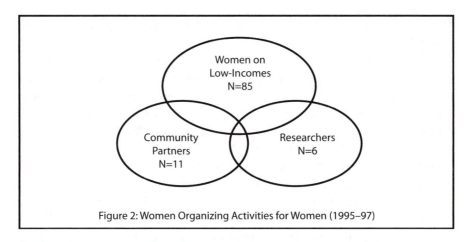

Figure 2: Women Organizing Activities for Women (1995–97)

outcomes included additional outreach efforts to low-income citizens, and a community-development approach where citizens are consulted and involved in the development of some recreation programs.

Important policy questions arising from this include whether the lessons learned in one community are sustainable and transferable to other communities. I have stories of "two wins and one loss" to share in this regard. The two wins occurred when other organizations picked up the WOAW model and developed communication tools and programs based on it that were distributed more broadly. For example, the British Columbia Parks and Recreation Association (BCRPA) released a publication for recreation leaders entitled *Poverty Matters* in 2008 that drew on the WOAW model. BCRPA has since funded several community recreation initiatives aimed at low-income populations. The second win occurred when CAAWS—the Canadian Association for the Advancement of Women in Sport and Physical Activity—drew, in part, on WOAW research to launch a social marketing initiative called *Mothers in Motion* that is designed to increase physical activity opportunities for mothers living on low income.

I do, however, have another story to tell that must be chalked up in the loss column. The lack of sustainability for WOAW became apparent when I got a call from the new leisure-access coordinator in the same municipality, who had heard that I had done some research on poverty and recreation inclusion. The new person was totally unaware that WOAW had taken place in her community for over five years. So, even though policy change did occur and we thought we were building capacity for the initiative to continue, once the research portion was over, the community-based organization was not sustained beyond the initial five years. This was likely due to the fact that the initial "idea champions," including several women on low income, community partners, and the researchers, had moved onto other projects, and insufficient support was given to those who remained.

We have learned that much more attention needs to be given to sustainability in the future.

There were other action insights gleaned from WOAW. First, it became clear that small-scale individual actions count. We heard over and over again that WOAW meetings and activities were "getting women out of their homes," thus breaking the cycle of social isolation. This reminded us that it is not only leisure-access policy change that counts in their daily lives (Reid et al., 2006). Second, there were political risks to taking action for all parties involved. For example, many of the women in WOAW were concerned about identifying themselves as on low income because of all the hurtful stigmas that go along with it—such as being called lazy welfare bums who are taking advantage of the system (Reid, 2004). In addition, some committed community partners had to engage in subversive activities to hide their involvement because their organizations were overloaded and recreation was not part of their mandates, just as poverty is often seen as someone else's mandate by recreation providers. And certainly, there are risks to researchers, including graduate students, as the time involved doing community-based research and communicating beyond traditional academic outlets are not always in line with traditional academic norms (Brydon-Miller, Maguire, & McIntyre, 2004). I recommend that these types of risks be discussed early on in FPAR projects so that participants will be in a better position to decide whether or not to get involved in action-oriented research that is infused with personal and political implications.

TALE #3:
BROKERING DIALOGUE BETWEEN IMMIGRANT WOMEN AND POLICYMAKERS

My third tale is about how we tried to build citizen engagement and policy change right into our latest FPAR project with Chinese immigrant women. We initiated this project because Canada, and Vancouver in particular, has a large immigrant population, and newcomer women were underrepresented in our previous projects. We were interested in the role that physical activity programs in municipal community centers might play in easing the stresses associated with settlement for new Canadians, a topic emphasized by the few immigrant women we had worked with previously. As indicated in Figure 3, the study involved interviews with 50 recent immigrant Chinese women, 36 local-, provincial-, and federal-level sport and recreation policymakers, and 5 staff from an immigration service agency.

While the Canadian government does have official policy on multiculturalism, we were unable to uncover related sport and recreation policy

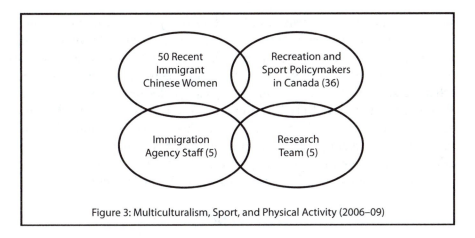

Figure 3: Multiculturalism, Sport, and Physical Activity (2006–09)

at the local, provincial, or federal levels. As a result, in 2009, we invited Chinese immigrant women to sit on a panel to tell their stories directly to the policymakers and staff. Translation in Mandarin and Cantonese was provided. In this way, the women could speak directly to the policymakers, rather than having the researchers summarize the results in a report that might collect dust on policymakers' shelves.[2] Several of the policymakers, particularly those at the provincial and federal level, admitted that they had never had direct contact with recent immigrants and were touched by the women's stories. Following the panel, we broke into small groups and spent another day discussing action strategies, including possibilities for policy development. This represents another example of Bryant's (2002) framework that is based on bringing experiential, instrumental, and academic knowledge together for policy change.

Our research team is now tracking to see what happens over the next two years to examine the factors that hinder or contribute to policy change. Similar to our first project, we are preparing another workbook, tentatively entitled *Multiculturalism, Sport, and Physical Activity Inclusion Workbook*, that captures the lessons learned in project #3. It will include "process-oriented worksheets" for thinking through the issues involved and identifying action strategies that other communities can adapt to meet their unique needs. We will continue to publish in traditional academic outlets, but we hope this type of "non-refereed" publication will be helpful to a broader audience as part of an overall action strategy.

NEXT COMPELLING QUESTIONS AND WAYS FORWARD

I remain highly committed to feminist participatory action research and think it has potential for widespread application in the leisure studies field. At the same time, studies like the three projects described in this chapter raise many questions that need to be addressed. Just a few of the myriad questions that we have wrestled with over the years include: 1) what counts as action? 2) who decides upon and takes action? 3) who benefits from actions taken and who does not? 4) when is taking action risky and in what ways? 5) how can action move beyond the local? 6) how can action be misappropriated and used in unintended ways? 7) how can action be sustained? and 8) how should action be evaluated and by whom? It is by collectively addressing these and other questions that action can be more adequately theorized and put into practice, which is essential when the goal is to promote gender equality and social justice in the leisure domain.

References

Brodie, J. (2005). The great undoing: State formation, gender politics, and social policy in Canada. In B. A. Crow & L. Gotell (Eds.), *Open boundaries: A Canadian women's studies reader* (pp. 87–96). Toronto, ON: Prentice Hall.

Bryant, T. (2002). Role of knowledge in public health and health promotion policy change. *Health Promotion International, 17*(1), 89–98.

Brydon-Miller, M., Maguire, P., & McIntyre, I. (2004). *Traveling companions: Feminism, teaching, and action research.* Westport, CN: Praeger.

Creese, G., Huang, X., Frisby, W., & Ngene-Kambere, E. (2011). Working across race, language, and culture with African and Chinese immigrant communities. In G. Creese & W. Frisby (Eds.), *Feminist community research: Negotiating contested relationships* (pp. 89–108). Vancouver, BC: University of British Columbia Press.

Davis, K. (2008). Intersectionality as buzzword: A social science perspective on what makes a feminist theory successful. *Feminist Theory, 9*(1), 67–86.

Frisby, W. (2006). Rethinking researcher roles, responsibilities and relationships in community development research. *Leisure/Loisir, 30*(2), 437–445.

Frisby, W., Alexander, T., & Taylor, J. (2010). Play is not a frill: Poor youth facing the past, present, and future of public recreation in Canada. In M. Gleason, T. Myers, L. Paris, & V. Strong-Boag (Eds.), *Lost kids:*

Vulnerable children and youth in Canada, the U.S., and Australia, 1900 to the present (pp. 215–229). Vancouver, BC: University of British Columbia Press.

Frisby, W., & Fenton, J. (1998). *Leisure access: Enhancing recreation opportunities for those living in poverty.* Vancouver, BC: British Columbia Health Research Foundation.

Frisby, W., Maguire, P., & Reid, C. (2009). The "f" word has everything to do with it: How feminist theories inform action research. *Action Research, 7*(1), 13–19.

Frisby, W., & Millar, S. (2002). The actualities of doing community development to promote the inclusion of low-income populations in local sport and recreation. *European Sport Management Quarterly, 3*, 209–233.

Frisby, W., Reid, C., Millar, S., & Hoeber, L. (2005). Putting "participatory" into participatory forms of action research. *Journal of Sport Management, 19*(4), 367–386.

Frisby, W., Reid, C., & Ponic, P. (2007). Leveling the playing field: Promoting the health of poor women through a community development approach to recreation. In K. Young & P. White (Eds.), *Sport and gender in Canada* (pp. 121–136). Don Mills, ON: Oxford University Press.

Gurstein, P. (2007). Creating digital public space: Implications for deliberative engagement. In P. Gurstein & L. Angeles (Eds.), *Learning civil societies: Shifting contexts for democratic planning and governance.* Toronto, ON: University of Toronto Press.

Gurstein, P., Pulkingham, J., & Vilches, S. (2011). Challenging policies for lone mothers: Reflections on and insights from longitudinal qualitative interviewing. In G. Creese & W. Frisby (Eds.), *Feminist community research: Case studies and methodologies* (pp. 127–146). Vancouver, BC: University of British Columbia Press.

Henderson, K. A., Bialeschki, M. D., Shaw, S. M., & Freysinger, V. J. (1996). *Both gains and gaps: Feminist perspectives on women's leisure.* State College, PA: Venture Publishing, Inc.

Lafleur, B. (2009). *Annual report card on social performance.* Ottawa, ON: Conference Board of Canada.

Lorber, J. (2005). *Gender inequality: Feminist theories and politics.* Los Angeles, CA: Roxbury.

National Council of Welfare. (2004). *Poverty Profile 2001.* Ottawa, ON: National Council of Welfare.

Reid, C. (2004). *The wounds of exclusion: Poverty, women's health, and social justice.* Edmonton AB: Qualitative Institute.

Reid, C., & Frisby, W. (2008). Continuing the journey: Articulating dimensions of feminist participatory action research. In P. Reason & H. Bradbury (Eds.), *Handbook of action research: Participative and practice* (2nd ed.) (pp. 93–105). London, UK: Sage.

Reid, C., Tom, A., & Frisby, W. (2006). Finding the "action" in feminist participatory action research. *Action Research, 4*(3), 313–330.

Taylor, J., & Frisby, W. (2010). Addressing inadequate leisure access policies through citizen engagement. In H. Mair, S. M. Arai, & D. G. Reid (Eds.), *Decentering work: Critical perspectives on leisure, social policy, and human development* (pp. 35–57), Calgary, AB: University of Calgary Press.

Thibault, L., Kikulis, L., & Frisby, W. (2004). Partnerships between local government sport and leisure departments and the commercial sector: Changes, complexities, and consequences. In T. Slack (Ed.), *The commercialisation of sport* (pp. 119–140). London, UK: Frank Cass.

Tirone, S. (2003–2004). Evening the playing field: Recreation in a low-income Canadian community. *Leisure/Loisir, 28*(1–2), 155–174.

Wang, C., Burris, M. A., & Ping, X. Y. (1996). Chinese village women as visual anthropologists: A participatory approach to reaching policymakers. *Social Science and Medicine, 42*(10), 1391–1400.

FOOTNOTES

[1] The first project is called the Kamloops Women's Action Project (1995–1997) and was funded by the British Columbia Health Research Foundation. The second project is Women Organizing Activities for Women (1999–2002), and the third project is Multiculturalism, Sport, and Physical Activity (2006–2009). The second and third projects were both funded by the Social Sciences and Humanities Research Council of Canada.

[2] An earlier study by Wang, Burris, and Ping (1996) provided the inspiration for this approach.

Chapter 31
Women's Leisure and the Gendered Politics of Health

Simone Fullagar

In this chapter, I explore the gendered politics of women's leisure, health, and well-being through a discussion of the literature and particular studies that illustrate the links between these fields of inquiry. Feminist scholars have made a significant contribution to the field by examining how women's and men's leisure experiences are shaped by gender power relations that inform social structures and cultural practices (Aitchison, 2003; Fullagar, 2003; Henderson, Bialeschki, Shaw, & Freysinger, 1996; Watson & Scraton, 2001; Wearing, 1998). Even in advanced liberal democracies, many women find that their access and sense of entitlement to leisure is a site of struggle, albeit one that usually remains hidden in the personal realm. For women with limited access to money, time, or space, and carrying multiple work and care responsibilities, leisure may seem like a redundant concept disconnected from their everyday reality. Yet as I have found in my own research, the important value of leisure has often been identified by women when they feel they have "lost" their leisure lives, identities, and sense of well-being (see also chapters by Frisby, Sullivan, this volume). Hence, the conceptualization of contemporary leisure practices requires a deeper understanding of particular tensions that arise between freedom and constraint in relation to the gendered expectations of work performance, family well-being, and identity construction. In a speech to young women, Germaine Greer made a particularly compelling comment about the gendered challenge of leisure in relation to feminist achievements: "Women worked and studied too hard and did not spend enough time on themselves. One of the things I cannot get women to understand is that they are entitled to leisure. . . . They don't have to justify their existence by working all the hours God sends'" (Stolz, 2006, p. 1).

The domain of feminist health research also has a strong history of identifying the gender inequities that underpin major health and illness problems facing women in both developing and developed countries—from poverty, war, malnutrition, and violence, through to "lifestyle" related issues that are identified with obesity, cancer, and heart disease (Irwin et al., 2006; Ussher, 2000). In addition, women have been identified as experiencing higher rates of mental health problems across the world (depression, anxiety, eating disorders, and related psychiatric conditions) (see also Parry's chapter, this volume). The World Health Organization has predicted that depression will become the second largest global health problem by 2020 (World Health Organization, 2000).

Gender differences in health and illness are significantly shaped by socioeconomic status and access to resources, services, and meaningful work, as well as leisure and community engagement. Women in developed countries on average live longer than men, yet women in developing countries die in far greater numbers at younger ages due to complications during childbirth, malnutrition, and a lack of public sanitation. Feminist researchers have also challenged the conceptualization of health and illness to consider the effects of biomedical "truths" about the mind and body that obscure the social context of women's everyday experiences. The women's health movement has also articulated a stronger focus on women's knowledge of their own minds, bodies, and emotions as a means of challenging the authority that had been historically invested in medical expertise and clinical services (see Boston Women's Health Book Collective, 1998, *Our Bodies, Our Selves*). Feminist perspectives have contributed greatly to reconceptualizing health and illness beyond the narrow confines of biomedicine, which focuses on the biology of disease. Importantly, gender, in conjunction with ethnicity, religion, age, disability, and sexuality, is now widely recognized as a significant social determinant of individual and population health and illness (Irwin et al., 2006).

The value of leisure as a preventative, restorative, or recovery-oriented domain of experience for women has gained some recognition within the public sphere, often due to the connection with health. The World Health Organization many years ago defined health in terms of "a state of complete physical, mental and social well-being and not merely the absence of disease or infirmity" (1948, p. 100). Over time there have been significant debates within the health literature about the need to move beyond a medicalized focus on treating illness in order to also explore the social conditions that also support prevention, health promotion, early intervention and recovery strategies (see also, Tirone & Gahagan, this volume). Building upon this holistic focus, the health-promotion movement further politicized health through the creation of the Ottawa Charter in 1986, which emphasized community engagement in the process of improving health outcomes and addressing inequality.

The shift towards understanding community health also enabled a stronger link between leisure and quality of life to generate greater recognition of the benefits of parks, active recreation, social connection, sport, and fitness (Godbey, Caldwell, Floyd, & Payne, 2005; Henderson & Bialeschki, 2005). The meaning of health and well-being was opened up through different political and discursive constructions, yet particular notions of health risk and benefit have also come to dominate everyday life within advanced liberal societies (Kline, 2004; Lupton, 1999). Crawford describes this permutation of health anxiety and desire through individual lives and state concerns as "healthism" (Crawford, 2000). For women, this process is highly gendered, as health is often equated with slimness and attractiveness, and it is implicated in problematic issues like anorexia, compulsive exercising, fad dieting, obesity, and a disengagement from pleasurable embodied activity (Moulding, 2007; Wright, O'Flynn, & Macdonald, 2006). In addition, women are positioned as the guardians of family health with increasing responsibility for children's emotional and physical well-being (Featherstone, 2004).

During an Australian study that I conducted on healthy family lifestyles, I can recall the disheartened comments of a mother with few financial resources talking about the exhausting work of managing her children's health (obesity, epilepsy, behavioral issues). She juggled the finances so they could enjoy some leisure together as a family amidst the routines of maintaining daily exercise regimes, monitoring the fridge, and searching for low-cost healthy food, while managing risk to ensure safe access to local parks and friendship networks. For this mother and other women in the study, a healthy family lifestyle depended largely upon women's material, temporal, and emotional resources; health was equated with work-like rather than leisure-like qualities (Fullagar, 2009a). Women's own leisure time and space was often sacrificed for the sake of family well-being, although women also desired to reclaim their own leisure time in order to maintain their own and their family's well-being. Family leisure was also something mothers worked at by facilitating emotional relationships, shared memories, and purposive goals related to children's skill, education, and moral development (Freysinger, 1997; Hallman, Mary, & Benbow, 2007; Harrington, this volume; Shaw & Dawson, 2001; Trussell & Shaw, 2007).

The well-being challenge for many women with families is creating leisure time and space for themselves, or leisure time with their families/ friends for more collectivist cultures, amidst the increasing expectation that they will assume responsibility for managing "risks" to their children's education, health, and future within a market-based economy (see also Backett-Milburn, 2004; McKie, Bowlby, & Gregory, 2004). This personal challenge is, of course, shaped by broader social norms that structure gender relations through a heterosexual matrix, where whiteness is also privileged and the nuclear family is still held as an ideal formation (Kay, 2003a and this volume). A promising area for future research would be leisure experiences within same-sex relationships and families, where gender difference does not structure power relations for women in the same way (Bialeschki & Pearce, 1997; Foster, 2005; Gabb, 2005). Sociological research has argued that gender, class, and ethnicity play a very significant role in the production of inequity within and between different families that directly affects health, well-being, and life opportunities (Howard, this volume; Van de Mheen, Stronks, & Mackenbach, 1998; Wardle & Steptoe, 2003; Warinm, Turner, Moore, & Davies, 2008; Wray, 2007). Like the complex gendered experience of leisure, the meaning of health and well-being is not self-evident and requires a reflexive exploration of its construction in different women's lives (Wray, 2007).

As a sociologist, I have had a long-standing interest in developing a more critical understanding of women's diverse leisure and health experiences through engagement with poststructural and feminist theories. Traditionally, the domains of leisure and health have been rather loosely affiliated in the social science literature, and there is a need to move beyond conventional disciplinary divides to open up a discursive space to "think and do" gender and leisure differently. This requires a more reflexive approach to thinking about how the gendered nature of power plays out within different research areas, policy and professional practice domains concerned with women's leisure, health and well-being (Alvesson & Skoldberg, 2000; Dupuis, 1999). Poststructuralist ideas help make visible equity issues in relation to leisure and also to problematize various "truths" espoused in research, policy, and service provisions about benefits of prescribed activities for individual and social well-being. As Foucault (1980) argues in relation to the power-knowledge nexus, "everything is dangerous": even the promotion of health benefits through leisure is never free from the effects of *truth regimes*. In the following discussion, I identify several studies that have contributed to the leisure studies literature and reflect upon different research projects that enabled me to explore the complex gender relations shaping women's leisure and health.

PROMOTING WOMEN'S HEALTH THROUGH LEISURE: REGULATING FREEDOM?

With the current policy push to prevent "lifestyle diseases" in many developed countries, women are being targeted as an "at risk" population due to their generally lower rates of physical activity. Various health messages and interventions have been developed to promote participation in active transport, recreation, exercise, and sport as a means of reducing the "burden of disease" (van Dam, Li, Spiegelman, Franco, & Hu, 2008). While the focus on physical activity benefits does go some way to addressing aware-ness of disease prevention for women, the connection to leisure-related experiences is problematic in several ways. Simply prescribing more physi-cal activity for individual women to reduce their "health risks" does little to address the gendered constraints that regulate their everyday choices and sense of identity (Fullagar, 2003). The extension of the logic of individual-ized responsibility for health is often blame and moral judgment that can further undermine women's own embodied self-care and desire to partici-pate (e.g., issues related to obesity, anorexia, compulsive exercising, and a disconnection between femininity and embodied activity). The exercise of freedom of choice through leisure is also compromised by health discourses that emphasize moral duty, self-discipline, and the obligation to work on oneself in the name of health outcomes or benefits (Smith Maguire, 2008; White, Young, & Gillett, 1995). The moralism implicit in health promo-tion is often guilt-inducing, and misunderstands the important connec-tions between embodied identity, pleasure/shame, and social relationships that inform women's everyday leisure choices.

I explored these tensions in an applied research project that I con-ducted with an Australian women's health center in a rural community in response to new policy directions on gender and health (Fullagar et al., 2004). The publicly funded women's center had traditionally focused on addressing key gender problems (domestic violence, sexual assault, self-esteem, depression), providing group and individual support to women, along with the provision of heath information, advocacy, and some child-care. The "women exploring leisure" project arose from the desire of staff to engage with women differently in promoting physical activity through an exploration of leisure choices and experiences. They had an overwhelming response from women over 50 years of age and found many participants had never been into the center before due to negative perceptions. Rather than prescribing activities and focusing on health benefits, the program worked with groups of older women and young mothers to support them to identify leisure experiences they would like to try and to address gen-der issues (fear of body judgment in gyms, shame felt from high-school activities, lack of confidence and desire to enjoy lost childhood pleasures like cycling or swimming). The staff at the center also worked to promote gender awareness with local service providers, particularly gyms, to create a more inclusive environment. While this project was on a small scale, it worked well to promote a different model of health promotion that was premised on exploring the experience of leisure through an understanding of gendered constraints and supports. In this way, a feminist leisure studies approach was shown to provide another way of conceptualizing health beyond the conventional physical/mental health dualism, and to include the sociocultural context of women's well-being as a mental, bodily, and emotional connection (Fullagar & Brown, 2003).

Leisure researchers have offered a more holistic exploration and political understanding of the links between women's leisure experiences and their own and family well-being. Anne-Marie Sullivan's chapter in this volume and Betsy Wearing's earlier study on the gendered experience of mothers with young babies found that leisure was crucial time and space away from the emotional and physical demands of care. Leisure could be emotionally restorative and enable women to continue with care roles, but it could also be a source of resistance to the imposition of gender ideologies that were premised on self-sacrifice (Wearing, 1990; Wearing & Fullagar, 1996). This theme of resistance to gender norms, expectations, and discourses has become a significant focus in much feminist leisure research that has identified the power relations shaping everyday freedom, and hence also experiences of health or illness. Shannon and Shaw's (2005) research with women who had breast cancer identified the role leisure played in creating new purpose with changes in consciousness and behavior that emphasized caring for oneself. Making such changes were difficult as women experienced guilt and struggled with a sense of entitlement to leisure in relation to domestic responsibilities. Yet, women desired to make the most of their lives and leisure time to enhance their well-being, connect with others, and enjoy everyday pleasures. The theme of enjoyment is also something Henderson and Ainsworth (2002) identified as a crucial link between physical activity, leisure, and health that is often undervalued in the promotion of benefits and outcomes to women. Pleasure, enjoyment, play, and idleness become almost radical concepts when contrasted with the weight of guilt, responsibility for others, and moral obligation to work on being healthy that women often feel. Life-threatening illnesses, such as breast cancer, often open up a reflective space for women to renegotiate gender expectations in order to put their own well-being first. In a study of dragon boat racing for survivors of breast cancer, this theme of existential reflection identified how women redefined themselves as physically and mentally strong (Mitchell, Yakiwchuk, Griffin, Gray, & Fitch, 2007). Women's collective experience of participation provides not only social support but also a pleasurable space of self–other interaction that opens up new possibilities to experience selfhood beyond the confines of conventional femininity.

In relation to mental health, Pondé and Santana's (2000) review of the literature also identified important connections across a range of studies. In my own research on women's recovery from depression, I was interested in looking beneath the medical "cover story" that emphasized medication and therapy as the prescribed treatment pathways to recover well-being (Fullagar, 2008, 2009b). The 80 women in the study had extensive experience with depression and its destructive recurrence in their lives (many also had mothers and/or daughters with depression). Women articulated stories about their transformation of self in recovery, where they learned how to manage feelings of distress (often linked to gender inequities in child and adulthood) and explored alternative sources of identity to the dominant illness narrative of depression. Creative, social, and active leisure practices were significant in supporting women's identity shift over time and in relation to family, work, and other aspects of everyday life. Recovery was connected to women's desire to have leisure time through which to practice a "playful" ethic of care for oneself, and leisure spaces to connect with others for social support and to question the gendered expectations that evoked deep feelings of failure (as mothers, workers, partners, and daughters). One of the key findings from this research was the social and psychological significance of leisure in creating emotional experiences that supported women's well-being. The everyday practical wisdom that women shared about what worked for them in recovery provided a different form of embodied "truth" to dominant forms of medical and psy-expertise. The importance of hearing different stories and meanings about dominant health concepts is particularly important for creating spaces for cultural difference to be valued. For example, Indigenous Australians tend not to use the individualized term "mental health," preferring instead to refer to "emotional well-being," which strongly foregrounds the spiritual, physical, and material relationship to country and kin (Tsey, Harvey, Gibson, & Pearson, 2009).

Across a range of studies that have explored the significance of leisure in experiences of recovery, there is a common theme that highlights the process of transforming the relation to self, where women challenge and make visible the gender norms that entrap them. For example, Hood's (2003) research on women's recovery from alcoholism identified how women held unrealistic expectations of themselves in terms of their ability to care for others, and were often highly critical of their own inability to do so. In examining the place of leisure in recovery, Hood argued that women learned to negotiate the risks of encountering alcohol and to experiment with leisure experiences that enabled them to find purpose, develop different "healthful" social relationships, and take new risks to develop skills, talents, and passions. Green has also examined the important role of friendship in relation to women's identities and leisure lives (Green, 1998; Hutchinson, this volume). Similarly Warner-Smith and Brown (2002) identified the significance of social connection through leisure in a study of Australian women's well-being in rural communities, where services were in decline and masculine sport dominated.

In the health and psychology literature, the importance of these social connections has also been explored in relation to "befriending" as helpful intervention in depression (Harris, Brown, & Robinson, 1999) along with the "therapeutic benefits of art and creative pursuits" (Heenan, 2006). Dupuis and Smale's (1995) study on the relationship between leisure, psychological well-being, and older adults importantly identified gender differences relating to leisure preferences. The positive associations between physical activity and mental health were identified less for women, or specifically in relation to activities such as aerobics. In contrast, social and indoor activities were more commonly reported by women as contributing to life satisfaction. However, these findings also identified the need to examine gender differences in relation to the meaning of leisure pursuits rather than a more narrow focus on activity or the stress buffering effect of leisure that tends to dominate the literature (Coleman & Iso-Ahola, 1993; Faulkner & Biddle, 2004). Psychologists have also called for a focus on gender in relation to the therapeutic benefits and positive emotions produced through leisure that assist individuals to overcome the legacies of inequality, abuse, and negative life events (Caldwell, 2005). Some even argue that feminist approaches to therapy can draw upon women's empowerment through leisure-related experiences that bring into question feminine norms of passivity (Chrisler & Lamont, 2002). The range of feminist leisure research perspectives highlights the importance of understanding how individual women experience leisure in different sociocultural, political, and economic contexts that shape their well-being and freedom to choose. While therapeutic discourses about the health benefits of leisure do promote individual well-being, they need to be encompassed within a human rights discourse that situates the understanding of women's leisure and health in the context of gender relations as they are mediated by cultural, religious, age, disability, sexuality, and class differences.

CONCLUSION

In this chapter, I have explored the complex interrelationships between gender, leisure, and the politics of women's health through many different research studies and disciplinary perspectives. This diverse range of academic voices suggests that there is great potential for further interdisciplinary work that examines the significance of leisure to women's individual and social well-being. The concepts of leisure and health are indeed slippery and problematic when applied in an uncritical way to women's lives. Hence, there is a need for further research that examines women's leisure experiences in terms of mind-body-emotions rather than dualistic thinking, as well as situating the personal within the social realm to examine the structural and cultural effects of gender inequities. One of the key areas that is still under-explored is the question of diversity in women's experiences of leisure and health to help us move beyond the limitations of whiteness, ableism, heterosexism, and middle-class assumptions about womanhood (as also addressed by a number of other chapters in this volume). In an era where "healthism" prevails, there is an even greater need for feminist reflexivity about how women's leisure freedoms and human rights are addressed in relation to health problems and solutions that are funded and promoted by governments and corporations with vested interests across the globe.

REFERENCES

Aitchison, C. C. (2003). *Gender and leisure: Social and cultural perspectives.* London, UK: Routledge.

Alvesson, M., & Skoldberg, K. (2000). *Reflexive methodology: New vistas for qualitative research.* London, UK: Sage.

Backett-Milburn, K. (2004). How children and their families construct and negotiate risk, safety and danger. *Childhood, 11*(4), 429–447.

Bialeschki, D., & Pearce, K. (1997). "I don't want a lifestyle—I want a life": The effect of role negotiations on the leisure of lesbian mothers. *Journal of Leisure Research, 29*(1), 113–131.

Boston Women's Health Book Collective. (1998). *Our bodies, ourselves for the new century.* New York, NY: Simon & Schuster.

Caldwell, L. (2005). Leisure and health: Why is leisure therapeutic? *British Journal of Guidance and Counselling, 33*(1), 7–26.

Chrisler, J., & Lamont, J. (2002). Can exercise contribute to the goals of feminist therapy? *Women and Therapy, 25*(2), 9–22.

Coleman, D., & Iso-Ahola, S. E. (1993). Leisure and health: The role of social support and self-determination. *Journal of Leisure Research, 25*, 111–128.

Crawford, R. (2000). The ritual of health promotion. In S. Williams, J. Gabe, & M. Calnan (Eds.), *Health, medicine and society: Key theories, future agendas* (pp. 219–235). London, UK: Routledge.

Dam, R. M. van, Li, T., Spiegelman, D., Franco, O. H., & Hu, F. B. (2008). Combined impact of lifestyle factors on mortality: Prospective cohort study in U.S. women. *British Medical Journal, 337*(2), 1440–1448.

Dupuis, S. (1999). Naked truths: Towards a reflexive methodology in leisure research. *Leisure Sciences, 21*(1), 43–64.

Dupuis, S., & Smale, B. (1995). An examination of relationship between psychological well-being and depression and leisure activity participation among older adults. *Society and Leisure, 18*(1), 67–92.

Faulkner, G., & Biddle, S. (2004). Exercise and depression: Considering variability and contextuality. *Journal of Exercise and Sport Psychology, 26*(1), 3–18.

Featherstone, B. (2004). *Family life and family support: A feminist analysis.* Hampshire, UK: Palgrave Macmillan.

Foster, D. (2005). Why do children do so well in lesbian households? Research on lesbian parenting. *Canadian Woman Studies, 24*(2–3), 51–56.

Foucault, M. (1980). *Power/knowledge: Selected interviews and other writings, 1972–1977.* Hemel Hempstead, UK: Harvester Wheatsheaf.

Freysinger, V. (1997). Redefining family, redefining leisure: Progress made and challenges ahead in research on leisure and families. *Journal of Leisure Research, 29*(1), 1–4.

Fullagar, S. (2003). Governing women's active leisure: The gendered effects of calculative rationalities within Australian health policy. *Critical Public Health, 13*(1), 47–60.

Fullagar, S. (2008). Leisure practices as counter-depressants. *Leisure Sciences, 30*(1), 1–18.

Fullagar, S. (2009a). Governing healthy family lifestyles through discourses of risk and responsibility. In J. Wright & V. Harwood (Eds.), *Biopolitics and the "obesity epidemic": Governing bodies* (pp. 108–126). London, UK: Routledge.

Fullagar, S. (2009b). Negotiating the neurochemical self: Anti-depressant consumption in women's recovery from depression. *Health, 13*(3), 389–406.

Fullagar, S., & Brown, P. (2003). Everyday temporalities: Leisure, ethics and young women's emotional well-being. *Annals of Leisure Research, 6*(3), 193–208.

Fullagar, S., Gattuso, S., et al. (2004). *Women exploring leisure: Final report.* Albury-Wodonga Women's Centre: NSW Health.

Gabb, J. (2005). Lesbian m/otherhood: Strategies of familial-linguistic management in lesbian parent families. *Sociology, 39*(4), 585–603.

Godbey, G., Caldwell, L., Floyd, M., & Payne, L. (2005). Implications from leisure studies and recreation and park management research for active living. *American Journal of Preventive Medicine, 28*, 150–158.

Green, E. (1998). "Women doing friendship": An analysis of women's leisure as a site of identity construction, empowerment and resistance. *Leisure Studies, 17*(3), 171–185.

Hallman, B. C., Mary, S., & Benbow, P. (2007). Family leisure, family photography and zoos: Exploring the emotional geographies of families. *Social and Cultural Geography, 8*(6), 871–888.

Harris, T., Brown, G., & Robinson, R. (1999). Befriending as an intervention for chronic depression among women in an inner city. 2: Role of Fresh-Start experiences and baseline psychosocial factors in remission from depression. *British Journal of Psychiatry, 174*, 225–232.

Heenan, D. (2006). Art as therapy: an effective way of promoting positive mental health? *Disability and Society, 21*(2), 179–191.

Henderson, K. A., & Ainsworth, B. (2002). Enjoyment: A link to physical activity, leisure and health. *Journal of Park and Recreation Administration, 20*(4), 130–146.

Henderson, K. A., & Bialeschki, M. D. (2005). Leisure and active lifestyles: Research reflections. *Leisure Sciences, 27*, 355–365.

Henderson, K. A., Bialeschki, M. D., Shaw, S. M., & Freysinger, V. J. (1996). *Both gains and gaps: Feminist perspectives on women's leisure.* State College, PA: Venture Publishing, Inc.

Hood, C. (2003). Women in recovery from alcoholism: The place of leisure. *Leisure Sciences, 25*(1), 51–79.

Irwin, A., Valentine, N., Brown, C., Loewenson, R., Solar, O., Brown, H., et al. (2006). The Commission on Social Determinants of Health: Tackling the social roots of health inequities. *PLoS Med, 3*(6), e106, 749–751.

Kay, T. A. (2003a). Leisure, gender and self in the analysis of family. *World Leisure Journal, 4*, 4–14.

Kline, S. (2004). *Fast food, sluggish kids: Moral panics and risky lifestyles* (No. 9). London, UK: Cultures of Consumption Research Programme, Birkbeck College.

Lupton, D. (1999). *Risk and sociocultural theory.* Cambridge, UK: Cambridge University Press.

McKie, L., Bowlby, S., & Gregory, S. (2004, July 3). Starting well: Gender, care and health in the family context. *Sociology, 38*, 593–611.

van de Mheen, H., Stronks, K., & Mackenbach, J. (1998). A lifecourse perspective on socioeconomic inequalities in health: The influence of childhood socioeconomic conditions and selection processes. *Sociology of Health and Illness, 20*(5), 754–777.

Mitchell, T., Yakiwchuk, C., Griffin, K., Gray, R., & Fitch, M. (2007). Survivor dragon boating: A vehicle to reclaim and enhance life after treatment for breast cancer. *Health Care for Women International, 28*, 122–140.

Moulding, N. (2007). "Love your body, move your body, feed your body": Discourses of self-care and social marketing in a body image health promotion program. *Critical Public Health, 17*(1), 57–69.

Pondé, M., & Santana, V. (2000). Participation in leisure activities: Is it a protective factor for women's mental health? *Journal of Leisure Research, 32*(4), 457–472.

Shannon, C., & Shaw, S. (2005). "If the dishes don't get done today, they'll get done tomorrow": A breast cancer experience as a catalyst for changes to women's leisure. *Journal of Leisure Research, 37*(2), 195–215.

Shaw, S. M., & Dawson, D. J. (2001). Purposive leisure: Examining parental discourses on family activities. *Leisure Sciences, 23*(4), 217–231.

Smith Maguire, J. (2008). Leisure and the obligation of self-work: An examination of the fitness field. *Leisure Studies, 27*(1), 59–75.

Stolz, G. (2006, March 9). Put life before career, says Greer. *Courier Mail,* p. 1.

Trussell, D., & Shaw, S. M. (2007). "Daddy's gone and he'll be back in October": Farm women's experiences of family leisure. *Journal of Leisure Research, 39*(2), 366–388.

Tsey, K., Harvey, D., Gibson, T., & Pearson, L. (2009). The role of empowerment in setting a foundation for social and emotional wellbeing. *Australian e-Journal for the Advancement of Mental Health, 8*(1), 2–10.

Ussher, J. (Ed.) (2000). *Women's health: Contemporary international perspectives.* Leicester, UK: British Psychological Society.

Wardle, J., & Steptoe, A. (2003, June 6). Socioeconomic differences in attitudes and beliefs about healthy lifestyles. *Journal of Epidemiology and Community Health, 57,* 440–443.

Warinm, M., Turner, K., Moore, V., & Davies, M. (2008). Bodies, mothers and identities: Rethinking obesity and the BMI. *Sociology of Health and Illness, 30*(1), 97–111.

Warner-Smith, P., & Brown, P. (2002). "The town dictates what I do": the leisure, health and wellbeing of women in a small Australian country town. *Leisure Studies, 21,* 39–56.

Watson, B., & Scraton, S. (2001). Confronting whiteness? Researching the leisure lives of South Asian mothers. *Journal of Gender Studies, 10*(3), 265–277.

Wearing, B. (1990). Leisure and the crisis of motherhood: A study of leisure and health amongst mothers of first babies in Sydney, Australia.

In S. Quah (Ed.), *The family as an asset: International perspectives on marriage, parenthood and social policy* (pp. 122–155). Singapore: Times Academic Press.

Wearing, B. (1998). *Leisure and feminist theory.* Thousand Oaks, CA: Sage.

Wearing, B., & Fullagar, S. (1996). The ambiguity of Australian women's family leisure. In N. Samuel (Ed.), *Women, leisure and the family in contemporary society* (pp. 15–34). London, UK: CAB International.

White, P., Young, K., & Gillett, J. (1995). Bodywork as a moral imperative: Some critical notes on health and fitness. *Society and Leisure, 18*(1), 159–182.

World Health Organization. (1948). *Preamble to the Constitution of the World Health Organization as adopted by the International Health Conference, 19–22 June, 1946.* New York, NY: World Health Organization.

World Health Organization. (2000). *Women's mental health: An evidence based review.* Geneva, Switzerland: Department of Mental Health and Substance Dependence, World Health Organization.

Wray, S. (2007). Health, exercise, and well-being: The experiences of midlife women from diverse ethnic backgrounds. *Social Theory & Health, 5*(2), 126–145.

Wright, J., O'Flynn, G., & Macdonald, D. (2006). Being fit and looking healthy: Young women's and men's constructions of health and fitness. *Sex Roles, 54,* 707–716.

CHAPTER 32
ACTIVIST SCHOLARSHIP: FIGHTING HOMOPHOBIA AND HETEROSEXISM

B. DANA KIVEL AND COREY W. JOHNSON

In her autobiography, *Pentimento*, Louisiana-born author and playwright, Lillian Hellman, explained that the title refers to a painting on a canvas that lies underneath another painting. Perhaps, she said, the painter repented, changed his mind, and thus he painted over the original work of art. The idea of pentimento captures the sentiment of this chapter which is about shifts—shifts in feeling that lead to certain paths, ones that were not necessarily anticipated or understood by others, and which incorporate shifts in thinking about our lives and the world in which we live. Pentimento is about seeing the world one way and then experiencing a shift, and seeing the world again, but from a different perspective. This chapter explores how we began our journey as activist-scholars who investigated and wrote about people who identified as lesbian/gay/bisexual, and how we then shifted our thinking to focus on how systems based in prejudice, discrimination, and fear operate to influence individuals and their interactions with others.

> *At the age of 15, I became good friends with a woman named Susan. She was the person I played tennis with several times a week, she was the person who took me joyriding in her MG and who took me to the First Baptist Church in an attempt to save my Jewish soul. She was also the first person I fell in love with—an unrequited love—during my adolescence. At the time, I didn't have a name for how I felt. I couldn't articulate what she meant to me and I intuitively knew that I couldn't tell others how I felt about her. At the age of 17, I befriended a young woman I met at the end of my junior year in high school. We fell in love, and then I knew what to name myself and what those feelings toward my friend had meant two years before. I also quickly learned that other people had a name for me, too. My girlfriend and I were called "dykes," queers, lezzies, weirdos. We were verbally harassed at school; students slashed the tires on her car; someone threw a rock through the front window of my house. One night, a carload of guys*

followed us to a dead-end road. They parked their truck perpendicular to ours, blocking us from leaving. They got out with clubs and sticks and came over to our car. They shook the car and then pressed their faces up against the windows and began to taunt us with: "dyke, cunt, lezzie, queer." They threatened to rape us and to hurt us. After awhile, they got bored and allowed us to leave. We lost them by speeding through a red light. Because we weren't supposed to have been together and because we thought no one would care or do anything about it, we never told anyone about that night. (one author's story)

According to Hunter (1990), these narratives, although a bit unusual, were not all that uncommon for someone who came out in the late 1970s and even in the 1990s. Coming out is a process of internalizing and publicly acknowledging one's sexual identity as being lesbian/gay/bisexual/transgender/transsexual (LGBT). In fact, the first story was a narrative recounting Dana's experience of "coming out" in Tyler, Texas, more than 30 years ago while a student at Robert E. Lee High School. Corey stayed closeted during high school because he witnessed events like those experienced by Dana and did not come out until his college years, when he was safely away from the "small-town mentality." Although both of us survived this, many have not been so fortunate. In 1993, a young man by the name of Nicholas West was murdered in Dana's hometown; although the initial motive for the crime was robbery, the three men said they shot 23-year-old West more than nine times because he was gay. One local sheriff described this murder as a "sadistic and cold-blooded" killing and "one of the most brutal killings I've ever seen" (Trejo, 1993, p. 5A). Young people, as well as adults, who identify as LGBT are more likely to find support for their sexual identity today than in the distant and recent past, but prejudice, discrimination, heterosexism (the unquestioned assumption that everyone is heterosexual) and homophobia (an irrational fear and hatred of LGBT people) are pervasive.

Dana's coming-out experience in east Texas had a profound impact upon her life. In 1988, she was living in San Francisco where she met Donna Ozawa, and together they, along with several young people and adults, created the first social/recreational program for LGBT youth in San Francisco, the Lavender Youth Recreation and Information Center (LYRIC), which celebrated its twentieth anniversary in 2008.

Corey's experiences also had a major impact on him. Because he spent so much time trying to mask his gay identity, and since he had access to a considerable amount of masculinity, he often resorted to being the bully and victimizing other youth. Now, 20 years later, and on the other side of a lot of internalized homophobia, he feels a responsibility to make school and recreation environments safer for LGBT youth. Consequently, he recently produced a documentary called *Be There for Me: Collective Memories of LGBT Youth in High School* and is a co-founder of the Georgia Safe Schools Coalition.

For us, our earlier life experiences of being lesbian and gay influence the research we have pursued, and continue to pursue, in our careers, and these experiences are the lens through which we do our work. Both of us have focused on issues of sexual identity and leisure—Dana primarily on youth and Corey on gay men. Clearly, we have personal experiences that influence how we speak about and research this issue. There is no way that we could have separated ourselves from this topic, nor would we have wanted to do so. And we encourage other researchers to find their voice and to use it as a way to frame how they see and research the world.

RESEARCH ABOUT LGB YOUTH

Beginning in the 1980s, researchers from across disciplines—psychology, sociology, and social work—began to examine the lives of lesbian/gay/bisexual (LGB) youth. Later, researchers would include young people who identify as transgender/transsexual. Educators Griffin and Ouellett (2003) identified the period 1980–1989 as "identification of lesbian and gay youth as a population at risk" (p. 108). In 1987, Hetrick and Martin published a study, "Development Issues and Their Resolution for Gay and Lesbian Adolescents," in the *Journal of Homosexuality* at the same time that Hunter and Schaecher published a study entitled "Stresses on Lesbian and Gay Adolescents in Schools" in the journal, *Social Work in Education*. Both studies began to make visible the lives and experiences of being young and being lesbian/gay/bisexual. Perhaps one of the most important studies about LGB youth was published two years later by a San Francisco social worker, Paul Gibson. Gibson (1989) conducted a study on LGB youth as part of a comprehensive investigation of teenage suicide in the United States. The report showed that suicide was the leading cause of death for LGB youth compared with non-LGB youth for whom suicide was the third leading cause of death. The report also highlighted higher rates of drug and alcohol abuse, truancy, and homelessness among LGB youth. Gibson's report (1989) served as a catalyst for those working to support and develop LGB-friendly youth programs across the United States. Although the oldest program for LGB youth, the Hetrick-Martin Institute, dedicated to the protection of lesbian/gay youth in New York City, had been in existence since 1979, numerous other programs emerged following the release of Gibson's report. Such programs include District 202, founded in 1991 in Minneapolis; Lambert House, founded in the late 1980s in Seattle; and Out Youth in Austin, founded in 1990. Since that time, many more programs for LGBT youth have been established.

Gibson's study was not only a catalyst for the creation of many more LGBT youth programs; it was also an important catalyst for researchers, because it served as the basis for justifying further research on this particular segment of the adolescent population. Research on lesbian/gay/bisexual youth and later, transgender/transsexual youth, could now be found in a variety of journals across many disciplines. In a 2003 study, Griffin and Ouellett identified four categories of research on lesbian/gay/bisexual issues in education since the 1990s. These categories included: "a) issues of visibility; b) studies of the climate of schools; c) studies identifying ways to improve educational organizations for lesbian/gay people; d) studies about lesbian and gay youth" (pp. 109–110).

Early Research about LGB Youth and Recreation and Leisure

In recreation and leisure studies, research about LGB youth began with an article by Arnold Grossman in 1992. His article was published in the *Journal of Physical Education, Recreation and Dance.* In this short but pivotal essay, Grossman spoke about the need for park and recreation professionals to acknowledge this segment of the adolescent population and the importance of providing services and programs, especially since research indicated that they were at greater risk than the general adolescent population for truancy, drug and alcohol abuse, HIV/AIDS, and suicide. He went on to explain that LGB youth were at risk not because of anything inherent in their being LGB, but because of the social stigma, prejudice, and homophobia that was often a part of their experience of growing up and coming out during the time period of this article's publication.

Grossman's article acknowledged the existence of LGB youth as a population to be considered with regard to the recreation and leisure profession and served as a springboard for Dana's research (Kivel, 1994). She conducted a qualitative study that focused on how LGB youth conceptualized leisure, and found that their leisure was linked with sexual identity, safety, and coming out. Participants felt that sexual identity was related to what they did in their free time and with whom; they felt that issues of safety influenced their leisure choices. In short, there was an association between the extent to which they could be "out"—they could be themselves—and the perception that they could participate in certain programs and/or activities. Antecedent constraints have been identified in other literature related to markers of identity (e.g., race, gender) as mitigating factors in terms of what individuals may and/or may not choose to do in their leisure time, as a number of other chapters in this volume attest. The third main theme in the study was "coming out and enjoyment in leisure," whereby participants noted that their "outness" influenced the quality of their leisure experience. Interestingly, this theme provided the following paradox: although coming out can be a difficult process for LGB youth because of prejudice, stigma, homophobia, and heterosexism, it could also be liberating because individuals no longer feel compelled to hide their "true" and "authentic" selves.

BROADENING THE RESEARCH PERSPECTIVE

Building on her 1994 study, Dana (Kivel, 1996) later examined the relationship between leisure, identity formation, and LGB youth while Corey (Johnson, 2000) focused on young adults. The bulk of research about LGB youth at that time focused on "coming out issues" and on pathological issues such as drug and alcohol abuse, suicide, truancy, and unsafe sex practices. Although researchers had examined identify formation among lesbian/gay and bisexual youth, very little research had examined contexts of identify formation such as schools, family, peers, work, and leisure. Interestingly, in the mid-1990s, developmental psychologists and theorists in North America were strongly arguing that leisure was a critical context for identity formation, along with school, family, work, and peers. So the purpose of these two studies was to broaden the previous research on LGB young people, to move away from "coming out" issues and to expand identity formation research to include the experiences of this segment of the adolescent population.

In our studies, participants used various leisure contexts—reading, media consumption, playing sports, participating in band—to help construct their personal identities, but their involvement in leisure contexts was less helpful than extant research suggested in terms of the construction of their social identities (the notable exception was the gay bar, discussed in the next section). Although they believed their engagement with these leisure contexts helped them develop a better sense of self, participants did not engage in various sporting and music events at a level that would allow them to internalize the identity associated with the activity. Further, they did not think such engagements helped them create a public "gay" identity. For example, when one young woman had been a cheerleader for most of her life came out, she stopped doing cheering because she feared that it would make her too much of a public figure and, therefore, open to scrutiny about her personal life and her internal identity of being a lesbian. That is, she stopped engaging in this activity and lost the identity that accompanied being known as a cheerleader. Another participant loved music and wanted to play the saxophone. He believed, however, that playing this instrument would lead others to question his sexual identity; thus he "chose" to play the trumpet. Consequently, he felt he never really internalized the identity of a musician. These few examples illustrate the disconnect experienced by LGB youth between engaging in a leisure activity and internalizing the identity that accompanies such an activity. This process of identity formation may have been compromised as a result of their fears of being publicly identified as lesbian/gay, even though they all said they were very comfortable with their internal lesbian/gay identities. Thus, both of our early studies led us to consider the following questions:

1. If an individual is so concerned about hiding her/his true identity to others, even though s/he is totally comfortable with her/his identity internally, to what extent can s/he fully engage and participate in leisure activities as her/his "authentic self"?

2. When an individual has to constantly negotiate others' perceptions, what effects would this have on his or her leisure experience?

3. How can leisure contribute to an individual's development and identity formation if leisure contexts are being compromised because of homophobia and heterosexism?

For both of us, our early work began to respond to the first question, but it is the second and third questions that remained unanswered because we had yet to begin to fully consider the implications of heterosexism and homophobia vis-à-vis LGBT youth and leisure spaces. It was also the third question that led us to consider a shift in how we were thinking about lesbian/gay youth and adults. Dana realized that she had focused attention on making visible the leisure experiences of LGB youth and on understanding leisure as it influenced their identity formation. She also realized that her thinking was grounded in what Griffin and Ouellett (2003) had referred to as "identification of lesbian and gay youth as a population at risk." This identification made it easier to pursue funding opportunities from foundations and state agencies to support LGB youth, but the process of pathologizing them was also disempowering. Clearly, there was and is a fine line between talking about the pathological behaviors that had dominated the research on LGB youth and perpetuating that pathology— something that we did not want to do with our research. By not directly examining homophobia and heterosexism in leisure contexts as factors which may have profoundly influenced the behaviors of LGB youth, we were not understanding the totality of their experiences. And if we wanted to understand how homophobia and heterosexism operate, we needed to spend less time talking with LGB youth and more time talking with those who do not identify as LGB, understanding the attitudes and perceptions they hold toward those who are LGBT. Thus, this early research could be categorized as "visibility" research, while the research we shifted to next explored the contexts of culture and power in which individual experience is situated.

RESEARCHING LGB PLACES

Although Dana's (Kivel, 1996) research did not indicate that leisure contexts were instrumental in identity development for LGB youth, Corey's (Johnson, 2000) study on LGB young adults had found the gay bar to be a central leisure context for LGB identity development, perhaps given the required age to participate. This pentimento was pivotal for Corey as he began to go beyond the lives of LGB *individuals* and to examine the *power relations and ideologies* around gay/straight and masculinity/femininity produced in and through leisure. However, because gender/sexual identity construction is fluid and must be situated according to cultural and historical contexts, examining leisure's influence on gender construction is a complex and dynamic process (Shaw, 1999b). In an effort to document and capture these processes, he wanted to focus on the cultural spaces, practices, and products of leisure to illuminate how multiple meanings are constructed in and around leisure and reveal how power and privilege serve the interests of the dominant culture and keep marginal the non-dominant populations of our society. Because the bar had been such a central feature in his earlier work, he turned his attention there first and on media later (see Johnson, this volume).

The shift away from visibility research and to cultural context was an important step because it led to many new questions about leisure spaces and how such spaces are gendered, racialized, and sexualized. In other words, it led to consideration of the ways in which leisure spaces are constructed so as to produce, reproduce, and reinforce socially sanctioned expectations of what it means to be a woman, a man, a person of European American descent, a person of African American descent, a person of Southeast Asian descent, etc., while at the same time retaining the focus on people who identify as LGBT and/or as heterosexual.

In terms of sexuality, the dominant societal presumption of individuals and of space was that of heterosexuality; hence, LGBT people continuously engage in processes of "coming out." If heterosexuality was not the presumption, such a process would not be so central in the lives of LGBT people. This, we felt, was where the shift in focus needed to occur at that time and where we should be going with regard to research on and with both LGBT youth and adults. Specifically, a central question at that point was: To what extent are leisure spaces homophobic and/or might be presumptively heterosexual?

LEISURE SPACES—
CHALLENGING OR REPRODUCING HETEROSEXISM

While Griffin and Ouellett (2003) characterized the 1980s as the "at risk" period for LGB youth research, they framed the years 1990–2002 as an era that "focus(ed) on schools as *a risk environment* for lesbian, gay, bisexual youth" (p. 109, emphasis added). A parallel shift was also occurring in youth development. Researchers were shifting away from looking at youth as a problem toward examining the assets that youth possess and then on examining community assets that exist to support young people. The new thinking was, if we are open to examining community assets and contexts that support young people, we should also be asking if and how these "assets" and contexts may also serve to hinder young people and their development. In schools, the "climate," not the individual, became the focus of the research.

During the late 1980s and early 1990s, teachers and other adults associated with schools developed programs to create more positive environments that would support LGBT young people. Peer and adult support programs were created; "safe zone" programs designed to identify teachers and/or administrators who were "safe" to talk to about LGBT issues were created; and more recently, young people have created Gay/Straight Alliances (GSAs) to build allies across sexual identity and to blur the lines between individuals based on sexual identity. Examples of such programs include Corey's Georgia Safe Schools Coalition (www.georgiasafeschoolscoalition.org).

The impetus for creating these programs was not wholly altruistic. A litigious trend in public education in the United States had resulted in million-dollar payouts to LGBT youth and their families, thereby encouraging schools to be more proactive around issues of safety. High school student Jamie Nabozny, for example, won a million-dollar settlement in a lawsuit against his school district in Wisconsin which "had failed to respond effectively to his family's repeated calls for his protection from harassment and physical violence from schoolmates" (Griffin & Ouellett, 2003, p. 110). Despite the lawsuits against school boards and despite safe zones and sensitivity training for teachers, homophobia and heteronormativity [the assumption that only heterosexuality is "normal"] are still pervasive. A 2003 study by Ngo argued that although "Dynamic High School [a fictitious name] seems to be doing all of the right things to address LGBQ issues . . . homophobia and heteronormativity remains an unyielding presence in the attitudes and culture of the school and student body. Teachers find Dynamic's students to be 'profoundly homophobic' and 'incredibly intolerant' towards the LGBQ community [Q stands for questioning or queer. In this instance, 'queer' is viewed as a positive, powerful identity]" (p. 121).

The insidiousness of homophobia cannot be tackled in education settings only. Rather, it must be addressed in all of the contexts that influence a young person's development and identity formation, including contexts such as work, religious institutions, family, peers, and most notably, leisure. This shift away from the individual toward the contexts that influence young people affected the direction of our and others' research.

FUTURE DIRECTIONS

The question of "where are we going with LGBT youth and leisure?" is a complicated one in terms of what focus or frame to employ (e.g., individual experiences and/or cultural contexts). It is further complicated because more and more young people are distancing themselves from narrowly defined categories of sexual identity and prefer instead to just be known as someone who loves someone of the same gender (Savin-Williams, 2005). This causes difficulties for researchers because of the loss of clearly defined identity categories. Despite Savin-Williams's (2005) prediction that these identity labels would disappear, this has not been the case. Rather, what more and more young people are doing is blurring the lines between the discrete categories. They want to live *postmodern lives* in this new century that allow them not to be "tied" to a label that in some way easily aligns them with a social and political movement. Also, ever-shifting and changing feelings may be more fluid than previously identified and/or acknowledged. More and more young people are identifying themselves as transgender, omnisexual, and pansexual. Hence, one of the complicating issues for future research may involve how to "identify" this population and how to do this in a way that takes into account the fluidity of identity and young people's resistance to being labeled (Savin-Williams, 2005).

A compelling issue for future leisure and recreation research has to do with "socially responsible" practice. Much can be learned from the field of education. Specifically, educators have focused on creating safe climates, and while there continues to be homophobia, heterosexism, and intolerance, the work of creating safe schools is having an impact. To what extent might this model be useful for recreation and leisure settings? To what extent have recreation agencies created safe zones? The opportunities for research on this topic abound. It is unlikely that there are very many public and/or nonprofit leisure services agencies across the United States that explicitly identify as providing "safe spaces" for LGBT youth (other than LGBT youth-based organizations and the public spaces marked as LGBT) Are there ways, however, in which city agencies can link with existing LGBT youth groups to learn how to make their own spaces safer and more welcoming?

Research that explicitly focuses on the extent to which LGBT youth and adults feel safe and welcome at non-queer identified youth programs is needed and could provide the basis for creating programs such as a gay/straight alliance (GSA) and/or a safe zone in recreation-based settings. Research on/with LGBT youth in sports reveals the critical role that coaches play in lending support for young people who may or may not be publicly "out." Perhaps we, too, could develop research projects that examine the role that "key" adults can play in supporting LGBT youth in recreation-based settings.

In our work, we have also made a shift away from separating ourselves in research and practice toward trying to understand how we, individually and as part of a social collective, construct ideologies around gender/race/sexuality and how these ideologies inform our worldview. Our belief is that the more individuals become conscious of how ideologies are shaped and constructed, the more open they will be to shifting how they view the world. We hope that this, in turn, will lead to different social and professional practices in terms of program planning and service delivery.

Griffin and Ouellett (2003) argued that in terms of education, the next step is to employ a social justice perspective that "focuses on organizational or systemic change principles that address the larger interrelated nature of systems of injustice and oppression" (p. 111). We encourage recreation and leisure researchers and practitioners to consider such a perspective as well. This will require us to examine how homophobia, heterosexism, and the intersection of other oppressions based on gender, race/ethnicity, class ability/disability operate to unknowingly and perhaps insidiously shape the leisure experiences of all young people. Working toward social change that results in a more just world means that we will need to address these issues at the level of the individual and at the level of society. To do that, we might all need to invoke Hellman's pentimento (1973) in order to really "see" what exists and what needs to be done to effect change.

REFERENCES

Gibson, P. (1989). Gay male and lesbian youth suicide. Alcohol, drug abuse, and mental health administration. *Report of the Secretary's task force on youth suicide. Volume 3: Prevention and Intervention in Youth Suicide.* DHHS Pub. No. (ADM) 89-1623. Washington, DC: Supt. Of Docs., U.S. Govt. Print Office.

Griffin, P., & Ouellett, M. (2003). From silence to safety and beyond: Historical trends in addressing lesbian, gay, bisexual and transgender issues in K-12 Schools. *Equity & Excellence in Education, 36*(2), 106–114.

Grossman, A. (1992). Inclusion not exclusion: Recreation service delivery to lesbian, gay and bisexual youth. *Journal of Physical Education, Recreation and Dance, 63*(4), 45–47.

Hellman, L. (1973). *Pentimento.* New York, NY: Signet.

Hetrick, E. S., & Martin, A. D. (1987). Developmental issues and their resolution for gay and lesbian adolescents. *Journal of Homosexuality, 14*(1/2), 25–43.

Hunter, J. (1990). Violence against lesbian and gay male youths. *Journal of Interpersonal Violence, 5*(3), 295–300.

Hunter, J., & Schaecher, R. (1987). Stresses on lesbian and gay adolescents in schools. *Social Work in Education, 9*(3), 180–186.

Johnson, C. W. (2000). Living the game of hide and seek: Leisure in the lives of gay and lesbian young adults. *Leisure, 24*(2), 255–278.

Kivel, B. D. (1994). *The paradox of coming out: Lesbian and gay youth and leisure.* Paper presented at the Leisure Research Symposium, Minneapolis, MN.

Kivel, B. D. (1996). *In on the outside, out on the inside: Lesbian/Gay/Bisexual youth, identity and leisure.* (Unpublished doctoral dissertation). The University of Georgia, Athens, GA.

Ngo, B. (2003). Citing discourses: Making sense of homophobia and heteronormativity at Dynamic High School. *Equity & Excellence in Education, 36*(2), 115–124.

Savin-Williams, R. (2005). The new gay teen: Shunning labels. *The Gay and Lesbian Review, 12*(6), 16–19.

Shaw, S. M. (1999b). Men's leisure and women's lives: The impact of pornography on women's lives. *Leisure Studies, 18*(3), 197–212.

Trejo, F. (1993, December 18). Family's grief intensified by gay bias seen in killing. *The Dallas Morning News*, pp. 1A, 5A.

Chapter 33
Reconstructing Masculinities, Migration, and Transnational Leisure Spaces

Ray Hibbins

Gender identities today are influenced by a wide range of unpredictable and rapid major changes. These include changes in global economies and climate, transnationalism, environmental destruction, loss of livelihoods and cultural heritage, international alliances, disruptions to traditional cultural continuities, cultural amnesia and loss of belongingness (cultural roots), death of "failed states," genocide, changing power relations in macro- and micro-systems, and changing ethical and legal practices and policies. These transformations are reflected in various individual, societal, and cultural behaviors and practices. Imagine the complex behavioral changes for the Indonesian, gay male as he moves *flaneur*-like (Wearing &Wearing, 1990) across different sociocultural spaces typified by, say, groups of other gay Indonesian males in one social space; or mixed ethnic groups of heterosexual males and transgendered individuals in another space; or monoethnic, non-Indonesian heterosexuals in yet another space. Such diverse spaces could involve behavioral "passing," constraints on spontaneity, identity experimentation, and experiences of homophobia or pleasure associated with identity recognition. Here we see accommodations, resistances, adaptations, and ritualisms. Gender, ethnic, and sexual identities are constructed and reconstructed in these global and transnational spaces. Different emphases are given to particular dimensions of identity as they intersect in diverse spaces (locales and milieus). As Connell (2003) argues, masculinities come into existence as people act—they are actively produced, using the resources and strategies developed over time.

In this chapter, an emphasis will be placed on the chameleon-like nature of gender identity as it is intersected by other dimensions of identity in leisure, as well as in domestic and business spaces, in a globalizing and transnational world. Particular reference will be made to the influence of the migration and transnational experience on reconstruction of gender identities situated in political, economic, and cultural contexts, where the *patriarchal dividend* (i.e., privileges that men accrue regardless of their sexuality in patriarchal societies) and its changing nature in the "gender order" (Connell, 1987, 1995) can be seen at play. The emergence and resilience or persistence of varieties of masculinities, and their changing relationship with "the other" (women, other men, and children), will be discussed briefly. Reference will be made to a number of significant events in my own life course that may provide some historical and biographical clues to my interest in the intersection of gender, sexuality, ethnicity, and leisure. Finally, the chapter will explore future research directions, including a discussion concerning whether there is an emergence of "the global man," the influence of gender traditions on the second and third generations of male and female migrants, and the effect of changing global power relations on gender identities.

MIGRATION AND MASCULINITIES

It is interesting how often migration studies largely ignore gender relations or treat them as irrelevant to the contexts in which migration takes place. Some studies, however, are documenting how men and women experience migration differently, how they reproduce cultures and transnational migration circuits, and how patriarchal systems, ideologies, and practices are reaffirmed, reconfigured, or challenged in the process of migration and settlement (Pessar, 2003). How pervasive are hegemonic variants of masculinities, given the diversity of possibilities to which men are exposed? One only needs to flip through popular men's magazines to see the variety of models of masculinity presented. They range from highly cut, tanned bodies of sporting physiques, to the boy-next-door, outdoor activity variant, to the highly effeminate, fair, slim (even skinny), unhealthy type, to the urbane, sophisticated metro male. Men, it seems, can choose from among these variants. Are these magazines attempting to appeal to a wide audience? Or do particular designers of men's fashion choose body types, color, and shape to suit their diverse clothing styles/designs? Or is there ambivalence about the projection of one masculine type? Perhaps one individual can take on different identities at different times, depending on the sociocultural context. Models are black, brown, or white, and of different ethnicities, at least objectively. Do particular ethnic groups model themselves on specific variants? If one were to extend this to the multiple ethnicities which exist in the West today, one becomes aware of the diversity within as well as between and across ethnic/cultural groups. Is there a model type, or does this fluctuate over space and time? The latter suggests that there is no one ethnic or gender mainstream variant that the individual male can model. At the same time, there may still be commonalities across variants that can be seen to reflect a hegemonic type.

VARIANTS OF MASCULINITIES

In an important book on migrant men, Richard Howson (2009) engages in a deconstructive examination of the notion of hegemonic masculinity as a configuration of practice. Of particular interest for Howson is the problem of "slippage," where he asks if hegemonic masculinity is about men or masculinity, practice or identification, the "real" or the "abstract"? Howson concludes that hegemonic masculinity expresses contextually what men "should" do and what men "should" be, based on navigation through the accumulation of contradictions that represent a cultural situation. In the process of acculturation, migrant men undertake this process of negotiation.

Another issue raised by Howson (2009) involves the way in which hegemonic masculinity distances itself from other variants of masculinity, for example subordinate and marginalized forms (Connell, 1987, 1995; see also Lyons, this volume). Howson argues that although dominant notions of masculinity encapsulate hegemonic principles around which is constructed the appearance of homogeneity and stability, this is only possible by imposing a frontier that marks the limit of inclusion/exclusion (Howson, 2009). One way the appearance of homogeneity and stability can be achieved is through domination by coercion (Howson, 2009). For instance, through fear of injury or a realization of the benefits of the *patriarchal dividend* (Connell, 1995), many men may become complicit in the process of producing this apparent homogeneity, though its stability may be rather tenuous.

A number of survival strategies may be employed by those who are not seen as fitting into the hegemonic masculinity. One way of adapting may be to remain in diasporic communities within the new country, where men can practice social relations without changing the position of power they have traditionally had. Others may practice *strategic hybridity*, where they adopt chameleon-like characteristics and emphasize a facet of their identity that will be advantageous in specific, though changing, contexts. Still others, particularly gay males, may need to be very circumspect in the selection of locales and milieu for socializing and for leisure because of fear of homophobic reactions of hegemonically masculine heterosexual groups.

LEISURE, GENDER, AND MIGRANT MALES?

Studies of recreation activities have consistently demonstrated gender difference in participation in particular activities. Of significance to this chapter is the way particular sports have been reported (Edgar, 1997) as the testing ground for masculinity. For some, sport is a key site in contemporary society for the acting out and reaffirming of gender identities

(Hargreaves, 1994; McKay, Messner, & Sabo, 2000). These are also social spaces for the development of homosociality (i.e., same-sex friendships). In Australia, sporting fields, the military (Australian & New Zealand Army Corps tradition), the pub (or hotel), and the beach (surfing, lifesaving) have been locales and milieus where masculinity has been played out. However, such locales are not necessarily typical of migrant populations. Older Asian male migrants rarely frequent these locales, since their markers of masculinity are quite different. My research indicates that Asian males in Australia generally refer to the importance of accumulation of educational qualifications, a prestigious professional occupation, and the accumulation of wealth, which will assist in their becoming good providers and protectors as important markers of their manhood (Hibbins, 2005). However, some younger Taiwanese males have reported (Hibbins, 2009) using sport as one means of acculturation.

Full-body contact sport and other highly physical sports (e.g., rugby league, rugby union) play a very different role. Here the focus is on the body, courage, the hard-hitting physical specimen, heterosexuality, sexual potency, and homosociality. Women are seen as fans who adulate male sporting stars, yet they are also objectified. There have been frequent reports of their exploitation (e.g., sexual assault and rape) by male sporting teams. This is known locally as the "gangbang" phenomenon. Reports of these kinds of assaults abound in the popular media, but are often difficult to prove to the law, because one doesn't "tell on" or "dob in a mate," especially in the public arena. Again, my research suggests these cultural contexts play a minimal role in the lives of Asian male migrants. Rather, sport and recreation are generally used by Asian males as a social space where information is exchanged about business opportunities, such as real estate developments, as well as recent changes in the local Chinese community (Hibbins, 2005).

SOME LIFE-COURSE EXPERIENCES—
PERSONAL REFLECTIONS

As a white, male child at elementary school in Australia, I soon discovered that physical appearance was an important marker of masculine status. To be "fat" was an opportunity for others to be critical by calling me names like "fatso" and by picking on me. This usually meant engaging in a fist-fight where physical dominance was a marker of masculinity. I personally found these situations emotionally, mentally, and physically stressful. I generally was able to escape a physical beating by arguing with my assailant (the use of brains [word power] over brawn [physical power]). On the one occasion where I had to fight, I "won" and then escaped to cry, since I thought I would be either beaten severely by the gang (bullied) on my way home from school or that I had hurt my assailant. My behavior surprised my assailant and his gang, because it was not the usual behavior associated with physical success in a fight. Bragging was much more common. I eventually engaged in swimming training and went to boxing lessons. I became physically fit, lost my "puppy fat," and had success in the swimming pool and in the boxing ring. I discovered that success in these domains meant I was no longer threatened by other men (boys), and that I became attractive to girls (women). For some, sports are a primary arena through which a boy establishes his (hyper-/hetero-) sexual status and through which hegemonic masculine identities are forged and reinforced (McKay, Messner, & Sabo, 2000). It was as if I had attained two of the important markers of masculinity: sporting prowess or physical dominance, and being attractive to the opposite sex (and the potential for "winning" and accumulating/collecting notches on my "gun-sexual prowess" belt).

Never one to conform for too long, I decided that I would play two codes of football, a very physical sport, but also developed an interest in live theatre and acting, an interest seen by hegemonic males as effeminate—an activity for "poofters," or gay men. This interest amazed both males and females in a rural community where I was teaching in a local high school. Yet, this was where I did meet gay males and developed some close relationships that were not physically intimate. Here I discovered a need to sort out what attracted me to males and/or females and vice-versa. Success in the educational sphere and communication skills helped me to escape some of the pressures of hegemonic masculinity.

I also recognized from a very young age that ethnicity, "color," and social class were important variables associated with constructions of gender. More importantly, they were frequently associated with ethnocentrism, stereotyping, prejudice, xenophobia, and racism. Of particular interest to me were the reactions of people (sometimes family acquaintances or friends) to an African American friend who my father met when he loaned his bicycle to him in the early 1950s, when this man arrived in our home city as a crewmember on a cargo vessel from the USA. This man was different from the locals in size, color, speech and accent, and general demeanor. I was a child, and he showered my sister and me with gifts. He treated us as if we were his children. Many of our friends and acquaintances displayed amazement and xenophobia when they saw this "larger-than-life" African American male. They were frequently speechless and gave our friend "the look" (the hate stare). Many of these people rejected us after this and refused to speak to my parents. Gossip abounded in our suburban neighborhood and church.

As a family, we experienced very similar reactions in the early 1950s from others when we made friends with members of the Italian and Sicilian communities in our neighborhood. This may have involved dimensions associated with gender, ethnicity, and religion. I discovered strong family and community ties in both of these communities, and ties that I had rarely experienced among members of the Anglo Celtic community. I enjoyed experiencing these strong ties with my Italian friends. Again, however, non-Italian friends and acquaintances reacted quite negatively to these friendships. These were exacerbated when some of my early girlfriends were Italian. They were described by other males as "warm-blooded," or "hot-blooded" women. It was as if I had moved to the "dark side."

Today, I reflect on these experiences with amazement, given the integration of Italian and Sicilian people socially, publicly, culturally, and economically into the broader Australian community. Many males and females from these communities occupy prestigious positions in the government, business corporations, sociocultural community organizations, and the visual performing arts. It is as if they have been legitimized. Nevertheless, there are some evident age and cultural differences that influence behaviors among these early migrant groups.

It is not uncommon to see among older Italians and Sicilians religious, social, and cultural practices similar to those practiced many generations ago. This is obvious in the wearing of black by women, males working outside the home while women are responsible for household activities and the rearing of children, women walking behind men in public, and the use of their first language in public and in private. This introduces two important variables that need to be considered in future work on gender and leisure: age and generational differences. The experiences discussed in this section and later reflections upon them have contributed to a deep interest in researching the intersectionality of gender, sexuality, and ethnicity among migrants. My research studies are discussed in the next section.

MY RESEARCH

The research that I have undertaken since the turn of the twenty-first century has concentrated on:

1. The influence of migration on (re)construction of gender identities among Chinese males.

2. Intergenerational differences in constructions of belongingness in the Chinese diasporas in Australia.

3. The emergence of the "new" Chinese entrepreneur in Australasia.

4. The influence of leisure context on the nature of gender, sexual, and ethnic identity among diverse Asian groups in Australia.

5. The role leisure plays in the process of acculturation and the development of social capital among Taiwanese migrants.

All of these studies have been qualitative in nature and have used a critical social constructionist theoretical perspective. The first two will be discussed in some detail.

Constructions of Gender Identity among Chinese Males in Australia

The first of these studies involved a sample of 40 Chinese males from a variety of countries of origin who were aged from 19 years to 58 years (Hibbins, 2003). They were part of the skilled and relatively highly educated Chinese middle-class professionals. Their socioeconomic status was very much influenced by the points system used by the Australian immigration department to filter levels of education and skill, economic status, English language proficiency, capacity, and so on, among those entering the country. Several of the males were gay and single, but the majority were heterosexual, married, and had children born either in Australia or overseas. Sexuality was used as one of the variables to differentiate the sample, because until this research, there had been an assumption of heteronormativity in migration research.

Unlike their non-Chinese peers in Australia, alcohol consumption, sport interests, sexual activity, the beach, and surfing activities were not central markers of masculinity among these males. Sport, leisure, and recreation were generally secondary in their lives, except as a diversion from hard work or as a form of social interaction assisting in the development of business networks. Most of these males had not become more sensitized to changing norms around sexual or gender identities since migration and had been able to protect the traditional patriarchy by remaining culturally insular during the settlement process. In a few cases, there had been a change in the domestic division of labor, but most of these males preferred to be the sole provider and were ambivalent about spouses working. Even the younger males who saw some economic necessity for their spouses working had negative attitudes to this activity. Previous migration experiences, especially for those who migrated elsewhere for educational purposes, appeared to be significant for those males who played sport and engaged in sexual activity with non-Chinese women. Most of these males, however, had returned to more traditional Chinese male practices in terms of involvement with Chinese women, sexual conservativeness, and being the sole provider. The diaspora for many of these males was a significant influence.

Except for the gay males, the Chinese men in this study placed no emphasis on large and well-muscled bodies or gender and sexual identities, and the Western concept of masculinity has little applicability for them. In most cases, these Chinese men in Australia appeared to be different from their Asian American peers (Chan, 2001), who seemed to be more sensitized to hegemonic sexual and gender identities.

The results of this study clearly demonstrated that a new sociology of masculinities must employ concepts that display a greater cultural awareness and sensitivity to the nuances of cultural difference. Otherwise, masculinity studies will remain ethnocentric and, on the whole, will be applicable to less than 5% of men (Connell, 1995). Further, I am convinced that this new direction must be led by work that concentrates on the subjective experiences of men in the context of their lived worlds in order to avoid the decontextualization of notions of identity.

A Study Comparing a Younger Chinese (Taiwanese) Sample and Older Chinese Males

In the second study, a sample of Taiwanese young people (average age 25 years) was used, and the data were then compared with the earlier study of 40 Chinese males (average age 38 years) from a diversity of country of origins (Hibbins, 2006). A purpose of this comparison was to explore the ways experiences of being an "immigrant" change over time. Specifically, the second study focused on the effects of transnationalism on the identities of these young Taiwanese people, rather than the effects of migration on male gender identity that had been the focus of the earlier study. All of the Taiwanese young people were permanent residents and had arrived more recently than the sample of Chinese males who had lived in Australia for between 2 and 40 years.

In both studies, *memories of home* (generally place of birth), customs, and cultural traditions were reinforced by an attraction to popular culture and mass media, either from place of origin or produced locally. There was a strong preference for videos, DVDs, movies and music with Chinese, Taiwanese, Asian, or Japanese influences (Hibbins, 2005) among the migrant men as a whole. However, among the younger men and the more permanently settled Chinese males, community-based leisure included karaoke, yum cha, and mah-jongg, as well as other activities such as attending church, shopping for groceries, or playing social sports. These could be seen as *community moments* (Raj, 2003), since they were contexts where people clustered and experienced collective feelings. The younger Taiwanese, however, were more inclined to go clubbing with their mixed ethnic friends than were the males in the older sample, suggesting a sharing of tastes in music and dance across ethnic divides.

Fragments of the past (Samuel & Thompson, 1990) also emerged in the interviews, for example, when older Chinese male migrants talked about childhood games, relationships with parents and siblings, friendships at school, workplace relations, and the Cultural Revolution, especially in terms of its effects on families. In addition, responses were often linked to particular aspects of gender behavior, like the effect of the frequent absence of fathers and the importance of grandparents, rather than explicitly linked to memories of home, ethnicity, or nation. These fragments of the past also provided a context for these men to talk about changes in their identities as a result of migration.

The young Taiwanese people identified themselves as either Taiwanese or Taiwanese Australian (Hibbins, 2006). They still retained mainly Taiwanese friends, so their social and physical contexts also enabled them to evoke memories of their place of origin (Samuel & Thompson, 1990). However, the linking of memories of home to identity was less evident among the young Taiwanese compared to the older generation of Chinese males. Another generational difference between the two samples was the preparedness to use participation in local sports as a way of developing social and cultural capital in the process of acculturation. This was typical of the young Taiwanese. The actual playing of local sports seemed secondary to having an opportunity to learn about Australian culture and mores. The older Chinese males, on the other hand, played social sports (rather than competitive and structured sports) usually with older males of similar ethnic backgrounds, to learn about business opportunities inside and outside the Chinese community.

Social events at work were also problematic for the migrants, particularly for the Chinese men. These older men found the non-Chinese workplace to be less hierarchical and more collaborative than what they experienced traditionally, although they did feel a need to be super-productive and to prove themselves in this new environment (Hibbins, 2005). However, they faced greater difficulties related to informal leisure activities at work. For example, Chinese engineers were not comfortable with the happy hours in their workplaces, where participants spent time telling sexist jokes, drinking heavily, and conversing about sports and sexual performance. They either absented themselves from the event, or attended but interacted socially only with Chinese colleagues or pretended to be drinking. These types of leisure spaces may be particularly significant in terms of the meeting of different masculinities and may have an influence on the social identity of male migrant workers.

Future Directions

My research has suggested a number of issues that need to be addressed in future research on gender identity and the reconstructing of masculinities through migration and transnational leisure spaces. Of particular interest for future work are generational differences between older migrant males and their offspring, especially their sons. Exploration of the interactions between older and younger males in the (re)constructions of masculinities is needed. The effects of acculturation on both groups of males should be considered. I predict that notions of hegemonic masculinity will be challenged in these new households, and this may be influenced by the presence or absence of older males in the family. The influence of the females entering the workforce is of interest too, because this may also affect gendered relations of power within the family. The centrality of work and family may be questioned by the new generations of immigrants, and this, in turn, may have implications for gender as well as for the constructions of gender identities.

Of equal significance to future research is the effect of transnationalism and the emergence of the global workplace on the development of what I shall call the "global man." The global man moves easily within and across cultures, is multilingual, has multiple passports, is urbane, and claims no particular culture or nation as home. In the global man, we may be able to see the intersections of cultural, social, and economic capitals on power relations in the corporation, in the domestic sphere, and also in leisure. This raises the question of the importance of the intercultural and cross-cultural influences in comparison with the monocultural influences on reconstructions of masculinity and the challenges to traditional hegemonic masculinity. The increasing geographic mobility of undergraduate and postgraduate students, especially those taking MBAs, could well commence this process of change. I am witnessing, however, something that may counter this, and that is an emergence of literature out of Asia surrounding the sexual activities of transnational businessmen who are predatory and highly exploitative of women. This suggests a reinforcement of hegemonic masculinities. These are some of the paradoxical issues and complex, but potentially significant, influences on male gender identities.

Several times in this chapter, reference has been made to the importance of the use of culturally sensitive concepts in studies of constructions of gender identities across cultures. Such cultural sensitivity presents a challenge to comparative studies and is particularly relevant in studies of the subjective accounts of the lived experiences of men in global marketplaces.

Finally, the importance of sexuality as it intersects gender and ethnicity among transnational and migrant males needs further exploration. My research has indicated that homosexual Asian migrant males still enjoy the patriarchal dividend, have similar constructions about the body and the importance of sexual performance as their Western heterosexual counterparts, hierarchicalize gay males by ethnicity, and enjoy the company and interests of women, but still have similar expectations about the status of women as do heterosexual, hegemonically masculine males (see also the chapters by Lyons and Johnson, this volume). Of particular interest for future research is the influence of the intersection of sexuality, ethnicity, and gender in transnational leisure spaces.

Despite the insights provided by the scholarship of gender studies and masculinities, male dominance in corporate salary scales, in leisure time within the family, in coverage given to sports in the popular media, and in positions of power in traditional professions and politics continues; the number of deaths of young males through military action, street violence, and other dangerous activities remains high; and the majority of men remain unwilling to challenge the "patriarchal bargain." This chapter suggests, though, that global leisure spaces may have a variety of influences on gender identities, on masculine gender display (McMahon, 1999), and on the construction and reconstruction of masculinities.

REFERENCES

Antze, P., & Lambek, M. (Eds.) (1996). *Tense past: Cultural essays in trauma and memory.* New York, NY: Routledge.

Chan, J. (2001). *Chinese American masculinities: From Fu Manchu to Bruce Lee.* New York, NY: Routledge.

Connell, R. W. (1987). *Gender and power.* Sydney, Australia: Allen & Unwin.

Connell, R. W. (1995). *Masculinities.* Sydney, Australia: Allen & Unwin.

Connell, R. W. (2003). Introduction: Australian masculinities. In S. Tomsen & M. Donaldson (Eds.), *Male trouble: Looking at Australian masculinities* (pp. 9–21). North Melbourne, Australia: Pluto.

Donaldson, M., Hibbins, R., Howson, R., & Pease, B. (Eds.) (2009). *Migrant men: Critical studies of masculinities and the migration experience.* New York, NY: Routledge.

Edgar, D. (1997). *Men, mateship and marriage: Exploring macho myths and the way forward*. Sydney, Australia: Harper Collins.

Hargreaves, J. A. (1994). *Sporting females: Critical essays in the history and sociology of women's sports*. London, UK: Routledge.

Hibbins, R. (2003). Male gender identities among Chinese male migrants. In K. Louie & M. Low (Eds.), *Asian masculinities* (pp. 197–214). London, UK: Routledge.

Hibbins, R. (2005). Migration and gender identity among Chinese skilled male migrants in Australia. *Geoforum, 36*, 167–180.

Hibbins, R. (2006). Leisure and identity formation among young Taiwanese transnational migrants. In World Leisure Organisation & Leisure Board of Malmo (Eds.), *Bowling together: Seven articles from the Malmo Conference* (pp. 25–38). Malmo: Textbryan.

Hibbins, R. (2009). "Home is where my family is": Intergenerational differences in constructions of belongingness in the Chinese diaspora in Australia. *Annals of Leisure and Recreation Research, 5*, 1–30.

Howson, R. (2009). Theorising hegemonic masculinity: Contradictions, hegemony and dislocation. In M. Donaldson, R. Hibbins, R. Howson, & B. Pease (Eds.), *Migrant men: Critical studies of masculinities and the migration experience* (pp. 23–40). New York, NY: Routledge.

Louie, K., & Low, M. (Eds.) (2003). *Asian masculinities: The meaning and practice of manhood in China and Japan*. London, UK: Routledge

McKay, J., Messner, M. A., & Sabo, D. (Eds.) (2000). *Masculinities, gender relations and sport*. Thousand Oaks, CA: Sage.

McMahon, A. (1999). *Taking care of men: Sexual politics in the public mind*. Cambridge, UK: Cambridge University Press.

Pessar, P. (2003). Transnational migration: Bringing gender. *The International Migration Review, 37*(3), 812–846.

Raj, D. S. (2003). *Where are you from? Middle-class migrants in the modern world*. Berkeley, CA: University of California Press.

Samuel, R., & Thompson, P. (Eds.) (1990). *The myths we live by*. London, UK: Routledge.

Wearing, B. M., & Wearing, S. L. (1990). "Leisure for all," gender and leisure policy. In D. Rowe & G. Lawrence (Eds.), *Sport and leisure: Trends in Australian popular culture* (pp. 161–190). Sydney, Australia: Harcourt, Brace, & Janovich.

CHAPTER 34
GENDER EQUITY AND GOVERNMENT POLICY: AN ANALYSIS OF TITLE IX

AMANDA L. PAULE-KOBA

WHAT IS TITLE IX?

Title IX is a United States federal law designed to prohibit sex/gender discrimination in educational institutions. The law is part of the Education Amendments of 1972 and states that "No person in the United States shall, on the basis of sex, be excluded from participation in, be denied the benefits of, or be subjected to discrimination under any education program or activity receiving federal financial assistance" (Office of Civil Rights, 1979, p. 3). Since nearly every public educational institution (including high schools, colleges, and universities) in the United States is a recipient of federal funds and, thus, is required to comply with Title IX (Reith, 2004), this amendment changed the landscape of education and athletics for men and women across the United States. It is important to note that in this chapter, the term "athletics" refers to sport and competitive sport and not just track and field, as is sometimes the case in other countries. This chapter examines the impact of this legislation on equity, including the provision of sport opportunities, and—more importantly—the reactions of different communities to the changes that occurred as a result of the legislation.

Analyzing the impact of this specific legislation is complex because the idea for Title IX grew and developed over a period of time. The Civil Rights movement of the 1950s and 1960s laid the framework for creating equality between the sexes. Several members of the United States House of Representatives, Martha Griffiths (Michigan) and Edith Green (Tennessee), along with Bernice Sandler (commonly known as the Godmother of Title IX), were instrumental in the debate about equality between men and women. They claimed that women were being discriminated against throughout higher education. The legislators borrowed the language that was used in Title IX from the Civil Rights legislation, which stated, "no person in the United States shall, on the ground of race, color, or national origin, be excluded from participation in, be denied the benefits of, or be subjected to discrimination under any program or activity receiving federal financial assistance" (Title VI of the Civil Rights Act, 1964, p. 1). The discussions and hearings associated with Title IX were held in June and July of 1970, and they focused predominantly on the hiring of women in higher education and women's access to advanced degrees. Sports, specifically football, were brought up in a brief moment but then the discussion returned to higher education as a whole. The House and the Senate approved early versions of the law in 1971.

Title IX was officially enacted on June 23, 1972, when President Nixon signed the law. The law extended beyond higher education and demanded equality in all levels of education. This version of the act covered drama, band, home economics, Spanish club, and all other curricular and extra-curricular activities associated with school. However, in the 1972 law there was no mention of athletics or athletic programs. In 1974, the government deliberated about how and whether to apply Title IX to athletics. It was not until 1979 that the Office for Civil Rights, the governing organization that enforces Title IX, created an Intercollegiate Athletics Policy Interpretation. This policy was issued on December 11, 1979, and it continues to be in effect today (Arens, 1999; Gavora, 2002).

According to Title IX legislation, schools and/or institutions do not have to have the same men's and women's sports, but they do need to offer equal participation opportunities for men and women. In addition, schools are required to give the same resources and consideration to female and male athletes in regards to scheduling of games and practice times, equipment and locker rooms, travel and daily allowances, access to tutoring, coaching, locker rooms, facilities, medical and training facilities and services, publicity and promotions, recruitment of athletes, and support services (Bonnette, 2000; Reith, 2004).

Providing equivalent resources for men's and women's teams is just one small part of Title IX. In order for institutions to be in compliance with Title IX, they are also required to meet one of three prongs. The first prong is proportionality. The proportionality prong asserts that the percentage of female and male athletes has to be within 1% of the percentage of female and male undergraduate students at the institution (Simon, 2001).

The second prong states that an institution is in compliance with Title IX if they can demonstrate a history and continuing practice of program expansion for the underrepresented gender. This prong allows institutions to prove that they have made, and are continuing to make, advances toward equality in athletics (de Varona & Foudy, 2002). Program expansion refers to the addition of female athletes on existing teams or the addition of women's teams at the institution and not the addition of walk-ons to existing women's teams solely for the sake of raising the number of female athletes (Bonnette, 2000). For example, you cannot have 50 women on a women's volleyball team.

The third prong requires an institution to demonstrate that it is effectively accommodating the interests of the underrepresented gender. This prong allows institutions to "customize equal opportunity requirements to their own campuses, by providing a lower level of opportunity to women where that lower level nonetheless satisfies the interests and abilities that exist" (de Varona & Foudy, 2002, p. 5). In other words, an institution can have a lower percentage of women participating in athletics if they can prove that there is no interest in creating women's teams or if they offer some women's sports and the institution believes (and can prove) there are no other varsity sports in which women want to partake.

Failure to comply with Title IX can result in the loss of all federal funding for the institution. The institutions that have been found in breach of Title IX have all arranged to accept specific plans to work toward compliance rather than having their federal funding eliminated. However, these institutions are continually monitored to ensure that they are in fact meeting the guidelines in the plan to gain compliance (Reith, 2004).

While meeting one of these prongs may seem simple, it is important to understand the structure of high school and collegiate sport in the United States. First, men's sports, specifically football and basketball, have always dominated funding, media coverage, and associated resources. Second, competitive sports in high schools and colleges are very important, highly regarded, and can be a place for community interaction. Finally, there are only a few programs that generate revenue for their institution.

High school sports are used by some athletes as a place to showcase their skills in hopes of being recruited to play collegiate sport. The National Collegiate Athletic Association (NCAA) recruitment process is multilayered and consists of many rules that coaches and athletes must follow. The end goal for many of these athletes is to receive an athletic scholarship that will pay for all or part of their college education. Thus, sport can provide the means to obtain a college education for some athletes. Further, in some sports, playing collegiate sport is the "feeder system" into recruitment into professional sport. Historically, those who have traditionally had the opportunity to obtain a scholarship were men. When Title IX was created, this new policy was designed to bring about gender equity not just in participation opportunities but in other areas, such as comparable facilities and resources, including recruitment and scholarship monies.

Title IX provided the foundation for greater opportunities for girls and women in athletics. Prior to the creation and passage of Title IX in 1972, there were only 32,000 women participating in collegiate athletics across the country (United States General Accounting Office, 2001). By 2008, that number had increased to 178,084 women (DeHass, 2009). In addition, in 1978, colleges and universities in the United States offered an average of 5.61 sports per school for women. By 2008, that number had improved to an all-time average high of 8.65 women's sports per school (Acosta & Carpenter, 2008). Further, between the years of 1998 and 2008, 2,775 new women's varsity athletic teams were added at colleges across the United States (Acosta & Carpenter, 2008).

In addition, since the enactment of Title IX, women's athletics at the collegiate level have received more scholarship dollars, increased recruiting and travel budgets, and had access to facilities that are more equivalent to those of men's athletics (Acosta & Carpenter, 2008; Bryjak, 2000). The increase in financial support and other resources for women's teams has improved the visibility of women's collegiate sports.

However, regardless of these many changes and gains, women's athletics still receive fewer scholarship dollars, smaller recruiting budgets and operating expenses, and lower salaries for coaches than their men's athletics counterparts (Kennedy, 2006). For example, in 2002, 54% of all college students were female; however, female athletic programs on average received only 36% of athletic departments' operating budgets. During the 2002–2003 academic year, "women received 42 percent of athletic scholarships, which in actual dollars amounted to $133 million less than men received" (Carpenter & Acosta, 2005, p. 177). In addition, during this same academic year, Division I-A institutions spent an average of $369,200 for the recruiting budget of men's sports, while women's sports received on average a recruiting budget of $159,300 (Carpenter & Acosta, 2005).

BLAMING THE VICTIM

The gains for women and girls under Title IX have been remarkable, but the law still has its detractors, who argue that the gains for women have come at the expense of men (Gavora, 2002). Those groups who believe that Title IX is responsible for the loss of opportunities for men at the collegiate level also blame the law for the regulations being placed upon collegiate athletic teams (Gavora, 2002; Mott, 1995; Zapler, 1995). In 1987, Sage argued that the NCAA was partly to blame for this problem because they had refused to confront the problem head on and instead framed the problem in the context of "blaming the victim." Blaming the victim involves making those individuals or groups with the least amount of power culpable for the injustices and wrongdoings that have occurred (Sage, 1987; Staurowsky, 1996)—in the case of interscholastic and intercollegiate sport, this meant blaming girls and women (those most disadvantaged to begin with) for the changes in boy's/men's sport. In the process of blaming the victim, the situation is reconstructed so that men appear to be the victims of women and of a law that leaves men seemingly vulnerable and powerless.

According to Staurowsky (1996), supporters of men's athletics do not focus on the fact of budget cuts in universities, increases in men's participation numbers, and the fact that a significant number of men's teams (specifically wrestling) were being eliminated before Title IX was being applied to athletics due to budgetary constraints. Instead these individuals blame women for the elimination of specific men's athletic teams, rather than the individuals who make these decisions at the university level (i.e., university presidents, athletic directors, members of the board of regents, etc.). It is easier, Staurowsky argues, to blame women than to blame senior university administrators. It is ironic that those people who believe Title IX legislation and women are hurting men's sports rarely mention the actions of athletic directors who are actually cutting the programs or refusing to consider creative alternatives (Staurowsky, 1996).

By framing men as the victims of Title IX, attention is taken away from the women who have been denied sporting opportunities for years. Further, by creating a dynamic of male athletes as victims and females as victimizers, the group that would ordinarily be thought of as the victims because of their underrepresented status (i.e., female athletes) is transformed into a group that is seen to be privileged, treated preferentially, and in control (Staurowsky, 1996). In the odd twist or paradox of how relations of power work, men are advantaged by appearing as the victim based on the idea that Title IX is unjust and is hurting men's chances to play sport.

RESEARCH IN TITLE IX AND GENDER EQUITY

As a young scholar studying in the area of gender equity, I first became interested in this topic when I observed the discourse surrounding Title IX and gender equity in sport at the university where I completed my undergraduate and Master's degree. It seemed a contradiction to me that gender-equity legislation could both promote opportunities for women, but also reproduce dominant gender ideologies. I conducted two research studies that examined the issues of Title IX and gender equity in athletics. These studies, *Community Perceptions of Title IX* (Paule-Koba, 2004) and *Gender Equity in Recruiting* (Paule-Koba, 2008), examined various issues of gender equity in high school and collegiate athletics.

The first study, *Community Perceptions of Title IX*, examined perceptions of Title IX from the viewpoints of 13 members of a college community that had recently made changes to its athletic programs. The participants in this case consisted of one university athletic administrator, two current collegiate athletes, one former collegiate athlete, two current student non-athletes, two residents of the town in which the university is located, and five head coaches (one of whom was a former collegiate athlete now coaching her former team). In this study, the stories participants told about Title IX included discussions of the role of football in collegiate athletics, the opportunities gained and lost as a result of attempting to achieve gender equity, and Title IX itself.

The second study, *Gender Equity in Recruiting*, examined the Division I intercollegiate athletic recruiting process. Through interviews with 25 head and assistant coaches from 19 universities across the country, insight was acquired into what these coaches believed about various aspects of the recruitment process, including the role of gender in Division I recruiting. Of these 25 coaches that participated in this study, there were 18 head coaches and 7 assistant coaches from 10 different athletic conferences: Atlantic 10, Atlantic Coast Conference, Big East, Big Ten, Big Twelve, Colonial Athletic Association, Mid-American Conference, Pacific 10, Patriot League, and Southeastern Conference. Twenty-one of the coaches were male, while four were female. Female coaches comprised 16% of the coaches in this study, which is comparable to the national proportion of female coaches in intercollegiate athletics (Acosta and Carpenter, 2008).

Qualitative, semi-structured interviews were used to guide these studies (Silverman, 2001). The interviews were recorded by the researcher with the permission of the participants, and the recordings were transcribed verbatim immediately after the interview.

Patton's (1990) strategies for analyzing data were adopted, and for each study a small research team (2–3 individuals) was used to conduct these analyses in order to reduce coding bias. Once all of the interviews were completed and transcribed, two to three individuals began the data-analysis procedure. The process of identifying and constructing themes continued between the research team until all the raw themes were combined to form the main themes.

The research studies revealed that:

1. Men's athletic and leisure opportunities are valued more than women's athletic and leisure opportunities.

2. Those in power reproduce gender ideologies.

3. Blaming Title IX and the victim are still occurring in athletics today.

Men's Athletic and Leisure Opportunities are Valued More than Women's Athletic and Leisure Opportunities

In both of the studies, the results indicated that men's sports and participation opportunities were more important than women's sports and participation opportunities. This was illustrated in the way participants changed the subject from women's sports to men's sports when being asked about opportunities to participate in collegiate athletics and recruiting differences of male and female athletes. For example, when asked about how Title IX has impacted women in the *Community Perceptions of Title IX* study, one community member switched the conversation to how it has impacted men. He stated:

> I am not opposed to things that make sense okay but . . . the perfect example, 200 spots for men, 200 spots for women. One hundred eighty spots get filled by women, the men are reduced to 180, okay . . . how could anybody who is truly being fair say, yes the men and the women have the same number of spots, but if the women can't fill it then the men have to be reduced accordingly.

This was further exemplified by the other participants in the *Community Perceptions of Title IX* study, when they spoke about the negative effects of Title IX on men and suggested that women should go to a school where their sport is offered, and universities should not have to create a sport just for the sake of having another sport for women. This view was illustrated by one of the college students. He believed that programs should not be created for women, and if a woman wanted to play a sport in college, she should go to a school that offered that program. He commented:

> *I don't particularly like it* [Title IX], *because if a girl wants to play basketball somewhere, she should go to a school that has the program available, not just put this program in place to make more programs available to women. All I can think about is women's NCAA basketball. You see the same basketball teams—Connecticut and Tennessee— in the finals all the time. I guess I don't really feel it's necessary.*

In each study, participants discussed the importance of women being able to participate in athletics; however, the participants also felt that women's participation should not come at the "expense" of men and men's athletic programs and opportunities. In fact, the perceived loss of opportunities for men and men's athletic programs because of having to share resources appeared to be the primary concern of many of the participants, while creating greater opportunities for women was secondary. That is, the supposed decrease in opportunities for men seemed to be of greater concern than the improved opportunities for women. This notion helped create and shape the meanings some participants had of Title IX.

Those in Power Reproduce Gender Ideologies

Ideologies are a "system of interdependent ideas that explain and justify particular political, economic, moral, and social conditions and interests, making them seem right or natural" (Sage, 1998, p. 2). Gender ideologies are those ideas related to the social relations between men and women.

In each of the studies of Title IX, those in power (coaches and administrators) could be seen to consistently reproduce the dominant gender ideologies that pervade American society. For example, in the *Community Perceptions of Title IX*, coaches and administrators suggested that when it comes to spectator interest, it would always be greater for men's sports than for women's sports. In their opinion, men are bigger, faster, and stronger, so spectators would rather watch men than women.

One of the participants, a community member, stated that he believed women's sports would never be as popular as men's sports. When asked to explain why he felt this way, he said:

> I just think it's skill level. I just think people want to see people jump really, really high. Anybody who doesn't jump that high, then they want to see a ball hit really, really far, and if it isn't, well, that really doesn't excite them. You know what I mean? It's just the way human nature is. They want to see someone jump a certain distance, throw a ball a certain speed, run a certain speed, hit really hard, you know. I just think that it's a male-dominated world.

For this participant, the "innate" difference in skill was the reason he believed women's sports would never be as popular as men's sports.

Similarly, in the *Gender Equity in Recruiting* study, some of the coaches reproduced gender ideology through their statements about the differences in recruiting male and female athletes. It was suggested that men make smart, well-thought-out decisions, while women are emotional, relying on "gut feelings" and did not make logical decisions based on "facts." These beliefs reproduce gender ideologies (e.g., stereotypes that men are "smarter" than women when it comes to sport) and assume that decisions that take into account emotions/feelings rather than "just facts" are somehow less well-thought-out or logical. In either case, these beliefs place men ahead of women.

An example of this occurring was when a women's basketball coach, who had previously coached men's basketball, discussed how young men and women approach decision-making in recruiting. He stated:

> I think with the girls . . . I think that they make very emotional decisions. Even though you can sit them down at 10 different occasions and tell them to list the positives and negatives of every school that's recruiting them. When it really comes down to making a decision, they rarely ever look at that list and make it with their gut.

In contrast, this coach believed that men made decisions very differently. He commented:

> I think the men make decisions much more . . . they're much less emotional and much more cut and dry. I think they make decisions based on a program's success. They make decisions based on things that are more tangible: media exposure, times on television.

These thoughts reproduce the gender ideologies and stereotypes that pervade American society, affecting how individual men and women think of themselves and others. As Coakley has argued, "sports [in American society] are sites for reaffirming beliefs about male/female difference and valorizing masculine characteristics. At the same time, women's sports often are marginalized because they are not seen as 'real' or as good as men's sports" (Coakley, 2007, p. 265).

Blaming Title IX and the Victim Are Still Occurring in Athletics Today

The third theme, consistent with the literature examined (e.g., Staurowsky, 1996), is about how female athletes are still being blamed for perceived inequalities that Title IX has created for male athletes. In the *Community Perceptions of Title IX* study, a former university athlete talked about Title IX in a way that favored men's athletics and marginalized women's athletics. She discussed the many opportunities she received due to Title IX, but then argued that Title IX is reverse discrimination because she, as a female, was able to play her sport in college. That is, she framed her brother's inability to play his sport because it was designated a "minor" sport and had been eliminated, as the inequality. In other words, during her interview this participant reasoned that while it was important for women to have athletic opportunities, they have been given "too much" opportunity because her brother and some of her male friends could not play their sport. That is, it was more important that her brother/these males be able to participate in his/their chosen sport than for females to have equal opportunity. She commented:

> I believe that it's good. I believe that I couldn't have been doing anything I am doing today or anything I have done in the past without it. I'm thankful that in 1972, it was brought about. I don't like how it's been misinterpreted lately. I don't like how it's giving me and my teammates and every other girl huge opportunities, I mean enormous opportunities. But my brother and my [male] friends, they're not getting the same opportunities as I am. I feel like it's totally doing the opposite of what it was intended to do. It has to be mended somehow, because it is flat out reverse discrimination when you're telling me that I can play because I'm a girl but my brother can't because he's a guy.

Similarly, a current varsity athlete had an interesting perspective about women's sports and Title IX. While she was in favor of Title IX, she also thought that the elimination of men's sports was unfair. She stated:

> I think it's . . . if you look at it in the way that men's sports are getting cut, I think it's unfair toward men sometimes because women's sports don't get cut. It's just the men's sports. So I think that's the only thing that is unfair.

Thus, even some of the women who have benefitted from Title IX believe that the law is unfair because, in their opinion, it discriminates against men. They do not look at it as a law meant to give women equality in all facets of education.

Discussion

The studies discussed in this chapter illustrate the contradictory effects of equity legislation. While Title IX has improved opportunities for women athletes, discourse surrounding this legislation serves to "naturalize" the superiority of men's sport and to devalue women's sport. In addition, this practice of blaming the victim takes the group that would generally be considered to be advantaged (men) and recreates the scenario so that men become victims of both women and the law. This discourse was evident not only among male athletes and coaches but also among female athletes and male and female community members. It also seemed to create some panic related to the elimination of some men's sports, as exemplified by one head coach who talked about the fear that it would be "my program next." A contradiction was also evident in the way that female athletes are not framed as the "victims" with regard to sports opportunities, but as less worthy because of their inferiority to men.

One of the concerns that this raises is whether the discourse among athletes, coaches, and community members can weaken or reduce the benefits that have accrued since Title IX came into effect. Further, since this discourse is evident among people in positions of power and authority (e.g., head coaches and university administrators), it may have a particularly powerful effect on others.

FUTURE RESEARCH DIRECTIONS

The findings of these studies, and especially the practice of making women's sports appear to be inferior and the "blaming of the victim," raise the question of how widespread these beliefs are, and whether they are common throughout the United States. These are questions that could be addressed in future research. In addition, the role that people in leadership positions play is of significance, too. University and community leaders, as well as media producers, play an important role in masking and/or challenging relations of power by how they frame the discourse around equity legislation related to education (in the United States, affirmative action legislation and its impact on college admissions and hiring would be another example). Further, additional research on this topic could lead to insights about how to address social inequalities though legislation—at universities or elsewhere—and how to disrupt discourses that undermine such legislation.

REFERENCES

Acosta, R. V., & Carpenter, L. J. (2008). *Women in intercollegiate sport: A longitudinal, national study thirty-one year update 1977–2008.* Retrieved from www.acostacarpenter.org

Arens, E. (1999). Title IX is Unfair to Men's Sports. In L. Egendorf (Ed.), *Sports and athletes: Opposing views* (pp. 127–135). San Diego, CA: Greenhaven.

Bonnette, V. (2000). *Title IX basics: NCAA achieving gender equity.* Indianapolis, IN: National Collegiate Athletic Association.

Bryjak, G. (2000, July 1). The ongoing controversy over Title IX. *USA Today*, pp. 62–63.

Carpenter, L. J., & Acosta, R. V. (2005). *Title IX*. Champaign, IL: Human Kinetics.

Coakley, J. L. (2007). *Sport and society: Issues and controversies* (9th ed.). Boston, MA: McGraw Hill.

DeHass, D. M. (2009). *NCAA sports sponsorship and participation rates report: 1981–82–2007–08*. Indianapolis, IN: National Collegiate Athletic Association.

de Verona, D., & Foudy, J. (2002). Minority views on the *Report of the Commission on Opportunity in Athletics. Gender Issues, 20*, 31–56.

Gavora, J. (2002). *Tilting the playing field*. San Francisco, CA: Encounter.

Kennedy, C. L. (2006). College sports and Title IX #3. *Gender Issues, 23*, 69–79.

Mott, R. D. (1995, May 10). Congress hears from all sides on Title IX. *NCAA News*, pp. 1, 12.

Office of Civil Rights. (1979). *A policy interpretation: Title IX and intercollegiate athletics*. Retrieved from http://www.ed.gov/print/about/offices/list/ocr/docs/t9interp.html

Patton, M. Q. (1990). *Qualitative evaluations & research methods*. Newbury Park, CA: Sage.

Paule-Koba, A. L. (2004). *Community perceptions of Title IX*. (Unpublished master's thesis). Miami University.

Paule-Koba, A. L. (2008). *The good, the bad, and the ugly: Examining intercollegiate athletic recruiting*. (Unpublished doctoral dissertation), Michigan State University.

Reith, K. (2004). *Playing fair: A guide to Title IX in high school and college sports* (4th ed.). East Meadow, NY: Women's Sports Foundation.

Sage, G. (1987). Blaming the victim: NCAA responds to calls for reform in major college sports. *Arena Review, 11*, 1–11.

Sage, G. H. (1998). *Power and ideology in American sport* (2nd ed.). Champaign, IL: Human Kinetics.

Silverman, D. (2001). *Interpreting qualitative data* (2nd ed.). London, UK: Sage.

Simon, R. (2001). Gender equity and inequity in athletics. In W. Morgan, K. Meier, & A. Scheider (Eds.), *Ethics in sport* (pp. 226–246). Champaign, IL: Human Kinetics.

Staurowsky, E. (1996). Blaming the victim: Resistance in the battle over gender equity in intercollegiate athletics. *Journal of Sport and Social Issues, 20*(2), 194–210.

Title VI of the Civil Rights Act of 1964. 42 U.S.C. § 2000d - 2000d-7 (1964).

United States General Accounting Office. (2011, March). Intercollegiate athletics: Four-year colleges' experiences adding and discontinuing teams. Washington, DC.

Zapler, M. (1995, January 6). Protecting men's sports: U.S. officials to consider complaints that male teams' existence in threatened. *Chronicle of Higher Education*, pp. A43–A44.

Chapter 35
"Developing" Women's and Girls' Participation in Dene Games at the Arctic Winter Games

Audrey R. Giles

As an avid leisure participant and feminist who spent summers during my undergraduate years working in Canada's North, I became interested in the ways in which beliefs pertaining to gender were reflected in one particular type of cultural practice: leisure activities. While in the North, I became aware that Western liberal feminism's ideals are not universal ideals; indeed, the very term "the West" assumes a kind of cultural coherence that is manufactured in such a way as to ignore important differences between and within cultural groups. Development studies and the discipline's associated literature have faced similar critiques—that they are unable to cope with difference. My interest in leisure, the North (particularly Dene culture), and feminist development combined to form the foundation for my doctoral studies, from which this chapter has emerged. In this chapter, I examine attempts at the development of girls' involvement in Dene games in the Northwest Territories (NWT) through the example of the addition of a Junior Girls' category to the Dene games component of the 2004 Arctic Winter Games (AWG). Specifically, I suggest that the difficulties that occurred in attempts at adding a girls' category reflect the conflicts that exist between different groups' perceptions of cultural practices and associated beliefs, and also understandings of gender equity. I examine the events that occurred and explain them in terms of three different feminist development models: women in development, women and development, and gender and development.

Geographic and Historical Context

The Dene are a First Nations group that inhabits a region they refer to as *Denendeh*, which is their homeland in the Canadian western sub-Arctic; together Dene individuals make up the membership of the Dene Nation. The Dene inhabit not only the NWT, but also northern areas of the

Western Canadian provinces. For the purpose of this chapter, however, I have chosen to focus on the NWT. In order to understand the ways in which Dene games (i.e., the games of the Dene) and their development reflect the highly charged political environment that can be found in the NWT, it is first important to conduct a brief examination of the NWT's history.

In general, the NWT has been treated as a colony within Canada. In fact, the NWT's administration operated out of Ottawa, which is thousands of kilometers away, until 1967. Coates (1985) noted that the NWT was largely developed according to the needs of people of European ancestry who lived in the southern parts of Canada and that Aboriginal peoples (First Nations, Inuit, and Métis) have had little opportunity for a say in changes in the region. Indeed, it was not until 1974 that the NWT Act was finally amended to allow for a fully elected Council of NWT residents (Coates & Powell, 1989).

The early Euro-Canadian- and southern-based models of decision-making that marginalized Aboriginal residents' voices in the NWT extended into sport and recreation programs. Paraschak (1985) noted that the government of the NWT had (and still has) a high proportion of workers from southern Canada and that "[s]ince it is government workers who establish the programs and services for recreation, very often those programs end up being based on southern Canadian rather than native standards, even though they are created to meet native needs" (p. 11). The AWG serve as a strong example of just such a program.

Arctic Winter Games (AWG) and the Development of Physical Practices

According to Paraschak (1983), the AWG "were conceived out of frustration by northerners involved in national sports competition" (p. 45) after the NWT and the Yukon were the worst-performing teams at the 1967 Canada Winter Games. The first AWG, a circumpolar sport and cultural festival, which originally included teams from Alaska, the NWT, and the Yukon (but have since grown to include teams from other regions), were held in Yellowknife, NWT in 1970. Sport development has been one of the AWG's primary objectives, as these games provide opportunities for experience in formal competitions for northern-based athletes, coaches, and officials (Paraschak, 1983). The AWGs consist of mostly European-derived sports, such as volleyball, hockey, basketball, curling, indoor soccer, skiing, and snowboarding. Two other categories of sports that are included are the so-called "cultural sports": Dene Games (sports played by the Dene) and Arctic Sports (sports played by the Inuit). Unlike the mainstream sports that are played at the AWG, Dene Games and Arctic Sports have mostly Aboriginal participants.

The Dene Games

Though unpopular throughout southern Canada, Dene games have been played by the Dene since time immemorial. Heine (1999) noted that Dene games were heavily influenced by the connection between travel and life on the land. Strength, endurance, speed, and accuracy were necessary for traveling and hunting on the land and were often practiced by playing traditional games.

Unlike Arctic Sports, which have been a part of the AWG since its inception (albeit as a demonstration sport in the early years), Dene games were only added in 1990. These games were comprised of five events: snow snake, pole push, stick pull, finger pull, and hand games (much like track and field and swimming consist of multiple events). At that time, these events were for senior men only, and thus no boys, girls, or women were able to participate. The inclusion of the Senior Men's category in 1990 and the 2002 debut of a Junior Men's category were accepted with relative ease. However, the same cannot be said of efforts to develop Dene games at the AWG for women and girls, which were plagued with difficulty and conflict.

The difficulties over attempts to include women and girls can be seen to relate not only to gender equity, but also to the role of feminist development models in bringing about social change. When gender equity is not present, as is the case with women's and girls' participation in Dene games, one needs to decide if change is warranted and, if so, how to bring about such change. Feminist development models have been used in many regions throughout the world to bring about such change and, as a result, an examination of them is necessary to understand what they bring to a leisure context. After presenting some of the details of my study, I turn to current debates pertaining to women and development to unpack and understand the emergence of a Junior Girls category in Dene games and to trouble the use of a "women in development" approach to obtaining gender equity.

METHODS

For this research, extensive consultations were conducted with the Aboriginal and non-Aboriginal governments within the Dehcho region of the NWT, as well as with the AWG International Committee, the Government of the NWT (GNWT), and Sport North. To conduct my research, I spent five months in Sambaa K'e/Trout Lake, NWT; four months in Thek'ehdli/

Jean Marie River, NWT; five months in Liidlii Kue/Fort Simpson; and two weeks at the 2004 AWG in the Wood Buffalo Region of Northern Alberta. In the communities, I participated in all aspects of community life, which included recreational activities, and I conducted interviews with a wide variety of community members. While at the AWG, I accompanied the Team NWT's Dene games participants to all of their competitions, spent some leisure time with the athletes, and also interviewed them, their coaches, a judge, and several spectators. In total, 89 individuals were interviewed, occasionally with the help of a trained local interpreter.

ANALYSIS

To understand my results, I analyzed them using three feminist development models. According to Visvanathan (1997), three distinct approaches have shaped and continue to shape development projects aimed at women: women in development (WID), women and development (WAD), and gender and development (GAD). Each of these approaches has been critiqued on various grounds. WID's "add women and stir" approach has been critiqued as only extending liberal discourses without challenging its patriarchal foundations (see chapter 3, this volume). Its successor, WAD, acknowledges that women's work in both the public and private spheres play a central role in the maintenance of social structures and inequality (Visvanathan, 1997). One of the main critiques of WAD is that it fails to address gender relations. GAD's emergence served as a critique of WAD in that it focuses on gender relations and not on women per se, and welcomes the contribution of male allies (Visvanathan, 1997). In particular, GAD scholars have looked at the oppression women experience in the private sphere and have noted that women act as agents of change and resistance and are not passive recipients of aid. As a result, with a GAD perspective, there exists the possibility and goal of transforming gender roles, such as the division of labor (Parpart & Marchand, 1995), as well as a fundamental reexamination of politics, institutions, social structures, and hierarchical gender relations (Rathgeber, 1995).

FINDINGS

Despite the fact that Dene games are quite popular in the NWT and have been played at annual Dene gatherings since time immemorial, by 2004, a Territorial Sport Organization for Dene Games had yet to emerge. As a result, the organization of Dene games for the AWG has been done on an ad hoc basis, with different groups of people taking the reins at different times. In 2002, a group calling itself the Denendeh Traditional Games

Association held a founding annual general meeting with the hopes of organizing something very similar to a Territorial Sport Organization. Ian Legaree, Director of the Sport, Recreation, and Youth Division of the Department of Municipal and Community Affairs (MACA) at the Government of the NWT explained,

> [i]t doesn't happen often, but when there's a group forming that wants to become a new [Territorial Sport Organization], the Department will typically fund a founding AGM for them, which we did with that association, and they had that founding AGM. Then they made some policy announcements that were contrary to Government policy and we subsequently withdrew our support. If they choose to . . . come back together and get themselves organized again, they can apply to Sport North like any [Territorial Sport Organization] does for funding support. (I. Legaree, personal communication, Jan. 29, 2004)

Importantly, though, the DTGA did not want to be like any other Territorial Sport Organization, and the policy announcements that it made illustrated that very point. As an Aboriginal organization, its founders wanted it to exist outside of the confines of Sport North, and they wanted their beliefs, in this case, that women should not participate in Dene Games, to be honored (Kay, 2002).

Despite opposition from members of the DTGA, in 2004 the AWG International Committee added a Junior Girls category to the Dene games component of the AWG. The junior girls competed in the same events as the senior men and junior men: stick pull, hand games, snowsnake, finger pull, and pole push. While some viewed the addition as a move towards gender equity, others believed that the addition ran against tradition and was thus wrong. Understanding the traditions behind girls' and women's exclusion thus became a major focus for my research.

Through my research I learned that in the past in the NWT, Dene games were played almost exclusively by men (Giles, 2004, 2005a, 2005b; Heine, 1999; Helm & Lurie, 1966). Although some examples of women's participation have been documented (e.g., Giles, 2005a), women's past involvement in Dene games, particularly a form of stick gambling known as hand games, was rare and to this day continues to be quite limited. I found that explanations for women's limited involvement in Dene games focused on two issues related to menstruation: power and pollution.

Menstrual practices and beliefs among the Dene have been documented by a number of authors (Abel, 1993; Giles, 2004, 2005a, 2005b; Goulet, 1998; Helm, 2000). In the past, Dene girls went through rites of passage when they had their first menses. Suza Tsetso, a Dene resident of Liidlii Kue/Fort Simpson who is an acknowledged cultural expert, explained that in the past at the start of her first period, a girl would build a shelter and stay in that shelter for up to a year. Relatives would go over to that spot and teach her the skills needed to be a Dene woman. Upon her return to the community, there would be a large celebration. For subsequent menstrual periods, girls and women would stay in one spot (either in the hut, or, later when homes were built, at home) and have separate dishes from the rest of her family. In many places in the NWT, menstrual practices have become less prevalent or less stringent. Nevertheless, though they are rarely practiced in other communities, residents of Sambaa K'e/ Trout Lake continue to follow several practices relating to menstruation, such as not participating in aquatic-based activities, eating fish, birds, or berries, or going anywhere they "don't have to" when menstruating (Giles, 2004).

Residents of Sambaa K'e/Trout Lake, Liidlii Kue/Fort Simpson, and Tthedzehk'edeli/Jean Marie River primarily drew on discourses of both pollution and power associated with menstrual practices as reasons why women have rarely participated in Dene games—especially hand games. Male participants in hand games are said to draw on their medicine power to have a favorable influence on the outcome of the game. Some research participants informed me that if a man were to come in contact with a menstruating woman in the context of hand games, it would have a negative impact on his hunting abilities (i.e., the pollution hypothesis). Others had a slightly different view. Suza Tsetso explained, "the woman has the power to give life and during that time when she's on her menstrual cycle, she has the power to take it . . . [at that time] you're closer to the spirit world than you are at your regular time" (Personal communication, Feb. 12, 2004). Thus, according to this view, women's medicine power is *stronger* than men's and, in order to keep the men safe, women abstain from participating in Dene games (i.e., the power hypothesis). In both cases, women's medicine power is seen as being in conflict with men's. In order to eliminate the conflict, in the past women would not participate in Dene games at all. The junior girls' participation in Dene games at the AWG thus represented for some a lack of respect of not only their own medicine power, but also of men's. Others, however, felt that it was entirely appropriate for girls to participate and believed that the traditions were outdated and that medicine power was no longer relevant to their lives.

Though there appeared to be a general level of agreement among research participants on the basic elements of menstrual practices, the extent and application of the practices themselves and the beliefs (e.g., power versus pollution versus relevance) behind them differed. It was evident that there was a continuum for the degree to which individuals within communities engage in menstrual practices and beliefs. As a result of the differences between and within communities and individuals pertaining to menstrual traditions, it becomes difficult to create rules and policies for Dene games that will recognize everyone's practices and beliefs. Finding ways in which to "develop" Dene games for women and girls thus becomes difficult.

Discussion

One of the pressing questions for leisure studies scholars and practitioners is, "how can we develop leisure programs and opportunities that are meaningful and desirable for a wide range of women?" I argue that the answers to these questions can be found in feminist development theory and practice. Feminist leisure development initiatives and those who implement them need to be cognizant of non-Western ways of knowing, their associated cultural practices, and the ways in which politics and power relations (between, for example, men and women, Indigenous and non-Indigenous peoples, governmental and non-governmental organizations) are embedded within something as seemingly apolitical as Dene games. I suggest that a postmodern and postcolonial approach (consistent with the GAD model) is one that ought to be used to provide direction in the creation of programs that address the challenges put forth by a postmodern world (see chapter 3, this volume).

The addition of the Junior Girls category to the AWG has generally taken a WID "add women and stir" approach, as girls now compete in the same events as boys and men. As a result, the addition does little or nothing to challenge existing power structures, and fails to pay attention to the reasons why girls and women are not participating in the first place. As a result, I argue that a different approach is necessary.

Postmodernism

In calling for a fundamental reexamination of many aspects of development, including gender, some development scholars and practitioners have begun to adopt a postmodern approach towards feminist development theory (e.g., Barriteau, 1995; Parpart & Marchand, 1995). Postmodernism's contributions to feminist development theory include critiques of modernity, Western universalism, and dualist/binary thinking, interrogations of power relations, and the surfacing of previously marginalized knowledge (Parpart, 1995). In particular, postmodernism's acknowledgment of difference between and within women is useful in creating development frameworks that are capable of dealing with the fact that, as Nzomo (1995) pointed out, "[g]ender subordination is . . . not uniformly experienced by all women in the same way with the same intensity at all times" (p. 136). Despite critiques that a postmodern attention to difference can result in the dilution of power, Barriteau (1995) has contended that a focus on the fluid nature of social relations and identities can result in coalition politics.

One of the great strengths of a postmodern GAD approach is that it can be used in conjunction with postcolonial theory. This is especially important for leisure development models that will be used with and applied to indigenous populations in Canada's North. According to McEwan (2001), "postcolonialism, like feminism, is a powerful critique of 'development'" (p. 94). As McEwan noted, postcolonial critiques are able to destabilize the dominant discourses of colonialism, including development, trouble the ways in which the world is and can be known, and can be used in attempts to recover "the lost historical and contemporary voices of the marginalized, the oppressed and the dominated, through a radical reconstruction of history and knowledge production" (p. 95). As a result, a postmodern GAD approach is able to provide a powerful critique of colonialism—a critique that is missing from WID and WAD. Through a postmodern and postcolonial GAD perspective, menstrual practices would not be viewed as impediments to "progress" and "development," but instead as important cultural practices that need to be acknowledged and brought into consideration when Dene games are being organized and delivered.

A postmodern and postcolonial GAD approach would also be able to acknowledge that there is no one right answer or approach to Dene games. By examining power relations and failing to attempt to meet a supposed universal standard (e.g., Western liberal notions of gender equity), such an approach opens up space for multiple interpretations of issues, while simultaneously allowing for the acknowledgment of the multifaceted, multilayered power relations at work. For example, it would be relatively easy to portray the issue of women's involvement in Dene games as relating only to issues of sexism/gender equity. As Ian Legaree from the Government of the NWT put it, "[the Denendeh Traditional Games Association] said no women, so no women means no support from the Government [of the NWT]" (Personal communication, Jan. 29, 2004). In a careful postmodern and postcolonial GAD reading of this statement, however, we also learn that Government of the NWT officials have the ability to exercise financial power over Aboriginal groups and also to direct the development of women's and girls' involvement in Dene games. Thus, women's involvement in Dene games becomes not only an issue of potential sexism and power relations between men and women, but also an issue of political struggles for cultural self-determination and unequal power relations between Aboriginal peoples and the GNWT, both of which are closely tied to/ remnants of colonialism.

A postmodern and postcolonial GAD framework could be used to bring about several changes in Dene games at the AWG. For example, it might be used to advocate for the inclusion of women, not just girls. It could also result in the addition of typically "women's games" (e.g., moose-hide ball games) to the current list of events offered, which would decenter male-dominated games as the only form of legitimate Dene games at the AWG. The use of substitutes for menstruating players or players who do not want to compete in certain events due to spiritual beliefs could also occur. Such an approach could also be used to advocate for the omission of gendered categories entirely. Importantly, at an organizational/administrative level, a postmodern and postcolonial GAD approach would result in the examination of power and political relations among men and women, the government of the NWT, Sport North, and Aboriginal organizations and would ensure that all organizations were involved in decision-making processes.

CONCLUSIONS

My research on girls' and women's involvement in Dene games made me realize the extent to which our understandings of gender and gender equity are rooted in culture, place, and society. I have gained a deep appreciation for the pitfalls involved in attempts to develop Aboriginal people's involvement in various activities in a manner that involves little to no consultation with stakeholders (i.e., Aboriginal peoples themselves) and which seek to merely transplant and develop programs/initiatives from southern Canada into a northern context.

Though not a panacea, I believe that a postmodern and postcolonial GAD approach enables the identification and appreciation of differences that are not offered by other feminist approaches to development. Such efforts will allow Dene games development initiatives once and for all to move beyond "add women and stir."

REFERENCES

Abel, K. (1993). *Drum songs: Glimpses of Dene history*. Montreal, QC: McGill-Queen's Press.

Barriteau, E. (1995). Postmodernist feminist theorizing and development policy and practice in the Anglophone Caribbean: The Barbados case. In M. Marchand & J. Parpart (Eds.), *Feminism/postmodernism/development* (pp. 142–158). New York, NY: Routledge.

Coates, K. (1985). *Canada's colonies: A history of the Yukon and the Northwest Territories*. Toronto, ON: James Lorimer.

Coates, K., & Powell, J. (1989). *The modern north: People, politics, and the rejection of colonialism*. Toronto, ON: James Lorimer.

Giles, A. R. (2004). Kevlar, Crisco, and menstruation: "Tradition" and Dene Games. *Sociology of Sport Journal, 21*(1), 18–35.

Giles, A. R. (2005a). A Foucaultian approach to menstrual practices in the Dehcho, Northwest Territories, Canada. *Arctic Anthropology, 24*(2), 9–21.

Giles, A. R. (2005b). The acculturation matrix and the politics of difference: Women and Dene games. *Canadian Journal of Native Studies, XXV*(1), 341–358.

Goulet, J.-G. (1998). *Ways of knowing: Experience, knowledge, and power among the Dene Tha*. Vancouver, BC: University of British Columbia Press.

Heine, M. (1999). *Dene Games: A culture and resource manual*. Yellowknife, NWT: The Sport North Federation & MACA (GNWT).

Helm, J. (2000). *The people of Denendeh: Ethnohistory of the Indians of Canada's Northwest Territories*. Montreal, QC: McGill-Queen's Press.

Helm, J., & Lurie, N. O. (1966). *The dogrib hand game*. National Museum of Canada Bulletin 205. Ottawa, ON: National Museum of Canada.

Kay, C. (2002, June 17). Tradition gains the upper hand. *News/North*, p. B19.

Legaree, I. (2004, January 29). Personal communication.

McEwan, C. (2001). Postcolonialism, feminism and development: intersections and dilemmas. *Progress in Development Studies, 1*(2), 93–111.

Nzomo, M. (1995). Women and democratization struggles in Africa: What relevance to post-modernist discourse? In M. Marchand & J. Parpart (Eds.), *Feminism/postmodernism/development* (pp. 127–130). New York, NY: Routledge.

Paraschak, V. (1983). *Discrepancies between government programs and community practices: The case of recreation in the Northwest Territories.* (Unpublished doctoral dissertation). University of Alberta, Edmonton.

Paraschak, V. (1985). A look at government's role in recreation in the Northwest Territories. In M. J. Patterson (Ed.), *Collected papers on the human history of the Northwest Territories* (pp. 11–27). Yellowknife, NWT: Prince of Wales Northern Heritage Centre.

Parpart, J. (1995). Deconstructing the development "expert": Gender, development and the "vulnerable groups." In M. Marchand & J. Parpart (Eds.), *Feminism/postmodernism/development* (pp. 221–243). New York, NY: Routledge.

Parpart, J., & Marchand, M. M. (1995). Exploding the canon: An introduction/conclusion. In M. Marchand & J. Parpart (Eds.), *Feminism/postmodernism/development* (pp. 1–22). New York, NY: Routledge.

Rathgeber, E. M. (1995). Gender and development in action. In M. Marchand & J. Parpart (Eds.), *Feminism/postmodernism/development* (pp. 204–220). New York, NY: Routledge.

Tsetso, S. (2004, February 12). Personal communication.

Visvanathan, N. (1997). Introduction to part 1. In N. Visvanathan, L. Duggan, N. Nisonoff, & N. Wiegersma (Eds.), *The women, gender and development reader* (pp. 1–32). Halifax, NS: Fernwood.

Chapter 36

Gender and Digital-Game Situated Play: Women, Girls, and the Multiple Constructions of Play

Fern M. Delamere and Shanly Dixon

As seen throughout this book, the challenges arising from the gendered nature of leisure are contextually situated. We live in a technologically mediated society. Digital games have become a ubiquitous part of our contemporary leisure landscape and represent a multibillion-dollar industry globally (Plunkett Research, 2004). The purpose of this chapter is to examine the specific context of digitally mediated game play and gender. Such explorations unveil the underlying ideological beliefs found within the social-cultural nexus of gender and leisure (Aitchison, 2003).

While market economics are one indicator of the popularity of digital games, more interesting are questions relating to who uses them, how are they used, and the nature of the gendered meanings constructed during play. Dovey and Kennedy (2006) state "it is the cultural context of gaming which makes it not only so interesting, but also so politically relevant" (p. 28). Gender and digital-game situated play is a powerful platform for the expression of gender, and aesthetically, interactively, and performatively, digital game play provides a fruitful context from which to understand gendered practices (Bryce & Rutter, 2006; Delamere, 2004; Walkerdine, 2006).

In this chapter, we share Fern's study of a group of women who are avid players of action and shooter-oriented games (Delamere, 2004; Delamere & Shaw, 2008) and Shanly's writing from her ongoing dissertation, as well as from her other research, which focuses specifically on girl culture and digital game play (Dixon & Boudreau, 2009; Dixon & Weber, 2007). As an overall starting point, we provide a brief discussion of leisure as a site for the social construction of gender. We then introduce some general ideas drawn from our collective research that act as a frame for discussion, as do the separate studies presented in the sections that follow.

Leisure and the Social Construction of Gender

Leisure contexts are shown to influence gender ideologies through participants' associated constructions of gender, often judged based on what is traditionally deemed gender-appropriate behavior (Henderson, Bialeschki, Shaw, & Freysinger, 1996; Shaw, 1999a, 2001, 2006). As noted by Shaw (1999a), "leisure activities, behaviors, and experiences . . . can function to reproduce or reinforce, or alternatively to challenge or resist patriarchal and dominant gender relations" (p. 277). Further, resistance can be contradictory, with varying degrees of intent and conscious deliberation (Shaw, 2001).

Our research explores the multiplicity of ways that females express and construct gender through digital game play. It also highlights the complex and sometimes contradictory nature of female player involvement. The women and girls we studied negotiated their participation, at times overtly challenging gender positions, while other times taking a more acquiescent stance and reproducing traditional gender ideologies. The women gamers in Fern's study were consciously aware of their overt resistance, fully recognizing that they were contesting masculine ideological boundaries. In contrast, the majority of the girls in Shanly's study were less overt in their resistance, yet they still played with their performances of gender, at times nudging traditional boundaries. Taken together, these studies indicated the complex nature of gendered constructions, as well as the simultaneous presence of resistance and reproduction as the players sometimes challenged traditional ideologies of femininity, but at other times reproduced them. Overall, our research indicates that the social construction of gender through leisure was not monolithic for these players. The gender terrain is still being charted by the women and girls who play and the boundaries they subvert or reinforce. Whether consciously aware or not, these constructions of gender impact the gaming culture and ideologies of gender, thereby also making shifts in the sociopolitical landscape.

Women Players:
Breaking through Masculine Territories

Fern's research was an examination of a group of adult women players and their gendered experience of digital game play (Delamere, 2004). This qualitative study consisted of in-depth, semi-structured interviews with five women who were avid players of what they self-defined as "violent video games." The age range of the female participants was 20 to 30, with the majority in their mid-20s. These women were "serious gamers" who played, on average, 35 hours per week. The complexity of their constructions of gender were evident through their differential readings of gender representation, their gaming culture struggles and responses to them, and the female-specific gained pleasures of play.

The social constructions of gender based on their interpretation of their own and the character representations of women in game culture were paradoxically complex. These women did not disapprove of the sexualization of female characters, even when acknowledging the aesthetic placement of them as male "eye candy." They enjoyed the type of female embodiment that emphasized a sexualized femininity, even making similar personal attire and styling choices. Their support of this was also evident by their team T-shirt logo, which depicted a sexually provocative woman holding a gun and featured the slogan, "Killing with a feminine touch!" Paradoxically, they also contested the sexualization of women in gaming culture as the singular representation. Instead they preferred more complex and multidimensional representations of women. They felt a better representation of women should include a mix of other attributes, such as being physically powerful, decisive, mentally tough, strategic, and aggressive. As such, they wanted to be seen as feminine and female first, but also seen as unapologetically competitive, strong, rough, smart, fearless, and capable of ruthlessly violent game play.

Their participation in violent video game play is a clear transgression of traditional ideologies of femininity. Breaking through existing norms of femininity and playing in a masculine space such as this did come with some social accounting and at some risk (West & Zimmerman, 1991). The fact that the space they were playing in was fortified by some male competitors as a "male only" location created a cold climate for these women. Game culture and the behaviors of some male competitors within it were discussed as a difficult and frustrating part of the female players' experiences. They faced numerous gender-based discriminations as part of game play, based solely on the fact that they were women. This included having their equipment sabotaged during tournaments, being called derogatory sexist names (bitch, whore, slut, fucking lesbian), being asked to perform sexual acts, and postmortem sexual attacks of the characters they played. While the participants in this study found these abusive behaviors to be a frustrating part of game play, it did not alter their desire to continue their involvement. The unwelcoming climate only acted as further catalyst for them to remain involved, continue their participation, and resist the gender ideologies perpetuated by it.

These experiences solidified their determination to stand up to those engaged in such behavior, and, in their terms, "kick some ass" along the way; perhaps adding additional pleasure to their game play through their acts of resistance? As an act of resistance, the female clan (team) in this study created a gaming Web server that monitored for any inappropriate gender-based behavior and banned any players from the server for such infractions. Through their act of resistance, the female players took control and empowered themselves, playing the game on their own terms and not the gaming culture's. The majority of these women also felt that they were breaking open new ground, blazing a new trail, and empowering other interested women to follow and play.

"Girl Culture" and Digital Play

While generationally different, the young girls in Shanly's ethnographic study of everyday engagement with digital media were also charting their own courses. These girls had been born into a "digital generation" (Buckingham & Willett, 2006; Jenkins, 1998; Livingstone, 2009) and were part of what Herring (2008) refers to as a "transitional generation," socialized as they were by a generation of adults who had not grown up immersed in digital culture.

The study involved 20 girls between the ages of 9 and 15, who were interviewed about their digital-play activities over the course of five years. The girls were also observed in a variety of game-play situations alone and with others. According to their parents, the girls began gaming very early on, around the ages of 4 or 5. Many of these girls began gaming on sites like Disney.com and other basic, quickly played, Flash-type games. As the girls got a little older—around age 9—their digital repertoire expanded to include other more complex games such as The Sims. The amount of gaming they engaged in varied throughout the year, depending on a range of factors, such as the amount of available free time that they were able to devote to video games, schoolwork, extracurricular activities, and the weather (particularly as the ethnography was done in Canada). There were often times when they could not go out, and so video-game play was something that they did to help pass the time while being "stuck" inside. Video-game play was fit in around other activities, when they had a group of friends over, or when a new game would be released. The majority of these girls were more casual players than the women in Fern's study, and they played a variety of different games.

The relationship between these girls and video-game culture was also complex. In general terms, young people increasingly acquire their game content by digitally downloading games from Web sites. This is especially true of girls who, particularly at younger ages, have less access to or freedom within public spaces to acquire games in any other way. Most of the girls in this study did not self-define as "gamers" for a variety of possible reasons—perhaps the pervasiveness of digital activities were a taken for granted part of contemporary play, or self-defining as a gamer may have been perceived as "uncool" and "geeky," or a gendered connotation. Self-defining as a "gamer" was a title often associated with gaming proficiency and males, something which Jenson and de Castell (2008) have noted girls are often reluctant to claim. Yet, with the addition of online video-game play, these girls were able to participate in large public spaces, unknown to previous generations of girls. As such, digital culture seemed to have had a profound impact and changed the ways in which these girls socialized, communicated, and played. Playing games online provided the girls with an opportunity to assume public roles and identities they may not have the opportunity to explore in offline spaces (Dixon & Weber, 2007). In addition, they could play at being super heroes and occupying powerful roles that traditional girls' play often does not encourage. Thus, the girls had opportunities to contest traditional notions of femininity by being action heroes or central lead characters, and breaking traditional ideologies about girls and game play. Games were a central part of this casual entertainment, as one among many digital-play opportunities through which to express themselves. Like the women players, at times these girls resisted traditional ideologies of gender while at other times they reproduced it. Overall, however, their involvement in game play allowed them opportunities for personal constructions of self that were empowering and not readily available through other types of play.

One of the girls in the study illustrated some of the points particularly well. Amy was an only child living in a luxury condo with her parents and attending an all-girls school. Her social circle and access to physical public space was limited and digital media opened this up. She was the only girl in this study to self-define as "a gamer" and was very proud of this distinction, even adopting "Gamer-girl" as a nickname among her close friends. Playing role-playing games online enabled Amy to interact with people of all ages outside of the confines of her sheltered environment. She embraced the identity of "geek gamer," perhaps because it enabled her to feel like she was part of a contemporary subculture. Her parents were not computer users, and while aware that their daughter played online, they were unaware of her life as a gamer, perhaps contributing to Amy's sense of independence and empowerment. This also provided Amy with control and autonomy in her digital life that she lacked in her everyday life experience. She, like the other girls in Shanly's study, played with digital culture in ways that afforded them unique opportunities for expressions of gender.

DISCUSSION

Typically digital games have been viewed as "boys' toys" and cultural artifacts that are produced and consumed by men (Taylor, 2007; Thornham,

2008). Female involvement, however, is substantive, with recent reports indicating that 40% of all gamers are female (ESA, 2009). Feminist critiques of science and technology endeavor to break down ideologies connecting machines (computers) to masculinity (Wajcman, 2004). Fern's and Shanly's research dissolves the games as a masculine-preserve discourse and erodes many preconceived notions of who plays, what is being played, and how games are being played.

As Walkerdine (2006) states, it is not the analysis of games as artifacts where gender meaning is constructed; rather, "it is in the game that subjectivity is constituted" and it is in the "subjectivity of play" that such meaning is produced (p. 521). Subjectivities of play for the females in Fern's and Shanly's research included complex negotiations and the development of multiple constructions of gender. Our research indicates that the social construction of gender within the context of digital game play is not monolithic, but rather the subjectivities of play are fluid, multiple, and complex. The female players negotiated their chosen positions, often resisting normative ideas of femininity while at other times reproducing them. As stated by Thornham (2008), positions of gender are always negotiated and multiple performances are part and parcel of gaming. The fact that *gaming culture* propagates what is thought to be gender-appropriate behavior simply added to the complexity of these players' constructions. As Yee (2008) expressed, it is often the "game culture rather than the game mechanics" that act as a deterrent for female players (p. 84). The discriminatory behaviors against the women in Fern's study or the social ideology that boys are "gamers" are two primary examples of deterrents. Also seen in this research, the social construction of gender for these players included the simultaneous presence of resistance and reproduction. This multiple construction of gender is not novel and can be found in other leisure contexts such as community gardens (Parry, Glover, & Shinew, 2005), women's folk dance (Du, 2008) and women and sport (Theberge, 2000) (see also, chapters by Berbary and Roster, this volume). The research in this chapter supports this notion that the construction of gender in leisure is non-unified, complex, and multiple.

Knowing that female players enjoy multiple constructions of gender as part of game play is sociopolitically significant and relates to game development and design. As Kennedy (2005) notes, providing opportunity to develop skills through playful engagement with technology is the foundation for the politically oriented "games for girls movement." Games are thought to be a good entry point for developing technological competencies necessary for today's job market, and there is ongoing concern that girls are missing out (Fullerton, Fron, Pearce, & Morie, 2008; Hayes, 2008). Cassell and Jenkins (1998a) report that designers of games continue to find it difficult to avoid essentializing gender, losing track of the fact that gender is a continuum rather than a set of binary oppositions. Based on the research presented in this chapter, it becomes important to challenge any essentialized views that result in perceiving girls, or boys for that matter, as a unified group. This research suggests that the range of girls' and women's tastes need to be accounted for, thus challenging the conventional thoughts that still dominate in today's programming and game design.

The women in our studies enjoyed digital game play, reaping many pleasures similar to those of their male counterparts. Taylor (2003) previously reported typical pleasures of digital game play to include social interactivity, identity, mastery and status, and team participation. What emerged from our studies, though, is that the women participants seemed to experience additional pleasures specific to gender that were not available to males. A prime example is the pleasure they found in challenging and resisting traditional ideologies of femininity. Moreover, they found pleasures through prowess specific to "beating the males" as a means of proving that they belonged in what is deemed to be a male social field of play. The female players' choices to persevere through the gender discriminatory behaviors they experienced, and to negotiate, resist, and contest some of the normative constructions of gender, paradoxically enhanced their pleasure of play. These pleasures are not part of the male play experience because, win or lose, males know they have the unspoken "privilege to play." However, actions such as creating a female-controlled game server, declaring yourself a "gamer," or playing powerful action heroes created subjectivities that were empowering for these female players. Thus it appears that there are female-specific pleasures of play founded on resistive social constructions of gender (see also Schmalz; Gibson et al., this volume).

As seen here, the players presented in this chapter also gained a great sense of pleasure based on challenging and changing the gaming culture through participating, competing, and proving that they belonged. Games were a site where they had opportunity to make their own constructions of what it is to be female. Wearing (1998) writes about how contemporary leisure offers counter-sites that act as a means of experiencing alternative subjectivities and forms of self-empowerment not typically available to women. In so doing, they "provide spaces for rewriting the script of what it is to be a woman, beyond definitions provided by males and the discourses propagated as truth" (Wearing, 1998, p. 147; see also Roster, this volume). The resistive actions of these players, conscious or not, have changed the social scripts about gaming and gender. Not unlike women in sport 35–40 years ago, their resistive choice to continue playing challenges the social notions of traditional femininity and gender-appropriate leisure participation. Also, the inclusion of emphasized femininity alongside aggressive game play actions, while retooling a more complex understanding of gender, may also be paradoxically used to counter-balance traditional ideologies of femininity with game-play transgressions. This aspect is an interesting avenue for further exploration. The reality is that females who choose to become digital game players are forging new territory (Bertozzi, 2008) and, as suggested here, making a place for themselves in the culture of gaming, changing it and themselves in the process.

Typical of any area of research, there are many future questions that arise. Further examination of female involvement as both casual and serious game players are interesting avenues of inquiry. There are a number of compelling questions could be examined in the gaming context. Leisure research has repeatedly shown that women have limited time available for leisure and what time they may have is found in short segments of time whereby they have to "fit" personal leisure "into" their busy lives (Henderson et al. 1996; Hilbrecht, this volume; Shaw, 1991). This is similar to the young girls in this chapter who were mostly casual players who often fitted games around other obligatory things such as schoolwork. Kafai, Heeter, Denner, and Sun (2008) support this, noting that an area worthy of more research is the significant portion of females whose busy, time-crunched lives dictate that they choose "quick play," casual types of games. Examples of such "quick play" games that might be a focus of research include many of the gaming applications found on social networking sites such as Facebook (e.g., Farmville, Mafia Wars, Café World) or other Flash games such as Diner Dash (which has been the focus of Soderman's recent research [2009]). Exploring serious game play and female player involvement with other competitive gaming communities such as e-sports and cybergames are also rich areas of gender research. For example, scholars at the IT University of Copenhagen Center for Computer Games Research are exploring gender and e-sports (IT University of Copenhagen, 2010). Other research possibilities include exploring experiences of elite female gamers in gaming culture, male gamer perspectives of female competitors, young players and mixed-gender play environments, family computer-game play (positive and negative aspects), digital games and persons with disability, and male constructions of gender in game play, to name but a few. All of these are potentially fruitful areas of future research.

Conclusion

The female players in Fern and Shanly's research are key examples of how gender influences the experience of digital game play and the related culture. This particular social nexus of gender and leisure also has sociopolitical implications. Digital game play enabled us to explore the multifaceted ways in which gender is expressed and constructed. The chapter shines light on the salience of the female players' gendered experiences and their multiple constructions of gender within this context. The women and girls' experiences of play and their differential readings of the games, their multiple constructions of gender, their overall response to and strategic negotiation of gender, and their empowering experiences not typically found in their day-to-day experiences all speak to the sociocultural understanding of gender, in and beyond the realm of the games.

As shown in this chapter, the consumption of digital games intersects with gender and the two mutually constitute each other (Royese, Lee, Undrahbuyan, Hopson, & Consalvo, 2007). Sociology of media recognizes leisure and game play as a context where gender influences the experience of technology (Green & Adam, 2001). We are currently at a critical juncture as digital games are beginning to be taken seriously not only as a means of leisure entertainment but also as potential resource to educate and socialize. As a powerful form of media, these games are changing the ways in which people think, learn, play, and understand the world around them. It is therefore particularly important that girls' and women's experiences be taken into account.

REFERENCES

Aitchison, C. (2003). *Gender and leisure: Social and cultural perspectives.* London, UK: Routledge.

Bertozzi, E. (2008). "You play like a girl!" *Convergence, 14,* 473–487.

Bryce, J., & Rutter, J. (2006). *Understanding digital games.* London, UK: Sage.

Buckingham, D., & Willett, R. (2006). *Digital generations: Children, young people, and the new media.* Mahwah, NJ: Lawrence Erlbaum.

Cassell, J., & Jenkins, H. (1998a). Chess for girls?: Feminism and computer games. In J. Cassell & H. Jenkins (Eds.), *From Barbie to Mortal Kombat: Gender and computer games* (pp. 2–45). Cambridge, MA: MIT Press.

Cassell, J., & Jenkins, H. (1998b). *From Barbie to Mortal Kombat: Gender and computer games.* Cambridge, MA: MIT Press.

Delamere, F. (2004). "It's just really fun to play": A constructionist perspective on violence and gender representations in violent video games.

(Unpublished doctoral dissertation). University of Waterloo, Waterloo, ON.

Delamere, F., & Shaw, S. (2008). "They see it as a guy's game": The politics of gender in digital games. *Leisure/Loisir, 32*(2), 1–24.

Dixon, S., & Boudreau, K. (2009, September 1–4). *Girl's play: Context, performance and social videogame play.* Paper presented at the DiGRA 2009: Breaking New Ground: Innovation in Games, Play, Practice and Theory. West London, UK.

Dixon, S., & Weber, S. (2007). Playspaces, childhood and videogames. In S. Weber & S. Dixon (Eds.), *Growing up online: Young people and digital technologies* (pp. 15–34). New York, NY: Palgrave MacMillan.

Dovey, J., & Kennedy, H. (2006). *Game cultures: Computer games as new media.* New York, NY: Open University Press.

Du, J. (2008). Women's leisure as reproduction and resistance. *Affilia: Journal of Women and Social Work, 23*(2), 179–189.

Entertainment Software Association. (2009). 2009: *Essential facts about the computer and video game industry.* Retrieved from http://www.theesa.com/facts/pdfs/ESA_EF_2009.pdf

Fullerton, T., Fron, J., Pearce, C., & Morie, J. (2008). Getting girls into the game: Towards a virtuous cycle. In Y. B. Kafai, C. Heeter, J. Denner, & J. Y. Sun (Eds.), *Beyond Barbie and Mortal Kombat: New perspectives on gender and gaming* (pp. 137–149). Cambridge, MA: MIT Press.

Green, E., & Adam, A. (2001). *Virtual gender: Technology, consumption and gender.* New York, NY: Routledge.

Hayes, E. (2008). Girls, games and trajectories of IT expertise. In Y. B. Kafai, C. Heeter, J. Denner, & J. Y. Sun (Eds.), *Beyond Barbie and Mortal Kombat: New perspectives on gender and gaming* (pp. 5–21). Cambridge: MIT Press.

Henderson, K., Bialeschki, D. M., Shaw, S., & Freysinger, V. J. (1996). *Both gains and gaps: Feminist perspectives on women's leisure.* State College, PA: Venture Publishing, Inc.

Herring, S. (2008). Questioning the generational divide: Technological exoticism and adult constructions of online youth identity. In D. Buckingham (Ed.), *Youth, identity and digital media* (pp. 71–92). Cambridge, MA: MIT Press.

IT University of Copenhagen. (2010). *Center for computer games research.* Retrieved http://game.itu.dk/index.php/about

Jenkins, H. (1998). Complete freedom of movement: Video games as gendered playspaces. In J. Cassell & H. Jenkins (Eds.), *From Barbie to Mortal Kombat: Gender and computer games* (pp. 262–297). Cambridge, MA: MIT Press.

Jenson J., & de Castell, S. (2008). Theorizing gender and digital game play. *Elumados: Journal for Computer Games Culture, 2*(1), 15–25.

Kafai, Y. B., Heeter, C., Denner, J., & Sun, J. Y. (2008). *Beyond Barbie and Mortal Kombat: New perspectives on gender and gaming.* Cambridge, MA: MIT Press.

Kennedy, H. W. (2005). Illegitimate, monstrous, and out there: Female Quake players and inappropriate pleasures. In J. Hallows & R. Mosley (Eds.), *Feminism in popular culture* (pp. 183–207). London, UK: Berg.

Livingstone, S. (2009). *Children and the Internet.* Cambridge, UK: Polity.

Parry, D., Glover, T., & Shinew, K. (2005). "Mary, Mary quite contrary, how does you garden grow?": Examining gender roles and relations in community gardens. *Leisure Studies, 24*(2), 177–192.

Plunkett Research. (2004). *Entertainment and media overview.* Retrieved from http://www.plunkettresearch.com

Royese, P., Lee, J., Undrahbuyan, B., Hopson, M., & Consalvo, M. (2007). Women and games: Technologies of the gendered self. *New Media & Society, 9*(4), 555–576.

Shaw, S. M. (1991). Women's leisure time: Using time budget data to examine current trends and future predictions. *Leisure Studies, 10*(2), 171–181.

Shaw, S. M. (1999a). Gender and leisure. In E. L. Jackson & T. L. Burton (Eds.), *Leisure studies: Prospects for the twenty-first century* (pp. 271–279). State College, PA: Venture Publishing, Inc.

Shaw, S. M. (2001). Conceptualizing resistance: Towards a framework for the analysis of women's leisure. *Journal of Leisure Research, 33*(2), 186–201.

Shaw, S. M. (2006). Resistance. In C. Rojek, S. Shaw, & A. J. Veals (Eds.), *Handbook of leisure studies.* New York, NY: Palgrave.

Soderman, B. (2009, September 1–4). *Killing time in Diner Dash: Representation, gender, and casual games.* Paper presented at the DiGRA 2009: Breaking New Ground: Innovation in Games, Play, Practice and Theory, West London, UK.

Taylor, N. (2007). Mapping gendered play. *Loading, 1*(1). Retrieved from http://journals.sfu.ca/loading/index.php/loading/article/view Article/21

Taylor, T. L. (2003). Multiple pleasures: Women and online gaming. *Convergence, 9*(1), 21–45.

Theberge, N. (2000). *Higher goals: Women's ice hockey and the politics of gender.* Albany, NY: State University of New York Press.

Thornham, H. (2008). "It's a boy thing." *Feminist Media Studies, 8*(2), 127–142.

Wajcman, J. (2004). *Techno feminism.* Malden, MA: Polity.

Walkerdine, V. (2006). "Playing the game": Young girls performing femininity in video game play. *Feminist Media Studies, 6*(4), 519–537.

Wearing, B. (1998). *Leisure and feminist theory.* Thousand Oaks, CA: Sage.

West, C., & Zimmerman, D. H. (1991). Doing gender. In J. Lorber & S. A. Farrell (Eds.), *The social construction of gender.* Newbury Park, CA: Sage.

Yee, N. (2008). Maps of digital desires: Exploring the topography of gender and play in online games. In Y. B. Kafai, C. Heeter, J. Denner & J. Y. Sun (Eds.), *Beyond Barbie and Mortal Kombat: New perspectives on gender and gaming* (pp. 51–65). Cambridge, MA: MIT Press.

CHAPTER 37
CULTURE SHOCK: CHALLENGES TO RESEARCH INTO WOMEN, GENDER, AND LEISURE

TESS KAY

BECOMING CULTURALLY AWARE IN THE STUDY OF WOMEN AND LEISURE: A PERSONAL RESEARCH JOURNEY

This chapter considers how we address issues surrounding cultural diversity—and cultural specificity—in research into women, girls, and leisure. Given the opportunities I have had to conduct research in diverse cultural contexts, my personal appreciation of such issues has been shamefully slow to evolve. In concentrating on the experiences of women and girls themselves at the individual level, and on the commonalities of gendered experience at the collective level, it has taken me some time to bring the larger issues surrounding cultural specificity into focus. This chapter is an attempt to do so, and to highlight what I believe is a potentially productive two-fold development for leisure sciences research: that applying awareness of cultural specificity will improve our understanding of the gender-leisure interrelationship, and that this in turn may help challenge cultural specificity in the wider leisure sciences.

In developing this argument, this chapter draws especially on my experiences during the last six or seven years. During this time, an increasing proportion of my work has been conducted in non-Western geographical locations and/or social milieus. These have not, however, been my first introduction to issues of cultural difference, which came when I participated in a series of research projects undertaken for the European Union in the late 1990s (Kay, 1999, 2000a, 2003b). This was a time of accelerated change in Europe, as the Union's membership expanded and diversified to include the emerging post-communist Eastern European states. An intensive debate was taking place about the extent to which EU social policy should converge across member states, given that these were not only so economically and culturally different from each other, but also so internally diverse. A range of research studies were commissioned to inform social-policy responses to these developments, including a series of studies into family dimensions of social and demographic change. Changes in women's employment patterns were very much to the fore, together with the implications these had for gender relations, intergenerational relationships, and systems of welfare support.

Working on these projects, with multinational research teams, at a time of rapid and multifaceted social transformations, influenced my research standpoint in a number of ways. The organization of family life varied dramatically between member states. I was struck by numerous examples of this, especially in relation to women's roles. In the United Kingdom, for example, it was believed that national government should not interfere in the "private" domain of the family—validating minimal levels of state childcare and making working motherhood an option only for women who could afford it. This produced dramatic divergence between women (and households) across social classes: by 1993, women in professional/managerial occupations were 30 times more likely to work full-time while they had a preschool-age child in the family than women in unskilled occupations (Kay, 1996). In contrast, in the Scandinavian countries, a strong belief in the positive value of socializing children into the wider community was supported by high levels of state-subsidized childcare provision and high maternal employment across all social groups. And differences were also evident within nations. The research team from the Mediterranean countries talked about the divergence between the lifestyles of the growing urban professional class of highly educated women who combined full-time employment with motherhood, compared to the homemaker and laboring roles women performed in the traditional, often heavily Catholic, rural communities. Elsewhere, those studying the pattern of social life in the newly reunified Germany spoke of the complex social, economic, political, and cultural issues that arose as the different social practices and ideologies of the previously communist East converged with the social democratic values of the West.

Through these experiences, I began to recognize family as a central social institution which both shaped and reflected different ideologies about the nature of social relationships; more specifically, I became particularly aware of how differences in family life were disproportionately manifest in the everyday lives of women. While men everywhere in Europe aspired to work full-time, women in the European Union displayed much more diverse, complex, fragmented and dynamic lifestyles as they balanced their reproductive/domestic and productive/labor-market roles across the life course. At this stage, however, my understandings of this diversity very much reflected the policy orientation of the research in which I was engaged. Working primarily in quantitative methodologies, I viewed these variations in family life mainly as a product of the interaction of different social histories, economic structures, and political ideologues at the aggregate level. This was probably a legitimate perspective, but only a partial one.

After more than five years of working on research that spanned 11 countries, it was, somewhat paradoxically, the more immediate experience of working in my own neighborhood, with young Muslim women, which finally widened my worldview! The opportunity to carry out research with a group which was so geographically proximate yet so ideologically distant from my own experience threw issues of cultural difference into sharp relief. I began to recognize culture not just as some intangible abstract, but as a phenomenon constructed and reproduced in the day-to-day minutiae of individual lives. The writings of the several contemporary analysts of multiculturalism reinforced this, and in particular placed family life at the heart of cultural identity. At the micro-level, women were therefore particularly instrumental in the (re)construction of culture.

In the sections that follow, I attempt to consider how this viewpoint may contribute to how we research women and leisure. I start by examining the institution that is pivotal to women's lives and to cultural identity—the family. From this, I move on to provide illustrative examples of recent research with young women in non-Western cultural contexts. I will conclude the chapter by considering what the implications may be for how we develop the study of women, gender, and leisure.

WOMEN'S EXPERIENCE OF CULTURE: THE SIGNIFICANCE OF FAMILY

However varied, contested, disputed, and sometimes downright dysfunctional it may be, "family" provides the bedrock of social life. Some form of organization based on parentage and marriage is present in every historical and contemporary human society, and in each of these it reflects culturally determined beliefs and values (e.g., Georgas, van de Vijver, & Berry, 2004; Smith, 2004). As a social institution, families are central to individual and collective social practice, and are regulated by political, legal, and religious institutions in accordance with the prevailing consensus on what family life "should" be. Family arrangements and values are therefore crucial distinguishing characteristics of different ethnic, racial, and cultural groups, with authors such as Elliott (1996) placing family very centrally at the heart of cultural identity per se. Writers such as Berthoud (2000), Bhopal (1999), and Harvey (2001) concur, emphasizing that family life is the domain in which different groups, such as immigrant minorities, deliberately maintain their identity by preserving their distinctive cultural traditions.

Although leisure researchers have addressed diversity in family life, they have not focused on cultural dimensions. They have instead concentrated on observable differences in family structures and formations— e.g., the emergence of "involved fathering" (Harrington, 2006b, 2009), dual-earner parenting (Such, 2006, 2009), and the growth of non-resident fatherhood (Jenkins, 2009; Jenkins & Lyons, 2006). Fundamental differences in the ideologies and practices around which family relationships are organized have rarely been considered. To do so involves considering the different *functions* families perform, and the different bases on which families are *structured*.

The functional dimension of family concerns how families satisfy members' physical and psychological needs and meet survival and maintenance needs (Smith, 1995). This encompasses the family's wider social role, as the basic unit of social organization upon which communities are founded. In Westernized states, families have moved from being units of production to units of consumption, the market and the state have usurped many traditional family functions, and the role of the family is relatively narrow in comparison to other times and cultures. In contrast, in non-industrial contexts, kinship units normally have a wider array of functions. They often serve as basic units of production, political representation, and even as religious bodies for the worship of spiritual beings.

Family structure is based on a culture's concepts of "kinship," which define the relationships between individuals who have family ties and provide the most basic principle of organizing social groups and roles. Kinship systems are based on two forms of relationship ties—marriage ties and "descent" (parentage) ties. It is instructive to consider the cultural differences in descent ties, which may be either unilineal, in which descent is traced through parents and ancestors of only one sex, or cognatic, in which it is traced through either or both parents. The majority of societies, including India and China, follow unilineal descent systems, which are almost universally based on descent through the male sex only. The gender basis of these societies is therefore fundamentally unequal, differing markedly from the principles of cognatic kinship with which people of European ancestry are more familiar but are followed by only 30% of the world's cultures. The normative assumptions that leisure researchers commonly make about the nature of family, and especially the relationship between male and female adult partners, are therefore only applicable to a global minority.

Differences in beliefs about kinship and family are evident in marriage and parenting practices. Marriage plays an important role in establishing social relationships that are the foundation for families and households and is very much a culturally defined process, institutionalized in civic and religious procedures. The current Western notion of marriage as an intense relationship between two individuals which emphasizes exclusive emotional attachments and independent households, often geographically distant from relatives, accords with Western values of individualism and independence, but it is seen from collectivist perspectives as socially isolating, separating people from wider family networks. Outside Western industrialized contexts, marriage is commonly considered a tool for wider social relations that can create economically and politically valuable links between families. In such contexts, marriage is seen as uniting two families, not just two people, with all of a family's members becoming obligated by the marriage of one of its members. Marriages are therefore valuable tools in creating alliances and must be considered carefully and even negotiated, as in the practice of arranged marriage.

Cultural differences are also manifest in parenting ideologies and practices. Among societies tending towards collectivism, "social" and collective parenting are practiced—an approach captured in the African saying, "it takes a village to raise a child." Millions of the world's children are therefore reared by multiple caregiving figures, contrasting with the Western expectation that parents should have virtually sole responsibility for raising a child. The nuclear two-parent model of the family therefore has limited applicability outside Westernized populations (Kurrien & Vo, 2004, p. 207), and has also been less fully adopted by minorities of other cultural heritages now living in such nations (e.g., black American fathers) (Connor & White 2006; Paschal, 2006).

Across all cultures, however, ideologies and practices of family are both dynamic and contested. Consciously and subconsciously, there is a continual reworking of the appropriate degree of accommodation and resistance to the cultural alternatives available. In a globalized world in which the mass consumption of the West is extending its penetration of the major economies of the East, it is the idealized portrayal of the "progressive" and "modern" Western nuclear family which is increasingly influential in this process. This assumes a family unit based on heterosexual parents living with their biological children; a permanent marital relationship that supports men and women's personal development through equitable gender roles; and an ideology of parenting that focuses on the nurturing of an independent child. But this model of family has limited appropriateness even within the North American and European societies in which it originates, embodying an ideology of parenting and family that is narrowly reflective of the white, middle-class values that are most familiar to media, and policy- and academic opinion-makers themselves. Such highly specific constructions obscure the diversity in family values and practices that characterizes multicultural and socially progressive societies, underplaying differences in family structures, including the existence of multigenerational households and households headed by lone parents and same-sex couples, and concealing alternative ideologies that emphasize collectivism, social parenting, and the mutual interdependence of family members. Yet notwithstanding these limitations, Western ideologies of family are exerting powerful influence across diverse socioeconomic and cultural groups beyond the societies in which they originate.

The way that cultural identity is expressed through family life has particularly strong implications for women's lives. Many of the most visible distinguishing characteristics of family arrangements lie in the roles ascribed to female members of the family. For minority groups that originally immigrated from South Asia, for example, the traditions of that region continue to be the dominant influences in defining strongly gendered ideologies and practices of family. Ballard's classic account (1982) highlights the privileged position of males in these traditions, describing how membership of a family unit consisted of a man, his sons and grandsons, together with their wives and unmarried daughters. Female children of a family were not, therefore, permanent members of their parents' household: at marriage, daughters left their natal home and became members of their husbands' family (Ballard, 1982, p. 3). Contemporary gender relations are therefore underpinned by a tradition of historically institutionalized gender inequity that is more explicit than Western experiences. For leisure researchers, it is important to understand this as a distinctive context within which women may attempt to negotiate their access to leisure (Delamere & Dixon, Scraton & Watson, this volume).

The two examples that follow feature leisure in the lives of young women of non-European culture. Both studies focus on sport and were undertaken as part of evaluation research for sports policymakers. This is a relatively narrow focus, but offers some initial insights to illustrate the themes raised above. In the account that follows, I focus on two particular dimensions: how the collectivist ideology of Indic societies is strongly evident throughout the young women's accounts of their experiences; and how we should assess the evidence that leisure challenges some of the gender constraints they encounter.

YOUNG MUSLIM WOMEN IN LOUGHBOROUGH, ENGLAND

My work with young Muslim women in my hometown of Loughborough began in 2003 when I became involved in a "Widening Participation" project. Funded by the European Social Fund, this initiative used sport as a vehicle for encouraging young people from ethnic minority groups to progress to higher education. The project offered a combined program of sport and education activities to local Muslim youth, one of the many minority groups underrepresented in university-level education in the United Kingdom. The teenagers participating in the program included daughters of recently immigrated Muslim families. These young women's day-to-day lives were subject to the varied and sometimes contradictory influences of their religion, the culture of their family's country of origin, and their exposure to Western values. The project offered them the opportunity to participate in sport in a culturally appropriate environment, and the girls and their families both reported multiple benefits as a result. In relation to sport, the girls increased their skills, enjoyed being active, and felt that they had shown that sport could be compatible with their culture and faith. They also reported personal development benefits, including increased self-knowledge, improved communication skills, and greater confidence to discuss their religion and culture with others. Despite these successes, daughters could only participate in the project with explicit permission from their parents, and at times permission had to be repeatedly renegotiated. We became interested in the role of the girls' families in influencing their participation in sport, and how this fitted within parents' wider views of their daughters' educational, employment, and domestic futures. An in-depth participatory research project was established within the girls' activity program and carried out in 2004 (Kay, 2006a). Five years later, we returned to the same young women to explore in more detail the longer-term impact of their involvement in the project.

By 2009, all but one of the original participants had progressed to university. All considered the sports project to have been significant in encouraging this, and in also contributing to wider shifts in attitudes which had broadened ideas about acceptable activities for young Muslim women. Since 2004, sport had become accepted by the local Muslim community as an appropriate activity for females: one young woman described it as a "new stereotype" for Muslim females, while others spoke about how it was now common to see young women in sportswear walking in the street.

The theme of impacting others was very prominent throughout the research, emphasizing how much the girls' lives were underpinned by a collectivist ideology. They rarely talked only about their personal learning, and made frequent references to passing lessons on to others. One participant described—in quite strong terms!—how she mentored her younger siblings:

> I mentor other people within the project and I actually mentor my own sisters and brothers. Like telling them, "oh you should come out and do sports, you're going to get unfit and then you're going to die young." (Project participant, 2009)

Another talked about educating her parents into accepting sport as a non-threatening activity. Her father was very protective of her, and would keep asking her if she was going to be all right: she would reply "It's alright Dada, I haven't even left the house yet!"

The collectivist theme evident in the girls' responses extended beyond the family context to a wider impact on Muslim women and girls in the town. Participants displayed strong consciousness of being members of a close-knit community, and talked about their duty under Islam to share any knowledge and skills that they developed. These examples challenge stereotypical views of Muslim women as confined to the immediate domestic zone, and limited in their wider social participation. They described how developing confidence through the project encouraged them and other women to be less dependent on and subservient to males—a potentially fundamental shift in gender relations and family arrangements in an ethnic group who can be among the most conservative in relation to gender roles and family arrangements (Berthoud, 2000). The research illustrated how change may be transmitted through female members of families, and beyond this to peers and the broader community.

Leisure researchers are familiar with examples of women's empowerment through leisure (e.g. Deem, 1986; Freysinger & Flannery, 1992; Green, Hebron, & Woodward, 1990; Henderson, Bialeschki, Shaw, & Freysinger, 1989, 1996; Kay, 2001; Pfister, 2001; Standing, 2001; Wimbush & Talbot, 1988). But a nuanced understanding is necessary. By contextualizing these young women's experiences within their family and cultural context, we see that they were not moving towards a Westernized model of gender equity, but creating a fusion between this and Islamic and South Asian traditions (e.g., Pilkington, 2003). Although sport was a leisure form that allowed them to explore and develop their ethnicity in ways which contributed to changing gender relations, it also reinforced their cultural identity and cohesion as a community. While the young women and their families were "constantly adapting and diversifying" (Parekh, 2000, p. 27), they were doing so only in ways that accorded with their own culture (Modood et al., 1997).

Young Women in New Delhi, India

This second example is from research undertaken into the social impact of sport on young women in Delhi, India, in May 2008 (Kay, Welford, Jeanes, Morris, & Collins, 2008). India is a strongly patriarchal society where women face multiple constraints on their lives, which are being addressed at the governmental level through policies to end oppressive practices such as female infanticide and forced marriage. The priority areas include education, which is regarded as a pivotal strategy to address gender inequity, and health, including fertility, sexual health, and HIV/AIDS education.

GOAL is a project which uses netball as a medium to engage young women, aiming to empower them to become leaders and social activists in their communities. GOAL is operated by the NAZ Foundation (India) Trust, a New Delhi-based NGO working on HIV/AIDS and sexual health. At the time of the research, GOAL ran twice-weekly netball sessions in Deepalaya and Aali Gaon, two impoverished neighborhoods in New Delhi, supplemented by educational modules that covered personal issues such as health and communication, social issues such as the environment, and economic issues such as micro-finance and computing.

The project's focus was on sustained, intense work with relatively small, close-knit groups of young women. The research involved 31 participants, who explained that their lack of education left them unable to safeguard their health and well-being and ill-equipped to challenge this situation. One described how previously, "Even though the body is mine, I was absolutely unaware of my own body." One of the key benefits GOAL offered was information relating to health and reproduction, which would allow the young women to protect their own well-being and share their knowledge with others, especially family members:

> Our mothers encourage us to go and once we get back home, they also look forward to us coming back home because we go home with a lot of information, which we share with them. (Aali Gaon girl H)

The importance of communicating what had been learned was mentioned very frequently. Participating in the project had built the girls' communication skills and confidence, allowing them to be more vocal in expressing their views. They believed that sharing knowledge was important for their communities and could contribute to change:

> I had no idea about [AIDS], and now I know what it is, and I can stand against it, because I have the knowledge, and probably this knowledge would also help me to help the people around me. (Aali Gaon girl D)

> If God wishes, if I have children, I'll at least try to pass on [*what I have learnt*] to them, and they'll pass on, and that's how it goes on. (Aali Gaon girl I)

> We would like to become people like you [*GOAL Project staff*], spreading the knowledge, and creating the chain, you know, the way you have. We want to create the ripple. (Aali Gaon girl H)

Several young women talked about the impact of the project on their aspirations, and described how the views of others had also been affected:

> The program has caused me to think on a different line that I really want to prove certain things, I don't have a dream as of now, I don't know where I will end up, but one thing is for sure that I want to do something. (Deepalaya girl E)

> People, families, when the sport came up, and the program was here, they said "clean, cook, and that's your life." And there was this line that was drawn that we could never cross. But now that line is going backwards. And we are just, you know, coming out, we have crossed it. And now we have realized that our life is not just limited to washing clothes, washing utensils, or cooking. And now we think that when we do everything we have done, this is the time we have for ourselves, and we don't want to compromise on that. [Aali Gaon girl C]

The school principal at Deepalaya, and the long-standing community coordinator at Aali Gaon, also commented on the wider significance of the young women's experiences, and the specific contribution netball made to this process as a team activity:

> (Now) they know how to assert their rights, they know how to speak within their family and be heard, which I think is a step in the right direction. They can be very active decision makers in the long run in the families. (School Principal, Deepalaya)

> One thing which is very important, these young women, during their sessions of the sports, they have developed team spirit, which is a very big thing for them. They will play a game, but team spirit is very, very important for their lives. As a team they can fight for their locality, as a team they can fight for any personal issues, now they know, that single person cannot do it, anything, you have to unite, to fight. (Community Coordinator, Deepalaya)

These findings from the research in New Delhi suggest that even in some very challenging settings, leisure can play a positive role in the lives of young women. Through having time for themselves, engaging in stimulating activities, and having the opportunity to develop relationships with each other, the participants in GOAL experienced forms of personal empowerment that also nurtured commitment to collective activity. In many respects these are familiar findings for leisure research—and these similarities provide a further argument for highlighting cultural difference, not ignoring it. They hint at leisure providing universal benefits for women—a possibility we can only appreciate if we acknowledge the very different worlds in which women live.

Addressing Cultural Specificity in Research into Women, Gender, and Leisure

This chapter has raised issues surrounding cultural specificity in research into women and leisure. Such concerns have been articulated by a number of leisure scholars who have highlighted the Western domination of leisure research. As Fox, Klaiber, Ryan, and Lashua (2006) have written, "the dominant meta-narrative, theoretical concepts, and conclusions of Euro-North American leisure scholarship" are inadequate for investigating the experiences and meanings of those who fall outside this cultural group (p. 456). When we focus on gender and leisure, both so centrally linked to the (re-)production of culture, this critique cannot be ignored.

Issues of cultural specificity are of course more obvious when confronting difference in an external "other" than they are as we pursue our own familiar everyday lives. It takes a conscious effort to be self-aware of our own social positioning—one of the reasons why activist movements from communism to the feminist movement start with "consciousness raising." As researchers, developing this awareness requires us to address issues surrounding methodology and the production of knowledge, as examined in the work of Linda Tuhiwai Smith. Smith (1999) is unequivocal in her rebuttal of Western research, describing "the word itself, 'research,' [as] probably one of the dirtiest words in the indigenous world's vocabulary" (p. 1). Her challenge, to the ontological and epistemological underpinning of Western research and its positivist empiricist roots, is fundamental:

> Many critiques of research have centred around the theory of knowledge known as empiricism and the scientific paradigm of positivism, which is derived from empiricism.... From an indigenous perspective, Western research is more than just research that is located in a positivist tradition. It is research which brings to bear, on any study of indigenous peoples, a cultural orientation, a set of values, a different conceptualisation of such things as time, space, and subjectivity, different and competing theories of knowledge, highly specialized forms of language, and structures of power. (Smith, 1999, p. 42)

Culture is not, therefore, something which researchers can address through tactical measures such as the modification of research tools and adoption of "appropriate" behavior, dress, and language. These types of adjustment are important, appropriate, and necessary, but also limited. They may even become counterproductive, misleading us into believing that through these simple measures we have "dealt with" culture. The traditional concerns of feminist research have, however, been more fundamental—to reject hierarchical relationships, reject the separation between researcher and researched, avoid treating research "subjects" as merely objects of knowledge, and allow women's own voices to emerge (e.g., Cook & Fonow, 1990). Pro-feminist research therefore embodies a commitment to democratize the academy and the process of knowledge production.

This approach has implications for the research process. It favors an orientation to participatory research that enables those outside the academic establishment to actively participate in its production of knowledge and ultimately claim membership of it (see Frisby, this volume). There are implications for method, with qualitative techniques often favored for supporting collaborative inquiry because the methods are "understandable, teachable, and usable by people without extensive research training" (Patton, 2002, p. 194). This is not to suggest that qualitative methodologies magically transform and democratize underlying power relationships between researchers and the researched: they clearly do not. They lend themselves to reflexive forms of research, however, which can provide a mechanism for the expression of local understandings that are crucial to culturally appropriate understandings of leisure.

In relation to subject matter, there is a simple need to be explicit in locating research with women within explicit consideration of its cultural context. This includes:

- Ensuring women, leisure, and gender are studied across a wide variety of cultural contexts;

- Reflecting critically on the cultural specificity of the extant body of research into women, leisure, and gender;

- Developing the implications of these approaches to inform understandings of gender relations, men's leisure, and family leisure; and

- Extending this debate to help challenge issues of cultural specificity across the breadth of leisure sciences.

One of the reasons for doing this is simply to address the greatly neglected gaps in our current knowledge base by identifying and making visible the missing populations. Within Western industrialized nations, demographic shifts have made populations more culturally diverse in ways that challenge taken-for-granted assumptions about central social institutions such as family. Scholarship is required which recognizes diversity between cultural groups and within them; responds to the different patterns produced as culture intersects with structural variables including gender, class, and ethnicity; and in societies in which "mixed race" is the fastest-growing category, is alert to the fluidity and complexities of any type of cultural heritage or identity. More fundamentally, extending research in this way enriches our current knowledge by encouraging deeper critical reflection on research findings and research processes that appear so familiar. Recognizing how differently ideologies and practices that surround leisure are constructed in other settings, and the challenge this presents to our concepts, theories, and methodological approaches, can liberate us from entrenched assumptions.

REFERENCES

Ballard, R. (1982). South Asian families. In R. N. Rapoport, M. P. Fogarty, & R. Rapoport (Eds.), *Families in Britain* (pp. 86–97). London, UK: Routledge and Kegan Paul.

Berthoud, R. (2000). *Family formation in multicultural Britain: Three patterns of diversity*. Working paper, Institute for Social and Economic Research, University of Essex.

Bhopal, K. (1999). South Asian women and arranged marriages in East London. In R. Barot, H. Bradley, & S. Fenton (Eds.), *Ethnicity, gender and social change* (pp. 117–134). London, UK: Macmillan.

Connor, M. E., & White, J. L. (2006). *Black fathers: An invisible presence in America*. Hillsdale, NJ: Erlbaum.

Cook, J. A., & Fonow, M. M. (1990). Knowledge and women's interests: Issues of epistemology and methodology in feminist sociological research. In J. McCarl Nielsen (Ed.), *Feminist research methods: Exemplary readings in the social sciences* (pp. 69–91). Boulder, CO: Westview.

Deem R. (1986). *All work and no play? The sociology of women and leisure*. Milton Keynes, UK: Open University Press.

Elliott, F. R. (1996). *Gender family and society*. Basingstoke, UK: Macmillan.

Fox, K. M., Klaiber, E., Ryan, S., & Lashua, B. (2006). Remixing, performing, and producing studies of leisures. *Leisure Sciences, 28*(5), 455–465.

Freysinger, V. J., & Flannery, D. (1992). Women's leisure: Affiliation, self-determination, empowerment and resistance? *Leisure and Society, 15*(1), 303–322.

Georgas, J., van de Vijver, F. J. R., & Berry, J. W. (2004). The ecocultural framework, ecosocial indices, and psychological variables in cross-cultural research. *Journal of Cross-Cultural Psychology, 35*, 74–96.

Green, E., Hebron, S., & Woodward, D. (1990). *Women's leisure, what leisure?* London, UK: Macmillan.

Harrington, M. (2006b). Leisure and sport as contexts for fathering in Australian families. *Leisure Studies, 25*(2), 165–184.

Harrington, M. (2009). Sport mad, good dad: Australian fathering through leisure and sport practices. In T. A. Kay (Ed.), *Fathering through sport and leisure* (pp. 51–72). London, UK: Routledge.

Harvey, C. (Ed.) (2001). *Maintaining our differences.* Aldershot, UK: Ashgate.

Henderson, K. A., Bialeschki, M. D., Shaw, S., & Freysinger, V. J. (1989). *A leisure of one's own: A feminist perspective on women's leisure.* State College, PA: Venture Publishing, Inc.

Henderson, K. A., Bialeschki, M. D., Shaw, S., & Freysinger, V. J. (1996). *Both gains and gaps: Feminist perspectives on women's leisure.* State College, PA: Venture Publishing, Inc.

Jenkins, J. M. (2009). With one eye on the clock: Non-resident dads' time use, work and leisure with their children. In T. A. Kay (Ed.), *Fathering through sport and leisure* (pp. 88–105). London, UK: Routledge.

Jenkins, J. M., & Lyons, K. D. (2006). Non-resident fathers' leisure with their children. *Leisure Studies, 25*(2), 219–232.

Kay, T. A. (1996). Women's work and women's worth: The leisure implications of women's changing employment patterns. *Leisure Studies, 15*(1), 49–64.

Kay, T. A. (1999). The family consequences of changing gender relations in the United Kingdom. In L. Hantrais (Ed.), *Changing gender relations and policy* (pp. 31–38). Cross-National Research Papers Fifth Series, Loughborough, UK: Loughborough University.

Kay, T. A. (2000a). Differentiation in mothers' employment patterns in the European Union. In L. Appleton (Ed.), *Spatio-temporal dimensions of economic and social change in Europe* (pp. 19–26). Cross-National Research Papers Sixth Series, Loughborough, UK: Loughborough University.

Kay, T. A. (2001). New women, same old leisure. In S. Clough & J. White (Eds.), *Women's leisure experiences: Ages, stages and roles* (pp. 113–128). Eastbourne, UK: Leisure Studies Association.

Kay, T. A. (2003b). The work-life balance in social practice. *Social Policy and Society, 2*(3), 231–239.

Kay, T. A. (2006a). Daughters of Islam: Family influences on Muslim young women's participation in sport. *International Review for the Sociology of Sport, 41*(3–4), 339–355.

Kay, T. A., Welford, J., & Jeanes, R., Morris, J., & Collins, S. (2008). *The potential of sport to enhance young people's lives: Sport in the context of international development.* Unpublished report to UK Sport and the Department for International Development.

Kurrien, R., & Vo, E. D. (2004). Who's in charge? Coparenting in South and Southeast Asian families. *Journal of Adult Development, 11*(3), 207–219.

Modood, T., Berthoud, R., Lakey, J., Nazroo, J., Smith, P., Virdee, S., & Beishon, S. (1997). *Ethnic minorities in Britain.* London, UK: Policy Studies Institute.

Parekh, B. (2000). *The future of Multiethnic Britain: The Parekh Report.* London, UK: Profile.

Paschal, A. (2006). *Voices of African-American teen fathers: I'm doing what I got to do.* New York, NY: Haworth.

Patton, M. Q. (2002). *Qualitative evaluation and research methods* (3rd ed.). Thousand Oaks, CA: Sage.

Pfister, G. (2001). The everyday lives of sportswomen: Playing sport and being a mother. In S. Clough & J. White (Eds.), *Women's leisure ex-*

periences: Ages, stages and roles (pp. 75–86). Eastbourne, UK: Leisure Studies Association.

Pilkington, A. (2003). *Racial disadvantage and ethnic diversity in Britain.* Basingstoke, UK: Palgrave.

Smith, L. T. (1999). *Decolonizing methodologies: Research and indigenous people.* Dunedin: University of Otago Press.

Smith, P. (2004). Nations, cultures, and individuals: New perspectives and old dilemmas. *Journal of Cross-Cultural Psychology, 35,* 6–12.

Smith, S. (1995). Family theory and multicultural family studies. In B. Ingoldsby & S. Smith (Eds.), *Families in multicultural perspective* (pp. 5–35). New York, NY: Guilford.

Standing, K. (2001). The absent spaces of lone mothers. In S. Clough & J. White (Eds.), *Women's leisure experiences: Ages, stages and roles* (pp. 65–74). Eastbourne, UK: Leisure Studies Association.

Such, E. (2006). Leisure and fatherhood in dual-earner families. *Leisure Studies, 25*(2), 185–200.

Such, E. (2009). Fatherhood, the morality of personal time, and leisure-based parenting. In T. A. Kay (Ed.), *Fathering through sport and leisure* (pp. 73–87). London, UK: Routledge.

Wimbush, E., & Talbot, M. (1988). *Relative freedoms.* Milton Keynes, UK: Open University Press.

SECTION 5
THE WAY FORWARD

Chapter 38
Gender and Leisure Policy Discourses: The Cultural Turn to Social Justice

Cara Aitchison

In this chapter, I seek to demonstrate the potential contribution of feminist and gender leisure research to a future research agenda of *gender justice* in leisure. This research agenda is designed to inform both theory *and* policy and is framed by critical reflection on three decades of feminist and gender research in leisure studies.

The purpose of engaging in this reflection and speculation is threefold. First, a review enables an assessment of the nature, extent, and impact of research undertaken to date. Second, an analysis of recent developments in the field gives rise to questions relating to the feminist underpinning, long-term efficacy, and policy relevance of the recent and influential *cultural turn* within social science. Third, by introducing the concept of *the social-cultural nexus*, together with more recent engagements with *social justice*, suggestions are made for future research agendas, priorities, and approaches. The research agenda advocated here is designed to embrace overarching and established feminist principles and practices, while also engaging with more recent critical and cross-cultural research to provide new perspectives on gender and leisure policy.

This moment is apposite to undertake such a review and discussion as the field of feminist and gender studies of leisure has reached a significant juncture in its development. Within the discussion, I map the terrain of gender and leisure studies by chronicling the major theoretical perspectives and associated literature that have informed thematic discussions in feminist and gender studies of leisure since the late 1970s. I then offer a synthesis and critique of the growing but fragmented field of gender and leisure research while seeking to contribute theoretical insights to produce a new critical discourse on gender justice in leisure studies/sciences. This chronology charts three distinct phases in the development of gender and leisure discourses:

- *Sex inequality in leisure participation and provision,* with research informed by liberal and socialist feminist approaches;

- *Gender, leisure relations, and the cultural turn in social science,* informed largely by poststructural theory in social science; and

- *Social and environmental justice in feminist and gender leisure research,* that seeks to develop a new phase or *third space* in feminist and gender research by adopting the concept of the social-cultural nexus to inform policy-relevant research.

This review provides a *context for* further discussion of recent calls for the *rematerialization* of social science, including gender and leisure studies. This questioning of the efficacy and *comprehensiveness of the cultural turn* (i.e., cultural rather than structural relations of power are foregrounded) has invited a return to previous research approaches informed by socialist feminism that investigated systemic structural (i.e., institutional) and material (i.e., economic) inequality (see section 1, chapter 3 for a discussion of socialist feminism). Rather than simply replacing recent cultural critiques with previous material critiques, my chapter turns to the development or synthesis of a theoretical critique that seeks to integrate cultural *and* material perspectives through a rematerialized gender project in leisure studies. Thus, I explore the third space between what can, in retrospect, be identified as the false dichotomy of the material analyses of socialist feminism in the 1980s and early 1990s and the cultural analyses of poststructural feminism in the late 1990s and 2000s.

Following earlier feminist critiques of dualistic thinking in wider social science put forward by writers such as Aitchison (2003), Butler (1990, 1993), Grosz (1994, 1995), Rose (1993), and Wearing (1998), exploring the neglected interface between the two seemingly polarized perspectives of the social/cultural, material/symbolic, structural/poststructural in leisure studies is timely. This exploration calls for the expansion of current research horizons by examining the social-cultural nexus of gender relations in leisure, and then applying this theoretical construct to policy and practice designed to bring about social justice. Rather than focusing on either the material *or* the cultural, I highlight the need for feminist and gender research that acknowledges and investigates the synergies between structural and poststructural perspectives.

This accommodation of the social and the cultural is constructed through the conceptualization of the social-cultural nexus, which is explained as both a site and process of construction, legitimation, reproduction, and reworking of gender relations. Thus, the concept engages with structural and poststructural theories to explore the social *and* cultural workings and reworkings of gender–power relations in the production, consumption, and *productive consumption* of leisure. Simultaneously, the concept acknowledges the value of material analyses of patriarchy and capitalism, or patriarchal capitalism, in shaping the power relations that construct, legitimate, and reproduce gender relations in leisure within an unequal world.

The social-cultural nexus, therefore, seeks to offer a critical and comprehensive frame for viewing gender relations in leisure. This frame of reference is designed to inform the next phase of the gender and leisure studies chronology, which I propose should center issues of gender justice. Informed by growing acknowledgment of discourses, policies, and practices of both social and environmental justice, the ground for gender justice is being prepared. Such a development also would facilitate greater collaborative work between feminist and gender researchers of leisure, inform and be informed by researchers in related fields such as sport and tourism studies, and lead to enhanced material and cultural change in provision, participation, and relations in leisure. Thus, research informed by the conceptualization of the social-cultural nexus will continue to develop the work of the two earlier phases of gender scholarship outlined below.

To develop new research agendas requires an understanding of the emergence, reworking, and even replacement of previous discourses. With over three decades of research, the gender and leisure project can be seen as one of accumulation of knowledge, where new knowledge formations have invited the reconsideration of the efficacy of previous epistemologies, methodologies, and interpretation of research findings. In discussing the development of post-1945 positivist human geography, Barnes and Gregory (1997) referred to the development of that particular body of knowledge as being the result of the *three Cs*, which they identified as *certainty*, *coherence*, and *cumulation*. In postpositivist social science, this stable and linear accumulation of knowledge has been disrupted such that the bodies of knowledge relating to gender and leisure studies have become increasingly fluid rather than certain, fragmented rather than coherent, and reflective of horizontal diversification rather than a vertical cumulation.

I do not advocate a return to the positivist research regime of the 1950s and 1960s, but I caution against the continual development of a fragmented knowledge base. In doing so, I reiterate Henderson's (2010) call for *defragmentation* of our research so that a coherent body of knowledge can be developed. In this regard, the course of gender and leisure research parallels that of tourism where:

> the gender project in tourism studies can be viewed as having moved from a period of relative internal coherence in the form of early feminist studies in tourism employment from two decades ago, to a larger and more fragmented set of discourses at the turn of the 21st century where, it could be argued, the break-up of

different feminist and gender perspectives has been in danger of fracturing the incomplete project of gender and tourism studies. (Aitchison, 2009, p. 632)

The challenge in developing an overarching research agenda for gender and leisure, therefore, is to establish internal coherence without losing sight of the individual contributions of specific discourses derived from sometimes competing perspectives. The identification of distinct theoretical perspectives, and emerging contestation among such perspectives, is part of the development of any discipline or subject field and should be welcomed as evidence of the maturing process that will ultimately give greater credibility to leisure studies within the wider academy. Where caution is urged, however, is in ensuring that the fragmentation of the discourse does not simply shatter any overall project and result in a severed community with separate shards of evidence too small to join together to have any overall or systemic impact.

SEX INEQUALITY IN LEISURE PARTICIPATION AND PROVISION

It is unsurprising that the first phase of feminist or gender research in leisure studies was concerned with identifying women's leisure participation levels, comparing and contrasting these data with those recorded in relation to men's participation, and then moving from exploration to explanation of the data. This mapping of the terrain is characteristic of early intervention by feminists within a discipline or subject field and tends to be associated with a liberal feminist approach that quickly develops into a more critical and policy-focused socialist feminist approach.

This typology of feminist epistemological evolution is typified within UK leisure studies where, between the late 1970s and mid-1980s, sex inequality in leisure participation was identified in a series of research projects and publications starting with *Women and Leisure: A State of the Art Review* (Talbot, 1979). Talbot's report resulted from 1 of 10 projects funded jointly by the then UK Sports Council and the Social Science Research Council (SSRC), the forerunner to the current UK Economic and Social Research Council (ESRC). In the United Kingdom, this report was followed by related research events and publications from key social research organizations including the Centre for Contemporary Cultural Studies, the Open University, and the Leisure Studies Association (Griffin, 1981; Hobson, 1981; McCabe, 1981; McIntosh, 1981). This early collection of feminist leisure studies research focused on equality of leisure opportunity and was central in accumulating evidence of unequal leisure participation patterns between women and men. Talbot (1981), for example, stated:

Not only do fewer women than men participate in leisure activities but women also participate in a narrower range of activities, and watch sport, both live and on television, less than men ... when data from surveys that include informal leisure activity are added to the knowledge gained from family and community studies, there emerges a picture of home-based, domestic leisure for women, especially for those from lower socioeconomic groups. (p. 35)

This emerging feminist leisure research of the late 1970s and early 1980s was informed by initial definitions of leisure as time, activity, space, and freedom, and it provided the early conceptualization of the *leisure constraints* that were studied later in greater depth by, among others, Henderson and Bialeschki (1991), Shaw (1994), and Samdahl (this volume). The excerpt from Talbot's report also highlighted two other discourses that became more visible within later feminist and gender leisure research. First, the reference to differential levels of participation between social groups provided an entrée for the subsequent socialist feminist analyses outlined below that addressed women's leisure participation related to a range of social and economic structures, including those of leisure policy and provision. Second, the contextualization of women's leisure within family and community studies, although not particularly prevalent in 1980s and 1990s research, has witnessed a resurgence following the earlier research by Rapoport and Rapoport (1975), and Hantrais, Clark, and Samuel (1984). Contemporary research on leisure and family relations now forms an important component of any future research agenda addressing issues of leisure and social justice and also engages with the overlap between research on women and research on gender (as evidenced by numerous chapters in this volume as well as Harrington, 2006a, 2006b; Kay 2000b, 2006b; Shaw 1992b, 1997; Shaw & Dawson, 2001; Willming & Gibson, 2000; Zabriskie & McCormick, 2001).

By the mid-1980s, a body of feminist leisure research comprising detailed case studies had begun to emerge in the United Kingdom. Three studies in particular provided data relating to women's leisure participation and experiences and began to mix and merge liberal feminist descriptions with socialist feminist analyses (e.g., Deem, 1986; Green, Hebron, & Woodward, 1987; Wimbush, 1986). For example, Deem's study, undertaken between 1980 and 1982, explored leisure participation among almost 500 women in Milton Keynes, in central England. The study explored women's leisure both outside and within the home. Deem identified constraints on women's leisure participation, including male attitudes, hours of employment, childcare, housework and domestic obligations, access to private transport, lack of money, and absence of close friends. Deem's work was also influential in centralizing the overlapping issues of *rights* and *power* in relation to gender and leisure participation. These concepts have subsequently become central to the critiques developed within the social and environmental justice discourse. The analysis of the data from the Milton Keynes study revealed that many women, and particularly those who were not in paid employment, did not feel entitled to leisure or the right to leisure, and were thus disempowered in relation to leisure (Aitchison, 2003). Issues of power, rights, and entitlement generally have not formed a central discourse within feminist and gender leisure research. I suggest that the discourse of social justice, now more established within academia, could form an anchor for floating more critical discourses of these concepts within future feminist and gender studies of leisure.

Deem's (1986) research was also significant in identifying differences between women in their access to leisure and this theme was given further prominence by Green et al. (1987) in their study, *Leisure and Gender: A Study of Women's Leisure Experiences*. They interviewed over 700 women between 18–59 years in the northern English city of Sheffield and concluded that:

> women's access to free time and leisure opportunities are structured by social class and income level, age and ethnic group, and their work and domestic situation. The main constraints took the form of a lack of resources such as time, money, safe transport, and childcare. Limitations on their access to leisure were experienced more acutely by the women not currently in paid work, those with unemployed partners, single parents, and married women with children under five. (Green, Hebron, & Woodward, 1990, p. 24)

Wimbush (1986) further highlighted these material constraints in her investigation of leisure participation by women with preschool-age children in two areas differentiated by social class in Edinburgh, Scotland. The study sought to "evaluate the importance and meaning that mothers attach to their existing leisure opportunities" and "to explore the ways in which social and recreational activities feature in their general health and well-being" (Wimbush, 1986, p. 2). The research identified factors that acted as enablers and constraints of women's leisure and the recommendations focused on the need for material change to leisure policy and practice by public-sector leisure providers. This shift in emphasis from leisure participation to leisure provision signaled the development of a new focus for feminist leisure policy research, particularly within a UK context.

Although feminist studies of leisure participation, and particularly the constraints affecting participation, continued to develop in North America throughout the late 1980s and 1990s, the situation in the United Kingdom was rather different. Preoccupied by the radical shift in public-sector policy resulting from the conservative policies of the Thatcher government (1979–1992), the focus in relation to leisure services was on the impact of commercial, privatized, or contracted-out provision. In spite of leisure being a predominantly market-led sector, the history of UK leisure is dominated by public-sector policy intervention. This discourse of political economy is heavily influenced by socialist approaches to reducing inequality and exclusion in leisure provision, including that affecting participation by women (Clarke & Critcher, 1985). Informed by legislation dating back to the Victorian era, equity, access, and inclusion have formed enduring themes within UK central and local government policy for over a century. Previous research has demonstrated, however, that the main beneficiaries of post-war, public-sector leisure, recreation, sport, and arts subsidies have generally been those groups already overrepresented in leisure-related participation figures (Aitchison, 2003; Coalter, 2001; Jowell, 2002; Long et al., 2002).

The provision of leisure services, of course, is in part a reflection of those who make the policies and manage their implementation. Like many service industries, leisure is a sector that is *dominated by women but managed by men* (Brockbank & Traves, 1996). In both North America (specifically, Canada and the United States), where public-sector leisure services have often developed as part of wider parks and recreation provision, and in the United Kingdom, where leisure services were more commonly developed as an addition to technical services, leisure services have evolved as part of heavily male-dominated departments. Notwithstanding the shift towards discrete leisure-services departments in the United Kingdom during the 1980s, the impact of Compulsory Competitive Tendering (i.e., the involvement of private-sector providers in the provision of UK local authority services from 1986) meant that many separate leisure-services departments disappeared or were subsumed within environmental services or economic development departments that, again, tended to be male-dominated areas of local government. This move contrasted with the relatively limited development of leisure services within education or youth and community services with their traditionally higher levels of representation of women.

The rapid change in leisure-service policy and provision during the 1980s and 1990s preoccupied many leisure studies and leisure management academics with an interest in gender relations on both sides of the Atlantic, and in Australia and New Zealand (e.g., Aitchison, 2000b, 2003; Aitchison, Jordan, & Brackenridge, 1999; Bacon, 1991; Frisby & Brown, 1991; Henderson & Bialeschki, 1993, 1995; McKay, 1996; Shinew & Arnold, 1998; Yule, 1997a, 1997b, 1998). In other academic disciplines, however, this same period witnessed a shift from the macro-analyses of public policy and political economy evident in materialist and socialist feminist analyses to micro-analyses of cultural relations and symbolic representation, captured in the writing epitomized in what has come to be known as *the cultural turn in social science*.

GENDER, LEISURE RELATIONS, AND THE CULTURAL TURN IN SOCIAL SCIENCE

Feminist leisure studies of the 1980s and early 1990s, and particularly research that can be categorized as reflecting a socialist feminist epistemology, was informed by critical theory, materialist, and structuralist approaches. In contrast, the last two decades of broader twentieth-century social science research are likely to be remembered as the period when disciplines became heavily influenced by poststructural theory and the cultural turn, which Evans (2003) pointed out, "persuaded many people that social life is now organized and regulated through culture" (p. 69).

By the late 1980s, the United Kingdom experienced a period of increasing cultural consumption related to both the materiality and symbolism of new forms of leisure, sport, and tourism. Geography and sociology engaged more quickly with the discourse of the cultural turn than did leisure studies, which, like many subject fields, tends to embrace theoretical and methodological change later than single disciplines. Strongly influenced by both sociology and cultural studies, the new social and cultural geographies of the 1990s began to rework Sauer's original cultural geography of the 1920s with the 1970s and 1980s sociological analyses of Bourdieu, de Certeau, Foucault, and others to offer sociospatial insights into the role of cultural capital, productive consumption, and the power of surveillance, respectively. Similarly, in sociology and reflecting the increasing proximity of sociology and geography since the 1990s, Barrett's (1992) assertion that the cultural turn led to the demise of the claims of materialism offered new scope for the development of cultural theory where, previously, critical theory had been dominant.

A number of writers by the turn of the twenty-first century were, however, urging caution regarding the wholesale adoption of the cultural over the social or the poststructural over the material. In social geography, Bondi (1992) urged against prioritizing the cultural over the social or the "unharnessing of the symbolic and the sociological" (p. 166), and this plea was reiterated almost a decade later by Valentine (2001), who asked "Whatever happened to the social?" in a paper exploring the impact of the cultural turn in British human geography. Evans (2003) also pleaded that "If the 'cultural turn' means anything, it must, I would argue, mean that as much as studying culture as an object, we also integrate the understandings offered to us by culture in our accounts of the social world" (p. 5). In addition to stressing the dangers of neglecting the social, such discussions emphasized the importance of maintaining the dual influences of the social and the cultural, the material and the symbolic, and the social sciences and the humanities in analyses of leisure as a site, form, and process that informs and is informed by social and cultural phenomena. At this site, or what can be termed the social-cultural nexus, such phenomena and their associated power relations are most powerfully produced, legitimated, identified, consumed, reproduced, and reworked (Aitchison, 2003, 2005a). The conceptualization of the social-cultural nexus as a response to the pleas of Bondi, Valentine, and Evans, is explained more fully in the next section, after some further discussion of the interrelationship between critical and cultural theory.

The cultural turn can be viewed as having the effect of disrupting the dualistic twentieth-century discourse between the social sciences, with their primary concern with economic production, and the humanities, with their greater focus on cultural consumption. Although the social sciences and humanities developed along largely separate but parallel tracks for much of the twentieth century, both critical and cultural theory that emerged between the 1920s and the 1980s encompassed a series of engagements *between* economic or material *and* cultural or symbolic forms of power (Jackson, 1998). These engagements formed the basis of the structural Marxism of Althusser (1971), the Marxian humanism of Adorno and Marcuse of the Frankfurt School, the critical theory of Habermas (1989), and Giddens's (1984) theory of structuration, with all pointing to the interrelationships between material power, ideology, and cultural conditions. Whereas most members of the Frankfurt School drew heavily on Marxist theory and saw cultural production as a consequence of material power, both Adorno and Giddens offered greater scope for individual agency through the conceptualization of a dialectic between societal structure and human agency. Later, and developing his work on "Third Way" politics, Giddens (1998) demonstrated that this focus on the significance of the dialectic and dynamic nature of social, cultural, economic, and environmental relations, rather than a preoccupation with the fixed and often polarized positions of adversarial ideologies or epistemologies, offered more scope for individuals to navigate the course of their life in relation to the major financial, personal, and environmental revolutions of late twentieth-century globalization. This emphasis on the economy, the sociocultural, the environmental, and the relations among these spheres not only reinforces the conceptual relevance of the social-cultural nexus, but also provides a platform from which to develop further the evolving discourse of social and environmental justice.

Earlier I asserted that the development of a new research agenda in social justice would enable feminist and gender researchers in leisure studies to collaborate more closely with those in the related fields of sport studies and tourism studies, where gender research has grown significantly in volume and strength during the last decade. In tourism studies, the *turn to culture* coincided with the turn into the new century, where subsequent developments have been evident in the publication of research embracing new theoretical perspectives, methodological approaches, and research techniques influenced by the developing poststructural literature in social science (Pritchard, Morgan, Ateljevic, & Harris, 2007). The cultural turn, with its emphasis on the symbolic and cultural nature of space, place, and identity, has informed new uses of discourse analysis, in-depth interviewing and diary keeping, observational analysis, and the role of actor-network theory (Ateljevic, Morgan, & Pritchard, 2007; Phillimore & Goodson, 2004). These approaches have developed cultural critiques from those of previously simplistic dualistic and linear approaches to *circuits of culture* (du Gay, 1996), cultural webs, networks, nexuses, and the *inbetweenness* of space (Aitchison, 2003; Heimtun, 2007b; Rose, 1997).

Both leisure and tourism studies have engaged with and benefited from the theoretical input associated with the turn to culture in single disciplines such as sociology and geography. Moreover, both fields also appear to have been cushioned from the excesses of the cultural turn experienced by the same disciplines in the early 1990s (Adkins, 1998; Jackson, 1998; Valentine, 2001). I offer two possible explanations, both relating to the timing of leisure and tourism studies' engagement with the cultural turn. First, the later development of the cultural turn within leisure and tourism studies has enabled researchers to become familiar with and learn from the ways in which the materialist-poststructuralist debate developed within geography, sociology, and subject fields such as gender studies. More significantly and relating only to tourism studies, the cultural turn developed *alongside* the critical turn, rather than evolving after the development of theoretical discourses that embraced critical theory, as was the case in leisure studies.

Thus, the relatively recent development of both cultural theory and critical social science within tourism studies, a subject field described only 15 years ago as lacking in theoretical sophistication (Apostolopoulos et al., 1996), has facilitated the possibility of developing new conceptual frameworks and theoretical directions, as evidenced in the new sub-discipline of critical tourism studies (Aitchison, 2006). The emerging discourse of environmental justice has begun to be established within tourism studies and, even more recently, linked to that of social and environmental justice through engagement with issues of environmental ethics, community development, and fair trade. In collaboration, feminist and gender researchers in leisure and tourism studies have the potential to contribute to a similar new research agenda in leisure studies centered on social and environmental justice and addressing Giddens's (2009) three areas of the global, the personal, and the environmental.

GENDER IN LEISURE STUDIES: TOWARDS SOCIAL AND ENVIRONMENTAL JUSTICE

The concept of the social-cultural nexus can be viewed as offering the potential to combine both critical and cultural analyses while simultaneously addressing the concerns raised by Bondi, Evans, and Valentine outlined above. Such a framework seeks to accommodate both the material and the symbolic in an integrated analysis that explores the mutually informing nature of social and cultural relations in shaping gender relations (Aitchison, 2003; Letherby, 2003). The rationale for such an approach is that while women and girls still suffer structural oppression within almost all social and cultural arenas, it is inappropriate to discontinue the research tradition embodied by socialist feminism, which has served feminism well in highlighting the material constraints, including leisure, that women and girls face as part of everyday life.

However, poststructural theory offers additional conceptual rigor and nuanced interpretation with which to interrogate and understand seemingly material constraints. The concept of the social-cultural nexus renders visible the connections *between* social and cultural relations and their respective material and symbolic representations of power. This way of seeing reveals that sites of exclusion and inequality are often most embedded where the two forms of exclusionary power relations (i.e., the material and the symbolic) coexist and mutually reinforce at the nexus of the social and the cultural. Thus the social-cultural nexus is explained as both a site and a process of construction, legitimation, reproduction, and reworking of power relations (Aitchison, 2005b).

A central focus of any future research agenda in feminist and gender leisure studies, therefore, must examine and explain the extent to which systemic economic power (i.e., capitalism as revealed and contested by Marxist and socialist feminism) and systemic male power (i.e., patriarchy as revealed and contested by radical feminism) exist in relation to policy, provision, and participation in leisure and/or the extent to which localized, contextualized, and pluralized power relations exert their influence on gender relations within leisure. I now turn to the development of a theoretical critique that has the potential to offer a new research agenda for feminist and gender leisure studies. This critique draws on and develops the concept of the social-cultural nexus in relation to the emerging discourse of social and environmental justice. Such a research agenda has the capacity to integrate material and cultural analyses, as outlined in the social-cultural nexus, with an integrated analysis of social and environmental justice. This discourse is informed by and further informs social and cultural geography in addition to the underpinning disciplines of sociology and geography and the subject fields of leisure and tourism studies.

I acknowledge the broader foundations of the social and environmental justice discourse within the disciplines of philosophy, divinity, and law. Philosophy informs the discourse on ethics, rights, and responsibilities. Divinity addresses the discourse on morality, and law provides discourse on legal conventions, international norms, and sanctions. Whether drawn from philosophical, religious, or legal origins, the act of seeking to define what justice is begins to question the moral and cultural relativity of the postmodernist discourse that expanded from the humanities into the social sciences at the end of the twentieth century. By defining what is *just* or in seeking to identify *justice,* what is seen as *unjust* or identified as *injustice* will be revealed simultaneously. This wider social science discourse then enables examination of the relationships between places, people, societies, and cultures, and related issues of equity, opportunity, cultural diversity, and global understanding of local situations.

This discussion foregrounds one of the most fundamental criticisms of the postmodernist discourse that gained ground during the 1990s: the debate between relativist and absolutist positions. The relativist position of postmodernism posed a significant challenge for the continued development of discourses relating to gender justice that had gained prominence during the late 1980s and 1990s. In particular, the discourse of leisure as a human right, which had begun to develop global discussion and a high level of acceptance, has not been developed further during the last decade. The notion of human rights has been challenged as absolutist and dominated by Western discourses of particular societal and cultural norms that should not be imposed on other societies and cultures. Pertinent discussions that developed around the discourse of *social capital,* however, have recently been applied to gender and leisure relations. These discussions inform a research agenda on gender justice that reengages with and reenergizes the debate on leisure and human rights (e.g., Adkins, 2005; Arai, 2006; Caiazza & Putnam, 2005; Heimtun, 2007b; Lin, 2001).

When the earlier discourse of gender, leisure, and human rights is combined with the emerging discourse of social and environmental justice and informed by the social-capital literature, a new discourse and research agenda in gender justice can be identified. This new discourse enables reengagement with debates that surfaced in gender and leisure literature during the 1980s and 1990s that remain incomplete or inconclusive relative to any clear identification of leisure policy and practice. Such a reengagement might serve to develop wider gender justice related to the participation and provision issues highlighted above. Drawing on the wider philosophical, religious and, most importantly, legal discourses of social justice, a reengagement with global definitions, policies, and practices of human rights relating to leisure becomes possible (Freeman, 2002; Sellers, 2002). For example, Articles 24 and 27 of the United Nations Declaration of Human Rights, and Article 13 of the Convention on the Elimination of All Forms of Discrimination Against Women, each highlights the significance of participation in and provision of leisure to all as part of a wider development of universal human rights and social justice:

> Everyone has the right to rest and leisure, including reasonable limitation of working hours and periodic holidays with pay. (Article 24: UN Universal Declaration of Human Rights) (United Nations, 1948)

> a) Everyone has the right freely to participate in the cultural life of the community, to enjoy the arts and to share in scientific advancement and its benefits.

> b) Parties shall take all appropriate measures to eliminate discrimination against women in other areas of economic and social life in order to ensure, on a basis of equality of men and women, the same rights, in particular: ...

> c) The right to participate in recreational activities, sports, and all aspects of cultural life. (Article 27: UN Universal Declaration of Human Rights) (United Nations, 1948)

In seeking to develop a new research agenda for gender and leisure in the twenty-first century, therefore, researchers need to be cognizant of the chronological development of earlier discourses of gender and leisure, and of the tensions between these differing epistemological and political positions. The development of a coherent agenda for change requires the development and acceptance of a conceptual framework for gender and leisure research. I have argued that such a framework needs to accommodate a broad alliance of epistemological positions focused on a shared objective. The concept of the social-cultural nexus and its application to the development of a new discourse of social and environmental justice could provide the framework around which a coherent alliance could be built. The objective of gender justice in relation to leisure participation and provision can, I argue, provide a sufficiently clear focus for the transition of theory into policy and practice. The identification of a shared objective, common framework, and coherent agenda for feminist and gender leisure research offers potential for academics, policymakers, and practitioners in leisure studies to collaborate in turning the cultural critique of the twentieth century into a new social justice for the twenty-first century.

References

Adkins, L. (1998). Feminist theory and economic change. In S. Jackson & J. Jones (Eds.), *Contemporary feminist theories*. Edinburgh: Edinburgh University Press.

Adkins, L. (2005). Social capital: The anatomy of a troubled concept. *Feminist Theory, 6*(2), 195–211.

Aitchison, C. C. (2000b). Women in leisure services: Managing the social-cultural nexus of gender equity. *Managing Leisure, 5*(4), 81–91.

Aitchison, C. C. (2003). *Gender and leisure: Social and cultural perspectives.* London, UK: Routledge.

Aitchison, C. C. (2005a). Feminist and gender perspectives in tourism studies: The social-cultural nexus of critical and cultural theories. *Tourist Studies, 5*(3), 207–224.

Aitchison, C. C. (2005b). Feminist and gender research in sport and leisure management: Understanding the social-cultural nexus of gender-power relations. *Journal of Sport Management, 19*(4), 222–241.

Aitchison, C. C. (2006). The critical and the cultural: Explaining the divergent paths of leisure studies and tourism studies. *Leisure Studies, 25*(4), 417–422.

Aitchison, C. C. (2009). Gender and tourism discourses: Advancing the gender project in tourism studies. In T. Jamal & M. Robinson (Eds.), *Handbook of tourism studies* (pp. 627–640). London, UK: Sage.

Aitchison, C. C., Jordan, F., & Brackenridge, C. (1999). Women in leisure management: A survey of gender equity. *Women in Management Review, 14*(4), 121–127.

Althusser, L. (1971). *Lenin and philosophy and other essays*. London, UK: New Left Books.

Apostolopolous, Y., Leivadi, S., & Yiannakis, A. (Eds.) (1996). *The sociology of tourism: Theoretical and empirical investigations*. London, UK: Routledge.

Arai, S. (2006). Where does social control end and social capital begin? Examining social space, conflict and the politics of difference. *Leisure/ Loisir, 30*(2), 329–340.

Ateljevic, I., Morgan, N., & Pritchard, A. (Eds.) (2007). *The critical turn in tourism studies: Innovative research methodologies*. Harlow: Elsevier.

Atkinson, A. B. (1982). *Social justice and public policy*. Brighton, UK: Harvester.

Bacon, W. (1991). *Women's experiences in leisure management*. Reading: Institute of Leisure and Amenity Management.

Barnes, T., & Gregory, D. (1997). *Reading human geography: The poetics and politics of inquiry*. London, UK: Arnold.

Barrett, M. (1992). Words and things: materialism and method in contemporary feminist analysis. In M. Barrett & A. Phillips (Eds.), *Destabilising theory: Contemporary feminist debates*. Cambridge, UK: Polity.

Bondi, L. (1992). Gender and dichotomy. *Progress in Human Geography, 16*(1), 98–104.

Brockbank, A., & Traves, J. (1996). Career aspirations—Women managers and retailing. In S. Ledwith & F. Colgan (Eds.), *Women in organisations: Challenging gender politics*. Basingstoke, UK: Macmillan.

Butler, J. (1990). *Gender trouble: Feminism and the subversion of identity*. London. UK: Routledge.

Butler, J. (1993). *Bodies that matter*. London, UK: Routledge.

Caiazza, A., & Putnam, R. A. (2005). Women's status and social capital in the United States. *Journal of Women, Politics and Policy, 27*(1–2), 69–84.

Carver, T. N. (1915). *Essays in social justice*. Cambridge, MA: Harvard University Press.

Charles, M., & Grusky, D. B. (2004). *Occupational ghettos: The worldwide segregation of women and men*. Stanford, CA: Stanford University Press.

Clarke, J., & Critcher, C. (1985). *The devil makes work: Leisure in capitalist Britain*. London, UK: Macmillan.

Coalter, F. (2001). *Realising the potential of cultural services: Making a difference to the quality of life*. London, UK: Local Government Association.

Cullen, P., Hoose, B., & Mannion, G. (Eds.) (2007). *Catholic social justice: Theological and practical explorations*. London, UK: Continuum.

Deem, R. (1986). *All work and no play? The sociology of women and leisure*. Milton Keynes, UK: Open University Press.

du Gay, P. (1996). *Consumption and identity at work*. London, UK: Sage.

Ely, R., & Padavic, I. (2007). A feminist analysis of organizational research on sex differences, *Academy of Management Review, 32*(4), 1121–1143.

Evans, M. (2003). *Gender and social theory*. Buckingham, UK: Open University Press.

Freeman, M. (2002). *Human rights: An interdisciplinary approach*. Cambridge, UK: Polity.

Frisby, W., & Brown, B. (1991). The balancing act: women leisure service managers. *Journal of Applied Recreation Research, 16*(4), 297–321.

Giddens, A. (1984). *The constitution of society: Outline of a theory of structuration*. Cambridge: Polity.

Giddens, A. (1998). *The third way: The renewal of social democracy*. Cambridge, UK: Polity.

Giddens, A. (2009). *Sociology* (6th ed.). Cambridge, UK: Polity.

Green, E., Hebron, S., & Woodward, D. (1987). *Leisure and gender: A study of Sheffield women's leisure experiences*. Sheffield: The Sports Council/ Economic and Social Research Council.

Green, E., Hebron, S., & Woodward, D. (1990). *Women's leisure? What leisure?* London, UK: Macmillan.

Griffin, C. (1981). Young women and leisure. In A. Tomlison (Ed.), *Leisure and social control*. Eastbourne, UK: Leisure Studies Association.

Grosz, E. (1994). *Volatile bodies: Towards a corporeal feminism*. Sydney, Australia: Allen and Unwin.

Grosz, E. (1995). *Space, time and perversion: The politics of bodies*. Sydney, Australia: Allen and Unwin.

Habermas, J. (1989). *The new conservatism: Cultural criticism and the historians' debate*. Cambridge, UK: Polity.

Hantrais, L., Clark, P., & Samuel, N. (1984). Time-space dimensions of work, family and leisure in France and Great Britain. *Leisure Studies, 3*(4), 301–317.

Harrington, M. (2006a). Family leisure. In C. Rojek, S. Shaw, & A. J. Veal (Eds.), *A handbook of leisure studies*. London, UK: Palgrave.

Harrington, M. (2006b). Sport and leisure as contexts for fathering in Australian families. *Leisure Studies, 25*(2), 165–183.

Heimtun, B. (2007b). *Mobile identities of gender and tourism*. (Unpublished doctoral dissertation). Bristol, University of the West of England.

Henderson, K. A. (2010, February). *Defragmenting leisure studies in the twenty-first century*. Keynote presentation given at the 9th Biennial Conference of the Australia and New Zealand Leisure Studies Association, Brisbane, Australia.

Henderson, K. A., & Bialeschki, M. D. (1991). A sense of entitlement to leisure as constraint and empowerment for women. *Leisure Sciences, 13*(1), 51–65.

Henderson, K. A., & Bialeschki, M. D. (1993). Professional women and equity issues in the 1990s. *Parks and Recreation, 28*(3), 54–59.

Henderson, K. A., & Bialeschki, M. D. (1995). Career development and women in the leisure services profession. *Journal of Park and Recreation and Administration, 13*(1), 26–42.

Hobson, D. (1981). Young women at home and leisure. In A. Tomlison (Ed.), *Leisure and social control*. Eastbourne, UK: Leisure Studies Association.

Jackson, J. (1998). Feminist social theory. In S. Jackson & J. Jones (Eds.), *Contemporary feminist theories*. Edinburgh: Edinburgh University Press.

Jowell, T. (2002, March). *The culture contribution: How culture and leisure help communities*. Presented at the Local Government Association Conference, Coventry, England.

Kay, T. A. (2000b). Leisure, gender and the family: the influence of social policy. *Leisure Studies, 19*(3), 247–265.

Kay, T. A. (2006b). Where's dad? Fatherhood and leisure studies. *Leisure Studies, 25*(2), 133–152.

Letherby, G. (2003). *Feminist research in theory and practice*. Buckingham, UK: Open University Press.

Lin, N. (2001). *Social capital: A theory of structure and action*. Cambridge, UK: Cambridge University Press.

Long, J., Melch, M., Bramham, P., Hylton, K., Butterfield, J., & Lloyd, E. (2002). Count me in: The dimensions of social inclusion through culture and sport. Leeds, UK: Leeds Metropolitan University. Retrieved from http://www.lmu.ac.uk/ces/lss/research/countmein.pdf

McCabe, T. (1981). Girls and leisure. In A. Tomlison (Ed.), *Leisure and social control*. Eastbourne, UK: Leisure Studies Association.

McIntosh, S. (1981). Leisure studies and women. In A. Tomlison (Ed.), *Leisure and social control*. Eastbourne, UK: Leisure Studies Association.

McKay, J. (1996). *Managing gender: Affirmative Action and organisation power in Australian, Canadian and New Zealand sport.* New York, NY: State University of New York Press.

Novak, M. (2000, December). Defining social justice. *First Things: A Monthly Journal of Religion and Public Life*, pp. 11–13.

Phillimore, J., & Goodson, L. (2004). *Qualitative research in tourism: Ontologies, epistemologies and methodologies.* London, UK: Routledge.

Pritchard, A., Morgan, N., Ateljevic, I., & Harris, C. (Eds.) (2007). *Tourism and gender: Embodiment, sensuality and experience.* Wallingford, UK: CAB International.

Rapoport, R., & Rapoport, R. N. (1975). *Leisure and the family life cycle.* London, UK: Routledge and Kegan Paul.

Rawls, J. (1971). *A theory of justice.* Cambridge, MA: Harvard University Press.

Rose, G. (1993). *Feminism and geography.* Cambridge, UK: Polity.

Rose, G. (1997). Situating knowledges: Positionality, reflexivities and other tactics. *Progress in Human Geography, 21*(3), 305–320.

Sellers, K. (2002). *The rise and rise of human rights.* Stroud, UK: Sutton.

Shaw, S. M. (1992b). Dereifying family leisure: an examination of women's and men's everyday experiences and perceptions of family time. *Leisure Sciences, 14*(3), 271–286.

Shaw, S. M. (1994). Gender, leisure, and constraint: Towards a framework for the analysis of women's leisure. *Journal of Leisure Research, 26*, 8–22.

Shaw, S. M. (1997). Controversies and contradictions in family leisure: An analysis of conflicting paradigms. *Journal of Leisure Research, 29*(1), 98–112.

Shaw, S. M., & Dawson, D. (2001). Purposive leisure: Examining parental discourses on family activities. *Leisure Sciences, 23*(4), 217–231.

Shinew, K. J., & Arnold, M. (1998). Gender equity in the leisure services field. *Journal of Leisure Research, 30*(2), 177–94.

Talbot, M. (1979). *Women and leisure.* London, UK: Sports Council/Social Science Research Council.

Talbot, M. (1981). Women and sport: Biosocial aspects. *Journal of Biosocial Science, Supplement, 7*, 33–47.

Tomlinson, A. (Ed.) (1981). *Leisure and social control.* Eastbourne, UK: Leisure Studies Association.

Valentine, G. (2001). Whatever happened to the social? Reflections on the "Cultural Turn" in British human geography. *Norsk Geografisk Tidsskrift (Norwegian Journal of Geography), 55*(3), 166–172.

Wearing, B. (1998). *Feminism and leisure theory.* Thousand Oaks, CA: Sage.

Willming, C., & Gibson, H. (2000). A view of leisure patterns of family life in the late 1990s. *Leisure and Society, 23*(1), 121–144.

Wimbush, E. (1986). *Women, leisure and well-being.* Final report to Health Promotion Research Trust. Edinburgh: Moray House College of Education.

Woodroffe, J. (2009). *Not having it all: How motherhood reduces women's pay and employment prospects.* London, UK: Fawcett Society.

Yule, J. (1997a). Engendered ideologies and leisure policy in the UK. Part 1: Gender ideologies. *Leisure Studies, 16*(2), 61–84.

Yule, J. (1997b). Engendered ideologies and leisure policy in the UK. Part 2: Professional ideologies. *Leisure Studies, 16*(3), 139–154.

Yule, J. (1998). Sub-cultural strategies in patriarchal leisure professional cultures. In C. Aitchison & F. Jordan (Eds.), *Gender, space and identity: Leisure, culture and commerce.* Eastbourne, UK: Leisure Studies Association.

Zabriskie, R. B., & McCormick, B. P. (2001). The influences of family leisure patterns on perceptions of family functioning. *Family Relations: Interdisciplinary Journal of Applied Family Studies, 50*(3), 66–74.

CHAPTER 39
REFLECTIONS ON LEISURE, WOMEN, AND GENDER

VALERIA J. FREYSINGER, SUSAN M. SHAW, KARLA A. HENDERSON, AND M. DEBORAH BIALESCHKI

This book has brought together a variety of voices, issues, insights, and perspectives related to leisure and gender with a primary emphasis on understanding women's lives. The issues are complex and multifaceted, and we have sought to shed light on some of those complexities. We are encouraged by the growing number of researchers working in this area of study, and the reinvigoration that occurs as new questions, new approaches, and new understandings develop.

The book has been organized around three central themes—namely, women's leisure activity participation and experiences; the social context of their lives and leisure; and the broader societal, cultural, and political (or macro-) environments that produce and reproduce gendered lives and leisure. Clearly, though, the division of individual, social, and cultural/societal/political are not and cannot be entirely separate or distinct. Rather, the categorization we have used can be seen as a heuristic that directs attention to these different ways of understanding leisure and gender in order to be inclusive and holistic in our orientation.

The primary focus in section 2 is on *personal lives* and experiences, including leisure meanings, personal identities, and the opportunities that leisure provides for making choices, for health and well-being, and for empowerment. Attention is also given to the notions of challenge and constraint, how constraints are experienced and negotiated, and how new opportunities can develop in response to constraints. Many of these discussions focus on specific types of leisure activity, such as sports, motorcycling, travel and tourism, and friendships. Nevertheless, the authors also take account of the broader social, cultural, and societal contexts within which these activities occur. That is, the significance of empowerment through leisure is essentially linked to notions of structured inequity, women's lack of power, and the unequal distribution of power and opportunity among women. Similarly, individual aspects of resistance are highly significant for the person involved, but they also have implications for others and potentially for broader societal change. Thus, the idea of gendered lives in a gendered society is central to understanding women's leisure opportunities, choices, and experiences, and it also links directly to constraints. Gendered ideologies and discourses influence what is seen as appropriate and what is seen as possible. Although these discourses can be challenged, systemic inequity persists in subtle and overt ways, influencing time use, leisure involvement, and leisure experiences. Moreover, while the concept of gendered lives implies some commonality of experience among women, other dimensions of power and ideological constructions, such as racism, heterosexism, and discourses surrounding obesity and appearance, also differentially affect women of color, older women, and women and girls who do not conform to the "ideal" body weight, body shape, or functioning. Similar processes also affect men in marginalized groups such as men who do not conform to the dominant norm of heterosexism.

In section 3 of the book, attention is directed to lives in *social contexts*. Exploration of different interactional and physical contexts such as family, home, and work environments adds new understanding to notions of women's gendered lives. Such explorations show how personal lives are enacted in specific contexts and environments, and further illustrate the many and complex connections among the individual, the social, and the systemic.

Not surprisingly, considerable attention is paid in this section to family issues and family contexts. The significance of parenthood and its dramatic influence on the lives of women is evident. Further, this influence ties directly to social expectations about parenthood and, in particular, ideologies of motherhood. The contradictions inherent in family life are also revealed, indicating a complex mixture of paid work, unpaid work, and family responsibilities. These contradictions also indicate the resultant loss of personal leisure alongside the pleasure and possibilities of family time. Moreover, this mix of positive and negative experiences, and of work, caregiving, and other responsibilities, continues into grandparenthood and affects women of all ages who provide care for others such as care for elderly, sick, or dependent others.

The chapters in this section help to explain the gendered nature of time and time-use that was first discussed in section 2. The chapters also cast additional light on the clear links between women's lives in context and the gendered nature of societal beliefs, expectations, and discourses of caregiving. Such gendered expectations continue despite increasingly similar rates of male and female engagement in the paid labor force, and despite widely expressed support for the idea of equal opportunities and equal rights.

The research discussed in section 3 adds to the notions of complexity in women's lives as well as diversity among women. The coexistence of positive meanings and negative constraints is again evident. However, challenge and resistance may be particularly difficult in family settings, where women are judged by their conformity to notions of being a "good mother," a "good daughter," or a "good caregiver." Again, it is clear that issues of social class, race, and ethnicity need to be taken into account too, particularly as they relate to discrimination at work and the combined effects of racism, classism, and sexism. For African American women and for women of color in many parts of the world, ideologies of equity in the workplace fly in the face of the reality of racism and sexism. Structured disadvantage affects all aspects of life including leisure.

In section 4 of the book, these issues of structured inequities are addressed more directly. Particular attention is paid to questions of *power* and to the idea of intersectionality of different dimensions of power. This concept links to notions of multiple oppressions related to able-bodiedness, class, race, sexual orientation, and age. At the same time, the individual and the social contexts are not lost but are incorporated into the discussion of multiple constraints and their impacts on women's lives. The focus on macro-issues in this section also necessitates further discussion of agency or individual power—ideas that can be seen to counterbalance the tendency towards structured determinism (see chapter 3). The idea of personal power is inherent in notions of resistance to male-dominated activities, contexts, and environments, and it is essential to activist scholarship designed to counteract oppression and bring about social change.

Issues of *politics* are addressed here, too. Although most, if not all, research can be seen to be political in its orientation and its interpretive stance, macro-level research is often more explicitly political. At this level, issues and discussion tend to fit more easily and directly with questions of social, political, and economic change. Such research may also deliberately address specific social, educational, or economic politics, arguing for and advocating for change. Some examples of this type of research in the leisure field are provided, although there seem to be relatively few researchers in the leisure and gender field who do explicit policy-related research.

For some of the authors featured in section 4, *culture* and *cultural diversity* is a central focus. These authors draw attention to cultural diversity within Western societies, as well as diversity across international settings around the world. Issues of racism and ethnocentrism are addressed, as well as the need for research that is sensitive to global and cross-cultural differences, inequities, and oppressions. This research reveals some of the complexities of addressing gender equity in different cultural contexts. For example, notions of equality, fairness, and equal opportunity are not necessarily universal, but may vary within and between specific contextual settings. Thus, white, Western views of feminist activist research and visions of social change need to be evaluated and reevaluated in terms of their applicability and acceptability in different global contexts. Again, these considerations point not only to the value of macro-research, but also to the importance of understanding the interconnections between individual, social-interactional, and societal components of women's gendered lives.

THEORETICAL AND METHODOLOGICAL ISSUES

In chapter 3 of the book, a variety of different theoretical approaches to feminist research were discussed, including early liberal approaches, structural and socialist approaches, cultural and multicultural feminisms, social constructionism, and postmodernism. In some ways, these theoretical positions can be seen to be divergent and conflicting, raising questions not only of political orientation, but also tensions between structuralist versus poststructuralist or more culturally based perspectives. This disjuncture also reflects the discussion in Aitchison's chapter in this final section of the book. With particular attention to feminist leisure scholarship in the United Kingdom, Aitchison documents the fragmentation of this body of research related to the growing conflict between *cultural* and *material* perspectives through the 1980s, 1990s, and into the first decade of the twenty-first century. Other researchers (e.g., Hesse-Biber, 2007) have also addressed the polarization that occurred among and between feminist scholars during this period of time, and particularly the conflicts related to the rise of postmodernism.

Yet, despite these problems, there seems to be some evidence that the period of theoretical fragmentation in feminist scholarship may be lessening or even coming to an end. In this book, the invited chapters reflect some theoretical diversity. The most commonly adopted approach seems to be social constructionism, which is typically associated with micro-social processes and how social interactions and contexts serve to construct meanings about leisure and leisure activities. At the same time, the authors who use this approach also incorporate an understanding of gender relations and the ways in which interactions, practices, and processes can reflect the gendered nature of society and the gendered nature of women's lives. Thus, these approaches might be better described as *critical constructionism*, rather than *social constructionism*, because of the incorporation of critical theory and a structured view of power alongside notions of socially constructed meanings. Similarly, researchers who take a more structuralist view of gender, power, inequity, and the intersectionality of different dimensions of power, also pay attention to individual and collective meanings, as discussed previously. Their studies are typically based within particular communities or settings and incorporate interpretations and responses to relations of power within these contexts. Sexism, racism, heterosexism, familism, and other ideologies are interrogated, and these ideologies are not seen as static but as contested domains. Leisure and everyday leisure practices are seen to have the potential to challenge, negotiate, and weaken ideological systems. Thus, notions of reproduction and resistance, and thereby notions of construction and reconstruction, point to the importance of individual agency and individual, collective, and culturally constructed meanings.

Other authors in this book have found *postmodernist* perspectives to be useful and valuable, providing additional insights and understandings related to women's leisure. Through a focus on the many subtleties of difference and diversity, postmodernism serves to alert researchers to the dangers of assuming commonalities of experience or meaning, such as a single meaning of gender equity in sport or leisure environments. Thus, although postmodernist research can help to reveal and illuminate nuanced understandings, feminist postmodernist scholars examine these nuances within a broader understanding of patriarchy and discrimination. They are also advocating for social change and for the empowerment of women, but typically focusing on specific localized and contextualized situations and settings.

To us, the variety of approaches used by feminist leisure scholars today is encouraging. Whether or not this situation represents a move towards the new emerging *social-cultural nexus* that Aitchison introduces in her chapter is yet to be determined. But the coexistence of a diversity of perspectives, along with some similarities related to ideas of patriarchy, sexism, and contextualization, seems to suggest that divisive tensions within feminist research circles may be waning. Instead, respect for difference and a valuation of diverse perspectives seem to be becoming more evident. Some feminist scholars have advocated for greater unity and more connections and interconnections among researchers (e.g., Aitchison, this volume; Bhavnani, 2007; Henderson, 2010; Hesse-Biber, 2007). Based on our shared objectives and mutual desire for social change, we think that some of these connections and interconnections may be already occurring within the feminist leisure research community, and we are hopeful that this book will contribute to that process.

Related to the question of theory are issues of epistemology and methodology. Again, some diversity of approaches is evident among the researchers featured in this book. Although the most common methodological approach used is qualitative interviewing, particularly one-to-one interviewing, some researchers used focus-group and family-group interviewing. In addition, there seems to be a growing interest in ethnographic approaches, especially *critical ethnographies*, in different cultural and sub-cultural settings. Further, a number of researchers explicitly incorporate *activist* methodological approaches and activist forms of scholarship, such as feminist participatory action research (FPAR).

This focus on essentially qualitative and interpretivist research is not surprising, since this epistemological approach is consistent with constructivist theorizing and cultural analysis. Moreover, previous debates about feminist methodologies (e.g., Harding, 1987) have drawn a clear link between feminist research and qualitative methods, which are seen to be more humanistic and less hierarchical than post-positivist approaches. However, while at one time there was considerable tension among feminist researchers about methodological imperatives, this debate—similar perhaps to the debate about theoretical imperatives—seems to have moderated in recent years. Feminist research is often described as building *emancipatory knowledge*, seeking to empower those involved in the actual research process as well as others (e.g., see Lather, 1991). This argument, however, does not necessarily link only to qualitative methodologies. According to Hesse-Biber (2007), feminist methods and feminist praxis incorporate notions of difference, power, and authority, reflect deep concern with ethical issues and adopt an ongoing practice of reflexivity. These goals and practices, it is argued, can be realized through quantitative research, or qualitative research, or through a combination of both.

What seems to be a growing acceptance of quantitative and mixed methods among feminist researchers may be linked to several issues. These issues include the desire to maintain a *macro* as well as a *micro* perspective on gender and gender relations, and a desire to influence *social and policy change*. Miner-Rubino, Jayaratne, and Konik (2007) argue that at least some quantitative research (i.e., research that reaches a larger population base and is more generalizable than qualitative approaches) is needed in order to argue effectively for policy change that is sensitive to women's needs. Quantitative research can also explore certain issues and questions that are less accessible to qualitative researchers, such as the economic and material conditions of women's lives, time use, social trends related to health and stress, and the need for improved parental leave, elder care, childcare, vacation leave, and other policies. Along these lines, this book includes some discussion of time-use data and the implications of time stress and caregiving activities on parents' access to leisure. Perhaps in future years, more feminist researchers might begin to incorporate quantitative epistemological and methodological approaches, or mixed methodological approaches, in their research on women's leisure.

Apart from specific theoretical and methodological paradigms, another feature of feminist research is the relatively common practice of incorporating the researcher's *voice* into the research process and into the final product or presentation of findings. We invited those contributing chapters to include a personal note or discussion of their relationship or connection to their research endeavors. Many have done so. This practice is often part of the process of reflexivity and of revealing the personal connections between the researcher, the topic, and/or the people involved in the study. This involvement of self or inclusion of voice is most typical among more subjectivist, qualitative approaches such as postmodernism, autoethnography, and narrative analysis, but it is sometimes advocated more widely. Such inclusion is seen to make the research process more transparent and accessible, and it is consistent with interpretive strategies that focus on the co-construction of meaning between the researcher and the researched.

Some feminist scholars also incorporate *self* into their research through creative ways of presenting ideas, concepts, and insights. Some examples are provided in this book, such as the use of narrative analysis and an ethnographic screenplay. Other possibilities include artistic or literary products. One of the values of this form of creative practice is the potential to reach different audiences and/or to appeal to a different type of understanding and knowledge, such as emotional knowledge, among members of the audience. These approaches are typically associated with qualitative methodologies, and particularly with more postmodernist approaches. Yet, the potential exists for these practices to be more widely used.

Overall, this discussion of theoretical and methodological issues leads us to advocate for an *expanded* vision of feminist research. The variety of theoretical and methodological approaches, as well as the variety of ways to disseminate knowledge and to advocate for change, provides a wide range of options. Although this suggestion could lead to contestation and division, we hope that the trend towards greater diversity of ideas and approaches will actually prevent the dissension and fragmentation that has happened in the past. Consistent with Aitchison's views, we advocate for new synergies, new insights, and a greater internal coherence that encourages debate and discussion, but which also rejects the notion that there is just "one way forward."

MISSING VOICES

As noted in the introduction to this book (section 1, chapter 1), this text brings together a *select* group of scholars. They are select in at least three ways. First, we (the editors of this book) were able to invite only some of the many researchers doing feminist work on leisure, women, and gender to contribute chapters to the book. Hence, Burke's (1935) contention that

"A way of seeing is always a way of not seeing" (p. 70) holds true for this book, as there are voices and perspectives missing. Responsibility for the missing voices lies to a great extent with us. Second, these individuals have built, or are building, research careers with a focus on leisure and women and/or gender. They are advancing a feminist agenda and a more just world. Third, they are a group who has, in one way or another, centered intersectionality in their work. By seeking to understand gendered leisure through an intersectional lens, the insights and thinking these scholars provide in this text illustrate, sometimes directly and other times more indirectly, the many-layered or contextualized *selves* of women and men. At the same time, their findings suggest and their calls for future research recognize that voices are missing and sometimes ignored in research, policy, and practice.

Feminist leisure research, for example, is rooted in the study of women's lives. Because research indicates the centrality of relationships and caring for others to girls' and women's emotional and material lives, *family* has been centered in much feminist research. Feminist researchers have found the *ethic of care* (Gilligan, 1982; Henderson & Bialeschki, 1991; Wearing, 1990a) to be a useful concept in seeking to understand gendered leisure and social inequality. However, as Shaw (1997) as well as chapters in this volume illustrate, *problematizing* notions of family and relationships of care in women's *and* men's lives is important. By doing so, insights into the nuances and complexities of how gender, sexism, and heterosexism work are gained.

Perhaps a next step in this family research is to not assume that family organizes all women's lives, at least not solely as the production and rearing of children and the making of a home with a partner or spouse. Nevertheless, the ideologies of femininity that are tied so centrally to heterosexual coupledom, and the bearing and rearing of children permeate all women's lives. The effect is evident in the *not doing* of traditional expectations. For example, *living apart together*, singledom, and not bearing/rearing children, whether by choice or circumstance, characterize a significant number of women's and men's lives. Further, family and gender are enacted in ways both similar and different based on age, culture, class, sexual orientation, able-bodiedness, and nationhood. While leisure researchers have begun to explore some of this diversity, much is yet to be considered.

Functionalist notions of the work/leisure (i.e., paid labor/non-work time and activity) relationship are also challenged by some of the research presented in this volume. On the one hand, echoes of socialist and radical feminists' contentions that the marginalization and control of women's reproduction is at the core of their unequal standing in society and oppression can certainly be heard. On the other hand, research has shown that for many women, work has elements of both pleasure and pain (Shaw, 1988;

Wearing, 1994). A dimension of women's (gendered) work and leisure that is little explored in leisure research (although tourism studies may be an exception) is that of sex. Consensual sex, glamour/beauty work, erotica, prostitution and sex tourism, expressions of sexuality, pornography, date rape, and sexual assault are clearly feminist concerns and are central to individuals' and cultures' leisure. The research that has explored these practices (e.g., Jeffreys, 2003, 2005, 2008, 2009; Johnson, 2005, 2008; Johnson & Samdahl, 2005; Pritchard, Morgan, & Sedgley, 2002; Shaw, 1999b; Skeggs, 1999) provides ample evidence that more analyses are needed. Many questions remain, such as in what sense these practices are work, oppression, freedom and self-expression, leisure, and/or exploitation. These questions are raised at least in part by the *feminist backlash* (Faludi, 1991), young women's femininities in an age of globalized media culture (Kehily & Nayak, 2008), free speech advocates, and religious fundamentalism.

In general, early thinking on the work/leisure relationship (e.g., spillover and compensation) has not developed much in leisure studies. Feminist research on women's work and leisure might help to positively complicate these functionalist models. Several chapters in this volume make clear that women's experiences of leisure and work cannot be separated from their experiences of racism, ageism, homophobia, classism, and disability.

Another material reality and relation of power that is underexplored in leisure research is age/aging. When Kaufman (1986) wrote about the *ageless self* over two decades ago, she referred to findings from her qualitative research that individuals who would be considered in many societies to be *old* did not see themselves as old, at least not in the way that society viewed "old." Rather, they saw themselves as they had always been, even if their physical self did not look or function the same as it did when they were chronologically younger. While the self is in many ways ageless, at the same time (and beginning at conception), social structures, processes, and cultural discourses inscribe aging bodies with meaning, opportunity, and constraint. Chronological age is one of numerous identities that intersects with gender and powerfully shapes gendered lives. Relatively little research conducted on age and aging, however, is feminist or recognizes feminist leisure research or considers age except as a categorical/descriptive variable. Several contributors to this volume are exceptions to that concern, but leisure and gerontological research, policy, and practice that view aging as a feminist issue are needed. When, many years ago, Gloria Steinem said that, "One day an army of grey-haired women may quietly take over the earth" (Steinem, n.d.) she could have been referring to now. Old age is a woman's issue in many ways, from the longer average life expectancy of women to their caretaking of those who are old and in need of assistance.

Chapters in this volume also illustrate how health and leisure are inextricably related. Leisure policy is health policy for individuals, families, and communities. However, despite the impact of poor health and disability on women's lives in particular, relatively little research in therapeutic recreation is overtly feminist. Looking through a feminist lens at issues of disability will help shed light both on how gender works and how social inequality is reproduced and resisted, as well as what must be considered in developing policy and practice with a feminist consciousness.

As much as family, work, aging, and health are gendered issues, they are also issues shaped by race, ethnicity, and nationhood. The centrality of culture and cultural diversity is evident through the discussions in many of the chapters. Yet, an evident gap remains with respect to women's lives and women's leisure in terms of the diversity of cultural settings around the globe. Most of the research to date on women and leisure has been conducted in Western and primarily white, Anglo geographic locations, such as North America, Europe, and Australasia. If the research is geographically limited in this way, though, we are focusing only on a *minority* of the world's population. Thus, we need to find ways to encourage broader global perspective and to become more sensitive to, and aware of, global inequities and global differences. Several chapters in this book clearly point to the need for new research, new approaches, and new questions that take up this challenge of enhancing global and cross-cultural understandings. They also provide compelling evidence for why researchers from the West, who produce most of the published research, need to locate themselves as the minority of the world's population and critically reflect on how and why they construct *otherness* and *marginality* in their research.

The chapters exploring girls' and women's leisure practices and participation also demonstrate that views of the opportunity and constraint, as well as pleasure and pain, of gendered leisure must allow for multiple and contradictory realities. A feminist lens helps to explain this multiplicity and seeming contradictions. For example, some of the research presented here found that while girls' participation in *nontraditional* (i.e., so-called masculine) leisure activity has expanded, boys' participation in *nontraditional* (i.e., so-called feminine) leisure activity has not. Boys, then, appear to be the *losers* as more gender equity in opportunity for leisure activity participation is legislated. A feminist lens, however, would ask to consider at least two issues. First, it would ask us to think about in what ways this discourse (re) produces inequity. In patriarchy, where *the masculine* is valued/centered and *the feminine* devalued/marginalized, little material or ideological benefit is gained by boys through participating in nontraditional activities. The opposite is true of girls who participate in nontraditional activities. Yet, that statement is not simple because new discourses of *othering* or marginalization are produced (e.g., heterosexism) as gender lines are renegotiated.

Second, a feminist lens would require us to recognize that boys' and men's lives are gendered, too. Not all boys and men reap benefits from hegemonic notions of masculinity and femininity, as several chapters in this volume illustrate (e.g., gay men, immigrant men, lower-income men, men of color, old men) (e.g., see Johnson, Richmond, & Kivel, 2008). Further research on the gendered lives of boys, men, and leisure is needed. While this issue has been addressed in sport (e.g., Kay, 2009a; Messner & Sabo, 1996), it has been given relatively little attention by researchers who study other practices of leisure, except perhaps the researchers in this volume.

Different men and different women are both differentially penalized and benefited by patriarchy. Further, individuals are not passive. They also challenge, negotiate, and resist hegemonic femininity and/or masculinity. That is, how gender works is highly complex, contested, and fluid. This is illustrated by some feminists who contend that we need to stay open to new ways of thinking about and understanding gender; we must *trouble* the ways of thinking about gender. Recent work on the femininities of young women (including that of some contributors to this volume), for example, provides insights into how gender is performed in *new times*. In these times, young women's participation in globalized media cultures is perhaps more central to their sense of self and other than their participation in schooling, the labor market, and family (Kehily & Nayak, 2008). Along the same lines, for many women and men around the globe, gender is not the only, or even the central, material, or cultural practice of inequality. Rather, nationhood, class or caste, ethnicity or race, and/or able-bodiedness are more important.

To advance a suggestion by Aitchinson (this volume), perhaps a way forward for feminist leisure research that focuses on family, work, health and disability, education, and sport, media, social groups, travel, and the many other leisure practices in which girls and women as well as boys and men engage, is through the notion of the *social-cultural nexus*. This nexus recognizes the usefulness of analyses of both structural and material inequality *and* cultural relations of power. As discussed earlier, feminist leisure research may already be moving in this direction through the incorporation of a variety of theoretical and methodological perspectives aimed at enhancing understandings of gendered lives and gendered leisure. Further, activist research is needed that focuses on gender, intersectionality, the local and the global, and social justice.

SOCIAL CHANGE AND SOCIAL JUSTICE

The Russian doll has many layers. As we have used the metaphor, the outside doll might be considered the national and international political and social worlds in which people live. Research conducted about women and gender from a feminist perspective must focus on these worlds and the social change that is necessary for equity, empowerment, *and* social justice. Concerns with equity and empowerment are evident in much of the research on individual lives and the social contexts of individual lives examined in this book. However, as the chapters in section 4 in particular indicate, more attention needs to be given to social change on political and policy levels as well. This attention is often difficult to address, especially in cultures where *rights of the individual* and *free market* economies are dominant ideologies, as well as in cultures where women's rights are given scant attention.

Praxis, or the combining of theory and action, ultimately, is the focus that makes feminist research, and some would say all research, meaningful (hooks, 1989). Praxis is based on the notion that the goal of research is to *change* the world, not just to study it. A feminist critique serves as a means for examining the underlying social structures and practices that produce and reproduce sexism specifically, and social inequality generally. A feminist critique contends that the totality of human interaction cannot be understood without interrogating the concept and practices of power. Further, researchers studying women and gender from a feminist perspective need to move beyond critique toward corrective action and the transformation of leisure research, practice, and policy.

Over 25 years ago, Bunch (1985) suggested that feminism could be the most important social force to address world problems. This social force and the changes it calls for, however, have been slow in coming, as documented in the introductory chapter to this book. When the status of girls and women around the globe is considered in relation to their access to education, employment, health and healthcare, pensions, reproductive rights, parental leave, and childcare, the profile that emerges likely tells much about the opportunities and constraints girls and women have in leisure. Although research has enhanced our knowledge about leisure, women, and gender, the linkages between social and economic policies and individuals' leisure require further exploration. This idea is supported by the layers of the Russian doll, suggesting that change in the individual self is best facilitated by a combination of social, environmental, organizational, and political/policy factors.

The change that results from feminist scholarship on leisure, women, and gender should focus on social justice. The research we do should help people to obtain a better quality of life *and* help them and us to critically reflect on what *a better quality of life* means or *looks like* and why. Justice refers to fairness, equity, and human rights. To quote Gloria Steinem, "Law and justice are not always the same. When they aren't, destroying the law may be the first step toward [creating justice]" (Steinem, n.d.). Social justice has been described as a vision of society where the distribution of resources is equitable and all members are physically and psychologically safe and secure. In this society, individuals are both self-determining and interdependent. Justice involves a sense of one's own agency and a sense of social responsibility toward and with others, and for society as a whole (Adams, Bell, & Griffin, 1997). Although many would subscribe to this definition, we also need to remain sensitive to different cultural perspectives on equity and justice. For example, the relative importance of self-determination versus social responsibility may vary in different global and cultural contexts. In addition, a diversity of opinions exists about how concepts of justice and fairness can and should be translated into practice through changes to specific policies, laws, and practices.

More research is needed on global or international policy and its impact on women's and men's gendered leisure. This research must take cultural diversity into account. Globalization has made our interdependence more visible, and an international mandate exists for research about leisure connected directly to policy. The *Universal Declaration of Human Rights*, passed in 1948 by the United Nations (UN) and still in effect today, calls for recognition that "the inherent dignity and the equal and inalienable rights of all members of the human family is the foundation of freedom, justice, and peace in the world" (Preamble). Further, this global document states that "everyone has the right to rest and leisure, including reasonable limitation of working hours and periodic holidays with pay" (Article 24). The *Convention on the Elimination of all Forms of Discrimination against Women*, ratified in 1979 by the UN, defines violence against women as "any act of gender-based violence that results in, or is likely to result in, physical, sexual or psychological harm or suffering to women, including threats of such acts, coercion or arbitrary deprivation of liberty, whether occurring in public or in private life." The document also states: "women are entitled to the equal enjoyment and protection of all human rights and fundamental freedoms in the political, economic, social, cultural, civil, or any other field." These examples are illustrative of the larger global practices and policies that could be further addressed in future research exploring the impact of policy on the lives of individuals, communities, and nation-states, especially as the study of leisure, women, and gender extends across the world beyond Western perspectives.

The *Charter for Leisure*, adopted by the World Leisure Organization (2000) at the turn of the century, also calls for action in direct support of leisure. The charter addresses the role that governments should play, stating: "all people have a basic human right to leisure activities" and "governments should ensure their citizens a variety of accessible leisure and recreational opportunities of the highest quality." As an advocacy document, this charter has merit. It focuses on leisure as a positive dimension of life that governments should support. Yet, the document largely reflects an industrialized, Western view of leisure. It does not take into account diverse cultural stances or the potential for leisure to be exploitative of women and/or men. Further, the document does not address the social inequalities that exist relative to leisure. It does provide, however, a basis for more research about women, gender, and inequality, as well as research on how policy *works* (or not) on national and international levels.

As noted earlier, relatively few researchers have addressed leisure and gender-related policy. This gap is unfortunate because policy can have direct and immediate outcomes, by addressing oppression and discrimination as well as enhancing and facilitating opportunities. Policy related to parks, recreation, media, and sport, as well as other broader issues such as employment, healthcare, parental leave and childcare, reproductive rights and freedoms, and discrimination in any form (e.g., race, ethnicity, religion, disability), are areas needing our attention. We advocate that future research about leisure, women, and gender should move toward being an intentional act deliberately designed to bring about the social changes that are required to realize social justice for individuals and local and global communities.

CONCLUDING THOUGHTS

When we first began to talk about this book, we felt strongly that we needed to conceptualize it in a way that captured the multidimensionality and diversity of women's/gendered lives. The Russian stacking doll, the many-layered matryoshka comprised of multiple selves, provided the guiding image. As we came to the end of this project, the work we and the book's contributors did led us to another way of thinking about the matryoshka— not as a single doll of many selves but as a multitude of dolls of different sizes and colors. That is, while the common shape that allows the many dolls to fit together and might represent the usefulness of thinking and working collectively with some broad common goals and understandings, the different sizes and colors of the dolls represent the necessity of diverse theories, research approaches, and specific interests. As noted, the heuristic categorization of our scholarship and that of our colleagues into personal lives, lives in social context, and culture, power, and politics—as well as the research presented in the various chapters—supplies evidence of the range of theory, approaches, and conceptual concerns informing recent work on leisure, women, and gender. We present this diversity (and this book) as a celebration of a growing field with new and established researchers focusing on new and continuing research interests and directions regarding leisure, women, and gender. We hope that our attempts to connect these ideas have honored the work of all involved.

When we invited the authors of the chapters of this book to participate in this project, we asked them to reflect on how they came to their research, what they have learned from their research, and the questions their research raises. This book provides evidence of some of the rich insights that they have recently produced about leisure, women, and gender. These insights both build upon and challenge previous understandings or ways of thinking about these topics. Further, those who have contributed to this volume directly and indirectly draw attention to what is little explored or understood, as well as missing altogether, in the research on leisure, women, and gender. That is, this book suggests directions for future research.

Some of the many issues and directions for future research identified include broadening our research to recognize the diversity of women and gender around the world. We further recognize that many people must be involved in this research, including men who can be feminists, too. We also hope that the diversity of epistemologies and methodologies that provide different ways of seeing and looking and different ways of asking and answering do not lead to fragmentation of our knowledge generation, but to a stronger collective voice.

The research presented in this volume also makes clear the necessity of thinking both locally and globally. Gendered lives and leisure of both women and men are experienced and performed in a world that is intricately interconnected. While we may celebrate the gains that girls and women in some parts of the world have made and the increasing leisure opportunities some of them have, we cannot ignore that the gains of some may be made at the expense of others. Perhaps more of us need to create and participate in collaborative research that cuts across not only disciplinary boundaries, but also other boundaries as well, so as not to lose sight of the fluidity, consistencies, and contradictions of power.

We believe the need for an increased focus on policy (i.e., both leisure policy and the many other areas of policy that affect leisure directly and indirectly), social change, and social justice in leisure research would also benefit from collaborative work. This collaboration should occur not only among researchers, but, as suggested by feminist perspectives, also through collaborations among researchers, practitioners, and those who are the *subjects* of leisure research, policy, and practices. Those subjects include *us*, as the research of all who have contributed to this book demonstrates. As feminists long ago pointed out, the personal is political and our research is personal and thus political.

We hope this book inspires and raises the consciousness of those who read it. As others have noted before, one of the most disturbing things learning can do is fill the mind with new ways of thinking. To the extent that this book raises new consciousness and inspires new thinking, we again thank those authors who contributed to it and those many others who disturbed and inspired us to ask the questions and do the work that we do.

REFERENCES

Adams, M., Bell, L. A., & Griffin, P. (Eds.) (1997). *Teaching for diversity and social justice.* New York, NY: Routledge.

Bhavnani, K. K. (2007). Interconnections and configurations: Toward a global feminist ethnography. In S. N. Hesse-Biber (Ed.), *Handbook of feminist research: Theory and praxis* (pp. 639–650). Thousand Oaks, CA: Sage.

Bryman, A., Teevan, J. J., & Bell, E. (2009). *Social research methods* (2nd Can. ed.). Don Mills, ON: Oxford University Press.

Bunch, C. (1985). *Bringing the global home.* Denver, CO: Antelope.

Burke, K. (1935). *Permanence and change.* New York, NY: New Republic.

Faludi, S. (1991). *Backlash: The undeclared war against American women.* New York, NY: Three Rivers.

Gilligan, C. (1982). *In a different voice.* Cambridge, MA: Harvard University Press.

Harding, S. (Ed.). (1987). *Feminism and methodology.* Bloomington, IN: Indiana University Press.

Henderson, K. A. (2010). *Defragmenting leisure studies in the 21st century.* Presentation given at Exploring New Ideas and New Directions, 9th Biennial Conference of the Australia and New Zealand Leisure Studies Association, Brisbane, Australia.

Henderson, K. A., & Bialeschki, M. D. (1991). A sense of entitlement to leisure as constraint and empowerment for women. *Leisure Sciences, 13*(1), 51–65.

Hesse-Biber, S. N. (2007). Feminist research: Exploring the interconnections of epistemology, methodology, and method. In S. N. Hesse-Biber (Ed.), *Handbook of feminist research: Theory and praxis* (pp. 1–26). Thousand Oaks, CA: Sage.

hooks, b. (1989). *Talking back: Thinking feminist, thinking Black.* Boston, MA: South End.

Jeffreys, S. (2005). *Beauty and misogyny: Harmful cultural practices in the West.* London, UK: Routledge.

Jeffreys, S. (2008). Keeping women down and out: The strip club boom and the reinforcement of male dominance. *Signs: Journal of Women in Culture and Society, 34*(1), 151–173.

Jeffreys, S. (2003). Sex tourism: Do women do it, too? *Leisure Studies, 22,* 223–238.

Jeffreys, S. (2009). *The industrial vagina: The political economy of the sex trade.* London, UK: Routledge.

Johnson, C. W. (2005). "The first step is the two-step": Gay men's negotiation strategies of a traditionally gendered dance. *International Journal of Qualitative Studies in Education, 18*(4), 445–464.

Johnson, C. W. (2008). "Don't call him a cowboy": Masculinity, cowboy drag, and a costume change. *Journal of Leisure Research, 40*(3), 385–403.

Johnson, C. W., Richmond, L., & Kivel, B. (2008). "What a man ought to be, he is far from": Exploring collective meanings of masculinity & race in media. *Leisure/Loisir, 32*(2), 1–28.

Johnson, C. W., & Samdahl, D. M. (2005). "The night they took over": Gay men's reaction to lesbian night in a country-western gay bar. *Leisure Sciences, 27*(4), 331–348.

Kaufman, S. R. (1986). *The ageless self: Sources of meaning in later life.* Madison, WI: University of Wisconsin Press.

Kay, T. A. (Ed.) (2009a). *Fathering through sport and leisure.* New York, NY: Routledge.

Kehily, M. J., & Nayak, A. (2008). Global femininities: Consumption, culture, and the significance of place. *Discourse: Studies in the Cultural Politics of Education, 29*(3), 325–342.

Lather, P. (1991). *Getting smart: Feminist research and pedagogy within/in the postmodern.* New York, NY: Routledge.

Messner, M. A., & Sabo, D. F. (Eds.) (1996). *Sport, men, and the gender order: Critical feminist perspectives.* Champaign, IL: Human Kinetics.

Miner-Rubino, K., Jayaratne, T. E., & Konik, J. (2007). Using survey research as a quantitative method for feminist social change. In S. N. Hesse-Biber (Ed.), *Handbook of feminist research: Theory and praxis* (pp. 199–222). Thousand Oaks, CA: Sage.

Pritchard, A., Morgan, N., & Sedgley, D. (2002). In search of lesbian space? The experience of Manchester's gay village. *Leisure Studies, 21,* 105–123.

Shaw, S. M. (1988, July). Gender differences in the definition and perception of household labor. *Family Relations, 37,* 333–337.

Shaw, S. M. (1997). Controversies and contradictions in family leisure: An analysis of conflicting paradigms. *Journal of Leisure Research, 29*(1), 98–112.

Shaw, S. M. (1999b). Men's leisure and women's lives: The impact of pornography on women's lives. *Leisure Studies, 18*(3), 197–212.

Skeggs, B. (1999). Matter of place: Visibility and sexuality in leisure spaces. *Leisure Studies, 18,* 218–232.

Steinem, G. (n.d.). Gloria Steinem quotes. Retrieved from http://www.goodreads.com/author/quotes/57108.Gloria_Steinem

United Nations. (1948). *Universal declaration of human rights.* Retrieved from http://www.un.org/en/documents/udhr/index.shtml

United Nations. (1979). *Convention on the elimination of all forms of discrimination against women.* Retrieved from http://www.un.org/womenwatch/daw/cedaw/

Wearing, B. (1990a). Beyond the ideology of motherhood: Leisure as resistance. *Australian and New Zealand Journal of Sociology, 26,* 36–58.

Wearing, B. (1994). The pain and pleasure of gendered leisure. *World Leisure and Recreation, 36*(3), 4–10.

World Leisure Organization. (2000). *Charter for leisure.* Retrieved from http://www.worldleisure.org/userfiles/file/charter.pdf

INDEX

Other books from Venture Publishing, Inc.